THE
END TIMES
CONTROVERSY

TIM LaHAYE
&THOMAS ICE
GENERAL EDITORS

HARVEST HOUSE™PUBLISHERS

EUGENE, OREGON

Unless otherwise indicated, Scripture quotations are taken from the New American Standard Bible®, © 1960, 1962, 1963, 1968, 1971, 1972, 1973, 1975, 1977, 1995 by The Lockman Foundation. Used by permission.

Verses marked KJV are taken from the King James Version of the Bible.

Verses marked NKJV are taken from the New King James Version. Copyright ©1982 by Thomas Nelson, Inc. Used by permission. All rights reserved.

Edited by Steve Miller

Cover by Terry Dugan Design, Minneapolis, Minnesota

Published in association with the literary agency of Alive Communications, Inc., 7680 Goddard Street, Suite 200, Colorado Springs, CO 80920

Harvest House Publishers, Inc. is the exclusive licensee of the trademark, TIM LAHAYE PROPHECY LIBRARY.

THE END TIMES CONTROVERSY
Copyright © 2003 by Pre-Trib Research Center
Published by Harvest House Publishers
Eugene, Oregon 97402

Library of Congress Cataloging-in-Publication Data
LaHaye, Tim F.
   The end times controversy / Tim LaHaye, Thomas Ice.
      p. cm – (The LaHaye prophecy library series)
   Includes bibliographical references.
   ISBN 0-7369-0953-2 (softcover)
   ISBN 0-7369-1264-9 (hardcover)
   1. End of the world. 2. Bible—Prophecies. I. Ice, Thomas. II. Title.
BT877 .L34 2003
236'.9—dc21

2002011963

Printed in the United States of America.

03 04 05 06 07 08 09 / RDC-MS / 10 9 8 7 6 5 4 3 2

In Memory of
Dr. John Walvoord

He was the dean of all twentieth-century prophecy scholars. As president and chancellor of Dallas Theological Seminary for over 50 years, he inspired and trained more ministers, teachers, and Christian college and seminary professors to teach the truth about prophecy than any other person. His voluminous writings on prophetic subjects were always true to Scripture and easily understandable by all. Through his writings he leaves able defenses of dispensationalism, the literal interpretation of prophecy, the rapture of the church before the Tribulation, and the differences between Israel and the church past, present and future, for future generations. The church of Jesus Christ enjoys a growing expectancy for our Savior's return because of John Walvoord's life.

He was a giant among men; physically, spiritually, and intellectually he "finished his course, he kept the faith," and was an example to all as a Christian, a loving husband, and a beloved father and grandfather. Consequently, there is laid up for him in heaven a crown of righteousness which the Lord will give him in that day for he "loved His appearance" and did everything he could to help others share that love and anticipation. We are honored to call him friend and mentor.

—Dr. Tim LaHaye, Dr. Thomas Ice, and all the contributors to this book

CONTENTS

INTRODUCTION

Has Jesus Already Come?

Tim LaHaye

Many Bible-believing Christians find it astounding that anyone would teach that our Lord Jesus Christ has already returned to this earth and that we are now living in the kingdom age predicted throughout the Bible. Yet that is what preterists believe and teach. And surprisingly, their numbers are growing—not because their arguments for what they are trying to believe are so convincing, but because many of their new followers have only heard one side of the argument. That is why we at the Pre-Trib Research Center are writing this book and seeking to expose some of the errors of this theory. Our purpose is to show that preterism is unscriptural and inconsistent, and to prove that the return of our Lord to this earth is yet future. What's more, the preterist notion that Christ returned spiritually in A.D. 70 would have come as a surprise to the early church fathers of the first three centuries, for they never mentioned that Christ's second coming was past. They invariably referred to it as a future event.

At the onset I would like to point out that most preterists are Bible-believing Christians who love the Lord and are striving to serve Him. Unfortunately, when it comes to the prophetic passages of Scripture, they do not interpret them literally, as they do those passages pertaining to the gospel and our Lord's deity. This is the cause of our difference. And in fairness to reformed theologians such as R. C. Sproul and Ken Gentry, who both assert they are preterists, we must point out that there are several degrees of preterism. In his book *The Last Days According to Jesus,* Dr. Sproul narrows down preterists to two main divisions: "Full Preterism and Partial Preterism."[1] Reduced to the most significant distinction between them, a full preterist is one who believes all prophecy was fulfilled at the destruction of Jerusalem in

A.D. 70, including the second coming of Jesus. Partial preterists such as Sproul and Gentry believe that even though Matthew 24 and the book of Revelation have largely been fulfilled, they still understand some Bible passages to teach a future second coming (Act 1:9-11; 1 Corinthians 15:51-52; 1 Thessalonians 4:13-18). They see the second coming of Jesus, the resurrection of the dead, the Judgment Seat of Christ, and heaven as yet future. Even Gentry points out that all the church creeds of history mention a future coming of Jesus Christ in power and glory,[2] clear evidence that the preterist view is of recent vintage. It is safe to say and easy to defend that the vast majority of the church has not identified the second coming of Jesus with the A.D. 70 destruction of Jerusalem. Instead, Christians have believed His coming will be physical and is still future!

We are justified in questioning the academic objectivity of some preterists when approaching this subject. One reason is that Revelation chapter 20 uses the phrase "a thousand years" six different times in reference to the kingdom age. These, of course, are not the only biblical references to the coming kingdom of the Messiah. The Hebrew prophets referred to His kingdom many times. Revelation is the only book that mentions the length of that period as "a thousand years." That the Holy Spirit repeated this phrase six times presents a strong case for accepting it as a literal 1,000 years. Preterists, like the reformed theologians from whence they come, try to allegorize prophecy and refuse to face the Bible's teaching of a millennial kingdom on earth when Christ shall reign as King of kings and Lord of lords. In so doing they rob the church of the "blessed hope" (Titus 2:13) we have in the rapture of the church before the Tribulation period and followed immediately by Christ's glorious return. And because some of them are amillennialists (believing there is no specific time when Christ will reign on the earth, as is described in the Bible), they find it convenient to instead promote the notion that Christ came spiritually in A.D. 70 and that we have been living in the kingdom of Christ for these many years.

If such a notion makes you feel cheated because no one is hammering "their swords into plowshares" (Micah 4:3), the curse has not yet been lifted, and we are not living in a world of peace (as the Bible promises for the millennium), do not be surprised. I am confident that if the prophets and apostles were still alive today, they would find such a notion equally confusing.

THE RETURN OF CHRIST

One of the most questionable teachings of preterists is their assertion that Jesus has already come. Admittedly, some have not accepted full-blown preterism yet and suggest instead that Christ came back spiritually in A.D. 70

when the temple and city of Jerusalem were destroyed. Both views fly in the face of the angels' promise in Acts 1:11: "This same Jesus, which is taken up from you into heaven, shall so come in like manner as ye have seen him go into heaven" (KJV). It cannot be contested that the disciples and other believers who witnessed the ascension saw Jesus taken up into heaven in His resurrected physical body, which could eat, be touched, and talk, and in short was a "flesh and bone body," as He Himself described. The angels' promise in Acts 1:11, then, must refer to a physical, literal return of the Savior to this earth.

When Jesus described His second coming, which was to be "immediately after the Tribulation of those days," He said it would be accompanied by "the sign of the Son of man in heaven: and then shall all the tribes of the earth mourn, and *they shall see the Son of man coming in the clouds of heaven with power and great glory*" (Matthew 24:27-30 KJV, emphasis added). That this could refer to anything other than a physical, visible return of Christ to this earth seems irrefutable, especially in light of Acts 1:11.

In a similar vein, John the Revelator in Revelation 1:7 says, "Behold, He is coming with the clouds, and every eye will see Him, even those who pierced Him; and all the tribes of the earth will mourn over Him. So it is to be. Amen." Note again the reference John cited from Jesus' words: "*every eye will see Him, even those who pierced Him*" (emphasis added). All men will see the Lord Jesus Christ at His coming—those in heaven, those on earth, and evidently, even those under the earth "who pierced Him." Again, this cannot refer to anything short of a physical, literal second coming.

Then there is the classic passage in Revelation 19:11-16:

> I saw heaven opened, and behold, a white horse, and He who sat on it was called Faithful and True, and in righteousness He judges and wages war. His eyes are a flame of fire, and on His head are many diadems; and He has a name written on Him which no one knows except Himself. He is clothed with a robe dipped in blood, and His name is called The Word of God. And the armies which are in heaven, clothed in fine linen, white and clean, followed Him on white horses. From His mouth comes a sharp sword, so that with it He may strike the nations, and He will rule them with a rod of iron; and He treads the wine press of the fierce wrath of God, the Almighty. And on His robe and on His thigh He has a name written: KING OF KINGS AND LORD OF LORDS.

How could the Bible possibly be any clearer? When Jesus returns to this earth, He will come physically to set up His long-promised kingdom.

There are, of course, other passages that teach a physical coming of Jesus—for example, 2 Thessalonians 2:8: "Then shall that Wicked be revealed, whom the Lord shall consume with the spirit of his mouth, and shall destroy with the brightness of his coming" (KJV). It should be obvious that for Christ to destroy Satan, who will be standing in the temple and blaspheming God, Christ will have to appear physically.

For preterists now to claim that Jesus has already come is incredible. It was a foreign idea during the first five centuries A.D. and then only possibly mentioned sporadically after that until about 400 years ago. That would require that the apostles, early church fathers, and most theologians until the seventeenth century were wrong! Not until the early seventeenth century—when preterist thinking was applied by the Jesuit Catholic scholar Alcazar to the book of Revelation—was it given much real consideration. LeRoy E. Froom, a painstakingly accurate historian, indicated that Alcazar put forth this theory as a means of counteracting the identification of the pope as the Antichrist. This assumption about the pope was becoming popular as the Bible spread throughout Europe and the common people could read the book of Revelation for themselves.

Dr. R. C. Sproul, for whom I have great respect as a writer and thinker, though we disagree on the literal interpretation of prophecy and whether Christ will return before the millennial kingdom, has not endorsed full preterism. In fact, he cites favorably his friend Ken Gentry as one who believes that "full preterism...falls outside the scope of orthodox Christianity."[3] That is a polite way of saying that those who teach Christ came physically in A.D. 70 are borderline heretics. Where I differ is that I would suggest that those who believe Christ came spiritually and somehow is in control of this messed-up world are also very close to that line, for Scripture teaches the contrary. Christ's second coming is yet future, as taught in Matthew 24:29-31 and Revelation 19:11-21. He will indeed rule this world as "King of kings and Lord of lords" (Revelation 19:16) in a kingdom in which He will enforce a cultural standard of righteousness. No kingdom of righteousness will permit crime, pornography in print or on the Internet, teach godless socialism in our public schools, or denigrate God the Father, our Lord Jesus Christ, or the Holy Spirit.

You can be sure of this: Jesus Christ will come to this earth in power and great glory to set up His kingdom as the Bible predicts, and His coming will be personal and physical!

When all the evidence is considered, we are forced to conclude that the case for a past fulfillment of the prophetic Scriptures is untenable. Too many unanswered questions still exist to make the rapture of the church, the Tribulation period, the second coming of Christ, the establishing of His kingdom on this earth, and other significant events be anything but future—just as the Bible teaches.

QUESTIONS PRETERISTS MUST ANSWER

Before preterism can be accepted by evangelical Christians, there are a number of questions preterists must answer. Many of them will be addressed in this book written largely by the executive director of the Pre-Trib Research Center, Dr. Thomas Ice, and several other scholar-members of the center, such as Dr. Arnold Fruchtenbaum, Dr. Randall Price, Dr. John MacArthur, Dr. Mal Couch, Dr. Larry Spargimino, Andy Woods, Gordon Frantz, and Mark Hitchcock. Each of these men are well qualified to write on the subject of preterism, and among the many points they will present is that preterism is a seventeenth-century invention. As Dr. Harry Ironside (one of my preacher heroes) often said, "Whenever you hear something new, examine it carefully because it may not be true." I have found preterist attempts to answer the following questions to be wanting.

1. How can preterists possibly prove Jesus came back in A.D. 70? Can they produce even one sign that He has been in charge of the world since then? If this has been the millennium He promised, a huge multitude of Christians through the past 2,000 years have been disappointed.

2. How do they prove Satan was bound for a "thousand years" (Revelation 20:1-3) in an evil world rampant with drugs, rape, and murder? When Jesus comes, He is going to be "King of kings and Lord of lords" (Revelation 19:16). Could anyone even suggest that for these last 1,900 years Jesus has been Lord and King over the kings of this earth—kings who have persecuted Christians by the millions (an estimated over 50 million martyrs have been slaughtered for their faith)? To say that Christ is ruler now is a statement that reaches almost blasphemous proportions. Had Christ been King of kings since A.D. 70, you can be sure the martyrs would have lived long and peaceful lives. The millennium that God promised through the Hebrew prophets, apostles, and the Lord Jesus will be like utopia. That is hardly an apt description of the last 1,900 years.

3. How do preterists explain that none of the events of the "end of the age" have ever happened, including the cataclysmic events that are supposed to take place in the heavens?

   For just as the lightning comes from the east and flashes even to the west, so will the coming of the Son of Man be. Wherever the corpse is, there the vultures will gather. But immediately after the Tribulation of those days the sun will be darkened, and the moon will not give its light, and the stars will fall from the sky, and the powers of the heavens will be shaken. And then the sign of the Son of Man will appear in the sky, and then all the tribes of the earth will mourn, and they will see the Son of Man coming on the clouds of the sky with power and great glory. And He will send forth His angels with a great trumpet and they will gather together His elect from the four winds, from one end of the sky to the other (Matthew 24:27-31).

4. What evidence can preterists marshal to show that Christ has been in charge of this world that has known 15,000 wars with millions dead, including the estimated 50 million or more of His followers mentioned earlier who were martyred for their faith? During the millennium, the only people who will die, according to Isaiah 65:17-20, will be sinners:

For behold, I create new heavens and a new earth; and the former things will not be remembered or come to mind. But be glad and rejoice forever in what I create; for behold, I create Jerusalem for rejoicing and her people for gladness. I will also rejoice in Jerusalem and be glad in My people; and there will no longer be heard in her the voice of weeping and the sound of crying. No longer will there be in it an infant who lives but a few days, or an old man who does not live out his days; for the youth will die at the age of one hundred and the one who does not reach the age of one hundred will be thought accursed.

Given the horrors of the past 2,000 years, they could not even come close to being the millennial kingdom of Christ. No, that kingdom is not behind us; it is yet future.

5. What evidence do preterists have that the tragic siege of Jerusalem in A.D. 70 was indeed a fulfillment of Jesus' description of the Great Tribulation? He said it would be a time that would be worse than any other in history, from "the beginning of the world until now, nor ever will" (Matthew 24:21). Anyone who reads history must admit that the Inquisition and Hitler's holocaust were far worse and occurred long after A.D. 70.

6. How can preterists possibly prove that Nero was the Antichrist, as they claim? He was never in Jerusalem, he did not desecrate the temple, nor was he destroyed by the "breath of His [Christ's] mouth at...the appearance of His coming" as Paul promised in 2 Thessalonians 2:8.

Actually, Nero is a poor excuse for an Antichrist. He was a wimpy emperor who preferred to act on the stage of his day and recite poetry than be the Caesar of Rome, and he died by suicide at 31 years of age. Admittedly, the man was evil, like most of his predecessors, but he doesn't even come close to being "a king of fierce countenance" (Daniel 8:23 KJV) or the king who makes a covenant with Israel for seven years and breaks it in three and one half years (Daniel 9:26-27). Nor could he be called the "man of sin" or "the son of perdition" mentioned in 2 Thessalonians 2:3-8. And, as we have seen, Nero was not destroyed by the coming of Christ, but committed suicide by cutting his own throat in A.D. 68. To make him the Antichrist takes intellectual gymnastics that makes a mockery out of both biblical and historical scholarship, for he died two years before the destruction of Jerusalem occurred, which is when preterists claim Christ returned.

Nero went down in history as the emperor who fiddled while Rome burned. Only those preterist "scholars" who need him desperately to fill the role of Antichrist (to keep from admitting that Revelation was written in A.D. 95) can even hold to this view. In truth, such a notion is historically ridiculous. No, the early church had it right: Revelation was written by John in A.D. 95, which means the book of Revelation describes yet future events of the last days just before Jesus comes back to this earth. This is what the early church believed for the first few centuries—a point made irrefutably clear by author Mark Hitchcock in chapter 6 of this book.

7. How can preterists prove from historical evidence that the 21 judgments of the Tribulation—the seal, trumpet, and vial (bowl) judgments—occurred during the seven years prior to the destruction of Jerusalem in A.D. 70? These judgments describe the turning of water to blood, three earthquakes (including the largest earthquake in the history of the world—Revelation 16:18), a worldwide war that wipes out 25 percent of the earth's population (Revelation 6:8), three plagues that wipe out one-third of the remaining population (Revelation 9:18), the Antichrist's demands to be worshiped, and the taking of his mark or being guillotined to death. If these judgments occurred, as preterists say, how did they escape any mention in the annals of history? The truth is, Revelation 6-19 has never even come close to happening in history. It is still future.

8. How do preterists explain the fact that their theory was never taken seriously by Bible scholars until the seventeenth century, when the Jesuit

priest Alcazar developed it to make people think the book of Revelation had been fulfilled back in the first 300 years of the church so people would stop calling the pope the Antichrist and the Catholic Church the Harlot of Babylon? To make matters worse, Alcazar's ideas were picked up by liberal scholars and perpetuated by those who reject the fact that the Bible was verbally inspired. The truth is, preterism is held only by those who allegorize or symbolize prophecy and, for the most part, is advocated by some in the reformed church who desperately need the tenets of preterism to keep their system of theology alive.

9. How can preterists state that Zechariah 12:3 has been fulfilled, saying that "all the nations of the world" came against Jerusalem when the Lord returned in A.D. 70, when only Rome came against Jerusalem in A.D. 70 and conquered it?

10. How can preterists possibly say Jerusalem's deliverance (prophesied in Zechariah 12:8) took place at the second coming of Christ after Jerusalem was destroyed in A.D. 70? Josephus, a Hebrew Roman citizen who wrote an account of the event, did not present it as a deliverance but as a wanton destruction. The deliverance Zechariah promised is yet future.

11. The preterist viewpoint says the events of the Tribulation took place before Christ's return in A.D. 70. But when did God destroy all the nations that came against Jerusalem? (Zechariah 12:9). Never—it is still a future event!

12. Did the Jews, as a nation, turn to Christ in A.D. 70 as Zechariah 12:10 promises? No—that is a yet future event.

13. Where is the evidence that two-thirds of the Jews were killed and one-third accepted their Messiah in A.D. 70, as required by Zechariah 13:8?

14. Zechariah 14:1-4 says the Mount of Olives will split in two at Christ's return. But that didn't happen in A.D. 70. And if He did return and split the Mount of Olives in A.D. 70, when was it moved back together, the way it is today? It's much easier to see Zechariah 14:1-4 as still in the future.

15. If Christ returned in A.D. 70 as preterists claim, then when were the "sheep" (believers) taken to heaven and the "goats" (unsaved) cast into hell? Who would have been left on earth in A.D. 71 to reproduce and bring the earth's population to today's six billion people?

16. If Christ returned in A.D. 70, when did the church go up in the rapture, or when was 1 Thessalonians 4:13-18 fulfilled? What about the judgment

of the nations as described in Matthew 25:31-46? Nothing even close to what is described in those passages has ever transpired. We insist that the judgment of the nations is yet future, when the "sheep" (believers) are permitted to go into God's kingdom and the "goats" are cast into hell.

17. If Christ returned in A.D. 70, then why aren't Christians in the Father's house, as Jesus promised in John 14:1-3?

And the list goes on! For example, when was Babylon destroyed "in one day" (Revelation 18:8), putting an end to the pagan religions that began in Babylon? Or when did the kings of the earth mourn over the death of Babylon? Or when was Satan bound in the bottomless pit for 1,000 years? And weren't most of those years when he supposedly couldn't tempt anyone known as "the dark ages"? How could the world become so void of Christianity and the light of the gospel while Satan was bound? Such a notion is preposterous on its face.

Recently, Dr. Thomas Ice debated one of the leading defenders of modern preterism at a well-known Christian university. Near the end of this debate, Dr. Ice asked his opponent, "If Christ returned in A.D. 70 as you claim, on what day did he come?" I submit that if Christ came back to this earth and all those who saw Him "mourned" as the Bible said they would, you can be sure it would have been a specific day we could point to in recorded history. Such a day would not have gone unnoticed by people. The only answer the preterist could give was, "The Bible says no man knows the day or the hour." That is an obvious reference to the future, not the past! Why would he use such an answer? Because preterists have none! They cannot point to a day and hour when Christ returned in A.D. 70—or any other year for that matter.

So far, I've mentioned only some of the many questions that remain unanswered in the preterist system of interpreting prophecy allegorically or spiritualizing it away. It is much easier to understand prophecy the way it was intended to be read—that is, literally, unless the facts of the immediate context clearly indicate otherwise. One important reason for interpreting Bible prophecy literally is because so many Old Testament prophecies have already been fulfilled literally, which serves as a precedent for the prophecies that have yet to be fulfilled. We know that 109 Old Testament prophecies of Jesus' first coming were fulfilled literally, and that is one reason we know without question that He is the Messiah. It stands to reason, then, that the 321 prophecies regarding His second coming will also be fulfilled literally.

When all the facts are considered, we are forced to conclude that the evidence for a fulfillment of the prophetic scriptures in A.D. 70 is untenable and that too many unanswered questions still exist to make the rapture of the church, the Tribulation period, the second coming of Christ, and the establishing of His kingdom on this earth and other significant events to be anything but future, just as the Bible teaches.

We would be better served by accepting the time-honored belief of the early church: that the apostle John did indeed write the book of Revelation in A.D. 95 while sentenced to the Isle of Patmos for "the testimony of Jesus Christ" (Revelation 1:2). A literal and the most sensible reading of the Scriptures renders the events of Revelation as being yet future, a perspective the evangelical church almost universally agrees upon. Certainly we who are members of the Pre-Trib Research Center are unalterably opposed to preterism, primarily because it is both scripturally and historically impossible.

I am confident that by the time you finish this book, you will agree!

Chapter 1

WHAT IS PRETERISM?

THOMAS ICE

The Olivet Discourse is not about the second coming of Christ. It is a prophecy of the destruction of Jerusalem in A.D. 70.
—David Chilton (preterist)[1]

The book of Revelation is not about the second coming of Christ. It is about the destruction of Israel and Christ's victory over His enemies in the establishment of the New Covenant Temple. In fact, as we shall see, the word *coming* as used in the book of Revelation never refers to the second coming. Revelation prophesies the judgment of God on apostate Israel; and while it does briefly point to events beyond its immediate concerns, that is done merely as a "wrap-up," to show that the ungodly will never prevail against Christ's Kingdom. But the main focus of Revelation is upon events which were soon to take place.
—David Chilton (preterist)[2]

Before we begin a careful examination of preterism and comparing its teachings to Scripture, it's necessary to have a clear definition of the preterist approach to prophecy. For a person who knows little or nothing about prophecy, preterist teachings might seem a legitimate and credible interpretation of biblical prophecy. It's not until you hold preterism up to careful scriptural scrutiny and historical facts that its shortcomings become obvious. We're going to begin by looking at preterism in relation to the other systems used for interpreting biblical prophecy. It is necessary to define and delineate these different systems because even theological scholars sometimes confuse preterism and what's known as historicism. This confusion is probably the result of lack of exposure to proponents of the various views. Simply put, there are four approaches to interpreting prophecy, and all relate to time: past, present, future, and timeless. These are known as preterism (past), historicism (present), futurism (future), and idealism (timeless).

FOUR MAJOR VIEWS

Preterism

Kenneth Gentry, a reconstructionist preterist, defines his view as follows:

> The term "preterism" is based on the Latin *preter*, which means "past." Preterism refers to that understanding of certain eschatological passages which holds that *they have already come to fulfillment*....
>
> The preterist approach teaches, for instance, that many of the prophecies of Revelation and the first portion of the Olivet Discourse have already been fulfilled. Matthew 24:1-34 (and parallels) in the Olivet Discourse was fulfilled in the events surrounding the fall of Jerusalem in A.D. 70. In Revelation, most of the prophecies before Revelation 20 find fulfillment in the fall of Jerusalem (A.D. 70).[3]

Preterist Gary DeMar says, "A preterist is someone who believes that certain prophecies have been fulfilled, that is, their fulfillment is in the *past*."[4] Thus, a preterist interpretation of a given prophecy would attempt to explain it as an event that has already taken place. Yet not all preterists are in agreement regarding certain prophecies, and we'll look at the spectrum of preterist viewpoints later in this chapter.

Historicism

Those who followed events surrounding David Koresh in Waco, Texas, may be interested to know that he, along with Adventists, are among the few historicists of contemporary times. This view was popular from the time of the Reformation to the beginning of the twentieth century, and has diminished since. "The historicist view, sometimes called the continuous-historical view, contends that Revelation is a symbolic presentation of the entire course of the history of the church from the close of the first century to the end of time."[5] This spiritualistic approach is built upon the day/year theory, whereby the 1260 days (literally 3 ½ years) mentioned in Daniel and Revelation cover the time (1260 years) of the domination of Antichrist over the church. Another variation is to apply the day/year theory to the 2,300 days of Daniel 8:14. Thus, the historicist attempts to figure out when Antichrist came to power (i.e., the Roman Church and the papacy) by adding 1,260 or 2,300 years to arrive at the time of the second coming and the defeat of Antichrist. So, if this time started some time during the reign of Constantine, say A.D. 350, then you add 1,260 years and you would come out with 1,610. American William Miller used a variation of the day/year theory by using the 2,300 days of Daniel 8:14 as the basis of his attempts to guess the date of the second coming.

Another feature of historicism is the attempt to correlate events described in Revelation with events occurring in the present church age. As the historicist interprets contemporary events as aligning with the description of the second coming of Christ in Revelation 19, he attempts to determine the precise year of Christ's return via use of the day/year scheme. An example of this can be seen in the following:

Albert Barnes' Historicist Interpretation of Revelation 6–19[6]

Item	Description	Barnes' Historical Interpretation
1st seal (Rev 6)	White horse— a conqueror	Peace and triumph in the Roman Empire from Domitian to Commodus (96–180)
2nd seal (Rev 6)	Red horse— war	Bloodshed from the death of Commodus onward (193–)
3rd seal (Rev 6)	Black horse— famine	Calamity in the time of Caracalla and onward (211–)
4th seal (Rev 6)	Green horse— death	Death by famine, etc., Decius to Callianus (243–268)
5th seal	Martyrs	Martyrdom under Diocletian (284–304)
6th seal (Rev 6)	Heavenly disturbances	Consternation at the threat of Barbarian invasions, Goths and Huns (365–)
1st trumpet (Rev 8)	⅓ earth smitten	Alaric and Goths invade the Western Roman Empire (395–410)
2nd trumpet (Rev 8)	⅓ sea smitten	Genseric and Vandals invade (428–468)
3rd trumpet (Rev 8)	⅓ rivers smitten	Attila and Huns invade (433–453)

4th trumpet (Rev 8)	⅓ sun, moon smitten	Odoacer and Heruli conquer Western Roman Empire (476–490)
5th trumpet (Rev 9)	Torment of locusts	Mohometan and Saracen powers rise in the East (5 months of Rev 9:5, 150 years!)
6th trumpet (Rev 9)	horsemen slay ⅓ men	Turkish power rises in the East
Angel and little book (Rev 10)	Angel gives book to John	The Protestant Reformation. The 7 thunders of Rev 10:3-4— Papal false doctrine
The beast and false prophet (Rev 13)	They blaspheme 42 months	The evil career of ecclesiastical and civil Rome, 42 months of Rev 13:5, 1,260 years!
First five bowls are poured out (Rev 16)	Wrath by sores; sea, rivers and sun smitten; darkness	The French Revolution and its aftermath strike at the Papacy
6th bowl of wrath poured out (Rev 16)	Way prepared for armies to come to Armageddon	The froglike spirits call Paganism, Muhammadanism, and Romanism prepare for their final struggle against the Gospel
7th bowl poured out (Rev 16)	Earthquake and hail; Babylon remembered for wrath	Papal power overthrown
Babylon destroyed (Rev 17-18)	Babylon destroyed	Destruction of Papal power
Battle of Armageddon (Rev 19)	Christ slays the beast and his armies	The Gospel finally triumphs morally over its foes who appear "as if" they're eaten by fowls

"The historicist is constantly confronted with the dilemma of a far-fetched spiritualization in order to maintain the chain of historical events," states Dr. Tenney, "or else if he makes the events literal in accordance with the language of the text he is compelled to acknowledge that no comparable events in history have happened."[7] The demise of historicism has resulted in less date-setting in our own day than had occurred during the era when historicism was popular.

Idealism

Idealists hold to an atemporal approach to Revelation and prophetic literature. While they may or may not believe that there will be/has been timing attached to eschatological passages, they do not think that it is important or knowable. Thus, they stress the *principles* or *lessons* that can be learned from prophecy. G. K. Beale, an idealist, describes his position as follows: "The book of Revelation is not merely a futurology but also a redemptive-historical and theological psychology for the church's thinking."[8] Idealist Raymond Calkins describes idealism through the following five propositions:

1. It is an irresistible summons to heroic living.

2. The book contains matchless appeals to endurance.

3. It tells us that evil is marked for overthrow *in the end*.

4. It gives us a new and wonderful picture of Christ.

5. The Apocalypse reveals to us the fact that history is in the mind of God and in the hand of Christ as the author and reviewer of the moral destinies of men.[9]

Futurism

Those who see predictive Bible prophecy as still being future are known as futurists. Futurists see eschatological passages being fulfilled during a future time, primarily during the seventieth week of Daniel, at the second coming of Christ, and during the millennium. While all dispensationalists are futurists, not all futurists are dispensationalists. Futurists are also the most literal in their interpretation of prophecy passages. Dr. Tenney says,

> The more literal an interpretation that one adopts, the more strongly will he be construed to be a futurist. The object like a burning mountain cast into the sea ([Revelation] 8:8), the opening of the bottomless pit (9:2), and many other episodes must be interpreted symbolically if they are to be taken as applying to current or to past history. If they are yet to come, they may be a more accurate description of actual phenomena than most expositors have realized, for the physical and psychical researchers of recent years have opened to the mind of man worlds that in John's time were completely unknown.[10]

Futurism is the view espoused by the contributors to this book.

THE TYPES OF PRETERISM

Generally, there are three kinds of preterism: mild, moderate, and extreme.

Mild Preterism

This was the earliest form of preterism to develop and the only kind to be put forth until the eighteenth century (see the chapter on the history of preterism). A Jesuit friar, Alcazar, is said to have provided the "first systematic presentation" in 1614.[11] Alcazar divided Revelation into two major sections (chapters 6–12 and 13–19), "which dealt respectively with the church's conflict against Judaism and against paganism."[12] Chapters 6–12 were said to focus upon an A.D. 70 fulfillment, while chapters 13–19 were seen as not being fulfilled until the fourth-century rise of Constantine and the Christianization of the Roman Empire. Mild preterism is really a blend of some A.D. 70 preterism (chapters 6–12) with historicism (chapters 13–19).

"Alcazar was the first to apply Preterism to the Apocalypse with anything like completeness," concluded LeRoy Froom. "It thus pioneered the way for acceptance first by Hugo Grotius of the Netherlands, and later by the German Rationalists."[13] Mild preterism, unlike the other two forms, does not see prophecy concluding with the destruction of Jerusalem in A.D. 70. Instead, "Alcazar made the church's millennium of rest to date from the downfall of old pagan Rome—his apocalyptical Babylon—with the destruction of Roman idolatry in the spiritual fires of the Catholic religion."[14] Mild preterism "contended that the prophecies of Revelation were descriptive of the victory of the early church, as fulfilled in the downfall of the Jewish nation and the overthrow of pagan Rome, and in this way limited their range to the first six centuries of the Christian Era, and making Nero the Antichrist."[15]

I am not aware of any on the contemporary scene who advocate mild preterism, even though historically it has been the most widely adopted form of preterism. Some commentators who were mild preterists include Moses Stuart,[16] R. H. Charles,[17] Henry Barclay Swete,[18] and Isbon T. Beckwith.[19]

Moderate Preterism

Moderate preterism has become, in our day, mainstream preterism. Today it appears to be the most widely held version of preterism. Simply put, moderates see almost all prophecy as fulfilled in the A.D. 70 destruction of Jerusalem, but they also believe that a few passages still teach a yet future second coming (Acts 1:9-11; 1 Corinthians 15:51-53; 1 Thessalonians 4:16-17) and the resurrection of believers at Christ's bodily return. Moderate preterism is more A.D. 70-oriented than mild preterism, but stops short of full preterism's insistence that all prophecy was fulfilled in A.D. 70.

Partial preterist R. C. Sproul describes his view as follows:

> While partial preterists acknowledge that in the destruction of Jerusalem in A.D. 70 there was *a* parousia or coming of Christ, they maintain that it was not *the* parousia. That is, the coming of Christ in A.D. 70 was a coming in judgment on the Jewish nation, indicating the end of the Jewish age and the fulfillment of a day of the Lord. Jesus really did come in judgment at this time, fulfilling his prophecy in the Olivet Discourse. But this was not the final or ultimate coming of Christ. The parousia, in its fullness, will extend far beyond the Jewish nation and will be universal in its scope and significance. It will come, not at the end of the Jewish age, but at the end of human history as we know it. It will be, not merely a day of the Lord, but the final and ultimate day of the Lord.[20]

In addition to R. C. Sproul, some well-known moderate preterists include Kenneth L. Gentry, Jr.,[21] Gary DeMar,[22] and the late David Chilton[23] (who converted to full preterism after all his books were published).

Extreme Preterism

Extreme or full preterists view themselves as "consistent" preterists (we will call this view full preterism throughout the book). If this is true, then where does their consistency lead? Extreme preterists believe that "the second coming MUST HAVE already occurred, since it was one of the things predicted in the O.T. which had to be fulfilled by the time Jerusalem was destroyed in 70 A.D.!"[24] This means there will never be a future second coming, for it already occurred in A.D. 70. Further, there will be no bodily resurrection of believers, which is said to have occurred in A.D. 70 in conjunction with the second coming. Full preterists believe that we now have been spiritually resurrected and will live forever with spiritual bodies when we die.

Full preterism does not see a prophesied end of history. In fact, full preterists say we are not merely in the millennium, but we are now living in what we would call the eternal state or the new heavens and new earth of Revelation 21–22. There are many other elements of full preterism, but needless to say, the proponents spiritualize the text of Scripture to an extreme degree while arguing that they are conservative, orthodox Christians.

Champions of this view include the originator of full preterism, the British Congregationalist J. Stuart Russell,[25] who taught the odd view that because Christ returned in judgment during A.D. 70, the rapture must have taken place in the year A.D. 66.[26] The modern-day American champion of full preterism is Max R. King and his son, Tim, of the Parkman Road Church of Christ in Warren, Ohio.[27] Formerly moderate preterist David Chilton converted to full preterism about a couple years before his death in 1997.[28] Other full preterists include Ed Stevens,[29] Don K. Preston,[30] John Noe,[31] and John L. Bray.[32]

Partial preterists like Dr. Gentry and Dr. Sproul believe that full preterism is heretical because it denies a future second coming and cannot hold to an orthodox view of the resurrection which is associated with Christ's return.[33] Dr. Sproul says of full preterist Max King, "For this schema to work, the traditional idea of resurrection must be replaced with a metaphorical idea of resurrection, dying to an old redemptive age or eon and 'rising' to the new eon."[34] Dr. Gentry lays out a number of problems with full preterism in an article entitled, "A Brief Theological Analysis of Hyper-Preterism."[35] "First, hyper-preterism is heterodox," declares Dr. Gentry. "It is outside of the creedal orthodoxy of Christianity."[36] (Dr. Gentry usually refers to full preterism as hyper-preterism.) Concerning the full preterists' faulty view of the resurrection, Dr. Gentry notes: "...there is a serious problem with the removal of the physical resurrection from systematic theology. Christ's resurrection is expressly declared to be the paradigm of our own (1 Cor. 15:20ff). Yet we know that His was a physical, tangible resurrection (Luke 24:39), whereas ours is (supposedly) spiritual. What happens to the biblically defined analogy between Christ's resurrection and ours in the hyper-preterist system?"[37]

In this book, our focus will be upon refuting partial preterism. If partial preterism is deemed untenable, then obviously the more extreme form will not be viable as well. What's more, we believe that when one ventures into extreme or full preterism, then he has moved away from orthodoxy into false teaching. Because full preterism believes that Christ's only coming (i.e., the second coming) occurred in A.D. 70 and because the translation and resurrection of believers are clearly connected with that event in Scripture (1 Corinthians 15; 1 Thessalonians 4:13-17), then that means full preterism is heretical.

THE IMPLICATIONS OF PRETERISM

Strange Preterist Implications

The preterist perspective of Bible prophecy greatly affects events, personalities, and chronologies. If preterism is true, then we would have a very different view of the past and future than Christendom has traditionally held to. We would have a vastly different view of Christianity altogether. The following list includes many of the conclusions that preterism yields:

- *The Great Tribulation* "took place in the Fall of Israel. It will not be repeated and thus is not a future event."[38]

- *The Great Apostasy* "happened in the first century. We therefore have no Biblical warrant to expect increasing apostasy as history progresses; instead, we should expect the increasing Christianization of the world."[39]

- *The Last Days* "is a Biblical expression for the period between Christ's Advent and the destruction of Jerusalem in A.D. 70: the 'last days' of Israel."[40]

- *The Antichrist* "is a term used by John to describe the widespread apostasy of the Christian church prior to the Fall of Jerusalem. In general, any apostate teacher or system can be called 'antichrist'; but the word does not refer to some 'future Führer.'"[41]

- *The Rapture* is "the 'catching up' of the living saints 'to meet the Lord in the air.' The Bible does not teach any separation between the second coming and the Rapture; they are simply different aspects of the Last Day."[42]

- *The Second Coming* "coinciding with the Rapture and the Resurrection, will take place *at the end* of the Millennium, when history is sealed at the Judgment."[43]

- *The Beast* "of Revelation was a symbol of both Nero in particular and the Roman Empire in general."[44]

- *The False Prophet* "of Revelation was none other than the leadership of apostate Israel, who rejected Christ and worshiped the Beast."[45]

- *The Great Harlot* of Revelation was "*Jerusalem* which had always been…falling into apostasy and persecuting the prophets…which had ceased to be the City of God."[46]

- *The Millennium* "is the Kingdom of Jesus Christ, which He established at His First Advent.…the period between the First and Second Advents of Christ; the Millennium is going on *now*, with Christians reigning as kings on earth."[47] "Other postmillennialists interpret the millennium as a future stage of history. Though the kingdom is already inaugurated, there will someday be a greater outpouring of the Spirit than the church has yet experienced."[48]

- *The First Resurrection* of Revelation 20:5 is a "spiritual resurrection: our justification and regeneration in Christ."[49]

- *The Thousand Years* of Revelation 20:2-7 is a "large, rounded-off number....the number *ten* contains the idea of a fullness of *quantity;* in other words, it stands for *manyness.* A thousand multiplies and intensifies this (10 x 10 x 10), in order to express great vastness.... represent a vast, undefined period of time....It may require a million years."[50]

- *The New Creation* "has already begun: The Bible describes our salvation in Christ, both now and in eternity, as 'a new heaven and a new earth.' "[51]

- *Israel* In contrast to the eventual faithfulness and empowerment by the Holy Spirit of the church, "ethnic Israel was excommunicated for its apostasy and will never again be God's Kingdom."[52] Thus, "the Bible does not tell of any future plan for Israel as a *special* nation."[53] It is said that the church is now that new nation (Matthew 21:43), and that Christ destroyed the Jewish state. "In destroying Israel, Christ transferred the blessings of the kingdom from Israel to a new people, the church."[54]

- *The New Jerusalem* "the City of God, is the Church, now and forever."[55]

- *The Final Apostasy* refers to Satan's last gasp in history (Revelation 20:7-10). "The Dragon will be released for a short time, to deceive the nations in his last-ditch attempt to overthrow the Kingdom."[56] This will be "in the far future, at the close of the Messianic age,"[57] shortly before the second coming.

- *Armageddon* "was for St. John a symbol of defeat and desolation, a 'Waterloo' signifying the defeat of those who set themselves against God, who obey false prophets instead of the true.... *There never was or will be a literal 'Battle of Armageddon,' for there is no such place.*"[58]

AN ATTEMPT TO HELP GOD

In the introduction of his book on prophecy, Dr. Sproul says he believes he is helping to save biblical Christianity from liberal skeptics like Bertrand Russell and Albert Schweitzer by adopting a preterist interpretation of Bible prophecy: "One of Russell's chief criticisms of the Jesus portrayed in the Gospels is that Jesus was wrong with respect to the timing of his future return," notes Dr. Sproul. "At issue for Russell is the time-frame reference of these prophecies. Russell charges that Jesus failed to return during the time frame he had predicted."[59] Dr. Sproul, along with many other preterists, answers this charge from liberals by saying that Jesus did return—in the first century. He returned spiritually through the acts of the Roman army, who destroyed Jerusalem and the Temple in A.D. 70.

However, when it comes to the Bible, we cannot fight liberalism with liberalism. Dr. Sproul believes that he is defending the integrity of Scripture by adopting the preterist viewpoint. However, in reality, I believe he is adopting a naturalistic interpretation that too many liberals feel at home with. While Dr. Sproul sees Matthew 24 as a prophecy that was fulfilled in the first century, liberal preterists join him in giving a naturalistic explanation even though they do so from a different framework. Ultimately, they both deny that our Lord prophesied a supernatural, bodily, visible return of Christ in fulfillment of Matthew 24.

Dr. Sproul and other preterists would not find it "necessary" to defend the Bible against liberal skeptics if they adopted the dispensationalist view, which distinguishes between the rapture, which could take place without warning at any moment, and the second coming, which will be preceded by the signs mentioned in Matthew 24. It's true that many of the post-apostolic church fathers believed that Jesus would come back possibly in their day, but the New Testament only teaches that Christ's coming in the clouds to rapture His church is *imminent* (1 Corinthians 1:7; Philippians 3:20; 1 Thessalonians 1:10; Titus 2:13; Hebrews 9:28; 1 Peter 1:13; Jude 21)—that is, an event that could have taken place at any time during the last 2,000 years. Scripture does not need to be rescued from critics by adopting the naturalistic preterist interpretation.

PRETERISTS AND THE OLIVET DISCOURSE

The crux of preterism is the belief that prophecy was declared and destined to be fulfilled within the generation of Christ's earthly ministry. Thus, the whole system is totally dependent upon what preterists consider the "timing" passages. Gary DeMar tells us that "one of the first things a Christian must learn in interpreting the Bible is to pay attention to the time texts. Failing to recognize the proximity of a prophetic event will throw off its intended meaning."[60] When challenged about details that do not seem to fit a first-century fulfillment, preterists fall back upon their belief that they have firmly established that the Bible teaches a first-century fulfillment of the debated passages. "The New Testament clearly states that the 'end of all things' was at hand....The last days were in operation in the *first century!*"[61] With this archimedean starting point established in their mind, which almost always starts with Matthew 24:34, preterists believe they are justified in spiritualizing prophetic texts so that they have an A.D. 70 fulfillment. For example, Kenneth Gentry declares, "The fulfillment of Matthew 24:4-33 in the destruction of Jerusalem is a most reasonable and even necessary conclusion....The past fulfillment of most of the prophecies in Revelation 4–19 is compellingly suggested by the various time indicators contained in its less symbolic, more didactic (instructional) introduction and conclusion."[62]

Thus, anyone who wants to understand the preterist position must begin by examining the number-one "time text" preterists believe lays the foundation for their system. Let's begin by reading about their belief about this "time-text" in their own words. Then in the upcoming chapters we'll learn how to respond biblically to this belief.

The Preterist Belief

Preterist Gary DeMar says, "Matthew 24:1-34 is a prophecy that was fulfilled in A.D. 70."[63] As we consider the way preterists interpret Matthew 24, we must first look at their understanding of Matthew 23. Gentry says, "Who could deny that Matthew 23, which introduces Matthew 24, relates to a soon coming judgment upon first century Israel?"[64] So, how *do* preterists interpret Matthew 24:1-34? The following list cites a preterist interpretation of each significant word or phrase found in Matthew 24:1-34:

The Preterist Interpretations

Verse 5—"*For many will come in My name, saying, 'I am the Christ,' and will mislead many.*"

"There are a number of examples of great pretenders who almost certainly made Messianic claims. Simon in Acts 8:9,10 may be an example of such.... Justin Martyr mentions Simon, and others....Such false Christs are mentioned in John's first epistle, where John calls them 'antichrists.'... These are the many (*polloi*) false christs mentioned in Matthew 24:5....such characters would play an important role in the religious and cultural foment that led to the A.D. 67–70 Jewish War with Rome....Josephus mentions the 'deceivers and impostors, under the pretense of divine inspiration fostering revolutionary changes' in the A.D. 50s, along with 'the Egyptian false prophet,' who even operated at the Mount of Olives (*Wars* 2:13:5; cp. Acts 21:38)."[65]

Verses 6-7—"*You will be hearing of wars and rumors of wars. See that you are not frightened, for those things must take place, but that is not yet the end. For nation will rise against nation, and kingdom against kingdom, and in various places there will be famines and earthquakes.*"

"The preterist approach to this passage, however, is quite relevant to the situation of Jesus' hearers.... 'Wars and rumors of wars' do serve as *significant* harbingers of the end of the temple....This is the era of the Jewish War, which resulted in the destruction of the temple stone by stone, and the Roman Civil Wars of the infamous 'Year of Four Emperors' (A.D. 68–69), when Rome almost collapsed. Consequently, as the events began unfolding up to the Jewish War, the Christians were to be forewarned of the coming devastation of Jerusalem, which would be the Great Tribulation. Thus, the 'wars and rumors of wars' were truly *significant* to that 'generation.'.... During the Roman Civil Wars, several nations revolted in an attempt to leave the Empire. It literally was 'nation against nation.'"[66]

"A major, large-scale famine is found prophesied and fulfilled in Acts 11:28....This is probably the famine mentioned by Josephus in Jerusalem.... There was also the famous famine that raged in Jerusalem during the Roman siege....Classical writers testify to the widespread, recurring famines of the era of the A.D. 50s through the 60s. For instance...Tacitus... (*Annals* 12:43). Pestilence, of course, follows especially fast in the train of famine... pestilential woes of Jerusalem during the siege...in Rome...."[67]

"A particularly dreadful earthquake shook Jerusalem in A.D. 67....Tacitus mentions earthquakes in Crete, Rome, Apamea, Phrygia, Campania, Laodicea...and Pompeii....Severe earthquakes plagued the reigns of the emperors Caligula and Claudius and in Asia, Achaia, Syria, and Macedonia. Of this era it has been observed: 'Perhaps no period in the world's history has ever been so marked by these convulsions as that which intervenes between the Crucifixion and the destruction of Jerusalem.'"[68]

Verse 9—*"Then they will deliver you to tribulation, and will kill you, and you will be hated by all nations because of My name."*

"This is a continuation and expansion of Matthew 23:34-36, which clearly applies to the first century....The pagan Roman historian Tacitus speaks of Christians in the era of Nero as universally 'hated for their crimes.'"[69]

Verse 11—*"Many false prophets will arise and will mislead many."*

False prophets were a problem then, as well as false Christs....Josephus records false prophets arising among the Jews. Because of this, Jesus urges His disciples to endurance through these troublesome times (Matthew 24:12). The chaos surrounding the Temple's destruction will eventually end."[70]

Verse 14—*"This gospel of the kingdom shall be preached in the whole world as a testimony to all the nations, and then the end will come."*

"The 'world' to which the 'gospel of the kingdom was preached' (the Roman Empire) was provided a 'witness' to all of its particular 'nations.' It is important to remember the contextual setting, again. The whole discourse was generated by Christ's reference to the destruction of the Jewish temple and the disciples' concern with the end of the Jewish age (Matthew 24:2-3). The 'witness' provided throughout 'all the nations' of the *oikumene* was a witness or testimony especially against the *Jews*, regarding the coming of the *kingdom* of Christ, which had been presented to and rejected by the Jews....Now let me point out the fulfillment of this prophecy in the first century. In Acts 2:5 we have a reference to the representation present at the pentecostal sermon of Peter....Here we have a gathering before the preaching of the gospel, a gathering that meets the requirements of Matthew 24:14, at least *representationally*....If Paul can state Romans 10:18 and Colossians 1:6 and 23 as fact in his lifetime, why can we not see these as fulfillments of Matthew 24:14?"[71]

Verse 15—*"Therefore when you see the abomination of desolation which was spoken of through Daniel the prophet, standing in the holy place (let the reader understand)...."*

"I believe an irrefutable case can be presented for the 'abomination of desolation' being fulfilled in the August/September, A.D. 70 destruction of the Temple by the armies of the Roman general Titus."[72]

Verses 21-22—*"Then there will be a great tribulation, such as has not occurred since the beginning of the world until now, nor ever will. Unless those days had been cut short, no life would have been saved; but for the sake of the elect those days will be cut short."*

"How are we to reconcile such dramatic statements to the A.D. 70 event?...*First*, Christ *did* say 'all these things' will happen to 'this generation' (Matthew 24:34). And He *did* say this in the context of dealing with the destruction of the very Temple then standing (Matthew 23:36–24:3).... *Second*, we must understand this passage from the Jewish perspective in Christ's day....1,100,000 Jews perished in the siege of Jerusalem.... 'throughout the whole history of the human race, we meet with but few, if any instances of slaughter and devastation at all to be compared with this.'...as awful as the Jewish loss of life was, the utter devastation of Jerusalem, the final destruction of the temple, and the conclusive cessation of the sacrificial system were lamented even more. The *covenantal significance* of the loss of the temple stands as the most dramatic outcome of the War. Hence, any Jewish calamity after A.D. 70 would pale in comparison to the redemptive-historical significance of the loss of the temple.... *Third*, we must understand the significance of the event from the divine perspective. It must be regarded as the holy judgment of God for the wicked crucifixion of His Son by the Jews....*Fourth*...the Lord mentions the Noahic Flood (verses 38-39), which *actually did* destroy the *entire* world, except for one family....Christ's language is *not* meant to be taken literally. It is dramatic hyperbole, justified by the gravity of the situation. Not every Jew was killed, but its devastation was such that had God not limited it, then surely *all of Israel* would have been totally destroyed (cp. Matthew 24:22)....*Fifth* this unique-event language of Christ is fairly common stock-in-trade terminology in prophetic writing....Clearly, the unique-event language is common parlance in prophetic literature. It is not to be pressed literally, as is evident from all the evidence above."[73]

Verse 27—*"Just as the lightning comes from the east and flashes even to the west, so will the coming of the Son of Man be."*

"Quite emphatically the Lord warned His disciples that there would be no *visible, bodily* coming by Him in those days. He twice states that any report of His physical presence would be erroneous…(Matthew 24:23)…. (Matthew 24:26)….If He were expected to appear visibly at some point in the narrative, then such universal prohibitions would have thwarted pointing to Him when He actually did come! Yet there was to be a 'coming' of Christ in that day… (Matthew 24:27). This, however, is a spiritual judgment-coming, rather than a bodily coming.…First, the local context demands that this coming occur in 'this generation' (Matthew 24:34)…. Second…the *direction* is clearly in view (given the spatial imagery of Scripture: heaven being up and hell being down). This directional factor probably is involved here, in that the destroying armies sent by Christ came at Jerusalem from an easterly direction.…Third, in the wider biblical context, we discover lightning being set forth as *that which is terrifying* (Ezekiel 19:16; 20:18) *because so violently destructive*.…The idea of terrifying destruction is surely involved in Matthew 24.…But even if the visibility aspect of lightning were intended here…that would not indicate that it spoke of the Second Advent. On this approach, the false christs that the Jews vainly looked for in various *hidden localities* (Matthew 24:26) would be overshone by the awesome and public *Israel-wide* destruction of the very visible Roman armies, whom the true Christ sent to do His bidding."[74]

Verse 28—*"Wherever the corpse is, there the vultures will gather."*

"The Roman ensigns, which were set up by Titus in the holy of holies in the Temple and sacrificed to, were *eagles!*…Certainly this was a grievous abomination. The presence of this gathering of eagles was indicative of the death of Israel.…Ultimately, upon Israel came 'all the righteous blood shed on the earth' (Matthew 23:35). This came through the providential instrument of God: Rome, with its eagle ensign. Israel was judicially dead, its carcass was devoured by the eagles of Rome."[75]

Verse 29—*"Immediately after the Tribulation of those days the sun will be darkened, and the moon will not give its light, and the stars will fall from the sky, and the powers of the heavens will be shaken."*

"How then shall we understand verse 29? Rather than interpreting it literally, we must interpret it covenantally!…By the very requirement of the context, *this passage speaks of the collapse of political Israel in* A.D. *70.* And since the immediate context demands that these events occur in Christ's generation, we should see if there is biblical warrant for speaking of *national catastrophe* in terms of *cosmic destruction*....Such imagery, then, indicates that the God of the heavens (the Creator of the sun, moon, and stars) is moving in judgment against a nation (blotting out their light). When a national government collapses in war and upheaval, it is often poetically portrayed as a *cosmic catastrophe—an undoing of Creation*....Consequently, we may see how easy it is to apply Matthew 24:29 to the destruction of Jerusalem in A.D. 70. The imagery that Christ employed in His prophecy (which limits itself to His generation, Matthew 24:34) is drawn from Old Testament judgment passages. These prophesied Old Testament-era judgments sound as if they were world-ending judgments, because, in a sense, it was 'the end of the world' for those nations judged."[76]

Verse 30—*"Then the sign of the Son of Man will appear in the sky, and then all the tribes of the earth will mourn, and they will see the Son of Man coming on the clouds of the sky with power and great glory."*

"It is easy to see how dispensationalists jump to the conclusion that this is referring to the Second Advent—*when we omit the historical episode designate (Matthew 24:2) and the time qualifier (Matthew 24:34)*....The Son of Man does not appear; the *sign* appears. Then He defines what the sign signifies: it is the sign 'of the Son of Man in heaven.'... Jerusalem's utter collapse and the Temple's final destruction, then, serve as *the sign* that the Son of Man is in heaven....In the smoky destruction of Jerusalem, these Jewish leaders should see the Son of Man's position of power in His cloud-judgment. The sign, then, is that the Son of Man is in heaven, where He came from.... neither was the 'coming of the Son of Man' that the Sanhedrin would see a physical coming."[77]

Verse 31—*"He will send forth His angels with a great trumpet and they will gather together His elect from the four winds, from one end of the sky to the other."*

"Matthew 24:31 portrays the ultimate Jubilee of salvation, decorated with imagery from Leviticus 25. Following upon the collapse of the Temple order, Christ's 'messengers' will go forth powerfully trumpeting the gospel of salvific liberation (Luke 4:16-21; Isaiah 61:1-3; cf. Leviticus 25:9-10). Through gospel preaching the elect are gathered into the kingdom of God from the four corners of the world, from horizon to horizon."[78]

Verse 34—*"Truly I say to you, this generation will not pass away until all these things take place."*

"We must recognize that a simple reading of Matthew 24:34 provides an unambiguous assertion that *all* of the things Christ the Great Prophet mentioned up to this point—i.e., in verses 4 through 34—were to occur *in the very* *generation of the original disciples....*The phrase 'this generation' is identical to the 'this generation' phrase of Matthew 23:36....The woes He had just pronounced on them cannot be catapulted 2000 years into the future....the whole impetus to this discourse is Christ's reference to the destruction of the historical Temple to which the disciples pointed....Just as surely as fig leaves indicate approaching summer (24:32), so do the events of Matthew 24:4ff. signify the destruction of the Temple."[79]

PRETERISTS AND THE BOOK OF REVELATION

The Preterist Belief

"The closer we get to the year 2000, the farther we get from the events of Revelation," says preterist Ken Gentry. "'Preterism' holds that the bulk of John's prophecies occurred in the first century, soon after his writing of them. Though the prophecies were in the future when John wrote and when his original audience read them, they are now in our past."[80] Dr. R. C. Sproul apparently agrees with Dr. Gentry's basic understanding of Revelation as fulfilled prophecy.[81] And in his commentary on Revelation, the late David Chilton, a preterist, said,

> The book of Revelation is not about the second coming of Christ. It is about the destruction of Israel and Christ's victory over His enemies in the establishment of the New Covenant Temple. In fact, as we shall see, the word *coming* as used in the book of Revelation never refers to the second coming. Revelation prophesies the judgment of God on apostate Israel; and while it does briefly point to events beyond its immediate concerns, that is done merely as a "wrap-up," to show that the ungodly will never prevail against Christ's Kingdom. But the main focus of Revelation is upon events which were soon to take place."[82]

Just as preterists view the Olivet Discourse (Matthew 24; Mark 13; Luke 21) as having past fulfillment, they view the prophecies in Revelation not as "things to come," but rather as "things that came." Why do they hold to this conclusion?

The Preterist Interpretation

Preterists are driven to a first-century fulfillment of Revelation because they, like the Olivet Discourse, believe the text says the events described in the book would take place soon (that is, in that era). What arguments do the preterists use to defend their view of Revelation?

Gentry argues for a first-century fulfillment of Revelation by noting its similarity to the Olivet Discourse:

> It is an interesting fact noted by a number of commentators that John's Gospel is the only Gospel that does not contain the Olivet Discourse, and that it would seem John's Revelation served as His exposition of the Discourse.[83]

> If, as seems likely, Revelation is indeed John's exposition of the Olivet Discourse, we must remember that in the delivery of the Discourse the Lord emphasized that it focused on Israel (Matthew 24:1,2, 15-16; cp. Matthew 23:32ff.) and was to occur in His generation (Matthew 24:34).[84]

Because preterists believe there is a parallel between what is taught in the Olivet Discourse and Revelation (I agree that both refer to the same events), they naturally would have to believe that Revelation was fulfilled in the first century (I disagree that either has been fulfilled).

"One of the most helpful interpretive clues in Revelation is...the *contemporary expectation of the author* regarding the fulfillment of the prophecies. John clearly expects the *soon* fulfillment of his prophecy,"[85] says Gentry. Preterist Gary DeMar has collected what he calls the "time texts" in Revelation, which lead him to believe that the fulfillment of the Apocalypse had to occur during the first century:

1. The events "must *shortly (táchos)* take place" (1:1).

2. "For the time is *near (eggús)*" (1:3).

3. "I am coming to you *quickly (tachús)*" (2:16).

4. "I am coming *quickly (tachús)*" (3:11).

5. "The third woe is coming *quickly (tachús)*" (11:14).

6. "The things which must *shortly (táchos)* take place" (22:6).

7. "Behold, I am coming *quickly (tachús)*" (22:7).

8. "For the time is *near (eggús)*" (22:10).

9. "Behold, I am coming *quickly (tachús)*" (22:12).

10. "Yes, I am coming *quickly (tachús)*" (22:20).[86]

It appears presumptuous at the outset of the interpretative process that these verses are labeled "time texts" by DeMar. The timing of a passage is determined by taking into account *all* factors in a given passage. I hope to show that these terms are more properly interpreted as *qualitative indicators* (not chronological indicators) describing how Christ will return. *How* will He return? It will be "quickly" or "suddenly."

Without a doubt, the exegetical survival of the preterist position revolves around the meaning of these timing passages. When preterists arrive at Bible passages that do not appear to harmonize with their view when taken plainly, they commonly revert to their timing passages and say, "Whatever this passage means, we have already established that it had to be fulfilled within the first century." In accordance with this belief, they search first-century "newspapers" for events that comprise the closest fit to a specific passage and usually cite it as a fulfillment of that passage.

The preterist viewpoints raised in this chapter are answered throughout the rest of this book by the various contributors, and the so-called "time text" arguments are answered in chapters 4 and 12.

Chapter 2

THE HISTORY
OF PRETERISM

THOMAS ICE

If preterism is true, then there is no doubt that the Olivet Discourse and the book of Revelation would have played a vital role in the life of the first-century church. Such relevance would be necessarily true because the events that had been prophesied would have been fulfilled in their day. It is strange that there is not one shred of evidence that anyone in the first century understood these prophecies to have been fulfilled when preterists say they were. You would think that if a large body of Bible prophecy were meant to relate to a specific generation, as preterists contend, then the Holy Spirit would have moved in such a way so that first-century believers would have reached such an understanding. However, there has not yet been found any evidence that indicates that the first-century church viewed Bible prophecy this way. This fact provides a major problem for preterism, which thus far has proved insurmountable.

Preterists love to boast how their interpretative approach makes prophecy relevant to the first century recipients of the New Testament. "The subject of the Revelation thus was *contemporary;*" insists preterist David Chilton, "that is, it is written to and for Christians who were living at the time it was first delivered."[1] Chilton concludes that, "the primary relevance of the book of Revelation was for its first-century readers."[2] "The original audience factor cannot be overlooked; the message of Revelation must be relevant to them,"[3] proclaims Dr. Kenneth Gentry. "With the particularity of the audience emphasized in conjunction with his message of the imminent expectation of occurrence of the events," continues Gentry, "I do not see how preterism of some sort can be escaped."[4]

Dr. Moses Stuart of the nineteenth century asserts, "I take it for granted, that the writer had a present and immediate object in view, when he wrote the book."[5] "The original readers of the Apocalypse, then, it would seem nearly if not quite certain, understood the Apocalypse,"[6] declares Dr. Stuart. By contrast, Englishman E. B Elliott, of the same era, rightly notes, "Not a vestige of testimony exists to the fact of such an understanding."[7] Yet Dr. Stuart admits, "We only know, that very soon after this age [first century], readers of the Apocalypse began to explain some parts of it in such a literal manner, as to throw in the way great obstacles to the reception of the book as canonical."[8] Dr. Stuart, of course, does not know that from historical evidence but merely on the basis of assumption, as noted earlier.

THE PRETERIST ASSUMPTION

It is a fallacy to think that something has to be fulfilled in one's lifetime in order for something to relate to or be important to an individual. This is what preterists are saying about prophecy. There are so many passages, especially in the Old Testament, which give distant prophecy but which also served as a comfort or admonition to those in the present age as well.

Almost all of the Old Testament prophetic books have a theme along these lines: A particular issue, problem, or sin is being address by the prophet at the time of writing; the prophet warns the people that, if they do not repent, God will send judgment; the judgment is described, but with the assurance that the Lord will one day fulfill the promises of blessing to Israel.

An example of this is seen in the book of Joel. The book concludes with a promise of millennial blessing in 3:18-21. Regardless of how one interprets Joel, there are clearly elements that are future to the time at which the book was written. So the futurist is taking prophetic literature in a way that is consistent with how believers have always understood it. Futurists are not coming up with a special, new way to deal with the Olivet Discourse and the book of Revelation as preterists have done.

How did such an approach relate to the people in 835 B.C., when much of the book of Joel was not fulfilled for at least 860 years? It works in the same way that the futuristic interpretation handles future prophecy like the book of Revelation and the Olivet Discourse. There is a particular current situation in which God's people need His Word. The encouragement for the present is to look to what God will ultimately do in the future. If Chilton and Gentry say that they can look back upon what God has done in the past and those past actions can nurture their faithfulness to Jesus Christ in the present, then why, at least in principle, can that not work in the other direction? It can, and does, throughout Scripture.

THE PRETERIST PROBLEM

When did the preterist approach to interpreting Bible prophecy first arise in the history of the church? That is, when do we find the first evidence of the teaching that Christ returned in A.D. 70 and the prophetic utterances in the Olivet Discourse were fulfilled in that era?

Interestingly, preterists themselves are not in agreement as to the answer. Some admit that a preterist witness is absent from the early church, while others point to what they believe to be evidence of preterism in the first-century church.

Full preterist Ed Stevens is among those who recognize a lack of support for the preterist viewpoint's presence in the early church. He asks, "How could it be that some of the apostles and their traveling companions lived through the events of A.D. 70 without recognizing the significance of it and saying something about it? This is the single most significant factor shaping the history of eschatological study that I am aware of."[9] In other words, if the preterist contention that the prophecies of the Olivet Discourse and Revelation were fulfilled in the first century is true, then why is there no evidence that the early church understood these prophecies in this way? There is zero indication, from known, extant writings, that anyone understood the New Testament prophecies from a preterist perspective. No early church writings teach that Jesus returned in first century. If we as God's people are to understand the prophecies of the New Testament in this way, you would think that the Holy Spirit would have left at least one written record of this. Preterist R. H. Charles noted: "Thus, since the real historical horizon of the book was lost, and its historical allusions had become unintelligible for the most part, the use of the Contemporary-Historical [his term for preterism], unless in isolated passages, had become practically impossible."[10]

Preterists have attempted to deal with this absent witness from the early church in various ways. Keep in mind we're talking about those who hold to the view that Christ returned in the first century via events surrounding the destruction of Jerusalem in A.D. 70. A preterist has to prove that the early church writings interpreted passages such as Matthew 24:27,30; 25:31, Acts 1:9-11, Revelation 1:7, and 19:11-21 as fulfilled in A.D. 70. A person isn't a real preterist unless he takes passages that futurists relate to the second coming as first-century events. For example, if someone interprets parts of the Olivet Discourse to refer to A.D. 70 (preaching of the gospel, false Christs, false prophets, etc.), yet considers Matthew 24:27-31) as a reference to a still-future second coming, he is not a true preterist. This kind of mixed approach to interpreting prophecy is still commonplace today.

Chrysostom (A.D. 347–407) is one example of someone who held to a mixed approach to interpreting Bible prophecy. In his commentary on Matthew 24:21, he said: "Seest thou that His discourse is addressed to the Jews, and that He is speaking of the ills that should overtake them?...And let not any man suppose this to have been spoken hyperbolically; but let him study the writings of Josephus, and learn the truth of the sayings."[11]

Clearly Chrysostom applies Matthew 24:21 to A.D. 70. However, he applies verses 27–31 to a future second coming, which means that he cannot be classified as a preterist:

> Because no small turmoil is then to prevail over the world.
> But how doth He come? The very creation being then transfigured, for "the sun shall be darkened," not destroyed, but overcome by the light of His presence; and the stars shall fall, for what shall be the need of them thenceforth, there being no night?...much more seeing all things in course of change, and their fellow servants giving account, and the whole world standing by that awful judgment-seat, and those who have lived from Adam unto His coming, having an account demanded of them of all that they did, how shall they but tremble, and be shaken?[12]

There are others in our own day who take a similar mixed approach to interpreting Matthew 24.[13]

THE PRETERIST RESPONSE

How do preterists deal with the fact that no early church writings confirm an A.D. 70 return of Christ? Generally, preterists deal with historical absence in two ways. Some admit that preterism did not exist until modern times, and see the recent development of preterism as a result of the church finally realizing the true teaching of Scripture, even though it had been there all along. Others try to interpret certain statements from the early church as if they supported preterism.

Full preterist Samuel M. Frost has written an entire book that sees preterism as a recent development. He concludes: "Modern Christian eschatology is based upon an early church error: assuming the second coming was delayed, by misunderstanding its spiritual fulfillment in A.D. 70. We need not remain in this wilderness of misplaced hope. Rather, through sound biblical scholarship, we can recover the transforming hope that the early church embraced. Herein lies our hope for the third Christian millennium."[14]

Ed Stevens says the reason there is no record of preterism in the early church is because a literal rapture occurred in A.D. 66, thus accounting for the silence.[15] Stevens says this view originated from the father of full preterism,

J. Stuart Russell,[16] and is also held by Milton S. Terry, Richard Weymouth, and Ernest Hampden-Cook.[17] Stevens speculates the following: "This ignorance of the left-behind folks also explains why the church went into immediate confusion and made so many departures from the NT patterns so soon after A.D. 70. Their leadership was gone. But at least they did have the writings of the NT to guide them, and those should have been sufficient to keep them on track. But they didn't follow them closely enough."[18]

Stevens even writes in response to early church documents that say the apostle John lived at least into the A.D. 90s.[19] He attempts to skirt this problem, but he is not successful in his efforts.[20]

Then there are the preterists who claim preterism was present in the early church, and they attempt to skew the actual evidence in their favor. Partial preterist C. Jonathin Seraiah assertively says, "At this point it is important to point to what the early Church believed in regard to eschatology. There is no doubt that many in the early Church held to a preterist perspective of various Scriptures, and the work of those who have shown this to be so will not be repeated here."[21] And whom does Seraiah cite as proof of his bold assertion? His footnote cites Dr. Kenneth Gentry's book *Before Jerusalem Fell*,[22] yet he does not provide any actual evidence to back up his statement. And when one looks at the supposed evidence cited by Seraiah in Gentry, all one finds is Dr. Gentry's treatment of the external evidence for his view of the date of Revelation. Dr. Gentry's material does not deal with evidence of early church preterism. Out of 68 pages that are said to present proof of preterism in the early church, there are perhaps only two pages that actually attempt to deal with this matter, and I will discuss those later.

Steve Gregg attempts to affirm early preterism when he declares that "elements of the preterist approach to both Revelation and the Olivet Discourse were held by some much earlier than Alcazar's time. In the early fourth century, the church historian Eusebius, after reviewing Josephus' description of the destruction of Jerusalem in A.D. 70...."[23] Gregg then cites the following statement from Eusebius: "...but it is worth appending to it the infallible forecast of our Saviour in which he prophetically expounded these very things—'Woe unto them that are with child and give suck in those days, but pray that your flight be not in the winter nor on a Sabbath day, for there shall then be great affliction such as was not from the beginning of the world until now, nor shall be.'"[24]

Those words do not indicate that Eusebius was a preterist in the contemporary sense. There is no evidence that he applied a preterist interpretation to second-coming passages such as Matthew 24:27-31 or Revelation 1:7 and 19:11-21. In addition to his *Ecclesiastical History*, Eusebius also wrote another book entitled *The Proof of the Gospel*.[25] This work is believed to have been written after earlier editions of *Ecclesiastical History*.[26] Eusebius, as in *Ecclesiastical History*, argues that the first-century destruction of Jerusalem by the Romans fulfilled biblical prophecy and was thus a "proof of the gospel." Yet nowhere does he apply second-coming passages such as Matthew 24:27-31 or Revelation 1:7 and 19:11-21 to Christ's coming in A.D. 70. Preterists need to find ancient references written by anyone who understood prophecy from their perspective, and so far they have not been able to find such references. As noted earlier, some early church writers apply part of Matthew 24 to A.D. 70 and other parts of the chapter to a still-future second advent. It is quite likely that Eusebius thought the same way about the Olivet Discourse. There is nothing that indicates Eusebius was clearly a preterist.

THE PRETERIST "EVIDENCE"

Early Church Era

Dr. Kenneth Gentry, in his work *House Divided*, attempts to paint a picture of the alleged antiquity of preterism in a section titled "The Historical Basis for Preterism," followed by a subhead that reads, "Nascent Preterism in Antiquity."[27] However, Dr. Gentry's claim of "Nascent Preterism in Antiquity" is virtually nonexistent, depending upon one's definition of *antiquity*. He claims Eusebius held to a nascent (budding, hopeful, growing) preterism.[28] Yet, as noted earlier, Eusebius's mere reference of some parts of the Olivet Discourse to A.D. 70 do not argue for nor prove he held to a preterist view at all.

The *Clementine Homilies*, (c. A.D. 200) according to Dr. Gentry, is "another ancient document that makes reference to the destruction of the temple based on Matthew 24:2-34."[29] However, as we've already seen, the first reference (Eusebius) did not refer to "the destruction of the temple based on Matthew 24:2-34," so Clementine cannot be said to be another. Dr. Gentry twists the evidence of Eusebius and Clementine by saying that they speak to the broader context of Matthew 24:2-34, when in reality Eusebius only commented upon Matthew 24:19-21 and Luke 21:20,23-24. Absent is any reference to Matthew 24:27-31, yet Dr. Gentry declares, without any basis, that verses 27-31 are included.

Clementine does likely reference Matthew 24:2 and 34 in the same paragraph,[30] but there is absolutely no indication that he interprets Matthew 24:27-31 as having a past fulfillment. In fact, Clementine does not provide commentary on Matthew 24:27-31. Thus, it seems unlikely that he should be viewed as containing a nascent form of preterism.

Of Cyprian (A.D. 200–258), Dr. Gentry claims that "we have a clear reference to Matthew 24 as referring to Jerusalem's A.D. 70 fall."[31] Yet when one examines the two references cited,[32] it's clear the two citations are really one, since the first reference is not to Matthew 24, but to Matthew 23:37-38.[33] The second reference is to Matthew 24:2.[34] Both references are verses that *everyone* (futurists, historicists, and preterists) interpret as a reference to A.D. 70. In other words, this second reference cannot be used to claim Cyprian was a preterist, for even futurists understand both passages exactly as does Cyprian. What's more, Cyprian said, "And when He was interrogated by His disciples concerning the sign of His coming, and of the consummation of the world, He answered and said…."[35] Cyprian then went on to quote Matthew 24:4-31 in its entirety, so we can see that he applies Matthew 24:4-31 to "the consummation of the world," contrary to Gentry. With Cyprian, Dr. Gentry wrongly asserts that just because a writer refers to the A.D. 70 destruction of Jerusalem or the temple, he must have been a preterist. I have shown that such is not the case.

That is the extent of the supposed evidence for preterism in the early church, according to Dr. Gentry. As we can see, it amounts to nothing. Unfortunately, Dr. Gentry even goes so far as to argue that those in the early church who saw a continual fulfillment of all of the 70 weeks of years in Daniel 9:24-27 "held a distinctly preteristic interpretation of Daniel 9."[36] To arrive at such a conclusion, he must be changing the nuance of the word *preterism* from referring to the system of preterism (as we have defined it in this book) and changing it to mean one who simply believes that something happened in the past. There are many historicists, futurists, and idealists who believe that the 70 weeks of Daniel 9 are past,[37] but this does not make them preterists, for they do not interpret other key passages as having been fulfilled in the past. In fact, Dr. Gentry basically follows the historicist premillennialist J. Barton Payne's view of the 70 weeks,[38] but that does not mean that Dr. Payne was a preterist.

Dr. Gentry concludes his presentation of "nascent preterism in antiquity" with a venture into a couple of early medieval citations. The first is that of Andreas of Cappadocia, whom Dr. Gentry says probably lived "near the commencement of the sixth century."[39] "It is clear from reading him that he prefers a Domitianic date for the Revelation," says Dr. Gentry. "He frequently challenges, however, other interpreters of his era who apply several of the prophecies of Revelation to the Jewish War under Vespasian and Titus."[40] Dr. Gentry says the following is a direct quote from Andreas: "There are not wanting those who apply this passage to the siege and destruction of Jerusalem by Titus."[41] Yet Dr. Gentry does not have an actual citation from Andreas's commentary, as he would lead us to believe. Instead, he has transposed a statement from Dr. Moses Stuart's summarization of Andreas's commentary on Revelation into an actual quote, as if it were from Andreas himself.[42] I will assume that it was an honest error done in haste, but nevertheless it is an error that can be copied by others as if these words were an actual quote from Andreas, and not a summary statement by Dr. Stuart.[43]

However, it *is* apparently true that Andreas said of Revelation 7:1, "These things are referred by some to those sufferings which were inflicted by the Romans upon the Jews."[44] Even though Andreas was not a preterist, it appears that he was interacting with a mild preterist position that had arisen by the sixth century. This appears to be the first real instance of an apparent mild form of preterism. Dr. Stuart says: "It is plain, then, from what Andreas says in these passages, that in his time there was one class of interpreters, who referred a part of the Apocalypse to the destruction of Jerusalem, and of course believed that this book was composed before that event took place."[45]

Dr. Gentry, apparently sourcing Dr. Stuart,[46] says, "Arethas specifically interprets various passages in Revelation in terms of the destruction of Jerusalem."[47] However, that is only half of the truth. What Dr. Gentry does not tell his readers[48] is that Dr. Stuart, also a preterist, characterizes Arethas not as a preterist, as does Dr. Gentry, but as one who sometimes found two fulfillments in the same passage—one past and one future.[49] Dr. Gentry gives the impression, especially in *House Divided*, that Arethas is a preterist. Dr. Stuart is not so sure and makes that clear when he says, "Nothing is plainer, here, than that Arethas admitted a double sense of prophecy; and in accordance with this he might consistently find *two fulfillments* of a prediction, as he seems to have done."[50] This begins to make sense when Dr. Stuart tells us that Arethas produced "a Greek commentary on the Apocalypse, which consists of little more than extracts from Andreas and other expositors."[51]

LeRoy Froom observed, "In his commentary on the Apocalypse, which is mostly a compilation, he follows Andreas in the main...and finds in each prominent word the possibility of reference to both past and future history."[52] Dr. Stuart adds, "...more than once seems to intimate that Revelation iv–xi. applies to the Jews and Jerusalem, although he would not exclude an ultimate reference to Antichrist."[53] Further, he tells us, "When Lucke (p. 409) speaks of him, in reference to these passages, as *confused* and *contradictory*, he could hardly have adverted sufficiently to the fact, that in the seemingly contradictory passages, Arethas only cites the opinion of others."[54] And E. B. Elliott says the following about Arethas:

> Under the *Sealing Vision* he suggests the possible reference of the four angels of the winds to the desolations of Judaea by the Romans; or, yet more probably, to the desolations by Antichrist: then, in speaking of the sealing itself, more distinctly and decid-

edly explains the sealed 144,000 as meaning the Jews converted to Christianity before the destruction of Jerusalem, asserting that Jerusalem was not destroyed when John received these revelations....Which passage has been naturally adduced by the advocates of an early date of the Apocalypse, in support of their opinion: but of which the value as an authority, small in itself because that of so late a writer, is rendered yet smaller by the fact of Arethas having not once only, but twice, stated from Eusebius, that it was under *Domitian's* reign that John was banished to Patmos.[55]

It does appear, then, in spite of Dr. Gentry's misrepresentations, that we see recorded in Andreas and Arethas some form of early preterism beginning to develop in relation to the book of Revelation.

Commentator Dr. Henry Alford summarized the early history of preterism this way: "The Praeterist view found no favour, and was hardly so much as thought of, in the times of primitive Christianity. Those who lived near the date of the book itself had no idea that its groups of prophetic imagery were intended merely to describe things then passing, and to be in a few years completed."[56] As we shall see later, the earliest form of distinct preterism, in relation to the book of Revelation, was that which saw the final book teaching God's defeat of His two ancient enemies—the Jews in the first half of the book (i.e., relating to A.D. 70) and Rome in the second half. Thus, the earliest and mildest form of preterism (as we will see later with Alcazar) saw the Apocalypse fulfilled in the early fourth century, when the Roman Empire became subservient to Christianity under Emperor Constantine.

The Middle Ages

There is no significant development of the preterist position—that we know of—during the middle ages. During this era, a moralistic interpretation of Revelation and Bible prophecy was dominant. Toward the end of this period, the historicist view began to rise and dominate prophetic studies under the influence of Joachim of Fiore (1135–1202).[57]

LeRoy Froom points out that a Spanish rabbi named Hayyim Galipapa (1310-1380), in his interpretation of the book of Daniel, "sought to throw all fulfillments back into the past."[58] For example, Galipapa applied the Little Horn of Daniel 7 to Antiochus Epiphanes. "In this he is unique among all Jewish expositors—a Jewish preterist in verity!—and antedates the Catholic preterist Alcazar by three centuries."[59] However, this is not preterism in the Christian sense because it does not relate New Testament passages, such as Matthew 24 or Revelation, to a past return of Christ.

The Post-Reformation Period

While preterism surfaced in only a small way during the early middle ages, as noted in the writings of Andreas and Arethas, it wasn't until the post-Reformation period that preterism began to truly show up on the church's radar screen. Dr. Stuart, speaking from the preterist perspective, says, "Looking back from the close of the eighth century upon what had been done by commentators in the way of explaining the Apocalypse, we find no real and solid advances were made."[60] Dr. Stuart argues that the Reformation itself did not do much to advance the preterist approach to interpreting Bible prophecy, but he believes that it "laid the foundation for such an exegesis, by substantially adopting it in the interpretation of the historical and doctrinal books of Scripture."[61] This paved the way for the Spanish Jesuit Luis Alcazar (1554–1613), whose commentary on Revelation first appeared in 1614 in Antwerp.[62]

Luis Alcazar

Dr. Henry Alford says that Alcazar was the first to promulgate preterism "in anything like completeness"[63] in his *Investigation of the Hidden Sense of the Apocalypse.*[64] "Alcazar was the first to apply Preterism to the Apocalypse with anything like completeness," echoes Froom, "though it had previously been applied somewhat to Daniel. It thus pioneered the way for acceptance first by Hugo Grotius of the Netherlands, and later by the German Rationalists."[65] Dr. Stuart agrees that Alcazar is the pioneer of a mild form of preterism when he notes: "Revelation v–xi, he thinks, applies to the Jewish enemies of the Christian church....This view of the contents of the book had been merely hinted at before....But no one had ever developed this idea fully, and endeavored to illustrate and enforce it, in such a way as Alcassar."[66]

Froom describes Alcazar's preterism as follows: "This scheme contended that the prophecies of Revelation were descriptive of the victory of the early church, as fulfilled in the downfall of the Jewish nation and the overthrow of pagan Rome, and in this way limited their range to the first six centuries of the Christian Era, and make Nero the Antichrist."[67]

More specifically, Alcazar took the following approach to Revelation:

> Revelation 1-11 he applied to the rejection of the Jews and the desolation of Jerusalem by the Romans. Revelation 12 to 19 Alcazar allotted to the overthrow of Roman paganism and the conversion of the empire to the church, the judgment of the great Harlot being effected by the downfall of pagan idolatry; Revelation 20 he applied to the final persecution by Antichrist, and the day of judgment; and chapters 21 and 22, referring to the

New Jerusalem, he made descriptive of the glorious and endless triumphant state of the Roman church.[68]

Isbon T. Beckwith wrote a preterist commentary on the book of Revelation in 1919 and said this concerning the origins of his own interpretative viewpoint: "His [Alcazar's] work is the first to attempt a complete exposition of the entire premillennial part of the book, as a connected & advancing whole falling within the Apocalyptist's age & the centuries immediately following. It becomes therefore important in the growth of a truly scientific method of exegesis."[69]

Alcazar's preterism is the mildest form for one applying that method of interpretation to the Apocalypse. Elliott notes that "Alcasar confesses the later Domitianic date of the Apocalypse."[70] His preterism, which was really a mix of preterism and historicism, was not widely received by fellow Catholics. Cornelius a Lapide (1567–1637), "the classical Jesuit exegete of the seventeenth century,"[71] was highly critical of Alcazar's work and "found 'much difficulty' in this approach."[72] "In the first place," warned Lapide, "because it was new and against the usual interpretations; in the second, because it seemed mystical rather than literal; and finally, 'because it makes history out of prophecy.'"[73] Froom says of Lapide that "he censured Alcazar, the Preterist, for making assertions without proof, and for his employment of allegorical interpretation."[74] Many historicists see the rise of preterism through Alcazar as a feeble attempt, on his part, to answer the charge by many Protestants who claimed that the Popes of the Catholic Church were the Antichrist.[75]

Hugo Grotius

Hugo Grotius (1583–1645) of Holland is considered "the first Protestant recruit to Preterism."[76] Grotius, a jurist, statesman, historian, and theologian, is one of the more interesting figures of the seventeenth century. He was condemned to life in prison in 1618 for being a member of the Remonstrates or Arminians, but escaped to Paris in 1621 in a book chest. He is viewed as the father of international and maritime law,[77] as well as the originator of a heretical view of the atonement called the governmental or Grotian view of the atonement.[78] Grotius was "extremely liberal in his religious views" and took a critical approach to interpreting Scripture, known as "the historical-philological method."[79] Grotius was also ecumenical in spirit: "He expressed a desire for the unity of the church and was willing to make such extensive concessions to restore union with Rome that he was accused of converting to Roman Catholicism. The reason for his irenic approach was his desire as a Christian and a statesman to bring peace and unity to a world torn by religious wars."[80]

It was through Grotius's friendliness with Catholics that he became exposed to the writings of Alcazar. Grotius originally introduced his preterist views through an anonymous work entitled *Commentary on Certain Texts Which Deal with Antichrist*, which was published in 1640. Once it was learned who wrote the clandestine work, he further developed his views in his work *Annotations on the New Testament*.[81] Froom summarizes Grotius's preterist view in this way: "He holds that Revelation 1 to 11 constitutes a history of the Jews and their overthrow in the early centuries, and that chapters 12 to 20 are limited to the Christian victory over pagan Rome, with the destruction of idolatry."[82]

Grotius had only marginal success in spreading his mild preterism within Protestantism. Nevertheless, he paved the way for preterism's entrance into the English-speaking world through the agency of Henry Hammond.

Henry Hammond

Henry Hammond (1605–1660) is "called the 'Father of English Biblical Criticism,'" and was a "member of the Westminster Assembly, but never sat with them."[83] Hammond first taught preterism in his *Paraphrase and Annotations upon all the Books of the New Testament* (1653). "This volume," notes Brady, "contained a brave but lonely attempt to introduce the preterist interpretation of the book of Revelation to English soil."[84] Hammond followed Grotius closely, and "acknowledged his indebtedness in this matter" to him.[85] Apparently both Grotius and Hammond knew the hostility that the reformed Protestant world would engender upon hearing of these new views. Brady notes the impact the Olivet Discourse had upon Hammond's preterist views: "Hammond in turn attached the words of Matthew 24:34 ('this generation shall not pass till all these things be fulfilled') to the events of the Apocalypse and suggested that chapters 4-11 described the infancy and growth of the Church of Christ up to its gaining possession of the Roman Empire."[86]

Froom provides this summary of Hammond's views:

> Employing the Preterist key in explaining the Apocalypse, he stressed the expression, "Things which must shortly come to pass."
>
> A brief fivefold summary will suffice to cover Hammond's main points. (1) The first beast of Revelation is... the seven heads to seven Roman emperors....(2) The two-horned beast, is applied to the heathen priests...[of] the early Christians. (3) Revelation 17 is...the seven heads, or kings, are specified Claudius, Nero, Galba, Otho, Vitellius, Vespasian (then reigning), and Titus (then yet to come). (4) Revelation 18...is a portrayal of the desolation of heathen Rome as barbarians....

(5) Revelation 20 is...portraying the thousand years of tranquility and freedom from persecution, after the conversion of Constantine, with the resurrection as the flourishing condition of the church under the Messiah. The loosing of Satan is set forth as the time of the Mohammedan incursions, Mohammedanism being also called Gog and Magog, and the comprising of the city is the siege of Constantinople, in 1453.[87]

It is easy to see from the above summary of Hammond's view that he, like Alcazar and Grotius, is actually more in the historicist camp when it comes to their views of Revelation, with preterism added on up front. In fact, Hammond clearly dates the book of Revelation *after* the destruction of Jerusalem. These early preterists are all mild in their use of preterism when compared with today's spectrum of partial and full preterists.

It should be noted also that what we have reviewed above as the preterist interpretation of the Revelation is not in fact the thoroughgoing preterism that we find in modern critical commentaries, the interpretation which applies the text to the events occurring about the end of the first century. The kind of preterism advanced by Alcazar, Grotius, and Hammond, on the other hand, viewed the events of the Apocalypse as past history from the standpoint of the seventeenth century, but they were nevertheless events stretching from the foundation of the Christian Church to the conversion of Constantine. Furthermore, the last two chapters of the Apocalypse were held to predict events still later than Constantine....In this respect they might be considered not as preterists in the true sense, but as historicists, albeit with a completely different time-scale to that of the leading Protestant expositors.[88]

Hammond did win at least one convert to his preterist position in Herbert Throndike (1598–1672), "who, like Hammond, assisted in the editing of Brian Walton's Polyglott Bible."[89] "It is therefore very rare to find any follower of Hammond in the succeeding two centuries."[90] Brady notes: "...those who argued for the preterist interpretation of the book of Revelation, and for that matter the futurist interpretation also, were playing to empty galleries, until at least the fourth decade of the nineteenth century. Their views were anything but popular and those who followed them could soon find themselves branded with the infamous mark of the papal beast."[91]

Jacques Benigne Bossuet

As noted above, very few Catholic scholars looked with favor upon Alcazar's preterist views. However, one scholar who was attracted to Alcazar's thoughts in 1689 was Cardinal Jacques Benigne Bossuet. "Bossuet was answering the Protestant Pierre Jurieu…the controversy was an important stimulation because it permitted Bossuet to organize a new system of historical reading which depended on recent progress in biblical criticism."[92] Bossuet's preterism pretty much followed that of Alcazar and Grotius.[93] Bossuet attempted to defend Alcazar and Grotius, who had precipitated strong responses from reformed Protestants. "Riberia and Alcazar were taken to task by the Puritan exegetes," notes Bernard McGinn, "who felt compelled to devote hundreds of pages to refuting the Jesuit rebuttal of standard Protestant arguments for the papal Antichrist."[94] Elliott depicts Bossuet's views as follows:

> The grand subject of the prophecy he conceives to be the triumph of Christianity over Judaism and Paganism—i.e. over Paganism as established in the Roman empire; and, in the *Jewish* part, with reference only to the later calamities of the Jews, not to the destruction of Jerusalem by Titus. For as Bossuet judged the Apocalypse to have been written under Domitian, that destruction by Titus had happened, in his opinion, before the giving of the Apocalypse.[95]

Even though Bossuet was generally preterist in orientation, like his predecessors, he still had many elements of historicism in his interpretative scheme. Nevertheless, he contributed to a small but growing trend that set the stage for a vigorous reaction primarily from Protestants.

It was at this time that we see a significant anti-preterist reaction develop. In Europe, Pierre Jurieu (1637–1713), a "distinguished Huguenot leader and noted controversialist," lead the way when he wrote *Exposition of the Apocalypse or the Coming Deliverance of the Church*[96] (1688) in order to combat the development of preterist thought: "Reacting against his coreligionists Grotius, Hammond, and others, Jurieu refused any preterite reading. Referring Revelation to the early centuries of the church's history, he says, dishonors its authors and constitutes "a shame and disgrace not only to the Reformation, but also to the name of Christian." Jurieu was a millenarian…."[97]

Brady cites Henry More, Matthew Poole, and Moses Lowman as fierce critics of preterism in England.[98] In fact, More claimed to have "found nearly eighty flaws in Grotius's commentary."[99]

In America, the Puritans were horrified at the implications of preterism and its allegorical interpretations of Scripture. The Mather dynasty sprang into action and penned a number of responses to the preterism of Grotius and Hammond:[100]

> Increase Mather "spoke for all of his Puritan colleagues in New England when he pleaded for the literal restoration of Israel in his book-length *Mystery of Israel's Conversion*" (London, 1669)… in response to several European colleagues who were prone to read Romans 11 as an allegory of the Christian church. Championed by Hugo Grotius, Henry Hammond, Jacob Batalerio (1593–1672), James Calvert (d. 1698), John Lightfoot (1602–1675)… these notable scholars adopted a preterist interpretation of Romans 11 and asserted with Grotius that St. Paul's prophecy had literally been fulfilled in the first two centuries of the Christian church when the churches of Palestine, Asia Minor, and Rome mostly consisted of Christian Jews. St. Paul's prediction, so they argued, must therefore be understood literally only of the Christian Jews and their offspring, who through intermarriage with their Gentile brethren lost their distinction. Any latter-day conversion of the Jews as a nation was therefore illogical and had to be understood of the surrogate Israel, the Christian church.[101]

Colonial-era Christians also battled with preterists over whether 2 Peter 3 refers to a physical burning up of the heavens and earth at the end of history, as Increase Mather asserted in his book *Threefold Paradise*, while preterists such as "Grotius and Hammond argued, the Petrine conflagration was applicable only to the historical destruction of Jerusalem."[102] Cotton Mather was also quite vocal in his opposition to preterist teachings.[103] Froom notes, "The Preterist concept of Antichrist, introduced in the eighteenth century by Grotius among certain Protestants in Europe, was flatly rejected in America during this century."[104]

John Lightfoot

John Lightfoot (1602–1675) was an English biblical and rabbinical scholar whose works are still useful and in print today. "In 1643 he became one of the original and more influential members of the Westminster Assembly."[105] Lightfoot's major work was *A Commentary on the New Testament from the Talmud and Hebraica,*[106] "which was originally published between 1658 and 1674, [and] was written in Latin. It was translated into English and published in four volumes in 1859."[107] These commentaries cover only Matthew, Mark, Luke, John, parts of Romans, and 1 Corinthians.

Lightfoot, in his commentary, focuses primarily on the Olivet Discourse. He said, in commenting on Matthew 24:34, "Hence it appears plain enough, that the foregoing verses are not to be understood of the last judgment, but, as we said, of the destruction of Jerusalem."[108] It is unmistakable that he understood all of Matthew 24 from a preterist standpoint. Lightfoot clearly interpreted the coming of Christ in Matthew 24:27-31 as relating to the first-century destruction of Jerusalem. Concerning Mark 13:32, Lightfoot declared: "That the discourse is of the day of the destruction of Jerusalem is so evident, both by the disciples' question, and by the whole thread of Christ's discourse, that it is a wonder any should understand these words of the *day and hour* of the last judgment."[109]

Unlike modern preterists, Lightfoot stepped to the plate and commented on Luke 21:24, which says in part, "Jerusalem will be trampled under foot by the Gentiles until the times of the Gentiles be fulfilled." He said, "...and what then? In what sense is the word *until* to be understood?...I am well assured our Saviour is discoursing about the fall and overthrow of Jerusalem; but I doubt, whether he touches upon the restoration of it: nor can I see any great reason to affirm, that the times of the Gentiles will be fulfilled before the end of the world itself."[110]

Lightfoot also held to a mild preterist interpretation of Revelation, as exhibited in his work *Harmony, Chronicle and Order of the New Testament* (1655). "His comments on the text," observes Brady, "appear to have been more greatly influenced by the exposition of Hammond than by that of Mede, particularly in the interpretation of the seals and vials."[111] However, Lightfoot's views on Revelation were not nearly as influential as his work on the Olivet Discourse.

Rationalist Preterism

The preterist approach to interpreting Bible prophecy was rarely found within Protestant scholarship until the 1800s. It gained a wide following among German liberals who did not believe that the Bible contained predictive prophecy. In the late eighteenth century, J. G. Eichhorn (1752–1827) introduced a version of Alcazar's preterism to the liberal German rationalists school. "Soon he was joined by other rationalist scholars, such as G. H. A. Ewald (1803–1875), G. C. F. Lucke (1791–1855), W. M. L. De Wette (1780–1849), Franz Delitzsch (1813–1890), and Julius Wellhausen (1844–1918)."[112] Elliott says that "the *German Praeterist School* that was about this time rising more and more into notice and influence [was] a School characterized by considerable mental acuteness, research, and philological learning; and at the same time by much of the hardihood and rashness of religious scepticism."[113]

The German liberals who gravitated to the preterist viewpoint did so because it allowed them to give a naturalistic explanation of John's revelation, which fit into their anti-supernaturalist presuppositions. Merrill Tenney tells us: "Alcazar's suggestion was followed by some Protestant expositors, but the rise of the modern preterist school came with the prevalence of the technique of historical criticism. Since preterism did not necessitate any element of predictive prophecy or even any conception of inspiration, it could treat the Revelation simply as a purely natural historical document, embodying the eschatological concepts of its own time."[114]

The advancing liberalism of the late nineteenth and twentieth centuries accounts for the attraction of many liberals to preterism. "Preterism," observes Froom, "had become well-nigh dominant in the rationalistic universities of Germany."[115] "The nearer we approach the time of the French Revolution," declares Froom, "the more the generation of rationalistic and higher critical expositors grows in influence, having adopted the Preterist School of interpretation."[116] Dr. James H. Moorhead explains how this liberal dynamic impacted the study of biblical prophecy during this era:

> After 1880, the acceptance of modern biblical criticism in major seminaries, universities, and pulpits made many Protestants even more uncomfortable with the notion that the Bible contained *any* literal predictions. This new scholarship was not so much a set of agreed conclusions—critics debated the "assured results" of their craft—as it was a new and sometimes disturbing angle from which to view the scriptures. Basic to that perspective was a commitment to analyze the meaning of scripture by placing it in temporal context through the tools of philology, comparative religion, literary analysis, or historical research, the new learning generally diminished the role of the supernatural as an explanatory device. Thus, the Bible often ceased to resemble a record of the unchanging faith once delivered to the saints and became instead a record of an ancient Near Eastern people's developing views of religion.[117]

That the rationalism of the Enlightenment was key to supporting the modern rise and acceptability of preterism is affirmed not only by futurists, but even by liberal preterist R. H. Charles:

> But the most important event connected with such subjects was the rise of historical criticism in this century [early 1900s]. It is remarkable that a century that gave birth to the most boundless

subjectivism should have also called the historic sense into active existence....

Under the influence of this rising critical spirit in rude collision with the dominate methods of interpretation the bold thesis was advanced, that the prophecies of the Apocalypse, so far from embracing the entire history of the world or even of the Jewish or Christian Churches, were directed firstly and lastly against Jerusalem.

Thus the Apocalypse was interpreted in this school by the Contemporary-Historical Method in a very limited sense. The chief advocates of this view were Abauzit, Harduin, Wetstein, Harenberg, Herder and Zullig, writing from 1732 to 1840.[118]

We find that most of the German rationalists saw the book of Revelation in the same light as the preterists who had gone before them. They tended to see the first half of the Apocalypse as relating to Israel and Jerusalem, which was fulfilled during A.D. 70 events. Chapters 12 through 19 are seen as referring to the destruction of God's other enemy, the Roman Empire, while the final three chapters are said to look to a heavenly future. However, within this pool of preterist interpreters, a new development arises: For the first time that we can document, an interpreter of the Apocalypse promoted the view "that the whole book [of Revelation] relates to the destruction of Judea and Jerusalem."[119] This marks the beginning of the kind of preterism that is held today by both partial and full preterists.

German Preterism

Firmin Abauzit (1679–1767) of Geneva, who was a friend of Rousseau and Voltaire, published a commentary on Revelation in 1730 titled *Historic Discourse on the Apocalypse*,[120] in which he advocated a more complete preterist view than his predecessors. Abauzit's work also broke new ground in that it was the first "in this period to attack the canonical authority of the Apocalypse."[121] Preterist Moses Stuart says of Abauzit that his "book is generally regarded as marking the commencement of a new period in the criticism of the Apocalypse."[122] Stuart describes Abauzit's views as follows: "His starting point was, that the book itself declares that all which it predicts would take place *speedily*. Hence Rome, in chap. xiii–xix. points figuratively to Jerusalem. Chap. xxi. xxii. relate to the extension of the church, after the destruction of the Jews."[123]

Johann Gottfried Herder (1744–1803) is credited with adopting Abauzit's understanding of the Apocalypse and also saw it as "emphasiz[ing] the Jewish catastrophe."[124] Herder expressed his views in his book entitled *Maranatha*, which was published in 1779.[125] Stuart said this about Herder's form of preterism: "Although he seems to move in a narrow circle, as to the meaning of the book, limiting it so generally to the Jews, yet he makes God's dealings with them, and with his church at that period, symbolical of the circumstances of the church in every age."[126]

In 1791, Johann Gottfried Eichhorn (1752–1827) produced a commentary on Revelation that was exalted, emulated, and admired in critical German circles for many years.[127] While Eichhorn did not see all of the Apocalypse being fulfilled in the first century, as did Abauzit and Herder, he did see a number of Jewish fulfillments in the second half of Revelation. Eichhorn was a typical German preterist—he did not believe the Bible was inspired by God, nor did it contain predictive prophecy. Stuart says, "I do not and cannot regard Eichhorn as a believer in Christianity, in the sense in which those are who admit the inspired authority of the Scripture."[128]

European preterism of the post-Reformation period, especially the German variety, was attractive to those of the liberal persuasion. Froom observes: "Preterist principles have been adopted and adapted by those of rationalistic mind as the easiest way to compass the problem of prophecy, throwing it into the past, where it does not affect life today. It has had a sizable following among rationalists, of which Modernism is the modern counterpart." [129]

Preterists in our own day may be pleased about the historical evidence for the spread of preterism in the eighteenth and nineteenth centuries in Europe. However, they cannot be happy that the foundational support for this growth of preterism was based upon German rationalism and unbelief.

English Preterism

The rise of preterism in the British Isles was preceded by a wave of German rationalism from the European continent. Froom tells us that "the influx of German rationalism into England was not without effect, with its Preterist apocalyptic scheme that had received great impetus under Eichhorn, Ewald, Heinrichs, and others."[130] "Probably the first British writer to revive preterism in the nineteenth century was Samuel Lee," says Brady, "the distinguished philologist and orientalist."[131] In 1830 Lee published his commentary on Revelation, called *Events and Times of the Visions of Daniel and St. John*.[132] Lee "placed great emphasis on the words of Revelation 1.1,3; 4.1; 22.6,10,12,20 ('things which must shortly come to pass,' 'the time is at hand,' etc.)."[133] He took the more traditional form of preterism that sees Revelation divided between the Jews of the first century and the later defeat of the Roman Empire. Though his work was not well received, Lee opened the way for preterism to spread in the English-speaking world.[134]

Even though preterism grew and thrived in the soil of German rationalism and liberalism, it was a British individual who came to develop the most extreme form of preterism possible—a Congregational pastor from Bays-water, England named J. Stuart Russell (1816–1895).[135] Russell was not a higher criticism scholar like virtually all the preterists who came before him. "Clearly Russell assumes that the text of Scripture is inspired," writes R. C. Sproul.[136] Russell released the first edition of his book in 1878, which he authored anonymously. One year before his retirement (1887), he released the second edition under his name.[137] Thus, J. Stuart Russell appears to be the father of full preterism, which sees the second coming as a fully past event that took place in conjunction with the Roman destruction of the Jewish Temple in A.D. 70. Russell summarizes his conclusion as follows:

> As the result of the investigation we are landed in this dilemma: either the whole group of predictions, comprehending the destruction of Jerusalem, the coming of the Lord, the resurrec-tion of the dead, and the rewarding of the faithful, did take place before the passing away of that generation, as predicted by Christ, taught by the apostles, and expected by the whole church; or else, the hope of the church was a delusion, the teaching of the apostles an error, the predictions of Jesus a dream....
>
> We are compelled, therefore, by all these considerations, and chiefly by regard for the authority of Him whose word cannot be broken, to conclude that the Parousia, or second coming of Christ, with its connected and concomitant events, did take place according to the Saviour's own prediction, at the period when Jerusalem was destroyed, and before the passing away of "that generation."[138]

I have not been able to find out if Russell's brand of preterism made much headway in Britain in the late 1800s. In his preface to the second edition of his book, Russell noted that the first edition "has not commanded a wide circle of readers." He went on to say that "the author must confess his disap-pointment that no serious attempt has been made to disprove any of his positions."[139] However, in the book's preface, it is clear that his colleagues had responded in some way to his views.[140]

American Preterism

No doubt the father of American preterism is clearly the aforementioned Moses Stuart (1780–1852) of Andover Seminary, who "introduced Preterism into the United States about 1842."[141] Dr. Stuart's commentary on the Apoca-lypse was a massive two-volume work that taught the milder form of preterism that prophesied the defeat of God's two ancient enemies: Israel and the Roman Empire.[142] Dr. Stuart says,

> It is Christianity as struggling first, and for a long time, with bitter Jewish enemies, who are in various ways weakened and ultimately destroyed; then it is Christianity struggling with the tremendous Roman power which governed the world—yea carrying on a death-struggle for a long time and with agonies often repeated—until finally victory lights upon the standard of the cross; it is Christianity not in the *abstract* (so to speak), but in the *concrete*, which John presents and holds up to our view, while she is bathed in blood and wrapped in flames, and finally comes out from all like gold from the fiery furnace.[143]

Contrary to the perspective of moderate preterists of our own day, Dr. Stuart is adamant that only chapters 6 through 11 of Revelation refer to the destruction of Jerusalem in A.D. 70. He says: "Not much better than this have those interpreters done, who have found in the Apocalypse little else but the Roman conquest of Judea and Jerusalem, excepting the final erection of a new and spiritual kingdom....Yet nothing less than absolute violence can make Revelation xii–xix. relate to Judea and Jerusalem. The great mass of commentators have regarded, and do still regard, such an exegesis as impossible."[144]

In relation to Revelation 1:1, Stuart remarked, "Now, although the closing part of the Revelation relates beyond all doubt to a distant period, and some of it to a future eternity, yet the portion of the book which contains this is so small, and that part of the book which was speedily fulfilled is so large, that no reasonable difficulty can be made concerning the declaration before us."[145]

Given these comments, there is no doubt that Dr. Stuart would not feel at home with the more extreme form of preterism that has become dominant today. Even moderate preterists of our time see the entire message of Revelation 6 to 19 as having been fulfilled by A.D. 70.

It is clear that Dr. Stuart adopted his view primarily from the German liberals whom he quoted constantly throughout his work. Enoch Pond said of Dr. Stuart's commentary on Revelation that it was "borrowed mostly from the Germans."[146] So even though he personally believed in the divine inspiration of the Bible, he still adopted the exegetical approach of liberal, German rationalists such as G. C. F. Lucke, whom he admitted his dependence upon.[147] While Dr. Stuart could be considered to have been within the sphere of some kind of evangelicalism, it is sadly true that he adopted a liberal method of interpretating of Bible prophecy—which is what preterism promotes. Dr. Stuart says: "The chance of substituting a better method of exegesis speedily, is probably but small. Yet it must come at last. It will come, whether we choose or refuse. The radical principles of hermeneutics are every year gaining ground; and inasmuch as they are founded in *reason* and *common sense*, they must sooner or later become triumphant."[148]

That Dr. Stuart adopted the liberal, critical approach to exegesis is confirmed by the fact that he used extracanonical sources in his endeavors to interpret the biblical text. He deemed important extrabiblical sources such as *The Ascension of Isaiah, The Sibylline Oracles,* and *The Book of Enoch.*[149] It is safe to say that Moses Stuart's concept of preterism originated from German rationalism, based on who it is that Dr. Stuart refers to time and again as his influences.

Recent American Preterists

Around the 1970s, preterism began its current rise in American evangelicalism. Before its recent upswing, contemporary forms of preterism tended to be found only within academic circles. The rise to a more popular visibility likely began simultaneously within the ranks of the Churches of Christ and as preterism received renewed attention within evangelical consciousnesses through those within the Reformed tradition by the publishing of Jay Adams's *The Time Is at Hand* (1966)[150] and J. Marcellus Kik's *An Eschatology of Victory* (1971).[151] However, the most significant impetus to the current rise of preterism has to be its widespread adoption and propagation by those within the Christian Reconstruction movement.[152] The Reconstructionist attraction to preterism appears to have been spurred by the late Dr. Greg Bahnsen and spread through him to many of his disciples, who, in turn, helped it to expand.

Max R. King

The recent rise of full preterism within American evangelicalism appears to have risen through the Churches of Christ in general and through Max R. King, the longtime pastor of the Parkman Road Church of Christ in Warren, Ohio, in particular. King, along with the influence of J. Stuart Russell's book, appears to be the fountainhead of full preterism in the United States. King's first volume on "fulfilled eschatology" (full preterism) was introduced to the public in his 1971 offering *The Spirit of Prophecy.*[153] King summarizes his view as follows:

> In conclusion of the time and manner of prophecy's fulfillment, it is the author's deepest conviction that God's redemptive purposes, as revealed and advanced through the typical and prophetical system of the Old Testament, were fully consummated in the time period of the Revelation message.... There is,

therefore, nothing more to be revealed through inspired writing, and nothing more to be fulfilled with respect to what God intended to accomplish within the volume of his word.[154]

King arrives at his full preterism through the most extreme form of what he calls a "spiritual interpretation" that besmirches any literal interpretation of future events.[155] From his perspective, there is no future second coming.

King's other works include his massive 784-page tome *The Cross and the Parousia of Christ* (1987)[156] and *Old Testament Israel and New Testament Salvation* (1990).[157] During the last few years, Max's son, Tim, has joined him in promoting their brand of full preterism, which they call "transmillennialism."[158] They also produce a full-color magazine called *Living Presence.*

Greg L. Bahnsen

It also appears that Reformed and Reconstructionist scholar Greg L. Bahnsen (1948–1995) is the source and inspiration for the rise and spread of partial preterism. In the 1970s, Dr. Bahnsen taught at Reformed Theological Seminary in Jackson, Mississippi. Four of his students during this time were David Chilton, James Jordan, Gary DeMar, and Kenneth Gentry.[159] I know from personal conversations over the years with these men that Bahnsen influenced their thinking toward a postmillennial form of preterism. In addition to influencing students in the classroom, during this time Dr. Bahnsen taught a class on the book of Revelation at a Presbyterian church in the Jackson area. The 64 lessons are still available on audiocassette tape.[160]

Dr. Bahnsen's views on Revelation and the Olivet Discourse were pretty much a milder form of partial preterism. He followed Marcellus Kik[161] by teaching that the first 35 verses of Matthew 24 refer to the A.D. 70 judgment, and that the events described after verse 35 relate to a yet-future second coming.[162] His view of Revelation was the more traditional form of partial preterism:

> Here then is the course of history according to the book of Revelation. (1) Jesus is with His Church and has established the kingdom. (2) The Jews who persecuted are going to be destroyed by God. (3) The Romans who persecuted are going to be destroyed by God. (4) Then the Word of God is going to conquer the nations. The Great Commission is going to be fulfilled. (5) At the very end of history, Jesus will come back in judgment and he will introduce the new heavens and the new earth, where every tear will be wiped from our eyes and everything will be perfect.[163]

David Chilton

The first of Dr. Bahnsen's students to begin propagating preterism was the late Dr. David Chilton (1951–1997). Chilton argued in support of preterism in his book on postmillennialism entitled *Paradise Restored* (1985).[164] A couple years later, Chilton produced his commentary on Revelation, *The Days of Vengeance* (1987).[165] That same year, a condensed version of his commentary was released, called *The Great Tribulation* (1987).[166] Dr. Chilton was a straight-shooting, direct communicator and expressed his preterist views in this way:

> The Olivet Discourse is not about the second coming of Christ. It is a prophecy of the destruction of Jerusalem in A.D. 70.[167]

> The book of Revelation is not about the second coming of Christ. It is about the destruction of Israel and Christ's victory over His enemies in the establishment of the New Covenant Temple. In fact, as we shall see, the word *coming* as used in the book of Revelation never refers to the second coming. Revelation prophesies the judgment of God on apostate Israel; and while it does briefly point to events beyond its immediate concerns, that is done merely as a "wrap-up," to show that the ungodly will never prevail against Christ's Kingdom. But the main focus of Revelation is upon events which were soon to take place.[168]

Dr. Chilton was a moderate preterist when he wrote his books on eschatology. Interestingly, his teacher, Dr. Bahnsen, considered Dr. Chilton to be guilty of using bad hermeneutics in his commentary on Revelation. Part of Chilton's error is what was termed "interpretive maximalism." Dr. Bahnsen calls this the first of three fatal flaws in Dr. Chilton's commentary on Revelation, *Days of Vengeance*. Bahnsen said: "David's commitment to the imaginative guesswork of interpretive maximalism renders his commentary on Revelation unsound.... Error is laid upon error to reach this height of imagination....These kinds of flaws and misreadings make the commentary unreliable for the reader....We must all realize that, while creativity is a virtue in an original author, it is a crime in an interpreter."[169]

In late 1996, a little over a year before his death, Dr. Chilton became a full preterist[170] and was looking forward to writing material in support of his convictions. Dr. Chilton's books still receive wide distribution, and his commentary on Revelation is still used by many preterists.

Kenneth L. Gentry, Jr.

The next of Dr. Bahnsen's disciples to enter the publishing world on behalf of preterism was Dr. Kenneth L. Gentry, Jr. Dr. Gentry's doctoral dissertation from Whitfield Theological Seminary in Florida was published in 1989 as *Before Jerusalem Fell,*[171] which attempted to state and defend the Neroian date of Revelation (a position required for modern preterism to be possible). Dr. Gentry produced a smaller version of his first work in *The Beast of Revelation* (1989).[172] The third book Dr. Gentry wrote promoting preterism was *House Divided,* with Dr. Bahnsen (1989).[173] Dr. Gentry has since produced a number of other publications relating to preterism,[174] including a book in which the two of us debate our prophetic viewpoints.[175]

Like Dr. Bahnsen, Dr. Gentry believes the Olivet Discourse applies to A.D. 70 only up to verse 36.[176] However, Dr. Gentry differs from Dr. Bahnsen in that he believes almost the entire book of Revelation was fulfilled by A.D. 70: "I believe that the judgment chapters of Revelation (chs. 6-19) focus almost exclusively on the events associated with the first imperial persecution of Christianity (A.D. 64–68), the Roman Civil Wars (A.D. 68–69), and the destruction of the Temple and Israel (A.D. 67–70)." [177]

Dr. Gentry is also writing a commentary on Revelation, which will carry the title *Revelation: A Tale of Two Cities.*[178]

Gary DeMar

Gary DeMar, another Bahnsen disciple, has a ministry called American Vision, which is based in the Atlanta area. DeMar has attempted to present preterism teaching in a more popular form with his writings, which include many articles in the periodical produced by his ministry, *Biblical Worldview.* While DeMar holds to a preterist view of the book of Revelation,[179] he has also focused on arguing for a first-century fulfillment of all of the Olivet Discourse (including Matthew 25). His books include *Last Days Madness* [180] (1991) and, more recently, an attack of Tim LaHaye's dispensational theology in a work titled *End Times Fiction.*[181] In this latter book, DeMar states,

> But how can we maintain that Jesus "came" in A.D. 70?...
>
> Jesus' "coming" in judgment upon Jerusalem (Matthew 24:27) and His coming "*up* to the Ancient of Days" (Daniel 7:13) were two events that occurred within the time span of the first generation of Christians. There is no future fulfillment of these events. Since Jesus left no doubt that He would "come" before the first-century generation passed away, we must conclude that the idea of "coming" in this context is different from the way many contemporary Christians understand the concept. Jesus' coming in judgment upon Jerusalem in A.D. 70 was an event that would occur within a specified time frame—the generation

between A.D. 30 and 70 would not pass away until all the events predicted in the Olivet Discourse took place.[182]

Others

There is no doubt that all forms of preterism, except mild preterism, are on the rise and at an all-time high in popularity in evangelical circles in North America. Part of the reason this is so is because preterism has never had a popular appeal until our own day. Evidence of a growing popularity is seen in the numerous Internet sites that advocate various forms of preterism.[183] In addition, there are probably hundreds of privately published books that have been produced over the last ten to fifteen years by preterists. Some of their works include *What Happened In A.D. 70?* by Edward E. Stevens,[184] *Who Is This Babylon?* by Don K. Preston,[185] *Beyond the End Times* by John Noe,[186] and *Matthew 24 Fulfilled* by John L. Bray.[187] These authors are all full preterists.

Another major reason for the contemporary growth of preterism is due to R. C. Sproul's conversion to partial preterism in the 1990s as expressed through his book *The Last Days According to Jesus.*[188] In February 1999, Dr. Sproul sponsored a conference on preterism at his annual Ligonier Ministries national conference in Orlando, Florida. About 4,000 people attended, and this exposure did a lot for the spread of preterism, especially in the Reformed community. The speakers at the conference included Dr. Kenneth Gentry and Gary DeMar.

THE PRETERIST-CHALLENGE

D. H. Kromminga has noted that "preterist and the futurist methods, or approaches stand at opposite extremes."[189] Perhaps this explains why the historicist and idealist approaches have receded into the background, while the futurist and preterist views are in the forefront. Until recently, futurism has enjoyed an unobstructed field. But over the last decade, preterism, the polar opposite of futurism, has grown to provide a challenge to the futurist dominance within evangelicalism.

The futurist-method of interpreting Bible prophecy is still overwhelmingly the most popular view today. Yet, it is doubtful that most who hold the position have thought much about why they are futurists. In the absence of any perception of a challenger, the futuristic position has been taken for granted with almost no need to learn how to defend it. But with the rise of preterism, futurists are now required to think more about the basis for their position.

In this chapter, we have seen that preterism arose and grew in a climate of theological and exegetical deviancy. The original proponents of preterism in recent centuries are among those who have practiced a critical or rationalistic approach to interpreting the Bible. For example, preterists interpret key prophetic passages such as Zechariah 12–14, Matthew 24, and the book of Revelation in the same way liberals approach the entire canon of Scripture. Thus, preterism is a toxic and dangerous framework in which to cast God's holy Word.

Dr. Gentry objects to preterism being characterized in this way, saying,

> The problem with such observations is that they have failed to recognize a critical distinction between preterists of radical, naturalistic liberalism (e.g., the Tubingen school) and those of evangelical, supernaturalistic orthodoxy (e.g. Moses Stuart, Milton Terry, and Philip Schaff). In point of fact, however, "there is a radical difference between those Preterists who acknowledge a real prophecy and permanent truth in the book, and rationalistic Preterists who regard it as a dream of a visionary which was falsified by events."[190]

There may be a difference in the motives of "evangelical preterists," as Gentry implies, but they still engage in the same interpretative approach or process as the liberal preterists. There is no other approach to interpreting Bible prophecy than the critical approach refined by German liberals from which even evangelical preterists such as Dr. Gentry have gleaned so much. The preterism of today is still naturalistic in its understanding of key biblical passages.

Elsewhere, Dr. Gentry states, "Unfortunately, evangelical scholarship in the last fifty years has been hesitant to adopt a preterist hermeneutic. This has left the impression—at least among many lay students—that preterism is intrinsically liberal."[191]

Yet Gentry fails to acknowledge that all preterists argue the same way about Matthew 24 and the Apocalypse, whether they are liberal or conservative. This is clear from the historical development of their interpretative approach—even the conservative preterists constantly refer to critical and liberal scholars as their sources. A classic example of this is Moses Stuart's reliance upon liberal German preterists all throughout his commentary on Revelation. Dr. Charles Hodge (1797–1878) of Princeton Theological Seminary warned against preterism in 1873 when he said, "…setting aside the school of rationalistic interpreters, there are among those who believe it to be a revelation from God entirely different methods or theories concerning its purport and structure. According to one class it relates exclusively to the past; it is a delineation of the struggles through which the Church passed during the early ages of Christianity, until its final triumph under Constantine the Great."[192]

This type of thinking may explain why none of the Reformed scholars adopted the preterist approach throughout the entire tenure of old Princeton, which ended in 1929. Westminster Theological Seminary, which began in 1929, was an extension of the theological tradition of Princeton. No faculty member from Westminster has adopted preterism except Jay Adams in the homiletics department. Why have those within the Reformed camp systematically avoided preterism until very recent times? I believe, as Dr. Hodge noted, they see it as a liberal approach to interpreting the Bible.

For years I have looked through journals and books written in the past 200 years for articles and chapters written to refute preterism. Very little has been written. Why would this be the case? Most likely because preterism was dismissed within conservative circles as a liberal approach to Scripture. Since conservative scholars have long been opposed to liberalism in all of its forms, the preterist approach was summarily dismissed as an invalid hermeneutic for Bible-believing scholars to adopt—that is, until recent years.

Why have a significant number of Reformed individuals been attracted to preterism as of late? Before I give an answer, I believe it is safe to say that the overwhelming majority of Reformed scholars do reject preterism. However, while preterists are still a small minority within the Reformed circles, they are making significant gains within the world of Reformed scholarship.

First, it appears that the Reformed individuals who adopt preterism do so primarily as a reaction to dispensationalism.[193] In fact, even people outside of Reformed circles appear to adopt preterism as a reaction to dispensationalism. R. C. Sproul, Jr. says,

> The sickness that is epidemic in the evangelical church is the disease of dispensationalism, and more particularly dispensational eschatology. These doctrines not only twist and distort the Scripture but bring the church to near paralysis. The harder we work to build Christ's kingdom, the more we delay it.
>
> Thankfully, God in his mercy has done a great work in waking up many people to their condition. The rapid spread of the doctrine of preterism has been a welcome tonic.[194]

THE PRETERIST DANGERS

By rejecting the historicism of previous Reformed exegetes, modern Reformed advocates believe that, in preterism, they have an interpretative system that can go up against a cogent system like futurism. However, as noted earlier, the cost of such an adoption is a break with traditional

Reformed exegesis. Dr. Gentry, in his introduction of the reprint of a book by David Brown on postmillennialism from the 1840s, writes, "Lest it be misunderstood by my endorsement of Brown, I would like to point out one major area of disagreement....Brown's approach to Revelation is along the lines of historicism....My interpretive approach to Revelation, as is evident in each of my three most recent works, is that of preterism." [195]

Second, Dr. Walt Kaiser suggested in the early 1980s that the church is "now going through a hermeneutical crisis, perhaps as significant in its importance and outcome as that of the Reformation." [196] The present-day crisis finds its historical roots in the writings of Friedrich Schleirmacher (1768–1834), Wilhelm Dilthey (1833–1911), Martin Heidegger (1889–1976), Rudolf Bultmann (1884–1976), and Hans Georg Gadamer (b. 1900). [197] With Gadamer, as Dr. Kaiser notes, "the meaning of the text lies in its subject matter, rather than in what an author meant by that text." [198] Dr. Kaiser explains further: "The process of exegesis of a text is no longer linear but circular—one in which the interpreter affects his text as much as the text (in its subject matter) somehow affects the interpreter as well. Clearly, there is a confusion of ontology with epistemology, the subject with the object, the "thereness" of the propositions of the text with the total cultural and interpretive 'baggage' of the interpreter." [199]

I believe that the spirit of our postmodern times, shaped by a dominant mysticism, has led some individuals to become more open to a less literal hermeneutic. This, in turn, has led some exegetical minds to see the supposed shadow of the biblical text instead of the letter, or what is actually written. Today's hermeneutical atmosphere is such that interpretative schemes such as preterism are made to seem feasible, when in the past they were dismissed as too farfetched. The zeitgeist of our day nudges the mind toward the allegorical and not the literal, the shadow instead of the clear, and the mystical rather than the physical. Dr. Kaiser notes, "The grammatical-historical method of exegesis has served us all very well. But in recent decades, the hue and cry has gone up from scholarship at large to allow the reader and the modern situation to have as much (or in some cases, more) to say about what the text means as has traditionally been given to the original speaker of the text." [200]

Just because a conservative scholar uses a liberal approach to biblical interpretation does not cleanse that interpretation of the fact that it is the result of a naturalistic hermeneutic. So it has been with preterism down through history.

Third, a movement often known as Christian Reconstructionism, in which Greg Bahnsen, David Chilton, James Jordan, Gary North, Gary DeMar, and Ken Gentry participated, served as a catalyst for the spreading of preterism.[201] While not all who are known as Reconstructionists are preterists (a notable exception was founder of the movement, the late R. J. Rushdoony), it appears that most have become ardent proclaimers and defenders of preterism. This movement helped to provide a ready audience for many who would come to form the backbone of the recent rise of preterism.

An additional observation about those who become preterists is that those who initially subscribe to small elements of preterism tend to quickly become more radical in applying more and more of that interpretative approach to an increasing amount of Scripture. Many proponents of preterism often rush from partial preterism to full preterism almost overnight. They seem to reason, *If part of Scripture can be preterized, then why not the whole?*

Another common observation by futurists who oppose preterism is the arrogant attitude that too often accompanies those of the preterist persuasion. When preterists present their position, much of their time is spent running down those who disagree with them, especially dispensationalists. It is rare to have a discussion with a preterist or read an article or hear a lecture by a preterist that declines to belittle the opposition. In fact, E. B. Elliott, back in 1851, made this comment about one preterist:

> Considering the self-sufficient dogmatism which pre-eminently characterized the School in question, even as if, a priori to examination, all other schemes were to be deemed totally wrong, and the Praeterist Scheme alone conformable to the discoveries and requirements of "*modern exegesis*" (a dogmatism the more remarkable, when exhibited by a man of calm temperament and unimpassioned style, like Professor Stuart, and which to certain weaker minds may seem imposing), the question is sure to arise, What the grounds of this strange presumptuousness of tone?[202]

Is such an attitude endemic to the position of preterism itself, as consistently evidenced in its contemporary advocates?

Preterism, both partial and full, is a dangerous perspective that will, over time, eat the heart of the biblical expectancy of our Lord's return. We have seen that while preterism has a murky beginning and past, if it continues to grow and exert increasing influence upon American evangelicalism, then it will deprive more and more of the comfort and motivation that the blessed hope has historically produced in the lives of an expectant church.

Chapter 3

HERMENEUTICS AND BIBLE PROPHECY

THOMAS ICE

Consistently literal or plain interpretation is indicative of a dispensational approach to the interpretation of the Scriptures," declared Charles Ryrie in 1965. "And it is this very consistency—the strength of dispensational interpretation—that irks the nondispensationalist and becomes the object of his ridicule."[1] "Consistently literal interpretation" was listed by Ryrie as the second most important *sine qua non* of dispensationalism, which forms the foundation for the most important essential, "the distinction between Israel and the Church."[2] Earl Radmacher, in 1979, went so far as to say that literal interpretation "is the 'bottom-line' of dispensationalism."[3]

Outside dispensational futurist circles, some would admit that dispensational hermeneutics "continues to exercise a widespread influence among evangelical Christians today."[4] However, there are those who ridicule the literal approach of interpreting the Scriptures. Among the louder voices of dissent against the consistent literal hermeneutic of dispensational futurism are those from the preterist movement. (*Hermeneutics* refers to how one interprets literature.) For example, Kenneth Gentry labels the dispensational claim to consistently literal interpretation as a "presumption" that "is unreasonable" and "an impossible ideal."[5]

A DEFINITION OF LITERAL INTERPRETATION

What do dispensational futurists mean when they speak of "literal interpretation"? Ryrie begins his discussion of literal interpretation by referring to Bernard Ramm, who wrote the standard hermeneutics textbook of his day:

67

"Dispensationalists claim that their principle of hermeneutics is that of literal interpretation. This means interpretation which gives to every word the same meaning it would have in normal usage, whether employed in writing, speaking or thinking."[6] He then provides a more extensive definition:

> This is sometimes called the principle of grammatical-historical interpretation since the meaning of each word is determined by grammatical and historical considerations. The principle might also be called normal interpretation since the literal meaning of words is the normal approach to their understanding in all languages. It might also be designated plain interpretation so that no one receives the mistaken notion that the literal principle rules out figures of speech. Symbols, figures of speech and types are all interpreted plainly in this method and they are in no way contrary to literal interpretation. After all, the very existence of any meaning for a figure of speech depends on the reality of the literal meaning of the terms involved. Figures often make the meaning plainer, but it is the literal, normal, or plain meaning that they convey to the reader.[7]

Ryrie concludes his statement of the dispensational futurist position by quoting Presbyterian E. R. Craven's oft-cited summary of literalism: "The *literalist* (so called) is not one who denies that *figurative* language, that *symbols*, are used in prophecy, nor does he deny that great *spiritual* truths are set forth therein; his position is, simply, that the prophecies are to be *normally* interpreted (i.e., according to received laws of language) as any other utterances are interpreted—that which is manifestly figurative being so regarded."[8]

I believe that Ryrie's statement is adequate and that literal interpretation still is (should be) a defining tenet of dispensationalism. Many scholars and teachers believe that they have been able to satisfactorily interpret the details of Scripture and harmonize their exegetical conclusions into a theology that is the product of consistent literal interpretation. Those who contributed to this book are among those who hold to such a view.

ATTEMPTS TO DISCREDIT LITERAL INTERPRETATION

Vern Poythress, in *Understanding Dispensationalists*, wrote two chapters discussing Ryrie, dispensational futurists, and literal interpretation.[9] Poythress presented dispensationalists as using the word *literal* in such a fluid manner that it is often difficult to know exactly what is meant. "Perhaps the word," he suggested, "has already unconsciously been loaded with some of the assumptions belonging to the theological system."[10]

He said literal interpretation can be used in four ways. First is "first thought meaning," which is said to describe "the meaning for words in isolation."[11] Second is "flat interpretation," by which he means an *a priori* commitment to an idea of "literal *if possible*."[12] Third, he said, the one who uses grammatical-historical interpretation "reads passages as organic wholes and tries to understand what each passage expresses against the background of the original human author and the original situation."[13] And fourth, is "plain interpretation," where one "reads everything as if it were written directly to oneself, in one's own time and culture." This, however, is opposed to grammatical-historical interpretation.[14] Poythress sees the dispensationalist reference to literal interpretation as "a confusing term, capable of being used to beg many of the questions at stake in the interpretation of the Bible."[15]

Though it is true that dispensational futurists have used the term *literal* in at least two ways, Poythress's charge that this has lead to confusion and not answered important questions is not justified. Apparently Ryrie's statement was clear enough for Poythress to work his way through it and break it up into categories. What's more, much of the verbiage used by dispensationalists (i.e., normal, plain, grammatical-historical) are attempts to spell out what is meant by *literal* in light of critical objections to approaching the Scriptures in this manner. And even though Poythress divided futurist literal interpretation into four categories, these "divisions" are as artificial as he claims futurist hermeneutics to be. Just because he has come up with a scheme that attempts to discredit literal interpretation does not mean that his observations are valid. Nor does his "unpacking" of the meaning of *literal,* even if justified, mean that Ryrie's definition of literal interpretation is still not valid. In fact, it is!

The Futurist Understanding of Literal Interpretation

The dictionary defines *literal* as "belonging to letters." Further, it says literal interpretation involves an approach "based on the actual words in their ordinary meaning,…not going beyond the facts."[16] "Literal interpretation of the Bible simply means to explain the original sense of the Bible according to the normal and customary usages of its language."[17] How is this done? It can only be accomplished through the grammatical (according to the rules of grammar), historical (consistent with the historical setting of the passage), contextual (in accord with the context) method of interpretation as noted by Ryrie earlier. This is what we mean by literal interpretation.

Elliott Johnson has noted that much of the confusion over literal interpretation can be eliminated when one properly understands the two primary ways the term has been used down through church history: "(1) the clear, plain sense of a word or phrase as over against a figurative use, and (2) a system that views the text as providing the basis of the true interpretation."[18] Thus, dispensational futurists, by and large, have used the term *literal* to refer to their system of interpretation (the consistent use of the grammatical-historical system), and once inside that system, *literal* refers to whether or not a specific word or phrase is used in its context in a figurative or literal sense. This helps us understand why Radmacher describes the system of literal interpretation (Johnson's second point) as "both plain-literal and figurative-literal"[19] (Johnson's first point).

Johnson's second use of *literal* (i.e., systematic literalism) is simply the grammatical-historical system consistently used. The grammatical-historical system was revived by the Reformers, especially John Calvin.[20] It was set against the spiritual (spiritualized) interpretation or deeper meaning of the text, an approach of interpretation that was popular during the middle ages. Those who used this approach used the literal meaning of a text as a springboard to a deeper ("spiritual") meaning, which was viewed as more desirable. For example, a classic spiritualized interpretation would see the four rivers of Genesis 2—the Pishon, Havilah, Tigris, and Euphrates—as representing the body, soul, spirit, and mind. Given that such spiritualizing could lead to all kinds of arbitrary interpretations of Bible texts, the Reformers saw the need to get back to the literal interpretation of the Bible.

The *system* of literal interpretation is the grammatical-historical, or textual, approach to hermeneutics. Use of literalism in this sense could be called *macroliteralism.* Within macroliteralism, the consistent use of the grammatical-historical system yields the interpretative conclusion, for example, that *Israel* always and only refers to national Israel. The church will not be substituted for Israel if the grammatical-historical system of interpretation is consistently used because there are no indicators in the text that such is the case. Therefore, one must bring an idea from outside the text by saying that the passage really means something that it does not actually say. This kind of replacement approach is a form of spiritualized, or allegorical, interpretation. So when speaking of those who do replace *Israel* with the church as not taking the Bible literally and spiritualizing the text, it is true, since such a belief is contrary to a macroliteral interpretation.

Consistently literal interpreters, within the framework of the grammatical-historical system, do discuss whether or not a word, or phrase, of a biblical book is a figure of speech (connotative use of language) or is to be taken literally/plainly (denotative use of language). This is Johnson's first use of *literal,* which could be called *microliteralism.* Ramm has said: "The literal meaning of the figurative expression is the proper or natural meaning as understood by students of language. Whenever a figure is used its literal meaning is precisely that meaning determined by grammatical studies of figures. Hence, figurative interpretation does not pertain to the spiritual or mystical sense of Scripture, but to the literal sense." [21]

Thus, within microliteralism, there may be discussion by literalists as to whether or not a given word or phrase is being used as a figure of speech, based on the context of a given passage. Some passages are quite naturally clearer than others and a consensus among interpreters develops, whereas other passages may find literal interpreters divided as to whether or not they should be understood as figures of speech. This is more a problem of application than of method.

THE PRETERIST SHELL GAME

Preterist Kenneth Gentry, in his attack on consistent literal interpretation, argues that "*consistent* literalism is unreasonable." [22] One way he attempts to prove this is by arguing that since dispensational futurists take some words and phrases as figures of speech, they are not consistently literal. [23] He asserts that "the dispensational claim to '*consistent* literalism' is frustrating due to its inconsistent employment." [24] Gentry seeks to discredit the dispensational futurist hermeneutic by giving examples of dispensationalists who interpret certain passages as containing figures of speech, citing this as inconsistent with the system of literal interpretation.

Since literal interpretation has been by and large adopted as the proper hermeneutic in the last couple hundred years, when opponents attack its consistent use throughout Scripture, they have traditionally argued that consistent literalism sometimes leads to absurdity. For example, in the early church, Augustine (354–430) argued for a "spiritual" interpretation against the literal when he said the following: "…for I myself, too, once held this opinion [millennialism]. But, as they assert that those who then rise again shall enjoy the leisure of immoderate carnal banquets, furnished with an amount of meat and drink such as not only to shock the feeling of the temperate, but even to surpass the measure of credulity itself, such assertions can be believed only by the carnal." [25]

However, Irenaeus (130–200) had earlier argued for the literal interpretation of prophecy and against allegorization. He said, "If, however, any shall endeavour to allegorize [prophecies] of this kind, they shall not be found consistent with themselves in all points, and shall be confuted by the teaching of the very expressions [in question]." [26]

According to Gentry, the dispensational futurist has to abandon literal interpretation when he realizes that Jesus refers to Himself figuratively as a door in John 10:9.[27] Yet Gentry is not defining literal interpretation the way dispensational futurists do. Therefore, his conclusions about literal interpretation are misguided because he commonly mixes the two senses described by Johnson. When speaking of the macroliteral, he uses an example from microliteralism, and vice versa, therefore only *appearing* to have shown an inconsistency in literal interpretation. In reality, the examples cited fall within the framework of how dispensationalists have defined what they mean by literal interpretation. Gentry is playing a shell game by which he confuses the two senses in his effort to make it appear that the literal interpretation method is organically inconsistent. The only inconsistency, however, is in Gentry's confusion of the different senses of literal interpretation. Gentry appears to deliberately mix senses of literal by constructing a straw man for the purpose of winning his argument against the consistent use of the grammatical-historical hermeneutic.

In John 10:9, when Jesus calls Himself a door, consistent literalists do believe that Jesus is using a figure of speech. That doesn't mean they are resorting to allegorical or nonliteral interpretation, for the hermeneutical approach involved is microliteralism, not macroliteralism. The issue here is whether or not a word or phrase is used denotatively or connotatively, as consistent literalists have always recognized. As noted earlier, the issue with consistent literalism is one's overall approach to Scripture and, in this instance, prophecy. This is what I am calling macroliteralism, which does argue exclusively for consistent literalism or always using the grammatical-historical hermeneutic. This Gentry does not do when he argues that the church has replaced Israel in the program of God.[28] It is wrong for Gentry to take an example from microliteralism in order to argue against macroliteralism.

IS LITERALISM PRIMARILY A PHILOSOPHICAL CONCEPT?

Vern Poythress has charged that "classic dispensationalists have 'hedged' on the idea of fulfillment. They possess an idea of fulfillment and an idea of literalness that make it almost impossible in principle for the opponent to give a counter example."[29] Gentry echoes Poythress when he says that aspects of dispensational interpretation are "a preconceived hermeneutic," and asks, "Why must we begin with the assumption of literalism?"[30] The implication is that, if it is an idea, then it is a subjective *a priori* that was not developed from Scripture and is thus suspect.

Ryrie did state his hermeneutic as ideals, but that is because he was summarizing principles. In the mind of the dispensational futurist, these principles have been verified and developed through volumes of specific exegesis from the text of Scripture. It would be hard to prove that literal interpretation is merely a form of idealism forced upon the text simply because some individuals have expressed principles of interpretation or tried to support the literal approach with a philosophical argument. How else can one present a summary of conclusions except as principles that include ideas?[31] Many dispensational futurists believe that a philosophical rationale could be removed from the defense of literalism and the approach could still be developed and defended inductively from Scripture.

No doubt, the human thought process involves an interplay between ideas and data, so nothing is purely the product of sheer inductive observation. Presuppositions can be tested and verified or rejected through the interplay of specific exegesis and the refinement of hermeneutical principles. But one cannot argue against literalism on the grounds that it is a form of idealism that masks the richness of God's Word.

In a related issue, some say dispensationalists reflect a "common sense" or "plain sense" *a priori* philosophical influence from eighteenth- or nineteenth-century rationalism when employing the "literal if possible" principle.[32] Bible teacher and author David L. Cooper gives a classic statement of this hermeneutical principle in his "Golden Rule of Interpretation": "When the plain sense of Scripture makes common sense, seek no other sense; therefore, take every word at its primary, ordinary, usual, literal meaning unless the facts of the immediate context, studied in the light of related passages and axiomatic and fundamental truths, indicate clearly otherwise."[33]

Cooper's "Golden Rule" should not necessarily be classified as one reflecting "Scottish Common Sense Realism" (as some have asserted) primarily because it is a literary not a philosophical statement. Cooper does not use the phrase "common sense," as critics suggest, by appealing to an abstract theory of common understanding latent in humanity. Instead, he defines it within a literary context. Common sense, for Cooper, is controlled by the context of Scripture, not some idea of common meaning residing supposedly within the mind of the reader of Scripture. Terms such as *primary, ordinary, usual,* and *literal* meaning are developed literarily from Scripture within Cooper's rule, as well as theologically (i.e., "axiomatic and fundamental truths"). The tactic of pouring a meaning not intended by users of a given text into "common sense" falls by the wayside upon close examination. Cooper's rule is a helpful guide for discerning the Bible's use of literal or figurative language within the consistently literal system of interpretation.

Gentry, who has charged dispensationalists with having a "preconceived hermeneutic" that builds upon "the assumption of literalism,"[34] could be accused of a similar fault. He says, "It should be the Christian's practice that: (1) the clearer statements interpret the less clear…and (2) our hermeneutic should not be *a priori*, but derived from Scripture itself, allowing Scripture to interpret Scripture."[35] While agreeing with these two canons of interpretation, the point to be made is that if a "flaw of dispensationalism is its *a priori* 'literal' hermeneutic,"[36] how do Gentry's two points escape the same problem? What one person may presume to be a clear statement might not be considered such by another person. If hermeneutics should not be *a priori*, how does one ever start the process of biblical investigation without at least assuming an approach that could then be verified? That is the approach commonly taken by literalists; they believe that their hermeneutic has been verified from the Scriptures themselves as a result of dealing with specific texts.[37]

LITERAL INTERPRETATION AND FIGURES AND SYMBOLS

Critics of consistently literal interpretation sometimes contend that such an approach is not always applicable because Scripture contains figures of speech and symbols. An example is seen in a series of questions from the pen of Kenneth Gentry: "May not so rich a work as the Bible, dedicated to such a lofty and spiritual theme (the infinite God's redemption of sinful man), written by many authors over 1,500 years employ a variety of literary genres? No symbols? No metaphors? No analogies?"[38] Gentry goes on to admit that dispensational futurists do recognize literary devices such as figures of speech. However, he then presents the consistently literal approach of many dispensationalists as unworkable.[39] By presenting the literal approach as not allowing for symbols, metaphors, and analogies, he blatantly misrepresents that approach.

In light of Gentry's characterization, it is interesting to note that the most extensive work we have in English on biblical figures of speech was written by the dispensational futurist E. W. Bullinger in 1898. *Figures of Speech Used in the Bible: Explained and Illustrated* is said to have "never been duplicated or equaled in point of thoroughness and detail." "No one has done more to open the eyes of Bible students to this key than has Bullinger." It is said that Bullinger "catalogs and discusses no less than two hundred fifteen distinct figures…giving full explanation of its use in each instance."[40] Bullinger's work demonstrates that literalists have at least thought about Scripture's use of figures in a detailed and sophisticated way and do not consider the presence of such to conflict with literalism. What Gentry claims to be true in principle is denied by the actual facts in the form of how literalists actually do handle the biblical text. He misrepresents consistent literalism in an apparent desperate attempt to dissuade his readers from an approach that has been shown to handle accurately the Word of God.

Figures of speech are used primarily for the purposes of illustration and ornamentation. While sports announcers can say that a defender tackled the quarterback, they usually resort to more colorful commentary, saying, "The blitzing linebacker killed the quarterback and almost decapitated him." Though figurative speech is used, it's still in reference to a literal event. That principle applies to figures of speech in Scripture. For example, Isaiah 55:12 says, "You will go out with joy and be led forth with peace; the mountains and the hills will break forth into shouts of joy before you, and all the trees of the field will clap their hands." This passage speaks of what will happen during the millennium, but the trees will not literally clap their hands, nor will the hills speak forth with shouts of joy. Here, the Bible uses figurative speech to say that the curse upon nature will be removed during this future time.

Paul Tan explains, "The presence of figures in Scripture…does not militate against literal interpretation. Since literal interpretation properly accepts that which is normal and customary in language—and figurative language is certainly normal and customary—literal interpreters are not hindered by that which is figurative. There is no necessity to change to a different method of interpretation."[41]

Tan provides the following list of the kinds of figures of speech:

Simile	Personification	Allegory
Metaphor	Apostrophe	Parable
Metonymy	Hyperbole	Riddle
Synecdoche	Irony	Fable[42]

Interestingly, in the single instance where an allegory—which is an extended metaphor—is used (Galatians 4:21-31), it can only be interpreted literally. Tan notes the following:

> In Galatians 4, Paul assumes the literal existence of Hagar, Sarah, Mount Sinai, Jerusalem, etc. He cites them as allegories *only* for the purpose of illustration. In fact, Paul himself mentions that he is about to depart from normal interpretation by adding the parenthetical statement, "which things are an allegory" (Gal. 4:24)….
>
> The allegorical method is unknown to all the other New Testament writers and is never once sanctioned by Christ during His earthly ministry. Although it is proper to *interpret* an allegory (as we may interpret Galatians 4), it is wrong to allegorize a plain text of Scripture.[43]

Consistent literal interpreters also recognize the biblical use of symbols. For example, "Lamb" is used symbolically 28 times in the book of Revelation to represent Jesus Christ. Yet that does not mean a symbol is not referring to an actual historical event. I believe this is the case with most of the uses of "Lamb" in Revelation. Likely, "Lamb" is used of Christ to counter the "beast" (used 36 times in Revelation), which is a symbol for the future person popularly known as the Antichrist. Similarly, just because a golfer is known as "the Shark," does not mean that Greg Norman does not actually play professional golf in real history. The same is true of biblical symbols. Revelation 12:9 says of the "dragon" that he is "the serpent of old who is called the devil and Satan." The dragon is a symbol for Satan, but it does not mean that the acts and events associated with him are not real, time-space events. They are! The symbols in Revelation 12 are to be interpreted in the same way in which they were used in Genesis 37, which spoke of a real, historical event. Richard Shimeall makes the following point:

> ...*symbols* are the *representatives* of the agents, objects, qualities, acts, conditions, or effects of others of a different and resembling class....
>
> In other words, figures are to the literal agents or objects illustrated, what *shadows* are to the *substance*. We cannot use a figure without having in view the *literal* thing from which the figure is derived. For example: If we speak of a man as the *pillar* of the state, we have in view the nature of a *literal column* at the same time.[44]

Shimeall concludes:

> That the advocates of the figurative theory of interpretation... convert *figures* into *symbols*, and thus employ the agents, acts, and events of which they treat, as though they were the *representatives* of those of another class: in other words, that their literal meaning is but the *shell*, under which a spiritual or mystical sense, which it is alleged is their *only true* sense, is *veiled*. For instance, take the prophecy of Isaiah ii. 1-5: the *subjects* of which the affirmation is made, viz., "the mountain of the Lord's house"—"all nations shall flow into it"—"many people"—"Jehovah's house," etc., are all interpreted and applied in a spiritual sense, to denote the *conversion* of the Gentiles to the Christian faith, and their *ingathering* into the Christian Church, etc.[45]

Preterists engage in the kind of allegorical interpretation just outlined by Shimeall when they take passages such as Matthew 24:27-31 to say "that the prophecy has something to do with the destruction of Jerusalem in A.D. 70."[46] Here they take a plain-literal statement of Christ's personal, bodily return and twist it into a shadowy reference to a "judgment coming" actually performed by the Roman army. This cannot be the case, since the term "coming" is not in any way, shape, or form a figure of speech or symbol. The passage says "they will see the Son of Man" (verse 30). This has to be a reference to the visible, bodily, physical return of Jesus Christ to planet earth! This did not happen in A.D. 70., for not even Josephus records any such event back then. This phrase in Matthew 27:30 cannot refer to a symbolic, naturalistic return of Jesus in conjunction with the Roman army in the first century. Jesus said, "They will see the Son of Man," and that's what He meant.

UNDERSTANDING SENSE AND REFERENT

A few years ago on a hot afternoon I arrived home from the office and sat down to eat dinner. Still perspiring from the heat, I began sprinkling pepper on my vegetables. My mother-in-law asked, "Is it hot?" Thinking that she was referring to the temperature outdoors, I gave an answer that did not make sense to her. She then pointed out she was referring to the pepper, not the weather. Once I understood what she had meant, I was able to answer her question correctly.

Because the word *hot* can have multiple meanings, it is important to consider how the word is used. So it is with symbols and figures. A phrase like *white house* can have different meanings. It could refer to the white house across the street from one's own house. Or, one could be speaking of any house painted white in contrast to another color. One could have in mind the building in Washington, D.C. that serves as the home and workplace of the president. Or, one could use *White House* as a figurative synonym for "office of the president of the United States." Building upon the basic sense of the phrase, the context serves to specify the possible meanings of a referent. "Sense and referent" are important to understand when it comes to biblical interpretation.[47]

Let's consider an example of preterist hermeneutics relating to sense and referent. In Matthew 24:29-30, which appears in the context of the Olivet Discourse, we read of the sun and moon being darkened, stars falling from the sky, the sign of the Son of Man appearing in the sky for all the world to see, and Christ "coming on the clouds of the sky with power and great glory" (verse 30). Preterists believe that these phrases do not describe a future coming of Christ; instead, they believe the passage refers to God's coming in judgment upon Israel in A.D. 70 through the Roman army's destruction of Jerusalem. "The sign that the Son of Man is in heaven was the smoking rubble of Jerusalem,"[48] declares Gentry. Gary DeMar agrees: "In speaking of the sun and moon going dark and stars falling (Matthew 24:29), Jesus is describing the nation of Israel under judgment."[49] Instead of seeing Matthew 24 as describing God's judgment during the future seventieth week of Daniel, preterists see the passage as depicting "a providential coming of Christ in *historical judgments upon men*."[50] Gentry explains:

> In the Old Testament, clouds are frequently employed as symbols of divine wrath and judgment. Often God is seen surrounded with foreboding clouds which express His unapproachable holiness and righteousness. Thus, God is poetically portrayed in certain judgment scenes as *coming in the clouds* to wreak historical vengeance upon His enemies. For example: "The burden against Egypt. Behold, the Lord rides on a swift cloud, and will come into Egypt; the idols of Egypt will totter at His presence, and the heart of Egypt will melt in its midst" (Isaiah 19:1). This occurred in the Old Testament era, when the Assyrian king Esarhaddon conquered Egypt in 671 B.C. Obviously it is not to be understood as a literal riding upon a cloud, any more so than Psalm 68:4: "Sing to God, sing praises to His name; Extol Him who rides on the clouds, By His name YAH, And rejoice before Him."
>
> The New Testament picks up this apocalyptic judgment imagery when it speaks of Christ's coming in clouds of judgment *during history*.[51]

Gentry cites the following passages as supporting his thesis: 2 Samuel 22:8,10; Psalm 18:7-15; 68:4,33; 97:2-39 (*sic;* Psalm 97 has only 12 verses); 104:3; Isaiah 13:9; 26:21; 30:27; Joel 2:1,2; Micah 1:3; Nahum 1:2ff; Zephaniah 1:14-15.[52]

Most likely all Bible interpreters would agree in principle that just because various passages have a similar sense does not mean that they have the same referent. It's possible, but each specific instance must be verified by the contextual usage. There is no question that divine judgment is related by the clouds mentioned in the passages cited by Gentry. The picture of smoke, fire, clouds, and darkness gives a universal sense of the Lord's wrath. However, certain differences exist, which supports the view that there are at least two referents.

First, there are those passages related to the Lord's judgment of Israel's enemies on behalf of Israel. These are events that have either taken place in the past or are taking place at the time of writing, in which the Lord is pictured as "riding" across the skies in a chariot of judgment (2 Samuel 22:8,11; Psalm 18:7-15; 68:4,33; "walks," Psalm 104:3). While the other passages cited by Gentry do speak of judgment, they do not employ the "cloud" motif, and/or a nonpreterist would locate their timing at the future Day of the Lord (Isaiah 13:9; 26:21; 30:27; Joel 2:1,2; Micah 1:3; Nahum 1:2ff; Zephaniah 1:14-15).

Second, Matthew 24:30 says that "all the tribes of the earth...will see the Son of Man coming on the clouds of the sky with power and great glory." Here we have a picture of Christ not just riding across the sky, as in the previously cited Old Testament passages, but One who is "coming" from heaven to earth. The picture here is of a different event, even though elements are present that characterize all of God's judgments. It may be that in the other passages, the Lord is pictured as "riding" or "walking" among the clouds in smaller, local judgments. Then when the time comes for the grand finale, the Bible continues along the theme of judgment, but this time Christ actually comes to the earth in a display of visible glory and power.

Third, preterists see Matthew 24 as describing the Lord's judgment upon Israel (the Lord being in the clouds) through the Roman army. A close examination of the passage, however, reveals that the Lord returns to earth to rescue His people Israel (see 24:31), and that His judgment is not poured out upon Israel, but upon the Gentile nations that are persecuting Israel. So again, just because a similar sense is painted in some passages does not mean that all passages with that same general sense refer to the same event. The interpretation of figures of speech must be controlled by their specific context.

For example, we understand that in Luke 21:20-24, Christ refers to the A.D. 70 destruction of Jerusalem because He says "when you see Jerusalem surrounded by armies, then recognize that her desolation is near" (21:20). Also, Jerusalem is said to be "trampled under foot by the Gentiles until the times of the Gentiles are fulfilled" (21:24). But in Luke 21:25-28 (a passage that's parallel to Matthew 24:30-34), there is a change of language in reference to God's intervention, which shifts from judgment upon Israel (as in A.D. 70 and Luke 21:20-24) to His judgment upon "the earth," where there is "dismay among nations" (*ethnon*, 21:25), and "the world" (*oikoumene*, 21:26) and to His rescue of Israel from her enemies (21:25-28). This is said to involve "signs in sun and moon and stars" (21:25).[53]

Finally, preterists such as Gentry do see some passages that have "cloud language" as referring to the second coming (Acts 1:9-11; 1 Thessalonians 4:13-17).[54] Further, Gentry interprets 2 Thessalonians 1:7-10 as a reference to the second coming,[55] for it contains many elements of judgment, such as "the Lord Jesus will be revealed from heaven with His mighty angels in flaming fire, dealing out retribution to those who do not know God" (1:7b-8a). Yet it would seem the grounds he uses to argue for a past fulfillment of Matthew 24:30 could be applied to these passages as well. This demonstrates that it is important to recognize the distinctions between sense and referent. Failure to do so may lead one to draw faulty conclusions and to overlook basic literary principles.

STAYING TRUE TO LITERAL INTERPRETATION

We suggest that it is wrong to abandon the use of a consistently literal hermeneutic when it comes to interpreting Bible prophecy, for this approach does not change the originally understood meaning of given Bible texts. And though the grammatical-historical hermeneutic approach is claimed by all evangelicals, we believe that only dispensational futurists attempt to apply it consistently from Genesis to Revelation. Preterists use a grammatical-historical-*theological* hermeneutic (a form of spiritualization, as they replace Old Testament Israel with the church based on what they wrongly believe are New Testament grounds).

When it comes to the role of pre-understanding, and *a priori* theological beliefs why do the critics of the older literal hermeneutic not invest some time examining the impact that the anti-rational, mystical ethos of today's culture is having on their own hermeneutical pre-understanding? To put today's skepticism in the language of a once-popular TV commercial, "Why ask why?" implying that one cannot really know. Paul Karleen notes,

> Poythress never questions this presupposition [covenant the-ology's covenant of grace]....He urges the dispensationalist over and over to examine cherished assumptions. Yet he does not do the same. Is it the case that everything is open to negotiation for him but the covenant? In spite of his appeal to all of us to look at the Bible, tradition may condition his thinking far more than he suspects.[56]

Walter Kaiser has warned,

> The grammatical-historical method of exegesis has served us all very well. But in recent decades, the hue and cry has gone up from scholarship at large to allow the reader and the modern sit-uation to have as much (or in some cases, more) to say about what a text means as has traditionally been given to the original speaker of the text....Can we profit from the insights of moder-nity without being sucked into its vortex? This will be the ques-tion of the next years.[57]

Perhaps some of the critics of the consistently literal hermeneutic (as defined in this chapter) are bothered by the certainty they see amongst older dispensational brethren because of the impact upon their hermeneutical pre-understanding that our modern culture represents. Today's climate is one of self-centered relativism, with no epistemological orientation to a concept of absolute truth. This mind-set is destructive of certainty and creates in people an attitude of tentativeness. While all evangelicals believe in absolute truth, at least to some degree, perhaps modernity has eroded a valid belief in the certainty that God's children can understand His Word in a detailed way.

Chapter 4

PRETERIST
"TIME TEXTS"

Thomas Ice

The whole system of the preterist interpretive approach revolves around when certain prophetic passages are to be fulfilled in history. If the preterist interpretation is wrong, then clearly, the whole view is wrong. I believe preterists are wrong about virtually every passage they cite as a "time text" in arguing their viewpoint. In fact, preterists are often wrong to assume that the many passages they put forward are even "time texts."

THE "TIME TEXTS" IN MATTHEW

Dr. R. C. Sproul and other preterists often teach that there are at least three major passages in Matthew that demand a first-century fulfillment.[1] The three verses are Matthew 10:23, 16:28, and 24:34. I will examine this triad of texts in the order in which they appear in Matthew and demonstrate why they were not fulfilled in the first century.

Matthew 10:23

> Whenever they persecute you in one city, flee to the next; for truly I say to you, you will not finish going through the cities of Israel until the Son of Man comes.

"Again, if Russell is correct in concluding that the coming referred to in this text is the parousia of Christ, then the primary time-frame for the parousia must be restricted to a forty-year period," writes Sproul. "It surely did not take the disciples much more than forty years to cover the boundaries of Palestine with the gospel message."[2] This view is not defended in Sproul's book; instead, Sproul merely asserts it as a supposition, taking J. Stuart Russell's word for it. Russell tells us "our Lord probably intended to intimate, that the apostles would not finish evangelizing the towns of Palestine, before He should come to destroy Jerusalem and scatter the nation."[3] Does the plain reading of this passage teach us what preterists say? I don't believe it does.

First, the time of fulfillment for this passage depends upon establishing the context for which our Lord envisioned its realization. Even J. Stuart Russell believes that there is "abundant warrant for assigning the important prediction contained in Matthew x. 23 to the discourse delivered on the Mount of Olives."[4] He explains that "it is an admitted fact that even the Synoptical Gospels do not relate all events in precisely the same order....Dr. Blaikie observes: 'It is generally understood that Matthew arranged his narrative more by subjects and places than by chronology.'"[5] I am in agreement at this point that the context is that of the Olivet Discourse, even though we disagree as to when that period takes place. Thus, to a large extent, a discussion of the time when Matthew 10:23 is to be fulfilled must be postponed until interpretative decisions are made in relation to other passages, such as Matthew 24.

Second, when consulting a harmony of the Gospels,[6] it becomes evident that the other uses of the vocabulary from the context of Matthew 10:16-23 parallels in the Synoptic Gospels the various versions of the Olivet Discourse (Matthew 24-25; Mark 13; Luke 17 and 21). In fact, the *New Geneva Study Bible*, of which Sproul is the general editor, says of this passage, "The 'coming' is the Second Coming of Christ to judge the earth. This view fits most of the other occurrences of the phrase (24:30; 25:31; 26:64; but see 16:28)."[7] This information supports the conclusion from the previous point that the timing of the fulfillment of this passage is tied to the Olivet Discourse.

Third, all agree there is no indication in Scripture that the disciples experienced the kind of persecution mentioned in this passage before the crucifixion of Christ. J. Stuart Russell admits, "There is no evidence that the disciples met with such treatment on their evangelistic tour."[8] Thus, this sustains the conclusion to which we are building: that our Lord has a future time in mind when He speaks the words of this passage.

Fourth, I believe that, because of the nature of the vocabulary, Matthew 10:21-23 refers to events that will take place during the Tribulation and climax in the glorious second coming of Christ. This point could not be made any clearer than has been stated by the Reformed commentator William Hendriksen:

> These explanations ignore the fact that in the other Matthew
> passages in which the coming of the Son of man is mentioned

and described the reference is linked with the second coming. It is a coming "in the glory of his Father," "with his angels," "to render to every man according to his deed" (16:27, 28); a coming when Christ shall "sit on the throne of his glory" (19:28); a coming that will be "visible" (24:27); "sudden and unexpected" (24:37,39,44); a coming "on clouds of heaven with power and great glory" (24:30; cf. 25:31; 26:64). It would be strange therefore if from 10:23 any reference to Christ's exaltation which attains its climax in the second coming would be wholly excluded....The destruction of Jerusalem is predicted not here in chapter 10 but in 22:7; 23:38; see also 24:2, 15 f."[9]

Fifth, the use of the title "Son of Man" "*has a definite doctrinal significa-tion—it always refers to the (Parousia) Second Coming.*' The phrase, so expressive of His *humanity, indicates a visible, personal Coming*, which was not exhibited at the destruction of Jerusalem. Beside this, all excepting John were deceased *before* the city was overthrown."[10]

John Calvin was correct when he noted that the suggestion that Matthew 10:23 was fulfilled in the destruction of Jerusalem is "too far-fetched."[11] It is noted that Matthew 21:9, speaking of Christ's triumphal entry, says, "Blessed is He who comes in the name of the Lord." Matthew 10:23 could not have been fulfilled then, because it does not handle the persecution aspects of the passage, which did not occur in relation to the triumphal entry. Instead, I believe that Matthew 10:21-23 refers to a still-future time of Tribulation and the second coming of Christ.

How should this passage be explained? Yeager explains it well: "The apostles never completed their kingdom ministry before they turned to the Gentiles. This was because Israel did not receive their message. This thought is developed throughout the remainder of chapter 10 and in chapter 11, in which Jesus finally castigates Israel, withdraws the message of national deliverance and turns to individuals with an offer of salvation in Matthew 11:28-30."[12]

Dr. Stanley Toussaint further explains, "The Messiah was simply looking past His death to the time of tribulation following. At the time the disciples would have the same message and possibly the same power. The narrow road leading to the kingdom leads through the tribulation (Matthew 10:16), and this persecution is to be of a religious and political nature (Matthew 10:16-19).... The Lord made no error and clearly had 'the coming' for judgment in mind. However, the coming is contingent upon Israel's acceptance of its King. Because even after His resurrection, that nation refused Him, it became impossible to establish the kingdom (cf. Acts 3:18-26). In fact, the tribulation period did not come; if it had, the promise of the soon coming of the Son of Man would have been of great comfort to the apostles." [13]

Matthew 10:23 does not support the preterist contention that the coming of the Son of Man occurred in A.D. 70 through the Roman army. Instead, Christ was looking ahead to another time, the Tribulation and the glorious second advent. I believe this will be made clearer as we investigate related passages.

Matthew 16:27-28

> The Son of Man is going to come in the glory of His Father with His angels, and will then repay every man according to his deeds. Truly I say to you, there are some of those who are standing here who will not taste death until they see the Son of Man coming in His kingdom.

Sproul and other preterists teach that Matthew 16:28 is another prophetic "time-text" that was fulfilled in the A.D. 70 destruction of Jerusalem by the Romans. Thus, coupled with a similar understanding of other so-called "time-texts," almost all Bible prophecies—including those in Matthew 24 and the book of Revelation—have already been fulfilled.

> The expression "shall not taste death" clearly refers to dying, so we may render the text to mean that some who were hearing Jesus' words on this occasion would not die before witnessing some kind of coming of Jesus....
>
> If Jesus had in mind a time-frame of roughly forty years, it could also be said that during this time-frame some of his disciples would not taste death. If the Olivet Discourse refers primarily to events surrounding the destruction of Jerusalem and if the word *generation* refers to a forty-year period, then it is possible, if not probable, that Jesus' reference to his coming in Matthew 16:28 refers to the same events, not to the transfiguration or other close-at-hand events. [14]

Preterists believe that Matthew 16:28 and its parallel passages (Mark 9:1; Luke 9:27) are all predictions of the destruction of Jerusalem as accomplished through the Roman army in A.D. 70. By contrast, I believe that Matthew 16:28 was fulfilled by events that took place on the Mount of Transfiguration.

Understanding the Transfiguration

To properly interpret Matthew 16:28, we need to observe the comparisons and contrasts of the three parallel statements found in Matthew 16:27-28, Mark 9:1, and Luke 9:26-27. All three accounts are descriptive of the same event, yet it is interesting to note the vocabulary and contexts of each inspired writer.

The Context

Matthew 16:27 is speaking of the future second coming, while verse 28 refers to the impending transfiguration. Why are these statements positioned in this way? Because earlier, Christ revealed clearly His impending death to His disciples (see 16:21). When Peter reacts to this (16:22), our Lord responded to Peter with His famous "Get behind Me, Satan!" statement (16:23). Then Jesus provided a lesson to His disciples on denial of self (16:24-26). Christ taught that the order for entrance into His kingdom, for both Himself and His followers, is the path of first the cross and then the crown. Suffering precedes glory! But the glory will one day come at Christ's second advent, when each individual will be required to give an account of his actions during the time of suffering (16:27). In order to encourage His followers, who would have to swallow the bitter pills of the impending death of Jesus and their own suffering and eventual deaths for Christ's sake, Christ provides a word of the promised future glory in 16:28 about some who will "see the Son of Man coming in His kingdom." "After Jesus predicted His own death, Peter and the other disciples needed reassurance that Jesus would ultimately triumph. His prediction that some of them would *see the kingdom of God present with power* must have alleviated their fears."[15] Thus, "verse twenty-seven looks at the establishment of the kingdom in the future, while a promise of seeing the Messiah in His glory is the thought of verse twenty-eight. They are two separate predictions separated by the words 'truly I say to you.' "[16]

The Preterist Objections

Preterists say that the phrase from Matthew 16:28, "there are some of those who are standing here who will not taste death," cannot be fulfilled by the immediately following transfiguration event. "But the transfiguration cannot be its fulfillment," insists Gary DeMar, "since Jesus indicated that some who were standing with Him would still be alive when He came but most would be dead."[17] DeMar misses the point of the passage in his attempt to prove too much, as noted by commentator William Lane, who counters such a view by noting: "…it is not said that death will exclude some of those present from seeing the announced event. All that is required by Jesus' statement is that "some" will see a further irruption of the power and sovereignty of God before they experience the suffering foreseen in Ch. 8:34-35."[18]

Some opposing the transfiguration interpretation say that a week is too short of a time frame to make proper sense of the statement. Ken Gentry says, "It was not powerfully to evidence itself immediately, for many of His disciples would die before it acted in power."[19] George N. H. Peters quotes a Dr. Kendrick who says that the disputed phrase "refers not to length of life, but to *privilege; some* shall have the privilege of beholding Him in His glory *even before they die*."[20] When we consider the force of the preceding context leading up to our Lord's statement, the futurist view makes the best sense. Randolph Yeager explains, "That Jesus should have suggested that some who had been standing there might die within the next week is in line with what He had been saying about taking up the cross, denying oneself, losing one's life, etc."[21]

A further problem with the preterist view is that our Lord said "*some* of those standing here...." It is clear that the term "some" would have to include at least two or more individuals, since "some" is plural and coupled with a plural verb, "to be." The word "some" nicely fits the three disciples—Peter, James, and John (Matthew 17:1)—who were participants at our Lord's transfiguration. On the other hand, Peters notes that "John only survived"[22] among the 12 disciples till the destruction of Jerusalem.

Further Support

All three instances of this parallel passage (Matthew 16:28; Mark 9:1; Luke 9:27) are immediately followed by an account of the transfiguration. This contextual relationship by itself is a strong reason to favor the futurist interpretation and shifts the burden of proof on the preterist view. In other words, Jesus made a prediction about a future event, and Matthew, Mark, and Luke record the fulfillment of that prediction in the passage that follows. The contextual fact is supported by the grammatical construction that connects these passages. Alva J. McClain notes that "the conjunction with which chapter 17 begins clearly establishes the unbroken continuity of thought between 16:28 and 17:1, as also in the accounts of Mark and Luke where no chapter division occurs."[23]

All three accounts of the prophesied event speak of *seeing* and *the kingdom*. Matthew says they will see "the Son of Man coming in His kingdom," emphasizing the person of the Son of Man coming. Mark says, "they see the kingdom of God" and he adds that it will come "with power." Luke simply says that "they see the kingdom of God." The transfiguration fits all aspects of the various emphases found in each of the three precise predictions.

Matthew's stress upon the actual, physical presence of the Son of Man is clearly met in the transfiguration because Jesus was personally and visibly present. Matthew says, "He was transfigured before them; and His face shone like the sun, and His garments became as white as light" (17:2). The preterist interpretation does not meet Matthew's criteria, since Jesus was not personally present at the later destruction of Jerusalem.

Mark's emphasis upon a display of the kingdom with "power" was certainly fulfilled by the transfiguration. No one could doubt that the transfiguration certainly fit the definition of a "power encounter" for the disciples. That Jesus appeared dressed in the Shechinah glory of God upon the Mount (Mark 9:3) was evidence to the disciples that He was God and that He acted with power.

Luke's simple statement about some who will "see the kingdom of God" is vindicated also by his account (17:28-36). Twice Luke records our Lord describing the transfiguration by using the term "glory" (17:31-32). "Why exclude the reference to Jerusalem's destruction? Because Luke does not associate the kingdom's power with this event.... Also, Jesus is not associated with Jerusalem's destruction directly, so it is not in view."[24]

Looking Back at the Transfiguration

The transfiguration made such an impression upon Peter and John that both provided a description of the glorified Christ in later writings (2 Peter 1:16-21; Revelation 1:12-20). Both describe the risen and glorified Christ in relation to His second advent (2 Peter 1:16; Revelation 1:7). In 2 Peter 1:16-18, no one doubts that Peter has in mind the transfiguration. I believe that Peter restates in his final epistle the same pattern established by our Lord in the passages we have been discussing above (Matthew 16:28; Mark 9:1; Luke 9:27). When encouraging believers to remain true to the faith (2 Peter 1:12ff.), Peter, like our Lord, reminds his readers of "the power and coming of our Lord Jesus Christ" (2 Peter 1:16). Peter follows Jesus' pattern of supporting the future second advent by citing the past transfiguration (2 Peter 1:16-18). In this way, Peter's second epistle supports the futurist understanding of Matthew 16:28.

George Peters says that 2 Peter 1:16-18 "is unquestionably, then, linking it with the still future Advent as a striking exhibition of the glory that shall be revealed—which is confirmed by Peter introducing this allusion to prove that Christ would thus again come."[25] William Lane further explains that

> Peter made known to his churches the power that was to be revealed at Jesus' coming in terms of the glory which had been revealed in the transfiguration. This expresses precisely the relationship between Ch. 8:38 (parousia) and Ch. 9:1 (transfiguration). The transfiguration was a momentary, but real (and witnessed) manifestation of Jesus' sovereign power which pointed beyond itself to the parousia, when he will come "with power and glory" (Ch. 13:26).[26]

The preterist contention that our Lord's prophecy in Matthew 16:28 predicts the destruction of the Temple in the first century has been proven to be off base. Instead, we have found that Matthew 16:27 refers to a yet-future second coming of Christ, while 16:28 was fulfilled only a week after the prophecy was uttered by our Lord. "The immediate sequel to Jesus' solemn promise is the account of the transfiguration (Ch. 9:2-8)," explains Lane.

> This indicates that Mark understood Jesus' statement to refer to this moment of transcendent glory conceived as an enthronement and an anticipation of the glory which is to come....The fulfillment of Jesus' promise a short time later (Ch. 9:2) provided encouragement to the harassed Christians in Rome and elsewhere that their commitment to Jesus and the gospel was valid. The parousia is an absolute certainty. The transfiguration constituted a warning to all others that the ambiguity which permits the humiliation of Jesus and of those faithful to him will be resolved in the decisive intervention of God promised in Ch. 8:38.[27]

Matthew 24:34

The Bible verse most widely used by preterists in their attempts to establish their thesis concerning Bible prophecy is Matthew 24:34. The much-debated passage says, "Truly I say to you, this generation will not pass away until all these things take place" (see also Mark 13:30; Luke 21:32).

The Preterist Interpretation

Examining the Preterist View

R. C. Sproul says, "I am convinced that the substance of the Olivet Discourse was fulfilled in A.D. 70...."[28] Ken Gentry declares of Matthew 24:34, "This statement of Christ is indisputably clear—and absolutely demanding of a first-century fulfillment of the events in the preceding verses, including the Great Tribulation."[29] Gary DeMar believes "that all the events prior to Matthew 24:34 referred to events leading up to and including the destruction of Jerusalem in A.D. 70."[30] DeMar continues, "Every time 'this generation' is used in the New Testament, it means, without exception, the generation to whom Jesus was speaking."[31] DeMar's assertion is simply not true! For example, "this generation" in Hebrews 3:10 clearly refers to the generation of Israelites who wandered in the wilderness for 40 years during the Exodus. In fact, DeMar spews forth another dogmatic assertion: "An honest assessment of Scripture can lead to no other conclusion. The integrity of the Bible is at stake in the discussion of the biblical meaning of 'this generation.'[32] It is true that the integrity of the Bible is almost always at stake in the discussion of what any biblical passage may mean. But why does DeMar make such a polarizing though misguided overstatement? I believe this can be better understood by Sproul's following explanation:

> The cataclysmic course surrounding the parousia as predicted in the Olivet Discourse obviously did not occur "literally" in A.D. 70....This problem of literal fulfillment leaves us with three basic solutions to interpreting the Olivet Discourse:
>
> 1. We can interpret the entire discourse literally. In this case we must conclude that some elements of Jesus' prophecy failed to come to pass, as advocates of "consistent eschatology" maintain.
>
> 2. We can interpret the events surrounding the predicted parousia literally and interpret the time-frame references figuratively. This method is employed by those who do not restrict the phrase...to Jesus' contemporaries.
>
> 3. We can interpret the time-frame references literally and the events surrounding the parousia figuratively.... All of Jesus' prophecies in the Olivet Discourse were fulfilled during the period between the discourse itself and the destruction of Jerusalem in A.D. 70.
>   The third option is followed by preterists.[33]

Sproul's "framing" of the possible interpretations of the phrase "this generation" distorts the first possibility with the perspective of liberalism. How so? Many interpreters, such as myself, interpret the entire discourse literally, but we dogmatically reject any notion "that some elements of Jesus' prophecy failed to come to pass." This does not mean that we have abandoned literal interpretation, nor does it "logically lead" to a failure in the fulfillment of Christ's prophecy.

Letting Scripture Interpret Itself

But how do we know that almost all of the other New Testament uses of "this generation" refer to Christ's contemporaries? We learn this by examining how each is used in its context. For example, Mark 8:12 says, "Sighing deeply in His spirit [Jesus is speaking], He said, 'Why does this generation seek for a sign? Truly I say to you, no sign will be given to this generation.'" Why do we conclude that "this generation," in this passage, refers to Christ's contemporaries? We know this because the referent in this passage is to Christ's contemporaries who were seeking for a sign from Jesus. Thus, it refers to Christ's contemporaries because of the controlling factor of the immediate context.

When interpreting the Bible, you cannot just say, as DeMar and many preterists do, that because something means XYZ in other passages that it has to mean the same thing in a given verse.[34] No! You must make your determination from the passage itself and how it is used in its context. *Context* is the most important factor in determining the exact meaning or referent under discussion.[35] That is how one is able to realize that most of the other uses of "this generation" refer to Christ's contemporaries.

Consider, for example, Matthew 23:36, which says, "Truly I say to you, all these things will come upon this generation." To whom does "this generation" refer? In this case, we know "this generation" refers to Christ's contemporaries because of the contextual support. "This generation" is governed or controlled grammatically by the phrase "all these things." "All these things" refers to the judgments that Christ pronounces in Matthew 22–23. So, in each appearance of "this generation," the meaning is determined by what it modifies in the immediate context.

The same is true for Hebrews 3:10, which says, "Therefore I was angry with this generation." "This generation" is governed or controlled grammatically by the contextual reference to those who wandered in the wilderness for 40 years during the exodus.

The Correct View
Regarding "This Generation"

Now, why does "this generation" in Matthew 24:34 (as well as Mark 13:30 and Luke 21:32), *not* refer to Christ's contemporaries? Because the governing referent to "this generation" is "all these things." Since Jesus is giving an extended prophetic discourse on future events, one must first determine the nature of "all these things" prophesied in verses 4 through 31 to know what generation Christ is referring to. Since "all these things" did not take place in the first century, then the generation whom Christ speaks of must still be future. It's as simple as that. Christ is saying that the generation that sees "all these things" occur will not cease to exist until all the events of the future Tribulation are literally fulfilled. Frankly, this is both a literal interpretation and one that was not fulfilled in the first century. Christ is not speaking to His contemporaries, but to the generation to whom the signs of Matthew 24 will become evident. Dr. Darrell Bock, in commenting on the parallel passage to Matthew 24 in Luke's Gospel, concurs:

What Jesus is saying is that the generation that sees the beginning of the end, also sees its end. When the signs come, they will proceed quickly; they will not drag on for many generations. It will happen within a generation.…The tradition reflected in Revelation shows that the consummation comes very quickly once it comes.…Nonetheless, in the discourse's prophetic context, the remark comes after making comments about the nearness of the end *to certain signs*. As such it is the issue of the signs that controls the passage's force, making this view likely. If this view is correct, Jesus says that when the signs of the beginning of the end come, then the end will come relatively quickly, within a generation.[36]

Preterists have *reversed* the interpretative process by declaring first that "this generation" *has* to refer to Christ's contemporaries, thus all these things had to be fulfilled in the first century. When one points out that various events described in Matthew 24 did not occur and thus those passages were not fulfilled, preterists merely repeat their mantra of "this generation," saying that all these things had to be fulfilled in the first century. In fact, when one compares the use of "this generation" at the beginning of the Olivet Discourse in Matthew 23:36 (which is an undisputed reference to A.D. 70) with the prophetic use in Matthew 24:34, a contrast becomes obvious. Jesus is contrasting the *deliverance* for Israel in Matthew 24:34 with the predicted *judgment* stated in Matthew 23:36.

Regarding All These Things

When challenged or threatened about the veracity of other interpretative details, preterists almost always fall back to what Gary DeMar calls the "time texts."[37] Their understanding of "this generation" (Matthew 24:34) in the Olivet Discourse becomes, for them, the proof text that settles all arguments and justifies their interpretation of many other details referred to by Christ as "all these things" in verse 34. Dr. Gentry explains: "We find the key to locating the great Tribulation in history in Matthew 24:34.… This statement of Christ is indisputably clear—and absolutely demanding of a first century fulfillment of the events in the preceding verses, including the great Tribulation (verse 21)."[38]

Yet "all these things"—that is, the things in Matthew 24:4-31—are allegorized to fit into the preterists' first-century fulfillment scheme. Since "this generation" is controlled by the meaning of "all these things," it is obvious that these things did *not* occur in and around the events of the Roman destruction of Jerusalem and the Temple in A.D. 70.

Contextual surroundings help us to determine the nuance of a specific word or phrase. It is true that all the other uses of "this generation" in Matthew (11:16; 12:41-42,45; 23:36) refer to Christ's contemporaries, but we arrive at that conclusion by observing each verse's context. Thus, if the contextual factors in Matthew 24 do not refer to the events of A.D. 70, then the text would have to refer to the future. This is the futurist contention—that the events described in Matthew 24 did not occur in the first century. When were the Jews, who were under siege, rescued by the Lord in A.D. 70? They were not rescued. Rather, they were judged, as noted in Luke 21:20-24. But Matthew 24 speaks of a divine rescue of those who are under siege (verses 29-31). This did not happen and thus was not fulfilled in the first century. In fact, the Jewish Christian community fled Jerusalem before the final siege.[39] Matthew 24 speaks about the deliverance of Jews who are under siege, and this did not happen in the first-century Roman siege.

Prior to His statement about "this generation," Jesus said "so, you too, when you see all these things, recognize that He is near, right at the door" (Matthew 24:33). The point of Christ's parable of the fig tree (Matthew 24:32-35) is that all the events noted earlier in Matthew 24:4-31 are signs that tell those under siege that help is coming in the person of Christ at His return to rescue His people. In contradiction to this, preterists teach that "all these things" refer to the non-bodily, non-personal coming of Christ through the Roman army in the first century. Because of how they interpret "this generation," they are forced to say the whole passage speaks of a coming of Christ via the events leading up to what Christ actually says will be His return. Yet, contra preterism, Christ says in the parable of the fig tree that preceding events instruct the reader to "recognize that He is near, right at the door." Had a first-century reader tried to apply a preterist understanding to Matthew 24, it would have been too late for him to flee the city. Instead, the people were told to flee the city when the siege first occurred, as noted in the first-century warning of Luke 21:20-24. And, the Jewish generation that sees "all these things" will be rescued as noted in Luke 21:27-28. Once again the question arises: "When were the people of Israel rescued in A.D. 70?" They were not. Neither were "all these things" (Matthew 24:33-34) fulfilled in the first century. These will all be fulfilled during the Tribulation, which will take place in the future. Thus, I have demonstrated that a futurist, literal interpretation is not only possible, but is to be preferred because of context.

Regarding the Return of Christ

Preterists argue that "all these things" had to have happened in the first century because of the phrase "this generation." So preterists use their very active imaginations, with a little help from Josephus, to try to explain why these passages speak about Christ's coming.

Matthew 24:29 says, "Immediately after the tribulation of those days the sun will be darkened, and the moon will not give its light, and the stars will fall from the sky, and the powers of the heavens will be shaken." Gentry says, "I will argue that this passage speaks of the A.D. 70 collapse of geo-political Israel. Let us note that there is biblical warrant for speaking of national catastrophe in terms of cosmic destruction."[40]

Now, if Matthew 24:29 is describing literal signs in the heavens, then these events have not happened yet. There is no record of such. Are we to interpret these signs as literal? Yes! One of the reasons the sun, moon, and stars were created is "for signs, and for seasons, and for days and years" (Genesis 1:14). What bigger event than the second coming of Christ would demand signs of a global magnitude? In this passage, Jesus is reporting what will actually happen in history. It will be a supernatural event, yet Gentry and other preterists attempt to "dumb down" this event with their naturalistic view that this has already happened.

Also, just as the sun was literally darkened as a sign, during Jesus' crucifixion, so will it be darkened at His return. And, the burden of proof is on preterists who do not take this passage literally as to why they don't. They need to come up with evidence that's more convincing than the argument that the words "this generation" requires it, because I have shown that it does not. Clearly, the passage is to be taken literally as a pronouncement that the Lord can control His creation and use it as a global sign that He is returning, as glorious Lord of all creation, to a world filled with unbelief.

Matthew 24:30 goes on to say, "Then the sign of the Son of Man will appear in the sky, and then all the tribes of the earth will mourn, and they will see the Son of Man coming on the clouds of the sky with power and great glory." Gentry says, "This verse, along with all other verses leading up to it from Matthew 24:1, applies to the A.D. 70 destruction of the Temple."[41] If this prophecy has something to do with the destruction of Jerusalem in A.D. 70, then Dr. Gentry has not been able to tell us exactly what it is.

I agree with Greek scholar A. T. Robertson that the sign is the coming of the Son of Man Himself.[42] The first sentence would be rendered as follows: "and then will appear the sign, *which is* the Son of Man in heaven." In Greek grammar, this is called the appositional use of the genitive case. The coming of the Lord Himself is the sign, which was the very point Jesus made to the high priest in Matthew 26:64 when He said people would see Him "coming on the clouds of heaven." This is what the angel told Christ's disciples in Acts 1:11. After the disciples watched Jesus being taken up to heaven in a cloud, the angel said, "This Jesus, who has been taken up from you into heaven, will come in just the same way as you have watched Him go into heaven." This means the next time Jesus comes, it will not be in the form of some "signless sign"—that did not actually exist—in the form of the Roman army, but instead we can expect a visible, bodily, physical return of Christ that mirrors His ascension.

Going back to Matthew 24:30, Jesus said, "Then all the tribes of the earth will mourn, and they will see the Son of Man coming on the clouds of the sky with power and great glory." Why will people mourn when they see the undeniable sign of the returning Christ? Gentry says this merely refers to the Jewish tribes of Israel in A.D. 70.[43] However, the phrase "all the tribes of the earth" is a universal term speaking of unbelievers everywhere. Every time this plural phrase is used in the parallel book of Revelation, it clearly refers to Gentiles. For example, Revelation 13:7 speaks of "every tribe and people and tongue and nation." Every use in the Old Testament of "all the tribes of the earth" has a universal meaning in the Septuagint. When referring to the Jewish tribes, the Old Testament uses the term "all the tribes of Israel" (about 25 times).

Note also that Matthew 24:30 says that when "the Son of Man [comes] on the clouds of the sky with power and great glory," the text clearly says "they will *see* the Son of Man." This event will be clearly visible. Jesus will return bodily and physically to planet earth. This did not happen in A.D. 70; Josephus did not record it, nor anyone else. We cannot resort to a symbolic, naturalistic interpretation that says Jesus somehow returned in conjunction with the Roman army in the first century. Jesus said, "They will *see* the Son of Man." And He said He will return on the clouds, just as Acts 1 says He will. He will return with power and great glory—the Shechinah glory that has been God's trademark throughout history.

Regarding the Evidence

If Jesus returned in A.D. 70, as preterists say, then on what day did He return? If this is a past event, we should be able to know the exact day our Lord supposedly returned. I have never read in any preterist material about the day and exact manner or event that supposedly marked Christ's return in A.D. 70. In fact, this was such a non-event, that it was not until the seventeenth century that we have an extant record of anyone suggesting anything like a preterist view that connects Matthew 24:27 and 30 to A.D. 70.

I do not believe that Christ's Olivet Discourse (Matthew 24; Mark 13; Luke 21) contains a single sentence, phrase, or term that *requires* a first-century fulfillment except for Luke 21:20-24. Since the timing of "this generation" is not innate in the phrase itself but is governed by the immediate context, I believe it refers to a future generation because the events described have yet to take place. This can be seen most clearly in Luke's account of our Lord's discourse because he documents Jesus' answers to all three of the disciples' questions. Matthew and Mark dealt only with the questions related to the future.

Luke's account includes the answer to the disciples' question (Luke 21:20-24) about *when* there will come a time when "there will not be left one stone upon another which will not be torn down" (Luke 21:6). Multiple time references are necessary; this is evident in the wording of the question in verse 7.

The first part of the question—"when therefore will these things happen?"—relates to the destruction of the Temple in A.D. 70. This explains the first-century section in Luke 21:20-24. Christ's answer to the second question—"what *will* be the sign when these things are about to take place?"—relates to "signs" preceding His second advent. Jesus is talking about a different event from that mentioned in response to the first question, and that event is still future to our day. The second question is answered in verses 25-28, which follows the long period of time described in the second half of verse 24: "Jerusalem will be trampled under foot by the Gentiles until the times of the Gentiles are fulfilled." Thus, verse 32—"this generation will not pass away until all things take place"—will be fulfilled in the future, for the scope of "all these things" refers to verses 25-28, not verses 20-24. Arnold Fruchtenbaum explains:

> Then Jesus stated that the generation that sees this event, the abomination of desolation, will still be around when the second coming of Christ occurs three-and-a-half years later....Verse 34 is intended to be a word of comfort in light of the world-wide attempt at Jewish destruction. It must be kept in mind that the abomination of desolation signals Satan's and the Antichrist's final attempt to destroy and exterminate the Jews. The fact that the Jewish generation will still be here when the second coming of Christ occurs shows that Satan's attempt towards Jewish destruction will fail, and the Jewish saints of the second half of the Tribulation can receive comfort from these words.[44]

Now that we've seen how to respond to the preterists' supposed "time texts" in Matthew's Gospel, let's shift gears and turn to the preterist interpretation of the book of Revelation. It should come as no surprise to learn that preterists believe that John's Revelation from Jesus Christ has already been fulfilled.

THE "TIME TEXTS IN REVELATION"

As we consider the preterist approach to Revelation as outlined in chapter 1, titled "What Is Preterism?" we will begin by examining their interpretation of Revelation 1:7: "Behold, He is coming with the clouds, and every eye will see Him, even those who pierced Him; and all the tribes of the earth will mourn over Him. So it is to be. Amen."

Revelation 1:7
What the Passage Says

Preterists believe Revelation 1:7 speaks only of the land of Israel and thus it refers to a local rather than global event that took place in A.D. 70. But if this passage refers to Gentiles and a global event, the preterists are wrong and the fulfillment is yet future.

We can analyze Revelation 1:7 by dividing it into four interpretive elements: 1) Christ's "coming"; 2) "with the clouds"; 3) "every eye will see Him, even those who pierced Him"; and 4) "all the tribes of the earth will mourn over Him." Since I will discuss the meaning of Christ's "coming with the clouds" later on, I will comment on the first two elements later. However, I, like almost all interpreters of Scripture before me, believe these words to be a clear reference to the bodily, personal return of Christ at a yet future time. This is supported by the final two elements of the passage, which include clear allusions to Zechariah 12:10-14. Having said that, let's start with element #3: "every eye will see Him, even those who pierced Him...."

This phrase plays a key role in helping us determine whether this passage refers to a global or local event. The first part, "every eye will see Him," does not appear in the Old Testament reference. The other part, "even those who pierced Him," is from Zechariah. It is clear in Zechariah that those "who pierced Him" are the Jewish people. On this, both preterists and futurists agree. The debate arises over whether "every eye" is a reference to just the Jewish nation (the preterist contention) or to the people of the whole earth (the futurist understanding). The way to resolve who is intended in the scope of the reference is to compare it to the subset "even those who pierced Him."

If the larger group of "every eye" refers to the Jewish nation, then it does not make sense that the smaller group "even those who pierced Him," would be a reference to the same exact people, as preterists contend. Their reading of the passage would be as follows: "every eye [Israel] will see Him, even those who pierced Him [Israel]." There would be no need to have a subgroup if both "every eye" and "even those who pierced him" mean the same thing. If "every eye" refers to all the peoples of the world as the larger group, then the qualifying phrase "even those who pierced Him" would be emphasizing the Jewish element as the smaller subgroup. Thus, it is not surprising that virtually everyone except preterists interpret this part of the passage in a global sense. It is obvious that bias, not the clear meaning of the text, is the only reason preterists interpret this part of the passage in a restricted manner.

Now let's look at element #4: "all the tribes of the earth will mourn over Him...."

The Greek word for "earth" can refer to either the "earth" as in "heavens and earth" (Genesis 1:1), or "land," as in the "land of Israel" (1 Samuel 13:19). The problem with interpreting Revelation 1:7 to refer to the land of Israel is that all the other uses of the exact phrase "all the tribes of the earth" in the original language always has a universal nuance (Genesis 12:3; 28:14; Psalm 72:17; Zechariah 14:17). G. K. Beale notes that "the phrases 'every eye' and 'of the earth' have been added to universalize its original meaning.... ('earth, land') cannot be a limited reference to the land of Israel but has a universal denotation, since the latter is the only meaning that ('all the tribes of the earth,' the full phrase here) has in the OT."[45]

This supports the futurist understanding of the text.

As we can now see, preterists have to restrict the meaning of clearly universal language in the Bible in order to make their approach to Bible prophecy appear to work. However, in doing so, they end up forcing the biblical text to say something it's not saying. Revelation 1:7 speaks of an event that will draw attention worldwide, yet preterists say otherwise.

What Preterists Say

I have now dealt with all of Revelation 1:7 except the part that deals with Christ coming on the clouds, or elements #1 and #2. Gentry attempts a most strained interpretation when he refers to this as "a providential coming of Christ in *historical judgments upon men*."[46] He says, "In the Old Testament, clouds are frequently employed as symbols of divine wrath and judgment. Often God is seen surrounded with foreboding clouds which express His unapproachable holiness and righteousness. Thus, God is poetically portrayed in certain judgment scenes *as coming in the clouds* to wreak historical vengeance upon His enemies."[47]

Gentry cites the following passages as examples: 2 Samuel 22:8,10; Psalm 18:7-15; 68:4,33; 97:2-39; 104:3; Isaiah 13:9; 19:1; 26:21; 30:27; Joel 2:1-2; Micah 1:3; Nahum 1:2ff; Zephaniah 1:14-15. He then concludes, "The New Testament picks up this apocalyptic judgment imagery when it speaks of Christ's coming in clouds of judgment *during history*."[48]

There are many problems with Gentry's declaration that Revelation 1:7 has a similar meaning as the Old Testament passages he cites. First, he cites no reasons from the context of Revelation 1:7 why it should be understood as a parallel to these Old Testament passages. He just declares them to be similar. Robert Thomas offers this insightful observation:

> Gentry interprets a reference to clouds in Revelation 1:7 as a nonpersonal coming of Christ. Christ never returned to earth in A.D. 70 personally, so explaining the fall of Jerusalem as his coming violates the principle of literal interpretation. All contextual indications point to a literal and personal-coming of Christ in that verse. Gentry calls this a "judgment-coming" of Christ, but the criteria of Revelation also connect a deliverance of the faithful with that coming. Preterism nowhere explains the promised deliverance from persecution that is associated with the coming, for example, in 3:10-11. Gentry's interpretation of 1:7 simply does not fulfill the criteria of literal interpretation of the text. The fact is, the church did not escape persecution in A.D. 70, but continued to suffer for Christ's sake long after that.[49]

Second, some of those Old Testament passages most likely are speaking of Christ's second coming. Gentry often assumes that because they are in the Old Testament they must have already been fulfilled. Such is often not the case. I believe that Isaiah 26:21; 30:27; Joel 2:1-2 and Zephaniah 1:14-15 have second-coming contexts. This means these passages look forward to a future fulfillment, not back to a past one. Nahum 1:2ff., although less clear, could also refer to an eschatological time.

Third, I do not think that a single one of the Old Testament passages cited by Gentry parallels Revelation 1:7. Upon clear examination, we see that they describe the Lord as "riding" upon a cloud in judgment against the Lord's enemies, much as Gentry has said. However, when compared to Revelation 1:7, there are too many differences. As Dr. Thomas noted earlier, Revelation 1:7 speaks of a coming to *rescue* someone, while the Old Testament references are all descriptive of judgment. Revelation 1:7 also mentions a different atmosphere than we see in the Old Testament passages. Christ's coming in Revelation 1:7, and in the parallel passage Matthew 24:30, builds upon the Old Testament fact that the Lord established His identity in cloud comings. But, in these two passages we also have a description of the Lord returning to the earth—an element not found in the Old Testament passages cited by Gentry. There are too many differences, as noted by Philip Edgcumbe Hughes:

> The clouds intended here are not dark storm-clouds which presage divine judgment…but the bright clouds of his transcendental glory. They stand for the *shekinah* glory of God's presence which caused the face of Moses to shine with supernatural bril-

liance...and they are to be identified with the "bright cloud" of Christ's divine glory witnessed by Peter, James, and John on the mount of transfiguration (Matthew 17:5), and with the cloud which received him out of the apostles' sight at his ascension....[50]

Fourth, the preterist view of Revelation 1:7 confuses a global event for a local event. Robert Thomas notes:

> Another hermeneutical shortcoming of preterism relates to the limiting of the promised coming of Christ in 1:7 to Judea. What does a localized judgment hundreds of miles away have to do with the seven churches in Asia? John uses two long chapters in addressing those churches regarding the implications of the coming of Christ for them. For instance, the promise to shield the Philadelphian church from judgment (3:10-11) is meaningless if that judgment occurs far beyond the borders of that city.[51]

Fifth, even if there were certain parallels between the cloud comings of the Old Testament and the text of Revelation 1:7, which I do not believe there are, as Gentry has suggested, they would be meaningless because of what happened at Christ's ascension as described in Acts 1:9-11. Notice what the passage says:

> After He had said these things, He was lifted up while they were looking on, and a cloud received Him out of their sight. And as they were gazing intently into the sky while He was going, behold, two men in white clothing stood beside them. They also said, "Men of Galilee, why do you stand looking into the sky? This Jesus, who has been taken up from you into heaven, will come in just the same way as you have watched Him go into heaven."

Because Christ will return the same way He ascended, we know we can expect Him to come on literal clouds and to return bodily and physically. This is what Matthew 24:30 and Revelation 1:7 refer to. In fact, all of the New Testament looks to Christ's return in this way. Thus, any future cloud coming has to be seen in light of the glorious promise in Acts 1:9-11.

Finally, accepting Gentry's preterist interpretation of Revelation 1:7 creates problems with the rest of the book of Revelation. This has been most clearly stated by Robert Thomas:

> This preterist view of 1:7...creates several unsolvable interpretive dilemmas within the verse itself, not to mention elsewhere in the

book: inconsistency regarding the identity of "those who pierced him," "the tribes of the earth," and "the land [or earth]." Are they limited to Jews and their land, or do they include Romans and the rest of the world? A preterist must contradict himself on these issues to have a past fulfillment of 1:7. They cannot limit "those who pierced him" to Jews only and elsewhere include the Romans as objects of Christ's "cloud coming." They cannot limit "the tribes of the earth [or land]" to Israel only, because in this case Zechariah 12:10ff. would require the mourning to be one of repentance, not of despair (as their interpretation holds). Their acknowledged worldwide scope of Revelation as a whole rules out their limitation of "the land" to Palestine in this verse.[52]

The preterist interpretation of Revelation 1:7 in relationship to Christ's coming is necessary if Revelation was fulfilled in the first century. However, the torturous interpretation of otherwise plain and clear language must be distorted beyond clear recognition in order to hold to such a view. When Revelation 1:7 is placed alongside of Revelation 19:11-21, it is more than clear that Revelation 1:7 speaks of a global, future, bodily, and literal return of Jesus the Messiah from heaven to planet earth. While the preterist notion that Revelation 1:7 had to be fulfilled in the first century is required of their view, they are not able to provide actual exegetical support for such a position. When we let Scripture interpret Scripture, it becomes clear that Revelation 1:7 speaks of a future event.

What "Quickly" and "Near" Mean

All through this chapter, we have seen that the error known as preterism is based upon the misinterpretation of a few key Bible passages. While Matthew 24:34 and the phrase "this generation" is their central passage, the preterists' dependence upon the so-called "time texts" of Revelation are also important in their attempts to "preterize" most of end-time Bible prophecy. They look to the terms "quickly" and "near" as the basis for their insistence that the book of Revelation was fulfilled during the A.D. 70 destruction of Jerusalem.

In reference to the term "quickly," Gentry says, "One of the most helpful interpretive clues in Revelation is…the *contemporary expectation of the author* regarding the fulfillment of the prophecies. John clearly expects the *soon* fulfillment of his prophecy."[53] However, as we'll see in a moment, the terms "quickly" and "near" are more properly interpreted as *qualitative indicators* describing how Christ will return. *How* will He return? He will come back "quickly" or "suddenly."

A form of the Greek word for "quickly" (*táchos*) is used eight times in Revelation (1:1; 2:16; 3:11; 11:14; 22:6-7,12,20). *Táchos* and its family of related words can be used to mean "soon" or "shortly," as preterists believe (relating to time), or they can be used to mean "quickly" or "suddenly," as many futurists contend (the manner in which action occurs). In the Bible, the *táchos* family is used both ways. On the one hand, 1 Timothy 3:14 is a timing passage, "I am writing these things to you, hoping to come to you *before long.*" On the other hand, Acts 22:18 is descriptive of the manner in which the action takes place: "I saw Him saying to me, 'Make haste, and get out of Jerusalem *quickly,* because they will not accept your testimony about Me.'"

The "timing interpretation" of the preterists teaches that the *táchos* word family, as used in Revelation (1:1; 2:16; 3:11; 11:14; 22:6-7,12,20) means that Christ came in judgment upon Israel through the Roman army in A.D. 70. But how would the "manner interpretation" of the futurist understand the use of the *táchos* family in Revelation? Futurist John Walvoord explains:

> That which Daniel declared would occur "in the latter days" is here described as "shortly" (Gr., *en tachei*), that is, "quickly or suddenly coming to pass," indicating rapidity of execution after the beginning takes place. The idea is not that the event may occur soon, but that when it does, it will be sudden (cf. Luke 18:8; Acts 12:7; 22:18; 25:4; Romans 16:20). A similar word, *tachys,* is translated "quickly" seven times in Revelation (2:5, 16; 3:11; 11:14; 22:7, 12, 20).[54]

Dr. Gentry is correct when he notes universal agreement among lexicons as to the general meaning of the *táchos* word family,[55] but these lexicographers generally do not support the preterist interpretation. Dr. Gentry's presentation of the lexical evidence is skewed and thus his conclusions are faulty in his effort to support a preterist interpretation of the *táchos* word family. Let's turn now to an examination of how the *táchos* word family is used in Revelation.

1. *The lexical use.* The leading Greek lexicon in our day is *Bauer, Arndt, and Gingrich (BAG),*[56] which lists the following definitions for *táchos:* "speed, quickness, swiftness, haste" (p. 814). The two times this noun appears in Revelation (1:1; 22:6), it is coupled with the preposition *en,* causing this phrase to function grammatically as an adverb revealing to us the "sudden" manner in which these events will take place.[57] They will occur "swiftly." The other word in the *táchos* family used in Revelation as an adverb is *tachús,* which all six times occurs with the verb *érchomai,* "to come" (2:16; 3:11; 11:14; 22:7,12,20). *BAG* gives as its meaning "quick, swift, speedy" (p. 814) and specifically classifies all six uses in Revelation as meaning "without delay, quickly, at once"

(p. 815). Thus, contrary to the timing assumption of preterists such as DeMar and Gentry, who take every occurrence as a reference to timing, *BAG* (and the other lexicons also agree) recommends a translation *descriptive* of the manner in which an event will happen (Revelation 2:16; 3:11; 11:14; 22:7,12,20).

A descriptive use of *táchos* is also supported by the 60-plus times it is cited as the prefix making up a compound word (according to the mother of all Greek lexicons, *Liddell and Scott* (p. 1762). G. H. Lang gives the following example:

> *tachy* does not mean *soon* but *swiftly*. It indicates rapidity of action, as is well seen in its accurate use in the medical compound *tachycardia* (*tachy* and *kardía=the heart*), which does not mean that the heart will beat *soon*, but that it is beating *rapidly*. Of course, the swift action may take place at the very same time, as in Matthew 28:7-8: "Go *quickly* and tell His disciples...and they departed *quickly* from the tomb": but the thought is not that they did not loiter, but that their movement was swift. Thus here also. If the Lord be regarded as speaking in the day when John lived, then He did not mean that He was returning *soon*, but swiftly and suddenly whenever the time should have arrived...it is the swiftness of His movement that the word emphasizes.[58]

2. *The grammatical use.* Just as *BAG* is the leading lexicon in our day, the most authoritative Greek grammar is the one produced by Blass, Debrunner, and Funk (Blass-Debrunner).[59] Blass-Debrunner, in the section on adverbs, divides them into four categories: 1) adverbs of manner, 2) adverbs of place, 3) adverbs of time, 4) correlative adverbs (pp. 55-57). The *táchos* family is used as the major example in the "adverbs of manner" category. Interestingly, no example from the *táchos* family is listed under "adverbs of time." In a related citation, Blass-Debrunner classifies *en táchei* as an example of "manner," Luke 18:8 (p. 118). Greek scholar Nigel Turner also supports this adverbial sense as meaning "quickly."[60]

Not only is there a preponderance of lexical support for understanding the *táchos* family as including the notion of "quickly" or "suddenly," there is also the further support that all the occurrences in Revelation are adverbs of manner. These terms are not descriptive of *when* the events will occur and our Lord will come, but rather, descriptive of the *manner* in which they will take place when they occur. These adverbial phrases in Revelation can more accurately be translated "that when these events begin, they will take place with 'rapid fire' sequence or 'speedily.' This is its contextual usage here."[61]

3. *The Old Testament (LXX) use.* It is significant to note that the Septuagint uses *táchos* in passages which even by the most conservative estimations could not have fulfillments within hundreds or even thousands of years. For example, Isaiah 13:22 says, "...her [Israel's] fateful time also will *soon* come." This was written around 700 B.C. and foretold the destruction by Babylon, which occurred at the earliest in 539 B.C. Similarly, Isaiah 5:26 speaks of the manner, not the time frame, by which the Assyrian invasion of Israel "will come with speed *swiftly*." Isaiah 51:5 says, "My righteousness is *near*, My salvation has gone forth, and My arms will judge the peoples; the coastlands will wait for Me, and for My arm they will wait expectantly." This passage will probably be fulfilled in the millennium, but no interpreter would place the fulfillment any sooner than Christ's first coming, or at least 700 years after the prophecy was given. Isaiah 58:8 speaks of Israel's recovery as "speedily spring[ing] forth." If it is a "timing passage," then the earliest it could have happened is 700 years later, but most likely it has yet to occur. And there are still other uses of *táchos* in the Septuagint that support the futurist interpretation of *táchos* in Revelation.

4. *The date of Revelation.* Gentry, as well as almost all other preterists, have to date the writing of Revelation before the destruction of Jerusalem in A.D. 70. The problems with their approach are discussed in chapter 13.

5. *A "timing" interpretation would require an A.D. 70 fulfillment of the entire book of Revelation.* Revelation 22:6 is passage #6 on DeMar's list of "time indicators" in Revelation: "And he said to me, 'These words are faithful and true'; and the Lord, the God of the spirits of the prophets, sent His angel to show to His bond-servants the things which must *soon* (*táchos*) take place." In contrast, Gentry cites Revelation 20:7-9 as a reference to the yet future second coming.[62] This creates a contradiction within Gentry's brand of preterism. Since Revelation 22:6 refers to the whole book of Revelation, it would be impossible to take *táchos* as a reference to A.D. 70 (as Gentry does) and at the same time hold that Revelation 20:7-9 teaches the second coming. Gentry must either adopt a view similar to futurism or shift to the extreme preterist view that understands the entire book of Revelation as past history and thus eliminates any future second coming and resurrection.

Revelation 1:3 and 22:10
The Meaning of "At Hand"

Preterists contend that the twice-used phrase "the time is near" (*eggús*— 1:3; 22:10) demands a first-century fulfillment and justifies an nonfuturist view of Revelation and the Tribulation. Gentry explains, "How could such events so remotely stretched out into the future be 'at hand'? But if the expected events were to occur within a period of from one to five years—as in the case with Revelation if the book were written prior to A.D. 70—then all becomes clear.[63]

Just as "quickly" is used in Revelation to teach imminence, so also is "near" or "at hand" (*eggús*) used to mean imminency and thus its usage does not support a first-century fulfillment. Philip E. Hughes rightly says, *"The time is near*, that is to say, the time of fulfillment is imminent. This interval between the comings of Christ is the time of the last days, and the last of these last days is always impending."[64] William Newell calls it, "the nearness, the *next*-ness, the at-hand-ness, of its time is given by our Lord."[65] (See chapter 12 for more on "at hand.")

I believe that the language of the "at hand" passages in Revelation, in concert with "quickly," teach the notion of imminence. This makes good sense, especially in light of Revelation 22:10, which says, " 'Do not seal up the words of the prophecy of this book, for the time is near [*eggús*].' " To what is John referring? He has in mind a period of time from the book of Daniel. The phrase "time of the end" occurs five times in Daniel (8:17; 11:35,40; 12:4,9). The "time of the end" refers to Israel's final period of history, which Daniel was told to seal but John is told not to seal. Since 22:10 is at the end of the book and refers to the total message of Revelation, it is inconsistent to interpret part of the message as having already been fulfilled and the other part as still future. It is better to see *eggús* as a term that teaches the imminency of a period of time that could begin to happen without the warning of signs. F. C. Jennings explains:

> In the one case the book is to be left open, "the time near"; in the other sealed up, for the time was still afar....There is nothing to come between in the former—much in the latter. Nor do the words we are considering at all necessitate the immediate fulfillment of *all* the words. They do, however (what the Lord ever seeks), put us in the attitude of immediate and constant expectancy and watchfulness. Oh, look at time with God. "Long" will not be long then; any more than when we actually look back at it from eternity.[66]

The expectancy Jennings speaks of is often labeled imminence.

The Promise of Imminence

A survey of the New Testament enables one to realize that there is an expectancy regarding the return of Christ and the consummation of His plan that is not found in the Old Testament. The passion of the Old Testament is for Israel to enter into her kingdom blessing with Messiah. I believe this is what Daniel was anticipating when he "observed in the books the number of years which was revealed as the word of the Lᴏʀᴅ to Jeremiah the prophet for the completion of the desolations of Jerusalem, namely, seventy years" (Daniel 9:2). The rest of Daniel 9 conveys Daniel's desire to see the culmination of the plan of God in our Lord's kingdom reign. Daniel apparently thought God would institute the messianic age upon Israel's return from the 70-year captivity. However, God had other plans. As revealed by an angel in the rest of Daniel 9, God was stretching out Israel's history. It would not be 70 more years, but 70 times 7, or 490 years until the culmination of Israel's history in the kingdom.

When we come to the New Testament we see the rejection of Jesus as Messiah by Israel and consequently, the postponement of the kingdom. God is prolonging the time of Israel's kingdom. However, this time God promises that when the current age of grace comes to an end, the next period of time will include the restoration of the kingdom to Israel (Acts 1:6,11; 3:19-21). Yet the length of our current church age is a mystery—part of the secret, unrevealed plan of God (Ephesians 3:2-13). The length has been preordained by God, but He has not told us how long this age will be. Peter explains that the duration of this age is based upon our Lord's great patience (2 Peter 3:9), which has thus far extended for almost 2,000 years.

The whole outlook of this current age is built upon the imminency of our Lord's return, which will at last trigger the final week of years for which Daniel so longed. Therefore, the events of the book of Revelation are said "to be at hand"—that is, they are to be the next season of events that will occur. God will not intervene with another new program like the church. We can be sure that the next phase of history is the Tribulation and then the millennial kingdom. John F. Walvoord is correct when he says,

> The expression "at hand" indicates nearness from the standpoint of prophetic revelation, not necessarily that the event will immediately occur....The time period in which the tremendous consummation of the ages is to take place, according to John's instruction, is near. The indeterminate period assigned to the church is the last dispensation before end-time events and, in John's day as in ours, the end is always impending because of the imminent return of Christ at the rapture with the ordered sequence of events to follow.[67]

Revelation is not the only book to speak about future events as imminent and "at hand." Paul admonishes godly living in light of the fact that the "night is almost gone, and the day is near" (Romans 13:12). Peter says, "The end of all things is near; therefore, be of sound judgment and sober spirit for the purpose of prayer" (1 Peter 4:7). This passage also makes the best sense when "at hand" is understood to mean "overhanging" or "the next imminent event." As in Romans 13:12, this also means that the practical admonitions to live a godly life are still in effect, since the end of all things has not yet come.

James joins the chorus of John, Paul, and Peter in his admonition that "you too be patient; strengthen your hearts, for the coming of the Lord is near" (James 5:8). Were believers only supposed to be patient towards those who wronged them until the destruction of Jerusalem in A.D. 70? Of course not! This passage is speaking about a still-future return of our Lord. Because it is imminent, ongoing patience is required by believers in our day.

THE INVALIDITY OF THE "TIME TEXTS"

Preterists attempt to create a kind of first-century "virtual reality"[68] in which they use the so-called "time texts" for the purpose of casting the reader of Scripture into a sense that the New Testament eschatology was fulfilled via events surrounding A.D. 70. Robert Thomas explains:

> Gentry…is a master in using words to take his readers back to the future, i.e., in creating virtual reality that many will not distinguish from reality itself. He does this by stating his "correct" view first, then often following it up with a long list of writers to support that view. This has the effect of blinding the reader on three sides so that he can see only what Gentry wants him to see in front of him. Only after the reader's exposure to the positive evidence for his view does the author turn to evaluate some of the weaknesses of that viewpoint. By this time, the merits of other viewpoints have become lost in the shuffle.[69]

Preterism rises and falls upon the validity of the preterists' so-called "time texts." Once preterists have confidently asserted that the texts are related to A.D. 70, they use that starting point to expand their preterist framework, until it has swallowed up the entire New Testament. However, I have shown that their starting point—the "time texts"—is not valid. Since their starting point is not valid nor accurate, it does not make any sense at all to preterize the other New Testament passages to which preterists desire to extend their understanding. If the infection is stopped at its source, then there is no danger of the gangrene spreading throughout the rest of the body. Hopefully, those who have been captured by the false reality of preterism will take a more careful look at the wonderful future plan that our Lord has in store for all of His people.

Chapter 5

SIGNS IN THE SKY

John MacArthur

A few years ago I taught a series on the doctrine of the church in a marathon-like, week-long series of all-day sessions in a conference for pastors in Kazakhstan. By Thursday morning we were deep into the pastoral epistles. During the morning break that day, one of the men who had helped organize the conference came to me and said, "Some of the pastors are asking when you're going to get to the *good* part."

"What's 'the good part'?" I asked.

"Why, it's the future of the church, the part where Jesus returns," he answered, utterly surprised that I did not instantly know what "the good part" is. "They're eager to hear about the return of Christ."

I certainly understand the desire to jump to "the good part." It's the same feeling I get whenever I study the Olivet Discourse. I suppose as the disciples sat on the Mount of Olives listening to Christ paint the bleak-sounding scenario of end-time events, they must have also been longing for Him to jump to "the good part."

So far the entire discourse has been filled with prophecies of doom and gloom. Christ started by predicting a long list of birth pangs. Those were bad enough, but things grew even worse after the abomination of desolation. And even now, as His prophetic account approaches the climax of the Great Tribulation, the world has yet to experience even more darkness before the visible dawning of Christ's glory.

THE LAST GREAT COSMIC SIGNS

Christ promised that His coming would be obvious to all: "As the light-ning comes from the east and flashes to the west, so also will the coming of the Son of Man be" (Matthew 24:27 NKJV).* One of the factors ensuring that no one misses Christ's return is the cosmic nature of the final signs: "Imme-diately after the Tribulation of those days the sun will be darkened, and the moon will not give its light; the stars will fall from heaven, and the powers of the heavens will be shaken" (verse 29). Luke's parallel account adds some grim details: "There will be signs in the sun, in the moon, and in the stars; and on the earth distress of nations, with perplexity, the sea and the waves roaring; men's hearts failing them from fear and the expectation of those things which are coming on the earth, for the powers of heaven will be shaken" (Luke 21:25-26).[1]

Such signs will have a sensational worldwide effect. Every person in every nation of the world will take note. Luke says some will even experience heart failure because of the sheer terror of these phenomena. The whole world's attention will immediately be drawn heavenward. The sense of dread and worldwide panic is scarcely imaginable. Finally, out of that same disquieted sky, Christ will reappear in all His glory.

Notice carefully how Christ leads up to this final great turning point in His discourse.

The sequence of events. Our Lord speaks expressly about the timing of these signs. He says the cosmic signs will occur at the very end of the Great Tribulation: "*Immediately* after the Tribulation of those days" (verse 29, emphasis added). These great signs in the sky seem to be to the second half of the Tribulation what the abomination of desolation was to the first—a clear and unmistakable signal that the era has reached an end and something sig-nificant is about to occur.

"The Tribulation of those days" in this context can only refer to the era Jesus has just been describing—and in particular, the time of the Great Tribu-lation launched by the abomination of desolation. Notice that these cosmic signs occur *immediately* after the Tribulation. Here is another powerful reason to reject the preterist interpretation of the Olivet Discourse: No great cosmic signs like this ever occurred in connection with the destruction of Jerusalem in A.D. 70.

Many preterists, undeterred by this, simply dismiss Jesus' language as metaphorical. They claim He is speaking symbolically about the collapse of

---

* All Scripture quotations in this chapter are taken from the New King James Version of the Bible.

the Old-Covenant era, not literally predicting vast signs in the sun and moon. For example, preterist Gary DeMar writes:

> The darkening of the sun and moon and the falling of the stars, coupled with the shaking of the heavens (24:29), are more descriptive ways of saying that "heaven and earth will pass away" (24:35). In other contexts, when stars fall, they fall to the earth, a sure sign of temporal judgment (Isaiah 14:12; Daniel 8:10; Revelation 6:13; 9:1; 12:4). So then, the "passing away of heaven and earth" is the passing away of the old covenant world of Judaism (1 Corinthians 2:8).[2]

In other words, DeMar believes that when Jesus says, "Heaven and earth will pass away" (verse 35), He is not speaking of any literal eschatological cosmic judgment that will really destroy the earth. Instead, the passing away of heaven and earth, according to DeMar, is merely metaphorical language that speaks of the transition from Old Covenant to New. Similarly, DeMar claims, the darkening of the sun and moon in Matthew 24:29 are merely metaphorical terms that refer to the passing away of the Jewish dispensation.

DeMar and other preterists impose a similar interpretive grid on most of the Olivet Discourse, employing allegory and symbolic language to make as many of the prophecies as possible fit the events of A.D. 70. In so doing, they utterly divest much of the discourse of any real significance, turning great cosmic signs into mere metaphors about the transition between covenants.

Most preterists stop short of allegorizing away the bodily return of Christ (the error of *hyper*-preterism).[3] But it is frankly hard to see how any preterist could ever give a credible refutation of hyper-preterism from Scripture, given the fact that the hermeneutical approach underlying both views is identical.[4] Hyper-preterists simply apply the preterist method more consistently to *all* New Testament prophecy. They start with the remainder of the Olivet Discourse, spiritualizing away not only the cosmic signs, but also the literal bodily return of Christ. Further imposing their interpretive grid on all of Scripture, most modern hyper-preterists ultimately defuse *every* biblical reference to yet-future events.

The typical preterist will claim that the apocalyptic language Christ employs in this passage gives sufficient warrant for interpreting the cosmic signs allegorically, symbolically, and spiritually. After all, they protest, imposing a strict literalism on all such passages throughout Scripture would have the moon literally turning to blood (Joel 2:31) and the stars literally falling from the sky to the earth (Revelation 9:1).

It is certainly true that the apocalyptic sections of Scripture are often filled with symbolic language. In Revelation 17:3, for example, the apostle John describes a woman riding a seven-headed beast. He later explains that "the seven heads are seven mountains on which the woman sits" (Revelation 17:9), forcing us to conclude that the "woman" is not a literal woman but a symbolic figure who represents either the city of Rome (well-known for being situated on seven hills) or, as John himself goes on to imply, the evil system behind seven successive world empires (verse 10). Symbolic language like that is sometimes clearly explained, sometimes not. But the context always makes clear when symbolism is being employed.

Most would agree there is a degree of symbolism in Matthew 24:29. Almost no one expects the stars to fall to earth literally. It's possible, too, that the sun might not be extinguished literally; rather, the sun's light could simply be partly or totally obscured from the earth (cf. Ezekiel 32:7). So I agree that *wooden* literalism is not necessary to get the right sense of Jesus' words.

But even granting a reasonable degree of obvious symbolism, the plain sense of these words still does not allow the preterist interpretation. Christ is predicting cosmic signs of some kind—signs so spectacular that no one on earth can possibly miss them. His whole point in this context is to reassure His people that when He returns, it will be spectacularly obvious to one and all. There will be no possibility of confusion about whether He has truly returned or not.

But the preterist interpretation utterly empties Jesus' words of that reassurance. If the preterists are right, not only did the whole world completely miss Christ's return on the clouds in glory, but so did virtually everyone in the church. Because with relatively few exceptions, practically every believer in 2,000 years of Christendom has believed Matthew 24:30 speaks of an event yet to happen.

The oldest extra-biblical Christian document known to exist is *The Didache*, which is a simple distillation of Bible doctrine from the early church. Most scholars believe it was written near the close of the first century, most likely after A.D. 80. It was certainly used and cited in the early centuries by many church fathers (as well as by the historian Eusebius).[5] So its early existence is well documented. The full text of *The Didache* was rediscovered little more than a hundred years ago, in a codex found in Constantinople in 1873. This document proves that those who actually lived through the events of A.D. 70 regarded Matthew 24:29-31—and the entire Olivet Discourse—as yet-unfulfilled prophecy.

For in the last days the false prophets and corrupters shall be multiplied, and the sheep shall be turned into wolves, and love shall be turned into hate. For as lawlessness increaseth, they shall hate one another and shall persecute and betray. And then the world-deceiver shall appear as a son of God; and shall work signs and wonders, and the earth shall be delivered into his hands; and he shall do unholy things, which have never been since the world began. Then all created mankind shall come to the fire of testing, and many shall be offended and perish; but they that endure in their faith shall be saved by the Curse Himself. And then shall the signs of the truth appear; first a sign of a rift in the heaven, then a sign of a voice of a trumpet, and thirdly a resurrection of the dead; yet not of all, but as it was said the Lord shall come and all His saints with Him. Then shall the world see the Lord coming upon the clouds of heaven (*Didache* 16:3-8).

Justin Martyr was probably born in the first century and certainly knew many believers who had lived through the events of A.D. 70. He also clearly regarded the second coming of Christ as a yet-future event. In his *Dialogue with Trypho*, Justin writes:

Two advents of Christ have been announced: the one, in which He is set forth as suffering, inglorious, dishonoured, and crucified; but the other, in which He shall come from heaven with glory, when the man of apostasy, who speaks strange things against the Most High, shall venture to do unlawful deeds on the earth against us the Christians.... The rest of the prophecy shall be fulfilled at His second coming (chapter 110).

So Justin, who could not have written much more than fifty years after the destruction of Jerusalem, still saw a future fulfillment of both the Tribulation prophecies and the return of Christ in glory.

That means if modern preterists are correct, some of the most astute students of Scripture and leaders in the early church utterly missed the fulfillment of the very prophecy Jesus indicated no one in the world would possibly be able to miss![6]

But it twists Jesus' words to turn them into mere allegory. What He was describing was an event long foretold in Scripture, an event so monumental that it would be a signal to the whole world. Moreover, Christ's coming was to usher in the final salvation of Israel, not the end of national Israel as the people of God.

The scene in the heavens. The cosmic signs Jesus gave in His discourse would have been thoroughly familiar to any student of Old Testament Messianic prophecy. These very same signs involving the sun, moon, and stars were well-known harbingers of the Messianic deliverance everyone in Israel looked for. The same signs were also heralds of the retribution he would mete out to His enemies. These were the emblems of the Day of the Lord.

> *Behold, the day of the* LORD *comes, cruel with both wrath and fierce anger, to lay the land desolate; and He will destroy its sinners from it.* For the stars of heaven and their constellations will not give their light: the sun shall be darkened in his going forth, and the moon will not cause its light to shine. *I will punish the world for their evil, and the wicked for their iniquity; I will halt the arrogance of the proud, and will lay low the haughtiness of the terrible. I will make a man more rare than fine gold; a man more than the golden wedge of Ophir. Therefore I will shake the heavens, and the earth will move out of her place, in the wrath of the* LORD *of hosts, and in the day of His fierce anger. It shall be as the hunted gazelle, and as a sheep that no man takes up. Every man will turn to his own people, and everyone will flee to his own land. Everyone who is found will be thrust through, and everyone who is captured will fall by the sword* (Isaiah 13:9-15, emphasis added).[7]

Later, describing the same scene of worldwide judgment, Isaiah wrote:

> *Come near, you nations, to hear; and heed, you O people! Let the earth hear, and all that is in it, the world and all that comes forth from it. For the indignation of the* LORD *is against all nations, and His fury against all their armies; He has utterly destroyed them, He has given them over to the slaughter. Also their slain shall be thrown out; their stench shall rise from their corpses, and the mountains shall be melted with their blood.* All the host of heaven shall be dissolved, and the heavens shall be rolled up like a scroll; all their host shall fall down as the leaf from the vine and as fruit falling from a fig tree. *For My sword shall be bathed in heaven; indeed it shall come down on Edom, and on the people of My curse, for judgment* (Isaiah 34:1-5, emphasis added).

The immediate context of Isaiah 34 describes the coming King of Israel reigning in His glory, building in Jerusalem "a tabernacle that will not be taken down," and making that city "a quiet home" (33:20)—a clear description of the millennial kingdom. The rest of Isaiah 34 describes the systematic judgment of all the nations. Then chapter 35 returns to the description of the earthly kingdom, in which "the desert shall rejoice and blossom as the rose" (35:1). "And the ransomed of the LORD shall return, and come to Zion with singing, with everlasting joy on their heads" (verse 10).

Joel foretold the same cosmic signs. "And I will show wonders in the heavens and in the earth: Blood and fire and pillars of smoke. The sun shall be turned into darkness, and the moon into blood, before the coming of the great and awesome day of the LORD" (Joel 2:30-31).[8] "The sun and moon will grow dark, and the stars will diminish their brightness" (3:15). Those words are set in the midst of millennial and end-times prophecies too. Joel 2:32 goes on to prophesy about the salvation of the Jewish remnant: "In Mount Zion and in Jerusalem there shall be deliverance, as the Lord has said, among the remnant whom the LORD calls." Joel 3 is filled with similar references: "For behold, in those days and at that time, when I bring back the captives of Judah and Jerusalem, I will also gather all nations, and bring them down to the Valley of Jehoshaphat; and I will enter into judgment with them there" (verses 1-2). Both the salvation of Israel and the judgment of the nations are constant themes wherever the cosmic-sign prophecies are found in Scripture.

The disciples' thoughts, when they heard mention of the cosmic signs, would have gone immediately to the Old Testament prophecies about the Day of the Lord. They knew Scripture had long foretold a time when God would shake the heavens, just as Jesus was prophesying here (cf. Isaiah 13:13; Joel 3:16). And they knew such signs were associated with the Day of the Lord.

What did Jesus mean when He said "the powers of the heavens will be shaken" (Matthew 24:29)? He made no explanation. But remember that He is the One who "uphold[s] all things by the word of His power" (Hebrew 1:3). He could merely speak the word, and gravity would weaken, the orbits of the planets would fluctuate, the very stars would appear to fall. None of that is beyond His power. In fact, if He but withdrew a fraction of His sustaining power, the entire universe would cease to function normally. The heavens and all the forces of energy would become unstable. Who knows what all the shaking of the heavens might entail? But one thing is certain: it will be terrifying when it happens.

Haggai wrote, "For thus says the LORD of hosts: 'Once more (it is a little while) I will shake heaven and earth, the sea and dry land; and I will shake all nations, and they shall come to the Desire of All Nations, and I will fill this temple with glory,' says the LORD of hosts" (2:6-7). There again, the Old Testament prophets connected these cosmic signs, including the shaking of the heavens, with the coming of the Messiah to judge the earth and establish His kingdom.

The sign in the sky. At that point there will be one remaining sign to come. It is the glorious appearing of Christ Himself. Here we finally reach "the good part": "Then the sign of the Son of Man will appear in heaven, and then all the tribes of the earth will mourn, and they will see the Son of Man coming on the clouds of heaven with power and great glory" (Matthew 24:30). Believers have long hoped for this moment (Titus 2:13).

This whole discourse had begun when the disciples asked Christ to tell them "the sign of [His] coming, and of the end of the age" (verse 3). This is that sign. His coming *is* what signifies the end of the age. It is the sign of signs—the glorious appearing of the Son of Man Himself.

Notice that Christ reiterates that His appearing will be universally visible. Every tribe on earth will see Him coming on the clouds of heaven. Bible students have long pondered how this will be possible. Some of the church fathers speculated that the whole world would see an enormous blazing cross in the darkened sky. They had no earthly idea how a single event could be witnessed by everyone on the globe at once. More recent students of prophecy have less to grapple with in that question, since His coming could easily be made visible worldwide via television.

Whatever the explanation, note that it is not a blazing cross or the *shekinah* glory or any other symbol of Christ's presence that appears in heaven; it is Christ Himself. *He* is the sign of signs. When the sun and moon are darkened, when the world's fear and hatred of God are elevated to unprecedented heights, suddenly Christ Himself will pierce through all that darkness and sin and return to win His final triumph.

He comes "on the clouds of heaven" (verse 30). When He ascended from earth into heaven, Scripture says, "A cloud received Him out of their sight" (Acts 1:9). An angel then appeared and told the disciples, "This same Jesus, who was taken up from you into heaven, will so come in like manner as you saw Him go into heaven" (verse 11). So it is fitting that He will return with clouds.

Revelation 1:7 perfectly echoes Jesus' words about His coming: "Behold, He is coming with clouds, and every eye will see Him, even they who pierced Him. And all the tribes of the earth will mourn because of Him." Earth's tribes will "mourn" His coming chiefly because they will know that He brings judgment for them, and that judgment is just. Moreover, He comes "with power and great glory" (Matthew 24:30). That is surely something of an understatement. His return will be the greatest display of power the earth has ever witnessed. Zechariah 14:3-4 describes it in these terms:

Then the LORD will go forth and fight against those nations, as He fights on the day of battle. And in that day His feet will stand on the Mount of Olives, which faces Jerusalem on the east. And the Mount of Olives shall be split in two, from east to west, making a very large valley; half of the mountain shall move toward the north and half of it toward the south.

Revelation 19 pictures the grand scene:

I saw heaven opened, and behold, a white horse. And He who sat on him was called Faithful and True, and in righteousness He judges and makes war. His eyes were like a flame of fire, and on His head were many crowns. He had a name written that no one knew except Himself. He was clothed with a robe dipped in blood, and His name is called The Word of God. And the armies in heaven, clothed in fine linen, white and clean, followed Him on white horses. Now out of His mouth goes a sharp sword, that with it He should strike the nations. And He Himself will rule them with a rod of iron. He Himself treads the winepress of the fierceness and wrath of Almighty God. And He has on His robe and on His thigh a name written: "KING OF KINGS AND LORD OF LORDS."

Then I saw an angel standing in the sun; and he cried with a loud voice, saying to all the birds which fly in the midst of heaven, "Come and gather together for the supper of the great God, that you may eat the flesh of kings, the flesh of captains, the flesh of mighty men, the flesh of horses and of those who sit on them, and the flesh of all people, free and slave, both small and great." And I saw the beast, the kings of the earth, and their armies, gathered together to make war against Him who sat on the horse and against His army. Then the beast was captured, and with him the false prophet who worked signs in his presence, by which he deceived those who received the mark of the beast and those who worshiped his image. These two were cast alive into the lake of fire burning with brimstone. And the rest were killed with the sword which proceeded from the mouth of Him who sat on the horse. And all the birds were filled with their flesh (verses 11-21).

The armies accompanying Christ in heaven will doubtless include both the redeemed who were caught up alive, as well as those who were raised from the grave, at the rapture. When Paul speaks of the rapture, he promises that all those who are caught up "shall always be with the Lord" (1 Thessalonians

4:17). Many passages of Scripture promise that when He returns, He will bring us with Him: "When Christ who is our life appears, then you also will appear with Him in glory" (Colossians 3:4). "The LORD my God will come, and all the saints with you" (Zechariah 14:5). "Behold, the Lord comes with ten thousands of His saints" (Jude 14).

And notice that He immediately executes vengeance on the Antichrist and the evil hordes of earth. As for the Antichrist, the lawless one, "The Lord will consume [him] with the breath of His mouth and destroy [him] with the brightness of His coming" (2 Thessalonians 2:8). The rest of the wicked are destroyed with the sword that proceeds from Christ's mouth (Revelation 19:21), possibly signifying that He judges and slays them merely by speaking the Word of God. Both the Beast and the False Prophet are cast alive into the lake of fire (verse 20). The rest of the dead are kept in the grave throughout the millennial kingdom, then resurrected for judgment and cast into eternal perdition (20:5,14-15).

THE GATHERING OF THE ELECT

Christ has more work than judgment to do at His appearing. This is not only a day of judgment; it is that glorious day when "all Israel will be saved, as it is written: 'The Deliverer will come out of Zion, and He will turn away ungodliness from Jacob'" (Romans 11:26). The elect will be gathered by the angels "from the four winds, from one end of heaven to the other" and brought before Christ (Matthew 24:31). For the wicked of the earth, Christ's coming will mean final judgment. For the elect, it will be the consummation of their redemption.

Zechariah had prophesied this day of judgment for the world and redemption for Israel long ago:

> It shall be in that day that I will seek to destroy all the nations that come against Jerusalem. And I will pour on the house of David and on the inhabitants of Jerusalem the Spirit of grace and supplication; then they will look on Me whom they pierced. Yes, they will mourn for Him as one mourns for his only son, and grieve for Him as one grieves for a firstborn. In that day there shall be a great mourning in Jerusalem, like the mourning at Hadad Rimmon in the plain of Megiddo (12:9-11).

Seeing with their own eyes the One whom Israel rejected and pierced, now fully realizing that He was the promised Messiah all along, the remnant will mourn. But it will be a short-lived mourning, for the Lord Himself will turn it into a day of joy: "In that day a fountain shall be opened for the

house of David and for the inhabitants of Jerusalem, for sin and for uncleanness" (13:1).

> And in that day it shall be that living waters shall flow from
> Jerusalem, half of them toward the eastern sea and half of them
> toward the western sea; in both summer and winter it shall
> occur. And the LORD shall be King over all the earth. In that day
> it shall be—"The LORD is one," and His name one. All the land
> shall be turned into a plain from Geba to Rimmon south of
> Jerusalem. Jerusalem shall be raised up and inhabited in her
> place from Benjamin's Gate to the place of the First Gate and
> the Corner Gate, and from the Tower of Hananel to the king's
> winepresses. The people shall dwell in it; and no longer shall
> there be utter destruction, but Jerusalem shall be safely inhab-
> ited (14:8-11).

That describes the millennial kingdom, which Christ will establish immediately in the wake of His coming. Revelation 20 describes it as a time of
unprecedented blessing on the whole world, during which Satan is bound
and the redeemed live and reign with Christ on earth.

Isaiah 11:6-9 describes the earthly kingdom in still more graphic terms:

> The wolf also shall dwell with the lamb, the leopard shall lie
> down with the young goat, the calf and the young lion and the
> fatling together; and a little child shall lead them. The cow and
> the bear shall graze; their young ones shall lie down together;
> and the lion shall eat straw like the ox. The nursing child shall
> play by the cobra's hole, and the weaned child shall put his hand
> in the viper's den. They shall not hurt nor destroy in all My holy
> mountain, for the earth shall be full of the knowledge of the
> LORD as the waters cover the sea.

Christ will eliminate all disease, drought, floods, crop failures, and hunger.
Bad weather and natural disasters will be things of the past. All wars, strife,
and persecution will end, and righteousness will rule. What child of God does
not long to see such a time?

All kinds of speculative questions arise about the millennial kingdom. If
the wicked are all annihilated, with whom is the world populated? The only
option would seem to be that the children of the elect remnant who emerge
from the Tribulation still alive will repopulate the earth over the thousand-
year period.[9]

Why is Satan turned loose at the end of the Millennium and permitted to
deceive the nations again (Revelation 20:7-8)? Scripture does not say, but we

can be confident that the Lord's purpose is a good one. It certainly will demonstrate that even in a perfect world, people born with depraved hearts cannot ultimately avoid the lure of evil and are desperately in need of redemption.

THE PARABLE OF THE FIG TREE

In the Olivet Discourse, however, Christ spends no time giving details about the millennial kingdom. Once He has reached the zenith of His message, once He has given them the final great sign of the end of the age, He gives a brief parable to underscore the lesson He has been teaching them:

> Now learn this parable from the fig tree: When its branch has already become tender, and puts forth leaves, you know that summer is near. So you also, when you see all these things, know that it is near—at the doors! Assuredly, I say to you, this generation will by no means pass away till all these things take place. Heaven and earth will pass away, but My words will by no means pass away (Matthew 24:32-35).

Many interpretations have been set forth to try to explain what Jesus meant here. It was popular for some time after the founding of the modern Jewish state to suggest that the fig tree is a reference to modern Israel. Therefore, many believed, from the time the "fig tree" started to bud—meaning 1948, when modern Israel declared statehood—it would be one generation until all the prophecies of the Olivet Discourse were fulfilled. By 1988, when the forty years thought to constitute a "generation" had passed since Israel's founding, that interpretation was not quite so popular.

Some suggest that "this generation" refers not to a particular *age* but rather to the Jewish *race*—employing the word *generation* (much the way Jesus used it in Luke 9:41 and 16:8) to speak of a class of people rather than a period of time. That's a possible interpretation, but it seems to conflict with the context, in which Christ is making a statement about the speed with which all these signs would unfold.

Preterists, of course, place much stress on this verse. They insist it guarantees that the generation alive during Jesus' time would be the same generation to see the complete fulfillment of all these signs, and they treat it as the key that unlocks the meaning of the Olivet Discourse. But the reasonable mind quickly sees the folly of having to allegorize so many passages of Scripture just for the sake of interpreting one verse (verse 34) with such rigid literalism. It is simply not necessary to insist that Christ meant that all the Olivet Discourse signs must be fulfilled in that current generation.

As we have seen throughout our study, many clues in the passage itself, including the cosmic signs and the abomination of desolation, indicate that these are end-time Tribulation prophecies, not merely historical warnings about A.D. 70. Furthermore, Christ says, "When you see *all* these things, know that it is near" (verse 33). The signs are a package. When they are truly fulfilled, they will be fulfilled all at once. That seems to be the gist of this parable, as well as the comment that follows it. Therefore, the most reasonable interpretation of verse 34 is this: Christ is saying that the generation alive when the true labor pains begin will be the same generation that sees the delivery. These things, when they happen, will not stretch out across generations.

In fact, this is the very meaning of the fig tree parable. When the fig tree starts to bud, you can virtually count the days until summer. Likewise, from the time when the actual birth-pang signs begin, there is a set time until all these things will be fulfilled—seven years, to be exact. The Olivet Discourse covers a relatively short period of time, not a long eschatological age. It is essentially a seven-year period, the seventieth week of Daniel's prophecy. And the generation that sees the start of it will be the same one that sees the fulfillment of all the things Christ predicted. So when the real birth-pang signs begin, when that is confirmed by the abomination of desolation and gives way to the trials of the Great Tribulation—"when you see *all* these things"—you can know that Christ's return is near.

The point of the parable is utterly uncomplicated; even a child can tell by looking at a fig tree that summer is near. Likewise, the generation that sees *all* these signs come to pass will know with certainty that Christ's return is near.

This exhortation is reminiscent of a rebuke Christ gave the Pharisees in Matthew 16:2-3: "When it is evening you say, 'It will be fair weather, for the sky is red'; and in the morning, 'It will be foul weather today, for the sky is red and threatening.' Hypocrites! You know how to discern the face of the sky, but you cannot discern the signs of the times."

Those who recognize the signs will realize that Christ's coming is at the door. Those living during the Tribulation can have absolute confidence that He will return soon, despite the viciousness of the persecutions, no matter how convincing the lies of the deceivers, regardless of how much it seems Satan, not God, is in control of things. In Christ's own words, "See, I have told you beforehand" (Matthew 24:25).

The reliability of His prophetic promises is confirmed by the unchanging authority of the Word of God. "Heaven and earth will pass away, but My words will by no means pass away" (verse 35). "The Scripture cannot be broken" (John 10:35). "The grass withers, the flower fades, but the word of our

God stands forever" (Isaiah 40:8). Therefore, those who are alive when these things come to pass can know with rock-solid certainty that His promises are true. And no matter how bleak things begin to look in the Tribulation, Christ will ultimately emerge as Victor over His enemies.

This chapter, "Signs in the Sky" by John MacArthur, is excerpted from John F. MacArthur, *The Second Coming* (Wheaton, IL: Crossway Books, 1999), pp. 119-34. Used with permission.

Chapter 6

THE STAKE IN THE HEART—THE A.D. 95 DATE OF REVELATION

MARK HITCHCOCK

The linchpin of the preterist view is the early date (A.D. 64–67) for the writing of the book of Revelation. Obviously, if Revelation was written after A.D. 70 when Jerusalem fell to Rome, then it cannot be prophesying this event. Preterists openly recognize the critical importance of the early date of Revelation to their own position.

In a review of fellow preterist David Chilton's commentary on Revelation, entitled *The Days of Vengeance*, Kenneth Gentry observes, "If it could be demonstrated that Revelation were written 25 years after the Fall of Jerusalem, Chilton's entire labor would go up in smoke."[1] Another preterist, R. C. Sproul, observes, "If the book was written after A.D. 70, then its contents manifestly do not refer to events surrounding the fall of Jerusalem—unless the book is a wholesale fraud, having been composed after the predicted events had already occurred."[2]

Over 150 years ago, a great Biblical scholar, Reverend E. B. Elliot, noted this fundamental weakness of preterism: "As to the date of the Apocalypse, how unfortunate are the Christian professors and critics…if this their fundamental foundation fails; and on what mere quicksand, in this respect, their structure is raised and in what mere imminent danger of being engulfed, the readers of my sketch of evidence on the Apocalyptic date will, I think, soon see."[3]

THE PRETERIST PROBLEM

The real problem preterists face is that their view is totally dependent on an early date for the writing of Revelation, but John does not specify when he receives his vision, except to say that it occurred on "the Lord's day" (Revelation 1:10). Therefore, their entire approach is built upon an assumption that is not stated in Revelation. This is bad news for preterists, for if their date is wrong, then their whole, elaborate system is worthless. The danger of dependence on a particular date for the writing of Revelation is aptly stated by Howard Winters:

> When the interpretation depends upon the date, the interpretation can never be more certain than the date itself—if the date is wrong, then, of necessity the interpretation is wrong. The whole business of making the interpretation depend upon the date is therefore built upon a sandy foundation. Consider this fact: if the understanding of the book depends upon the date, then it depends upon something that is not in the book itself, something that is not revealed, and something that is now impossible to establish beyond a reasonable doubt.
>
> But besides this, the force of the evidence, whether internal or external, is against an early date.[4]

Indeed, the foundation of preterism is sandy. If the date for Revelation is so central to its understanding, why didn't John clearly state the time of its composition somewhere in its 404 verses?

Unlike the preterist view, the futurist approach does not depend on any specific date for the writing of the book. Even if the early date were true, the futurist view of Revelation could still be correct and the preterist view could still be incorrect. This is a fundamental weakness of the preterist view.

THE RELEVANT EVIDENCE

Since the book of Revelation does not give the date of its writing, we are left to look for clues as to the most likely date of its composition. When attempting to date a biblical book, there are two main kinds of evidence: external and internal. External evidence examines material from outside the Bible to gain insight into the book's date, and internal evidence considers material within the text of the book itself for clues that point to the time of writing.

In this chapter, we will examine both the external and internal evidence, and I am asking you, the reader, to sit as a judge or juror and weigh the evidence as it is presented and, at the conclusion, to render your verdict. However, before the external and internal evidence are presented, as in any presentation of evidence, we need to establish some ground rules.

First, we must establish who carries the burden of proof. In American criminal trials, the prosecution carries the burden of proof beyond a reasonable doubt, and in civil trials, the plaintiff carries the burden of proof by a preponderance of the evidence. In proving the date of Revelation neither early nor late date advocates can claim that the case is beyond any doubt at all. However, I do believe the case for the late date (A.D. 95) can be proven at least by a preponderance of the evidence, if not beyond a reasonable doubt. Keep this in mind as you consider the evidence. Ultimately, we must ask: Which view is more likely to be true than the other in light of the evidence?

Another key point related to the burden of proof is that in this case, it lies with those who hold the early date. The late date is the dominant, established view. As R. C. Sproul admits, "The burden for preterists then is to demonstrate that Revelation was written *before* A.D. 70."[5]

A second important fact to keep in mind is that preterists consistently mention the pre-70 date of Revelation and make a great deal of the fact that many other scholars who are not preterists also hold to a pre-70 date for Revelation. Kenneth Gentry gives long litanies of these pre-70 proponents that he calls "early date advocates."[6] Gentry does not use this as a proof per se for his view, but apparently to lend credibility to his position. According to him, these lists show the "number of noted scholars who have discounted the late-date for Revelation in favor of an earlier date."[7]

While it is true that many scholars do hold to a pre-70 date for Revelation, it is critical to observe that the preterist position requires more than just a pre-70 date. According to Gentry, Revelation anticipates the destruction of Jerusalem (August A.D. 70), the death of Nero (June A.D. 68), and the formal imperial engagement of the Jewish War (spring A.D. 67).[8] Therefore, for preterists, the earliest Revelation could have been written (the *terminus a quo*) is the beginning of the Neronic persecution in November A.D. 64, and the latest possible date (the *terminus ad quem*) is spring A.D. 67. The date Gentry favors is A.D. 65.[9]

This point is critical because on closer examination, almost all the early-date advocates Gentry lists hold to a date for Revelation during the reign of Galba, Nero's successor, in A.D. 68–69.[10] This view was actually the dominant view of New Testament scholars in the nineteenth century.[11]

Therefore, the problem Gentry faces is that almost all of the scholars he lists in support of his position do not actually support his position at all. These early-date advocates hold an early date, but not an early-enough date to support the preterist position. Almost none of Gentry's "early date advocates" would accept his necessary pre-spring A.D. 67 position. While this by itself certainly does not dismantle the preterist date for Revelation, it does reveal that Gentry's effort to show the broad scholarly support for his dating of Revelation is without merit.

Preterists have painted themselves into a very narrow corner for dating the book of Revelation that has scant support outside their circle. If the date of Revelation is outside their narrow three-year window, their position is doomed. As was noted earlier, R. C. Sproul says "the burden for preterists then is to demonstrate that Revelation was written before A.D. 70."[12] Actually, this is incorrect. The burden is on preterists to show that Revelation was written before spring, A.D. 67 and after November, A.D. 64. This is a burden that, as we will see, they cannot meet.

The External Evidence

In the spring of 1998 I had the privilege of spending three days on the island of Patmos, where the apostle John received the book of Revelation. I spent one entire afternoon in the Monastery of St. John. During that time, I had the opportunity to talk at length with one of the most distinguished Greek Orthodox priests at the monastery. I asked him some questions about his understanding of the book of Revelation. When I raised the subject of the date of the book, he wasn't even aware of any contrary tradition to the A.D. 95 date for Revelation. He scoffed at the idea that Revelation was written at any time other than the end of Domitian's reign.

Let's examine the external evidence to see if this longstanding tradition of the late date is correct.

Examining the Evidence
Hegesippus (A.D. 150)

Hegesippus is an important historical source in the early church. He seems to have already held an important place in the church when he made his journey to Rome in A.D. 155. He may have been just a few years younger than Papias of Hierapolis. His best-known writing is his *Memoirs*, which consisted of five treatises. The *Memoirs* were an apology for the faith against unbelievers.

A careful examination of the writings of Eusebius (c. A.D. 300–340) reveals that Eusebius relied upon the *Memoirs* for some of his historical information. Hegesippus is specifically cited as a source by Eusebius two times in the section of Eusebius's *Ecclesiastical History* where the banishment of John to Patmos is discussed.[13]

After discussing the cruelty of Domitian, Eusebius is clearly referring to some source when he writes, "At this time, *as the story goes*, the Apostle and

Evangelist John was still alive, and was condemned to live in the island of Patmos for his witness to the divine word"[14] (emphasis added). Since Hegesippus is specifically mentioned as Eusebius's source in the very next section, it makes sense that he was his source concerning the banishment of John to Patmos under Domitian.

Hugh Lawlor believes that Hegesippus was in the mind of Eusebius, if the *Memoirs* were not actually open before him, as he wrote chapter xvii.[15] Lawlor believes that all of *Ecclesiastical History* 3.11-20 was taken from Hegesippus's *Memoirs*. Lawlor says,

> On that hypothesis we find ourselves able to give a reasonable account of the construction of this part of the *Ecclesiastical History*. Eusebius acted, it would seem, exactly as we might expect that a historian would act whose design was to give a narrative of a series of events, which should practically consist of extracts from earlier writers. He took as his basis Hegesippus, who had the fullest account known to him of the history of the Church during the period with which he was concerned. And here and there he added to his Hegesippean narrative illustrations from other authorities—Irenaeus, Tertullian, Brettius, and the rest. Thus...we have arrived once more at our former conclusion, that Eusebius drew from Hegesippus the account of Domitian in chapter xvii and the statement of chapter xviii that the Apostle St. John was banished under Domitian to Patmos; and we have extended it by tracing to the same source the further statement in chapter xx that the apostle returned to Ephesus in the reign of Nerva.[16]

Eusebius says,

> After Domitian had reigned fifteen years, Nerva succeeded. The sentences of Domitian were annulled, and the Roman Senate decreed the return of those who had been unjustly banished and the restoration of their property. *Those who committed the story of those times to writing relate it.* At that time, too, the story of the ancient Christians relates that the apostle John, after his banishment to the island, took up his abode at Ephesus"[17] (emphasis added).

The key phrase here is, "Those who committed the story of those times to writing relate it." To whom is Eusebius referring? The context indicates he is referring to Hegesippus, whom he has just referred to twice as a source for his information.

Hugh Lawlor concludes:

> Now evidence from the second century in regard to the date and authorship of the canonical Apocalypse is both scanty and, in some respects, difficult to interpret. But if the two passages referred to are really from Hegesippus we have his testimony that St. John was banished to Patmos under Domitian, and resided at Ephesus under Nerva. That is to say, he must be added to the small band of early witnesses to the late date and apostolic authority of the Apocalypse, and this is full of significance.... Hegesippus is the earliest writer who can be quoted in favour of that view. That, indeed, we may well claim for him."[18]

Irenaeus, Bishop of Lyons (A.D. 120–202)

While Hegesippus is the earliest witness to the late date of Revelation, without question the most important ancient witness is Irenaeus. Irenaeus is Exhibit A for late-date advocates. The importance of his testimony cannot be overemphasized because his credibility as a witness is outstanding.

Irenaeus spent his youth in Smyrna and claims to have been a pupil of Polycarp, bishop of Smyrna, who in turn was a student of the apostle John. Therefore, a more knowledgeable, reliable witness could hardly be imagined.[19]

Irenaeus's compelling statement is found in his comments on Revelation 13:18 in his work *Against Heresies,* which was probably written about A.D. 180: "For if it were necessary that the name of him [antichrist] should be distinctly revealed in this present time, it would have been told by him who saw the apocalyptic vision. For it was seen no long time ago, but almost in our generation, toward the end of Domitian's reign."[20]

That statement is straightforward and unambiguous to the unbiased reader. Nevertheless, Gentry reinterprets Irenaeus, maintaining that John is the subject of *eorathe* ("it was seen"), not the Apocalypse. In other words, for Gentry, Irenaeus was commenting on *how long* John lived, not on *when* he wrote Revelation.

There are four simple points that render Gentry's position highly suspect. First, the nearest antecedent to the verb "it was seen" is "the apocalypse" (*apokalupsis*) or "apocalyptic vision," and the Latin translation of Irenaeus supports this understanding of the clause.[21] David Aune observes, "Further, the passive verb *eorathe,* 'he/she/it was seen,' does not appear to be the most appropriate way to describe the length of a person's life; it is much more likely that *eorathe* means, 'it [i.e., 'the Apocalypse'] was seen,' referring to the time when the Apocalypse was 'seen' by John on Patmos."[22]

Second, the verb "was seen" fits perfectly with the noun *apokalupsis*. An *apokalupsis* is an uncovering, revelation, or disclosure often revealed through visions.[23] The *apokalupsis* is clearly something that John saw; therefore, the verb "was seen" refers to what John saw (the apocalypse) rather than someone seeing John.[24]

Third, if John were the intended subject of this statement, Irenaeus, who was trying to bring the matter as near to his own time as possible, would surely have said that John lived into the reign of Trajan, a fact that Irenaeus knew well.[25]

Fourth, the vast majority of scholars, ancient and modern, have accepted the fact that this statement refers to the time the Apocalypse was seen.[26] Even most of the early-date advocates do not agree with Gentry's exegesis of Irenaeus. For example, John A. T. Robinson, who dates Revelation in late 68 after the death of Nero, accepts Irenaeus's statement as a reference to the Apocalypse, not John. He says, "The translation has been disputed by a number of scholars, on the ground that it means that *he* (John) was seen; but this is very dubious. One must assume that Irenaeus believed the Apocalypse to have come from c. 95."[27]

Philip Schaff, another early-date advocate, calls Irenaeus's testimony of the Domitianic date "clear and weighty testimony."[28]

J. Ritchie Smith summarizes the issue well:

> It is a sufficient answer to all these forced interpretations, that the early church always understood the words of Irenaeus in their plain and obvious meaning, nor would any other have been suggested if his testimony had not been a stumbling-block in the way of modern exposition. That Irenaeus refers the Apocalypse to the reign of Domitian is generally admitted by scholars of all shades of opinion.[29]

As convincing as Irenaeus's testimony remains, the dating of the Apocalypse does not rest upon his testimony alone. There are many more witnesses that can be called upon.

Publius Papinius Statius (A.D. 92)

Publius Papinius Statius was a Roman poet born in Naples around A.D. 40. Beginning in A.D. 92, five books he authored were published. This collection is called Statius's *Silvae*. The word *Silvae* is from the Latin *silva*, which means "pieces of raw material." This five-volume work contains 32 poems addressed to friends as they celebrated various events in life.

One key poem in Statius's *Silvae* is an adulation of the emperor Domitian. Deane James Woods has demonstrated that Statius's *Silvae* and

John's Apocalypse contain numerous parallels.[30] Woods's thesis is that "in Statius's *Silvae* and John's Apocalypse, eleven common, yet parallel contrastive motifs are discernible, and which, on inherent, circumstantial grounds, suggest that John may have written his distinctive apocalyptic work with purposive resolve in the light of Statius' 'adulatio' emphases of Domitian in his *Silvae*."[31]

This is significant for establishing the date of the writing of Revelation because it is further external evidence that helps substantiate the A.D. 95 date.[32]

Clement of Alexandria (c. 150–215)

Clement of Alexandria is known as the Father of Alexandrian Christianity. His pertinent testimony concerning the date of Revelation is in his *Quis Salvus Dives* (*Who Is the Rich Man That Shall Be Saved?*), Section 42:

> And to give you confidence, when you have thus truly repented, that there remains for you a trustworthy hope for salvation, hear a story that is no mere story, but a true account of John the apostle that has been handed down and preserved in memory. When after the death of the tyrant he removed from the island of Patmos to Ephesus, he used to journey by request to the neighboring districts of the Gentiles, in some places to appoint bishops, in others to regulate whole churches, in others to set among the clergy some one man, it may be, of those indicated by the Spirit.

The key phrase in this section is the chronological indicator "after the death of the tyrant." Since both Nero and Domitian were tyrants during the later half of the first century, the word "tyrant" could refer to either of them. However, there are two key facts that strongly favor Domitian as the tyrant. First, Eusebius understood that Clement meant Domitian when he referred to the tyrant, citing him along with Irenaeus as a witness.[33]

Second, later in the same section of *Who Is the Rich Man That Shall Be Saved?* Clement tells a story that corroborates the identity of the tyrant as Domitian. In this account, John, on horseback, chases a young church leader who has forsaken the faith. The relevant portion says, "But when he recognized John as he advanced, he turned, ashamed, to flight. The other followed with all his might, forgetting his age, crying, 'Why, my son, dost thou flee from me, thy father, unarmed, old? Son, pity me.'"[34]

Gentry says this strenuous activity is much more believable activity for a man in his sixties.[35] He notes that Paul referred to himself as "aged" (Philemon 9) when he was in his late fifties.

However, what does the text say? The text says that when John gave chase to the young man he forgot his age and appealed to the young man to have pity on him because he was old. A man of 60, who lived to be about 100, would not have to forget his age to jump on a horse and chase someone down. And a healthy 60-year-old man is hardly old enough to ask for a favor based on pity.

Moreover, the word Paul used of himself in Philemon 9 ("aged") is the word *presbutes;* whereas, in Clement, the word John used to describe his age is *geron*. While the age parameters for these different words are not precise, *presbutes* was normally used for a man between the ages of 49–56 who was a senior or aged, while *geron* was the term for an "old man" over 60 years of age.[36] Therefore, the word *geron* could be used by John to describe himself during the reign of Nero or Domitian. However, the fact that he asks the young man to have pity or mercy on him strongly suggests that he was very advanced in years when this event transpired.

The wording of the text, then, supports the thesis that the "tyrant" is Domitian not Nero. These statements are further evidence for Clement as a late date advocate.

Tertullian (c. A.D. 160–220)

Tertullian, or Quintus Septimius Florens Tertullianus, was born near the middle of the second century at Carthage, where his father was a centurion of the proconsular cohort. He was a Latin scholar with equal skill in Greek.

While Tertullian does not specifically say that John was banished to Patmos during the reign of Domitian, he is credited by Jerome with doing so.[37]

In addition, Eusebius quotes Tertullian's *Apology* 5, which was written in A.D. 197, and then follows with his own statements that reveal he interpreted Tertullian as following the prevailing tradition of placing John's exile under Domitian.[38]

Tertullian does mention the liberation of those who were banished by Domitian.[39] Again, while he does not mention John, the connection of Domitian with banishment corroborates the exile of John to Patmos. The word Tertullian used for banishment is *relegaverat*—a word often used elsewhere of John's banishment by Domitian.[40]

Early-date proponents seize upon another statement by Tertullian that they believe supports their view:

> But if thou art near to Italy, thou hast Rome, where we also have an authority close at hand. What a happy Church is that! on which the Apostles poured out all their doctrine, with their

blood: where Peter had a like Passion with the Lord; where Paul hath for his crown the same death with John; where the Apostle John was plunged into burning oil, and suffered nothing, and was afterwards banished to an island.[41]

Gentry cites this statement as evidence that John's banishment occurred at the same time as the martyrdom of Peter and Paul.[42] But this is making the statement say more than was intended. The focus in this quote is on three events that all occurred in the same *place* (locality), not on *when* they occurred (chronology). In the context, the focus is on the city of Rome. As J. Ritchie Smith notes, "The words obviously contain no indication that the martyrdom of Peter and Paul and the persecution of John occurred at the same time, but only that they occurred at the same place."[43]

The Muratorian Canon (c. 170)

This manuscript states in lines 47-59,

> ...since the blessed Apostle Paul himself—following the pattern of his predecessor John—writes, giving their names, to not more than seven churches, in this order: To the Corinthians a first; to the Ephesians a second; to the Philippians a third; to the Colossians a fourth; to the Galatians a fifth; to the Thessalonians a sixth; to the Romans a seventh. But although there is one more each to the Corinthians and to the Thessalonians, for the sake of reproof, nevertheless it is obvious that one church is dispersed over the whole globe of the earth. For also John, in his Apocalypse, while writing to seven churches, yet speaks to all.

Gentry asserts this means that John wrote to the seven churches in Asia before Paul wrote to the seven churches he addressed.[44] Gentry follows the Muratorian Fragment and lists the seven churches addressed by Paul as Rome, Corinth, Galatia, Ephesus, Philippi, Colossae, and Thessalonica.[45] However, following Gentry's argument would mean that Revelation must have been written earlier than the last of these seven Pauline epistles, which would be the epistle to the Philippians, which is normally dated near the end of Paul's two-year period of house arrest in Rome in A.D. 60–62.[46] Therefore, Revelation would have to have been written in A.D. 62 at the latest, yet in his own writings, Gentry contends that Revelation could not have been written earlier than November 64. His own argument here goes against him.

The point of the Muratorian Canon in referring to John as Paul's predecessor is not that John wrote before Paul, but simply that John was an apostle before him.[47]

Origen (185–253)

Origen was a disciple of Clement of Alexandria. His relevant statement on the date of Revelation is, "The King of the Romans, as tradition teaches, condemned John, who bore testimony, on account of the word of truth, to the isle of Patmos."[48] The difficulty, as with Tertullian, is that Origen does not identify who he means by "the King of the Romans," but the tradition to which he alludes must have been handed down from Irenaeus, because at this time there was no other tradition in the church.[49] Knowing this tradition, had Origen intended someone other than Domitian, he certainly would have named that person in order to correct any perceived mistake.[50]

R. H. Charles correctly says, "Neither in Clement nor Origen is Domitian's name given, but it may be presumed that it was in the mind of these writers."[51]

Dio Cassius (150–235)

Dio Cassius was a Roman historian. While he does not mention John's banishment, he does reference the liberation of those Domitian had banished after his assassination on September 18, A.D. 96.[52] This testimony corroborates with the ecclesiastical tradition of John's liberation when Domitian died.

Victorinus, Bishop of Pettau or Petovium (d. c. A.D. 304)

Victorinus, who wrote the first commentary on Revelation, suffered martyrdom under Diocletian. In his *Commentary on the Apocalypse* at Revelation 10:11 he notes:

> He says this, because when John said these things he was in the island of Patmos, condemned to the labor of the mines by Caesar Domitian. There, therefore, he saw the Apocalypse; and when grown old, he thought that he should at length receive his quittance by suffering, Domitian being killed, all his judgments were discharged. And John being dismissed from the mines, thus subsequently delivered the same Apocalypse which he had received from God.[53]

Commenting further upon Revelation 17:10, Victorinus states, "The time must be understood in which the written Apocalypse was published, since then reigned Caesar Domitian; but before him had been Titus his brother, and Vespasian, Otho, Vitellius, and Galba. These are the five who have fallen. One remains, under whom the Apocalypse was written—Domitian, to wit."[54]

Eusebius Pamphili (260–340)

Eusebius was bishop of Caesarea in Israel, and is known as "the father of church history" due to his classic work *Ecclesiastical History*. Several times in his writings he expressly dated the Apocalypse to the reign of Domitian. His witness is especially weighty because he had all the early Christian literature at his disposal. Apparently he was not even aware of a contrary tradition to the Domitianic date.

Concerning Domitian's cruelty, Eusebius wrote, "It is said that in this [Domitian's] persecution the apostle and evangelist John, who was still alive, was condemned to dwell on the island of Patmos in consequence of his testimony to the divine word."[55]

Eusebius wrote about Revelation as follows:

> But after Domitian had reigned fifteen years and Nerva succeeded to the empire, the Roman Senate, according to the writers that record the history of those days, voted that Domitian's honors should be cancelled, and that those who had been unjustly banished should return to their homes and have their property restored to them. It was at this time that the apostle John returned from his banishment in the island and took up his abode in Ephesus, according to an ancient Christian tradition.[56]

In another section he continues:

> At that time the apostle and evangelist John, the one whom Jesus loved, was still living in Asia and governing the churches of that region, having returned after the death of Domitian from his exile on the island. And that he was still alive at that time may be established by the testimony of two witnesses. They should be trustworthy who have maintained the orthodoxy of the Church; and such indeed were Irenaeus and Clement of Alexandria.[57]

In the *Chronicle*, Eusebius lists these events in the fourteenth year of Domitian: "Persecution of Christians and under him the apostle John is banished to Patmos and sees his Apocalypse, as Irenaeus mentions."[58]

It is true that Eusebius maintained doubts concerning Johannine authorship of Revelation, but this in no way impairs his ability to accurately reflect the traditions of the church on the date of its composition.

Gentry points out that in his *Evangelical Demonstrations*, Eusebius speaks of the martyrdom of Peter and Paul in the same sentence that he mentions the banishment of John. He contends this means these events were contemporaneous and thus demonstrates that Eusebius later held to a Neronic date for John's banishment.[59] However, this statement by Eusebius does *not* say John was banished at the same time Peter and Paul were martyred. Rather it simply states in one sentence the fact of the suffering of these three great apostles.

In light of Eusebius's numerous clear statements about John's banishment under Domitian, to hold, based on this one statement, that Eusebius later changed his mind is weak at best and desperate at worst.

Jerome (340–419)

Jerome is a giant of the ancient church. He was proficient in several languages. At the direction of Pope Damascus he translated the Scriptures into Latin (the Vulgate).

In two places, Jerome stated clearly that John was banished under Domitian. First, in his *Against Jovinianum* (A.D. 393), Jerome wrote that John was "a prophet, for he saw in the island of Patmos, to which he had been banished by the Emperor Domitian as a martyr for the Lord, an Apocalypse containing boundless mysteries of the future."[60]

Second, Jerome's most specific statement is found in his *Lives of Illustrious Men,* where he writes about John's banishment:

> In the fourteenth year then after Nero, Domitian having raised a second persecution, he was banished to the island of Patmos, and wrote the Apocalypse, on which Justin Martyr and Irenaeus afterwards wrote commentaries. But Domitian having been put to death and his acts, on account of his excessive cruelty, having been annulled by the senate, he returned to Ephesus under Pertinax and continuing there until the time of the emperor Trajan, founded and built churches throughout all Asia, and, worn out by old age, died in the sixty-eighth year after our Lord's passion and was buried near the same city.[61]

Jerome is another strong link in the steady chain of late-date supporters.

Sulpicius Severus (c. 400)

Sulpicius Severus was a historian and hagiographer. In his *Sacred History* he states, "Then, after an interval, Domitian, the son of Vespasian, persecuted the Christians. At this time, he banished John the Apostle and Evangelist to the island of Patmos. There he, secret mysteries having been revealed to him, wrote and published his book of the holy Revelation, which indeed is either foolishly or impiously not accepted by many."[62]

Orosius (early fifth century)

Paulus Orosius also supports the late date of Revelation:

> In the eight hundred and thirtieth year after the founding of
> the City, Domitian, the ninth emperor after Augustus, suc-
> ceeded his brother, Titus, to the throne....But Domitian, elated
> by the most distorted form of vanity, held a triumph nominally
> over the enemy who had been overcome, but actually over the
> loss of his legions. This same emperor, crazed by his pride
> because of which he wished to be worshiped as a god, was the
> first emperor after Nero to order a persecution against the
> Christians to be carried on. Also at this time, the most blessed
> Apostle John was banished to the island of Patmos. Also among
> the Jews, an order was given that the race of David be searched
> out and killed by cruel tortures and bloody inquisitions, since
> the holy prophets were both hated and believed, as if some day
> there would be One from the seed of David who could acquire
> the throne.[63]

Primasius, Bishop of Hadrumentum (c. 540)

Primasius was bishop of Hadrumentum in North Africa until his death in
about A.D. 560. In the preface to his commentary on the Apocalypse he stated
that John received his apocalyptic visions while he was banished and impris-
oned in the mines on the island of Patmos under Caesar Domitian.

Andreas of Cappadocia (c. 600)

Andreas or Andrew was a bishop of Caesarea in Cappadocia. He authored
a commentary on Revelation c. A.D. 600 that clearly favors a Domitianic date
for Revelation.

The Acts of John (c. 650)

This is an apocryphal work of the fifth or sixth century A.D. attributed to
Prochorus that supports the Domitianic exile of John. The entire work
assumes John's exile under Domitian.

> And the fame of the teaching of John was spread abroad in
> Rome; and it came to the ears of Domitian that there was a cer-
> tain Hebrew in Ephesus, John by name, who spread a report
> about the seat of empire [sic] of the Romans, saying that it
> would quickly be rooted out, and that the kingdom of the
> Romans would be given over to another. And Domitian, trou-
> bled by what was said, sent a centurion with soldiers to seize

John, and bring him.…And Domitian, astonished at all the wonders, sent him away to an island, appointing for him a set time. And straightway John sailed to Patmos.[64]

Venerable Bede (700)

Baeda Bede, known as Bede the Venerable, was a famous church leader (672-735) considered to be "the father of English history." His *Homilies on the Gospels* are considered one of the masterpieces of monastic literature. They were probably written late in his career sometime in the 720s. In his *Homilies* he wrote,

> And it is told in church history how he was put by the emperor Domitian into a tub of boiling oil, from which, since divine grace shielded him, he came out untouched, just as he had been a stranger to the corruption of fleshly concupiscence. And not much after, on account of his unconquerable constancy in bringing the good news, he was banished in exile by the same prince to the island of Patmos, where although he was deprived of human comfort, he nevertheless merited to be relieved by the frequent consolation of the divine vision and spoken message. Accordingly, in that very place he composed with his own hand the Apocalypse, which the Lord revealed to him concerning the present and future state of the church.[65]

Writing on John's Apocalypse, Venerable Bede stated, "John wrote his epistles, and his gospel, all about the same time; for after the death of Domitian, being returned from his exile, he found the church disturbed by heretics, which had arisen in his absence, whom, in his epistles, he often called antichrists."[66]

The Syriac Version of the New Testament (A.D. 550)

A subscription in two Syriac versions of Revelation states that John was exiled by Nero: "The Revelation which was made by God to John the Evangelist in the island of Patmos, whither he was banished by the Emperor Nero." It is of paramount importance to note that this one sentence is the first unambiguous testimony that supports a Neronic date for Revelation, and it appears 450 years after the Apocalypse was written![67]

Arethas (c. 850–944)

Arethas, a native of the Peloponnesus, became the bishop of Caesarea in 902. He wrote a commentary on Revelation that was a revision of the commentary of Andreas of Caesarea. He favored a pre-A.D. 70 date for Revelation.

Theophylact (d. 1107)

Theophylact was bishop of Achrida during the eleventh century A.D. In the preface to his commentary on the Gospel of John he placed John's exile during the reign of Nero (PG CXXIII.1133-34) .

Summarizing of the Evidence

The external evidence has now been presented. Let's put the findings side by side. Only the witnesses that are clear and unambiguous for each date are presented.

Witnesses for the Domitianic Date	Witnesses for the Neronic Date
Irenaeus (A.D. 180)	
Victorinus (c. 300)	
Eusebius (c. 300)	
Jerome (c. 400)	
Sulpicius Severus (c. 400)	
The Acts of John (c. 650)	
Primasius (c. 540)	Syriac Version of NT (550)
Orosius (c. 600)	
Andreas (c. 600)	
Venerable Bede (A.D. 700)	
	Arethas (c. 900)
	Theophylact (d. 1107)

As you can see, the first clear, accepted, unambiguous witness to the Neronic date is a one-line subscription in the Syriac translation of the New Testament in A.D. 550. There are only two other external witnesses to the early date: Arethas (c. 900) and Theophylact (d. 1107).

The late date, on the other hand, has an unbroken line of support from some of the greatest, most reliable names in church history, beginning in A.D. 180. And don't forget that Clement of Alexandria, Tertullian, and Origen all support the late date; however, they are not included in the chart because they don't specifically say that John was banished by Domitian.

Amazingly, in light of this overwhelming evidence in favor of the late date, Gentry says, "that the Domitianic date cannot be certainly established from the external evidence. Indeed, when carefully scrutinized the evidence even tilts in the opposite direction."[68] He also states, "There simply is no 'voice [singular] of church tradition concerning the late date of Revelation.'

It is time for late date advocates to admit this. Neither is there an 'overwhelming voice of the early church' in this regard."[69]

It is no surprise that few scholars agree with Gentry. Read what other scholars of various backgrounds and eschatological viewpoints have to say about the external evidence.

Philip Schaff, who dates the book of Revelation in A.D. 68–69, admits that the external evidence points to the reign of Domitian.[70]

Paton Gloag addresses the external evidence for the Neronic date: "The external evidence in favour of this view is acknowledged by all to be weak; indeed it is scarcely worth mentioning. There is not the slightest trace of it in the writings of the Fathers. The earliest direct statement to this effect is a subscription attached to a manuscript of a Syrian version of the sixth century."[71]

G. K. Beale, who adopts an eclectic view of Revelation, refers to "the firm tradition stemming from Irenaeus."[72]

William Hendricksen, an amillennialist, says flatly, "One cannot find a single really cogent argument in support of the earlier date. The arguments produced are based on late and unreliable testimonies."[73]

R. H. Charles states, "The earliest authorities are practically unanimous in assigning the Apocalypse to the last years of Domitian....The external evidence is, as we have already seen, unanimous in favour of the latter [the late date] as against the former [the early date]."[74]

Arthur S. Peake observes, "And on the other side we have the external evidence which is almost all in favour of the later date."[75]

Barclay Newman, who rejects the Domitianic date, says, "The earliest authorities are almost unanimous in dating the Apocalypse during the last years of Domitian."[76]

F. J. A. Hort, one of the most eminent supporters for an early date calls the external evidence for the late date "undoubtedly weighty." He concludes, "On the one hand the tradition as to Domitian is not unanimous; on the other it is the prevalent tradition, and goes back to an author likely to be the recipient of a true tradition on the matter....If external evidence alone could decide, there would be a clear preponderance for Domitian."[77]

In light of this evidence and testimony, it stretches the limits of credulity for any preterist to assert that the external evidence actually favors the early date. To any unbiased mind, the external evidence overwhelmingly favors the A.D. 95 date for Revelation.

The Internal Evidence

Preterists marshal three main internal arguments from the book of Revelation for the Neronic date. Before presenting the positive evidence for the Domitianic date, let's briefly consider each of these arguments.

Internal Evidence for the Neronic Date
The Temple in Revelation 11:1-2

The chief preterist argument for the Neronic date from Revelation is the mention of the temple in Revelation 11:1-2. In this text John is told to measure the temple: "There was given me a measuring rod like a staff; and someone said, 'Get up and measure the temple of God and the altar, and those who worship in it. Leave out the court which is outside the temple, and do not measure it, for it has been given to the nations; and they will tread under foot the holy city for forty-two months.'"

Preterists contend this is a reference to the Second Temple period or Herod's Temple in Jerusalem before its destruction in A.D. 70. Therefore, they conclude Revelation must have been written before A.D. 70 while the Temple was still standing. There are three arguments against this point.

First, this interpretation completely fails to take into account the Old Testament prophetic parallels. It is recognized by scholars of every stripe that Revelation relies heavily on the Old Testament, especially Daniel and Ezekiel.[78] In both of these Old Testament prophetic books a Temple is mentioned that is not in existence at the time the author is writing.

Daniel wrote after the destruction of the Temple in 586 B.C. and before the temple was rebuilt in 520–516 B.C. When Daniel wrote, there was no Temple standing in Jerusalem. However, he refers to Temple sacrifices and Temple desecration on several occasions, in Daniel 8:11-14; 9:27; 10:31; 12:11. Daniel must have been referring to a future Temple when he wrote.

Ezekiel also describes a Temple. G. K. Beale says that the measuring of the temple in Revelation 11:1-2 "is best understood against the background of the temple prophecy in Ezekiel 40–48."[79]

Ezekiel received news of the destruction of the temple in Jerusalem in Ezekiel 33. However, after receiving that news, in Ezekiel 40–48, Ezekiel, like John, receives a vision of a Temple that, if taken literally, has never existed up to this day. Moreover, Ezekiel, like John, is told to measure the Temple he sees in his vision. The words "measure" and "measured" occur 44 times in Ezekiel 40–48. Ezekiel is measuring a Temple that must be future to his day because no Temple is standing on earth in Jerusalem for him to measure.

Some preterists also recognize that Revelation 11:1-2 cannot be used to argue an early date. Preterist and early-date proponent Chris Schlect declares: "Gentry, Russell, and others devote a good deal of space arguing that the integrity of the temple (assumed in Revelation 11:1-2) is a strong evidence that Revelation was written before the temple's destruction. They don't consider that Ezekiel was commanded to measure the temple (Ez. 40) fourteen years *after* the temple was burned by the Babylonians (2 Ki. 25:9)."[80]

These examples show it is common for Old Testament prophetic writings to refer to a Temple that is future from the perspective of the writer. If Daniel and Ezekiel both discussed a Temple when there was no temple standing in their own day, and Ezekiel even measured this future Temple, couldn't we expect John, a New Testament prophet, to follow the same pattern?

Second, Revelation 11:2 says the Temple John measured would be overrun by the nations for 42 months. Then in Revelation 11:3-14, John describes the work of the two witnesses who will fulfill their ministry during this same period. Revelation 11:3 says the two witnesses will prophesy for 1,260 days, which is the exact same time period mentioned in 11:2 for the treading down of the Temple.

The problem for preterists is this: When did anything like the ministry of the two witnesses occur in the first century while the Temple was standing in Jerusalem? The obvious answer is that it didn't. The setting of Revelation 11 is future. The Temple John measured is the future Tribulation Temple (cf. Matthew 24:15; 2 Thessalonians 2:4), and the two witnesses are two Spirit-empowered men who will do great signs and wonders, be murdered by the Beast in Jerusalem, and then rise again three-and-one-half days later.

Just as Satan will have his two men during the Tribulation, the Beast and the False Prophet, the Lord will have his two men—the two witnesses.

Third, Clement of Rome, whom most scholars believe wrote in the A.D. 90s, refers to the Temple as though it were still standing in 1 *Clement* 41. If Clement can write after A.D. 70 about a Temple that is standing in Jerusalem, why can't John do the same thing?

Gentry's response to this argument is to assign a pre-A.D. 70 date to Clement as well. But again, to make his case, he must swim upstream against the convincing majority of scholars, who date Clement in the 90s.[81]

The Number of the Beast ("666") in Revelation 13:16-18

The second internal argument for the early date of Revelation centers on "666," or the number of the Beast. Preterists maintain that the gematria value of "Neron Kaiser" in Hebrew is 666.[82] Therefore, they conclude that the Beast of Revelation 13 is Nero; thus, indicating that John wrote the Apocalypse during his reign.

Several arguments have been raised against this position. Gentry lists these objections and deals with each of them.[83] However, there are two arguments that make the identification of Nero with the Beast in Revelation 13:16-18 highly doubtful.

First, for the number 666 to fit the gematria value of Nero, the title Nero Caesar must be used. This is important to note at the outset because there are many names and titles for Nero one could choose. Choosing this title seems too convenient for the Nero view.[84] How can one be sure this is the form of the name that should be adopted? While Nero's name can certainly be rendered in this way, it could be a case of adapting the facts to fit a predetermined solution.

Second, for the gematria value to fit Nero Caesar, the Greek form of his name must be transliterated into Hebrew (*nron qsr*). The sum of 666 can be reached only by transliterating the Greek form of this one title for Nero into Hebrew. If the Latin form of the name Nero Caesar is transcribed in Hebrew characters (*nro qsr*), then the total adds up to only 616.[85] One wonders why John, writing to a primarily Greek audience in western Asia Minor, would not use a Greek form instead of a Hebrew form?

However, even if one agrees that this specific title (Nero Caesar) is the correct one and that the correct form is the Greek transliteration into Hebrew (*nron qsr*), there is still another hurdle—should the vowels be included? The calculation for Nero Caesar from Hebrew equals 666 only if the Hebrew letter *yodh* is omitted from the word Caesar (*qsr*). This is a defective spelling.[86] Robert Mounce summarizes the problems preterists face on this issue: "What is not generally stressed is that this solution asks us to calculate a Hebrew transliteration of the Greek form of a Latin name, and that with a defective spelling."[87]

G. Salmon has developed three rules that have been used throughout the centuries for making any desired name equal 666. His rules are appropriate for the attempts by preterists to make Nero fit the number of the Beast: "First, if the proper name by itself will not yield it, add a title; secondly, if the sum cannot be found in Greek, try Hebrew, or even Latin; thirdly, do not be too particular about the spelling....We cannot infer much from the fact that a key fits the lock if it is a lock in which almost any key will turn."[88]

A third serious problem with identifying Nero with 666 is that this view is not corroborated by the early church fathers, as one would expect, if this view were correct. Irenaeus wrote extensively about the number 666. He warned against people falsely presuming to know the name of the Antichrist.[89] He was aware of many candidates for the number 666 and mentions three of them by name: Evanthas, Lateinos, and Teitan.[90] However, he himself never identified anyone with the number 666. Irenaeus said, "We will not, however, incur the risk of pronouncing positively as to the name of Antichrist; for if it were necessary that his name should be distinctly revealed in this present time, it would have been announced by him who beheld the apocalyptic vision."[91]

Amazingly, the first mention of the name Nero Caesar in connection with the number 666 didn't come until the nineteenth century, when it was suggested by four German scholars.[92] If Nero Ceasar is such an obvious connection to the number 666, then why did it take almost 1,800 years for someone to see it?

Fourth, even if it can be proven that there is an allusion to Nero Caesar in 666 it does not necessarily follow that Revelation had to be written during his reign. John could have referred back to him from a date after his death.[93]

The fifth and strongest argument against identifying Nero with the Beast of Revelation 13 is that Nero did not fulfill the activities of the Beast as recorded in that chapter. Gentry and other preterists take the reference to 666 literally as the gematria value of the name Nero Caesar. However, when it comes to taking the rest of the information about the Beast in Revelation 13 literally and applying it to Nero, this view falls flat.

Revelation 13 states that the Beast will rule the world for 42 months, that all who dwell on the earth will worship him, that he will be killed and come back to life,[94] that he will be supported by another beast who will do great miracles (including making fire come down from heaven), that an image of the Beast will be constructed that will be animated and speak, that all who do not worship this image will be killed, and that all the people on the earth must take his mark of 666 on their right hand or forehead if they went to engage in any form of commerce. None of these things were literally fulfilled during the reign of Nero from A.D. 54–68.[95]

Simply stated, preterists are not consistent in their method of interpreting Revelation 13. If the Beast is a literal world ruler (Nero) and the numerical value of his name is 666, then the other facts presented in Revelation 13 must be taken literally. And if they are, we find none of them were fulfilled in Nero.

Revelation 13 refers not to Nero but to the future Antichrist, whose name will equal 666 and who will literally fulfill all the other statements mentioned in this chapter.

The Sixth King in Revelation 17:9-11

The third main internal argument preterists rely upon is that the "sixth king" in Revelation 17:9-11 is Nero. Revelation 17:9-11 says, "Here is the mind which has wisdom. The seven heads are seven mountains on which the woman sits, and they are seven kings; five have fallen, one is, the other has not yet come; and when he comes, he must remain a little while. The beast which was and is not, is himself also an eighth, and is one of the seven, and he goes to destruction."

Preterists adopt a historical approach and identify the kings in this text with specific Roman emperors, and on that basis, suggest that Revelation was written during the reign of Nero. They begin the count with Julius Caesar and list the six kings in this order:

1. Julius Caesar (101–44 B.C.)

2. Augustus (27 B.C.–A.D. 14)

3. Tiberius (A.D. 14–37)

4. Caligula (37–41)

5. Claudius (41–54)

6. Nero (54–58)

The real problem for the preterist position here is that there are many different schemes for counting these kings. David Aune lists nine alternate ways of counting the Roman emperors.[96] G. K. Beale gives five different schemes of enumerating the emperors in Revelation 17:9-11.[97] The reason for these different schemes is that there are many ways to count the Roman emperors, depending upon several factors.[98] This forces us to ask some questions:

1. With which emperor should one begin counting—Caesar Augustus, Julius Caesar, or Caligula?

2. Are all the emperors to be counted or only those deified by an act of the Senate?

3. Should the brief reigns of Galba, Otho, and Vitellius, who all reigned during the 18 months between Nero's death and Vespasian's capture of Rome (December 21, 69), be excluded from the count?

As you can see, one must be absolutely correct in all three of these introductory decisions or the final identification becomes suspect. Moreover, each of these decisions is purely arbitrary.[99] As Robert Mounce concludes, "However one tries to calculate the seven kings as Roman emperors, he encounters difficulties which cast considerable doubt on the entire approach."[100]

To avoid this problem and make the interpretation more reliable, the preferred view is to see the seven heads as seven successive empires represented by seven kings. This view goes all the way back to Andreas of Caesarea. He saw the seven kings as representing seven successive kingdoms, each of which was associated with a specific king: 1) Assyria (Ninus), 2) Media (Arbakus), 3) Babylon (Nebuchadnezzar), 4) Persia (Cyrus), 5) Macedonia (Alexander), 6) the old Roman Empire (Romulus), and 7) the new Roman Empire (Constantine), followed by 8) the kingdom of Antichrist. There are minor variations of this scheme, but all include Assyria, Babylon, Persia, Greece, historical Rome, and Rome II or the reunited Roman Empire under Antichrist.[101]

The preferred scheme is that the five who have fallen are kingdoms of the past which have persecuted God's people: Egypt, Assyria, Babylon, Persia, and Greece. The one that remains is Rome, the persecutor of God's people when John was writing. The seventh is the final great persecutor, the reunited Roman Empire headed up by Antichrist, and the eighth is the final form of Gentile world rule—the final empire of Antichrist, which will arise from the seventh after the Antichrist dies and comes back to life (Revelation 13:3,12,14). In this case, the seven heads span the entire history of Gentile world empires who have oppressed and will oppress the people of God.

This is the best view for two main reasons: First, the seven heads are seven mountains, and in the Bible, "mountains" or "hills" often symbolize kingdoms or empires (Psalm 30:7; 68:15-16; Isaiah 2:2; 41:15; Jeremiah 51:25; Daniel 2:35; Habakkuk 3:6,10; Zechariah 4:7).

Second, this view fits the Old Testament imagery of the Beast and its heads as seen in Daniel 7. The imagery of the Beast in Revelation 13 and 17 clearly alludes to Daniel 7, where there are four beasts.[102] Daniel 7:17 and 23 state that the four beasts are four kings, although they in fact represent four kingdoms or empires: Babylon, Medo-Persia, Greece, and Rome. The translated Aramaic text of Daniel 7:17 reads, "These great beasts, which are four in number, are four kings who will arise from the earth." But the Septuagint translates "kings" in Daniel 7:17 as "kingdoms" in harmony with verse 23. This translation is followed in numerous English translations as well (NCV, NIV, NLT, REB).

Since Revelation 17 draws its imagery from Daniel 7 and the kings there are successive kingdoms, it makes sense that the same principle of interpretation should be applied in Revelation 17:9-11 and the kings there should be interpreted as kingdoms. G. K. Beale supports this conclusion:

> The angel now gives the interpretation of the beast's "seven heads," which he initially identifies as "seven mountains." The mountains are sometimes identified as the seven hills of Rome, and, therefore, with the Roman Empire....This usage points beyond a literal reference beyond Rome's "hills" and to a figurative meaning, "kingdoms," especially in the light of 8:8 and 14:1. Mountains symbolize kingdoms in the OT and Jewish writings, for example, Isa. 2:2; Jer. 51:25; Ezek. 35:3; Dan. 2:35, 45; Zech. 4:7; I *En.* 52; *Targ. Isa.* 41:15.[103]

Third, the verb "to fall" (*pipto*) in Revelation 17:10 is much more applicable to empires or kingdoms than to individual kings. Bauer gives the meaning as "the five have perished, disappeared, passed from the scene."[104]

Fourth, those who argue that Nero is the sixth king run up against a serious problem with their view. They maintain that Nero is the Beast out of the sea in Revelation 13 and that Nero is the sixth king in Revelation 17. The problem, however, is that the Beast is the *eighth* king in Revelation 17:11, not the sixth king. Early-date proponents can't have it both ways. If Nero is the Beast in Revelation 13 as they maintain, then he must be the Beast in Revelation 17 who is the eighth king, not the sixth. However, if the Beast of Revelation 13 is the future Antichrist and the eighth king in Revelation 17 and his kingdom is the future reign of Antichrist, then the two passages can be reconciled.

Having answered the preterists' internal arguments for the Neronic date, let's turn now to examine the internal evidence for the Domitianic or late date.

Internal Evidence for the Domitianic Date

There are three key lines of internal evidence that favor the Domitianic date.[105]

The Condition of the Seven Churches

One of the key internal arguments for the late date of Revelation is the condition of the seven churches of Asia Minor in Revelation 2–3. These churches all show the signs of being second-generation churches. The period of Paul's great mission seems to lie in the past. Let's consider the clues from three of these churches.

The Church at Ephesus

If John wrote Revelation in A.D. 64–67, then the letter to the church at Ephesus in Revelation 2:1-7 overlaps with Paul's two letters to Timothy, who was the pastor of the church when Paul wrote to him. In fact, if Revelation was written in 64–66, then it is very likely that Paul wrote 2 Timothy after John wrote to the church. Yet Paul makes no mention of the loss of first love or the presence of the Nicolaitans at Ephesus in his correspondence with Timothy. Neither does he mention these problems in his Ephesian epistle, which was probably written in A.D. 62. Jesus' statement to the church at Ephesus in Revelation 2:2 that it had guarded itself well against error does not fit what we know of this church in Nero's day (Acts 20:29-30; 1 Timothy 1:3-7; 2 Timothy 2:17-18).[106]

Gentry's response to this point is that error can erupt very quickly in a church. As an example he cites the churches of Galatia, which had, "so quickly desert[ed]...the grace of Christ, for a different gospel" (Galatians 1:6). But there is a great difference between the condition and maturity of the Galatian churches after Paul's brief visit there on his first missionary journey and the church at Ephesus, where Paul headquartered for three years, where Apollos taught, where Priscilla and Aquila ministered, and where Timothy pastored for several years.

Moreover, Revelation 2:1-7 makes no mention of the great missionary work of Paul in Asia Minor. On his third missionary journey Paul headquartered in Ephesus for three years and had a profound ministry there. If John wrote in A.D. 64–67, then the omission of any mention of Paul in the letters to the seven churches of Asia Minor is inexplicable.[107] However, if John wrote 30 years later to second-generation Christians in the churches, then the omission is easily understood.

The Church at Smyrna

Apparently the church at Smyrna did not even exist during Paul's ministry. Polycarp was the bishop at Smyrna. In his letter to the Philippians, written in about A.D. 110, Polycarp says that the Smyrnaeans did not know the Lord during the time Paul was ministering. "But I have not observed or heard of any such thing among you, in whose midst the blessed Paul labored, and who were his letters of recommendation in the beginning. For he boasts about you in all the churches—those alone, that is, which at that time had come to know the Lord, for we had not yet come to know him."[108]

Polycarp is saying that Paul praised the Philippian believers in all the churches, but that during Paul's ministry the church of Smyrna did not even exist. R. C. H. Charles says,

> The church of Smyrna did not exist in 60–64 A.D.—at a time when St. Paul was boasting of the Philippians in all the Churches. Cf. Polycarp (*Ad Phil...*). But though Polycarp's letter tells us that the church of Smyrna was not founded in 60–64 A.D., he gives no hint as to when it was founded. Hence several years may have elapsed after that date before it was founded. When, however, we turn to Revelation 2:8-11 we find that our text presupposes a Church poor in wealth but rich in good works, with a development of apparently many years to its credit. This letter, then, may have been written in the closing years of Vespasian (75–79) but hardly earlier.[109]

Gentry's reply is that Smyrna must have been evangelized before A.D. 60, based on Act 19:10,26.[110] Because Paul was headquartered in Ephesus, because Acts 19:10 says "that all who lived in Asia heard the word of the Lord, both Jews and Greeks," and because of the statement in Acts 19:26, Gentry assumes that a church must have been founded in Smyrna during Paul's three-year Ephesian ministry, which lasted about A.D. 55–57.

However, just because the gospel came to Smyrna during Paul's third missionary journey does not necessarily mean that a church was founded during this time. Scripture specifically states that churches were founded in the Asian cities of Ephesus, Colosse, Hierapolis, and Laodicea by the time of Paul's first Roman imprisonment in A.D. 60 (Colossians 4:13). However, there is no mention of any church at Smyrna. In the face of this scriptural silence and the specific statement of Polycarp, it seems best to let Polycarp's statement stand.

The Church at Laodicea

The church at Laodicea was the only one of the seven churches (and possibly Sardis) that did not receive any commendations in Revelation 2–3. In his letter to the Colossians, probably written in A.D. 60–62, Paul indicates that the church was an active group (Colossians 4:13). He mentions the church three times in his letter (2:2; 4:13,16). It would certainly take more than two to seven years for the church to depart so completely from its earlier acceptable status such that absolutely nothing good could be said about it in Revelation.[111]

Laodicea is also described in Revelation as flourishing economically. Jesus quotes the church as saying, "I am rich, and have become wealthy, and have need of nothing" (Revelation 3:17). Yet the city suffered devastation in the earthquake of A.D. 60. After the earthquake the Laodiceans refused all aid and assistance from Rome, preferring to rebuild their devastated city from their own resources. Tacitus, the Roman historian, describes this independent spirit: "In the same year, Laodicea, one of the famous Asiatic cities, was laid in ruins by an earthquake, but recovered by its own resources, without assistance from ourselves."[112]

The extent of the damage to Laodicea and the length of time it took to reconstruct the city are powerful evidence of a late date for Revelation. Archaeological excavations in the cities of the Lycus Valley (Laodicea, Colosse, and Hierapolis) reveal a marked interruption of numismatic (coin) evidence from A.D. 60–79. Colin Hemer notes that from A.D. 60–69 there are no coins at all from Laodicea in the *Catalogue of the Greek Coins in the British Museum*. There are only two coins from Laodicea during the reign of Vespasian (A.D. 69–79). However, there is a much richer series of coinage under Domitian. Hemer says, "the abrupt numismatic poverty of Hierapolis, Laodicea and perhaps Tripolis is sufficiently marked to be suggestive."[113]

Moreover, most of the main ruins that exist today in Laodicea are from buildings constructed during the time of earthquake reconstruction. The great public buildings destroyed in the earthquake were rebuilt at the expense of individual citizens and were not finished until about the year A.D. 90. The completion date of the stadium can be precisely dated to the latter part of A.D. 79, and the inscriptions on several other buildings indicate that they too can be dated to this same period.[114] New gates and fortifications seem to have culminated the rebuilding of Laodicea. It is likely that the great triple gate (Syrian gate) and towers were not finished until A.D. 88–90.[115]

Because the rebuilding of Laodicea after the earthquake occupied a complete generation, and because there is no numismatic evidence from the decade of the A.D. 60s, it is highly problematic for preterists to claim that Laodicea was rich, wealthy, and in need of nothing in A.D. 64–67. During those years the city was in the early stages of a rebuilding program that would last another 25 years. However, if Revelation was written in A.D. 95, the description of Laodicea in Revelation 3:14-22 would fit the situation exactly. By this time the city had been completely rebuilt and was enjoying prosperity and prestige and basking in the pride of its great accomplishment.[116]

The Banishment of John to Patmos

Church history consistently testifies that both Peter and Paul were executed in Rome near the end of Nero's reign. Preterists maintain that during this same time the apostle John was banished to Patmos by Nero. Why would Nero execute Peter and Paul and banish John? This seems inconsistent. The different punishments for Peter and Paul as compared with John argue for the fact that they were persecuted under different rulers. Moreover, there is no evidence of Nero's use of banishment for Christians.

Since Domitian was the second Roman emperor after Nero to persecute Christians, and since banishment was one of his favorite modes of punishment, John's exile to Patmos is much more likely under Domitian than Nero.[117]

The New Jerusalem

Revelation 21:9–22:5 focuses on the New Jerusalem coming down out of heaven from God. The fact that John mentions a New Jerusalem points to the fact that the Old Jerusalem had already been destroyed.[118]

Fourth Ezra 9:28–10:28, which was written about A.D. 100, contains a similar vision of the heavenly New Jerusalem, but only after a description of the destruction of the old Jerusalem and the Temple.[119] While Revelation does not mention the destruction of the Old Jerusalem, this parallel of New Jerusalem with 4 Ezra points to a late date for the writing of Revelation.

THE OVERWHELMING VERDICT

While preterism has many weaknesses, the Achilles' heel of this view is the early date the proponents assign to Revelation. The external evidence for the late date of Revelation is overwhelming. And the internal evidence for the late date, while not as overpowering as the external evidence, nevertheless is strong and convincing.

It is my prayer that those who hold the preterist position will admit the serious problems with their view and adopt an approach to dating Revelation that is not dependent upon the sandy foundation on which their defense now stands.

Chapter 7

THE OLIVET DISCOURSE

THOMAS ICE

> The Olivet Discourse, delivered shortly before Jesus' crucifixion,
> is the most important single passage of prophecy in all the Bible.
> It is significant because it came from Jesus Himself immediately
> after He was rejected by His own people and because it provides
> the master outline of end-time events.
>
> —Dr. Tim LaHaye[1]

A proper understanding of the Olivet Discourse is absolutely essential for anyone who wants to gain a clear picture of God's plan for the ages. This discourse is so significant that the way a person interprets it will impact his understanding of the rest of the prophecy passages in the Bible. In the battle between preterists and futurists, for the preterist, the Olivet Discourse is their most important passage. The preterist view either rises or falls depending on whether preterists can make their case based on our Lord's prophetic sermon. And we can find this discourse recorded in three of the Gospels, in Matthew 24–25, Mark 13, and Luke 21.

THE SETTING

The Contextual Setting for Christ's Discourse

The setting for the Olivet Discourse, at least for Matthew's account, is found in the events leading up to Matthew 24. Christ had presented Himself to the nation of Israel as their Messiah, but both the leaders and the people rejected Him. In Matthew 22–23, Jesus rebuked the Jewish leaders' hypocrisy and unbelief. He noted that the leaders were like the leaders from previous generations, who had killed the prophets (23:29-36). Christ then told the leaders, "Truly I say to you, all these things shall come upon this generation" (23:36). What things? He was referring to the judgment that would come upon the Jewish people through the Roman army in A.D. 70. "All hope for a turning of Israel to God in repentance has gone," notes Dr. Stanley Toussaint. "The King therefore has no alternative but to reject that nation for the time being with regard to its kingdom program. The clear announcement of this decision is seen in these verses of Matthew's Gospel."[2]

In spite of the fact that the Jewish people deserved the approaching judgment, like a caring parent about to administer a just punishment, Christ cried out, "O Jerusalem, Jerusalem, who kills the prophets and stones those who are sent to her! How often I wanted to gather your children together, the way a hen gathers her chicks under her wings, and you were unwilling" (23:37). Jesus wanted to gather His people (as He will in 24:31); instead, He would scatter them via the A.D. 70 judgment (Luke 21:24).

Jesus then declared in verse 38, "Behold, your house is being left to you desolate!" What house was Jesus talking about? The context of this passage tells us He had to be referring to the Jewish Temple, for in Matthew 24:1-2 Jesus and His disciples discuss the Temple. It is there that Jesus startled them by saying, "Do you not see all these things? Truly I say to you, not one stone here shall be left upon another, which will not be torn down" (24:2). What Jesus stated in Matthew 23:38 is described more precisely in Matthew 24:2: both verses refer to the same thing: the Temple.

Next, Christ said, "For I say to you, from now on you shall not see Me until you say, 'Blessed is He who comes in the name of the Lord!'" (24:39). Not only does this verse affirm the certainty of upcoming judgment, but it also promises future hope and blessing upon the Jewish nation. Alfred Edersheim, a son of the present remnant of Israel, said of this passage:

> Looking around on those Temple-buildings—that House, it shall be left to them desolate! And He quitted its courts with these words, that they of Israel should not see Him again till, the night of their unbelief past, they would welcome His return with a better Hosanna than that which had greeted His Royal Entry three days before. And this was the "Farewell" and the parting of Israel's Messiah from Israel and its Temple. Yet a Farewell which promised a coming again; and a parting which implied a welcome in the future from a believing people to a gracious, pardoning King.[3]

So, this verse not only speaks of the judgment that surely came in A.D. 70, but looks to a future time of redemption for Israel. We know this because the passage contains the forward-looking word "until." Luke 21:24 records another use of "until" by our Lord. "They will fall by the edge of the sword, and will be led captive into all the nations; and Jerusalem will be trampled under foot by the Gentiles until the times of the Gentiles be fulfilled." Hebrew Christian Bible teacher Arnold Fruchtenbaum says that based upon Matthew 23:39, as a condition for the second coming, Israel must call for the Lord to rescue them.[4] Fruchtenbaum explains:

> But then He declares that they will not see Him again until they say, *Blessed is He that cometh in the name of the Lord*. This is a messianic greeting. It will mean their acceptance of the Messiahship of Jesus.
>
> So Jesus will not come back to the earth until the Jews and the Jewish leaders ask Him to come back. For just as the Jewish leaders lead the nation to the rejection of the Messiahship of Jesus, they must some day lead the nation to the acceptance of the Messiahship of Jesus.[5]

Bible teacher David Cooper echoes Fruchtenbaum's understanding when he says, "Since Jesus came in the name of the Lord, and since He will not return until Israel says, 'Blessed is he that cometh in the name of the Lord,' it is clear that the people of Israel will see and recognize that Jesus was and is their true Messiah."[6] The last few verses of Matthew 23 reveal that judgment was coming in the near future, but beyond that, according to Matthew 24, deliverance and redemption awaits the Jewish nation.

THE HISTORICAL SETTING FOR CHRIST'S DISCOURSE

Matthew 24:1-3 describes for us the setting in which Christ delivered His prophetic sermon. Jesus went from the Temple (24:1) to the Mount of Olives (24:3), which means He most likely traveled down the Kidron Valley and then up to Olivet. As He was departing from the Temple, "His disciples came up to point out the temple buildings to Him" (24:1). This statement leads us to believe they were talking to Jesus about how beautiful the Temple complex was. Herod had spent years remodeling and refurbishing it, and it still wasn't finished. This emphasis is borne out in the parallel references—Mark 13:1-2 and Luke 21:5-6—where the disciples speak of the beauty of the Temple buildings. The Lord must have startled His disciples by His response to their gloating when He said, "Do you not see all these things? Truly I say to you, not one stone here shall be left upon another, which will not be torn down" (24:2).

At the end of Matthew 24:2, there is a break in the narrative. The narrative picks up again in 24:3, where we read that "the disciples came to Him privately." Mark 13:3 tells us that the disciples who came to Jesus privately were Peter, James, John, and Andrew, and that they were sitting on the Mount of Olives looking at the Temple. This is the same vista many visitors see today when they stand on the Mount of Olives and look toward the Temple Mount and the Dome of the Rock upon it.

That the disciples came to Jesus privately is consistent with the fact that Jesus limited His teaching only to His believing disciples from Matthew 13 onward because the nation had rejected Him as their prophesied Messiah (in Matthew 12). Starting in Matthew 13, Jesus spoke only in parables to the rejecting nation (Matthew 13:10-17). "Therefore I speak to them in parables; because while seeing they do not see, and while hearing they do not hear, nor do they understand" (Matthew 13:13). However, after telling a parable in public, Jesus would explain it in private to His disciples (see, for example, Matthew 13:10-23). In the Olivet Discourse, Christ is following this same pattern. The Olivet Discourse is a private explanation of future history for the benefit of believers.

THE QUESTIONS

A Key Distinction

While sitting on the Mount of Olives, the four disciples with Jesus asked Him, "Tell us, when will these things happen, and what will be the sign of Your coming, and of the end of the age?" (24:3). Now there is some debate over whether the disciples asked two questions or three. Even if one takes the first option, there is still no doubt that the second question contains two parts to it. I believe that there are two basic questions because of the grammar of the passage as explained by Craig Blomberg: "'The sign of your coming and of the end of the age' in Greek reads, more literally, *the sign of your coming and end of the age*. By not repeating the definite article ('the') before 'end of the age,' Matthew's rendering of Jesus' words is most likely linking the coming of Christ and the end of the age together as one event (Granville Sharp's rule)."[7]

This means that in the minds of the disciples, the two phrases are closely related to one another.

Clearly the first question relates to the destruction of the Temple, which was fulfilled in the Roman invasion and destruction of A.D. 70. It is equally clear that the two aspects of the second question have yet to occur in history, even though some want to see Christ's second coming in this passage (I'll explain more on the errors of preterism as I progress through the passage).

It appears likely to me that the disciples believed that all three aspects of their two questions would occur around the same event—the coming of Messiah. Why would they have thought this way? Toussaint is correct to note that the disciples were influenced by the prophet Zechariah:

> In their minds they had developed a chronology of events in the following sequence: (1) the departure of the King, (2) after a period of time the destruction of Jerusalem, and (3) immediately after Jerusalem's devastation the presence of the Messiah. They had good scriptural ground for this since Zechariah 14:1-2 describes the razing of Jerusalem. The same passage goes on to describe the coming of the Lord to destroy the nations which warred against Jerusalem (Zechariah 14:3-8). Following this the millennial kingdom is established (Zechariah 14:9-11).[8]

In other words, the disciples thought that all three events were related to a single event—the return of the Messiah, as taught in Zechariah 14:4. As we shall see, they were right to think of Zechariah 12–14 and his teaching about Messiah's coming. However, they were wrong to relate the impending judgment upon Jerusalem and the Temple with the return of Messiah.

A Certain Misunderstanding

The disciples' question in Matthew 24:3 is divided into two parts. The first question relates to the destruction of the Temple, which took place in A.D. 70. The second question, composed of two parts but related to one another, refers to events that are still yet to come. The disciples apparently thought that all three elements—the destruction of the Temple, the sign of Christ's coming, and the end of the age—would occur at the same time. Yet this is not what Jesus was saying.

It was common for Jesus to correct the disciples, and in this case, their misunderstanding represented the popular belief of their day.[9] J. Dwight Pentecost tells us:

> The questions showed that they had arrived at certain conclusions....To these men Christ's words concerning the destruction of Jerusalem was the destruction predicted by Zechariah that would precede the advent of the Messiah. In Jewish eschatology two ages were recognized: the first was this present age, the age in which Israel was waiting for the coming of the Messiah; the second was the age to come, the age in which all of Israel's

covenants would be fulfilled and Israel would enter into her promised blessings as a result of Messiah's coming.[10]

Stanley Toussaint echoes this notion:

> This sequence is so clearly in view that Luke records the question concerning the destruction of Jerusalem only (Luke 21:7). That is, the disciples took the destruction of Jerusalem to be completely eschatological. Therefore, Luke records this question only, as though Jerusalem's destruction would mark the coming of the King to reign. Bruce is correct when he asserts, "The questioners took for granted that all three things went together: destruction of temple, advent of Son of Man, end of the current age."[11, 12]

While the disciples merged these three events into a single time period, Christ did not. In fact, Matthew and Mark do not deal with the destruction of Jerusalem in their accounts of the Olivet Discourse. Rather, they focus upon the future days of tribulation leading up to Christ's return. Only in Luke's account do we find Christ's comments about Jerusalem's impending destruction (21:20-24). But Luke goes on to deal with future days of tribulation and Christ's return as well (21:25-36). For whatever reason, Matthew and Mark's entire focus is upon Jesus' answer regarding "the sign of [His] coming, and of the end of the age."

A Careful Examination

The disciples asked, "Tell us, when will these things happen...?" (Matthew 24:3). Since Christ had been speaking about the Temple and a time when "not one stone here will be left upon another, which will not be torn down" (Matthew 24:2), it is clear that He had prophesied the destruction of the Temple in Jerusalem by the Romans in A.D. 70.

Earlier, Jesus had spoken of Israel's "house [Temple]...being left to you desolate" (Matthew 23:38). Luke records another prediction of judgment upon Israel, as in Matthew 23:37-39, preceded by Christ's weeping over the city of Jerusalem (Luke 19:41). This prophecy occurred at the time of Christ's triumphal entry on Palm Sunday and is based upon Israel's rejection of Jesus as their Messiah (Luke 19:42). Jesus prophesied in Luke 19:43-44:

> The days will come upon you when your enemies will throw up a barricade against you, and surround you and hem you in on every side, and they will level you to the ground and your children within you, and they will not leave in you one stone upon

another, because you did not recognize the time of your visitation.

Here are some key observations about this prophecy: First, "your enemies" undoubtedly refers to the Romans who destroyed the city in A.D. 70. Second, the phrase "will throw up a barricade against you and surround you and hem you in on every side" is a clear description of the Roman siege used to defeat Jerusalem. Third, the Roman siege resulted in a total destruction of the city and of life within the city. Usually in wartime, if anyone is spared it will be the children, but even most of them were killed. Fourth, the very words of Christ from Matthew 24:2 were used by Him earlier in this passage when He said, "They will not leave in you one stone upon another." Fifth, the reason for the Roman destruction of Jerusalem was because the people "did not recognize the time of [their] visitation."

Fulfillment of the First Question

Comparison with Luke's Account

Since I will not be dealing specifically with Luke's version of the Olivet Discourse in my exposition, I will now look at Luke 21:20-24 because it records the prophecy about the first question of the disciples. The passage reads as follows:

> When you see *Jerusalem surrounded by armies*, then recognize that *her desolation is near*. Then those who are in Judea must flee to the mountains, and those who are in the midst of the city must leave, and those who are in the country must not enter the city; because *these are days of vengeance*, so that all things which are written will be fulfilled. Woe to those who are pregnant and to those who are nursing babies in those days; for *there will be great distress upon the land* and *wrath to this people*; and *they will fall by the edge of the sword*, and *will be led captive into all the nations*; and *Jerusalem will be trampled under foot* by the Gentiles until the times of the Gentiles are fulfilled.

Preterists and futurists do not agree on much when it comes to the Olivet Discourse. However, when it comes to the interpretation of Luke 21:20-24, both agree that it is a literal prophecy of the A.D. 70 judgment. Preterist Kenneth Gentry says, "The context of Luke demands a literal Jerusalem (Luke 21:20) besieged by literal armies (Luke 21:20) in literal Judea (Luke 21:21)—which as a matter of indisputable historical record occurred in the events leading up to A.D. 70."[13] However, when expounding on Luke 21:25-28, preterists resort to massive doses of *symbolic* interpretation in their attempt to give these verses a first-century fulfillment. The futurist does not need to make such adjustments and instead, continues a *plain* or literal reading of the text. I believe that Luke 21:25-28 is a brief prophecy that parallels Matthew 24 and Mark 13, as I will explain in the upcoming pages.

It is clear that Luke 21:20-24 speaks of the first-century Roman invasion of Jerusalem. In the aforementioned quote, I placed in italics all the key phrases that support the A.D. 70 fulfillment. The entire passage speaks over and over again of judgment and wrath upon the Jewish people and their city, just as Christ prophesied in Matthew 24:2 and the other passages noted earlier. Yet when one searches the prophecies in Matthew 24 and Mark 13, this language is missing. Instead of "great distress upon the land and wrath to this people," Matthew 24 speaks of the rescue of the Jewish people, who are under great distress (Matthew 24:29-31).

Contrasts Between A.D. 70 and a Future Temple

Preterists, unfortunately, misuse Luke 21:20-24 and say that all of Matthew 24 was a prophecy of the Roman conquest in A.D. 70. Randall Price has noted six major differences between the A.D. 70 Temple and the Temple of the future Tribulation period, which is found in Matthew 24:

> During this time Jesus speaks of a signal event connected with the Temple—its desecration by an abomination which was prophesied by the prophet Daniel (Matthew 24:15; Mark 13:14). What Temple is being spoken of here by Jesus? Was the Temple that was to be desecrated the same Temple as the one predicted to be destroyed? There are a number of contrasts within this text that indicate that Jesus was talking about *two different* Temples:
>
> (1) The Temple described in Matthew 24:15 is not said to be destroyed, only desecrated (see Revelation 11:2). By contrast, the Temple in Jesus' day (or Matthew 24:2) was to be completely leveled: "not one stone would be left standing on another" (Matthew 24:2; Mark 13:2; Luke 19:44).
>
> (2) The Temple's desecration would be a signal for Jews to escape destruction (Matthew 24:16-18), "be saved" (Matthew 24:22) and experience the promised "redemption" (Luke 21:28). By contrast the destruction of the Temple in Matthew 24:2 was a judgment "because you did not recognize the time of your visitation [Messiah's first advent]" (Luke 19:44b) and resulted "in the Temple being level[ed] to the ground and your children [the Jews] within you" (Luke 19:44a).
>
> (3) The generation of Jews that are alive at the time that the Temple is desecrated will expect Messiah's coming "immediately after" (Matthew 24:29), and are predicted to not pass away until they have experienced it

(Matthew 24:34). By contrast, the generation of Jews who saw the Temple destroyed would pass away and 2,000 years (to date) would pass without redemption.

(4) The text Jesus cited concerning the Temple's desecration, Daniel 9:27, predicts that the one who desecrates this Temple will himself be destroyed. By contrast, those who destroyed the Temple in A.D. 70 (in fulfillment of Jesus' prediction)—the Roman emperor Vespasian and his son Titus—were not destroyed but returned to Rome in triumph carrying vessels from the destroyed Temple.

(5) The time "immediately after" (Matthew 24:29) the time of the Temple's desecration would see Israel's repentance (Matthew 24:30), followed by, as Matthew 23:29 implies, a restoration of the Temple. By contrast, the time following the destruction of the Temple only saw a "hardening" happen "to Israel," which is to last "until the fullness of the Gentiles has come in" (Romans 11:25)—still 2,000 years and counting.

(6) For the Temple that is desecrated, the scope is of a worldwide Tribulation "coming upon the world" (Luke 21:26; compare Matthew 24:21-22; Mark 13:19-20), a global regathering of the Jewish people "from one end of the sky to the other" (Matthew 24:31; Mark 13:27), and a universal revelation of the Messiah at Israel's rescue (Matthew 24:30-31; Mark 13:26; Luke 21:26-27). This scope accords with the prophesied end-time battle for Jerusalem recorded in Zechariah 12–14, where "all nations of the earth will be gathered against it" (Zechariah 12:3). By contrast the A.D. 70 assault on Jerusalem predicted in Luke 21:20 is by the armies of one empire (Rome). Therefore, if there are two different attacks on Jerusalem, separated by more than 2,000 years, then two distinct Temples are considered in Matthew 24:1-2 and Matthew 24:15.[14]

The above points demonstrate certain preterist problems that have no resolution—problems that arise in the attempt to cram still-future prophetic events into a past mold. The details of Matthew 24 cannot be made to fit into a first-century fulfillment.

Context for the First Question

Let's look more closely at the first question. After observing the Temple, Christ said to the disciples, "Do you not see all these things? Truly I say to you, not one stone here will be left upon another, which will not be torn down" (Matthew 24:2). The disciples asked Jesus, "Tell us, when will these things be…?" (Matthew 24:3). Thus, the first question relates to the destruction of the Temple in A.D. 70.

As we saw earlier, according to Gentry, "The context of Luke demands a literal Jerusalem (Luke 21:20) besieged by literal armies (Luke 21:20) in literal

Judea (Luke 21:21)—which as a matter of indisputable historical record occurred in the events leading up to A.D. 70."[15] This demonstrates that preterists take Scripture literally unless it contradicts their presupposed system of theology, at which time they usually come up with a more pliable, deeply spiritual meaning of the text. But because both preterists and futurists believe that Luke 21:20-24 was fulfilled literally in A.D. 70, this passage can be used as a template that demonstrates how Scripture speaks of the destruction of Jerusalem in the first century.

Christ's Prophecies

Before we look at Luke 21:20-24, let's examine Jesus' prophecies referring to the first-century destruction of Jerusalem and the Temple:

> Truly I say to you, all these things will come upon this generation. Jerusalem, Jerusalem, who kills the prophets and stones those who are sent to her! How often I wanted to gather your children together, the way a hen gathers her chicks under her wings, and you were unwilling. Behold, your house is being left to you desolate! (Matthew 23:36-38; see Luke 13:34-35 for parallel passage).

> When He approached Jerusalem, He saw the city and wept over it, saying, "If you had known in this day, even you, the things which make for peace! But now they have been hidden from your eyes. For the days will come upon you when your enemies will throw up a barricade against you, and surround you and hem you in on every side, and they will level you to the ground and your children within you, and they will not leave in you one stone upon another, because you did not recognize the time of your visitation" (Luke 19:41-44).

Here, Christ speaks clearly about the coming Roman destruction of Jerusalem and the Temple. He describes a siege in verses 43-44 that came because the nation of Israel "did not recognize the time of [their] visitation." The Jewish people rejected Jesus as their Messiah. Notice that not once does Jesus describe this as a "judgment coming" as do preterists.[16] In fact, "coming" is not used in any of these prophecies relating to A.D. 70 in the way that it is used to speak of Christ's future return.

Luke 21:20-24 and A.D. 70

When we look at Jesus' prophecy about the destruction of Jerusalem and the Second Temple, He uses words and phrases that clearly correspond to what the Romans did in A.D. 70:

> When you see Jerusalem surrounded by armies, then recognize that her desolation is near. Then those who are in Judea must flee to the mountains, and those who are in the midst of the city must leave, and those who are in the country must not enter the city; because these are days of vengeance, so that all things which are written will be fulfilled. Woe to those who are pregnant and to those who are nursing babies in those days; for there will be great distress upon the land and wrath to this people; and they will fall by the edge of the sword, and will be led captive into all the nations; and Jerusalem will be trampled under foot by the Gentiles until the times of the Gentiles are fulfilled (Luke 21:20-24).

Note how the following words and phrases support the notion of judgment upon Israel in the first century:

- Jerusalem surrounded by armies, then recognize that her desolation is at hand

- flee to the mountains (the admonition to flee indicates Jerusalem would be destroyed—if the Jews were to defeat the Romans, then the safe place to be would be inside the walled city)

- these are days of vengeance

- there will be great distress upon the land

- wrath to this people (Israel)

- they (Israel) will fall by the edge of the sword

- (Israel) will be led captive into all the nations

- Jerusalem will be trampled under foot by the Gentiles

There is not a single phrase in Luke 21:20-24 that suggests anything other than the A.D. 70 destruction of Jerusalem, which was clearly a judgment upon the Jewish people for their national rejection of Jesus as their Messiah (Matthew 23:38; Luke 19:44). This passage is our Lord's answer to the disciples' first question, which relates to the statement about there not being one stone of the Temple left upon another. Yet when we compare Luke 21:20-24 with other sections of the Olivet Discourse, the kind of language listed above is missing completely (see Matthew 24:4-31; Mark 13:5-27; Luke 21:25-28). Instead, in general, the language of the Olivet Discourse, except for Luke 21:20-24, does not speak of Israel under God's judgment, but of Israel under threat from the Gentile nations and God's rescue of the Jewish people. This overall thrust of the passage is even clearer when one looks at the parallel passage of Zechariah 12–14.

Luke 21:24 ends by saying that Jerusalem will be under Gentile domination "until the times of the Gentiles are fulfilled." The little word "until" clearly denotes there will be a time when the current domination of Jerusalem by the Gentiles will come to an end. We are now living in "the times of the Gentiles," which will indeed come to an end in the future. Thus, the end of verse 24 serves as a transition between the prophecy that refers to the past event in A.D. 70 (Luke 21:20-24) and the prophecy that looks to a future fulfillment at Christ's second coming (Luke 21:25-28).

There is also a clear connection between Luke 21:24, which speaks of the current era of "the times of the Gentiles" being fulfilled and coming to an end, and Romans 11:25, which speaks of "the fullness of the Gentiles" having "come in." Both passages speak of Israel's redemption (Luke 21:28; Romans 11:26-27). When we consider the Old Testament pattern that says Israel will pass through the Tribulation, the Jewish people will repent toward the end of the Tribulation when they recognize Jesus as the Messiah, they will experience conversion, and then the second coming will occur to rescue them from their enemies, it follows that "all Israel will be saved" (Romans 11:26) in connection with the Tribulation. This is exactly the pattern of Luke 21:25-28. Gentry believes Romans teaches a future conversion of Israel, yet he does not associate it with the Tribulation as Scripture repeatedly does. Gentry declares, "The future conversion of the Jews will conclude the fulfillment (Romans 11:12-25)."[17] Yet only a futurist interpretation harmonizes these passages, which are clearly connected.

Luke 21:25-28 and the Future

> There will be signs in sun and moon and stars, and on the earth dismay among nations, in perplexity at the roaring of the sea and the waves, men fainting from fear and the expectation of the things which are coming upon the world; for the powers of the heavens will be shaken. Then they will see the Son of Man coming in a cloud with power and great glory. But when these things begin to take place, straighten up and lift up your heads, because your redemption is drawing near (Luke 21:25-28).

J. C. Ryle says of this passage, "The subject of this portion of our Lord's great prophecy is His own second coming to judge the world. The strong expressions of the passage appear inapplicable to any event less important than this. To confine the words before us, to the taking of Jerusalem by the Romans, is an unnatural straining of Scripture language."[18]

The focus of Luke 21:25-28 reveals a distinct shift from the first-century description of 21:20-24. The differences include the local focus of Jerusalem in the first-century judgment versus the global perspective of the future Tribulation. The Tribulation will involve heavenly and global events that did not literally occur in A.D. 70. If preterists such as Gentry would interpret verses 25-28 in the same way they did verses 20-24, then the events of 25-28 would be understood to be global, and if they are global, then they did not occur in the first century. Since they did not occur in the first century, then they must take place in the future. These are future Tribulation events.

The basic message of Luke 21:25-28 is the opposite of that found in Luke 21:21-24, which speaks of God's judgment upon Israel. Instead, verse 28 tells Israel that "your redemption is drawing near." We find the night (God's judgment) in verses 20-24 and the day (salvation and deliverance) in verses 25-28. William Kelly describes some aspects of the differences in this way:

> Hence, too, the reader may notice that, in spite of a considerable measure of analogy (for there will be a future siege, and even a twofold attack, one of which will be partially successful, the other to the ruin of their enemies, as we learn from Isaiah xxviii, xxix, and Zechariah xiv), there are the strangest contrasts in the issue; for the future siege will be closed by Jehovah's deliverance and reign, as the past was in capture and destruction of the people dispersed ever since till the times of the Gentiles are full. Accordingly we hear nothing in this Gospel of the abomination of desolation, nor of the time of tribulation beyond all that was or shall be; we hear of both in Matthew and Mark, where the Spirit contemplates the last days.[19]

When one examines the entire Olivet Discourse as recorded in Matthew 24 and Mark 13, there is no reference to wrath or judgment upon the nation of Israel. Instead, Israel is delivered from its invader, as noted in Matthew 24:31: "He will send forth His angels with a great trumpet and they will gather together His elect from the four winds, from one end of the sky to the other" (see also Mark 13:27). The question arises: "When was Israel rescued in A.D. 70?" There was no rescue! The events of Matthew 24 and Mark 13 (and Luke 21:25-28) will all be fulfilled during the Tribulation, which will take place in the future.

So, the first question at the introduction of the Olivet Discourse relates to the destruction of Jerusalem in A.D. 70. The fulfillment of this prophecy is recorded only in Luke 21. Matthew 24–25 and Mark 13 deal only with the disciples' latter question, which leads Jesus to prophesy events that are still future.

Two Major Views

The Inter-Advent Age View

There are two major views that futurists hold in regard to the inter-advent age, which is the time period between Christ's first coming and the beginning of the Tribulation. Some believe that Matthew 24:4-14 refers to the inter-advent age, while others say that verses 4-14, especially verses 4-8, refer to the first part of the Tribulation and correspond with the first four seal judgments of Revelation 6:1-8. I think that the second view is correct.

John F. Walvoord is among the futurist interpreters who believe verses 4-14 describe the general signs of the inter-advent age. He says verses 4-14 are "describing the general characteristics of the age leading up to the end, while at the same time recognizing that the prediction of difficulties, which will characterize the entire period between the first and second coming of Christ, are fulfilled in an intensified form as the age moves on to its conclusion."[20]

Walvoord believes that verses 15-26 have to do with specific signs that describe the Tribulation, while verses 27-31 relate to the second coming.[21]

Within the inter-advent age view is a variation of this perspective. Some believe that verses 4-8 describe general signs of the inter-advent age, leading up to the Tribulation, while verses 9-14 have to do with the first half of the Tribulation. "The events concerning the first half of the Tribulation are recorded in Matthew 24:9-14," says Arnold Fruchtenbaum. This "passage begins with the word *then*, pointing out that what Christ is describing now will come *after* the event of nation rising against nation and kingdom against kingdom."[22]

If the inter-advent age view is the correct interpretation, then wars, earthquakes, famines, and the appearance of false Christs would be constantly on the increase as we approach the Tribulation. However, if these events describe the first half of the Tribulation, then wars, earthquakes, famines, and false Christs during any part of the church age would not constitute prophetic signs. This explains why some futurists believe that an increase in wars, earthquakes, and famines, are prophetically significant, while others, like myself, do not think that they are prophetically significant because these verses refer to global events that take place during the seven-year Tribulation.

The Tribulation View

I believe that Matthew 24:4-41 refers to the seven-year period (Daniel 9:24-27) that many commonly call the Tribulation. The Tribulation period is divided in half by the abomination of desolation, which is mentioned by Jesus in verse 15. Thus, verses 4-14 describe the first half of the Tribulation and are parallel to the first five seal judgments, which are found in Revelation 6.

Bible commentator Arno Gaebelein insists, "If our interpretation is the right one there must be perfect harmony between these three: Old Testament Prophecy: Matthew xxiv:4-44, and Revelation vi-xix."[23] I believe such a harmony exists, especially between the Olivet Discourse and Revelation. That's what convinces me verses 4-14 refer to the first half of the Tribulation. Gaebelein continues:

> If this is the correct interpretation, if Matthew xxiv:4-14 refers to the beginning of that coming end of the age and if Revelation vi refers to the same beginning of the end and that which follows the sixth chapter leads us on into the great Tribulation, then there must be a perfect harmony between that part of the Olivet Discourse contained in Matthew xxiv and the part of Revelation beginning with the sixth chapter. *And such is indeed the case.*[24]

"The acceptance of this view, in part," observes John McLean, "is dependent on how much weight is given to the parallels between the synoptics and Revelation."[25] Since all futurists see the Olivet Discourse as parallel to Revelation to some degree, it makes sense that these two portions of Scripture are seen to be focusing on the same basic time period—the Tribulation. McLean has displayed the aforementioned parallels in the following chart.[26]

Parallels Between the Olivet Discourse and the Seal Judgments of Revelation

	Revelation 6	Matthew 24	Mark 13	Luke 21
False messiahs, false prophets	2	5,11	6	8
Wars	2-4	6-7	7	9
International discord	3-4	7	8	10
Famines	5-8	7	8	11
Pestilences	8			11
Persecution, martyrdom	9-11	9	9-13	12-17
Earthquakes	12	7	8	11
Cosmic phenomena	12-14			11

THE EVENTS

Birth Pangs

Matthew 24:8 characterizes the events of verses 4-7 as "the beginning of birth-pangs." The Greek word for "birth-pangs" is *dinon*, which means "the pain of childbirth, travail-pain, birth-pang." It is said to be "intolerable anguish, in reference to the dire calamities which the Jews supposed would precede the advent of the Messiah."[27] Another authority agrees and says the "Messianic woes" are "the terrors and torments that precede the coming of the Messianic Age."[28]

Most likely our Lord had in mind the Old Testament reference to birth pangs in Jeremiah 30:6-7, which says, "Ask now, and see if a male can give birth. Why do I see every man with his hands on his loins, as a woman in childbirth? And why have all faces turned pale? Alas! for that day is great, there is none like it; and it is the time of Jacob's distress, but he will be saved from it." Randall Price explains the birth pangs of Messiah as follows:

> The birth pangs are significant in the timing of the Tribulation, as revealed by Jesus in the Olivet Discourse (Matthew 24:8). Jesus' statement of the "birth pangs" is specifically that the events of the first half of the Tribulation (verses 4-7) are merely the "beginning," with the expectation of greater birth pangs in the second half (the "Great Tribulation"). Based on this analogy, the entire period of the seventieth week is like birth pangs. As a woman must endure the entire period of labor before giving birth, so Israel must endure the entire seven-year Tribulation. The time divisions of Tribulation are also illustrated by the figure, for just as the natural process intensifies toward delivery after labor ends, so here the Tribulation moves progressively toward the second advent (verses 30-31), which takes place "immediately after" the Tribulation ends (verse 29). As there are two phases of the birth pangs (beginning labor and full labor), so the seven years of Tribulation are divided between the less severe and more severe experiences of terrestrial and cosmic wrath, as revealed progressively in the Olivet Discourse and the judgment section of Revelation 6–19.[29]

Paul also uses the motif of birth pangs in 1 Thessalonians 5:3, where he says, "While they are saying, 'Peace and safety!' then destruction will come upon them suddenly like labor pains upon a woman with child, and they will not escape." The context of this passage relates to the Tribulation period, which fits the other uses of "birth pangs."

Raphael Patai, in his helpful book *The Messiah Texts,* has dozens of references to extrabiblical commentary from Jewish writings in a chapter entitled "The Pangs of Times."[30] Patai tells us that "the pangs of the Messianic times are imagined as having heavenly as well as earthly sources and expressions.... Things will come to such a head that people will despair of Redemption. This will last seven years. And then, unexpectedly, the Messiah will come."[31] This widespread Jewish idea fits into the exact framework Jesus expresses in the Olivet Discourse. The birth pangs of Messiah, also known as "the footprints of the Messiah,"[32] support the notion that Matthew 24:4-14 relates to the Tribulation period leading up to the second advent of the Messiah, since it is known as a time of great Tribulation that results in Messiah's earthly arrival.

I have often been asked on radio talk shows if I believe that events such as earthquakes, famines, wars, and so on are telling us that the end is near. Of course I always say no. This usually surprises the hosts, who frequently hear from other prophecy teachers that such phenomena have current prophetic significance. As you can see, if these events don't appear in context to the church age, then they must have reference to the Tribulation. While it is likely that we stand on the verge of the Tribulation, we are not yet in that time period. And because Matthew 24:4-14 cannot happen until after the rapture and the start of the Tribulation, it is wrong to say that such events are prophetically significant in our own day. The birth pangs do not start until Israel faces her time of trouble.

As we move into the next section, I take it that in Christ's discourse "the disciples were the representatives of godly Jews, and were warned of what should befall their nation."[33] Thus, the fulfillment of this passage will take place in the future, after the rapture of the church, at the beginning of the Tribulation.

Deception

Since the Tribulation begins with the arrival of the Antichrist on the scene, it is not surprising that this passage also begins with a warning to believers about his arrival. Jesus begins answering the disciples' question with a warning about false messiahs. "And Jesus answered and said to them, 'See to it that no one misleads you. For many will come in My name, saying, "I am the Christ," and will mislead many'" (Matthew 24:4-5).

I believe William Kelly is correct to note that this passage is not referring to Christians in the current church age. "In the epistles of Paul it is never exactly such a thought as warning persons against false Christs. For there the Holy Ghost addresses us as Christians; and a Christian could not be deceived by a man's pretensions to be Christ. It is most appropriate here, because the disciples are viewed in this chapter, as representatives, not of us Christians now, but of future godly Jews."[34]

The first thing Jesus says is to make sure no one misleads you. One of the Antichrist's primary goals during the Tribulation will be to deceive people spiritually. "This warning was prompted by their eagerness for a sign. The danger of being misled was increased if one was too enthusiastic or anticipated some symbolic indication of the event."[35] Stanley Toussaint tells us:

> The key to understanding the discourse is found in this first sentence. The disciples thought that the destruction of Jerusalem with its great temple would usher in the end of the age. The Lord separates the two ideas and warns the disciples against being deceived by the destruction of Jerusalem and other such catastrophes. The razing of the temple and the presence of wars and rumors of wars do not necessarily signify the nearness of the end.[36]

False Christs

Why did Jesus warn about being on guard against deception? Because during the Tribulation, many will claim to be the Messiah, and many will believe them. But the Jewish believers during the Tribulation are not to fall for that line.

The emphasis in Matthew 24:5 is upon "many." Not just a single person will come claiming to be the Messiah, but a whole host of individuals will make this claim. That's one of the reasons we know this passage is not referring to the time leading up to the A.D. 70 destruction of Jerusalem. A. H. M'Neile says, "No such definite claim to Messiahship is known till that of Barkokba in the reign of Hadrian."[37] The Barkokba revolt was put down by the Romans in A.D. 135 when Hadrian lead the Roman legions to once again destroy Jerusalem and the surrounding area, which resulted in the deaths of half a million Jews.[38] Robert Gundry notes the following:

> The lack of evidence that anyone claimed messiahship between Jesus and Bar-Kokhba a hundred years later militates against our seeing the discourse as a *vaticinium ex eventu* [a prophecy of an event] concerning the first Jewish revolt (A.D. 66–73). False prophets figured in that revolt (Josephus *J.W.* 6.5.2 §§285-87; 7.11.1 §§437-39; *Ant.* 20.5.1 §97); but one did not have to claim messiahship to be a false prophet. Cf. Acts 5:36; 8:9; 21:38.[39]

James R. Gray tells us, "Strict claims to the Messianic office in the strictest sense are almost nonexistent in history."[40] However, in the future, such claims will be rampant.

Preterists like to say, "False messiahs made regular appearances in Israel."[41] Gentry is more careful, but nevertheless says, "There are many examples of great pretenders who almost certainly make Messianic claims."[42] Gentry and DeMar say such activity occurred during the first century. Gentry lists the following individuals as those whom he says made messianic claims: Theudas in Acts 5:36, Simon Magus in Acts 8:9-10, and "the Egyptian false prophet."[43] DeMar adds to the list with, "Josephus tells of 'a certain impostor named Theudas...' Dositheus, a Samaritan, 'pretended that he was the lawgiver prophesied of by Moses.'"[44] DeMar contends all these individuals made claims to be the Messiah. However, upon closer examination, we find that none of these people actually claimed to be Messiah. Some of them could be described as false prophets, but not false messiahs. These preterists are playing fast and loose with the data because they have such a large investment in their view that all this took place in the first century. H. A. W. Meyer clarifies the issue when he notes,

> We possess no *historical* record of any false Messiahs having appeared *previous to the destruction of Jerusalem* (Barcochba did not make his appearance till the time of Hadrian); for Simon Magus (Acts viii. 9), Theudas (Acts verse 36), the Egyptian (Acts xxi. 38), Menander, Dositheus, who have been referred to as cases in point (Theophylact, Euthymius Zigabenus, Grotius, Calovinus, Bengel), did not pretend to be the *Messiah.* Comp. Joseph *Antt.* Xx. 5. 1; 8. 6; *Bell.* Ii. 13. 5.[45]

Another says, "The first and second centuries saw quite a few famous false prophets who made eschatological claims." However, upon further reading we find this: "That any of them (before Bar Kochba) said, in so many words, 'I am Messiah,' is undemonstrated by the sources."[46] Finally, Leon Morris tells us, "In this place the meaning is rather that they will claim for themselves the name *Messiah,* Jesus' own title." Morris explains: "This will surely be a reference to the last days, for there is little evidence that any of the turbulent men so active preceding the fall of Jerusalem ever claimed to be the Messiah. Some claimed to be prophets, but that is not the same thing."[47]

"The statement that such persons will come, 'in my name,' means either that they will come using the name of Jesus or that they will come assuming the messiahship of Jesus, as is spelled out in the explicit claim that follows," says Donald Hagner. "The claim to be the Christ means here the claim to be the eschatological Messiah."[48]

Even if some first-century individuals did claim to be the Messiah—which they did not—it would not fulfill this passage. This is one of the many reasons we know this passage looks to the future Tribulation and the coming of the beast of Revelation, popularly known in Christendom as the Antichrist.

The First Seal Judgment

It's important to note that the judgments of Matthew 24:4-11 parallel, in order, the first five seal judgments of Revelation 6:1-11. "The first seal depicts a false Messiah,"[49] as observed in Revelation 6:1-2. "I saw when the Lamb broke one of the seven seals, and I heard one of the four living creatures saying as with a voice of thunder, "Come." I looked, and behold, a white horse, and he who sat on it had a bow; and a crown was given to him, and he went out conquering and to conquer."

Arno Gaebelein, that great Bible teacher from a former generation, says this about this similarity:

> The rider upon the white horse under the first seal is a counterfeit. He is a false Christ, who goes forth to conquer. His conquest is a bloodless one, as he has only a bow. He will bring about a false peace among the nations, which for a time may have been alarmed by the supernatural removal of the church. The second rider "takes peace from the earth," from which we would conclude that the first rider upon the white horse (white emblem of peace) has established peace.
>
> And as we turn to Matthew xxiv we find that the first thing our Lord saith, is about the deceivers who will come with the beginning of the age ending saying: "I am Christ," and succeeding to lead away many.[50]

Wars and Rumors of Wars

Verse 6 begins with an interesting Greek word, *mell* (which is usually not translated into English, but it carries the idea of "about to"). Because it is in the future tense, this opening phrase has the sense of saying, "You are going to be about to hear…"[51] This indeed is the case!

The Greek word *polemos* is a general word for war and connotes the "whole course of hostilities" rather than just the individual battles that comprise the larger war campaign.[52] This is a reference to actual wars that will take place in the future and involve the Jewish people. Meyer says this phrase is a "reference to wars near at hand, the din and tumult of which are actually heard, and to wars at a distance, of which nothing is known except from the reports that are brought home."[53]

Here we have the parallel to Revelation 6:4 and the red horse judgment, which is said "to take peace from the earth, and that men would slay one another; and a great sword was given to him." The first seal judgment of

Revelation 6:2 is the rider on a white horse, who is a counterfeit Christ, which corresponds to verses 4-5 of Matthew 24. This means that Antichrist begins the Tribulation with a false peace that soon turns into multiple wars breaking out all over the globe. There will also be war that those in Jerusalem will see themselves and those further away will only hear about.

To whom is the Lord addressing His comments in this discourse? I believe it is not to the church, but "to the Jewish disciples as they then were, and as they will be."[54] William Kelly expounds upon this:

> ...the Lord is predicting about the Jewish remnant....And this, because many things must yet be accomplished before the Jews can come into their blessing. But for Christians, all things are ours in Christ even now; the blessing is never put off, though we await the crown at His coming. Again, many parts of scripture speak of scenes of anguish before the Lord's coming; others make Christians to be expecting Christ at any time. These scriptures cannot be broken, nor can they contradict one another; and yet they must do so, if they be applied to the same people.[55]

These wars of the Tribulation are described in verse 7 as bringing nation against nation and kingdom against kingdom. This description depicts multiple struggles taking place on various levels internationally. Nations will fight against other nations, as if, for example, the national entities of France and Germany were to fight one another. Kingdom will rise against kingdom, as if, for example, NATO were to fight the former Warsaw pact nations. These are the kinds of geopolitical conflicts we see depicted in Daniel and Revelation, and they are described within the context of a future Tribulation. This is *not* what took place in A.D. 70. Rome was an empire that fought against Israel— a single nation. This first-century conflict does not resemble nation against nation and kingdom against kingdom. M'Neile notes, "The horrors described are not local disturbances, but are spread over the known world; nations and kingdoms are in hostility with one another."[56]

Do Not Be Frightened

In Matthew 24:6, Jesus tells His disciples that they should not be frightened. The Greek word for "frightened" is used only here, in the parallel passage Mark 8:15, and by Paul in 2 Thessalonians 2:2. A. T. Robertson says it "means to cry aloud, to scream, and in the passive to be terrified by an outcry." He renders this passage as follows: "Look out for the wars and rumours of wars, but do not be sacred out of your wits by them."[57]

All three uses of this word are found within the context of the Tribulation. Apparently this is going to be a very scary time for those who do not understand that God is in control of these events. In 2 Thessalonians 2:2 Paul endeavored to comfort the believers when he says, "that [they] may not be quickly shaken from [their] composure or be *disturbed* either by a spirit or a message or a letter as if from us, to the effect that the day of the Lord has come." The Thessalonian believers thought they were in the day of the Lord or the Tribulation. Paul told them not to be disturbed because they were not in the day of the Lord.

Both our Lord and the apostle Paul describe the human reaction to thinking that one is in the Tribulation as the temptation to cry out in pain. We can understand why people would react this way as we come to realize from the seal judgments of Revelation 6 that during this time, over a quarter of the earth's population will be killed (Revelation 6:8).

What is the antidote to this frightening knowledge? Simply to know that "those things *must* take place" (verse 6). Meyer says, "The reflection that it is a matter of necessity in pursuance of the divine purpose (xxvi. 54), is referred to as calculated to inspire a calm and reassured frame of mind."[58] Believers are comforted to know that "if God says that something shall be, then it must be."[59] Morris explains: "They have one thing going for them that the general public has not: they know that God is over all and that his purpose will in the end be worked out. This is the significance of *it is necessary*."[60] This phrase lets us know that God is in control of what is seemingly out of control—His judgment.

Judgment is a necessary part of God's plan because there is evil in the world. Before the Lord can usher in His kingdom, which will be a righteous kingdom, He must purge out evil through judgment. This can be scary if one does not know God and His plan. Knowing what Bible prophecy says about the predetermined plan of God is what will offer comfort to the people of God during this time of global upheaval.

James R. Gray has the following excellent summary of this passage:

> Matthew 24:6 and Revelation 6:3-4 are parallel. The red horse symbolizes war. The purpose of the rider is "to take peace from the earth, and that they should kill one another" (Revelation 6:3). Many perceive the first half of the Tribulation as a time of great peace. That is not so. The Antichrist will be perceived as a man of peace because of his great deceptive ability. The fact is he comes to power and stays in power because of war (Daniel 7:8,24). The Tribulation will bring wars and more wars. The book of Revelation prophesies of many wars, not only in chapter 6, but also in 16:12-15, 17:14, 19:1ff, and 20:8. These will not only be

in invasions of Palestine (Daniel 9:26-27, 11:40-45, Zechariah 12:2-11, Revelation 12:9-17).[61]

THE GOSPEL OF THE KINGDOM

The next significant passage in Matthew's version of the Olivet Discourse is Matthew 24:14: "This gospel of the kingdom shall be preached in the whole world as a testimony to all the nations, and then the end will come."

Through the years, there have been some who, in discussions about Bible prophecy, say, "The details don't really matter since everything will pan out in the end." This perspective is sometimes called *panmillennialism*. There is a lot wrong with this perspective. Perhaps the most significant problem is this: What if the details have already happened? What if most or all of Bible prophecy was fulfilled by A.D. 70, as those who hold to a preterist (past fulfillment) view of Bible prophecy think? In fact, in their zeal to show that Christ's prophetic sermon, the Olivet Discourse, was fulfilled during the apostolic era, they claim that the whole world was evangelized within 25 to 30 years of Christ's ascension.

The Preterist Claim

Preterists claim that the Olivet Discourse, the book of Revelation, and many other New Testament prophetic passages were fulfilled in the events surrounding the Roman destruction of Jerusalem and the Temple by A.D. 70, and they include passages such as Matthew 24:14 and Revelation 14:6-7 as part of that fulfillment. "Matthew 24:14 clearly shows that the gospel would be preached throughout the Roman Empire before Jesus returned in judgment upon Jerusalem,"[62] insists preterist Gary DeMar. He further claims:

> The word translated "world" in 24:14 is the Greek word *oikoumene*. It is best translated as "inhabited earth," "known world," or the "Roman Empire" (Acts 11:28; 17:6)....
>
> This translation helps us understand that Jesus was saying the gospel would be preached throughout the Roman Empire before He would return in judgment upon Jerusalem. In fact, this is exactly what happened, and that is what the Bible says happened.[63]

DeMar supposes to provide biblical proof for his claim by citing such passages as Colossians 1:6,23 and Romans 16:25-27.[64] Do these passages support the preterist understanding of Matthew 24:14? I insist they do not. Preterists have distorted the meaning of these passages in order to defend their view of Matthew 24.

The Futurist Response
The Meaning of World

While it is true that "world" *oikoumene* is used in the New Testament to refer to "the Roman Empire of the first century," its basic meaning is that of "the inhabited earth."[65] This compound word contains the prefix from *oikos*, which means "house," or the "inhabited" or "lived-in" part of the world. The inhabited world could refer to the Roman Empire if supported by the context (for example, Luke 2:1), since Roman arrogance thought that nothing of significance existed outside of their realm. However, this word was earlier "used of the Greek cultural world."[66]

Since the core meaning of *oikoumene* is "inhabited world," then the scope of its meaning has multiple possibilities depending upon the referent. If the contextual referent is Roman, then it will mean the Roman Empire, as in Luke 2:1. However, if its referent is global, then it must include the entire world, as in Acts 17:31, which says, "He has fixed a day in which He will judge the world in righteousness." Surely this speaks of the whole globe since not a single individual will escape God's judgment. Clearly *oikoumene* can be used globally, even though it may have a more restricted use. The deciding factor is the context. Thus, if Matthew 24:24 was fulfilled in A.D. 70, then it would have a localized meaning, as noted by DeMar. However, if it will be fulfilled in the future, then it has the meaning of the entire inhabited world at some future date, which would clearly include much more than the old Roman Empire.

The Understanding of the Passages
Colossians 1:6,23

DeMar uses Colossians 1:6,23 to teach that the New Testament itself supports a first-century fulfillment of Matthew 24:14. "Paul, without inching and need of further explanation," claims DeMar, "declares that the gospel had been preached in his day to 'every creature under heaven' (Col. 1:23). This is probably hyperbole, but it certainly fulfills what Jesus said would happen within a generation."[67] But is that really what Jesus was saying?

Let's take a closer look at Paul's words: "the gospel, which has come to you, just as in all the world...." (Colossians 1:6). The verb "to come," *páreimi*, is the word from which the noun *parousia* is derived. It has the core meaning of "to be present" with an emphasis upon the fact that the person, usually a dignitary, is present or has arrived.[68] "Paul uses the vb. *paremi* with the meaning of to be present."[69] Paul is saying that the gospel has come, or been introduced to the Colossian believers, just as it has come, or been introduced, in all the world. So this is not a statement about whether the gospel has been preached to a certain area per se; rather, it is a statement about the arrival of the gospel as a global message. "The Colossians are to remember that its range is worldwide," says Lenski, "the very opposite of the little Judaistic sectlet that has somehow appeared in their midst."[70]

Paul makes a similar statement in Colossians 1:23, where he speaks of "the gospel that you have heard, which was proclaimed in all creation under heaven." Does this passage teach that Matthew 24:14 was fulfilled? No, it does not. "The phrase 'in all creation,'" says Ernest R. Campbell, "is probably best understood as being in the locative case, i.e., it was preached *in the sphere of* or *in the midst of* all creation."[71] In context, Paul is explaining why the Gentiles now have the gospel coming to them. It is because its purpose has now been introduced and presented as a global message. J. B. Lightfoot says, "The motive of the Apostle here is at once to emphasize the universality of the genuine Gospel, which has been offered without reserve to all alike...."[72] James R. Gray sums up the point well when he explains: "Paul's claim is to the universal appeal and scope of the gospel. That it is bearing fruit in the world—not that the gospel has been preached in all the world....Paul is talking about the sphere of preaching, not that every creature was preached unto."[73]

Romans 16:26

"We also learn from Paul that the gospel 'had been made known to all the nations' in his day (Romans 16:26)," claims DeMar. "This, too, is a fulfillment of what Jesus said would happen in Matthew 24:14."[74] He also says, "Paul declared that the gospel had 'been made known *to all the nations*,' a direct fulfillment of Matthew 24:14 (Romans 16:26, emphasis added). Notice the verb tense, '*has been* made known.' All the requirements of a pre-A.D. 70 fulfillment are met when we let the Bible interpret the Bible."[75]

However, Romans 16:26 is *not* "a direct fulfillment of Matthew 24:14." In Matthew 24:14, Jesus said that the gospel would be *preached* to all nations. Paul, by contrast, said that "the mystery...has been made known to all the nations." The grammar of Romans 16:25-26 is broken down as follows: First, "has been made known" is an aorist, passive, adjectival participle that is in agreement with the noun "mystery" in verse 25. It is the third of three adjectival participles that are describing things about the mystery. The first two participles are "kept secret" and "is manifested." So where does this passage actually say what DeMar contends it means? Instead, as virtually every commentary affirms, the purpose of Paul's mystery about the gospel is so that "it reaches throughout the world."[76] H. P. Liddon says that "to all the nations" speaks "of the *range* of destination among all the heathen peoples."[77] "Having revealed this truth to Paul, God ordered it preached to all the Gentile nations."[78] This passage informs us that the gospel message has been introduced into the entire world and was intended for every human being throughout all creation. This statement could have been made on the day of

Pentecost when the church was born because it speaks to the fact that the gospel mystery tells us that it is not just for Jews, but also for Gentiles as well.

Acts 17:16-31

I believe that Colossians 1:6,23 and Romans 16:26 are speaking about the new revelation, called by Paul a mystery, that salvation is now going to include select Gentiles from all the nations. Thus, the gospel should be taken to all nations throughout the world. That is why in both contexts, Paul speaks of the mystery about the Gentiles (see Romans 16:25-27; Colossians 1:24–2:4). The fullest explanation of this mystery is found in Ephesians 2 and 3.

Paul explains the concept of a global message in his sermon on Mars Hill. "Therefore having overlooked the times of ignorance, God is now declaring to men that all people everywhere should repent" (Acts 17:30). This passage has many of the same elements found in Paul's epistles, where he explains to the church what he meant by that statement. Paul's phrase "the times of ignorance" is a parallel concept to God's having not revealed the mystery in past times (see Romans 16:25; Ephesians 3:6; Colossians 1:26). Paul's declaration that "God is now declaring to men that all everywhere should repent" is similar to his statements that the gospel message is now going global (see Romans 16:26; Ephesians 3:6; Colossians 1:27). Paul is now announcing a new global accountability for all men because of the introduction of the gospel. This parallels the concepts taught by Paul in Romans, Ephesians, and Colossians.

The Great Commission

If DeMar's view of Matthew 24:14 is true, then one could legitimately assign a similar first-century fulfillment to the phrase "all the nations" in Matthew 28:19. If DeMar's logic is followed, it would have required the total fulfillment of the Great Commission by A.D. 70. Why? Our Lord says in the Great Commission that He will be with us "always, even to the end of the age" (Matthew 28:20). This is very similar to the phrase "end of the age" in Matthew 24:3. DeMar teaches that the end of the age occurred in A.D. 70,[79] and since he applies almost all other uses of the phrase to the first century, then why not apply it to Matthew 28:20? In fact, fellow preterist Don Preston has written a whole book using just such preterist logic, saying that the Great Commission was in fact fulfilled by A.D. 70.[80] Apparently DeMar does not like the implications of his preterist position when it is consistently applied to the whole New Testament.

The preterists' arguments for a first-century fulfillment of Matthew 24:14 are much less than compelling. Their insistence that *oikoumene* in Matthew 24:14 must refer to the ancient Roman Empire has no traction. If Matthew 24:14 is a future event, then the gospel will be preached across the globe as described in Revelation 14:6-7, which I believe is a parallel passage. Both passages are set in contexts that tell us that this global evangelization will take place just before the middle of the seven-year Tribulation. This passage was no more fulfilled during the nativity of the church than was the Great Commission. The prophecy of Matthew 24:24, like the other passages in that context, awaits a future fulfillment during the future Tribulation.

THE ABOMINATION OF DESOLATION

In Matthew 24:15, Jesus said, "Therefore when you see the abomination of desolation which was spoken of through Daniel the prophet, standing in the holy place (let the reader understand)...."

Predictably, Gentry believes that the famous "abomination of desolation" in Matthew 24:15 (cf. Mark 13:14) was fulfilled in the first-century destruction of Jerusalem.[81] Even though there are a few similarities between the past destruction of Jerusalem and a future siege, there are enough differences to distinguish the two events.

One of Gentry's arguments for the preterist position is his confusion of Luke 21:20-24 with Matthew 24:15-22. Luke 21:20-24 does refer to the A.D. 70 destruction of Jerusalem, yet all of Matthew 24 describes the future (see chapter 13 on the seventieth week of Daniel for a statement and defense of the futurist view on this matter).

The key passages in Daniel that mention the term "abomination of desolation" are Daniel 9:27, 11:31, and 12:11. This is a technical term, which means that it has a precise and consistent meaning in all three passages. The phrase refers to an act of abomination that renders, in this case, the Temple, something unclean. Daniel 11:31 speaks of an act that was fulfilled in history before the first coming of Christ. John Walvoord explains:

> In Daniel 11:31, a prophecy was written by Daniel in the sixth century B.C. about a future Syrian ruler by name of Antiochus Epiphanes who reigned over Syria 175–164 B. C., about 400 years after Daniel. History, of course, has recorded the reign of this man. In verse 31, Daniel prophesied about his activity: "...they shall pollute the sanctuary of strength, and shall take away the daily sacrifice, and they shall place the abomination that maketh desolate." This would be very difficult to understand if it were not for the fact that it has already been fulfilled. Anyone can go back to the history of Antiochus Epiphanes and discover what he did as recorded in the apocryphal books of 1 and 2 Maccabees. He was a great persecutor of the children of Israel and

did his best to stamp out the Jewish religion and wanted to place in its stead a worship of Greek pagan gods....

One of the things he did was to stop animal sacrifices in the temple. He offered a sow, an unclean animal, on the altar in a deliberate attempt to desecrate and render it unholy for Jewish worship (cf. 1 Macc. 1:48). First Maccabees 1:54 specifically records that the abomination of desolation was set up, fulfilling Daniel 11:31. In the holy of holies Antiochus set up a statue of a Greek god....In keeping with the prophecy the daily sacrifices were stopped, the sanctuary was polluted, desolated and made an abomination.[82]

This passage sets the pattern and provides details about what the abomination of desolation consists of. Daniel 9:27 says that this abomination is to take place in the middle of a seven-year period. The passage says, "In the middle of the week he will put a stop to sacrifice and grain offering; and on the wing of abominations will come one who makes desolate." "In other words, the future prince will do at that time exactly what Antiochus did in the second century B.C."[83] But Daniel goes on to say that the one who commits this act will be destroyed three and a half years later. Daniel 12:11 provides "the precise chronology."[84] The text says, "And from the time that the regular sacrifice is abolished, and the abomination of desolation is *set up*, there will be 1,290 days."

In addition to the three passages in Daniel are the two references by our Lord in Matthew and Luke, Paul in 2 Thessalonians 2:4, and John in Revelation 13:14-15. Based on these passages, the abomination of desolation includes the following elements:

1. It occurs in the Jewish Temple in Jerusalem (Daniel 11:31; 2 Thessalonians 2:4).

2. It involves a person setting up a statue in place of the regular sacrifice in the holy of holies (Daniel 11:31; 12:11; Revelation 13:14-15).

3. This results in the cessation of the regular sacrifice (Daniel 9:27; 11:31; 12:11).

4. There will be a time of about 3½ years between this event and another event and the end of the time period (Daniel 9:27; 12:11).

5. It involves an individual setting up a statue or image of himself so that he may be worshiped in place of God (Daniel 11:31; 2 Thessalonians 2:4; Revelation 13:14-15).

6. The image is made to come to life (Revelation 13:14).

7. A worship system of this false god is thus inaugurated (2 Thessalonians 2:4; Revelation 13:14-15).

8. At the end of this time period the individual who commits the act will himself be cut off (Daniel 9:27).

Despite this specific information about the abomination of desolation, Gentry identifies it as simply the Roman invasion and destruction of Jerusalem and the Temple in A.D. 70.[85] Rather than going to Daniel for an explanation of what our Lord wanted the reader to understand, Gentry goes to Luke 21:20-22, with a little help from Josephus, to conclude that Christ is warning of Jerusalem's devastation by military assault, not just the Temple's desecration by profane acts.[86] Let's see if this interpretation measures up to the biblical explanation of the abomination of desolation.

As noted earlier, Luke 21:20-24 does refer to the A.D. 70 destruction of Jerusalem. Therefore, when verse 20 says, "When you see Jerusalem surrounded by armies, then recognize that her desolation is near," it is describing in clear language the destruction of Jerusalem. This is vindicated by the language of the rest of the passage, especially verse 24: "and they will fall by the edge of the sword, and will be led captive into all the nations; and Jerusalem will be trampled under foot." In context, the desolation refers to the destruction of Jerusalem; it's not a technical term relating to the Temple, as Gentry suggests.

In contrast, the Matthew 24:15 passage has a context of its own that differs from the Luke account. Matthew says, "When you see the abomination of desolation which was spoken of through Daniel the prophet [not Luke], *standing in the holy place....*" Comparison of the description in Matthew and Daniel with the passage in Luke yields differences that prove they are two separate events.

In the A.D. 70 destruction of Jerusalem there was...

- no image set up in the holy place.

- no worship of the image required.

- no 3 ½ year period of time between that event and the coming of Christ. This is especially true since the destruction of Jerusalem occurred at the end of the siege by Rome. It was over in a matter of days. D. A. Carson notes, "By the time the Romans had actually desecrated the temple in A.D. 70, it was too late for anyone in the city to flee."[87]

- no image came to life and beckoned men to worship it.

Josephus tells us that Titus did not want the Temple burned. However, the Roman soldiers were so upset with the Jews that they disobeyed his orders and burned the Temple anyway. All Titus was able to do was to go in and tour the holy place shortly before it burned.[88] This does not comport with the biblical picture of the image to be set up on the altar in the middle of Daniel's seventieth week, resulting in cessation of the regular sacrifice and a rival worship system set up in its place for three-and-a-half years. Toussaint says,

> Because Christ specifically related the prophecy of the abomi-nation of desolation to Daniel's prophecy, it seems best to see some correspondence between the abomination of desolation committed by Antiochus Epiphanes and that predicted by Christ. If this is so it would entail not only defilement on the altar by sacrifices offered with impure hearts, but also an actual worship of another god using the Temple as a means for such a dastardly act. Those preterists who agree with this take it to be the worship of the Roman standards in the Temple precincts. However, if this interpretation is taken, Matthew 24:16-20 is dif-ficult if not impossible to explain. By then it would be too late for the followers of the Lord Jesus to escape; the Romans had already taken the city by this time.
>
> If the abomination of desolation spoken of by Daniel 9:27 and 12:11 is foreshadowed by Antiochus Epiphanes (11:31), it would be best to say it is a desecration carried out by a person who sacrilegiously uses the Temple to promote the worship of a god other than Jehovah. This is what is anticipated in 2 Thessa-lonians 2.[89]

Another major dissimilarity between Gentry's preterism and Matthew 24 is that according to Matthew, "neither the city nor the temple is destroyed, and thus the two situations stand in sharp contrast."[90] Luke 21:20-24, of course, does record the "days of vengeance" that befell Jerusalem.

Let's look at some other details related to the fact that the future fulfill-ment of Matthew 24 is one in which Christ delivers the Jews, rather than destroying them, as happened in A.D. 70.

First, as Jesus shifts from the A.D. 70 destruction of Jerusalem in Luke 21:20-24 to His second coming in 21:25-28, He says in verse 28 to "straighten up and lift up your heads, because your redemption is drawing near." This is the language of deliverance from the threat of the nations, not destruction. This language of deliverance is reflected in Zechariah 12–14, as noted in chapter 11 of this book. These three chapters in Zechariah include three important facts: 1) Jerusalem will be surrounded by the nations who are seeking to destroy it (12:2-9; 14:2-7); 2) the Lord will fight for Israel and Jerusalem and defeat the nations who have set up a siege against the city (14:1-8); 3) at this same time the Lord will also save Israel from her sins and she will be converted to Messiah—Jesus (12:9-14).

Fact #1 fits very well into the language of Matthew 24. The nations have surrounded Jerusalem. That does *not* describe the A.D. 70 destruction of Jerusalem because that was accomplished by one nation—Rome. Zechariah 14:2 says, "I will gather *all the nations* against Jerusalem to battle...."

Fact #2 also fits Matthew 24 and not the preterist view. Zechariah 14:3 says, "Then the LORD will go forth and fight against those nations, as when He fights on a day of battle." Matthew 24:22 speaks of God's intervention into the affairs of that time when it says, "Unless those days had been cut short, no life would have been saved; but for the sake of the elect those days shall be cut short." Luke 21:28 tells the Jews to look up for the redemption that is near. This interventionist language parallels the Zechariah account, but not the A.D. 70 destruction of Jerusalem.

The third fact speaks of the conversion of Israel. This certainly did not happen in A.D. 70, for the whole purpose for the destruction of Jerusalem was because of the nation's rejection. As already cited earlier, the picture in the Gospels is one of conversion: The people are to "look up" to the coming of the Lord for their redemption. This later occurs when the elect are gathered from the four winds of the earth (Matthew 24:31). And it's the entire Jewish nation that is under siege, not just the first-century Hebrew Christians, as Gentry supposes,[91] because in the A.D. 70 event, the remnant had already fled the city by this point in the siege. Furthermore, Zechariah 14:5 describes the Lord as coming with all His holy ones. The next verse (14:6) says that "in that day there will be no light; the luminaries will dwindle." Similar language appears in Matthew 24:29-31, which pictures the darkening of light and luminaries as the Lord comes in the clouds to rescue his people and the city of Jerusalem. There is no judgment here except upon the armies that have laid siege.

In addition, Daniel 9:27 says that the one leading the siege of Jerusalem will himself be cut off: "...even until a complete destruction, one that is decreed, is poured out on the one who makes desolate." This did not happen in A.D. 70. The Roman general Titus went back victoriously to Rome and lived a number of years after the destruction of Jerusalem. Daniel 9:27 speaks of one being *cut off* in the course of the siege.

There are great parallels between Matthew 24 and Zechariah 12–14. I believe that our Lord's discourse in Matthew 24 and the siege of Zechariah 12–14 speak of the same future event. Both prophesy a time when Jerusalem is surrounded by armies and the Lord moves to rescue His people and judge the invaders. By contrast, Gentry wrongly attempts to equate Luke 21:20-24 with Matthew 24. So that we can better note the differences between the two scenarios, J. Randall Price has provided the following helpful chart:

Contrasts Between Luke 21:20-24 and Zechariah 12–14

Luke 21:20-24	*Zechariah 12–14*
• Past fulfillment—"led captive to all nations" (verse 24)	• Eschatological fulfillment—"in that day" (12:3-4,6,8,11; 13:1-12; 14:1,4,6-9)
• Day of the desolation of Jerusalem (verse 20)	• Day of deliverance of Jerusalem (12:7-8)
• Day of vengeance against Jerusalem (verse 22)	• Day of victory for Jerusalem (12:4-6)
• Day of wrath against Jewish nation (verse 23)	• Day of wrath against Gentile nations (12:9; 14:3,12)
• Jerusalem trampled by Gentiles (verse 24)	• Jerusalem transformed by God (14:4-10)
• Time of Gentile dominion over Jerusalem (verse 24)	• Time of Gentile submission in Jerusalem (14:16-19)
• Great distress upon the land (verse 23)	• Great deliverance for the land (13:2)
• Nations bring the sword to Jerusalem (verse 24)	• Nations bring their wealth to Jerusalem (14:14)
• Jerusalem destroyed (A.D. 70) "in order that all things which are written [concerning the Jewish people] may be fulfilled" (in the future—verse 22)	• Jerusalem rescued *and redeemed* that *all things* written (concerning Jewish people) may be fulfilled (13:1-9; cf. Romans 11:25-27)
• Jerusalem's desolation is given a time limit: "until the times of the Gentiles are fulfilled" (verse 24); this implies that a time of restoration for Jerusalem will then follow	• The attack on Jerusalem is the occasion for the final defeat of Israel's enemies, thus ending the "times of the Gentiles" (14:2-3,11)
• The Messiah comes in power and glory to be seen by the Jewish people only *after* "these things"— the events of verses 25-28—which are yet future to the events of verses 20-24	• The Messiah comes in power and glory *during* the events of the battle (14:4-5)[92]

In spite of a few similarities, such as the fact that both passages are set in Jerusalem, there is a Gentile siege, and so on, it is the *differences* that are determinative. Once again, we see that the events of Matthew 24 and the Tribulation have yet to occur.

THE GREAT TRIBULATION

Jesus then went on to say this in Matthew 24:21-22: "Then there will be a great tribulation, such as has not occurred since the beginning of the world until now, nor ever will. Unless those days had been cut short, no life would have been saved; but for the sake of the elect those days will be cut short."

Predictably, Gentry, following the normal preterist approach, teaches that the Tribulation and Great Tribulation are past, having already occurred in the first century, while admitting that Matthew 24:21-22 "seems to preclude an A.D. 70 Great Tribulation."[93] Gentry insists, however, that this passage has already been fulfilled. The core of Gentry's argument on this, and a number of other points, is that it had to have a first-century fulfillment; thus, I believe, preterists have to find some explanation. Gentry asks, "Is the destruction of first century Jerusalem a disaster 'such as has not occurred since the beginning of the world until now, nor ever shall'?"[94] He concludes concerning this passage that "we should not interpret Christ's language literally after all. It is dramatic hyperbole, well justified by the gravity of the situation."[95]

Before I respond on this issue, I want to examine more closely a statement by Gentry. He says, "The Lord is not referring to his Second Advent, or else we should wonder why his disciples should pray about fleeing from Judea (Matthew 24:16): what good would running to the hills be at the Return of Christ?"[96] It is hard to know why he would come up with a point like this. There are no futurists who believe this will occur "at the Return of Christ." Clearly, futurists believe this will occur "in the middle of the week" (Daniel 9:27), which is 3½ years before the second coming. Such a scenario makes sense in light of the biblical text; Gentry's "straw man" argument does not.

In support of his "prophetic hyperbole" argument Gentry cites Exodus 11:6, Ezekiel 5:9; 7:5-6, and Daniel 9:12[97] as examples of other passages using similar language. Further, Gentry argues that the Flood (in Noah's day) was a worse judgment than that described in Matthew 24 since it "destroys the entire world except one family."[98]

I believe there is a very serious error preterists frequently commit in their interpretations. Preterists tend to generalize many of the specifics of a given text and thus limit the scope of these descriptions. In other words, that which Scripture says will involve massive tribulation or destruction is limited, by the preterists, to some smaller-scale event. I wrote Hebrew Christian scholar

Arnold Fruchtenbaum regarding this and presented some of these same arguments made by Gentry's fellow preterist DeMar a few years ago. Here is Fruchtenbaum's able response:

> As for Exodus 11:6, the focus here is specifically on one country which is the nation of Egypt. Furthermore, the verse is not saying that what happened with the ten plagues was the worst judgment that Egypt will ever experience and, therefore, the correlation between 14 million and 55 million is irrelevant. The text is saying that there was not such a great cry in all the land of Egypt in the past, nor will there be such a great cry in the land of Egypt in the future. The emphasis is not on the judgment itself but on the Egyptian response to the judgment. The firstborn son of every Egyptian family died, but the remainder of the family was spared, so every single family was affected. In the Tribulation, there is no need to assume that every family will be affected and, furthermore, rather than merely one or two members of the family, whole families might be destroyed; and if whole families are destroyed, there will be no one to mourn for that particular family. Another point is the Bible says that one quarter of the world's population will be destroyed, but mentions the world population in general and does not apply that exactly 25 percent of the Egyptian population will be destroyed. In other words, whether we speak of 25 percent or 75 percent of the earth's population destroyed, most of it is among the nations outside of the Middle East and, therefore, will not affect Egypt to the same degree as it would affect, let's say, North America or Europe. Therefore, there might be a lot less death in Egypt than there would be elsewhere, and it still might be less than those who died in the tenth plague. In other words, Exodus 11:6 simply does not present such a great problem.
>
> Finally, concerning Ezekiel 5:9-10.... There are two implications. The first implication is that what happened in A.D. 70 was far more severe than what happened in 586 B.C. That point is true. But the point of Ezekiel 5:9 is that God, in this case, is going to perform a judgment of the type that He has not done before and will not do again, and the type of judgment was that one third will die by plague and famine, one third will die by the sword, and one third will be scattered to the four winds. It did not happen that way in A.D. 70, and it will not happen that way in the Tribulation. What Ezekiel is describing is something that happened uniquely in the Babylonian destruction of Jerusalem when the inhabitants were equally divided into thirds with two thirds dying in two different ways, and one third surviving but under divine judgment were scattered. No such threefold division equally happened in A.D. 70. Even [in regard to] the Tribulation, where it does mention in Zechariah 13:8-9

that two thirds will die and one third will survive, it does not say that the two thirds will die in an equal two halves by sword and by famine. Furthermore, the remaining surviving third is not under divine judgment and scattered, but rather, they are saved and regathered. So, Ezekiel's words can be taken as literally true; what he said did happen to Jerusalem and was unique to the Babylonian destruction.

The second implication is his statement under point 4: "The flood was obviously a greater Tribulation." This is true as far as Tribulation in general. However, here we are dealing specifically with the Jewish people and Jerusalem. The focus of the flood was not on the Jewish people, since Jewish history had not begun as yet. Nor was the focus on Jerusalem since that city had not existed yet. The Noahic flood destroyed the world in general and was the worst flood that ever was or will be. But Ezekiel's prophecy focuses specifically on the Jewish people and Jerusalem, which was not or will not be destroyed by flood. And while God will once again destroy the mass of humanity, according to Isaiah 24, it will not be by means of water but by means of fire.

So, none of these "problems" that Gary DeMar is presenting are in any sense a great problem. They are all solvable if we remain with their own context and we move carefully through the actual words and to what they are referring.[99]

These issues are not a problem if one follows the context that governs the words of these passages. But another objection can be raised to the preterist handling of these verses, as noted by Toussaint:

> ...the Tribulation referred to in Matthew 24:21 is explained further in verse 22. "And unless those days had been cut short no life would have been saved; but for the sake of the elect those days shall be cut short." This verse must be considered along with verse 21. What is meant by "life" in the clause "no life would have been saved"? DeMar explains this as referring "to life in the land of Israel." The noun translated "life" is *sarx.* It should be noted, however, that the Greek construction is *pasa sarx* or all flesh, a technical term which refers to all humanity. The following are all the occurrences of "all flesh" in the Greek New Testament text—Matthew 24:22; Mark 13:20; Luke 3:6; John 17:2; Acts 2:17; Romans 3:20; 1 Corinthians 1:29; 15:39; Galatians 2:16; 1 Peter 1:24. In every case except 1 Corinthians 15:39 the expression describes all humans. In the passage Paul is discussing the nature of the resurrection body, "All flesh is not the same flesh, but there is one flesh of men, and another of beasts...." Here he is using it in an even broader sense, all human and animal life.

BAG takes *pasa sarx* to mean *every person, everyone.* With the negative they take it to mean *no person, nobody* and list Matthew 24:22 and Mark 13:20 as instances of this meaning. The expression *pasa sarx* comes from the Septuagint, which in turn looks at the Hebraism *kol basar,* "all flesh." Gesenius says this Hebrew construction means "all living creatures...especially *all men,* the whole human race...." Therefore, to interpret "all flesh" in Matthew 24:22 and Mark 13:20 as referring to Jews living in Judea in A.D. 70 is too limiting. "All flesh" describes all humanity. In other words, the Tribulation described in Matthew 24:21 is of such huge proportions that human life stands in jeopardy on planet earth. This could not be said in A.D. 70 as horrible as the decimation of life was in Judea at that time. Matthew 24:21-22 must look beyond the past destruction of Jerusalem.[100]

It is quite clear, then, that once again, if the plain meaning of the text is allowed to stand, then a first-century interpretation is precluded. Preterists must revert to sophistry in order to say why the text does not mean what it says so they can suggest a meaning in support of their view. Interestingly, they tend to take this approach only with passages that do not appear to support their thesis, yet they still interpret plainly the verses that appear to support their views, even when figures of speech are embedded in the text. No, the Great Tribulation has not yet happened, but the world is now being prepared for this future time (2 Thessalonians 2:6-7).

Coming As Lightning

Going back to our text in the Olivet Discourse, Jesus then went on to tell us about how He would return: "Just as the lightning comes from the east and flashes even to the west, so will the coming of the Son of Man be" (Matthew 24:27).

Since Christ did not return to earth bodily in A.D. 70, Gentry and his fellow preterists are bound by their system to say that Matthew 24:27 "is a providential *judgment-coming,* a Christ-directed judgment, rather than a miraculous visible bodily coming."[101] Gentry continues, "It is not *Christ Himself* who is *corporally present.* Rather He directs the Roman armies by his providence...."[102] The logic of such an approach would demand that Christ comes many times every day through the vehicle of His providence. Yet, such an approach strips the significance from the hope of our Lord's actual return. Instead of looking for a future event, preterist logic suggests that we should be seeking the many mystical comings of Christ.

There are a number of issues to be dealt with in regards to this passage. First, Gentry compares Christ's coming in Matthew 24:27 with a statement to Israel's Sanhedrin in Matthew 26:63-64 "that they will 'see' his coming. Obviously, they are not still alive today! Jesus must be referring to an event in their first century life spans."[103] The preterist misuse of Matthew 26:63-64 is better explained as an event that will literally take place. The Sanhedrin will see Christ's glorious return, even if it is a few thousand years after their time, just as all men of all ages will see this event, whether alive are not. Paul says the same kind of thing in Philippians 2:9-11: that all will bow the knee to Christ, whether alive at His moment of glorification or not. Paul says "that at the name of Jesus every knee will bow, of those who are in heaven and on earth and under the earth, and that every tongue will confess that Jesus Christ is Lord, to the glory of God the Father" (Philippians 2:10-11). Further, it is very likely that hardly any of the Sanhedrin would have lived another 40 years to see a coming in the sense that the preterists describe. Instead, Christ was saying that even though He was in a position of humiliation before them, He would not always be that way. One day He would return as the very Jewish Messiah in power and great glory. The Sanhedrin, and all of us, will one day see this great event.

Gentry, in all his effort to say why "the coming of the Son of Man" in Matthew 24:27 was not a literal coming of Christ, fails to tell his readers that the Greek word *parousia* is used in this verse. Three of the four times that *parousia* is used in Matthew 24, Gentry admits that it refers to the yet future second coming.[104] The *Bauer-Arndt-Gingrich Greek Lexicon (BAG)* says that *parousia* means "presence," "coming, advent," and "of Christ, and nearly always of his Messianic Advent in glory to judge the world at the end of this age."[105] *BAG* cites all four uses of *parousia* in Matthew 24 as a reference to Christ's second advent. In fact, *BAG* does not even recognize Gentry's stated meaning as a possibility. It appears that the preterist "mother" is the "necessity of invention" in this instance. Kittel's dictionary, in concert with *BAG*, tells us that the core idea of the word means "to be present," "denotes esp. active presence," "appearing."[106] Kittel describes *parousia* as a technical term "for the 'coming' of Christ in Messianic glory."[107] Thus, *parousia* carries the idea of a "presence coming," contra the preterist notion of a "non-presence coming," or an invisible coming. Our Lord's use of *parousia* demands His physical, bodily presence.

Toussaint provides further reasoning for the futurist understanding of *parousia* in this passage:

> …"What will be the sign of your coming?" (Matthew 24:3). What does "coming" (*parousia*) mean? That term is filled with significance. This noun occurs four times in the Olivet Discourse (the only times Matthew uses *parousia* and the only occurrence in the Gospels). The first occurrence is in the question asked by

the disciples. Very interestingly, the remaining three are in identical clauses, "thus, shall be the coming of the Son of Man"... (Matthew 24:27, 37, 39).

...The problem with this interpretation is the meaning of parousia before verse 36 and after. If the coming of the Son of Man in Matthew 24:37, 39 is the Second Advent, one would expect *the identical clause* in 24:27 to refer to the same event. The word would also have the same meaning in 24:3. It must be the Second Advent in each case.

Furthermore, the word *parousia* as found in the New Testament is always used of an actual presence. It may be employed of the presence of persons as in 1 Corinthians 16:17; 2 Corinthians 7:6-7; 10:10; Philippians 1:26; 2:12 and 2 Thessalonians 2:9. In each of these above cases the person is *bodily* present. In all the other cases *parousia* is used of the Lord's presence at His second coming, cf. 1 Corinthians 15:23; 1 Thessalonians 2:19; 3:13; 4:15; 5:23; 2 Thessalonians 2:1, 8; James 5:7, 9; 2 Peter 1:16; 3:4, 12; 1 John 2:28. The only occurrences in the Gospel of *parousia* are in Matthew 24. It would seem that they, too, refer to a yet future coming of Christ.[108]

Gentry attempts to say that the use of the term "lightning" in Matthew 24:27 "reflects the Roman armies marching toward Jerusalem from an easterly direction."[109] Yet lightning is very swift, and it is hard to imagine that the time-consuming march of the Roman armies is the true interpretation of this passage. Once again, I follow Toussaint's explanation of the text:

What then is Matthew 24:27 saying? It is simply saying people should not be misled by false teachers or counterfeit messiahs who make their deceptive claims in some wilderness or inner sanctum (24:26). They may even fortify their pretensions by fantastic miracles (24:24). The reason the Lord's followers should not be drawn aside is because the coming of the Lord Jesus will be so spectacular no one will miss seeing it. It will be like a bolt of lightning that streaks from one horizon to the other. This is why the Lord used the correlatives *hosper....* *houtos;* He is simply using an analogy or comparison. His Second Advent will be as obvious as a brilliant sky-spanning bolt of lightning. So will be the unmistakable and actual presence of the Lord Jesus Christ in His second coming to earth.[110]

Cosmic Disturbances

Continuing the description of His return, Jesus says, "Immediately after the tribulation of those days the sun will be darkened, and the moon will not give its light, and the stars will fall from the sky, and the powers of the heavens will be shaken" (Matthew 24:29).

"Here we encounter remarkable cosmic disturbances that seem too catastrophic for applying to A.D. 70," says Gentry. He believes "this portrays historical divine judgment under the dramatic imagery of a universal catastrophe."[111] How does he arrive at such a conclusion? "To understand it properly we must interpret it covenantally, which is to say biblically, rather than according to a presupposed simple literalism."[112] Gentry believes that this verse "draws upon the imagery from Old Testament judgment passages that sound as if they are world-ending events."[113] Would that Gentry actually drew upon the Old Testament prophetic pattern!

Gentry admits that this passage "seems too catastrophic" to apply to the first century. This is why, by his own admission, he must introduce his theology (if *covenant* were a true synonym for *biblical*, why must he tell us?) as a factor for interpreting this text. Those who follow the normal canons of *sound* hermeneutics—the historical, grammatical, contextual approach—cannot find Dr. Gentry's view taught from the passage. Because the preterist erroneously believes that these events had to occur in the first century, he is forced to adhere to views that are not supported by the words, phrases, and context of the passage.

When I study the Old Testament figures that preterists say speak of the passing of a great political power, I wonder how they know what the original figures mean? I do not see a textual basis either in the Old Testament or in Matthew 24. There are no biblical passages that establish the preterists' use of these figures. In 1857 Reverend D. D. Buck made the following hermeneutical points about interpreting Matthew 24:29:

> (1.) The use of metaphoric language implies a knowledge or idea of what would be understood if such language were applied literally. No one ever uses figures without having in view the literal things from which the figures are derived....If we say Christianity is the sun of the world, it implies that we have a previous understanding of the nature and fact of the sun.
>
> (2.) Now, whence did this ancient figurative use of the darkening of the luminaries arise? How did it happen that it was so common for the prophets to speak of ordinary, limited judgments, in language which all admit would, if used literally, apply to the general judgment? How became it so common to speak

metaphorically of the darkening of the sun, moon, and stars, and the passing away of the heavens? Figures are the shadow of the literal. Where is the substance that originates the shadow? Metaphors are borrowed from literal speech. Where is the literal speech, and the revelation of the literal idea, of the blotting out of the bright heavens, and the downfall of the world?

(3.) This question is to be settled by those who seize upon every reference to these great events, and pronounce them figurative. Will they please to tell us where there is a spot in all the Bible where the literalist may plant his feet, and stand up in defense of orthodoxy, and give a philosophical explanation of the commonness of such language as appears to refer to the day of Judgment?[114]

Matthew 24:29 is not a new revelation by our Lord. Old Testament passages such as Isaiah 13:9-10 and Joel 2:31; 3:15 also mention this "blackout" that will occur "immediately after the tribulation" in preparation for Christ's second coming as mentioned in Matthew 24:30. These Old Testament passages refer to the same future events that Christ spoke of in Matthew 24:29. In conjunction with the theme that I have noted throughout this book—that is, that Israel will be rescued from her tribulation by Christ Himself—we see support from the contexts of these Old Testament passages, especially Joel 2 and 3:

> The sun will be turned into darkness and the moon into blood before the great and awesome day of the LORD comes (Joel 2:31).
>
> For behold, in those days and at that time, when I restore the fortunes of Judah and Jerusalem, I will gather all the nations and bring them down to the valley of Jehoshaphat. Then I will enter into judgment with them there on behalf of My people and My inheritance, Israel, whom they have scattered among the nations; and they have divided up My land (Joel 3:1-2).

In Matthew 24:39, it is clear that our Lord has quoted part of His declaration about the sun and moon from Joel 2:31: "Immediately after the tribulation of those days the sun will be darkened, and the moon will not give its light." Both verses speak of the same time and events—the future Tribulation. Thus it is interesting to take note of Joel 3:1-2, which provides a "time text" saying that the "blackout" (Joel 2:31) will occur "in those days and at that time" (Joel 3:1). In conjunction with this is described a time when the Lord will "restore the fortunes of Judah and Jerusalem" (Joel 3:1)—that is, a time of deliverance and not judgment, as in Matthew 24. In this deliverance, the

Lord "will gather all the nations" (Joel 3:1) in the Valley of Jehoshaphat just north of Jerusalem. Israel will also have been regathered from among the nations (Joel 3:2). It is at this time that the sun and moon will be darkened.

Luke 21:24—"and they will fall by the edge of the sword, and will be led captive into all the nations; and Jerusalem will be trampled under foot by the Gentiles until the times of the Gentiles are fulfilled"—provides an outline of the history of Jerusalem from the time of its destruction until Israel's redemption at the second coming (Luke 21:25-29). The time in which the sun and moon will be darkened will follow the end of "the times of the Gentiles," according to Luke 21:25. The fact that the blackout of Matthew 24:29 is to come at the end of the times of the Gentiles—"immediately after the tribulation of those days"—makes it clear that it could not have happened in the first century, since, according to Luke 21:24, the Roman destruction of the Holy City would commence at that time, which has gone on now for almost 2,000 years. This event must be future and in conjunction with a time in which the Lord will deliver His people, not judge them (as in A.D. 70).

If the preterist interpretation of Matthew 24:29 is left to stand then it creates tremendous contradictions between the text and the historical records of the Roman siege. Reverend Richard Shimeall explains the preterist problem in this way:

> Historically, therefore, the state of the case amounts to this:
>
> (1.) The high-priest of the Jewish nation and many of his associates had been murdered, and the whole body of the priesthood overthrown; and, if there were any religious services, they were conducted by such wretches as the robbers saw fit to appoint.
>
> (2.) Their temple was changed into a citadel and stronghold of an army of the vilest and most abominable robbers and murderers that ever disgraced the human race.
>
> (3.) Their "holy houses" (synagogues) throughout the land had been pillaged and destroyed by the ruthless and bloody Sicarii.
>
> (4.) Their judiciary and temple officers had either fled for their lives to the Romans, or had been murdered by the robber-gangs of the city, while their nobles and men of-wealth perished by myriads. And finally,
>
> (5.) Whether within the capital or throughout the borders of Judea, east, west, north, and south, the *ecclesiastical* and *civil* institutions of the nation were exterminated, and the country conquered and laid waste by the Romans, or ravaged by organized banditti.
>
> And thus, reader, it continued to the end. These, we repeat, are the *historical facts* of the case. And yet, our commentators have trusted the interpretation of some of the most important parts of the Bible to the theory, the principal argument to sustain which lies in the assumption

that the Jewish ecclesiastical and civil governments were destroyed *"after"* the destruction of Jerusalem!

What shall the writer say more? He claims to have settled the question by *undeniable* historic facts. If anything, let it be in the form of the following appeal to logic:

1. If by the heavenly luminaries be meant the ecclesiastical and civil States and rulers of the Jews, and the darkening of them refers to their destruction; and if this was effected by the Roman legions, it follows that it must have occurred either *before* or *during* the Tribulation that resulted in their ruin.

2. But, inasmuch as the *object* of the war was to reduce the nation to obedience, or to bring it to ruin, it could not have *preceded* it.

3. It must therefore have occurred *during* the war. Recollect we are now speaking of the darkening of the sun, moon, and stars, as denoting the so-called *Jewish Tribulation* at the hands of the Romans. We repeat, then, it must have occurred during the war. Now, it is undeniable, that that war did not cease until its object was effected. It is also undeniable, that the nation was in ruins *before* the war was ended. And it is a fact, also, that the predicted Tribulation continued undiminished, if indeed it did not increase in severity, *to the last.*

It is, therefore, we submit, settled—historically and logically settled—that it was during, and *not* after, that time of trouble, that the so-called Jewish luminaries were darkened. And, what is decisive of this point, are those notable words of Christ, *"Immediately after* Tribulation of those days, the sun shall be darkened,"* etc.; which shows conclusively that our Lord was not speaking of *that event* in the 29th verse of this chapter.[115]

Preterists admit that if Matthew 24:29 requires a literal blackout, then it did not happen in A.D. 70. Is a literal fulfillment of Matthew 24:29 so far-fetched as preterists insist? Stars do literally fall from heaven. They are called "falling stars," "shooting stars," "comets," or "meteors." The Greek word for "star" in Matthew 24:29 can be used in this way.[116] "Stars" that fall to the earth often disintegrate and burn up as they enter the earth's atmosphere. Robert Gundry has said, "The falling of the stars refers to a shower of meteorites, and the shaking of the heavenly powers of God's displacing 'the spiritual forces of wickedness in the heavenly places' (Eph. 6:12)."[117] In a similar passage, this is what causes the people of the earth to hide in caves (Revelation 6:12-17). Perhaps this is similar to the Lord's raining down of fire and brimstone upon Sodom and Gomorrah (Genesis 19:23-26)?

It makes sense that the heavens and earth are physically affected by man's sin at the end of history, just as they were when man fell at the beginning of history. With the literal view, Genesis and Revelation recount the beginning and ending of history. Revelation notes the magnitude of the shaking of the heavens and the earth in judgment. Noah's flood had physical effects, and so too will the judgment of the Tribulation prior to Christ's return.

I believe Gentry takes a number of similar, yet smaller in scale, incidents of biblical history to be literal. These other events do not put his preterism at risk. The questions must be raised: Did the sun literally not shine over the land of Egypt and at the same time shine in the land of Goshen during the ninth plague (Exodus 10:21-29)? Of course. Similarly, during the crucifixion of our Lord, did darkness really fall over the whole land of Israel about the sixth hour until the ninth hour (Luke 23:44-45)? Certainly. That was a pattern of the final darkness that will accompany the final judgment at the end of the world. "When He died, the sun refused to shine (Luke 23:45). When He comes again it will not shine (Matthew 24:29)."[118] Why shouldn't grandiose, super-natural phenomenon accompany the glorious return of our Lord? Only a naturalist mentality would say that a literal occurrence of Matthew 24:29 is impossible. After all, God said in Genesis 1:14 that one of His purposes for the sun, moon, and stars is to serve as "signs" in the heavens. It would be absurd to think that these references to the sun, moon, and stars are to be taken merely as symbolic with no physical referent. Why shouldn't the One who created the heaven and earth have the heavens reflect His global judgment upon a sinful world?

THE SIGN OF THE SON OF MAN

Jesus then goes on to describe His appearance at the second coming: "Then the sign of the Son of Man will appear in the sky, and then all the tribes of the earth will mourn, and they will see the Son of Man coming on the clouds of the sky with power and great glory" (Matthew 24:30).

Gentry's preterist interpretation of this passage, once again, is an exercise in why the text does not mean what it appears to say. Gentry teaches that

> "...the sign" of verse 30 is when the Romans lay waste the temple (verse 6 and 15 anticipate this) and pick apart Jerusalem (verse 28). That is, when the government of Israel utterly collapses (verse 29), then it will be evident that the one who prophesies her destruction is "in heaven." The "sign" is not a visible token in the sky. Rather, the sign is that the "Son of Man" rejected by the first century Jews is in heaven. The destruction of Israel vindicates Christ.[119]

It is hard to believe that such an interpretation is what Christ intended when He prophesied this event. Since Gentry wants the passage to teach that the sign appeared in heaven (i.e., the throne room of God), rather than as a sign in heaven to be seen by humanity, he insists upon a certain word order for the verse. The word order of the Greek text is as follows: "And then shall appear the sign of the Son of Man in the heaven." It is true that this allows for the possibility of Gentry's understanding that there was a sign in heaven. However, the Greek *also* allows for the possibility that the intent of the passage is that the sign of the Son of Man will appear in the heavens or the sky. To understand this passage as speaking of a humanly visible sign in the sky, as I do, Gentry says, "requires a restructuring of the text."[120] It does not *require* a restructuring, even though many who take a futurist view do put forward translations that do not retain the original word order. The difference amounts to whether "in heaven" refers to the preterist invisible sign that takes place in the throne room of God in heaven, or to a sign in the sky that is seen by humanity. Grammarian Nigel Turner says, "Matthew 24:30 is ambiguous, either *the sign which is the S.M.* (appos.), or *the sign which the S.M. will give* (possess.)."[121]

I believe the context of the passage argues in favor of the futurist interpretation that the sign is visible to the human eye looking up to heaven, or the sky. First, the Greek word *ouranós* can mean either "throne room," as preterists believe, or the visible heaven or sky that can be seen by the human eye, as understood by futurists. The majority of New Testament uses fall into this latter category.[122] *BAG* classifies it as the latter and says "*then the sign of the Son of Man (who is) in heaven will appear;* acc. to the context, the sign consists in this, that he appears visibly in heavenly glory Matthew 24:30."[123]

Second, surrounding verses focus upon heavenly meteorological disturbances (cf. verses 27,29,31) that are visible to humanity. The appearance of a sign in the sky would certainly fit the contextual theme of a focus on heavenly phenomena.

Third, "it must, in the nature of the case, be *luminous*. This is indicated by the original word for *appear*. But it must be luminous from this single consideration: it will appear, or shine, at a time of *total darkness*," declares Reverend Buck. "The sun will be previously turned to darkness, and the moon and the stars will have withdrawn their shining. All the great sources of light being thus totally obscured, whatever shall *appear* must be luminous in its nature."[124]

Fourth, the time relationships of the passage support a visible, and thus a future understanding. Matthew 24:30 begins "and then," referring back to the meteorological events of verse 29, which will occur "immediately after the tribulation of those days." Thus, verse 30 tells us that "the sign…will appear"; "and then" there will be human mourning in response to the sign, followed by Christ's glorious return. Amazingly, Gentry says that the sign of verse 30 means that the Jews "must flee the area if they are to preserve their lives."[125] How can this happen if the sign is the Roman conquest of Jerusalem? It would be too late. Such assumption does not fit an A.D. 70 sequence of events, as noted by Shimeall:

> Yes, reader. This is the theory of our Lord's *second* coming.… Briefly, then, as it respects the *first* branch of this theory, its inconsistency, we submit, will become apparent, from the following arguments and facts:
>
> (1.) *If* the coming of the Lord at the time here specified was merely "the coming of the Roman army to destroy Jerusalem and the unbelieving Jews," then it will follow, of necessity, that it occurred at the same time, since, in fact, it is affirmed to be the *same event.*
>
> (2.) Again. The destruction of the Jewish Church and State, and city, and people, resulted from the coming of the Romans, and must, of course, have been *after* that coming, because results must be subsequent to the causes which produce them. Accordingly, as our blessed Lord delivered the whole of this remarkable prophecy with special regard to the *chronological* order of the events,
>
> (3.) He describes the appearance of the "sign" of His coming, of the mourning of all the tribes of the earth, and of His actual coming in the clouds of heaven, as being "*after* the tribulation of those days," and subsequent, in the order of time, to the darkening of the sun, moon, and stars.

Reader, which shall we believe—the comments and opinions of men, or the teachings of Christ?[126]

Fifth, I believe that "the sign" will likely include a display of the Shechinah glory that has been manifested throughout history.[127] After all, it was the sign of Christ's first coming—the Shechinah glory—that flashed upon a darkened sky announcing His birth to the shepherds. It was the Shechinah glory star that led the wise men from the East. So it is that His sign, the sign of the Son of Man, will once again be His trademark, the Shechinah glory cloud. Fruchtenbaum explains:

> At this point Matthew states that the sign of the second coming will appear (verse 30a); and since this sign is coupled with God's

glory, it is obviously the Shechinah Glory light that will signal the second coming of Christ. So the answer to the second question, "What will be the sign of the second coming?" is the Shechinah Glory. So *immediately after the tribulation of those days* there will be a total blackout with no light penetrating at all, followed by a sudden, glorious, tremendous light that will penetrate through the blackout. This Shechinah light will be the sign of the second coming of Christ. The light will be followed by the return of Christ Himself (verse 30b).[128]

Gentry argues that "they will see…" Christ's "…coming on the clouds" is once again not visible sight (the eyes of faith) nor a physical coming.[129] He goes so far as to evidence "exegetical vertigo" when he says that Christ's "coming on the clouds" "actually speaks of his ascension."[130] At this point, preterists confuse coming with going. This is in spite of the fact that Gentry, unlike some preterists, understands Acts 1:11 as a second-coming passage.[131]

> After He had said these things, He was lifted up while they were looking on, and a cloud received Him out of their sight. And as they were gazing intently into the sky while He was departing, behold, two men in white clothing stood beside them; and they also said, "Men of Galilee, why do you stand looking into the sky? This Jesus, who has been taken up from you into heaven, will come in just the same way as you have watched Him go into heaven" (Acts 1:9-11).

The language in Acts 1:9 clearly states Christ ascended *upward* to heaven. It is equally clear that verse 11 speaks of His return as a *coming down* from heaven on a cloud. Further, the Greek word for "coming" in both Matthew 24:30 and Acts 1:11 is *erchomai*. Thus, once Christ has ascended into heaven, His next act of coming could not be up, but only down—down from heaven to earth. This is clearly the picture our Lord paints, not only in the specific passage (verse 30), but throughout the overall context (verses 27-31). Toussaint adds:

> It will be conceded by all that the first part of Matthew 24:30 looks back to Zechariah 12:10. However, it is important to notice that in Zechariah the mourning of 12:10 is explained by the verses that follow. It is a repentant lamentation by Israel because it results in the purification of the nation (Zechariah 13:1). The context of Zechariah 12:10 is most significant. Rather than prophesying the destruction of Jerusalem, it is predicting the opposite. "And it will come about in that day that I will set about to destroy all the nations that come against Jerusalem" (Zechariah

12:9). This is the tenor of Zechariah 12:1-8. It looks ahead to God's future deliverance of Israel when Jerusalem will again be surrounded by enemies. "In that day" is prophetic of a time of deliverance of Israel, not judgment. (Note the constant repetition of "in that day" [12:3, 4, 6, 8 (2x), 9, 11; 13:1, 2, 4]). It is clear that the context of Zechariah is a mourning that results in cleansing and deliverance for Israel. Whatever the sign of the Son of Man is, it results in the national repentance of Israel. This parallels perfectly what Paul says in Romans 11:25-27. This explanation of Matthew 24:30a sets the stage for the understanding of the last half of the verse.

It is true that in the vision of Daniel 7:13 as it is translated in the NASB the Son of Man came up to the Ancient of Days to receive the dominion to rule. However, the Hebrew verb has no idea of direction; it simply means to arrive or to reach. This specific verb is only used in Daniel where it may refer to something reaching up as Nebuchadnezzar's greatness did in 4:22, or it may describe something going down as in 6:24 where the detractors of Daniel were thrown into the lion's den. It has no intrinsic sense of direction. Nor does the following preposition indicate direction in itself. The construction simply means the Son of Man approached the Ancient of Days. But even if it describes the Son of Man coming up to the Ancient of Days, it only looks at the bestowment of authority. The question is where is the authority expressed? Keil says it well when he writes:

> In this very chapter before us there is no expression or any intimation whatever that the judgment is held in heaven. No place is named. It is only said that judgment was held over the power of the fourth beast, which came to a head in the horn speaking blasphemies, and that the beast was slain and his body burned. If he who appears as the son of man with the clouds of heaven comes before the Ancient of Days executing the judgment on the earth, it is manifest that he could only come from heaven to earth. If the reverse is to be understood, then it ought to have been so expressed, since the coming with clouds of heaven in opposition to the rising up of the beast out of the sea very distinctly indicates a coming down from heaven. The clouds are the veil or the "chariot" on which God comes from heaven to execute judgment against His enemies; cf. Psalm xvii;10f., xcvii 2-4, ci verse 3, Isaiah xix 1, Nah. i. 3. This passage forms the foundation for the declaration of Christ regarding His future coming, which is described after Daniel vii. 13 as a coming of the Son of

man with, in, on the clouds of heaven; Matthew xxi verse 20,
xxvi. 64; Mark xiii. 26; Revelation 1.7, xi verse 14.[132]

In summary, Matthew 24:30 describes a visible appearance of the sign of
the Son of Man, the repentance of Israel, and the triumphant return of Christ
to reign on planet earth.[133]

THE ANGELIC GATHERING

Christ then ends Matthew chapter 24 with these words: "And He will send
forth His angels with a great trumpet and they will gather together His elect
from the four winds, from one end of the sky to the other" (Matthew 24:31).

In keeping with his localized and nonsupernatural interpretation, Gentry
teaches that "Matthew 24:31 continues the poetic imagery."[134] He explains the
verse as "the gathering of the saints into local assemblies or churches (Heb.
10:25; Jms. 2:2) and the universal assembling of the saints into the body of
Christ, the church universal (cp. Matthew 22:7-13)."[135] The reference to "a
great trumpet" speaks of "the destruction of the temple trumpets in the *ultimate* Jubilee Year."[136] Finally, angels do "not seem to refer to the supernatural
heavenly beings here, but to those who now proclaim the message of full salvation."[137]

This section in Gentry's argument[138] provides us with another blatant
example of the hermeneutical error termed by James Barr as "illegitimate
totality transfer."[139] While totally ignoring contextual uses, Gentry seeks to
establish his own context for trumpets, the gathering, and angels. For
example, he fails to note that the Greek verb "they will gather together" is
used earlier in this passage. Other than an insignificant use in verse 28, the
phrase "they will gather together" is used twice in Matthew 23:37, where
Jesus weeps over Jerusalem as He pronounces the A.D. 70 judgment and
declares, "How I wanted to *gather* your children together, the way a hen
gathers her chicks under her wings, and you were unwilling." Matthew
chapter 24 is about a future time when Jerusalem is again in peril, but this
time the Jews are willing for the Lord to *gather* His elect (saved Jews at the
end of the Tribulation) from around the world and bring them to Jerusalem,
instead of scattering them as He did in A.D. 70 (Luke 21:24).

Preterists such as Gentry often talk about "interrupting passages" in accordance with the Old Testament, yet he misses an opportunity when it comes to
the phrase quoted from the Old Testament "they will gather together." Such a
regathering was predicted in the Old Testament:

> So it shall be when all of these things have come upon you, the
> blessing and the curse which I have set before you, and you call

them to mind in all nations where the LORD your God has banished you, and you return to the LORD your God and obey Him with all your heart and soul according to all that I command you today, you and your sons, then the LORD your God will restore you from captivity, and have compassion on you, and will gather you again from all the peoples where the LORD your God has scattered you. If your outcasts are at the ends of the earth, from there the LORD your God will gather you, and from there He will bring you back" (Deuteronomy 30:1-4).

He will lift up a standard for the nations and will assemble the banished ones of Israel, and will gather the dispersed of Judah from the four corners of the earth (Isaiah 11:12).

The only element missing from the Old Testament passages that our Lord expands upon in His discourse is that He will use angels to accomplish this task. In Deuteronomy 30:1-4 the Lord made an important covenantal promise to His people Israel, and in Matthew 24:31 He affirms that the same One who made the promise in Deuteronomy will fulfill His promise in history, even if it requires a miraculous solution.

Surely Gentry does not have a bias against our Lord's use of the supernatural and the angelic beings in this way in order to support the naturalistic explanations of preterism. We know that Elijah was translated to heaven without dying. Second Kings 2 records this interesting event with an emphasis upon the mode of Elijah's transportation to heaven, explaining that he was taken "by a whirlwind to heaven" (verse 1). In verse 11 the whirlwind is further described as "a chariot of fire and horses of fire." There's no doubt this was an appearance of the Shechinah glory of God, as Hebrews 1:7 says, "Of the angels He says, 'Who makes His angels winds, and His ministers a flame of fire.'" If an individual, Elijah, could be taken to heaven by angels (mere human messengers could not accomplish such a task), then why is it not possible for a group to be gathered and returned to the Land of Israel? This is exactly what we find in conjunction with an important event such as Christ's second advent.

Deuteronomy 30:1-4 also provides an answer for why our Lord used the term "elect" in Matthew 24:31 to characterize His people. It is because at this pivotal point in history, the Jews will fulfill the requirements of Deuteronomy 30:2 and will turn "to the LORD your God and obey Him with all your heart and soul according to all that I command you today." This was also our Lord's own requirement for the second coming in Matthew 23:39. The passage makes great sense with such a futuristic interpretation and is also in harmony with clear Old Testament teaching about Israel and that wonderful day when the

Jewish people will be converted to Messiah and receive in history their long-awaited blessing. Fruchtenbaum says,

> In the New Testament, the final regathering revealed by the Old Testament prophets is summarized in Matthew 24:31 and Mark 13:27. In this passage, Jesus stated that the angels will be involved in the final regathering and they will bring the Jews back into the land. As to locality, the emphasis is on the worldwide regathering. The two passages are a simple summary of all that the prophets had to say about the second facet of Israel's final restoration. The Matthew passage is based on Isaiah 27:12-13 and the Mark passage is based on Deuteronomy 30:4. Its purpose was to make clear that the worldwide regathering predicted by the prophets will be fulfilled only after the second coming.[140]

In this careful review of the Olivet Discourse, we have seen that not only does Christ's prophetic sermon not fit with the events that took place in the first century, but it must be fulfilled literally and it has yet to be fulfilled. Consequently, it must still be future to our own day.

Chapter 8

HOW PRETERISTS MISUSE HISTORY TO ADVANCE THEIR VIEW OF PROPHECY

Larry Spargimino

One doesn't have to read very many preterist writers to realize they rely heavily on specific ancient historians to support their view of a past fulfillment of certain Bible prophecies. In particular, they rely on Josephus's work *The Jewish War*. Any apparent similarities between its record of events that transpired around the time of the Roman invasion of Jerusalem in A.D. 70 and the statements found in the Olivet Discourse, and to a lesser degree in the book of Revelation, are cited as proof for a first-century fulfillment of these prophecies. Reformed theologian R. C. Sproul writes:

> Josephus's record of Jerusalem's fall indicates the radical fulfillment of Jesus' prophecy in the Olivet Discourse. As we have seen, preterists see in this event not only the destruction of the temple and its attending circumstances, but also the parousia of Christ in his judgment-coming. Radical preterists see in this event the fulfillment of all New Testament expectations for the return of Christ and for the last things of eschatology. But here we find sharp disagreement among preterists. Moderate preterists, such as those who hold to a postmillennial view of eschatology, insist that though the bulk of the Olivet Discourse was fulfilled in A.D. 70, there still remains a future coming or parousia of Christ....[1]

Preterist Kenneth L. Gentry believes that using Josephus in this manner is valid and was the procedure of many of the church fathers:

Nor does the preterist principle arise in these relatively recent centuries. In fact, a preteristic understanding of the Great Tribulation appears among early church writers. For instance, Origen (A.D. 185-254) and Eusebius (A.D. 260-340) clearly hold this position. When speaking about the Great Tribulation passage in Matthew 24, Eusebius points to "the infallible forecast of our Savior in which He prophetically expounded these very things" (*Eccl. Hist.* 3:7:1)—after citing many paragraphs "from the history written by Josephus" (*Eccl. Hist.* 3:5:4) to document the A.D. 70 fulfillment of this discourse.[2]

Gentry takes pains to demonstrate Josephus's credibility as a historian by referring to the ancient historian's accurate reporting of first-century events. For example, he cites the famines and earthquakes of Matthew 24:7 and the prophecy of Agabus in Acts 11:28, which took place during the reign of Claudius. "This seems to be the famine that strikes Jerusalem," writes Gentry. "According to Josephus, 'a famine did oppress them at that time, and many people died for want of what was necessary to procure food withal' (*Antiquities* 20:2:5). He later calls it 'the great famine' (*Antiquities* 20:5:2). He mentions others (*Antiquities* 20:2:6; 20:4:2; *Wars* 6:3:3)."[3]

One can maintain, of course, the relative accuracy of Josephus and other ancient historians without becoming a preterist. Belief in preterism requires the bold assumption that what Jesus described in the Olivet Discourse finds its fulfillment in the events recorded by Josephus. To accomplish this, preterism erroneously assumes that similarity equals identity.

THE PRETERIST USE OF HISTORICAL ACCOUNTS

Josephus and the Great Tribulation

Since the Olivet Discourse and the book of Revelation describe a time of "great tribulation" (Matthew 24:21; Revelation 7:14) preterists must search the writings of the historians to find a first-century event that could also be considered indicative of a time of great tribulation. The writings of Josephus provide such material. Preterist Gary DeMar quotes William Whiston, the English translator of the *Works of Josephus*, to show how Josephus described those "days of vengeance" (Luke 21:22). Whiston writes: "That these calamities of the Jews, who were our Savior's murderers, were to be the greatest that had ever been since the beginning of the world....Josephus is here a most authentic witness."[4]

Josephus is known to have exaggerated numbers. In *The Jewish War* (4:55) Josephus claims that Mt. Tabor was "thirty stadia" in height (18,200 feet) when in reality it rises only 1,920 feet.[5]

Maier observes that one of Josephus's weaknesses—one that he shares with almost all of the ancient historians—was his "propensity to exaggerate, particularly with numbers. Casualty lists after some of the battles are so impossibly high that even to note such overstatements would clutter too many pages in the text. The reader must also discount such hyperboles as, for example, the claim that so much blood was shed in Jerusalem during its conquest that streams of gore extinguished fires there."[6]

Is it possible that the exaggeration we see in Josephus's historical reporting was an attempt to glorify the military might of Rome in the face of the maniacal hostility of the zealots whom Josephus despised? To be sure, Josephus makes much mention of the valor of key Roman leaders. On one occasion Josephus cites Titus's bravery and how he seems to have been miraculously preserved in a most desperate situation: "Although he [Titus] wore neither helmet nor breastplate, none of the hail of arrows aimed at him touched his body, while he slashed the Jews on all sides, riding his horse over fallen enemies."[7]

Josephus records that at one point in the battle, the Roman forces were thrown into disarray. However, "Titus, still pressing on those who opposed him, ordered the legion back to resume their fortifications, while he and his band kept the enemy in check. Thus Caesar twice personally rescued the entire legion from jeopardy and enabled them to entrench their camp unmolested."[8] In a note Maier comments on Josephus calling Titus "Caesar": "Josephus uses 'Caesar' proleptically for Titus, since his father was Caesar at this time."[9]

Josephus also seems to glorify Rome when he voices the view that Jewish resistance was futile because God was with the Romans: "Titus, anxious to preserve the city from destruction, sent Josephus to negotiate with the Jews....Their forefathers, men far superior to them, had yielded because they knew God was on the Roman side, and it was now hopeless to fight famine and the imminent conquest."[10] Maier reports that Josephus won Titus's favor and was accepted into the inner circle of Roman officials, as evidenced in these words about the fall of Jerusalem:

> The scene was graphic: Josephus below the walls of Jerusalem, lecturing his countrymen in Aramaic from Roman lines and evoking curses from them but gratitude from Titus. Vespasian's son and successor both as commander and as Roman emperor became Josephus' closest friend in the Flavian dynasty. He would sail to Rome with Titus and greatly benefit from his patronage and advocacy there. Josephus even claimed that Titus "...was so anxious that my books should be the sole authority

from which the world should derive the facts of these affairs that he added his own signature to them and ordered that they be published" *(Vita,* 363).[11]

Josephus, Suetonius and the Beast

In Revelation 13, the New Testament Greek text speaks about the *therion*—the Beast. Gentry writes, "*Therion* is often used of wild, carnivorous animals employed in the cruel Roman arenas." He cites *The War of the Jews* (7:38) for substantiation, and then, after citing the Arndt-Gingrich *Lexicon,* adds that the term is also used figuratively of people who exhibit "a 'bestial' nature, *beast, monster.*"[12]

Further evidence from an early writer is brought forth to demonstrate Nero's animal-like ferocity. "His bestial cruelty," writes Gentry, "is evidenced in the writings of the Roman historian Suetonius (A.D. 70–160), who speaks of Nero's 'cruelty of disposition' evidencing itself at an early age....He also mentions that Nero was a sodomist, who is said to have castrated a boy named Sporus and married him. He enjoyed homosexual rape and torture...."[13] Gentry affirms that "Nero was one who was possessed of a 'bestial nature'" and cites evidence showing that Nero "killed his parents, brother, wife, aunt, and many others close to him....'[he] so prostituted his own chastity that after defiling almost every part of his body, he at last devised a kind of game, in which, covered with the skin of some wild animal, he was let loose from a cage and attacked the private parts of men and women, who were bound to stakes.'"[14]

It should be observed, however, that there is no indication in Revelation 13 that the beasts described in this passage expressed anything like these kinds of sexual deviations. Indeed, there is not a single clear reference to sexual perversion.

The reference to the "sword" (Revelation 13:10,14) is another item that, according to preterists, supposedly points a finger at Nero as being the Beast. Gentry writes:

> That Nero did in fact kill by the sword (and by many other means) is well-attested fact. Paul, for example, is said to have died under Nero by decapitation by means of the sword. Tertullian credits "Nero's cruel sword" as providing the martyr's blood as the seed for the church. Just as well attested is the fact of Nero's own death by sword. According to Suetonius, he "drove a dagger into his throat, aided by Epaphroditus, his private secretary." He not only killed others by the sword, but himself, as Revelation mentions.[15]

In reply, it is important to recognize that the sword was an instrument of death in the first century. The mention of the sword in Revelation 13 need not prove a first-century Antichrist or Neronic identification of the beast of Revelation 13. The apostle Paul speaks of the civil magistrate and writes that he "does not bear the sword for nothing; for it is a minister of God, an avenger who brings wrath on the one who practices evil" (Romans 13:4). On the basis of a preteristic hermeneutic, "sword" here cannot mean "gallows" or "gas chamber." Moreover, Revelation 13 does not match Gentry's statement, cited above, that Nero "not only killed others by the sword, but himself, as Revelation mentions." Revelation 13 says nothing about the beast killing both himself and others with the sword. Verse 10 states very simply that "if anyone kills with the sword, with the sword he must be killed." It doesn't say that he will be killed with his own sword or the sword of his servant.

Premillennial authors are often chided by preterists for their "newspaper exegesis" and dogmatic assertions that a certain individual—Hitler, Mussolini, Kissinger, Bill Clinton—*is* the Antichrist. Preterists, however, proceed in much the same fashion. "Clearly," concludes Gentry, "Nero fits the bill of the beast. He was a destructive 'beast' of the worst and most horrible sort— far worse than the paranoid Domitian."[16]

The way in which Gentry proceeds is a sterling example of first-century newspaper exegesis. He goes to great lengths to demonstrate how Nero is associated with a "serpent." "Not only is Satan himself called a 'serpent' in Revelation (Revelation 20:2), but his cohort, the Beast, is so designated. The sound of the number 666 even in English sounds hauntingly like a serpent's chilling hiss." Gentry proceeds to explain that the three Greek letters indicating 666 are significant because "phonetically their eerie sound is that of a serpent's hiss. What is more, the middle-number-letter even has the appearance of [a] writhing serpent."[17] It seems strange that while preterists ridicule the grammatical-historical approach that allegedly turns the book of Revelation into a massive hallucination, they themselves escape into flights of fancy and find significance in the shape of a Greek letter that allegedly looks like a snake.

To drive home his point, Gentry quotes Suetonius, who relates that when Nero was three years of age he was taking a nap and "would-be assassins were frightened away be [sic] a snake which darted out from under his pillow." Gentry also cites Tacitus and Dio, who wrote, "As time went on, the finding of a serpent's skin around Nero's neck while he was still a child caused the seers to declare that he would receive great power from an old man...."[18]

Gentry's approach shares the same weakness evidenced by sensationalistic prophecy writers who seek to identify a contemporary individual as the

Antichrist: There are simply too many coincidental correspondences that can be predicated of all evil rulers with charismatic personalities. Such people often have sexual problems. They are often masters of the spoken word and can sway multitudes with their oratory—and all of them seem to leave legends about their strange powers and mental prowess. In a fascinating book entitled *Hitler: Diagnosis of a Destructive Prophet*, Franz Redlich, professor emeritus of psychiatry at UCLA, brings to light the darkest recesses of the mind of one of the world's most evil leaders. Indeed, one could claim the man was demon-possessed and that he had many similarities to the Beast mentioned in Revelation. However, we gain some perspective when we consider these words from Redlich: "Hitler has been falsely credited for inventing an automatic rifle, new anti-tank guns, and super-tanks. In fact, he did not possess the technical knowledge to invent such military weapons."[19]

Josephus and the Demon Hordes of Revelation 9

Preterists, in defending their view of a past fulfillment of certain Bible prophecies, seek to relate chronological references in the book of Revelation to chronological references given by Josephus. Time periods—such as 5 months or 3 years—found in both Jewish history and in the text of Revelation are interpreted literally and matched. Other aspects of the prophetic text, however, are allegorized by preterists. For example, in Revelation 9 we read, "And they [the 'locusts'] were not permitted to kill anyone, but to torment for *five months*.... They have tails like scorpions, and stings; and in their tails is their power to hurt men for *five months*" (verses 5,10). Gentry comments: "Remarkably, we have record of a five-month episode in the Jewish War that serves well as fulfillment of such prophetic expectations."[20]

Gentry believes that a "good case can be made for the era of the final siege of Jerusalem by Titus, after his legions hemmed in the defenders of Jerusalem in A.D. 70." To make his point he quotes F. F. Bruce: "Titus began the siege of Jerusalem in April, 70. The defenders held out desperately for five months, but by the end of August the Temple area was occupied and the holy house burned down, and by the end of September all resistance in the city had come to an end." E. W. G. Masterman's article, printed in the *International Standard Bible Encyclopedia* in 1915, is also cited by Gentry: "...'the siege commenced on the 14th of Nisan, 70 A.D., and ended on the 8th of Elul, a total of 134 days.' This is a period, less just a few days, of virtually five months' duration. And surely it was the most grim and distressing period of Jerusalem's resistance...."[21]

While the five months time-span is taken literally, what about the locusts? They are said to come out of the smoke that issues forth from the bottomless pit (9:3). From a reading of the text of Revelation Gentry believes that this involves a demonic horde: "Although Josephus makes no express reference to demonical possession, that the period was a demon-enhanced era seems evident from the record of the case. Josephus does record the extreme barbarity and iniquity of Jerusalem during these final days. The cruelty especially of the seditious leaders of the revolt (the *sicarii,* or zealots) increased rapidly as the final pall of doom settled over the exhausted, terrified, starving, dying, and doomed masses...."[22]

Equating the final five months of the Roman siege of Jerusalem with what is described in Revelation 9 can be accomplished only by reading one's eschatology into the text of Revelation. Gentry admits that "Josephus makes no express reference to demonical possession," yet he believes that the historical record demonstrates that it was "a demon-enhanced era." Frankly, it depends on your definition of demon possession.

The New Testament is quite graphic regarding demonic activity—so graphic in fact that even the most hardnosed allegorizer laboring under a cloud of liberal presuppositions must wince upon giving anything other than a literal interpretation of the text. In the account of the Gadarene demoniac (Mark 5:1-20), the demoniac was so overwhelmingly energized by demonic entities that he had his dwelling among the tombs and possessed superhuman strength. Mark 9:14-29 relates the account of the demon-possessed son who was thrown into water and fire by the unclean spirit, and who convulsed and foamed at the mouth because of the spirit. The evidences of demon-possession in the New Testament, then, are open and evident. One does not need a magnifying glass, so to speak, to find them. Given this fact, how does Gentry know the last days of the Roman siege was a "demon-enhanced era"? He seeks to make his case by giving three quotations from Josephus's *Wars:*

> The madness of the seditious did also increase together with their famine, and both those miseries were every day inflamed more and more...(5:10:2). It is therefore impossible to go distinctly over every instance of these men's iniquity. I shall therefore speak my mind here at once briefly:—That neither did any other city ever suffer such miseries, nor did any age ever breed a generation more fruitful in wickedness than this was from the beginning of the world...(5:10:5).
>
> And here I cannot but speak my mind, and what the concern I am under dictates to me, and it is this:—I supposed that had the Romans made any longer delay in coming against those villains, the city would either have been swallowed up by the ground opening upon them, or been overflowed by water, or

else have been destroyed by such thunder as the country of Sodom perished by, for it had brought forth a generation of men much more atheistical than were those that suffered such punishments; for by their madness it was that all the people came to be destroyed (5:13:6).[23]

These references from Josephus are supposed to show how the final months of the siege of Jerusalem in A.D. 70 were a "demon-enhanced" period of time, and therefore the fulfillment of Revelation 9. It is doubtful, however, that these quotations from Josephus support the preterist position. We must ask: What is particularly demonic about "the madness of the seditious"? How is demonic activity indicated in the phrase that says this was "a generation more fruitful in wickedness" than any other "from the beginning of the world"? Is demonic activity the only explanation for such evil behavior? We must further ask: Are there any parallels between Josephus's account and the New Testament accounts of demonic possession that lead us to believe that Josephus was describing a particularly "demon-enhanced era"?

The account given in Revelation 9 is so obviously superhuman and goes far beyond the general miseries of war that it takes an extreme allegorizer to conclude that Revelation 9 is a description of the fall of Jerusalem. In Revelation 9:1 a star is seen falling from heaven and we are told literally that "the key of the bottomless pit was given to him." The "star" is a volitional being ("him," not "it") and the key opens the place in which the demonic spirits are incarcerated (Revelation 9:1-2,11; 11:7; 17:8; 20:1,3). The locusts that are released upon the earth are commanded not to harm the grass or trees, but only those men who have not been sealed by God (Revelation 9:4). How this can be equated with the Romans and the events of the final months of the siege of Jerusalem is beyond the comprehension of any reasonable expositor of Scripture. Moreover, the degree of detail given in Revelation 9:7-10 strongly suggests that all of this is to be regarded far more literally than preterists want to admit.

Gentry's attempt to see a flurry of demonic activity in the evils associated with the siege of Jerusalem and to connect that with Revelation 9 is not at all surprising. Believing that Revelation 20:1-6 indicates a "Gospel-age millennium," preterists must maintain a "realized eschatology" that doesn't leave much room for demonic activity subsequent to the resurrection of Christ. Jay E. Adams, a preterist for example, in writing on Christian counseling, makes an amazing statement about demonic activity:

Paul said that extensive demonic activity would characterize the last days of the Old Testament era (1 Timothy 4:1). It was during that period that John predicted that Satan's rage would be intensified because he had been cast down upon the earth (Revelation 12:13)....The eschatological timetable and the nature of the present millennial era [!] adequately account for the failure of the modern church to encounter demon possession as a common daily contemporary phenomenon....This, and the other considerations about the cessation of demonic activity mentioned above has important implications for Christian counselors....[24]

The observant reader will notice there is a total disparity between Josephus's account of the last five months of the siege and Revelation 9. It takes more than exegesis and historical study to claim that they describe the same events. What is recorded in Revelation 9—locusts that produce torment resembling the sting of a scorpion and whose leader is "Abbadon" (in Hebrew) and "Apollyon" (in Greek)—can only be explained in terms of chimeric evil forces. But what is recorded by Josephus can be attributed solely to the natural course of events that develop during a protracted siege. Josephus, for example, records an incident that occurred in August of A.D. 70. Mary of Bethezuba, who had fled to Jerusalem from Perea, "killed her infant son, roasted his body, and devoured half of it, hiding the remainder."[25] This was certainly an evil deed and, in common parlance, we might want to call it "demonic." But to say that it is the fulfillment of a prophecy describing an intense demonic infestation is without exegetical warrant. When people are starving, they do strange things.

The kind of behavior Josephus recorded during the first revolt also occurred at other periods in the history of Jerusalem. This city has been subjected to several periods of grievous suffering and woe. Eusebius's account of the Bar Kokhba revolt (A.D. 132–135) and the consequent barbarity of the Roman invasion under Hadrian are similar to the account of the siege of Jerusalem some 60 years earlier. Eusebius notes some of the same features recorded by Josephus:

> When the Jewish rebellion again grew formidable, Rufus, the Governor of Judea, received military assistance from the emperor and moved against their madness with no mercy. *He destroyed thousands of men, women, and children,* and—under the laws of war—confiscated their lands. The Jews at the time were led by a certain Bar-Kokhba, which means 'star,' a murderous bandit who, on the strength of his name, *claimed to be a luminary come down from heaven to shed light on those in misery,* as if they were slaves.

In Hadrian's eighteenth year, the war reached its climax at Betthera, a strongly fortified little town not far from Jerusalem. After a long siege, *hunger and thirst drove the rebels to destruction*, and the instigator of their madness paid the penalty he deserved[26] (emphasis added).

Clearly, there were other periods of woe for the city of Jerusalem that brought untold misery to the people. And false messiahs were not limited to the first century. In fact, Bar Kokhba fits the description given by Jesus (Matthew 24:5). Bar Kokhba's effectiveness as a dynamic pseudo-messiah is brought out by Randall Price:

This revolt was successful in liberating Jerusalem. In recognition of the victory, the leading sage of the time, Rabbi Akiva, heralded Shimon as the Messiah and renamed him *Bar Kokhba*.... Shimon seemed to fit this role, for he not only had managed to repulse the Roman garrisons but ruled as king of an independent Jerusalem for the next three years. He, too, was apparently convinced of his Messianic status, for he announced that his conquest of Jerusalem had begun the Messianic era and he began a new calendar system of counting the years from the date of his victory. However, the capstone of Messianic identity, as later the sage Maimonides would affirm (*Melochim* 11:4), was rebuilding the Temple.

According to the nineteenth-century Lithuanian rabbi, Samuel Shtrashun (R'shash), who claimed his source was the Roman historian of the period, Dio Cassius, Bar Kokhba rebuilt the Temple and resumed the sacrificial system....[27]

All wars have their share of barbarism and cruelty, whether ancient or modern. The attempt to make the First Jewish Revolt and the Roman efforts to suppress it a particularly grievous and demonically inspired event referenced in biblical prophecy as "the great tribulation" is totally unconvincing. In writing *The Rape of Nanking*, which documents an event often called "The Forgotten Holocaust of World War II," author Iris Chang recounts the gruesome deeds of the attackers:

The Japanese also waged ruthless experiments in biological warfare against the Chinese....entire cities were targeted for disease. We now know that Japanese aviators sprayed fleas carrying plague germs over metropolitan areas like Shanghai...and that flasks of disease-causing microbes—cholera, dysentery, typhoid, plague, anthrax, paratyphoid—were tossed into rivers, wells, reservoirs, and houses. The Japanese also mixed food with deadly germs to infect the Chinese civilian and military population. Cakes laced with typhoid were scattered around bivouac sites to entice hungry peasants; rolls syringed with typhoid and paratyphoid were given to thousands of Chinese prisoners of war before they were freed.[28]

All wars provide ample evidence of what happens when human depravity is unrestrained by civil government and the canons of decency and order. It is in such situations that the unseen forces of evil readily manipulate fallen human nature. Thus, with this in mind, there is no historical or biblical reason to believe that the events described by Josephus in his *Wars of the Jews* were specifically a fulfillment of Revelation 9. The fact that preterists have to arbitrarily switch between a literal understanding of the "five months" of Revelation 9:5,10 and an allegorized understanding of the demonic infestation mentioned in that same chapter provides sufficient warning that such an approach leaves much to be desired.

Josephus and the 42 Months of Revelation 11

Revelation chapter 11 mentions another significant time period—one that lasts 42 months. Predictably, preterists go to great lengths to show how Jerusalem was downtrodden by the Gentiles for precisely 42 months and thus Revelation 11:2 was literally fulfilled in the past. For example, Gentry writes, "If, indeed, the pre-A.D. 70 date is correct [for the composition of the book of Revelation], then this time-frame must somehow comport with the Jewish war."[29]

Gentry attempts to show how it comports "with the Jewish war" by referring to Josephus's account of Cestius Gallus, the Roman governor of Syria, who, in A.D. 66, had to retreat from Judea because the Jewish forces had gained the upper hand there. This discredited the moderates and leaders of the pro-peace party. The Jews, greatly emboldened by their successes, prepared to make war with the Romans. This led Nero to commission his seasoned general, Vespasian, to put down what had turned out to be rebellion against Imperial Rome and the *Pax Romana*. Gentry explains the timing of the events as follows: "Now from the time of this official imperial engagement in the Jewish War (early spring A.D. 67) until the time of the Temple's destruction and Jerusalem's fall (early September, A.D. 70) is a period right at the symbolic figure of 1260 days (or 42 months or 3½ years). Indeed, counting backward from early September, A.D. 70, we arrive 42 months earlier at early March—in the spring of 67!" Gentry understands this as the period referenced in Revelation 11:2 when "the holy city shall they tread under foot forty and two months."[30]

This deduction is highly subjective and lacks valid textual controls. Gentry finds 3½ years in the late 60s that he believes fits the chronology of Revelation 11:2, but, again, he finds what he needs to support his preterist understanding of the text. He makes the time frame "comport with the Jewish war," but the fact is there are other equally valid ways of looking at the historical data that make the period of Gentile domination in the first century *longer* than 3½ years and therefore not compatible with Revelation 11:2.

For example, Josephus, in his *Wars*, relates that in May of A.D. 66 Gessius Florus, whom Nero sent to Judea as successor to Albinus, provoked the Jews, who "extracted seventeen talents from the temple treasury, claiming government necessity." This so infuriated the people that they "rushed to the temple, shouting contempt for the procurator. Some passed around a basket begging coppers for the 'poor beggar Florus.'"[31]

Florus was incensed and wanted to retaliate by pillaging Jerusalem. He marched into the city and brought death and destruction. The following account from Josephus relates what took place in early June of A.D. 66:

> Florus stayed at the palace, and in the morning summoned the chief priests and leaders before him. He demanded that they hand over those who had insulted him, or face his vengeance. They asked his pardon for any who had spoken disrespectfully, blaming a few indiscreet youths who were impossible to identify. If he wanted to preserve the city and the peace of the nation, they said, he should forgive the few offenders on behalf of the many who were innocent.
>
> Florus became all the more incensed, and shouted to his soldiers to plunder the upper market and kill any they met. The troops not only sacked the market, but broke into houses and massacred the occupants. The city ran with blood, and 3,600 men, women, and children were cruelly slaughtered or crucified.[32]

Notice Josephus states that Jerusalem "ran with blood, and 3,600 men, women, and children were cruelly slaughtered or crucified." It is impossible to be honest with history and to ignore the significance of this assault by a Gentile oppressor. Should not this, too, be considered a part of Jerusalem's being downtrodden by the Romans? If not, can we give a good reason other than it doesn't fit with the 3½-year time span demanded by Revelation 11:2? Gentry seems to think that the start of the 3½-year period was Nero's commissioning of "a seasoned general, Vespasian," which marked "the official entry of Roman imperial forces into the campaign."[33] No doubt Florus was somewhat of a renegade procurator, and his slaughter of 3,600 men, women, and children may not have had imperial sanction. However, while Revelation 11:2 limits the period to 3½ years, it says nothing about the period beginning with some kind of "imperial sanction." Those who were slain by the Romans were murdered irrespective of whether or not it was by official decree. Indeed, the victims and their families would find it a moot point.

While Gentry takes the 3½-year period of Revelation 11:2 literally, what, we might wonder, does he do with the following verses, which speak of the two witnesses? Fire spews forth out of their mouths, they are raised from the dead, and they ascend into heaven—does Gentry understand these things literally?

On page 247 of Gentry's *Before Jerusalem Fell*, footnote 46 states: "Revelation 11:3 will not be treated. Almost certainly its time frame is concurrent with the one in 11:2 and the events are simultaneous." A glance at the Scripture Index in his book shows that the two witnesses receive scant attention in the 353-page volume.

This may be because the two witnesses present a problem for preterists. One preterist, J. Stewart Russell, for example, acknowledges that the passage represents "one of the most difficult problems contained in Scripture, and one that has exercised, we may even say baffled, the research and ingenuity of critics and commentators up to the present hour."[34] Some preterists believe that the two witnesses represent a group of divinely commissioned witnesses endowed with miraculous powers, or that they represent a line of prophets culminating with John the Baptist. Interestingly, despite his statement that the witnesses are problematic, Russell is dogmatic about their identification: "*We have no hesitation in naming St. James and St. Peter* as the persons indicated."[35]

This simply brings to light a major problem of preterism: Its fluid hermeneutic. The preterists' sudden and often unannounced switch from literalism to a spiritualized understanding of a biblical text can be justified only on the grounds that their system requires it. The proper approach to interpreting Scripture, however, is exegesis. Preterism, by contrast, practices "eisegesis" and reads its system into a text before it is willing to commit to an interpretation of a prophetic text.

Eusebius and Revelation 7

Revelation 7 speaks about the 144,000 and the sealing activity of the angel. Gentry feels sure that there is a connection here with Jesus' warning in Matthew 24:16: "Then those who are in Judea must flee to the mountains." While explaining Revelation 7:1-8, Gentry writes:

The fact that an angel intervenes in order to prevent their being destroyed along with the Land surely indicates the era prior to the devastation of Israel in A.D. 70....Were "the Land" already destroyed (as it was in August A.D. 70), such a promised protection would have been embarrassingly anachronistic.

In the Olivet Discourse Jesus spoke of the destruction of the very temple to which the disciples could physically point (Matthew 24:1-2). He warned His disciples that they should flee *Judea* (Matthew 24:16) when it was time for these things to come to pass (which occurred in A.D. 70). He added further that they should accept His promise that these horrendous events would be cut short (Matthew 24:22), and that he who endured to the end would be saved through it all (Matthew 24:13). He also clearly taught that all of these things would happen to "this generation" (Matthew 24:32). Indeed, this coming event was to be "the great tribulation" (Matthew 24:21)— the very tribulation in which John finds himself enmeshed even as he writes (Revelation 1:9; cp. 7:14).

The protection of Jewish Christians in Jerusalem is thus indicated in Revelation 7:1-7 via the symbolism of sealing. This refers to the providential protection of those Christians of Jewish lineage who were "in the land."[36]

Gentry argues that Revelation 7 speaks about a miraculous preservation of God's people. If the identification of Revelation 7 with the events of A.D. 70 is to stand, Gentry must find an example of God's people being miraculously preserved during the siege of Jerusalem. He finds "proof" of such miraculous preservation in "an extremely interesting and famous piece of history" recorded by the church historian Eusebius (260–340):

> But the people of the church in Jerusalem *had been commanded by a revelation,* vouchsafed *to approved men there* before the war, to leave the city and to dwell in a certain town of Perea called Pella. And when those that believed in Christ had come thither from Jerusalem, then, as if the royal city of the Jews and the whole land of Judea were entirely destitute of holy men, the judgment of God at length overtook those who had committed such outrages against Christ and his apostles, and totally destroyed that generation of impious men[37] (emphasis added).

Do Revelation 7:1-4 and this "extremely interesting and famous piece of history" really have valid parallels, or are there just surface similarities? In Revelation 7:1-4, the wind is held back from harming the earth until the sealing of the 144,000 is accomplished. In the statement from Eusebius, however, the people of the Jerusalem church are "commanded" by some kind of a "revelation" to leave the city. By contrast, Revelation 7 says nothing about any revelation commanding the saints to leave. The miracle of protection is not in a miraculous command, or in a miraculous flight out of the city, but in a divine suspension of judgment *until* the sealing is accomplished. Moreover, while Eusebius's account speaks about a special warning given to the inhabitants of the *city* of Jerusalem and deliverance is provided for them, Revelation 7 speaks about something that is far more extensive: "Do not harm *the earth or the sea or the trees.*" A fair reading of both Eusebius and Revelation 7 clearly shows they are not describing the same event.

Neither Eusebius nor Scripture verifies a first-century fulfillment of Revelation 7. To assert that "the protection of Jewish Christians in Jerusalem is thus indicated in Revelation 7:1-7" and that the passage refers "to the providential protection of those Christians of Jewish lineage who were 'in the land'"[38] at the time of Titus's invasion is without sound warrant.

The Preterist Misinterpretation of Scripture

What Preterists Say About the Hailstones

Some statements from preterists can easily give the impression they have an authority that is higher than that of Scripture. Gentry writes about the 100-pound hailstones referenced in Revelation 16:21 and makes a categorical statement about the impossibility of such large hailstones: "It is quite impossible that such gargantuan hailstones can be accounted for under the most aggravated of meteorological conditions." Rather than accepting Scripture at face value he turns to Josephus and offers what he believes is a better understanding of the passage: "Josephus records for us an event so visually and effectually similar that what he records must be the fulfillment of the Revelational prophecy."[39] It "*must be* the fulfillment of the Revelational prophecy"? He explains that Josephus relates how the Roman Tenth Legion used 100-pound white boulders in their catapults, and this, says Gentry, is really the fulfillment of Revelation 16:21.

There are several problems with Gentry's position. First, as Gordon Franz has observed, stones thrown in a catapult are surface-to-surface missiles, while hailstones are air-to-surface missiles.[40] And second, Scripture itself provides a better explanation.

Dr. Gentry believes, at least in theory, that, "Scripture interprets Scripture."[41] Yet when it comes to dealing with the large hailstones, Dr. Gentry prefers Josephus to God's Word. This is true in spite of the fact that Scripture has a fair amount to say about this subject. However, when one takes into account what Scripture actually says on this matter, it does not support preterism. This is likely the reason Josephus is to be preferred by Gentry and other preterists.

It is interesting to note that Gentry selectively quotes Josephus and does not include Josephus's comment that when the Romans left their stones white, the Jews saw them coming and were able to dodge them. It was only after the Romans blackened the stones that they were able to inflict damage on the Jews.[42] Thus, in the later and effective use of the stones by the Romans, they did not actually resemble white hailstones, as Gentry contends. Is this what Gentry means when he says the prophecies of Revelation were fulfilled "in almost literal fashion in the Jewish War"? Hardly! When biblical prophecy is fulfilled, it is always clearly and evidently fulfilled.

What Scripture Says About Hailstones

What does the Bible have to say about the Lord fighting with hailstones? First, the oldest book in the canon of Scripture says, "Have you entered the storehouses of the snow, or have you seen the storehouses of the hail, which I have reserved for the time of distress, for the day of war and battle?" (Job 38:22-23). This passage clearly teaches that God has a storehouse of hail, specifically for "the time of distress," and "for the day of war and battle." Is this just metaphor or "almost literal" language?

When you look at biblical accounts of occasions on which God used hail against Israel's enemies, they start to add up. God used hail against Egypt during the seventh plague (Exodus 9:22-26). In this instance it was clearly literal hail and not just a metaphor for bad weather. This plague was not a result of human agency. Only God was involved in fighting for Israel against Egypt. And there are additional Old Testament passages that refer to God's use of hail in a battle context (Psalm 18:12-13; 78:47-48; 105:32; 148:8; Isaiah 28:17; 30:30; 32:19; Ezekiel 13:11-13; 38:22).

Meteorologist and Bible teacher Charles Clough says, "The proper way to understand prophecies of catastrophes is to follow the apostle Peter's approach and look at the true record of God's past historical judgments (2 Pet. 3:5-7)."[43] The most significant passage for our study is the hailstone incident in Joshua 10:11: "As they fled from before Israel, while they were at the descent of Beth-horon, the LORD threw large stones from heaven on them as far as Azekah, and they died; there were more who died from the hailstones than those whom the sons of Israel killed with the sword." This is a clear example of the implementation of the purpose stated in Job—that the Lord has a storehouse of hail ready for "the time of distress" and "for the day of war and battle." In Joshua 10, God fights with divinely directed hailstones during a time of distress and on the day of war and battle on behalf of Israel. John Calvin notes:

> In the second slaughter the hand of God appeared more clearly, when the enemy were destroyed by hail. And it is distinctly stated that more were destroyed by hail than were slain by the sword, that there might be no doubt of the victory having been obtained from heaven. Hence again it is gathered that this was not common hail, such as is wont to fall during storms. For, in the first place, more would have been wounded or scattered and dispersed than suddenly destroyed; and secondly, had not God darted it directly, part would have fallen on the heads of the Israelites. Now, when the one army is attacked separately, and the other, kept free from injury, comes forward as it were to join auxiliary troops, it becomes perfectly clear that God is fighting from heaven. To the same effect it is said that God threw down great stones of hail from heaven: for the meaning is that they fell with extraordinary force, and were far above the ordinary size.[44]

A point of similarity between Joshua 10:11 and Revelation 16:21 is found in the fact that both passages describe the hailstones as large in size. They are said to be "large" in Joshua and "huge" in Revelation. Clearly Joshua 10:11 describes a supernatural event, and I believe that Revelation 8:7 and 16:21 will prove to also be direct miracles from the hand of God.

Not only do preterists such as Gentry mistakenly interpret future prophecies to be past events, they also interpret supernatural events to be the result of natural causes. When it comes to interpreting the details of Revelation, preterists, more often than not, pull out the equivalence of their first-century newspapers—Josephus—and start reading the headlines to find a correspondence which they say has already fulfilled certain Bible passages. Inevitably their interpretations have naturalistic explanations that do not require God to do anything. When it comes to A.D. 70, they say that the Romans fulfilled what the Bible says God would do.

For example, the only similarity between Revelation 16:21 and an event recorded by Josephus in his *Wars of the Jews* is the phrase "one talent." Yet preterists latch onto that similarity in spite of the fact that there is no contextual correspondence between Josephus and the other words and phrases in Revelation 16:21. E. W. Bullinger notes that "Josephus says that stones of a talent's weight were thrown by the Romans against Jerusalem (*Wars* iii. vii. 9). Surely God can send from heaven what man could send on earth."[45] In fact, earlier in Revelation, God used hail and fire as a judgment upon mankind: "The first [trumpet] sounded, and there came hail and fire, mixed with blood, and they were thrown to the earth; and a third of the earth was burned up, and a third of the trees were burned up, and all the green grass was burned up" (Revelation 8:7). Did Josephus record an event that corresponds to this passage?

Both Revelation 8:7 and 16:21 describe real, supernatural events, as both correspond to the regional plague of hail in Exodus 9:22-26. As Bullinger reasons, "The plague of hail in Egypt was real (Exodus ix. 18-21). So is this. Why not?"[46] It's important to note that Revelation 16:21 describes the hailstones as a "plague," just like in Exodus. How could the use of catapults by the Romans in A.D. 70 be viewed as a plague from God? Every plague that God sends, either in Exodus or Revelation, is something that God does Himself. Not one plague in either Exodus or Revelation is said to be mediated through human agency. All are direct miracles wrought by God Himself. The preterists' naturalistic interpretation shifts the glory from God to man, which is not good for anyone to do!

Gentry's naturalism is evident when he says, "It is quite impossible that such gargantuan hailstones can be accounted for under the most aggravated of meteorological conditions."[47] Quite right! These are specially prepared hailstones from the heavenly storehouse in heaven, as Job 38:22-23 tells us. Scientist Dr. Henry Morris says of Revelation 16:21, "This hail will not be the usual form of hail—that is, ice produced by violent updrafts in atmospheric storm cells."[48] If anyone has a problem with such a view, then they will likely have problems with other miraculous events described in the Bible, both past and future.

Gentry's naturalistic and thus symbolic interpretation of Revelation 16:21 is questionable for yet another reason. Revelation 16:21 states that men will blaspheme God "because of the plague of the hail." Dr. Robert Thomas notes, "It is doubtful that men would blaspheme God because of something symbolic only. The Egyptian plague of hail was literal, so this one must be too."[49] Thus, preterists fail in their interpretation of Revelation 16:21 not only in relation to one aspect of the passage, but the entire verse.

Revelation 16:21 is just one example of passages that preterists explain using a naturalistic interpretative approach whereas futurists give a supernatural explanation. If we let Scripture interpret Scripture, we must conclude with Dr. Thomas that "the Egyptian plague of hail was literal, so this one must be too."[50] What's more, the fact that the Lord threw down great hailstones from heaven and hit only the Amorites in the days of Joshua provides a precedent that He does such things. That the great hailstones hit only the enemy and not the Israelites is proof of God's divine intervention. It would also be the envy of modern-day smart weapons technology.

Charles Clough concludes, "The same fire, smoke, hail, thunder, plague, and earthquake of the Old Testament judgments once again appear in Revelation 6-18. These terms are not exaggerations and metaphors. They point to a final culmination in God's program of separating good from evil throughout all creation. God's past judgments thus model His future judgments."[51]

Even if we did not have the Old Testament precedents of Job, the Exodus, Joshua, and others, I believe Revelation 16:21 is clear enough for us to understand it as a literal, future, supernatural event. Given the Old Testament support, it is mere sophistry to attempt any other interpretation.

THE PRETERIST APPROACH TO PROPHECY

No doubt many preterists have a high view of Scripture and seek to honor the biblical teachings regarding the sovereignty of God and other key doctrines, but when it comes to prophecy, they seem to be controlled by a spirit of unbelief. Because of their first-century template for interpreting Bible prophecy, preterists come close to investing certain historians with canonic authority. Gary DeMar, for example, cites Josephus, who recounts how the Idumeans and the Zealots entered Jerusalem and murdered 8,000 people in their attempt to assassinate the chief priest Ananus. He had invoked their ire because he tried to persuade the people to rise up against the Zealots. Along with Ananus, many other priests were murdered and their bodies were mocked by those who stood on them. DeMar quotes Josephus, who adds a personal "insight": "I should not mistake if I said that the death of Ananus was the beginning of the destruction of the city, and that from this very day may be dated the overthrow of her wall, and the ruin of her affairs, whereon they saw their high priest, and the procurer of their preservation, slain in the midst of the people." DeMar comments, "If Josephus believed that the destruction of the city was due to the execution of Ananus the high priest, is it not probable that God would take his 'vengeance' (Luke 21:22) on the city because of the death of His Son—the Greater High Priest—Jesus (Hebrews 5:6,10; 6:20; 7:11,17)?"[52]

Notice DeMar's reasoning: If Josephus *believed something* then it is "probable" that God would take His "vengeance." It would be better, however, to leave Josephus's opinion out of the explanation, for there are plenty of scriptures that show that Jerusalem was being judged for her sins (e.g., Matthew 23:31-37)—unless, of course, one deems that Josephus's opinion has some theological weight. One must ask: Why does DeMar reference Josephus? Does he believe that what Josephus believes gives some added credibility to his preterist assumptions? Should Josephus's writings become the sixty-seventh book of the Bible?

In conclusion, this study demonstrates that preterists seek to bolster their views by appealing to ancient historians, especially Josephus. However, rather than supporting their views, the misapplication of both the historical accounts of historians and the prophetic texts of Scripture show that preterism fails to live up to its claims of being historically and biblically sound.

Chapter 9

WAS "BABYLON" DESTROYED WHEN JERUSALEM FELL IN A.D. 70?

GORDON FRANZ

In the ongoing debate over systems of Bible prophecy, one of the points on which preterists differ from futurists is the identification of Babylon in Revelation 17 and 18.[1] Preterists propose that Babylon was Jerusalem, and they see the fulfillment of Revelation 17–18 in the destruction of the city in A.D. 70. This chapter will address two issues: Was "Babylon" destroyed when Jerusalem fell in A.D. 70? And, are the "fulfillments" of the preterist view historically accurate?

Dr. Stanley Toussaint gave a paper at the 1995 Pre-Trib Study Group meeting entitled "A Critique of the Preterist View of the Olivet Discourse." In the question-and-answer session that followed, someone asked if there was a good book that refuted the preterist position from a historical perspective. The questioner observed that preterists were "historical revisionists" who took history and made it fit their viewpoint. When no book was mentioned, he went on to challenge one of the "history buffs [in the group] to dig into it." Having worked on archaeological excavations in Jerusalem, and given my familiarity with the history of the First Jewish Revolt, I accepted the challenge. This chapter is part of the fruit of that challenge.

THE PRETERIST VIEW OF REVELATION

One of the key tenets of the preterist position is that the Babylon mentioned in the book of Revelation is Jerusalem of A.D. 70. They say that the judgment that was poured out on this Babylon was fulfilled with the destruction of the city of Jerusalem in A.D. 70. Kenneth Gentry summarizes the evidence for Jerusalem as being the harlot Babylon in a footnote in his book *Before Jerusalem Fell:*

> (1) Both are called "the great city" (Revelation 14:8; 11:8). (2) The Harlot is filled with the blood of the saints (cp. Revelation 16:6; 17:6; 18:21,24; with Matt. 23:34-38; Luke 13:33; Acts 7:51-52). (3) Jerusalem had previously been called by pagan names quite compatible with the designation "Babylon" (cp. Revelation 14:8 and 17:5 with 11:8). (4) Rome could not fornicate against God, for only Jerusalem was God's wife (Revelation 17:2-5, cp. Isa. 1:20; Jer. 31:31). (5) There is an obvious contrast between the Harlot and the chaste bride (cp. Revelation 17:2-5 with Revelation 21:1ff) that suggests a contrast with the Jerusalem below and the Jerusalem above (Revelation 21:2; cp. Gal. 4:24ff.; Heb. 12:18ff.). The fact that the Harlot is seated on the seven-headed Beast (obviously representative of Rome) indicates not identity with Rome, but alliance with Rome against Christianity (cp. Matt. 23:37ff.; John 19:6-16; Acts 17:7).[2]

In the preface of the new edition of his book, Gentry expands on these ideas.[3] There are also other studies that elaborate on this subject.[4]

THE DATING OF REVELATION

Another key tenet of preterism is dating the book of Revelation to before A.D. 70. The strongest defense for the pre-A.D. 70 date in recent years has come from Kenneth Gentry in his book *Before Jerusalem Fell: Dating the Book of Revelation* (1998, rev. ed.). This book is a reworking of his doctoral dissertation from Whitefield Theological Seminary in Lakeland, Florida.

It is not the purpose of this chapter to discuss the date of the book of Revelation. That has already been done in the previous chapter. I will, however, make a few observations about the early date view. I myelf believe the best evidence points to a late date writing of the book during the reign of Emperor Domitian (about A.D. 95).[5]

The Acts of John

The apocryphal book *The Acts of John* clearly states that John wrote the book of Revelation on Patmos during Domitian's reign. Gentry acknowledges a Domitianic exile for John, but suggests that "the *rationale* for the exile is suggestive of a prior publication of Revelation. It could be that John was banished twice, once under Nero and later under Domitian (which would explain the two traditions of a Neronic and Domitianic exile)."[6] He then gives selective quotes from *The Acts of John* in an attempt to show that Revelation was written earlier. Let's look at the account: "And the fame of the teaching of John was spread abroad in Rome; and it came to the ears of Domitian that there was a certain Hebrew in Ephesus, John by name, who spread a report about the seat of empire of the Romans, saying that it would quickly be rooted out, and that the kingdom of the Romans would be given over to another."

It should be noted that there is no reference to the book of Revelation in this passage. The sayings could well have been from the oral teachings of John that worked their way to Rome. After all, Rome was at the other end of the Ephesus–Rome maritime trade route. The teachings of John would have been based on the Old Testament prophets and the parables and discourses of the Lord Jesus. Interestingly, Gentry left out a very important part of the passage. The text just cited goes on to say that when John arrived in Rome, Domitian asked him about his teachings:

> Art thou John who said that my kingdom would speedily be uprooted, and that another king, Jesus, was going to reign instead of me? And John answered and said to him: Thou also shalt reign for many years given thee by God, and after thee very many others; and when the times of the things upon earth has been fulfilled, out of heaven shall come a King, eternal, true, Judge of living and dead, to whom every nation and tribe shall confess, through whom every earthly power and dominion shall be brought to nothing, and every mouth speaking great things shall be shut. This is the mighty Lord and King of everything that hath breath and flesh, the Word and Son of the living One, who is Jesus Christ.

It is obvious why Gentry does not quote this portion of the text—it sounds pretty futuristic!

After John demonstrated his power by drinking deadly poison (cf. Mark 16:18), and raising a couple of people from the dead, Domitian banished him to an island. The last part of Gentry's quote is, "And Domitian, astonished at all the wonders, sent him away to an island, appointing for him a set time. And straightway John sailed to Patmos...." Unfortunately for Gentry, the sentence does not end there. It goes on to say, "where also he was deemed worthy to see the revelation of the end."[7] *The Acts of John* clearly supports the late date for the writing of Revelation and a futuristic view of prophecy. Yet Gentry is selective with his quotes in an effort to prove his perspective.

The Seven Stars on the Coins of the Emperors

In relation to the matter of dating the book of Revelation, David Chilton comments on the phrase, "In His right hand He held seven stars," which appears in Revelation 1:16:

> The symbolic use of seven stars was quite well known in the first century, for the seven stars appeared regularly on the Emperor's coins as a symbol of his supreme political sovereignty. At least some early readers of Revelation must have gasped in amazement at St. John's audacity in stating that the seven stars were in *Christ's* hand. The Roman emperors had appropriated to themselves a symbol of dominion that the Bible reserves for God alone—and, St. John is saying, Jesus Christ has come to take it back. The seven stars, and with them all things in creation, belong to Him. Dominion resides in the right hand of the Lord Jesus Christ.[8]

Chilton is generally very good about documenting his statements with reliable sources; most serious preterist works abound with footnotes. This is very helpful for readers who want to follow up on the writer's statements. However, this statement is not footnoted at all.

In response to Chilton, a few points should be clarified. First, the coins of emperors along with seven stars on them did not appear regularly until the end of the first century and beginning of the second century A.D. Second, the stars on coins generally symbolize the "idea of divinity or of mortals who have joined the stars, as it were, and become gods."[9] The idea of sovereignty comes from a coin featuring Emperor Domitian's deceased and deified son sitting on a globe (representative of the earth) and reaching for seven stars.[10] Third, Chilton also has a problem with the dating of the seven-star coins. The first seven-star coins minted during the Imperial period were struck on the island of Crete during the reigns of Caligula (A.D. 37–41), Claudius (A.D. 41–54), and Nero (A.D. 54–68).[11] A monumental work on Roman provincial coins states the seven stars "represent the Septentriones, the Great Bear; this constellation had a particular connection with Crete as the nurses of Zeus, Helice and Kynosoura, were placed in the heavens as the Great and Little Bear. Therefore the seven stars linked with the cult image of Augustus brought him into a close relationship with Zeus Cretagenes."[12] These coins, however, were for local circulation and were not widely circulated off the island of Crete.[13] It is doubtful most people in the Roman world would have been aware of them.

A second coin was struck in Spain and Gaul during the Civil War (A.D. 68–70). According to Chilton's dating system, this was after the book of Revelation was written. This denarii coin, of the "Divvs Augustus" type, had a crescent and seven stars on the reverse side with Augustus on the obverse side.[14] It was observed by Sutherland that "the stars and crescent of no. 95…are borrowed from Republican times."[15] The meaning of the seven stars in the Republican period is unclear, but at that time, there were seven known planets, and some have suggested that the stars represented the planets and the crescent represents the moon.

Most of the seven-star coins minted in that era come from the end of the first century A.D. The coin featuring Domitian's son sitting on a globe with his hand stretched out to the seven stars is unique.[16] Others coins with seven stars and a crescent were struck during the reign of Trajan[17] as well as Hadrian in the year A.D. 119.[18] Mattingly and Sydenham, two numismatic experts, interpret the seven stars and crescent as "natural symbols of immortality in an age which sought immortality in the stars. It is probably the memory of Trajan that is here honoured. The seven stars of the second type may be purely conventional—a representation of the 'Septenttiones,' the seven stars of the Great Bear."[19] The evidence connected with the seven-star coins, then, better fits a late date for the book of Revelation, not an early date.

Historical Fulfillment?

Under the subtitle "The Ease of Application to the Jewish Wars," Gentry notes that "much of Revelation's vivid imagery lends itself admirably to the catastrophic events of the Jewish War."[20] He ends the paragraph with the statement, "But, with a number of the distinctive elements, there are simply too many converging lines of evidence pointing to the Jewish Wars to allow for this argument's hasty *a priori* dismissal."[21] Is this really the case, or can we dismiss the "fulfillments" as historically inaccurate?

Before we look at the "historical fulfillments" we should consider Josephus and his writings. First, Josephus was a witness to the events surrounding the fall of Jerusalem. He was born into a priestly family on his father's side and the royal Hasmonean family on his mother's side.[22] Raised in the city of Jerusalem, he knew the geography and buildings of the city well. After he pulled his "Benedict Arnold" act at Yotapata in Galilee, he became a historian for the Flavian family, which included the soon-to-be emperor Vespasian and his son, Titus. Josephus was also an eyewitness to the fall of Jerusalem with a very good vantage point, sitting in the tent of Titus Caesar! One should also acknowledge his bias. Josephus was a beneficiary of the Flavian family (Emperor Vespasian and his sons Titus and Domitian), he also received Roman citizenship from Vespasian as well as compensation for his land in Jerusalem by Titus. He had a privileged position in Rome.[23]

Second, the references to the book, chapter, section, paragraphs, and verses of Josephus's works can sometimes be confusing. It is my observation that most preterists (and most evangelicals, for that matter) use the William Whiston edition of *The Life and Works of Flavius Josephus*. Within the scholarly community, however, most use the ten-volume Greek and English Loeb Classical Library edition. The different numbering systems in the two editions can be confusing. Fortunately there is a helpful tool for cross-referencing these works. In 1984, H. Douglas Buckwalter and Mary Keil Shoaff compiled a *Guide to the Reference Systems for the Works of Flavius Josephus* for the Department of Theological Studies at the Wheaton Graduate School. It was recently published in the ETS (Evangelical Theological Society) monograph series.[24] In this chapter, I will use the Loeb Classical Library reference numbers and translation. Let's look now at some examples of preterist arguments that draw their support from Josephus, and see whether they hold up to careful scrutiny.

The Third Seal (Revelation 6:5,6)

The judgments in the book of Revelation begin with the seal judgments, of which there are seven. The third seal judgment involves a man riding a black horse and holding a pair of scales in his hands. A voice says, "A quart of wheat for a denarius, and three quarts of barley for a denarius; and do not damage the oil and the wine." The preterists see this as the famine that resulted from the siege of Jerusalem prior to its destruction. Several passages from Josephus are quoted in attempt to prove their point.[25] This judgment does describe a famine, but what causes the famine? The answer lies in the phrase "do not harm the oil and wine." J. M. Ford, in the Anchor Bible commentary on Revelation, attributes the warning to an order from Titus not to disturb the olive groves and vineyards.[26] Ford is actually quoting a French book but gives no primary source for the statement. Gentry suggests that the phrase "may even be that the reference to 'the oil and the wine' finds expression in the adulteration of the sacred oil and wine by the Jews themselves; *Wars* 5:13:6."[27]

The proper understanding of the phrase "do not damage the oil and the wine" is found in an event recorded in 1 Samuel 12. The context of 1 Samuel 12 is Israel's call for a king "like the other nations" and the rejection of the Lord as King. "Is not the wheat harvest today? I [Samuel] will call to the LORD, that He may send thunder and rain. Then you will know and see that your wickedness is great which you have done in the sight of the LORD by asking for yourselves a king" (12:17). The people cried out, "Pray for your servants to the LORD your God, so that we may not die…" (12:19). Samuel was threatening to call upon the Lord to bring thunder and rain as punishment. Why? The people were evil in their rejection of the Lord as their king. Heavy rains at the time of harvest would destroy all the wheat, thereby bringing a famine.

The people were not pleading to be saved from death from the rain, but for the wheat to be preserved from it. As Nogah Hareuveni of Neot Kedumim, the Biblical Gardens in Israel, has pointed out:

> The ripe, heavy-eared wheat can suffer from a downpour not only through physical damage from the force of the wind-driven rain, but also by rotting from the sudden moisture combined with the high temperatures that prevail in Israel by *Shavuot* (in late May-early June). This interpretation explains why the Israelites cried out to Samuel to "pray...to save us from death" (I Sam. 12:19)—from death by starvation that would follow the destruction of the grain crop.[28]

In Scripture, we see that mildew is one of the results of disobedience to the Word of God (Deuteronomy 28:22; 1 Kings 8:28; 2 Chronicles 6:28; Amos 4:9; Haggai 2:17).[29]

During a trip to Israel in June 1992 I witnessed one of these devastating rainstorms. For two days Israel was hit with heavy rains during the wheat harvest, and the wheat was devastated by mildew. Ironically, it was right before the national elections, when people were crying out "Itzhaq, melek Yisrael! Itzhaq, melek Yisrael!" (Itzhaq, king of Israel) at their election rallies!

The third seal judgment is an untimely rainstorm during the wheat harvest that destroys a great portion of the crop in Israel and the rest of the Mediterranean world. The demand for wheat, plus the shortage in supply, will lead to higher prices for all. The olive trees and grapevines, "the oil and the wine," will not be affected by this rainstorm because they will have already been pollinated. In fact, the water might even help them, thus giving oil and wine for all, rich and poor alike.[30]

The First Trumpet (Revelation 8:7)

After the seven seal judgments come the seven trumpet judgments. The first trumpet judgment appears in Revelation 8:7: "The first [angel] sounded and there came hail and fire, mixed with blood, and they were thrown to the earth; and a third of the earth was burned up, and a third of the trees were burned up, and all the green grass was burned up.

Chilton interprets this passage as follows:

> St. John sees hail and fire, mixed with blood, and they were thrown onto the Land. The blood of the slain witnesses [I assume the martyrs of the fifth seal, Revelation 6:9-11] is mixed with the fire from the altar, bringing wrath down upon the persecutors. The result of the curse...is the burning of a third of the

Land and a third of the trees, and all the green grass (i.e., all the grass on a third of the Land; cf. 9:4). If the trees and grass represent the elect remnant (as they seem to in 7:3 and 9:4), this indicates that they are not exempt from physical suffering and death as God's wrath is visited upon the wicked.[31]

A couple of observations should be made at this point. First, Chilton does not indicate if the hail is literal or not. If it is not, he neglects to identify what it represents. Later in his book he identifies the hail as something other than hailstones.[32] Second, Chilton makes a qualifying statement, "if the trees and grass represents the elect remnant," and then refers to two passages elsewhere in the book of Revelation. Do the trees and grass represent the elect remnant? Revelation 7:3 makes a distinction between the earth, sea, and trees and the "bond-servants of our God." The apostle John uses the word "and" to distinguish the trees from the servants. In Revelation 9:4 the demonic "locusts" were commanded not to harm the grass and trees but "only the men who do not have the seal of God on their foreheads." In an actual plague of locusts, the locusts would eat vegetation only (i.e., grass or leaves of trees), and not attack human beings. The demonic "locusts," however, were not to attack vegetation, but human beings, and in particular, those who did not have the seal of God. In either case, it's clear that the grass and trees do not represent the elect remnant.

Chilton tries to find a literal fulfillment of Revelation 8:7 during the siege of Jerusalem in A.D. 70. He says, "Literally, the vegetation of Judea, and especially of Jerusalem, would be destroyed in the Roman scorched-earth methods of warfare."[33] He then quotes a passage from *Wars* 6:6-8 describing the desolation of Jerusalem and the surrounding countryside caused by the war. What Chilton does not say is why the Romans cut down the trees. The passage before the one quoted by Chilton says, "The Romans, meanwhile, though sorely harassed in the collection of timbers, had completed their earthworks in one and twenty days, having, already stated, cleared the whole district around the town to a distance of ninety furlongs."[34] Elsewhere, Josephus says "the trees were felled and the suburbs rapidly stripped; but while the timber was being collected for the earthworks and the whole army busily engaged in the work, the Jews on their side were not inactive."[35] Later on, Josephus writes that "timber was now procured with difficulty [for the erection of earthworks]; for, all the trees round the city having been felled for the previous works, the troops had to collect fresh material from a distance of ninety furlongs."[36] The Romans cut down the wood in order to build earthworks for the siege of Jerusalem. They didn't burn as part of a "scorched earth" policy.

The actual explanation for the cutting of the trees stands in marked contrast with the description of the first trumpet judgment: "a third of the trees were *burned up*, and all the green grass was *burned up*" as a result of hail and fire, mixed with blood, thrown to earth (apparently from heaven). The first trumpet judgment, then, was not fulfilled literally in A.D. 70.

The Second Trumpet (Revelation 8:8-9)

In the second trumpet judgment, John sees a great mountain burning with fire thrown into the sea and a third of the sea became blood and a third of the sea creatures died. Also, a third of the ships were destroyed.

Chilton identifies the mountain as the nation of Israel because it is "the mountain of God's inheritance (Ex. 15:17)."[37] A careful reading of Exodus 15:17 shows that Israel is separate from the mountain: "You [the LORD] will bring them [Your people = Israel, of verse 16] and plant them in the mountain of Your inheritance, the place, O LORD, which You have made for Your dwelling, the sanctuary, O LORD, which Your hands have established." The mountain, in the context, is Mount Zion in Jerusalem, where God would eventually dwell (Psalm 48).

Chilton does not interpret the sea becoming blood or the sea creatures dying, or the ships being destroyed. It would be better to see this "burning mountain" as a volcano somewhere in the Mediterranean Sea during the Tribulation period. The descriptions that follow—the sea turning to blood, sea creatures dying, and the ships destroyed—are phenomena known to be connected with volcanic activity.[38]

The Sixth Trumpet (Revelation 9:13-21)

The sixth trumpet judgment begins with the sixth angel releasing four angels who are bound at the Euphrates River. Their job is to kill one third of mankind. The army lead by the angels will have "myriads of myriads" horsemen. The NASB and NKJV give the number as "two hundred million" horsemen. Chilton argues that the number "simply means *many thousands*, and indicates a vast host that is to be thought of in connection with the Lord's angelic army of thousands upon thousands of chariots."[39] Yet he goes on to say, "As it actually worked out in history, the Jewish rebellion in reaction to the 'locust plague' of Gessius Florus during the summer of 66 provoked Cestius' invasion of Palestine in the fall, with large numbers of mounted troops from the regions near the Euphrates (although the main point of St. John's reference is the symbolic significance of the river in Biblical history and prophecy)."[40] He cites Josephus's *Wars* ii.xviii.9-xix.7[41] and J. M. Ford's commentary on Revelation (in the Anchor Bible Commentary [New York:

Doubleday, 1975], p.154). She, in turn, cites a French work by S. Giet. Does this argument hold up? I do not think so.

Dr. M. Gichon has given a good overview of the Cestius Gallus campaign against Judea.[42] Josephus records Cestius' preparation in Antioch[43] for the "invasion of Palestine" (Chilton's words).[44]

> He accordingly left Antioch, taking with him the twelfth legion in full strength [5,400 infantry and 120 cavalry], two thousand picked men from each of the other legions [6,000 more men from the third, sixth, and tenth Legions] and in addition six cohorts of infantry [500 soldiers in a cohort, so another 3,000 men], and four squadrons of cavalry; [45] beside these he had the auxiliary contingents furnished by the kings, of which Antiochus supplied two thousand horse [2,000] and three thousand foot [3,000], all archers, Agrippa an equal number of foot [3,000] and rather less than two thousand horse [-2,000], Soaemus following with four thousand, of which one-third were cavalry [1,333] and the majority archers [2,666].... Further auxiliaries in very large numbers were collected from the towns."[46]

The organized army, then, had just over 23,000+ infantry and about 5,500 cavalry. The 5,500 does not come close to the 200 million stated in the biblical text, which is why Chilton interprets it as "many thousands"!

The horsemen are instructed to kill one-third of all "mankind" (Revelation 9:15) and are successful in this task (9:18). Chilton ignores this number and attributes no fulfillment to it. If he were consistent with his position, the Roman army, under Cestius, would have had to kill one-third of "Israel" in their attack against Jerusalem. Is this the case? I do not believe so. Of the Jews he records, "Their [the Jews'] own losses had been quite inconsiderable."[47] At one point Josephus records 22 being killed in a skirmish with the Romans.[48] The irony is that the Romans and their allies lost "five thousand three hundred infantry and four hundred and eighty of the cavalry."[49] That was one-fifth of the Roman forces! But one-third of mankind or Israel were not killed.

Chilton realizes this problem and makes a creative excuse for the Jews:

> The retreat of Cestius was of course taken to mean that Christ's prophecies of Jerusalem's destruction were false: The armies from the Euphrates had come and surrounded Jerusalem (cf. Luke 21:20), but the threatened "desolation" had not come to pass....The Jews recklessly plunged ahead into greater acts of

rebellion, unaware that even greater forces beyond the Euphrates were being readied for battle."[50]

The problem with this interpretation is that the text does not say what Chilton tries to make it say!

Earthquakes in the Book of Revelation

The word "earthquake" is used seven times in the book of Revelation to describe five different earthquakes (Revelation 6:12; 8:5; 11:13 [twice], 19; 16:18 [twice]). The first earthquake occurs during the sixth seal (Revelation 6:12). It is called a "great earthquake" and is connected with other cosmic disturbances (6:12-17). Chilton calls this seal judgment a "de-creation," or "God ripping apart and dissolving the fabric of creation."[51] The pattern of this judgment is based on the order of creation (i.e., earth, sun, moon, stars, firmament, land, and man). The first judgment is the earthquake, and its imagery is the destabilization (of earth?). A number of Scriptures are quoted, but Chilton does not say if this earthquake actually occurred. Another preterist says that earthquakes are "the symbol of revolution, the shaking up of the nations in their various places. It is the figure of the agitations, upheavals, resulting in the revolutions and wars of Matthew 24:29. It is the symbol of divine judgment on the nations persecuting the cause of the Lamb."[52]

The second earthquake occurs during the seventh seal judgment: "Then the angel took the censer and filled it with the fire of the altar, and threw it to the earth; and there followed peaks of thunder and sounds of flashes of lightning and an earthquake" (Revelation 8:5). Again, Chilton does not say if this is a literal earthquake or not.[53]

The third earthquake occurs in conjunction with the martyrdom and resurrection of the two witnesses in Jerusalem (Revelation 11:13): "In that hour there was a great earthquake, and a tenth of the city fell; seven thousand people were killed in the earthquake, and the rest were terrified and gave glory to the God of heaven." Chilton understands this to mean the defeat of the Lord's enemies, but does not take this as a literal earthquake.[54]

The fourth earthquake is mentioned at the end of chapter 11: "The temple of God which is in heaven was opened; and the ark of His covenant appeared in His temple, and there were flashes of lightning and sounds and peals of thunder and an earthquake and a great hailstorm" (verse 19).

The fifth and final earthquake in Revelation is after the gathering of the armies of the nations at Armageddon (Revelation 16:16). This occurs during the seventh bowl judgment: "Then the seventh angel poured out his bowl upon the air, and a loud voice came out of the temple from the throne, saying, 'It is done!' And there were flashes of lightning and sounds and peals of thunder; and there was a great earthquake, such as there had not been since man came to be upon the earth, so great an earthquake was it, and so mighty" (Revelation 16:17-18). This earthquake, John writes, is like none that has ever occurred "since man came to be upon earth." If the preterist position is true, then this earthquake would have been the most devastating earthquake ever to hit the earth and Jerusalem in particular (verse 19, "the great city" = Jerusalem). Yet preterists do not take this as a literal earthquake. Chilton says, "Seven times in Revelation St. John mentions an earthquake (6:12; 8:5; 11:13 [twice]; 11:19; 16:18 [twice]), emphasizing its covenantal dimensions. Christ came to bring the definitive earthquake, the great cosmic earthquake of the New Covenant."[55] Another preterist comments, "These [the voices, thunder, lightnings, and earthquakes] are symbolic of the great energies of God's throne being loosed in accomplishment of His purpose. The great earthquake symbolizes the great change in the earth that took place when Israel as a nation under God was destroyed."[56] Preterists do not take this prophecy literally, but rather symbolically. Why? Because they have no historical event recorded by Josephus or any Roman historian that corresponds with this prophecy. Remember that Josephus was sitting in Jerusalem as an eyewitness to the siege of the city by Titus Caesar. If any earthquake had occurred, for sure Josephus would have mentioned it—especially one of the magnitude that John predicted.

Historical records document only three earthquakes in Jerusalem during the first century A.D. One occurred in A.D. 30 in connection with the death and resurrection of the Lord Jesus (Matthew 27:51-54; 28:2). Another earthquake in A.D. 33, caused slight damage to the Temple, and another one in A.D. 48 caused slight damage as well.[57] Since there was no earthquake during the events of A.D. 70—much less a devastating quake—preterists have had to interpret the earthquake as symbolic!

Consider again the fact that preterists date the book of Revelation to before A.D. 70. If they were to take Revelation 16:17-18 as referring to a literal earthquake, Pliny the Elder would have put the lie to John's statement "such a mighty and great earthquake as had not occurred since men were on the earth." Pliny was a Roman of equestrian rank and a prolific researcher and writer. His best known work is the 37 books of his *Natural History*. Ironically, Pliny died while investigating the eruption of Mount Vesuvius in A.D. 79. Writing in A.D. 77, Pliny described the earthquake that destroyed a portion of Asia Minor (now western Turkey) in A.D. 17 as "the greatest earthquake in human memory occurred when Tiberius Caesar was emperor, twelve Asiatic cities being overthrown in one night."[58]

Tacitus, in his *Annals*, described this earthquake as well.

> In the same year, twelve important cities of Asia collapsed in an earthquake, the time being night, so that the havoc was the less foreseen and the more devastating. Even the usual resource in these catastrophes, a rush to open ground, was unavailing, as the fugitives were swallowed up in yawning chasms. Accounts are given of huge mountains sinking, of former plains seen heaved aloft, of fires flashing out amid the ruin. As the disaster fell heaviest on the Sardians, it brought them the largest measure of sympathy, the Caesar promising ten million sesterces, and remitting for five years their payments to the national and imperial exchequers."[59]

Pliny wrote this statement in A.D. 77. If preterists are correct that John penned the book of Revelation before A.D. 70, and Pliny said the A.D. 17 earthquake was the greatest in human memory rather than the quake John said would strike Jerusalem, then John—and God's revelation—would have been wrong. And if the quake in Jerusalem right before A.D. 70 had indeed been the largest, Pliny would have said so in his statement in A.D. 77.

Earthquakes create a big problem for the preterist position because none occurred during the time of the Jewish revolt. Thus, preterists have to view the quakes in Revelation as symbolic, and not literal.

Hailstones (Revelation 16:19-21)

After the greatest earthquake ever recorded in the history of humanity (Revelation 16:17-18), the great city (Jerusalem) is divided into three parts. Chilton, quoting Carrington, attributes this historically to the three rival Jewish leaders within Jerusalem during the siege by Titus.[60] "Babylon the great" (Jerusalem) was remembered before God and He poured out His wrath (16:19). "And every island fled away, and the mountains were not found" (16:20). Rather than seeing this as seismic activity resulting from the greatest earthquake to hit the face of the earth (cf. 16:18), Chilton sees this symbolically as the disappearance of false refuge for the wicked to hide.[61]

Then, "huge hailstones, about one hundred pounds each, came down from heaven upon men, and men blasphemed God because of the plague of the hail, because that plague was extremely severe" (16:21). Chilton correctly sees the connection between this judgment and the seventh plague during the exodus from Egypt (Exodus 9:18-26), and the hailstones that fell on the Canaanites at Beth Horon (Joshua 10:11). In both cases literal hailstones fell, and in modern-day military parlance, hail would be considered *air*-to-surface projectiles. Yet how do Chilton and other preterists, understand these hailstones? "Hailstones" = stone missiles (ballista stones) shot from Roman catapults against the Jewish defenders of Jerusalem![62] Josephus describes the Roman "artillery engines" (or "stone projectors") as "wonderfully constructed" and "the rocks which they hurled weighed a talent and had a range of two furlongs or more."[63] Elsewhere, Josephus mentions the 160 artillery engines that the three Roman legions employed against Jerusalem and ballista stones that weighed one talent.[64] However, in modern military jargon, these would be "*surface*-to-surface" projectiles.

The differences between hailstones and ballista stones are drastic. One is made of ice and the other is made of stone, and in Jerusalem, limestone. One is air-to-surface and divinely poured out, while the other is surface-to-surface man-made artillery shot by the Romans. The only similarities between the hailstones of Revelation 16 and the ballista stones of the Roman siege are that they both weighed one talent. While Chilton observes that a talent is equal to 100 pounds, others point out that, "no precise weight is intended by the talent-sized hailstones poured out of the bowl of the seventh angel in Revelation 16:21, but they would have been formidable, weighing, even by the late Jewish definition of the talent, at least 20.4 kg."[65] An object weighing 20.4 kg would equal 49.982 pounds, half what Chilton states.

A good example of ballista stones found in an archaeological context in Jerusalem can be seen in the area of the Citadel Museum at Jaffa Gate. However, these stones are not from the First Jewish Revolt, but most likely from "the siege of Jerusalem by Antiochus VII Sidetes during the reign of John Hyrcanus (133–132 B.C.E.)."[66]

In June of 2000, I guided a field trip to the Herodian, which is south of Bethlehem. In Herod the Great's bedroom was a pile of ballista stones. As I sat on top of them, I read Revelation 16:21 to the group of seminarians from The Master's Seminary. I pointed to the stones and said, tongue-in-cheek, "Folks, these are the hailstones mentioned in this passage!" The students, all good pre-Tribbers, looked at me in bewilderment until someone in the back asked, "Why haven't they melted?!" I smiled and responded, "Good question. Next time you talk to a preterist, ask him."

Revelation 16:17-21 illustrates a glaring problem in the preterist position. When is the text to be taken literally, and when is it to be taken symbolically? The earthquake in verse 18 is symbolic and the hailstones (which, according to preterists, are really ballista stones) are taken literally as having been historically fulfilled in A.D. 70. Consistent hermeneutics would prove helpful to preterists in determining literal meaning from symbolic meanings.

The Man of Sin

Full preterist James Stuart Russell, in his book *The Parousia*, gives 12 criteria for identifying the "man of sin" (KJV) in 2 Thessalonians 2:1-12.[67] They are:

1. He will be an individual.

2. He is a public person.

3. He holds the highest rank in the State.

4. He is a Gentile, not Jewish.

5. He claims divinity.

6. He pretends to exercise miraculous power.

7. His character is wickedness.

8. He is a lawless ruler.

9. When the epistle was written, he had not come to power.

10. He was "hindered" by someone known to the Thessalonians.

11. He was doomed to destruction.

12. His "manifestation" was prior to the Parousia.

Russell then goes on to identify the man of sin as Nero and his stepfather, Claudius, as the "restrainer."

The biggest problem with this view is that the list of criteria leaves out a very important point. Paul writes that the "man of sin" would sit "in the temple of God, displaying himself as being God" (2 Thessalonians 2:4). While Nero claimed divinity, he never sat in the Temple of God in Jerusalem and declared himself God.

John Noe, a full preterist, following a booklet written by fellow full preterist, John Bray,[68] has recently suggested that the "man of sin" was John of Gischala, one of the commanders of the Zealot forces defending Jerusalem and the Temple Mount during the Jewish revolt. He also says the "restrainer" was the Jewish priesthood lead by Ananus, the high priest. They were removed when John of Gischala had them all murdered.[69]

The shortcoming of this view is that John of Gischala never declared himself to be God. If he had, Josephus would have picked up on it and accused him of blasphemy. There was no love lost between the two. In fact, they hated one other.

The preterist views regarding Nero and John of Gischala were not a fulfillment of "the man of sin." Nero proclaimed himself to be divine, but never sat in the Temple of Jerusalem. John of Gischala, on the other hand, was in the Temple in Jerusalem, but never declared himself to be God. Thus both preterist candidates for the "man of sin" fail to fulfill the prophecy in 2 Thessalonians 2. It is better, then, to see this passage as having a future fulfillment in a rebuilt Temple in Jerusalem. John Noe should be commended for showing the comparison between Matthew 24 and 2 Thessalonians 2,[70] but it makes more sense to see the two passages as future rather than fulfilled in A.D. 70.

Some Final Observations

The biggest problem with the preterist position is the lack of consistent hermeneutics. They work hard to find historical evidence of prophetic fulfillment in the destruction of Jerusalem in A.D. 70. Any time an event described in a prophecy cannot be linked to an actual historical event, preterists immediately resort to a symbolic interpretation of the text. It would be helpful if someone in the preterist camp would write a hermeneutics for this position. What are the criteria for taking something literally? When does something become symbolic?

In some cases, they do not give a complete interpretation of a passage. For example, in regard to the second trumpet judgment, Chilton fails to identify or interpret all the things in the passage. He makes no mention of the blood, the sea life that died, or the one-third of the ships that were destroyed (Revelation 8:8-9). And, as we have seen, preterists are also selective in their use of the material they use to prove their point, as evidenced by their use of *The Acts of John*. We've also seen them use the historical data incorrectly, as demonstrated by the ancient coins with the seven stars.

THE FUTURIST RESPONSE REGARDING REVELATION

This chapter began by asking two questions: Was "Babylon" destroyed when Jerusalem fell in A.D. 70? and, Are the "fulfillments" of the preterist view historically accurate? These questions must be answered two ways—prophetically and historically. Prophetically, the prophecies were *not* fulfilled in A.D. 70 with the destruction of Jerusalem. Historically, the "fulfillments" do *not* fit the historical record. The answer to both questions, then, is a resounding *no!* The "historical fulfillments" of the destruction of "Babylon" were not "fulfilled" in A.D. 70.

Chapter 10

REVELATION 13 AND THE FIRST BEAST

ANDY WOODS

Recently, leading preterist Kenneth L. Gentry devoted an entire book to attempting to prove the thesis that the prophecies in Revelation 13 regarding the first beast were fulfilled in the person of the first-century Roman emperor Nero.[1] Gentry and other preterists maintain that the contextual, hermeneutical, and exegetical clues found within the text of Revelation 13 favor a Neronic interpretation of the first beast. These textual clues include the beast's character, death, revival, reception of worship, 42-month war with the saints, number, and relationship with the second beast. In this chapter, we will see why these textual clues could not have been fulfilled in the person of Nero and, instead, they convincingly argue for a futuristic interpretation of the beast of Revelation 13.

A REVIEW OF REVELATION 13

The Character of the Beast

Much of the preterist Neronic interpretation of the first beast is built upon associating the evil character of the first beast (as alluded to in Revelation 13:1-2) with Nero's "beastly" character as described by ancient historians.[2] Preterists contend that the beast's evil character is communicated by the fact that he is described as a composite of various destructive animals—a leopard, a bear, and a lion (Revelation 13:2). This portrait is reminiscent of Daniel's vision of the four beasts as recorded in Daniel 7. Preterists claim that John demonstrates the evil nature of the beast by compounding three of Daniel's beasts into one beast.[3] In this regard, Gentry explicitly makes the connection between the fourth beast of Daniel 7 and the first beast of Revelation 13 by observing that "John's beast even has ten horns like Daniel's fourth beast (Dan. 7:7; Rev. 13:1)."[4]

Preterists are correct in relating the beast of Revelation 13 with the fourth beast of Daniel 7. Many interesting parallels exist between the two.[5] For example, both have a worldwide empire (Daniel 7:7,23; Revelation 13:8), both rule for three-and-one-half years (Daniel 7:25; Revelation 13:5), both dominate the saints for three-and-one-half years (Daniel 7:25; Revelation 12:14; 13:7), and both are characterized by their arrogant and blasphemous words (Daniel 7:8, 11,20,25; Revelation 13:5). Because of these parallels, many scholars have concluded that both beasts are one and the same.[6]

However, the preterist admission that the beast of Revelation 13:1-2 is an allusion to the fourth beast of Daniel 7 actually does far more to further the futurist interpretation than it does the preterist Neronian interpretation due to the fact that many of the details regarding the fourth beast of Daniel 7 have obviously not yet come to pass. For example, ancient Rome never crushed the entire earth (Daniel 7:23),[7] never came to power through the assistance of a ten-king confederacy (Daniel 7:7,24),[8] never experienced instantaneous destruction (Daniel 7:11,26),[9] and was never immediately replaced by a subsequent eternal political kingdom following its sudden demise (Daniel 7:27). Because these details do not fit the known facts of history, they obviously await a future fulfillment. In sum, the admission that the first beast of Revelation 13 is identical to the fourth beast of Daniel 7 requires a futuristic interpretation of the first beast of Revelation 13, as opposed to the preterist Neronian interpretation, because many of the details regarding the fourth beast of Daniel 7 await a future fulfillment.

The Death of the Beast

Revelation 13:10 says, "If anyone is destined for captivity, to captivity he goes; if anyone kills with the sword, with the sword he must be killed. Here is the perseverance and the faith of the saints." Preterists believe that John was encouraging his audience, the persecuted seven churches of Asia Minor (Revelation 1:4,11), by promising them that the person who is persecuting them with the sword will experience the same fate.[10] Preterists believe this prophecy fits Nero because not only did believers experience martyrdom under Nero's persecution, but Nero himself also perished by the sword.

However, this interpretation overlooks the fact that the Neronic persecution was confined to Rome and never reached modern-day Turkey, which was the geographical locale of the seven churches of Asia Minor. Imperial persecution did not reach Asia Minor until the empire-wide persecution under the reign of Domitian.[11] Therefore, how could Revelation 13:10 be understood as a word of encouragement to the persecuted churches of Asia Minor during the Neronic reign when, in actuality, the Neronic persecution never reached these churches? Preterist Steve Gregg argues that the churches of Asia Minor did experience persecution during the Neronic reign, although not as a direct result of the emperor's decree. Gregg contends that because Nero persecuted Christians in Rome, Christians in other parts of the empire may have faced local persecution at the same time because their local enemies were taking advantage of the general anti-Christian sentiment ushered in by the emperor's persecution of believers in Rome.[12] However, even if such a scenario transpired, it still removes Nero as the primary culprit of persecution against the churches of Asia Minor. Removing Nero as the primary conduit makes it difficult to argue that Revelation 13:9-10 was written to encourage the seven churches in the midst of directly receiving persecution from Nero.

In addition, a textual clue found in Revelation 13:9 has led many Bible interpreters to the conclusion that those addressed in Revelation 13:10 are not the seven churches of Asia Minor but rather, consist of a different group all together. When Christ addressed the seven churches of Asia Minor in Revelation 2–3, He always used the phrase, "He who has an ear, let him hear what the Spirit says to the churches" (Revelation 2:7,11,17,29; 3:6,13,22). However, the verse that immediately precedes Revelation 13:10 departs from this standard formula. Instead, Revelation 13:9 says, "If anyone has an ear, let him hear." Conspicuously missing from this phrase are the words "what the Spirit says to the churches."

Why would John use an identical phrase seven times in reference to the seven churches of Asia Minor and yet use a different phrase in Revelation 13:9? This discrepancy has led many interpreters to the conclusion that those addressed in Revelation 13:9-10 are a different group than the seven churches of Asia Minor addressed in Revelation 2–3.[13] Some futurists believe that the absence of the phrase "what the Spirit says to the churches" in Revelation 13:9 furnishes support for the teaching that the church, the body of Christ, will have been raptured and is not on earth during the Great Tribulation depicted in Revelation 4–19.[14] At any rate, the fact that a group other than the seven churches may have been addressed in Revelation 13:9-10 detracts from the preterist view that Revelation 13:9-10 was written to encourage the suffering churches of Asia Minor in the midst of the Neronic persecution.

The Revival of the Beast

Preterists argue that the verses predicting the beast's revival (Revelation 13:3,14) speak of either the Nero Redivivus Myth (Nero's return symbolically in the incarnation of subsequent Roman emperors), or Rome's political revival under Vespasian. Before explaining why these three options are implausible fulfillments of Revelation 13:3,14, it should be noted that the language of Revelation 13:3 itself makes it difficult to argue that the verses depicting the beast's revival were fulfilled locally in the first-century events following Nero's death. Revelation 13:3 predicts global worship of the beast following his revival: "and the whole earth" *(holē ē gē)* "was amazed and followed after the beast." This language argues against a local fulfillment and instead favors a global fulfillment.

Preterist David Chilton's interpretation of the phrase "and the whole earth" *(holē ē gē)* as pertaining to apostate Israel[15] alone is unsatisfactory. Although the term "earth" *(gē)* can have a local meaning by referring to the nation of Israel (1 Samuel 13:19; Zechariah 12:12; Matthew 2:9), the phrase can also have a universal meaning by referring to all the earth (Genenis 1:1). Thus, the meaning of the term depends upon the context in which it is used. The word "whole" *(holē)* before "earth" *(gē)* does not naturally lend the term to the limited meaning "land of Israel." Also, Revelation 13:7 reinforces the global nuance by mentioning every tribe, people, language, and nation. Thus, the global emphasis of this immediate context also argues for *gē* to be given a global rather than local understanding.[16] Because such universal worship did not take place following the Neronic reign, or any other time in world history, it obviously awaits a future fulfillment.

Some of the earlier preterists, such as J. Stuart Russell, believed that these verses are speaking of the Nero Redivivus Myth.[17] Nero died in June A.D. 68. Because Nero had terrified his world, legends began to quickly proliferate and infiltrate the minds of the Roman populace that Nero was still alive and in hiding.[18] Historians refer to these rumors as the Nero Redivivus Myth.[19] However, it is unlikely that Revelation 13:3,14 is speaking of the Nero Redivivus Myth. One reason is because it is unlikely that John or other Christians believed the myth. In fact, this view was unknown to the earliest church fathers. Irenaeus, who was the disciple of Polycarp, who in turn was the disciple of John,[20] had no knowledge of the Nero Redivivus Myth.[21] Because Nero has never returned from the dead and never will,[22] the theory that John refers to the Nero Redivivus Myth in Revelation 13:3,14 "ascribes to John a false prophecy based upon a silly superstition."[23]

Some preterists point to the many similar attributes and behavioral patterns between Nero and subsequent Roman emperors as fulfillments of Revelation 13:3,4.[24] However, viewing these parallels as the fulfillment of the revival passages is unsatisfactory. Even Gentry admits that such parallels would not be sufficient to cause the world to be "amazed" and follow after the beast.[25] Furthermore, Revelation 13:3,14 and 17:8,11 seem to indicate that the same beast who is wounded will also be the same beast who is revived. Preterists reject this straightforward reading of the text and opt instead for an interpretation that requires both Nero's literal death and a symbolic resurrection through subsequent emperors.

Finally, preterists view the political instability that Rome suffered following Nero's death and the political resurgence that the empire enjoyed after Vespasian's enthronement as the fulfillment of Revelation 13:3,14.[26] However, understanding Rome's political revival as the fulfillment of the revival passages is not persuasive. The weakness of this view resides in its failure to recognize that the pronoun "his" (*aútou*) in the phrase *tou qanatou aútou* (Revelation 13:3) limits the wounding and healing to one of the heads representing a king, and not the whole kingdom.[27] Moreover, Revelation 13:3,14 and 17:8,11 seem to indicate that the same beast who is wounded will also be the same beast who is revived. If the beast's death was personal and individual, then his revival must also be personal and individual rather than national. Therefore, it is unnatural for preterists to interpret the prophecies regarding the beast's death as finding their fulfillment in Nero's individual, personal death while simultaneously interpreting the prophecies regarding the beast's revival as finding their fulfillment in Rome's political revival. Such repeated reliance upon a dual hermeneutic exposes preterism's inability to adhere to a consistent method of interpretation.

The Worship of the Beast

Those holding to a Neronian interpretation of the first beast of Revelation 13 believe that the verses describing the worship of the beast (Revelation 13:4,8,12,15) were fulfilled through the emperor worship Nero received during his reign.[28] However, such a localized understanding of worship seems improper in light of the context in which these verses were written. A careful scrutiny of just one of these verses depicting the worship of the beast is sufficient to demonstrate that reference is being made to *global* worship rather than local. Revelation 13:8 says, "All who dwell on the earth will worship him, everyone whose name has not been written from the foundation of the world in the book of life of the Lamb who has been slain." Although the terms "earth" (*gē*) and "world" (*kosmos*) can have a localized interpretation in some contexts (1 Samuel 13:19; Zechariah 12:12; John 12:19; Colossians 1:16), these same terms also evidence a global interpretation in other contexts (Genesis 1:1; John 1:29; 3:16; 1 John 2:2). Thus, the meanings of these terms are dependent upon the context in which they are used. The emphasis of Revelation 13:8 is clearly global. For example, the word "all" (*pantes*) that modifies the participle "who dwell on the earth" (*katoikountes*) indicates the universality of this beast worship.[29] By assigning the phrases "earth" (*gē*) and "world" (*kosmos*) in Revelation 13:8 the same localized meaning that these terms have in a few other isolated contexts (1 Samuel 13:19; Zechariah 12:12; John 12:19;

Colossians 1:16), preterists are guilty of committing a hermeneutical error known as "illegitimate totality transfer." This error arises when the meaning of a word as derived from its use elsewhere is then automatically read into the same word in a foreign context.[30]

Moreover, the phrase in Revelation 13:8 that reads, "everyone whose name has not been written…in the book of life of the Lamb" is also used in Revelation 20:15 to describe all of unsaved humanity's participation in the final judgment. Because partial preterists believe that the events of Revelation 20 will be fulfilled in the future,[31] they believe that Revelation 20:15 refers to the final judgment at the end of history for all of humanity. Now, if the concept of "everyone whose name has not been written…in the book of life of the Lamb" has a futuristic, universal meaning in Revelation 20:15, then why don't preterists allow the same futuristic, universal meaning in Revelation 13:8? That partial preterists say this same concept can simultaneously have a futuristic, universal meaning in Revelation 20:15 and a historical, localized meaning in Revelation 13:8 unnecessarily bifurcates the book of Revelation, thus causing internal inconsistency within the book. Such a bifurcation would be justified if the context of Revelation 13 was local. However, nothing in the context of Revelation 13 justifies a local interpretation.

Revelation 13:15 says, "It was given to him to give breath to the image of the beast, so that the image of the beast would even speak and cause as many as do not worship the image of the beast to be killed." Preterists believe Revelation 13:15 was fulfilled in A.D. 66 when Tiridates paid homage to images of Nero.[32] However, details of Tiridates's reverential activities do not adequately fulfill the details of Revelation 13:15. For example, Tiridates paid homage to several images, while the image of Revelation 13:15 is singular rather than plural. Moreover, unlike the image of Revelation 13:15, there is no record that the images Tiridates revered spoke or received breath. Those seeking to find a first-century fulfillment for Revelation 13:15 often attribute the image's ability to speak to ventriloquism and magic tricks practiced in the ancient world.[33] However, such conjecture is invalid because John's language implies genuine miracles rather than sleight-of-hand deceptiveness.[34]

Moreover, many scholars associate the worship of the beast's image in Revelation 13:15 with the "abomination of desolation" spoken of in Daniel 9:27. This same terminology, "abomination of desolation," also appears in Daniel 11:31 in relation to the intertestamental activities of Antiochus Epiphanes, who desecrated the Jewish Temple by putting an end to the Jewish sacrifices and setting up a pagan image in the Temple. Because Daniel 9:27 applies the identical phrase "abomination of desolation" to the work of the man of sin, many scholars believe he will do exactly what Antiochus did by setting up a pagan image in the Jewish temple.[35] Many of these same scholars believe the beast's image in Revelation 13:15 is the same pagan image that will be established in the Temple.[36] If this analysis is correct, then Tiridates's first-century homage does not satisfy the criteria of Revelation 13:15, because there is no record of him paying tribute to an image erected in the Jewish Temple.

In addition, the image of the beast is not only mentioned in Revelation 13:14-15, but also six other times in Revelation, including Revelation 20:4. Both partial preterists and futurists agree that Revelation 20:4 appears in a futuristic context.[37] The fact that the image mentioned in Revelation 20:4 is the same image described in Revelation 13:14-15 is evidenced by the fact that the initial reference to the image is anarthous while the remaining references to the image retain the article. This retention of the article in the subsequent references indicates that all of the later references to the image point back to the initial reference.[38] Therefore, all subsequent references to the image are referring to the same image as in the initial reference. Unfortunately, partial preterists ignore this grammatical reality. Instead, they cause unnecessary internal inconsistency within the book of Revelation by insisting that the image of the beast has a historical meaning in Revelation 13:14-15 and a futuristic meaning in Revelation 20:4.

The 42-Month War and the Beast

Revelation 13:5,7 predicts, "There was given to him a mouth speaking arrogant words and blasphemies, and authority to act for forty-two months.... It was also given to him to make war with the saints and to overcome them, and authority over every tribe, and people and tongue and nation was given to him." Preterists believe these verses focus on the Neronic persecution of A.D. 64–68. One of the main reasons for maintaining that view concerns the assertion that the Neronic persecution lasted roughly 42 months, just as the persecution in Revelation 13:5 does.[39]

The preterists' adherence to a literal hermeneutic regarding the 42-month period mentioned in Revelation 13:5 is at variance with how preterists interpret other numbers in Revelation. The book's numbers include 2, 3, 3½, 4, 5, 6, 7, 10, 12, 24, 42, 144, 666, 1,000, 1,260, 1,600, 7,000, 12,000, 144,000.[40] Preterists are inconsistent when they interpret Revelation's numbers. On one hand, they interpret the numbers 42 (Revelation 13:5), 666 (Revelation 13:18), and 1, 5, and 7 (Revelation 17:10) in a straightforward, literal fashion.

On the other hand, preterists contend that the numbers 1,000, 12,000, and 144,000 are purely symbolic. Regarding the number 12,000 that is used 12 times in Revelation 7:4-8, Gentry observes, "Inarguably, an elevated symbolism is here presented. If nothing else, the prefect rounding of numbers along with the exact identical count in each of the tribes bespeak a symbolic representation."[41] And Chilton comments, "The number 144,000 is obviously symbolic...."[42] Regarding the number 1,000 that is used six times in Revelation 20, Chilton states, "...the thousand years of Revelation 20 represent a vast undefined period of time..."[43] Later, Chilton quotes Milton Terry, who said, "The thousand years is to be understood as a symbolical number, denoting a long period of time. It is a round number, but stands for an indefinite period, an eon whose duration it would be a folly to attempt to compute."[44]

Why is it that preterists interpret the numbers 1,5,7,42, and 666 literally while they interpret 1,000, 12,000, and 144,000 symbolically? Gentry attempts to answer this question by contending that the larger rounded numbers of Revelation, such as 1,000 and 144,000, should be understood as symbols while the smaller numbers should be understood literally.[45] However, because he also indicates that the two prophets of Revelation 11 "probably represent a small body of Christians who remained in Jerusalem to testify against it,"[46] it appears that Gentry is unwilling to consistently adhere to even his own interpretive method. Gentry's inconsistency illustrates preterism's inability to offer a consistent hermeneutic in interpreting Revelation's numbers. It also demonstrates the preterists' need to selectively apply a literal hermeneutic only to those numbers in Revelation that fit their preconceived system.

Even if these hermeneutical inconsistencies are overlooked, the preterist interpretation cannot be sustained because the Neronic persecution did not last the same length of time as the 42-month period predicted in Revelation 13:5. Preterists themselves indicate that the Neronian persecution did not last exactly 42 months. After identifying the time of the beginning and end of the Neronian persecution, Gentry claims this "represents, but for a few days, a period of 42 months."[47] Regarding the length of the Neronian persecution, Russell states, "...that is as nearly as possible three years and a half."[48] By using language such as "but for a few days" and "as nearly as possible," preterists tacitly admit that the duration of Neronian persecution is not an exact or precise fulfillment of the 42-month period prophesied in Revelation 13:5. Such an admission is problematic for preterist interpreters because the fulfilled prophecies of Scripture demonstrate a precise, exact fulfillment.[49] The fulfilled prophecies that involve a time indicator have been fulfilled to the exact day.[50] Why would the prophecy of the 42-month period in Revelation 13:5 be any different?

Preterists' inability to demonstrate that the Neronian persecution is the precise fulfillment of Revelation 13:5 is further compounded by their insensitivity to Revelation's use of 360-day prophetic years as opposed to 365-day calendar years. The fact that Revelation utilizes 360-day years is apparent from a careful study of the numbers used in the book. For example, Revelation 13:5

says the beast will rule for 42 months. It can also be inferred from Revelation 12:6 that his rule will last 1,260 days. Because 1,260 days divided by 42 months equals 30 days, each month consists of 30 days. Because 30 days times 12 months equals 360 days, a year in Revelation consists of 360 days.[51] Thus, any attempt to find a precise fulfillment of the 42-month period of Revelation 13:5 must demonstrate an appreciation for the fact that each month consists of 30 days. Such an appreciation is never demonstrated in the writings of preterists. In sum, the inability of preterists to demonstrate that the Neronian persecution lasted exactly 42 months disqualifies this persecution from being the fulfillment to Revelation 13:5.

In addition, the universal scope of the language found in Revelation 13:7 makes it difficult to interpret the verse as having a Neronic, local fulfillment. Revelation 13:7 says, "…authority over every tribe and people and tongue and nation was given to him." Such terminology clearly describes *universal* authority.[52] This all-inclusive scope prohibits any application of this verse to a past ruler.[53] Interestingly, the same four groups mentioned in Revelation 13:7 to describe the universality of the beast's authority are the same four groups mentioned in Revelation 5:9 to indicate those for whom Christ died.[54] Both verses mention every (*pashs*) tribe (*fulhs*), tongue (*glwsshs*), people (*laou*), and nation (*éqnous*). Viewing these four groups as pertaining only to those within the sphere of Nero's first-century local governance logically leads to the conclusion that Christ died only for those within this same sphere rather than the whole world. In other words, if the benefits of Christ's death were indeed universal, then consistency would dictate that the authority of the beast must be universal as well. In sum, neither the duration nor scope of the Neronic persecution fully satisfies the details given in Revelation 13:5,7.

The Number of the Beast

Preterists believe the beast's number as given in Revelation 13:18 clearly identifies the beast as Nero. They believe the sum of the numerical equivalents of the letters of Nero's name, "Caesar Nero," when transliterated into Hebrew, equals 666.[55] Although this relationship between Nero's name and the number 666 is interesting at first glance, the notion that Nero's name yields the number 666 is plagued with numerous problems. First, preterists' adherence to a literal hermeneutic regarding the number 666 in Revelation 13:18 raises the same interpretive questions that are posed when preterists insist upon a literal interpretation of the 42 months in Revelation 13:5. Why is the number 666 given a literal interpretation in the preterist system while the numbers 1,000, 12,000, and 144,000 are to be understood allegorically or symbolically? Their handling of the number 666 furnishes yet another example of the dual hermeneutic inherent in the preterist system as well as more evidence of preterism's inability to provide a consistent method of interpretation when approaching Revelation's numbers.

Second, the suggestion that the riddle can be solved only through a shift to the Hebrew letters is suspect because Revelation was written in Greek to a Greek-speaking audience.[56] Gentry attempts to counter this assertion by pointing out the Hebraic character of Revelation, other uses of Hebrew names found in Revelation such as "Abbadon" (Revelation 9:11) and "Armageddon" (Revelation 16:16), the Greek spelling of Hebrew names found throughout the New Testament (Mark 13:18), the partial Jewish composition of John's original audience, and the fact that John himself was a Jew sent to the circumcised (Galatians 2:9).[57] However, the use of Greek numbers for the purpose of decoding the riddle would not be out of character for John because elsewhere in Revelation he employs Greek letters as symbols (Revelation 1:8; 21:6; 22:13). Moreover, when John uses Hebrew words in Revelation, he makes a special note of it in order to bring it to the attention of his readers (see Revelation 9:11; 16:16). No such special designation is even hinted at in Revelation 13:18 regarding the number 666. Furthermore, the earliest Christian commentators never looked to a solution in any language other than the Greek.[58]

Also, Revelation's Hebraic character poses no obstacle for the use of Greek gematria. For example, the *Sibylline Oracles,* which is a Jewish document composed in Greek, does its gematria in Greek rather than Hebrew.[59] Also without merit is the idea that John, in an attempt to avoid detection, used Hebrew letters in order to hide behind a disguise that was easily penetrable by a believing Jew. There were unbelieving Jews in Asia Minor who were hostile to the early church (Revelation 2:9; 3:9) who could have easily deciphered such a Hebrew code. The presence of hostile unbelieving Jews in Asia Minor is confirmed by the fact that Jews played a prominent role in the martyrdom of Polycarp in that region in the middle of the second century.[60]

Third, Nero had many other names and titles.[61] Thus, there is no conclusive evidence that the title Nero Caesar is the name that John had in mind in Revelation 13:18. It appears that preterists have selected this particular title solely on the basis of its ability to fulfill their desired interpretive outcome.

Fourth, the preterists' calculation is built upon a defective spelling of the word *Caesar*. Preterists rely upon the abnormal spelling *rsq,* while the usual spelling is *rsyq*.[62] The addition of the *yod* would obviously damage the Neronic gematric calculation.

Fifth, in transliterating a foreign word into Hebrew, there is considerable latitude in including, omitting, or varying vowel letters. What's more, there are three possible Hebrew equivalents for the Greek letter for s.[63] Thus, any vowel letter arrangement or equivalent other than the one selected by the preterists would injure the Neronic calculation.

Sixth, a Neronic identity of the first beast was never suggested as a solution by any of the ancient commentators.[64] Not even Irenaeus, who was discipled by Polycarp, who in turn was discipled by John, suggested a Neronic identity.[65] There is not a trace of the Neronic interpretation found in the early church.[66]

Seventh, according to Zahn, the Neronic gematric calculation was not even suggested as a solution until Fritzsche first proposed it in 1831.[67] If the preterist interpretation of Revelation 13:18 is accurate, then the discovery of 666 as a prophecy concerning Nero was made roughly 1,800 years too late to assist John's original audience. Smith summarizes the issue well by noting, "If John's purpose was concealment, certainly he succeeded admirably, for his meaning was hidden not only from the enemies of the church, but from the church itself, for 1800 years. It is simply incredible that if this solution is so simple, and if it was ever known to the church, it should have been absolutely forgotten until our time."[68]

Eighth, because it appears that almost anything can be done with the number 666, all attempts to use these numbers in order to identify a specific person in history should be viewed with suspicion. For example, George Eldon Ladd observes that if A=100, and B=101, and C=102, and so on, then the name Hitler totals 666.[69] Throughout church history the gematric method has been used to identify the beast as Teitan, Lateinos, Julius Caesar, Domitian, Vespasian, Caligula, the Nicolaitans, and the German Kaisers.[70] Johnson notes that "the sheer disagreement and confusion created through the years by the gematria method should have long ago warned the church that it was on the wrong track."[71] Such confusion probably exists because the meaning of the number may not be evident until the Antichrist appears.[72] Thus, the best approach is to avoid all guessing and allow God to give the understanding when it is needed.[73]

The First Beast's Relationship with the Second Beast

Most preterists believe the second beast, depicted in Revelation 13:11-18, represents the Roman imperial cult that flourished under Nero's reign.[74] Several reasons cause this interpretation to be suspect. First, the universal language found within Revelation 13:11-18 makes it difficult to apply the passage to the local Neronic reign. Rather, the passage's universal language naturally leads the interpreter to a futuristic understanding of the passage. For example, Revelation 13:12 uses the phrase "the earth and those who dwell in it." Several commentators have observed the universal nuance associated with this phrase. Mounce observes that the phrase is a comprehensive designation indicating the totality of mankind.[75] Bullinger notes that the phrase is a Hebrew figure of speech called a *pleonasm* or *redundancy* used to speak of all the earth's inhabitants.[76]

Moreover, Revelation 13:14 uses the phrase "those who dwell on the earth." According to Mounce, this phrase is a semi-technical designation for the entire body of unregenerate humanity.[77] Furthermore, Revelation 13:16 uses the terms "small" and "great," "free" and "slave," "rich" and "poor" in order to describe those under the influence of the second beast. Such a coupling of opposites is a way of stressing the totality of human society.[78] In all, John mentions six classes of people from social, cultural, and economic categories. Because "all" (*pantas*) probably refers to all the classes rather than all the individuals, these groups taken together speak of the entire human population.[79] They should be understood to communicate universality due to the fact they encompass every civic, class, and cultural rank,[80] and commentators recognize this.[81]

Second, many of the words and concepts found in Revelation 13:11-18 are also found in Revelation 20, which both partial preterists and futurist interpreters agree involve a universal, futuristic context.[82] For example, the notion of people receiving a "mark" (*caragma*) on their right hand or forehead is found not only in Revelation 13:16 but also in Revelation 20:4. In addition, the personality known as the "false prophet" who performs miracles in the presence of the first beast (Revelation 19:20) is found not only in Revelation 13:13 but also in Revelation 20:4. The categories "the great and the small" (*tous mikrous kai tous megalous*) are not only used to describe those under the authority of the second beast in Revelation 13:16, but they are also used to depict those involved in the final judgment in Revelation 20:12. If these same words and concepts have a universal, futuristic nuance in Revelation 20, why should they not also have the same universal and futuristic meaning in Revelation 13:11-18?

Third, the details of Revelation 13:11-18 fit better with the interpretation that the second beast is a specific individual rather than a religious institution. For example, it is more likely that the singular phrase "beast" (*thērion*) or "false prophet" (*pseudoprophētēs*) refers to an individual rather than a religious institution.[83] Moreover, because he spends eternity in the lake of fire (Revelation 19:20; 20:10), the false prophet is characterized as possessing an eternal soul. Such an attribute and eternal fate is descriptive of individuals rather than institutions.[84]

Furthermore, if the preterist understanding that the first beast as an individual is accurate, then consistency would dictate that the second beast should also be understood as a person. Such a consistent interpretive approach is justified in light of the fact that the Greek word for "beast" *(thē-rion)* is used to describe both the first and second beasts (Revelation 13:1,11). In addition, the personal pronoun *aútou* is used to describe both the first and the second beasts (Revelation 13:1,12). The preterist interpretation that the first beast is a person and the second is a religious institution is inconsistent hermeneutically. Because the preterist has the luxury of vacillating between hermeneutical methods, he is able to interpret items in Revelation either literally or non-literally based upon what best fits his preconceived theology.

Fourth, although those seeking a first-century fulfillment of the miracles performed by the second beast in Revelation 13:13-15 often point to the contrived wonders performed by the imperial cult, the text indicates the miracles are genuine rather then mere chicanery. For example, in his Gospel, John employs the combination *poieō* and *simeion* to speak of Christ's miracles.[85] John also employs this same combination in Revelation 13:13, which indicates the miracles performed by the false prophet are just as genuine as the miracles wrought by Christ.

Moreover, other miracles involving fire nearly identical to the miracle recorded in Revelation 13:13 are similarly described in Revelation 11:5 and 20:9. In neither Revelation 11:5 nor Revelation 20:9 is it ever hinted that a contrivance or sleight-of-hand deceptiveness is employed. Because all three of these miracles are described in a similar manner, it is inappropriate to interpret Revelation 13:13 differently by unnecessarily reading contrivances into the context of the verse.[86] Furthermore, some commentators have observed the connection between the false prophet and Elijah. Just as Elijah called down fire from heaven (1 Kings 18:38; 2 Kings 1:10-12), the false prophet will imitate Elijah's miracle by also calling down fire from heaven (Revelation 13:3).[87] If this comparison is correct, then it stands to reason that the false prophet's miracle will be just as genuine as Elijah's miracle was.

Fifth, although there are many examples of people receiving a mark in the first century, none of these instances fully satisfies the details of Revelation 13:16-17. For example, the widespread use of documents stamped with a seal containing the name of the emperor and granting permission to buy or sell does not satisfy the criteria that the mark must be placed upon *(épi)* the right hand or forehead. Moreover, the Jewish custom of wearing phylacteries on the left hand or forehead also fails to satisfy the details given in Revelation 13:16-17. Not only is it doubtful that an anti-Christian authority would use portions of the law or prayer scrolls as its insignia, but also, phylacteries were worn on the left hand rather than the right. And, the practice of Christians wearing the first letter of Christ's name is also an implausible explanation due to the fact that the practice was not known well enough at the time John wrote.[88] At any rate, none of the first-century examples of people receiving a mark comes even close to matching the description in Revelation 13:16-17.

A RESPONSE ON REVELATION 13

The partial preterist Neronian views regarding the first beast of Revelation 13 cannot be sustained, especially in light of the text of Revelation 13. As has been demonstrated, the events of the Neronic reign do not completely satisfy the universal descriptions that appear in Revelation 13. In order to make their interpretations fit, partial preterists must selectively apply a literal hermeneutic only to those parts of Revelation 13 that are consistent with their preconceived system while, at the same time, applying a non-literal method of interpretation to the rest of Revelation 13. Partial preterists must also resort to interpreting words, phrases, and concepts found in Revelation 13 historically and locally while, at the same time, interpreting these same words, phrases, and concepts universally and futuristically in Revelation 20. In sum, the hermeneutical, contextual, and exegetical details of Revelation 13 should cause any unbiased interpreter to reject the idea that the prophecies about the first beast were fulfilled by Nero. Rather, the language of Revelation 13 is sufficient to lead interpreters to the conclusion that the beast of Revelation has yet to appear in world history.

Chapter 11

THE LITTLE APOCALYPSE OF ZECHARIAH

Arnold G. Fruchtenbaum

Our understanding of Zechariah 12–14 can have a significant impact on how we understand the other prophetic passages of Scripture. For that reason, in this chapter, we'll consider a basic exposition of Zechariah 12–14, and then we will examine the timing of the fulfillment of these prophecies. Were they already fulfilled during the Maccabean period, or the Roman period (A.D. 70), or the Holocaust? Or is the fulfillment of these prophecies still future?

THE EXPOSITION OF ZECHARIAH 12–14

The word "apocalypse" is the Greek title for the book of Revelation, the last book of the Bible, a book that deals with the subject of prophecy, the subject of eschatology, the study of the events of the last days. The last three chapters of Zechariah (12, 13, and 14) deal with the same or similar material as found in Revelation, or the Apocalypse. Therefore, these three chapters can be called "The Little Apocalypse of Zechariah." Zechariah 12–14 is also important because both futurists and preterists believe this passage speaks of the same events that our Lord expounded upon in His Olivet Discourse (Matthew 24–25; Mark 13; Luke 21). Therefore, all three passages (Zechariah 12–14, the Olivet Discourse, and Revelation) are said to refer to the same prophesied events.

Zechariah chapters 12–14 discuss three major topics: first, the final campaign against Israel, frequently referred to as the Campaign of Armageddon; second, the fact that Israel is going to be purged, saved, and redeemed from her enemies; and, third, the establishment of the messianic kingdom. The focus is clearly on Israel and the Jewish people. Not only is the term "Israel" used, but also "Judah," "Jerusalem," and other key geographical places are specifically named.

The timing is pinpointed as being "in that day," a very common prophetic term used to speak of the prophetic future. In these three chapters, the phrase is used a total of 17 times (12:3-4,6,8 [twice], 9,11; 13:1-2,4; 14:4,6,8-9, 13, 20-21). Dods observed, "It is obvious from the beginning of the twelfth chapter to the end of the book it is one period that is described."[1] In attempting to find the timing of these events in history, Dods also stated, "We look in vain for any historical occurrences in which the letter of this prophecy has been fulfilled to Israel after the flesh, unless it be in the Maccabean period."[2]

Feinberg makes the following observations:

> Hengstenberg is frank to admit that "we are introduced here to a state of things such as never existed under the Old Testament." Wright feels certain of his ground, for his position is that "the prophecy…is a prediction of what actually occurred in the glorious days of Israel's revival under the Maccabee chieftains." We invite the reader to peruse the deeds and events of Maccabean days in order to find there a fulfillment of the things predicted here. The only manner in which the two can be made to speak of the same thing, is to spiritualize in large measure the actual statements of the text. Such men demand of us a more than rigid literalism (such as the actual gathering of all the populations of all peoples against Jerusalem) and yet will in no wise abide by a consistent literal interpretation of the text themselves. As we have intimated above in the course of our remarks, we place the entire passage in the time of the Great Tribulation and more specifically in the Battle of Armageddon, when the nations of the earth will make their last frantic effort to blot Israel out of existence, only to be met by the most crushing defeat at the hands of the Lord of hosts Himself.[3]

The Campaign of Armageddon—12:1-9

This first section provides some of the details concerning the Campaign of Armageddon. These verses emphasize the physical deliverance of Israel.

Introduction—12:1

The Little Apocalypse begins by describing the God who is in control: "The burden of the word of Jehovah concerning Israel. Thus says Jehovah, who stretches forth the heavens, and lays the foundation of the earth, and forms the spirit of man within him...."*

With this verse Zechariah introduced a new theme of his book and he called it "the burden." This is the second burden in the book of Zechariah; the first was given in chapters 9–11. The word "burden" in Hebrew means "a heavy weight." In this prophetic context it means that the message, which God gave forth through Zechariah, was a heavy message. It was heavy for it was the Word of God, and it contained prophetic truth that was both negative and positive. Furthermore, he stated in the first part of verse one that this was "the burden of the word of Jehovah concerning Israel." The message concerned Israel in particular. While it mentioned other nations, it only mentioned them in connection with their relationship to the people of Israel. The second part of this verse describes the omnipotent God, the God who established all things, who created the heavens and the earth and who formed the spirit of life in man. Because of who God is, because of what He has done, and because of what He is able to do, all the things that are about to be prophesied in this "burden of the word of Jehovah" concerning Israel will surely be accomplished.

The Attack on Jerusalem—12:2-3

After introducing His message, God then gave the content of this heavy message in verses 2-3, where He says the Gentile nations will come against Jerusalem: "Behold, I will make Jerusalem a cup of reeling unto all the peoples round about, and upon Judah also shall it be in the siege against Jerusalem. And it shall come to pass in that day, that I will make Jerusalem a burdensome stone for all the peoples; all that burden themselves with it shall be sore wounded; and all the nations of the earth shall be gathered together against it."

As God described the nations coming against Jerusalem during the Campaign of Armageddon, he said two things about Jerusalem. First, Jerusalem will become "a cup of reeling" (verse 2). Here he pictured Jerusalem as a huge, vast bowl around which the Gentile nations would gather together to drink. When the word "cup" is used symbolically in the Old Testament, in the majority of cases it is used as a symbol of divine judgment (Psalm 75:8; Isaiah 5:17,21-23; Jeremiah 25:14-16; 51:7). As these Gentile nations come against Jerusalem, which has become a huge, vast cup, they will begin to drink from it, hoping to derive pleasure from it; but after having drunk from it, they will run away, reeling and staggering, no longer in control as they thought they

---

* All biblical quotations are taken from the American Standard Bible of 1901. The archaisms have been modernized.

would be. And not only will Jerusalem suffer in this siege, Judah will also suffer. God mentioned Judah separately from Jerusalem because the majority of the people of Judah will no longer be in the environs of Jerusalem. By this time, the majority of the Jews will no longer be in the land but will have been scattered out of the land, having fled to the *mountains* of Matthew 24:15-16 and the *wilderness* of Revelation 12:5,13-14. There will still be a number of Jews living in Jerusalem, and the Gentile nations will come against them in this siege; but the Jews elsewhere will also feel the siege in due course.

Second, Jerusalem will also become "a burdensome stone" (verse 3). It will become a very heavy stone, one that is not smooth, but rather one that has many jagged, pointed edges. Those who try to lift this heavy stone with their hands will be able to lift it just a little bit; but as they do so, it will be so heavy that it will begin to slip through their hands. As it does so it will lacerate and cut the hands to shreds. That is what is meant by making Jerusalem a burdensome stone; those who burden themselves with it will be lacerated.

So, Jerusalem will become two things to the Gentile nations in the Campaign of Armageddon: a cup of reeling that will cause them to stagger, and a burdensome stone by which they will be lacerated. Just how Jerusalem becomes these two things is detailed in verses 4-9.

Verse 3 ends with the statement that "all the nations of the earth shall be gathered together against it." The Campaign of Armageddon will not be one group of nations fighting a second group of nations. Rather, all the Gentile nations of that day will come together against one nation, Israel, and they will come against Jerusalem. This fact is repeated in Zechariah 14:1-2. (Other relevant passages include Joel 3:9-13 and Revelation 16:12-16.)

The Battle for Jerusalem—12:4-9

Just how Jerusalem will become a cup of reeling and a burdensome stone is detailed in 12:4-9:

> In that day, says Jehovah, I will smite every horse with terror, and his rider with madness; and I will open mine eyes upon the house of Judah, and will smite every horse of the peoples with blindness. And the chieftains of Judah shall say in their heart, The inhabitants of Jerusalem are my strength in Jehovah of hosts their God. In that day will I make the chieftains of Judah like a pan of fire among wood, and like a flaming torch among sheaves; and they shall devour all the peoples round about, on the right hand and on the left; and they of Jerusalem shall yet again dwell in their own place, even in Jerusalem. Jehovah also shall save the tents of Judah first, that the glory of the house of David and the glory of the inhabitants of Jerusalem be not mag-

nified above Judah. In that day shall Jehovah defend the inhabitants of Jerusalem; and he that is feeble among them at that day shall be as David; and the house of David shall be as God, as the angel of Jehovah before them. And it shall come to pass in that day, that I will seek to destroy all the nations that come against Jerusalem.

These verses describe the physical deliverance of Jerusalem as well as how the city will become the cup of reeling and a burdensome stone. First will come God's judgment upon the enemies' horses (verse 4).[4] As the enemies come against Jerusalem upon their horses, God will strike the horses with terror, madness, and blindness. God said that these judgments, under the Mosaic Covenant, would come upon the Jews for disobedience (Deuteronomy 28:28). If Israel disobeyed the Lord and did not keep the Law, they would be smitten with terror, madness, and blindness. What God once announced upon the Jews, He now announces upon the Gentiles because of their movement against the Jews (see also Deuteronomy 30:7), and this judgment is based on the principle in Genesis 12:3: "I will bless them that bless you, and him that curses you will I curse." As a result of being stricken with blindness, the Gentile armies will rush to their own destruction. At the same time, God said His eyes will be upon Judah. While the eyes of the enemy are blinded, the eyes of God, which are never blinded, will be upon the people of Israel, not merely to see where they are, not merely to see how things are going, but to look out for their protection. He will keep His eyes upon them in order to protect them from these Gentile armies.

Second, God will energize the Jewish forces (verses 5-6). He will miraculously and supernaturally energize the Jewish forces so that they will inflict tremendous losses upon the Gentile armies that come against them. The battle cry will be, "The inhabitants of Jerusalem are my strength." God will energize the Jews of Jerusalem and they will become like fire among wood, like a flaming torch among sheaves. The Gentile armies are pictured as dry wood and as sheaves, and when the fire is applied to the dry wood or sheaves, a quick burning and destruction are the result. By this means, the forces will be further lacerated—and that is how Jerusalem will become a burdensome stone and a cup of reeling.

In verse seven we read that: "Jehovah also shall save the tents of Judah first, that the glory of the house of David and the glory of the inhabitants of Jerusalem be not magnified above Judah." While the Jews of Jerusalem will be energized, causing great havoc among the enemies, God is not going to save the inhabitants of Jerusalem first but will instead save "the tents of Judah first." The term "tents" points to a temporary abode or place of dwelling. The point Zechariah is making is that the people of Judah will no longer be living in permanent abodes. They will not be living in their homes in the land of Judah; rather, they will be living in temporary abodes outside of the land. According to Micah 2:12-13, the place where the bulk of the Jewish remnant will be living is Bozrah (ASV reading). According to Micah, God intends to rescue the Jews in Bozrah first before He rescues the Jews in Jerusalem. But until then, the Jews of Jerusalem will be greatly energized. Nevertheless, Jerusalem will fall after inflicting tremendous losses upon of the enemy (Zechariah 14:1-2).

In verse eight, God again points out the means He will use to rescue the Jews of Jerusalem. Again, He says the Jews of Jerusalem will be energized so that the "feeble" and lame ones will be able to fight like King David did, and those who are like King David will be able to fight like "the Angel of Jehovah," who once killed 185,000 enemy soldiers in one night (Isaiah 37:36). In biblical revelation, it is obvious this angel is not a common, ordinary angel, but the unique Angel, the second person of the Trinity, the Messiah Himself. So the Davids among the Jews will be able to fight with the power of the Messiah Himself.

Zechariah 12:9 concludes with the statement that God is going to pass judgment upon the Gentiles. God's intent is to destroy those nations that come against Jerusalem. All the nations of the earth will come against the Jews, and God will pass judgment against them. Once again, this affirms the principle found in Genesis 12:3: "I will bless them that bless you, but him that curses you will I curse." First God will rescue the Jews in Bozrah and destroy many of the armies there. Then He will go to Jerusalem to rescue the Jews. As a result, He will destroy the final portions of the armies just outside Jerusalem in the Valley of Jehoshaphat (Joel 3:12-13).

The Salvation of Israel—12:10–13:1

The second main division of the Little Apocalypse of Zechariah is 12:10–13:1, which deals with the salvation and spiritual deliverance of Israel:

> I will pour upon the house of David, and upon the inhabitants of Jerusalem, the spirit of grace and of supplication; and they shall look unto me whom they have pierced; and they shall mourn for him, as one mourns for his only son, and shall be in bitterness for him, as one that is in bitterness for his first-born. In that day shall there be a great mourning in Jerusalem, as the mourning of Hadadrimmon in the valley of Megiddon. And the land shall mourn, every family apart; the family of the house of David apart, and their wives apart; the family of the house of Nathan

apart, and their wives apart; the family of the house of Levi apart, and their wives apart; the family of the Shimeites apart, and their wives apart; all the families that remain, every family apart, and their wives apart. In that day there shall be a fountain opened to the house of David and to the inhabitants of Jerusalem, for sin and for uncleanness.

Verses 10-14 speak specifically of the mourning for the Messiah. According to verses 10-11, Israel will mourn and plead for the Messiah to return to them. This mourning will result from an outpouring of the Holy Spirit upon the nation of Israel (Isaiah 32:13-20; 44:3-5; Joel 2:28-32; Acts 2:16-21). When the Holy Spirit is poured out upon all of Israel, the people will be spiritually regenerated and saved. As a result of their spiritual salvation, they will begin to mourn for the Messiah to return so that Messiah can rescue them physically as was predicted in 12:1-9: "They shall look unto me whom they have pierced." The Hebrew word for pierced is *dakar*, which is used 11 times in the Old Testament, twice in Zechariah (12:10; 13:3). It means "to thrust through." "They shall look unto me whom they have thrust through." This refers to the spear that pierced Jesus' side (John 19:57). The time is coming, after Israel is saved and the Spirit has been poured out upon the nation, that the people will begin to look *unto* the One whom they have thrust through. The King James Version erroneously translated this to read that they shall look *upon* whom they have pierced. Consequently, many have interpreted this to mean that Jesus will come first. The Jews will see Jesus, and only then will they be saved. However, the Hebrew word used here does not mean "upon," but "unto." When believers look *unto* the Lord, they do not visibly and physically see the Lord. That is the way this passage should be interpreted. When the Holy Spirit is poured out upon the whole house of Israel, the people will then *look unto* (not upon) the One whom they have pierced, mourning for Him to return. Only then will He return. It is not the second coming that will result in Israel's salvation, but Israel's salvation is the prerequisite and the cause of the second coming (Leviticus 26:40-46; Jeremiah 3:12-18; Micah 5:15-6:3; Matthew 23:37-39). After they are saved, they will look unto the One whom they have thrust through. "They... shall be in bitterness for him, as one that is in bitterness for his first-born"[5]—this emphasizes the intensity of the mourning. In that day, there was greater mourning for the loss of a firstborn son than for any other loss of a child. The fact that Israel will mourn for the Messiah as one mourns for his firstborn shows the intensity of that mourning. This mourning is not only a mourning over loss, but also a mourning that this son might come back and be restored to life. The Jewish people will mourn over the fact that they rejected Christ's Messiahship, and they will mourn that He might come back. Indeed, in this case, He will come back.

According to verse 11, the mourning for the Messiah will be similar to "the mourning of Hadadrimmon in the valley of Megiddon." The mourning referred to was the mourning over the death of King Josiah, a good king. Josiah was killed in a battle against the Egyptians in the Valley of Megiddon, the Valley of Jezreel, or the Valley of Megiddo (2 Chronicles 35:22-25). Israel, according to Jeremiah, mourned the loss of Josiah because he was such a good king. Jeremiah also mourned, knowing that this was the last of the good kings and Judah was now destined for a series of wicked kings who would in turn bring about the destruction of Judah. So just as the people mourned bitterly over King Josiah, they will mourn again for the Messiah to return.

Verses 12-14 list three specific groups of mourners. First, the royal house (verse 12), from the greatest (David) to the lowest (Nathan). Nathan was the third son born in Jerusalem (2 Samuel 5:14; 1 Chronicles 3:5), but the house of Nathan never saw any kings upon the throne. Yet of this line, the pierced Messiah came (Luke 3:27). Second, the priestly house (verse 13), from the greatest (Levi) to the lowest (Shimei). Shimei was the grandson of Levi through Gershom (Exodus 6:16-17; Numbers 3:17-18). No one from this line ever served as priest because the priestly line came through his brother Kohath (1 Chronicles 6:1-3). Third, all the people will be mourning (verse 14). In keeping with the Jewish customs observed during mourning, the sexes will be separated so that nothing can detract from the main business at hand, the business of mourning.

Finally, in 13:1, Zechariah spoke of the spiritual cleansing of Jerusalem. There is going to be a "fountain opened." In the Old Testament, the fountain was a symbol of cleansing. The fountain in the Tabernacle and the fountain in the Temple compound were the means of cleansing from ceremonial uncleanness. Here the word "fountain" is used symbolically of an outpouring of water. The outpouring of water is the symbol for the outpouring of the Holy Spirit (John 7:37-39). As a result of the outpouring of the Holy Spirit in Zechariah 12:10, the nation of Israel will be saved and look unto the Messiah. As a result of this, there is going to be a spiritual cleansing from their sinful state. Zechariah says the cleansing will be of both sin and uncleanness. The word "sin" refers to the active expression of sin, to the judicial guilt resulting from violation of the law, whether the Mosaic Law or the Law of Christ, and this requires justification. As a result of this fountain of the Holy Spirit, Israel will be justified, judicial guilt will be removed, and the people will be declared righteous. The word "uncleanness" refers to the passive result of sin and has to do with moral guilt, the condition or state of defilement due to the violation of holiness and which requires sanctification. As a result of the outpouring of the Holy Spirit and of Israel's national salvation when they look unto the Messiah, Israel as a nation will be cleansed from sin (judicial guilt) and uncleanness (moral guilt). The people will be both justified and sanctified.

The Cleansing of the Land—13:2-6

The third segment comprises Zechariah 13:2-6, which deals with the spiritual cleansing of the land:

> It shall come to pass in that day, says Jehovah of hosts, that I will cut off the names of the idols out of the land, and they shall no more be remembered; and also I will cause the prophets and the unclean spirits to pass out of the land. And it shall come to pass that, when any shall yet prophesy, then his father and his mother that begat him shall say unto him, You shall not live; for you speak lies in the name of Jehovah; and his father and his mother that begat him shall thrust him through when he prophesies. And it shall come to pass in that day, that the prophets shall be ashamed every one of his vision, when he prophesies; neither shall they wear a hairy mantle to deceive: but he shall say, I am no prophet, I am a tiller of the ground; for I have been made a bondman from my youth. And one shall say unto him, What are these wounds between your arms? Then he shall answer, Those with which I was wounded in the house of my friends.

Following Israel's spiritual and physical deliverance will come the cleansing of the land (verses 2-6). Three things can be pointed out from these verses.

First, there will be a judgment against all sources of pollution (verse 2). Zechariah mentions three sources of the pollution of the land—idolatry, false prophets, and demons—and all three of these will be removed. Idolatry will be removed once and for all when the image of the Antichrist is destroyed (Daniel 12:11). Demons will also be removed from the land. During the messianic kingdom, all demons will be confined in one of two places: some will be confined in Babylon (Isaiah 13:21-22; Revelation 18:2), and others will be in Edom (Isaiah 34:8-15). Both places will be a continuously burning wasteland throughout the messianic kingdom. In that way, demons are going to be removed from the land. The third thing that will be removed are false prophets (verses 3-6). The false prophets caused and led the people to worship idols, and demons, in turn, are the source of false prophecy.

The second point in this passage concerns the killing of the false prophets (verse 3). There will be such a national transformation of the people of Israel that they will have a zeal against the sins in which they once participated. Once they were involved in idolatry and demonology, listening to false prophets; now there will be a zealousness to do away with these things, in particular with the false prophets that led them astray in the course of the Great Tribulation. Indeed, the Old Testament law clearly demanded that false prophets be destroyed (Deuteronomy 13:6-10; 18:20-22). And it is the parents of the false prophets who will "thrust [them] through" when they prophesy. The word that is used for killing the prophets in 13:3 is the same word used in 12:10. Just as the Messiah was "thrust through," even so these false prophets are going to be "thrust through." In Numbers 25:8, this same word is used to speak of thrusting a sword or spear through two people engaged in pagan sexual intercourse. So, the false prophets will be executed by being thrust through by a sword or spear.

Third, the people will hunt out these false prophets. These false prophets will be ashamed because their prophecies did not come true (verse 4). As a result, they will try to discard the "hairy mantle." The wearing of a hairy mantle was the mark of a prophet, and God's prophets often wore them (1 Kings 19:13; 2 Kings 1:8; 2:8,13; Matthew 3:4; Mark 1:6). The false prophets will attempt to imitate the true prophets by wearing hairy mantles, but when they are discovered as false prophets, they will discard the mantles so that they are not recognized as prophets any longer. While they can remove the hairy mantle, there are other marks these false prophets will not be able to remove (verses 5-6). The prophets will be interrogated (verses 5-6). When they are asked, "Were you not a false prophet?" (verse 5), they will answer, "No, I was never a prophet and never claimed to be one; but I have always been *a tiller of the ground*, a farmer, from the time that I was a boy." Then will come a second question: "What are these wounds between your arms?" (verse 6). The phrase "between your arms" was an idiom for "chest" (see 2 Kings 9:24). It was a practice of false prophets to not only imitate a true prophet by wearing a hairy mantle, but also to do things that true prophets never did: mark their bodies and cause scars. For example, in the contest between Elijah and the prophets of Baal, the prophets of Baal cut themselves (1 Kings 18:28—an act forbidden to true prophets, according to Leviticus 19:28 and Deuteronomy 14:1). While the false prophets will be able to cast away their hairy mantles, they will not be able to remove the scars from their bodies. They will try to say they received the wounds while partying in the house of friends; but the truth will be discovered, and these prophets will lose their lives anyway.

Sometimes Zechariah 13:6 is pulled out of its context and is made to refer to Christ. But verse 6 is part of the context, which began with verse 2 on the subject of false prophets. It is part of the dialogue that began with verse 5. Thus, verse 6 is not a reference to the true Messiah, but rather, it is a reference to the false prophets of the Tribulation who will be executed at that time as part of the spiritual cleansing of the land.

Israel and the Messiah—13:7-9

The fourth division in the Little Apocalypse is Zechariah 13:7-9, which summarizes Israel's relationship to the Messiah:

> Awake, O sword, against my shepherd, and against the man that is my fellow, says Jehovah of hosts: smite the shepherd, and the sheep shall be scattered; and I will turn my hand upon the little ones. And it shall come to pass, that in all the land, says Jehovah, two parts therein shall be cut off and die; but the third shall be left therein. And I will bring the third part into the fire, and will refine them as silver is refined, and will try them as gold is tried. They shall call on my name, and I will hear them: I will say, It is my people; and they shall say, Jehovah is my God.

As Zechariah prophesied of the Campaign of Armageddon, Israel's turning to the Messiah, and the national cleansing of the land, before he proceeded with further details concerning the second coming and the establishment of the kingdom (chapter 14), he summarized Israel's relationship to the Messiah. In this summary he made three points.

First in verse 7, he summarizes what he detailed in 11:4-14, Israel's rejection of the Good Shepherd, the rejection of the Messiah at His first coming: "Awake, O sword against my shepherd, and against the man that is my fellow, says Jehovah of hosts: smite the shepherd...." The first thing to notice in this verse is the nature of the Messiah: He is both God and man. By stating "against my shepherd," Zechariah emphasized the humanity of the Messiah. But then he added, "...against the man that is my fellow." The word "fellow" is not a good translation of the Hebrew word, which is *amiti* and means "my equal." "Awake, O sword, against my shepherd, and against the man that is my equal." The term *amiti* as a noun is used 11 times and the other instances appear only in the book of Leviticus (5:21[twice]; 18:20; 19:11,15,17; 24:19; 25:14 [twice]; 25:17), referring to common, equal physical descent. For this One to be God's equal means that He must be God Himself. Here the deity is stressed: The Messiah is both God and man. Then the word "sword" is used, which is often a symbol of death. The "sword" is not necessarily the manner of execution (the Messiah was not killed by means of a sword), but a symbol of a violent death. Indeed, the Messiah died a violent death, as symbolized by the sword. Zechariah 13:6, then, speaks of the rejection of the Messiah at His first coming, and the rejection was by means of a violent death. The violent death came by means of crucifixion.

Second, Zechariah revealed the two results of the rejection (verses 7-8). The immediate result is the scattering, the dispersion of the flock (verse 7). In Zechariah 11:4-14, Zechariah gave a detailed pictorial prophecy concerning the Good Shepherd who is rejected. As a result of this rejection, the sheep, the flock of Israel, were scattered. What Zechariah detailed in 11:4-14 is summarized here in 13:7. The shepherd was smitten, he died a violent death, and the result was that the sheep, the flock of Israel, were scattered. This was fulfilled by the two Roman invasions of A.D. 66–70 and 132–135. (This verse is often applied to the scattering of the disciples when Jesus was arrested in the Garden of Gethsemane in Matthew 26:31-32, but the actual fulfillment came when the Good Shepherd, the Messiah, was smitten and died a violent death, and the flock of Israel was dispersed.) The distant result of the smiting of the shepherd is that in the course of time "in all the land two parts therein shall be cut off and die" (verse 8). The second result of the rejection of the True Shepherd is the death of two-thirds of the flock. This will be fulfilled during the persecutions of the Great Tribulation when Israel will suffer tremendous persecution (Matthew 24:15-28; Revelation 12:1-17). As a result of this persecution of the Jewish people, two-thirds are going to be killed. Yet what is meant by the phrase "in all the land"? The Hebrew word can be translated to mean the land of Israel, and if that was the intent, then it means that two-thirds of the Jewish people in the land of Israel will be killed. However, the same word is often translated in reference to the whole world, and if that is the meaning, it means that two-thirds of the Jewish population worldwide will be killed. By the time Armageddon begins, only one-third will be left.

The third point Zechariah makes in this passage (verse 9) relates to the salvation of the remaining one-third of the Jewish people. This remnant is going to be saved, both spiritually and physically. God is going to refine them by means of the outpouring of the Holy Spirit (12:10), their mourning (12:11-14) and the cleansing of their sins (13:1). He will refine them just as silver and gold are refined. As a result of the fiery furnace of refinement (a reference to the fires of persecution of the Great Tribulation) they will call on His name, and all who call upon his name will be saved. This calling upon the name of the Lord in Zechariah 13:9 results from the outpouring of the Holy Spirit in 12:10. When the Jewish remnant calls upon the name of the Lord, God will hear them and will save them, and they will truly become the people of God.

When they say, "Jehovah is my God," He will say, "They are my people." So all Israel will be saved (Romans 11:25-26).

It should be noted that the one-third who survive and are saved are of the same generation as the two-thirds who die. Those who interpret the two-thirds as dying in A.D. 70 must explain why the remaining one-third of Israel did not come to faith at that time. And those who believe the two-thirds died during the Holocaust must explain why the one-third of surviving Jews did not become believers at that time.

The Campaign of Armageddon—14:1-5

The fifth segment of the Little Apocalypse is comprised of Zechariah 14:1-5, which deals with the Campaign of Armageddon and gives details that were not covered earlier:

> Behold, a day of Jehovah comes, when your spoil shall be divided in the midst of you. For I will gather all nations against Jerusalem to battle; and the city shall be taken, and the houses rifled, and the women ravished; and half of the city shall go forth into captivity, and the residue of the people shall not be cut off from the city. Then shall Jehovah go forth, and fight against those nations, as when he fought in the day of battle. And his feet shall stand in that day upon the mount of Olives, which is before Jerusalem on the east; and the mount of Olives shall be cleft in the midst thereof toward the east and toward the west, and there shall be a very great valley; and half of the mountain shall remove toward the north, and half of it toward the south. And ye shall flee by the valley of my mountains; for the valley of the mountains shall reach unto Azel; yea, ye shall flee, like as ye fled from before the earthquake in the days of Uzziah king of Judah; and Jehovah my God shall come, and all the holy ones with you.

When will the Campaign of Armageddon take place? We're told, "Behold, a day of Jehovah comes" (verse 1). In the Hebrew text, we do not see the usual form *Yom YHVH* (The Day of Jehovah) but *yom Le YHVH*, meaning "a day to Jehovah." As such, it refers to a specific time within the period of *yom YHVH*, the Day of Jehovah—in this case, at the end of the Tribulation. As in Zechariah 12:2-3, Zechariah 14:1-2 describes all the nations coming against Jerusalem. When these armies attack, they will suffer tremendous losses (12:4-9). However, in spite of the tremendous losses the Jewish forces inflict upon the enemy, in the course of time, the city will fall. Jerusalem's spoil will be divided among these Gentile armies (verse 1). The same point is made in

Micah 4:9–5:1, where Micah also explains how the Gentile nations will come against the Jewish people and how the Jewish forces will be supernaturally energized so as to cause heavy losses against the enemy. But eventually the enemy will win, and the judge of Israel shall be "smitten with a rod upon his cheek," which is a sign of defeat. Zechariah states that the spoil will be divided right in the presence of the Jews after the city falls. That which normally happens in war after a city is taken will occur: the houses will be rifled and the women will be ravished as the armies take the spoils.

Verse 3 states that at some point after Jerusalem falls, "then shall Jehovah go forth, and fight against those nations, as when he fought in the day of battle." It should be noted that the fighting will *precede* the standing upon the Mount of Olives, and this is crucial. Too often, teachers of prophecy have taught that at the second coming, Jesus will first come to the Mount of Olives to fight against the enemy. However, that is not the order given in Scripture. The second coming will occur not upon the Mount of Olives initially, but at the city of Bozrah (Micah 2:12-13; Isaiah 34:1-7; 63:1-6). It is at that point that the Lord will begin fighting with the forces of the Antichrist who have come down to the city of Bozrah to try to destroy the remnant located there. As we learned in Zechariah 12:7, Judah will be saved before the inhabitants of Jerusalem. The fight will finally end in the Valley of Jehoshaphat (Joel 3:12-13), just outside the east walls of Jerusalem and below the Mount of Olives. That is where the winepress of blood will be located (Revelation 14:19-20).

Verse 4 says, "His feet shall stand in that day upon the mount of Olives," that takes place after the fighting in verse 3. So one should not picture Jesus descending upon the Mount of Olives at the second coming. Rather, after He finishes the fight in the Valley of Jehoshaphat, which is at the foot of the Mount of Olives (in fact, the Valley of Jehoshaphat separates the Old City of Jerusalem from the Mount of Olives), He will then ascend to the Mount of Olives. This will conclude the Campaign of Armageddon. When Jesus ascends the Mount of Olives, He will cause a tremendous earthquake that will, in turn, bring about a number of geographical changes in preparation for the messianic kingdom, which will have a somewhat different geography than Israel has today.

Among the results of this earthquake will be the creation of a new valley that will split the Mount of Olives. The Jewish people who are still in Jerusalem will flee through this valley to escape the earthquake that will destroy the city of Jerusalem as she stands now. While half of the Jewish population of Jerusalem will be taken into slavery, the other half will still be within the city, though under subjugation (verse 2). These people will escape through the valley. The way the Mount of Olives stands now, it serves as a blockade to an easy and quick escape so that one would have to ascend a rather steep hill to get away. However, with the creation of this new valley, the Jews will be able to flee through the cleft, through this valley, and escape from the city before it collapses as a result of the earthquake.

Finally, when the Messiah returns, He will be Jehovah Himself (verse 5): "Jehovah my God, shall come with the holy ones." These holy ones will include the good angels, who will return with Jesus (Matthew 16:27; 25:31), and will include the church saints, who will return with Him at the second coming (Jude 14).

The Results of the Second Coming—14:6-11

The sixth section comprises Zechariah 14:6-11, which deals with various results of the second coming:

> It shall come to pass in that day, that there shall not be light; the bright ones shall withdraw themselves: but it shall be one day which is known unto Jehovah; not day, and not night; but it shall come to pass, that at evening time there shall be light.
>
> And it shall come to pass in that day, that living waters shall go out from Jerusalem; half of them toward the eastern sea, and half of them toward the western sea: in summer and in winter shall it be. And Jehovah shall be King over all the earth: in that day shall Jehovah be one, and his name one. All the land shall be made like the Arabah, from Geba to Rimmon south of Jerusalem; and she shall be lifted up, and shall dwell in her place, from Benjamin's gate unto the place of the first gate, unto the corner gate, and from the tower of Hananel unto the king's wine-presses. And men shall dwell therein, and there shall be no more curse; but Jerusalem shall dwell safely.

This passage mentions five results of the second coming. The first result will be changes in the light sources (verses 6-7). There will no longer be an interchange between day and night every 12 hours as we have today. Rather, there shall be one long, continuous day. The same truth is taught in Isaiah 30:26. This may refer only to the day of the second coming, and not the whole Millennium.

The second result will be a new river of living waters, which will go out from Jerusalem (verse 8). Half of these waters will empty into the "eastern sea" (the Dead Sea) and the other half will empty into "the western sea" (the Mediterranean Sea). There are two other passages in Scripture that speak of this river: Joel 3:18 and Ezekiel 47:1-12. By combining all three of these passages together, it is clear that this millennial river will begin to gush out from the threshold of the Millennial Temple, which at that time will be located approximately 35 miles north of Jerusalem. It will initially flow eastward from the threshold of the Temple, but then it will turn south. It will then make its way to Jerusalem. Once it reaches Jerusalem it will then split in two, half of it flowing into the Mediterranean Sea and the other half flowing into the Dead Sea. Today the Dead Sea is just that—a dead sea so thick with minerals that it cannot sustain life. Even salt-water fish cannot survive there. However, this river of living waters will change the nature of the western shore of the Dead Sea, which will host a major fishing industry.

The third result is that Jehovah will be the king of the world and the One God (verse 9). The "Jehovah" here is the same as the Jehovah of verse 5 who comes, and He is the same as the Messiah of verses 3-4. Again, the Messiah is God Himself, and He will be the one king over all the earth. There will be no other God that is worshiped and no other king equal to Christ. There will be kings in the messianic kingdom besides Jesus, but all the others will be subservient to the Messiah. He will truly be the King of kings.

The fourth result will be a number of geographical changes (verse 10). These tremendous changes in the land will result from the earthquake mentioned in verses 4-5. They will cause some things to remain as they are, but other things will be totally different. Jerusalem will end up being exalted above all. Today Jerusalem is not the highest city in the world, but it will be in that future day (Isaiah 2:2; Ezekiel 40:1; Micah 4:1). The changes will be from Geba, north of Jerusalem, to Rimmon, south of Jerusalem.

The fifth result will be the safety of Jerusalem (verse 11). Zechariah emphasizes two things: first, the curse will be removed; and second, the people of Jerusalem will dwell safely and will not be intimidated any further.

The Destruction of the Enemy—14:12-15

The seventh main division of Zechariah's prophecy is Zechariah 14:12-15, in which he gives more details as to how the enemy will be destroyed:

> This shall be the plague wherewith Jehovah will smite all the peoples that have warred against Jerusalem: their flesh shall consume away while they stand upon their feet, and their eyes shall consume away in their sockets, and their tongue shall consume away in their mouth. And it shall come to pass in that day, that a great tumult from Jehovah shall be among them; and they shall lay hold every one on the hand of his neighbor, and his hand shall rise up against the hand of his neighbor. And Judah also shall fight at Jerusalem; and the wealth of all the nations round about shall be gathered together, gold, and silver, and apparel, in great abundance. And so shall be the plague of

the horse, of the mule, of the camel, and of the ass, and of all the beasts that shall be in those camps, as that plague.

Having described the events of the Great Tribulation, the Campaign of Armageddon, the second coming, and some of the results of the second coming, Zechariah next describes four specifics about how the enemy will be destroyed.

First, their flesh will melt away (verse 12). Their eyes will suddenly begin to melt within their sockets and their skin will melt away from their bones. Just how this will occur is stated in Habakkuk chapter 3, which discusses the events of the second coming and states that from the fingers of the Messiah death rays will shine forth and by means of these rays the enemy's flesh will melt.

Second, there will be civil strife (verse 13). The enemy will begin fighting among themselves. This fighting will probably result from the sudden confusion that arises during the second coming and from the fact that different armies from the various nations will have disagreements amongst themselves and begin killing each other.

Third, God will supernaturally energize the Jewish forces so they inflict heavy losses upon the enemy (verse 14).

And fourth, God will inflict a plague upon the animals (verse 15). Even the various forms of transportation used by the enemy armies will suffer from the same type of plague that was mentioned in verse 12, the plague of melting. Whether this is to be understood as literal animals or more modern forms of travel, the conclusion is the same: the transports used by the enemy against the Jews will melt.

The Messianic Kingdom—14:16-21

The eighth section is Zechariah 14:16-21, which concerns the messianic kingdom:

> It shall come to pass, that every one that is left of all the nations that came against Jerusalem shall go up from year to year to worship the King, Jehovah of hosts, and to keep the feast of tabernacles. And it shall be, that whoso of all the families of the earth goes not up unto Jerusalem to worship the King, Jehovah of hosts, upon them there shall be no rain. And if the family of Egypt go not up, and come not, neither shall it be upon them; there shall be the plague wherewith Jehovah will smite the nations that go not up to keep the feast of tabernacles. This shall be the punishment of Egypt, and the punishment of all the nations that go not up to keep the feast of tabernacles. In that

day shall there be upon the bells of the horses, Holy unto
Jehovah; and the pots in Jehovah's house shall be like the bowls
before the altar. Yea, every pot in Jerusalem and in Judah shall be
holy unto Jehovah of hosts; and all they that sacrifice shall come
and take of them, and boil therein: and in that day there shall be
no more a Canaanite in the house of Jehovah of hosts.

In this final segment of the Little Apocalypse, Zechariah reveals two major
truths concerning the messianic kingdom.

First, it will be obligatory among all Gentile nations to celebrate and
observe the Feast of Tabernacles (verses 16-19). Once a year, every year,
throughout the 1,000-year kingdom, it will be mandatory for every Gentile
nation to send a delegation to Jerusalem in order to observe the feast (verse
16). Should any nation fail to send a delegation to Jerusalem, God will punish
it by inflicting a plague of drought, and no rain will fall for that year upon that
nation (verse 17). The lack of rain will cause a lack of necessities of life. Egypt
is then cited as an example (verses 18-19). If Egypt decides to not send a delegation, then God will punish the Egyptians by not sending them any rain.

It is interesting that Zechariah brings up the Egyptians as an example. If
anyone would be tempted to dispense with observing the Feast of Tabernacles
in the millennial kingdom, it would be the Egyptians. The Feast of Tabernacles was one of the seven holy seasons of Israel inaugurated as part of the
observance of God's deliverance of Israel from the land of Egypt. Perhaps one
day the Egyptians will say to themselves, "Why should we send a delegation to
Jerusalem to observe a festival that commemorates an Egyptian defeat?" And
if they refuse to send a delegation to Jerusalem for the Feast of Tabernacles,
God will punish them with a lack of rain. Any nation that experiences this
punishment will probably learn from it and send a delegation from then on.
Under the Law of Moses, the Feast of Tabernacles was obligatory for Jews
only; but under the system of millennial law, it will be obligatory for every
Gentile nation as well.

The second truth Zechariah revealed about the messianic kingdom is that
everything in the land will be holy (verses 20-21). He emphasized the holiness
of everything in the land of Israel during the kingdom period. Under the
Mosaic system, there was a division between that which was for holy use and
that which was for mundane, earthly, secular, or common use. Under the Law
there were divisions between holy bells and non-holy bells, holy bowls and
non-holy bowls, and so on. This did not mean that the "unholy" items were
sinful; rather, that which was declared holy was that which could be used for
various observances in the Tabernacle and the Temple. The other items were
to be for mundane uses in private homes—such as cooking pots and pans. By

contrast, *everything* in the land will be holy during the millennial kingdom. That includes the bells upon the horses (verse 20) and all the pots and pans (verses 20-21). Zechariah stated that the same pots and pans that a Jewish woman might use to cook supper could also be used for special sacrifices, for special observances in relationship to the Millennial Temple. Under millennial law, there will be no distinction between the holy and the profane. Everything will be holy.

Zechariah closed his book by saying, "In that day there shall be no more a Canaanite in the house of Jehovah of hosts." God commanded the Jewish people to totally exterminate the Canaanite population because of the extreme degree of their sinfulness. But never in Israelite history were they able to accomplish it. There were Canaanites living in the land after Joshua died. There were Canaanites living in the land even during the days of David and Solomon. In fact, David and Solomon had agreements with the Phoenicians, who were Canaanites. So there were Canaanites present throughout biblical history. However, once the kingdom is established, only then will God's will be carried out to its fulfillment and there will be no more Canaanites anywhere in the land, let alone in the house of Jehovah. As a result of the total extinction of the Canaanites, everything in the land will be holy.

THE FULFILLMENT OF ZECHARIAH 12–14

As we carefully review Zechariah 12–14, one thing becomes obvious very quickly. If these prophecies are interpreted literally or normally, then it is obvious they have never been fulfilled. Therefore, those who claim all this was fulfilled in the past must resort to a non-literal, non-normal hermeneutic.

David Baron, a Jewish believer writing in the early 1900s, well before Israel became a state, had the following to say:

> Perhaps in connection with no other scripture do the contradictions and absurdities of the allegorising commentators appear so clearly as in their interpretations of this 14th chapter of Zechariah. Thus, according to Hengstenberg, Keil, and others of the older German expositors, who are followed by such English scholars as Pusey and C. H. H. Wright, to whose works I have so often referred in this exposition, "Israel," in this last section of Zechariah, "denotes the people of God in contradistinction to the peoples of the world; the inhabitants of Jerusalem with the house of David, and Judah with its princes, as the representatives of Israel, are typical epithets applied to the representatives and members of the new-covenant people, namely, the Christian Church; and Jerusalem and Judah, as the inheritance of Israel, are types of the seats and territories of Christendom."

And yet, when it is a question of judgment, as, for instance, the statement that "two thirds shall be cut off and die in the land," then, of course, they are agreed that those "cut off" are literal Jews, and "the land" Palestine.

Or again, when it is a prediction *which has already been fulfilled*, such as the piercing of the Messiah in chap. xii. 10, or the smiting of the shepherd and the scattering of the flock in chap. xiii. 7, then it is to be understood literally; but when the prophet speaks of things of which no fulfillment can yet be found in history, then the words, however definite and particular, must be spiritualized, and "Jerusalem" is no longer the capital of the Promised Land, but "the Church," and "Israel" no longer the literal descendants of Abraham, Isaac, and Jacob, but "the people of God," by which, as is seen in the quotation given above, is meant "Christendom."

But that is not really a spiritual way of interpreting Scripture, which robs it of its simple and obvious sense.

Kielfoth, Keil, etc., speak of the views expressed by Koehler and Hoffmann in their works on Zechariah, that this chapter refers to a yet future siege of Jerusalem after the return of the Jews in a condition of unbelief, and of their deliverance by the appearing of Christ, as "Jewish Chiliasm," but Jewish Chiliasm was not *all* wrong. *There is* a Messianic Kingdom—a literal reign of peace and righteousness on the earth, with Israel as its centre; but where Jewish Chiliasm erred was that it overlooked, or explained away, the sufferings of the Messiah which precede the glory. The question is if these allegorising commentators are not as much in the dark in relation to the second coming and the glory that should follow, as the Jews were in relation to His First Advent and His atoning suffering and death.

In the words of a true master in Israel: "The literal fulfillment of many prophecies has already taken place. It belongs to history. But the Christian has no more difficulty in believing the future fulfillment of prophecy than in crediting the record of history. He believes because God has spoken, because it is written. To believe that the Jews are scattered among all nations, that Jerusalem was destroyed by the Romans, that of the Temple not one stone was left upon another, requires no spiritual faith—it requires only common information. But to believe that Israel will be restored, Jerusalem rebuilt, and that all nations shall come up against the beloved city and besiege it, and that the Lord Jehovah shall appear and stand on the Mount of Olives, requires faith, for it is as yet only written in the Bible. But what difference does it make to the child of God whether the prophecy is fulfilled or not? Can he for a moment doubt it?

"And when we remember how literally prophecy has been fulfilled, we cannot but expect as literal a fulfillment in the future.

"How natural it would have been for those who lived before the First Advent, to think that only the spiritual features of the Messiah's Coming and Kingdom could be the object of inspired prophecy, and that the outward and minute circumstances predicted were either allegorical and figurative, or only the drapery and embellishment of important and essential truths. And yet the fulfillment was minute even in subordinate detail." For our own part, it is unnecessary to say, after what we have already written on chaps. xii. and xiii., that we have here a great and solemn prophecy which will yet be literally fulfilled in the future. And when it is objected by some of the modern writers that the literal fulfillment is "impossible," because it would involve not only national upheavals, but physical convulsions of nature, our answer is that *this is just what the prophet declares as most certainly to take place;* and, as if to anticipate the objection on the ground of its being naturally "impossible," or, according to human judgment, "improbable," he reminds us at the very outset of this section of his prophecy that it is *the word of Jehovah,* "*Who stretcheth forth the heavens, and layeth the foundation of the earth, and formeth the spirit of man within him,*" *with whom nothing is impossible.*[6]

Now, to repeat, we believe, in a literal fulfillment of this prophecy in Zechariah, and when we are told by a scholarly English writer that a literal fulfillment is out of the question because "the physical nature of the whole land would have to be changed to permit literal rivers to flow forth from Jerusalem," our answer is, "Certainly; *this is just what the prophecy says will be the case.* The physical nature of the whole land will be changed through the convulsions of nature, which are described here and in other scriptures, and which will be brought about by the Almighty power of God, with whom nothing is impossible. But while this literal fulfillment cannot be emphasized too strongly in order to be a true understanding of these prophecies, it is important also to note that the literal, material river will be at the same time the visible symbol of the mighty river of God's grace and salvation, which, during the millennial period dividing itself into full streams of Messianic blessings, will start from Jerusalem as its source and centre, and carry life and salvation to all nations.[7]

Feinberg, referring to the view that the prophecies were fulfilled by the Romans, states:

The prophecy has been understood by some of the Church Fathers to refer to the destruction of Jerusalem by the Romans. This cannot be the overthrow of the city of Titus, because he was not at the head of all nations, nor did he leave half of the population. Too, the passage cannot be speaking of the Babylonian conquest of Jerusalem, because the greater part of the people were exiled and later the remnant suffered the same treatment. Compare II Kings 25:11. Half of the population will go into captivity, but the other half will constitute the remnant. To the literal interpretation of this prophecy it has been objected that it would be a physical impossibility for all nations to assemble in battle against Jerusalem. Newton correctly states: "It should be observed that when nations are described as being gathered *as nations*, it is not meant that every individual comes, but they who are governmentally and executively the constituted representatives of their power."[8]

Even within the Reformed camp, there is the minority that cannot simply allegorize these three chapters away. James Montgomery Boice states:

> The chief problem is that nothing in this chapter fits historical events. So either the chapter is descriptive of events yet future, or it is to be considered figuratively as describing this present age. H. C. Leupold takes chapter 14 in this second sense. "Our verses do not, therefore, apply to any one situation. They do not describe a siege, capture and captivity which actually occurred. By means of a figure they describe a situation which obtains continually through New Testament times. God's people shall continually be antagonized and suffer bitter adversity at the hands of their foes and shall in consequence be brought low; but there shall always be an imperishable remnant, and that not so extremely small."
>
> This will not do. Scholars who apply these prophecies to God's people in this age take "Israel" as meaning "true Israel (or the church)." Yet when a statement of judgment occurs, as in the prophecy that two-thirds of the people will be struck down or cut off (Zechariah 13:8), they usually view them as literal Jews and the land as literal Palestine. When it is a question of a prophecy which has already been fulfilled, such as the piercing of the Messiah (Zechariah 12:10) or the scattering of the sheep (Zechariah 13:7), they take it literally. It is inconsistent to do this and then give spiritual meanings to portions of the book which have not been fulfilled. If one portion of these last chapters

refers to literal events, the other portions must refer to literal events too, even if, from our particular viewpoint, we are not able to explain all the details accurately.[9]

Next we will need to see precisely what the passage teaches. There are a number of items. First, the passage presupposes that there will be a Jewish nation centered about Jerusalem in the last days. Today, with the existence of the modern state of Israel a reality, this does not seem to be terribly remarkable. But we forget how improbable it seemed for the thousands of years that passed between the final scattering of the Jews by the Romans in the first Christian century and the establishing of the modern state of Israel in 1948.

Before World War II many commentators mocked even the possibility of a reestablished Israel. But David Baron, whom I have been quoting favorably and who wrote in 1918 (between the world wars), predicted the regathering of the Jews on the basis of this prophecy:

> "It seems from Scripture that in relation to Israel and the land there will be a restoration, before the second advent of our Lord, of very much the same state of things as existed at the time of his first advent, when the threads of God's dealing with them nationally were finally dropped, not to be taken up again 'until the times of the Gentiles shall be fulfilled.' There was at that time a number of Jews in Palestine representative of the nation; but compared with the number of their brethren, who were already a diaspora among the nations, they were a minority, and not in a politically independent condition. So it will be again. There will be at first, as compared with the whole nation, only a representative minority in Palestine, and a Jewish state will be probably formed, either under the suzerainty of one of the Great Powers, or under international protection....Around this nucleus a large number more from all parts of the world will in all probability soon be gathered." Since the conditions for the events described in Zechariah 14 seem to be receiving a literal fulfillment, why should we not expect that the events themselves will be literal when they unfold?[10]

Moore has a puzzling comment at this point, saying,

> "It is impossible for us to take this whole passage literally, for God cannot literally place his feet on the Mount of Olives." But surely God has already done it in the person of Jesus Christ. What is more, the angels who appeared at Christ's ascension said, "Men of Galilee...this same Jesus, who has been taken

from you into heaven, will come back in the same way you have seen him go into heaven" (Acts 1:11). What is more natural than that the second coming of Christ should be at this place and at the moment of a desperate need on the part of the Jewish people?[11]

Probably the primary promoters today of the view that Zechariah 12–14 was fulfilled in A.D. 70 are those who expose Dominion Theology, or Kingdom Now Theology, or Neo-Postmillennialism and take the preterist view of these prophecies. They have influenced others to adopt the preterist view, such as Sproul, although they do not necessarily accept the post-millennial view (Sproul, for example, is undecided on the millennial issue). The remainder of this chapter will interact with the leading proponents of this view.

Gary DeMar has a two-page treatment on Zechariah 14.[12] He is a good example of how preterists resort to certain methods in their interpretation of prophecy: first, resort to extreme allegorizing of the text; second, ignore or amend the details of the text (a literalist cannot ignore the details but an alle-gorist need not worry about such details and he can ignore them since they will destroy his case); third, resort to a *non sequitur* argument, meaning, bring in issues or passages which are irrelevant to the issue or passage under discussion.

Concerning Zechariah 14:2, where the prophet predicts that all nations will come against Jerusalem, DeMar interprets the verse as follows:

> This happened when the Roman armies, made up of soldiers from the nations it conquered, went to war against Jerusalem. Rome was an empire consisting of all the known nations of the world (see Luke 2:1). The Roman Empire "extended roughly two thousand miles from Scotland south to the headwaters of the Nile and about three thousand miles from the Pillars of Hercules eastward to the sands of Persia. Its citizens and subject peoples numbered perhaps eighty million." Rome was raised up, like Assyria, to be the "rod of [His] anger" (Isaiah 10:5). "So completely shall the city be taken that the enemy shall sit down in the midst of her to divide the spoil. *All nations*, generally speaking were represented in the invading army, for Rome was the mistress of many lands." Thomas Scott, using supporting references from older commentators and cross references to other biblical books, writes that Zechariah is describing the events surrounding Jerusalem's destruction in A.D. 70.[13]

This is a good example of what happens if one ignores the literal meaning and approaches a text with a preconceived theological bias, in this case, post-millennial preterism. It is true that the Roman army was made up of different nationalities, but it was still the army of only one nation: Rome. To claim that this fulfills Zechariah's "all nations" is purely "contrived and unnecessary," something DeMar accuses dispensationalists of doing. Furthermore, according to Zechariah 14:3, God will go forth to fight against the very same nations that came against Jerusalem, and the context shows that it is the very same armies that attack Jerusalem that God will fight against. DeMar interprets this as follows: "After using Rome as His rod to smite Jerusalem, God turns on Rome in judgment. It is significant that the decline of the Roman Empire dates from the fall of Jerusalem."[14] But the fact is that Rome continued to thrive for several more centuries and the barbarian hordes that finally sacked Rome did not punish the same army that destroyed Jerusalem. On the contrary, the victors over Jerusalem in A.D. 70, Vespasian and Titus, both became emperors; this is hardly a divine judgment.

DeMar is also guilty of what I call the fallacy of irrelevant contexts. What I mean by irrelevant contexts is the attempt to establish an interpretation of one text by using another text that does not deal with the same issue. One common example of such a fallacy is the attempt to extend the dates of Genesis 1 by using Psalm 90:4 and claim that each day in Genesis is equal to 1,000 years. But the two contexts are dealing with different issues and they do not qualify as "related passages" that the Golden Rule of Interpretation[15] requires. DeMar succumbs to this fallacy in his interpretation of Zechariah 14:4:

> It is this passage that Dispensationalists use to support their view that Jesus will touch down on planet earth and set up His millennial kingdom. Numerous times in the Bible we read of Jehovah "coming down" to meet with His people. In most instances His coming is one of judgment; in no case was He physically present. Notice how many times God's coming is associated with mountains.
>
> - "And the LORD *came down* to see the city and the tower which the sons of men had built....Come, let Us *go down* and there confuse their language, that they may not understand one another's speech" (Gen. 11:5,7).
>
> - "So I have *come down* to deliver them from the power of the Egyptians, and to bring them up from that land to a good and spacious land, to a land flowing with milk and honey..." (Exodus 3:8).

- "Then Thou didst *come down* on Mt. Sinai, and didst speak with them from heaven..." (Neh. 9:13a).

- "Bow Thy heavens, O LORD, and *come down;* touch the mountains, that they may smoke" (Psalm 144:5).

- "For thus says the LORD to me, 'As the lion or the young lion growls over his prey, against which a band of shepherds is called out, will not be terrified at their voice, nor disturbed at their noise, so will the LORD of hosts *come down* to wage war on Mount Zion and on its hill'" (Isa. 31:4).

- "Oh, that Thou wouldst rend the heavens and *come down,* that the mountains might quake at Thy presence—" (Isa. 64:1).

- "When Thou didst awesome things which we did not expect, Thou didst *come down*, the mountains quaked at Thy presence" (Isa. 64:3).[16]

It should be noted that every passage DeMar quotes uses the phrase "come down" or a variation of the same. Even if one concedes (and I do not) that all of these uses are figurative, are they really relevant to 14:4? The verse does not use any form of the phrase "come down." On the contrary, Zechariah's wording is far more specific and states, "His feet shall stand in that day upon the mount of Olives...." Whatever the other passages may be saying, they are not relevant to this one. Furthermore, His feet standing on the Mount of Olives occurs "in that day" when He goes forth to fight the nations that came against Jerusalem (verse 3). But, as we have noted, the judgment described for the invading armies in Zechariah 14:12-15 did not happen to the Roman army in A.D. 70. A dispensational theology does not allow the exegete to ignore such details, but DeMar's theology obviously does. This is convenient, but it is not honest.

And what about the earthquake that is to split the Mount of Olives? DeMar interprets this as symbolizing the breaking down of the partition between Jews and Gentiles as stated in Ephesians 2:14. Not only is this rather imaginative exegesis, it is once again employing the fallacy of irrelevant contexts. In the context of Ephesians 2:14, the breaking down of the wall of partition occurred with the death of the Messiah about 40 years before the events of A.D. 70.

DeMar totally ignores many other details in the text. He says nothing about Israel looking to the One whom they pierced and the mourning of all segments of Jewish society for Him. None of this happened in A.D. 70. While he implies that the deaths of the two-thirds took place in A.D. 70, he says absolutely nothing about the remaining one-third all coming to saving faith—which we know did *not* happen in A.D. 70. DeMar simply ignores the context in which these verses are found and tries to interpret them on the basis of irrelevant contexts. This is not exegesis but theologizing.

In addition, while DeMar implies that only dispensationalists believe that Jesus will literally come to the Mount of Olives, the fact is that this view is held by many non-dispensationalists, as well.

Another modern preterist is Kenneth L. Gentry, Jr. In reference to Zechariah 12:10 he states: "The Zechariah 12:10 passage indisputably refers to the land of Israel."[17] This is true, but to be more specific, it refers to those in Jerusalem, since Zechariah, more than once in the context, distinguishes between Judah and Jerusalem. Gentry then tries to relate the passage to the events of A.D. 70. But there was no outpouring of the Holy Spirit upon all segments of Jewish society resulting in them looking unto Him whom they had pierced. The context speaks of a national revival of Israel that did not happen in A.D. 70.

Gentry declares, "But Zechariah is greatly misunderstood in dispensationalism."[18] However, Gentry's interpretation of Zechariah 12–14, like DeMar's, requires ignoring the details that are necessary to arrive at a proper understanding of Zechariah. In fact, he seems to disclaim a need to be concerned about such details when he states, "…Dispensationalists interpret literalistically, with all the topographical and redemptive historical absurdities intact."[19] And we plead guilty as charged but disclaim that it is absurd! We dispensationalists really do take every word of Scripture seriously and refuse to ignore all those topographical notations just because they will not fit a specific preconceived and forced theology.

Beyond this, Gentry's treatment of Zechariah 12–14 differs little from DeMar's. The "all nations" are said to be the one Roman army comprised of various ethnic groups,[20] but this would hardly fulfill what Zechariah meant by "all nations." Also, the Lord standing on the Mount of Olives is not literal but symbolic of God rescuing His people, which ignores the fact that no such rescue of Israel occurred in A.D. 70. Gentry ignores the same details of the context that DeMar did.

David Chilton, although also a preterist, seems to take a slightly different view on Zechariah 12:10:

> Jesus had said also that "all tribes of the Land will mourn" on the day of His Coming (Matthew 24:30), that "weeping shall be there and the gnashing of teeth" (Matthew 24:51). St. John repeats this as part of the theme of his prophecy: *all the tribes of the Land*

[the Jews] *will mourn over Him.* Both Jesus and St. John thus reinterpreted this expression, borrowed from Zechariah 12:10-14, where it occurs in an original context of Israel's mourning in repentance. But Israel had gone beyond the point of no return; their mourning would not be that of repentance, but sheer agony and terror.

Yet this does not negate the promises in Zechariah. Indeed, through Christ's judgment on Israel, by means of her excommunication, the world will be saved; and, through the salvation of the world, Israel herself will turn again to the Lord and be saved (Romans 11:11-12, 15, 23-24). Because Christ comes in the clouds, in history, judging men and nations, the earth is redeemed.[21]

Chilton appears to waver as to whether the passage refers to A.D. 70 or to a future national salvation and seems (he is very unclear) to resort to a double fulfillment view. What Chilton does ignore is that Israel's national salvation described in this passage takes place during the time all the nations war against Jerusalem. If the war occurred in A.D. 70, then Israel's salvation should have occurred in A.D. 70. But if the salvation of Israel described by Zechariah is still future, so is the war of all the nations against Jerusalem.

We see more of the same confusion again in the same work:

Perhaps the most significant event that took place there in terms of St. John's imagery, was the confrontation between Judah's King Josiah and the Egyptian Pharaoh Neco. In deliberate disobedience to the Word of God, Josiah faced Neco in battle at Megiddo and was mortally wounded (2 Chronicles 35:20-25). Following Josiah's death, Judah's downward spiral into apostasy, destruction, and bondage was swift and irrevocable (2 Chronicles 36). The Jews mourned for Josiah's death, even down through the time of Ezra (see 2 Chronicles 35:25), and the prophet Zechariah uses this as an image of Israel's mourning for the Messiah: After promising to "destroy all the nations that come against Jerusalem" (Zechariah 12:9)....

This is then followed by God's declaration that He will remove from Israel the idols, the false prophets, and the evil spirits (Zechariah 13), and that He will bring hostile armies to besiege Jerusalem (Zechariah 14).[22]

All that Chilton said above is correct. But none of this happened in A.D. 70. The weaknesses of the preterist interpretation of Zechariah 12–14 can be summarized as follows:

1. Preterists use a highly inconsistent hermeneutic in that they take literally what fits their premise and what does not is allegorized or symbolized away, and to accept those elements as literal is rendered "absurd."

2. That highly inconsistent hermeneutic, in turn, leads to an inconsistent view of Israel by which the negative statements about Israel are applied to the "Jews" while the positive statements are applied to "the people of God" though the text never indicates that there has been a change of subjects.

3. The passage is interpreted in broad sweeps while the details are ignored or simply dismissed (i.e., the geographical and topographical notations have no meaning; "all nations" loses its meaning and dilutes to different ethnic groups in only one army; while 12:1-9 is interpreted to refer to A.D. 70; 12:10–13:1, speaking of Israel turning to the Messiah in the same time period is ignored; the two-thirds dying is said to take place in A.D. 70 but the salvation of the one-third is ignored; the coming of the Lord to the Mount of Olives is the coming of judgment but the context that shows Him coming for the purpose of rescuing Israel is ignored; and so on).

4. Much of the preterists' interpretation requires a large amount of subjectivity and imagination—such as the belief that the split of the Mount of Olives represents the breaking down of the partition between Jews and Gentiles, an interpretation one must read into Zechariah 14:4-5 since it is simply not there.

5. Preterists do not exegete a Bible text in its own context, but simply impose their theology on the text and conveniently ignore numbers of details that simply do not fit.

Thomas Ice has made the following observations:

> A preterist cannot give a textual interpretation of Zechariah 12–14 because they believe it is to be equated with God's judgment upon Israel at the hands of the Romans in A.D. 70—error number one. Greg Beale notes that, "Zechariah 12 does not prophesy Israel's judgment but Israel's redemption." Zechariah 12–14 clearly speaks of a time when Israel is rescued by the Lord from an attack by "all the nations of the earth," not just the Romans—error number two. In this context, Israel must refer to Israel. Since that is true, then the event of Zechariah 12–14 has not yet happened in history. This means that it is a future event. Dr. Beale makes a comment about Daniel that applies to Zechariah as well:
>
> > The burden of proof rests on these preterists to provide an exegetical rationale both for exchanging a pagan nation with Israel as the primary object of

> Daniel's final judgment and for limiting the last
> judgment mainly to Israel and not applying it uni-
> versally.[23]

Ice has also observed the preterist tendency to ignore the context of
Zechariah 12–14 and interpret it by irrelevant contexts and presupposing
replacement theology:

> Preterist Gary DeMar recently attempted an interpretation of
> Zechariah 14. Predictably, he says that Zechariah 14 "describes
> events leading up to and including the destruction of Jerusalem
> in A.D. 70." DeMar cannot show from the text of Zechariah the
> destruction of Jerusalem. DeMar approached the passage in
> what I would call a thematic approach. He hopped-skipped-
> and-jumped around the passage, denuding it of its context.
> Worse, he repackaged it into a false context. Dealing only with
> chapter 14, DeMar fails to produce any evidence that God is
> judging Israel, as is clearly used in Luke 21:20-24. In fact, the Lord
> is judging the nations, for the text says, "I will set about to destroy
> all the nations that come against Jerusalem" (12:9), and "I will
> gather all the nations against Jerusalem to battle...the LORD will
> go forth and fight against those nations" (14:2-3). Instead, the
> Lord is defending (12:8) and rescuing (14:3) Israel from those
> nations....
>
> The only way that preterists can attempt to deal with
> Zechariah 12–14 is not by taking the words and phrases of the
> passage in its literary context, but by simply declaring—as done
> by Chilton and Gentry—that the church replaces Israel. The
> text of Scripture is supposed to be the basis upon which we
> develop sound theology. Instead, preterists have to impose their
> false theological beliefs upon God's inerrant Word.[24]

As has been stated, the preterist must ignore the context and details of
Zechariah 12–14 itself. Instead, they resort to the fallacy of irrelevant context
by referring to Luke 21:20-24. Luke, of course, does speak of A.D. 70—a passage, by the way, the preterists have no difficulty taking literally. But preterists
then use the Luke passage to interpret Zechariah 12–14 rather than interpret
Zechariah 12–14 in its own right. As stated, they must ignore the details and,
in turn, the contrasts between the two passages, as the chart on page 182
shows.

THE EVIDENCE REGARDING ZECHARIAH 12–14

When it comes to interpreting Bible prophecy, the strength of dispensationalism is its high view of Scripture, which in turn leads the dispensationalists to take every text seriously, interpret it in its own context, and not ignore the context of any passage. Using that approach, it's clear that Zechariah 12–14 is to be understood as a future event. Since Zechariah 12–14 is linked to the Olivet Discourse and some events in Revelation as references to the same events, then it means that this passage supports a futurist understanding of the other related passages.

Chapter 12

THE WAR OVER WORDS

MAL COUCH

Many preterists are driven in their belief that the New Testament uses certain words and phrases to indicate that Christ would return sometime during the first century. They argue that certain "timing" passages spoken by Christ and referenced in the book of Revelation indicate a soon rather than a delayed return. Preterists focus on words that they see as "immediate" chronological indicators, such as *tachos* ("must *shortly* take place"), *engys* ("the time is *near*"), and *mello* ("*about to*"). But are they correct in their assessment?

Some preterists admit that they have arrived at their view, in part, because leading liberals and atheists have attacked these "timing" words and their meanings, and thus the credibility of Christ's promises of the New Testament is smeared. Preterists believe one way to counter such critical attacks is to reinterpret these "timing" passages and offer a different view about the Lord's return.

One critic, atheist Bertrand Russell, a leading intellectual of his day, denigrated the words of Christ on the basis that He seemed to make significant errors about His soon return. Nowhere in history do His predictions come to pass, Russell argued. He wrote, "[Jesus] thought that His second coming would occur in clouds of glory before the death of all the people who were living at that time."[1] In addition to referring to Russell's criticisms, preterist author R. C. Sproul cites critic Albert Schweitzer's critical book against the Gospels, *The Quest of the Historical Jesus.*[2]

Schweitzer was a German rationalist scholar who criticized the teachings of the Lord. Arguing from a humanistic and biblically destructive position, he said Jesus "underwent a series of crises" and that Jesus expected soon the dramatic coming of His kingdom. However, Christ ended up having to face the postponements of His own expectations. Schweitzer called Jesus' eschatology "parousia-delay," which required the apostolic church to adjust their thinking about Christ's imminent return.

Sproul shows how such criticism of the Bible and futurist eschatology impacted his thinking as a young theologian studying for the ministry. He writes,

> In seminary I was exposed daily to critical theories espoused by my professors regarding the Scripture. What stands out in my memory of those days is the heavy emphasis on biblical texts regarding the return of Christ, which were constantly cited as examples of errors in the New Testament and proof that the text had been edited to accommodate the crisis in the early church caused by the so-called parousia-delay of Jesus. In a word, much of the criticism leveled against the trustworthiness of Scripture was linked to questions regarding biblical eschatology.[3]

Full preterist John Noe also quotes Bertrand Russell and Albert Schweitzer in his call for the renewal of preterism, the theory concerning the *spiritual* return of Christ that he believes has already taken place. Agreeing with Sproul, Noe writes, "We must 'counterattack' the liberals and skeptics and give 'a loud wakeup call to a slumbering Church' about its mistaken doctrine of Christ's return."[4] Noe goes one step further than Sproul and quotes even Muslim writings and the venerable C. S. Lewis, who argued that Christ was wrong in His statements about the timing of His second coming.[5]

Sproul and Noe believe the time-restrictive predictions of the Lord need to be re-interpreted because "this perceived weakness was, and still is, the crack that let the liberals in the door to begin their systematic criticism and dismantling of Scripture with its inevitable bankrupting of the faith."[6] Preterist David Chilton also wrote about how damaging it is for the church to look for a future second coming of Christ and millennium. He said believers should not teach an apostasy of the church and the future reign of Christ: "For too long, Christians have heeded the false doctrine which teaches that we are doomed to failure, that Christians *cannot* win—the notion that, until Jesus returns, Christians will steadily lose ground to the enemy."[7] He then added, "A futuristic interpretation is completely opposed to the way John himself [in Revelation] interpreted his own prophecy."[8]

Preterist Gary DeMar also ties the "time texts" issue to the dating of the book of Revelation. He writes, "The Bible states without equivocation that the time was near for God to pour out His wrath on those who persecuted the saints. Since the book of Revelation was written prior to the destruction of Jerusalem in A.D. 70, the time texts makes perfect sense."[9]

Preterists say these prophetic statements were fulfilled in the first century, thereby silencing those critics who say Jesus and the Bible were in error in regard to His second coming. But is that really what the Lord Jesus, in the Gospels, and the apostle John, in Revelation, really taught—that the second coming had happened or was about to take place?

Do the phrases such as "must shortly take place" and "the time is near" really mean that Jesus was returning in a few decades, or sooner? Are these so-called "time texts" or "timing passages" *qualitative indicators* or *chronological indicators?* "Without a doubt, the exegetical survival of the preterist position revolves around the meaning of these passages" and others.[10]

Examining the Meaning of Words

To understand the key timing words and phrases (which include the words *engys, tachos,* and *mello*), we will look at their 1) root meanings, 2) contexts, and 3) finally, in terms of a larger picture, how the early church understood the second coming of Christ.

Each word will be examined separately.

The Meaning of Engys, Engizo[11]

Considering the Meaning

This family of Greek words is a compound with a preposition and a noun, meaning "in [the] hand." As an adverb, it carries the thought that something "is certain, it is a sure thing," "one has it in his hand." The *Exegetical Dictionary of the New Testament* Greek lexicon gives the meaning of the related word *engyos* as "standing as surety, guaranteeing."[12] In Hebrews 7:22, the word is used to foster *full assurance* "of the more excellent covenant made by God with us, and of the truth and stability of the promises connected [to the verse]."[13] The NASB rendering of Hebrews 7:22 is, "Jesus has become the *guarantee* of a better covenant." In other words, *certainty* is one of the most compelling meanings for the word. And though the word *engyos* may imply in some contexts nearness in the sense of location and even time, are these the ways it is always used in the New Testament prophetic passages? Or, because of the contexts, should the word be translated more accurately to say that "these prophetic happenings are *certain* to take place"?

One of the most important prophetic passages in which *engyos* appears is Matthew 24, where Jesus teaches about the coming Tribulation and His second coming, after which He will reign on earth. The parallel teaching is found in Luke 21. Let's take a closer look at how *engyos* is used.

Matthew 24:32-33. Jesus has just told His disciples that a terrible day, "a great Tribulation, such as has not occurred since the beginning of the world until now," is going to come (verse 21). It will be so awful that "unless those days had been cut short, no life would have been saved" (verse 22). He speaks of a day of tribulation in which "the heavens will be shaken" with the sun and moon darkened (verse 29). Finally He, the Son of Man, will appear and "be seen" by all the tribes of the earth (verse 30). With such global-encompassing language, and by normal standards of interpretation, this passage is seen as speaking about a far-off traumatic period that will have physical consequences upon the entire world. To take any other view is to twist the meaning of the passage.

Then Jesus mentions the budding of the fig tree and reminds His disciples that when the tender leaves start coming forth, "you know that summer is *near*" (verse 32). He adds, "When you see *all these things,* recognize that He is *near,* right at the door" (verse 33). Though one may argue that time is involved, the point is that the budding leaves is a *sure* sign that summer will come. Many commentators who realize that Christ is talking about far-off events see this clearly in the passage.

The leaves speak of the experiences of the Jewish remnant during the Great Tribulation. When they see and pass through all these events, they must recognize that their Messiah is about to come forth. Leon Morris states, "The fig tree does not bring the summer, but the appearance of its new leaves is a *sure* and *certain* indication that summer is now at hand."[14] Charles J. Ellicott adds, "What our Lord teaches is that as *surely* as the fresh green foliage of the fig-tree is a sign of summer, so shall the signs of which He speaks portend the coming of the Son of Man"[15] (emphasis added).

Surprisingly, many of the older amillennial commentators understood that *certainty* is the main thought of the passage. For example, in reference to the leaves budding, one commentator wrote, "We rely with such *certainty,* that we speak with *certainty* of all it implies....of the whole procession of events.... Insomuch that when we see the first of them, we feel as *sure* of the rest of them as though we saw them as well"[16] (emphasis added). Though not a premillennialist, R. C. H. Lenski realized that *engys* could not mean that the events Jesus described were about to fall on the generation that heard these words. Lenski wrote about this verse, "Just when the end will come no one knows."[17]

Luke 21:25-31. There are some important elements to be aware of in this parallel teaching about the future Tribulation and the coming of the Son of Man. In these verses, Jesus adds that there will be dismay among the nations because the sea and the waves will be roaring in perplexity (verse 25); men will faint from fear of the things coming upon the world (verse 26); and then the Son of Man will be observed coming with "power and great glory" (verse 27).

If Christ had returned in A.D. 70, then why didn't the nations see the sea and the waves in physical upheaval? And, why didn't the whole world see Him coming in His messianic power and glory? How was Christ's great glory manifested if He simply returned to earth *spiritually* as some preterists say? What's more, in Luke 21:35, Jesus makes it clear He is speaking about a terrible *global* tribulation that is going to take place: He says it will come upon all those who dwell on the face of the earth."

In Luke 21:28, Jesus said, "When these things begin to take place, straighten up and lift up your heads, because your redemption *is* drawing near" (verse 28). What redemption took place in A.D. 70? Can anyone honestly say this really happened in the sense of people *truly* experiencing redemption, as preterists argue? Of course not! Jesus, then, must be speaking of some far-distant generation who, when it sees "these things happening, [can] recognize that the kingdom of God *is near*" (verse 31). He then says "this generation" who sees and experiences all these terrible calamities falling upon the earth "will not pass away until all things take place" (verse 32).

Considering Location

Though there are some differences of opinion on the subject, more than likely the expressions "the kingdom of God" and "the kingdom of heaven" are but two sides of the same coin. They both probably refer to the future earthly millennial reign of Christ.

Engys is used in reference to the kingdom (with both the verb and adverb) in Matthew 3:2; 4:17; 10:7; Mark 1:15; Luke 10:9,11; 21:31. But before we examine how *engys* is used in these kingdom passages, we need to make some additional observations about how the word is used. There is little doubt that *engys* may, by context, be used to convey a *locational* meaning, or in a *chronological* way. For example:

Locational: "Now Bethany was *near* Jerusalem, about two miles off" (John 11:18); and "since Lydda was *near* Joppa…" (Acts 9:38).

Chronological: "The Feast of Unleavened Bread, which is called the Passover, *was approaching*" (Luke 22:1); and "the Feast of the Jews, the Feast of Booths, was *near*" (John 7:2).

Also, based on the grammar and context of a given passage, *engys* may simply mean that something is *coming near, approaching,* or *being brought near.*[18]

But does this guarantee that the referred-to event will take place immediately? If John the Baptist and Christ said the "kingdom of heaven *is at hand*" (Matthew 3:2; 4:17; 10:7), is it inherent in the verb that the kingdom will come right then? Could the kingdom be *near or certain* but not *actually arrive* because of some other factors? As well, could the verb tenses simply be telling us that the kingdom *is certainly on its way?* Could it be that the Jewish rabbis understood that the kingdom would be announced yet not arrive because the nation of Israel was unworthy—that it was not inaugurated because of the sins of the nation? Can it be shown by the writings of the church fathers that they understood this problem? The church fathers indicate that this kingdom was yet to arrive—perhaps in their day, or beyond.

Considering the Term "Near"

Key Places Where "Near" Is Used

Most contemporary American preterists believe that the Bible is the inspired Word of God. They would agree that it is not an accident that, when the Gospels say "the kingdom of heaven *is near,*" that this expression is found solely in the perfect verb tense in the Greek text. The phrase "the kingdom of God" is used in the present tense only once (Luke 2:31—more on this later). If the words "the kingdom of heaven *is near*" is in the perfect tense in nearly every case, what does this mean? The great New Testament Greek grammarians Dana and Mantey say, "It is best to assume that there is a reason for the perfect [tense] wherever it occurs."[19] The perfect tense usually implies "[a] process as having reached its consummation and existing in a finished state."[20] For example, when John the Baptist said "the kingdom of heaven *is at hand*" (Matthew 3:2), we would probably classify his statement as a *consummative perfect tense,* meaning that it "is not an existing state, but a consummated process which is presented."[21]

Putting it simply, the process of the kingdom of heaven coming *was consummated.* That *coming* ended with the presentation of Christ to the nation of Israel. Colin Brown, one of the most respected authorities on New Testament Greek, confirms this when he writes that the phrase "is near," with the perfect tense, "express[es] the end of the time of preparation. God's kingdom *has* drawn near, i.e. in the proclamation and work of Jesus...."[22]

Though difficult to translate into English, the clause could read, "The kingdom of heaven has certainly and completely drawn near." Does this indeed mean it was right then taking place? The answer is, no! The kingdom had *come* near, but it had not yet been inaugurated.

We must remember that John had also said, "*Repent,* for the kingdom of heaven is at hand." In other words, if Israel did not abandon her sinful ways, the kingdom would not arrive. This is why orthodox Jewish rabbis say the Messiah has not yet come to establish His earthly kingdom! More on this later.

Lenski translates Matthew 3:2 as "the kingdom of heaven *has come near*."[23] He adds, "The perfect tense…is durative-punctilliar…has been drawing near and is thus now at hand."[24] Jesus told the disciples that they were to go forth to the Jewish people and communicate the same message. "Say to them, 'The kingdom of God has come near to you'" (Luke 10:9), and, "Be sure of this, that the kingdom of God has come near" (verse 11).

The kingdom was at hand; it was certain to take place. But when? That answer is not given in the context. And when the kingdom does arrive, is it going to be the promised messianic reign, or the church? Commentator John A. Broadus states: "Much error has diffused itself through the Christian world from confounding 'the kingdom' with what is popularly called 'the church.'… We must dismiss the notion that the expression Kingdom of Heaven refers to the church, whether visible (according to the Roman Catholic view) or invisible (according to certain Protestant writers)."[25]

Though the kingdom was presented, would some of the most important actors in the drama—the Jewish people—come on stage? Would they accept the King and His reign? By their lack of repentance, would the Davidic kingdom of Christ be set aside for a period? History shows that is exactly what happened!

Other Places Where "Near" Is Used

Luke 21:7-36. Again, let's look a little closer at this passage that is parallel with Matthew 24. In Luke 21, Jesus focuses on the destruction of Jerusalem that will take place in A.D. 70. However, in verses 25-36, he also elaborates on the fact of His far-future coming. He speaks of "the Son of Man coming in a cloud with power and great glory" (verse 27). He mentions the fig tree leaves bursting forth (verse 30) and says, "When you see these things happening, recognize that the kingdom of God is near" (verse 31). Then He adds, "Truly I say to you, this generation will not pass away until all things take place" (verse 32).

"This generation" is a reference to those who will witness all the terrors Jesus has previously described: "signs in sun and moon and stars, and on the earth dismay among nations, in perplexity at the roaring of the sea and the waves" (verse 25). No matter what preterists say, these are not localized or regional happenings. They are global in scope—that is clear in the context.

In the context, the "near" ("certain") kingdom will arrive in the lifetime of that future generation that sees Christ's coming, and they will "stand before the Son of Man" (verse 36). New Testament scholar Walter Liefeld shows that the word "generation" and the expression "is near" come together and refer to the people in the end times who are present when these final terrible events transpire. *They* are the ones who will see the end come.[26]

Earlier in Luke 21, Jesus warned of the coming destruction of the Temple that would take place almost 40 years later in A.D. 70. He said of that great edifice, "There will not be left one stone upon another which will not be torn down" (verse 6). Using *engys*, Christ adds, "The time *is near*. Do not go after them" (verse 8). He continues, "For these things must take place first, but the end does not follow immediately" (verse 9). Thus, when the Lord talked about the destruction of the temple, while this event *was at hand*, there was still a period of almost four decades before Jerusalem and the Temple fell. Being *at hand*, then, does not mean *immediate*. That these events were *certain* and *sure* seem to be the best way to translate these passages.

Mark 1:15. Here, John the Baptist says, "The time is fulfilled, and the kingdom of God *is at hand*; repent and believe in the gospel." It's important to recognize that while the gospel would later refer to the message of personal salvation through Christ, at the beginning of John's ministry, it had to do with the Davidic reign of the Messiah. The able Greek scholar Alexander agrees and writes that John was "proclaiming, publishing the good news that the reign of the Messiah, so long promised by the prophets and expected by the people, was begun."[27] It is also important to note the clause with another perfect tense, "The time *(kairos)* is fulfilled" (Mark 1:15). On this Alexander adds, "*The time is fulfilled,* i.e. the set or appointed time for the Messiah's advent has arrived; *his reign…has approached,* is at hand."[28]

J. Dwight Pentecost concurs and says, "by the term 'at hand' the announcement is being made that the kingdom is to be expected imminently. It is not a guarantee that the kingdom will be instituted immediately, but rather that all impending events have been removed so that it is now imminent."[29] Louis Barbieri adds, "The fact of the institution of a messianic Davidic kingdom on the earth was clearly within the expectations of the nation. That kingdom was the focus of many Old Testament prophecies (cf. 2 Samuel 7:8-17; Isaiah 11:1-9; Jeremiah 23:4-6; Zechariah 9:9-10; 14:9). However did not the offer of that kingdom necessitate an affirmative response?"[30]

As the Gospel accounts unfold, it is obvious that the Jews had come to a wrong understanding of the promised messianic kingdom. They thought that when the Messiah arrived, He would set up His kingdom, of which they would automatically become a part. "They would be allowed entrance simply because they were the offspring of Abraham."[31] However, they also believed there would be a change of heart required, a repentance, before the Messiah would actually begin to rule. There is no question this was the orthodox Jewish perspective during the time of Christ and for generations after, and this helps us to recognize that simply because the kingdom had been brought to the people didn't mean it would be consummated right at that moment!

Other prophetic passages. Other passages using *engys* also appear to have the force of *certainty.* Writing about final redemption, the apostle Paul says, "For now salvation is nearer to us than when we believed. The night is almost gone, and the day *is near*" (Romans 13:11-12). Paul was saying, "The day of deliverance *is certain,*" even though many years may pass before it is accomplished. Ellicott says of this passage, "Every hour brings the expected end nearer."[32]

The apostle Peter adds to what Paul says in Romans 13: "The end of all things *is near;* therefore, be of sound judgment and sober spirit for the purpose of prayer" (1 Peter 4:7). The phrase "the end of all things" apparently refers to more than the arrival of the kingdom of God. What did Peter have in mind?

We find Peter's explanation in 2 Peter 3:1-14. Here, he refers back to 1 Peter 4:7 and adds, "This is now, beloved, the second letter I am writing to you in which I am stirring up your sincere mind by way of reminder" (verse 1). He then picks up his discussion of end-time events. Though he does not deal with the messianic kingdom, Peter elaborates on the final judgments that will come upon the earth:

- "Know…that in the last days mockers will come with their mocking… saying, 'Where is the promise of His coming?'" (verses 3-4).

- "The present heavens and earth are being reserved for fire, kept for the day of judgment and destruction of ungodly men" (verse 7).

- "The day of the Lord will come like a thief, in which the heavens will pass away…and the earth and its works will be burned up" (verse 10).

- "According to His promise we are looking for new heavens and a new earth" (verse 13).

Peter concludes, "Therefore, beloved, since you look for these things, be diligent to be found by Him in peace, spotless and blameless" (verse 14). Now, all of these dramatic future happenings are connected with what Peter said in 1 Peter 4:7. What does he mean, then, by, "The end of all things is at hand" in 1 Peter 4:7? Clearly, he is saying that these phenomena are coming nearer—but when, no one can predict.

It must be conceded that the Jews of New Testament times understood something in this expression that we do not comprehend. They did not measure time as we do. Their view of the timing of events was drastically different than ours. In fact, the problem of "at hand" seems to be solved by what Peter says in 2 Peter 3:8-9. The apostle must have heard the same criticisms we hear today about Christ's return, for he writes, "Do not let this one fact escape your notice, beloved, that with the Lord one day is like a thousand years, and a thousand years like one day. The Lord is not slow about His promise, as some count slowness." Some people have attempted to use these verses to discount the idea of the 1,000-year kingdom. But Peter is not discussing the kingdom here. Rather, he is talking about the ultimate final day of world history as we know it. His point is that God does not calculate time as we do.

The respected Greek scholar A. T. Robertson says of 1 Peter 4:7, "How near Peter does not say, but he urges readiness (1:5f.; 4:6) as Jesus did (Mark 14:38) and Paul (I Thessalonians 5:6), though it is drawing nearer all the time (Romans 12:11), but not at once (II Thessalonians 2:2)."[33] Ellicott says on 2 Peter 3:8-9,

> What is insisted on is simply this—that distinctions of long and short time are nothing in the sight of God; delay is a purely human conception....By ["is not slow"] is meant "does not delay beyond the time appointed." There is no dilatoriness; He waits, but is never slow, is never late....["about His promise"]—the Greek construction is peculiar, formed on the analogy of a comparative adjective—"is not slower than his promise."[34]

However, DeMar would probably object. In Appendix 1 of his book *Last Days Madness,* he merely mentions 1 Peter 4:7, but does not deal with the point of the verse.[35] Peter uses *engizo* in the perfect tense, which is the tense used most often with this word. With a broad, sweeping statement, Peter says, in essence, "The end of all things has become certain."

Similarly, James says, "The coming of the Lord *is near*" and adds, "The Judge is standing right at the door" (James 5:8-9). John also writes, "Children, it is the last hour; and just as you heard that antichrist is coming, even now many antichrists have appeared; from this we know that it is the last hour" (1 John 2:18).

Whether DeMar and other preterists like it or not, the fact is that these passages are clearly telling us that we have entered into the final period of world history. It is a fact that we have seen the beginning of the final days. The end is near, the coming of the Lord is certain, and we are in the last hour before the rapture and Tribulation events begin. The challenge is for preterists to put all the facts together in light of the prophetic scenario laid out in the Old Testament. We are waiting expectantly for the conclusion of all things. Everything is in place, but the timing will be determined by the Lord. We cannot rewrite the prophetic scriptures and spiritualize away the literalness of impending events.

The Book of Revelation. Engys is used twice in the book of Revelation. In fact, the word *engys* bookends Revelation in 1:3 and 22:10. The apostle writes, "Blessed is he who reads and those who hear the words of the prophecy, and heed the things which are written in it; for the time is *near*" (1:3). At the end of the book an angel speaks to John and says, "Do not seal up the words of the prophecy of this book, for the time is *near*" (22:10). DeMar argues, "If the book of Revelation is 'meant to be understood,' and its first-century readers expected the 'imminent return of Christ,' then Jesus' return should have been 'near' for *them.*"[36]

In the original Greek text, both Revelation 1:3 and 22:10 read nearly the same way. The verses do not say the kingdom of God (or heaven) is at hand, but *the season ("kairos") is sure.* Here in Revelation, why did John not use the Greek word *kronos,* which would have indicated a nearness in a certain *chronological* sense? Also, why in these verses did he not use the verb *engyzo* (with the perfect tense), but instead, simply the noun *engys?* John is simply focusing on the fact of the *certainty* about the season someday coming, and is not emphasizing the closeness of these events. Many respected Greek scholars concur; we are not certain *when* the last season may fall upon the world.[37] J. A. Seiss adds that when these prophecies in Revelation were written, they were "first pressed upon the study of the Church by the solemn consideration that the period of their fulfillment was rapidly approaching. But if this argument was [in] force then, how much more now?"[38]

Kairos always denotes a season or a period, longer or shorter, that is marked by what it contains. But *chronos* simply speaks of time as extended. The end had not yet occurred, and the season was still in the process of coming.[39] "The season (*kairos*) for Christ's return is always imminent—now as it has been from the days of his ascension (John 21:22; Acts 1:11)."[40] Commentator Albert Barnes writes

> The word "time" (*kairos*) refers not to time in general (as would *chronos*), but to a season as marked out by certain conditions.... Several grammarians have pointed out that in scripture the use of the expression "the time" takes on a special meaning.... Prophecy up to the cross and the death, burial, resurrection and ascension of Christ has all been fulfilled. The next prophecy awaiting fulfillment is the rapture of the church which is thus imminent (i.e. it does not await the fulfillment of any intervening event). The rapture thus opens the way for the end-time events on earth.... The intervening centuries since this was written have done nothing to lessen the imminence of the

end-time crises. It is still impending and the words "shortly" and "at hand" bring it very near.[41]

He further explains,

> It is customary to speak of a succession of events or periods as near, however vast or interminable the series may be, when the commencement is at hand....So Christians now speak often of the millennium as near, or as about to occur, though it is the belief of many that it will be protracted for many ages....Though the end might be remote, for the series of events might stretch far into the future.[42]

It is important to differentiate between the words *immediate* and *imminent*.[43] *Immediate* speaks of taking effect without delay, which does not allow for any intervening events. But *imminent* speaks of impending—that is, it may happen at any time. Some other events can intervene, but this does not affect the fact of the return. In the New Testament, the coming of Christ is set forth as imminent rather than immediate. If the Bible had meant immediate, the saints of the Lord would certainly have been disappointed as they waited for Christ to come right away—which He didn't.

The imminent return of Christ has been the hope of the church since apostolic times and down through the centuries. And God has all events in His own hands (Acts 1:7). The return of Christ does not have to be immediate, but it is certainly imminent. (Also, the doctrine of imminence requires a moral response in the life of the believer [1 John 3:3].) Unfortunately, theories such as preterism have robbed the church of the joy and anticipation of the actual historical, glorious hope of the Lord's coming. What R. C. H. Lenski writes on 1 Peter 4:7 is certainly relevant to Revelation 1:3:

> Since Christ's first coming there is nothing more to expect except his coming to judgment, and this may occur at any time. The apostles had no revelation as to the date of it. They were in the same position in which we are at this date; they spoke as we must now speak. None of us knows but what we may live to see the end. We have the advantage of knowing that it has been delayed for centuries, but we know this, not from Scripture, but from the fact, from history. To charge Paul or Peter with false prophecy for saying 1900 years ago that the end is near, is to treat them unfairly. They, as we, had to live in constant expectation of Christ's sudden return.[44]

The Meaning of Tachos

Preterists like to continue their argument by saying that the Greek word *tachos*—and the family of words that go with it—also implies that something is going to happen soon, or right now. However, as we will see in a moment, the more common way of translating the word is "hastily, with speed, swift, swiftly, without delay," or "fast" in relation to movement, and as a comparative adverb, "more swiftly, quicker."[45] On Revelation 1:1 and 22:6 and the expression "must shortly take place," preterist Chilton writes, "The words *shortly* and *near* simply cannot be made to mean anything but what they say."[46] Preterist DeMar says, "'Soon,' 'near,' and 'at hand' are explicit time indicators that are meant to describe a period of time in the near future. While days, weeks, months, and years are not specified, we can be certain that the events that are said to be 'near,' 'soon,' and coming 'quickly' are not far off in time."[47]

Considering the Lexical Meaning

The internationally known lexicographers Liddell and Scott, in showing the descriptive use of *tachos* with compound words, confirm that in most cases, the overwhelming meaning of *tachos* is "speediness of action."[48] Many if not most of the descriptions Liddell and Scott illustrate read "swiftness, hastiness, velocities, fast-walking, talking fast, burning quickly, working quickly, fast-rowing, rapid, sudden death, quickly changing, swift to anger."

Swiftness of motion is the compelling and most common meaning of *tachos:* "quickness, haste, speed."[49] Bauer, Arndt, and Gingrich (BAG) list the meaning of *tachos* as "speed, quickness, swiftness, haste."[50] See chapter 4 for more on *tachos*.

Considering the Use of Tachos *in the Book of Revelation*

Not only is there a preponderance of lexical support for understanding the *tachos* family as including the notion of "quickly" or "suddenly," but there is also the fact that all the occurrences in Revelation are adverbs of manner. Such terms are not used as descriptives of *when* the events will occur and Christ will return, but instead, they are descriptive of the *manner* in which they will take place when they occur. Such adverbial phrases in Revelation can more accurately be translated "with swiftness, quickly, all at once, at a rapid pace."

Consider, for example, Revelation 1:1: "The Revelation of Jesus Christ, which God gave Him to show to His bond-servants, the things which must *soon* take place...."

Many Greek scholars, both futurists and nonfuturists, agree that the idea of *tachos* here has to do with *swiftness* of execution when the prophetic events begin to take place. *Tachei* ("shortly") "is a relative term to be judged in the light of II Peter 3:8 according to God's clock, not ours. And yet undoubtedly the hopes of the early Christians looked for a speedy return of the Lord Jesus."[51] The much-respected author and teacher Joseph Seiss translates the phrase, "that which must come to pass speedily."[52] Alford argues that it is wrong for critics of the Scriptures to press *en tachei* "to furnishing a guide to the interpretation of the prophecy [of Revelation]" and he criticizes those who try to create a false argument and scenario for preterism with such prophetic schemes.[53]

En tachei is translated by Lange "in swift succession," who adds that other scholars "correctly interpret it as referring to the rapidity of the course of the events prophesied."[54] Swete argues that *near fulfillment* is really in view here, and the Ritchie Commentary agrees: "This [*en tachei*] phrase, which if literally translated would be 'in brief (time),' is used seven times in the NT....the primary thought is not so much the proximity of the event, but the absolute certainty of the event and the rapidity of fulfillment once the action is commenced....Both certainty and rapidity of action are involved here. Whatever seeming delay there is, action is certain and it will be swift."[55]

The adverb *tachu* is translated in almost every case as "quickly, suddenly, speedily, without delay." The meaning is "do not procrastinate, do not hesitate." In the Gospels we read, "Make friends *quickly* with your opponent at law while you are with him on the way" (Matthew 5:25); "go *quickly* and tell His disciples that He has risen from the dead" (28:7); "they left the tomb *quickly*" (verse 8); "when [Mary] heard [of Lazarus' resurrection], she got up *quickly* and was coming to [Jesus]" (John 11:29).

This meaning is carried over into the Apocalypse. The Lord said to the church at Pergamum, "Therefore repent; or else I am coming to you *quickly*, and I will make war against them with the sword of My mouth" (Revelation 2:17). To the church at Philadelphia He said, "I am coming *without delay*; be hanging on [present imperative] then to what you have, so that no one should suddenly take away [aorist subjunctive] your crown" (3:11, translation mine).

The book of Revelation ends with the same thought. When the terrible events described in the book begin, they will come about with rapidity. John goes on and uses from the *tachos* family the adverb *tachu* and closes the book of Revelation by writing, "Behold, I am coming *quickly*" (22:7,12), and finally at the very end of the book, "Yes, I am coming *quickly*" (verse 20).

How did the early church understand these verses in chapter 22? Did those early believers think that "quickly" meant Christ had already arrived in a spiritual sense in A.D. 70? Or did they understand the Lord's words to mean that His arrival was yet to take place? In the *Didache,* written in the second century, the church used Jesus' words in the prayer used at the close of every observance of the Lord's Table and said, "Amen, come, Lord Jesus."[56] They apparently understood the word "quickly" in a full eschatological context that's different than the understanding of preterists today. "The church in every age has always lived with the expectancy of the consummation of all things in its day. Imminency describes an event possible any day, impossible no day. If this sense is followed, we are neither forced to accept a 'mistaken apocalyptic' view as Schweitzer advocated nor a preterist interpretation."[57]

The Meaning of Mello
Considering the Meaning

It is important to remember that words must be seen in the light of how they are used in their context. And the greater context of prophecy passages must be looked at with the backdrop of the entire prophetic scenario in mind, as pointed out at the beginning of this chapter. When it comes to the Greek word *mello*, preterists are quick to say they believe *mello* ("to be about to, going to happen, intend to"), as used in certain prophetic passages, proves that second coming events were imminent. However, the word is seldom used in passages that support the preterist arguments about the second coming, or in a way that would point to *an instant and sudden happening*. The lexicons BAG and Balz and Schneider confirm this fact. BAG hardly mentions a future use of *mello* that would specifically prove the preterist case.[58] The word is most often translated "be destined, inevitable, intend."

According to the prestigious Liddell and Scott Greek-English lexicon, the main way the word is to be translated is "to be destined," or "likely to," "indicating an estimated certainty or strong probability" and an "expectation."[59] The respected Greek lexicon by Thayer says the word is used "of those things which will come to pass...by fixed necessity or divine appointment...*are* to be, *destined* to be."[60]

In certain prophetic passages where *mello* is used in a future sense, immediacy is not implied. Balz and Schneider show that the word "can express the necessity of an event that is based on the divine will and thus is certain to occur."[61] When used in a prophetic passage, the word "is used with reference to the suffer[ing] (of Christians, 1 Thessalonians 3:4) and for the anticipated future, the judgment, the new aeon, the future life, and other 'blessings' that are objects of hope...."[62]

Considering the Context

Jesus said of Himself, "The Son of Man is going to come in the glory of His Father with His angels" (Matthew 16:27). The phrase "is going" is a present tense form of *mello*, and "to come" is a present infinitive of *erchomai*. The verse could read, "The Son of Man *is certain to be coming.*" Broadus translates it, "He is coming, and there is no mistake about it."[63]

Was this the actual coming of the kingdom of the Lord? Or was it simply meant to be a revelation of the messianic glory and majesty of Christ, who will indeed someday come and reign on earth? It's important to note that Peter, James, and John do not call this event the fulfillment of the kingdom. In their writings, they still looked forward to a future establishment of the literal Davidic reign.

Reminiscing about what he saw, Peter wrote, "We were eyewitnesses of His majesty. For when He received honor and glory from God the Father, such an utterance as this was made to Him by the Majestic Glory, 'This is My beloved Son with whom I am well-pleased,'—and we ourselves heard this utterance made from heaven when we were with Him on the holy mountain" (2 Peter 1:16-18). In the same letter, Peter mentioned the mockers who ask, "Where is the promise of His coming?" (3:4). James, in his epistle, also wrote, "Be patient, brethren, until the coming of the Lord" (5:7). John, writing about A.D. 90, said to "not shrink away from Him in shame at His coming" (1 John 2:28). Though the Transfiguration was certainly a revelation to the fact that Jesus was indeed the Messiah, the Son of Man, none of these disciples in their later writings called this mountaintop experience "the coming of the kingdom."

What was the purpose, then, of this glorification of the Lord before these three disciples? Did it mean that the messianic reign had begun?

In the chapter prior to the Transfiguration, Jesus had said that when the Son of Man came in the glory of His Father, He would come with His angels, and then would "repay every man according to his deeds" (Matthew 16:27). If the kingdom had come in chapter 17, or even in A.D. 70 or sometime after, then when were His angels seen, and when did He carry out the judgment for every man's deeds? It is obvious that the phrase "is going to come" (Matthew 16:27), using the Greek word *mello*, should not be interpreted to mean that the messianic kingdom was about to arrive at that very moment.

Preterists use Matthew 24:6 to argue their case that Tribulation events are about to come on the world. There, Christ said, "You *will* be hearing of wars and rumors of wars. See that you are not frightened, for those things must take place, but that is not yet the end." The word "will" is the present infinitive translated in Thayer's lexicon as "what is *sure* to happen."[64]

Considering the Use in the Book of Revelation

The word *mello* is used thirteen times in Revelation, and is to be translated "will" in most cases. Again, the idea of *when* specific events are to take place is not the point. That they are *certain* is the most common meaning. After the apostle John wrote about seeing the glorified Christ in chapter one and listed the problems in the seven churches of Asia Minor in chapters two and three, he then is told by the Lord to write down "the things which *will* take place after these things" (1:19).

The *chronological* order and the concept of *certainty* continues with the word *mello* in most of its uses in the book of Revelation. For example, because of faithfulness, the church at Philadelphia was promised protection from the hour of judgment that was "*about* to come upon the whole world, to test those who dwell on the earth" (3:10); John "was *about* to write" what he heard (10:4); when the "angel *is about* to sound" the trumpet, then the mystery of God is finished (verse 7); the dragon stood before the woman [Israel] "who *was about* to give birth" to the Messiah (12:4); "she gave birth to a son, a male child [Christ], who *is sure* to rule all the nations" (verse 5, translation mine). From what Thayer has already said about *mello*, he adds concerning this verse "…used also of those things which we infer from certain preceding events will of necessity follow."[65]

Understanding How the Kingdom Will Arrive

In Luke 17:20-21, Jesus told His disciples and the Pharisees how the messianic kingdom would come: "The kingdom of God is not coming with signs to be observed; nor will they say, "Look, here it is!" or, "There it is!" For behold, the kingdom of God is in your midst."

This is a much-misunderstood passage of Scripture. Jesus is not saying that people at that time were saying the kingdom of God was in their midst. Rather, He was quoting what certain Jews *might* incorrectly say at some point in the future. By saying the kingdom would not be observed with signs, He meant signposts or specific indicators leading up to the coming of the kingdom. The Lord continued with His argument and turned to His disciples and warned them, saying, "The days shall come when you will long to see one of the days of the Son of Man, and you will not see it" (verse 22), because *other* people will say, "Look there! Look here!" But He went on and added, "Do not go away, and do not run after them" (verse 23).

Jesus then reminded His disciples that His coming will be instant, dramatic, and visible to the entire world: "For just like the lightning, when it flashes out of one part of the sky, shines to the other part of the sky, *so will the Son of Man be [coming] in His day*" (verse 24). Matthew added to what Jesus said in Luke: "Then the sign of the Son of Man will appear in the sky, and then all the tribes of the earth will mourn, and they will see the Son of Man coming on the clouds of the sky with power and great glory" (Matthew 24:30).

Preterists say this happened in a *spiritual sense* in A.D. 70. But such an argument is ludicrous and completely destroys any normal meaning and the principles of interpretation! There's a little verse often overlooked in the Luke passage that gives us a better sense as to how this prophecy would unfold. After saying that His coming would happen dramatically, as a flash of lightning across the sky, Jesus then said, "First [the Son of Man] must suffer many things and be rejected by this generation" (Luke 17:25). This is repeated by the Gospel writers elsewhere. "The Son of Man must suffer many things and be rejected by the elders and chief priests and scribes, and be killed and be raised up on the third day" (Luke 9:22; see also Matthew 16:21). In other words, Jesus was saying that 1) His death would come before the kingdom reign, and 2) that kingdom reign, when it came, would be literal, dramatic, and visibly observed by all the people on earth.

How does all this play out in the Gospels? Where does the fact that Jesus must first die fit in with the promise of a coming, literal earthly messianic kingdom? More on this later in the chapter.

Understanding the Jewish Hope

In the New Testament we find many indications that the Jews were looking for the coming of the Messiah and His earthly reign. Just before the birth of John the Baptist, the angel told his father Zacharias that his son will be "a forerunner before [the Lord] in the *spirit* and *power* of Elijah" (Luke 1:17). It was prophesied in the Old Testament that Elijah would come to earth to herald the arrival of the King and His earthly kingdom (Isaiah 40:3-5; Malachi 4:5-6). John the Baptist would announce the first coming of the King, but Elijah would arrive to announce the second coming. If John the Baptist was a literal and actual prophet, would we not expect Elijah to be the same when he points to the coming messianic kingdom?

Zacharias recognized prophetic fulfillment in the birth of his son when he said that God "remember[ed] His holy covenant, the oath which He swore to Abraham our father" (Luke 1:72-73). He remembered that God had promised national and earthly deliverance for Israel from their enemies through the house of David, as spoken by the mouths of the prophets (verses 69-70). Elizabeth, who was the mother of John and the cousin of the mother of Jesus, Mary, called Mary "blessed [since she] believed that there would be a fulfillment of what had been spoken to her by the Lord" (verse 45); that is, because through her the Messiah will come and "will reign over the house of Jacob forever, and His kingdom will have no end" (verse 33).

In the Temple at Jerusalem there was an elderly man named Simeon who was told by the Holy Spirit that he would not die until he saw "the Lord's Christ" (or Messiah) (2:26). This devout man was then looking for the birth of the Messiah who would initiate the messianic "consolation of Israel" (verse 25). Anna, an elderly prophetess at the Temple, also realized instantly upon seeing the infant that the Messiah had been born. She continued to speak about Him "to all those who were looking for the redemption of Jerusalem" (verse 38). This verse shows there were also others who were expecting the coming birth of the Messiah, who would someday establish His earthly reign.

Even the evil king Herod knew of the promises of the coming Messiah. When the wise men were brought before Herod, they asked, "Where is He who has been born King of the Jews?" (Matthew 2:2). Herod then asked his chief priests and scribes "where the Christ was to be born" (verse 4).

As Jesus began His ministry and started gathering His disciples, some of them also quickly realized He was the promised Messiah. Andrew said to his brother Simeon, " 'We have found the Messiah' (which translated means Christ)" (John 1:41). Philip said they had found the One (the great Prophet) whom Moses (Deuteronomy 18:18) and the other prophets had spoken about (John 1:45). Nathanael added, "Rabbi, You are the Son of God; You are the King of Israel" (verse 49).

The Samaritan woman said to Christ, "I know that Messiah is coming (He who is called Christ); when that One comes, He will declare all things to us" (John 4:25), and then urged those in her village to "come, see a man who told me all the things that I have done; this is not the Christ, is it?" (verse 29). The villagers were finally convinced after hearing Jesus speak, that "this One is indeed the Savior of the world" (verse 42).

All the above responses tell us that there was a great anticipation, an expectation of the arrival of the King and His kingdom. The kingdom had *been brought before* the people of Israel, but something would stop it from being established. That *something* was the nation's lack of repentance from their sinful ways.

A Call to Repentance

Both John the Baptist and Jesus began their ministries by proclaiming to the Jewish people that they must "repent, for the kingdom of heaven is at hand" (Matthew 3:2; 4:17). This was the prerequisite for the kingdom's arrival. Remember that at the beginning of this chapter we saw that "is at hand" is a perfect tense in the Greek that means "the coming of the kingdom has been completed," but this does not mean that the kingdom has begun, or that it must necessarily begin. The kingdom had arrived, but certainly had not started!

Studying Jewish rabbinical thought helps us gain a better understanding about the issue of repentance and about how and when the kingdom would start. For example, one of the most respected writings on what the Jews thought during the time of Christ is found in the classic volume *Society and Religion in the Second Temple Period*[66] and in *The Messiah Texts*,[67] both written by respected Jewish scholars. Raphael Patai writes in *The Messiah Texts* that from before the time of Christ, and even during the last two thousand years, "the expected and hoped-for Coming [of the Messiah] was simply indispensable for the continued existence of Israel.…The Messiah was prevented from coming because the generation was unworthy; because there was too many sinners in Israel."[68] Pharisaic Judaism believed "in the futility of 'forcing' the millennium" and said the Messiah could not come while Israel was under foreign domination. "All depended on repentance, on a fundamental change in men's souls."[69]

In *Society and Religion in the Second Temple Period*, Baras and Avi-Yonah argue that during the period of the Gospels, Jesus taught that the kingdom of heaven was at hand and all that was needed and necessary was for the people to repent.[70] These authors add that "as the herald of the Messiah, John [the Baptist] had to prepare the way for the Messiah's coming by preaching repentance and pious deeds. He exhorted the people to repent, for the kingdom of heaven was near."[71] But the kingdom did not come because such a change of heart did not take place among the vast majority of the Jewish people.

Because Israel did not repent, orthodox rabbis have argued from the Old Testament that

> the pangs of the Messianic times…must come upon Israel because of its wickedness.…the pangs of the Messianic times are imagined as having heavenly as well as earthly sources and expressions.…awesome cosmic cataclysms will be visited upon the earth: conflagrations, pestilence, famine, earthquakes.… These will be paralleled by evils brought by men upon themselves.…Things will come to such a head that people will despair of Redemption. This will last seven years. And then, unexpectedly, the Messiah will come.[72]

With the Old Testament in view, the orthodox Jews of the New Testament era held to the scenario just described: 1) The Messiah could not come if the Jews did not repent of their sins; 2) If Israel did not repent, the people would face great persecution; 3) the people would come to face a terrible period of seven years of Tribulation on earth; and 4) finally, the Messiah would come.

In contrast to preterists, futurists see the same prophetic plan unfolding in the Old Testament that some orthodox Jews have always observed. The Jewish people held to correct beliefs about end-time events in Christ's day; the only difference is that they refused to believe that indeed He was the promised Messiah!

But what does all this have to do with the preterists' charge that the kingdom of God must have already come or else the words of Jesus and the prophet John are invalid? And, what does all this mean in light of the little expressions "at hand, quickly, about to"? We can find our answer in Isaiah 60.

A Promise of Hastening

Isaiah 60 contains one of the more significant messianic prophecies in the Old Testament, and verse 22 may be the key to what this chapter is all about. In Isaiah 60, the prophet predicts the glory of God coming upon Israel (verse 2), of the nations coming to Israel's light (verse 3), of the return of the Jews from afar (verse 4), and of Jerusalem being named "the city of the LORD, the Zion of the Holy One of Israel" (verse 14). The chapter relates how the Jews will be called the "righteous," and will "possess the land forever" (verse 21). In all this, God will be glorified (verse 21).

Verse 22 then concludes: "The smallest [person] will become a clan, and the least one a mighty nation. *I, the LORD, will hasten it in its time.*" What does Isaiah mean? How can something be done in haste, but yet in its own time? The last sentence seems to be a contradiction—and this is exactly how Jewish scholars have taken it! To figure out what Isaiah meant, it is first important to translate the verse. From the Hebrew text it reads: "I, [the] Ever-existing One [Yahweh], in its *time*, I will cause it to hurry."

The Hebrew noun for "time" is *gehth*, which can be translated a "point of time, a lapse of time."[73] The verb *ghoosh* means "to hurry, hasten" and is in the future or Hiphil causative tense.[74] The passage could mean, "When the time is right, I will cause [that messianic day of blessing] to happen quickly." How could something be held back for just the right moment but yet be coming about quickly? For centuries the Jewish rabbis pondered this. The Jewish scholar I. W. Slotki wrote that this refers to the time "the appointed hour of deliverance has struck. The rabbis detected an apparent contradiction in the last clause: if an event is to happen *in its time,* how can God *hasten it?* They explain: if Israel is worthy, God will hasten its coming; if not, it will happen *in its* (destined) *time.*"[75]

Merrill Unger wrote that God "pledged to expedite the prediction contained in this chapter of Jerusalem's restoration, which is so widely denied in the scholarly world [today]."[76] John Gill said, "As there was a fixed appointed time for Christ's first coming, so there is for his second coming, when this state and dispensation of things will commence; and when that time comes, it will be deferred no longer; as soon as ever it is up, the Lord will hasten the accomplishment of what he has promised."[77] The renowned Hebrew scholar

J. A. Alexander said, "*I will hasten it* has reference to the time ordained for the event, or may denote the suddenness of its occurrence, without regard to its remoteness or the length of the intervening period."[78]

In Harry Bultema's commentary on Isaiah we read, "Finally, the assurance is given that God *in his time* will materialize this salvation for Israel. He has already been waiting for many centuries, but once He begins to deliver Israel, He will do so speedily."[79] And John N. Oswalt offers this excellent observation:

> Although it may take a long time for all things to be ready, nevertheless, when they are ready, God will suddenly bring it to pass. This is the way it was with the first coming. It seemed that the Messiah would never come; but when the time was right, he was suddenly present, and those who were not prepared had no time to get prepared. So it will be in the consummation of all things. Suddenly the sun will leap over the horizon, and God's everlasting day will be here.[80]

In order to be worthy the Jews must confess and repent. This is what John the Baptist and Jesus preached, but Israel refused! Following Pentecost, and after the church had been established, Peter proclaimed the same message of repentance. Besides repentance, his sermon now exhorted people toward belief in the Lord Jesus as Savior. He reminded the Jews that if they repented, the messianic promised "times of refreshing" would begin. He said,

> The things which God announced beforehand by the mouth of all the prophets, that His Christ would suffer, He has thus fulfilled. Therefore, repent and return, so that your sins may be wiped away, in order that times of refreshing may come from the presence of the Lord; and that He may send Jesus, the Christ appointed for you, whom heaven must receive until the period of restoration of all things about which God spoke by the mouth of His holy prophets from ancient time (Acts 3:18-21).

THE MESSAGE OF PROPHECY

When Christ presented Himself as Israel's king, it was incumbent upon the Jews to repent of their sins in order for the messianic rule to begin. The issue of repentance overrides such expressions as "the kingdom of God is at hand." However, even with this expression, the more basic idea is that the coming of the kingdom of God is certain to come someday. Likewise, the expression "I come quickly" seems to be more accurately translated, "I come speedily, swiftly" as with *quickness* of movement.

In the larger contextual picture of Bible prophecy, there seems to have been little misunderstanding as to what was being communicated actually happening with these expressions. In the great mystery of the providence of God, we can now look back upon specific verses of Scripture that remind us that Christ *must* first suffer and die before He would reign. Most Bible teachers, except preterists, seem to comprehend that because Israel refused to repent of their sins, the Messiah did not take the throne. But following the seven-year Tribulation, He will return, regather the people of Israel, and begin His 1,000-year reign in Jerusalem!

Chapter 13

THE 70 WEEKS OF DANIEL

Thomas Ice

Let the postmillennial and amillennial commentators look long
and steadily at this fact. This prophecy is a prophecy for Daniel's
people and Daniel's city. No alchemy of Origenistic spiritualizing interpretation can change that.

—Robert Culver[1]

It has been well observed by various writers that if the seventy
weeks are *to end* with the death of Christ and the incoming
destruction of Jerusalem, it is simply *impossible*—with all ingenuity expended in this direction by eminent men—to make out
an accurate fulfillment of prophecy from the dates given, for the
time usually adduced being either too long to fit with the crucifixion of Christ or too short to extend to the destruction of
Jerusalem.

—George N. H. Peters[2]

One of the most important prophecy passages in the whole Bible appears
in Daniel 9:24-27. If worked out logically, this text is both seminal and determinative in the outworking of one's understanding of Bible prophecy. Especially for those of us who believe that prophecy should be understood
literally, it is essential that a right understanding of this central text be developed and cultivated. In this chapter, we're going to take a close look at Daniel
9:24-27 via a consistently literal interpretation of the passage.

THE INTERPRETATION

Critics of the literal interpretation of Bible prophecy recognize that in order to uphold their perspective of certain prophetic passages, they must strike down the plain meaning of Daniel's prophecy. Critic Gary DeMar defines the key issue in these words:

> While nearly all Bible scholars agree that the first sixty-nine weeks of Daniel's prophecy refer to the time up to Jesus' crucifixion, only dispensationalists [who interpret Bible prophecy literally] believe that the entire seventieth week is yet to be fulfilled. Without a futurized seventieth week, the dispensationalist system falls apart. There can be no pretribulational rapture, great tribulation, or rebuilt temple without the gap. How do dispensationalists find a gap in a text that makes no mention of a gap?[3]

I agree with DeMar that much rides on Daniel's prophecy, and I hope to demonstrate here that the only interpretation of Daniel's 70-weeks prophecy that remains true to this passage and others is the consistently literal approach. And if we approach this prophecy literally rather than allegorically, then this would mean that the numbers given by Daniel should be taken literally as well. Yet some believe that's not the case: "This facilitates the adoption of the symbolical interpretation of the numbers, which....we regard as the only possible one, because it does not necessitate our changing the seventy years of the exile into years of the restoration of Jerusalem, and placing the seven years, which the text presents as the first period of the seventy weeks, last."[4]

In contrast, Harry Bultema observes: "The angel himself gives a literal explanation and it would be nonsensical to insist on giving a symbolical interpretation of a literal explanation. If the exegetes had always obeyed the angel's interpretation as is evident from practically every word he speaks, then this text would never have been so obscured by all kinds of human conjectures and imagined 'deep' insights."[5]

There are solid reasons why the numbers in Daniel's prophecy should be taken literally. First, chapter 9 opens with Daniel realizing from Jeremiah's writings that Israel's captivity would last 70 years. These were literal years. Since the prophecy delivered by Gabriel to Daniel in 9:24-27 is related to the 70-year captivity, it follows that the 70 weeks of years are equally literal. Second, definite numbers are given to us in the prophecy (7 weeks, 62 weeks, and 1 week), and it would be strange indeed for such specific numbers to not have literal meaning. Leon Wood asks, "Why should definite numbers be applied to periods of indefinite lengths?"[6] Nothing in the context suggests that we should not take the numbers literally.

THE CONTEXT

We know from the beginning of chapter 9 (verse 2) that Daniel had read about "the number of the years which was revealed as the word of the LORD to Jeremiah the prophet for the completion of the desolations of Jerusalem, namely, seventy years." The two passages Daniel studied most likely were Jeremiah 25:11-12 and 29:10-14. Both texts clearly speak of Israel's Babylonian captivity as limited to a 70-year period. Both passages also blend into their texts statements that look forward to a time of ultimate fulfillment and blessing for the nation of Israel. This is why Daniel appears to think that when the nation returns to their land, then ultimate blessing (the millennial kingdom) will coincide with their return. Daniel's errant thinking about the timing of God's plan for Israel occasioned the Lord's sending of Gabriel "to give [him] insight with understanding" (Daniel 9:22).

God was not yet ready to bring history to its destined final climax. Thus, He told Daniel that He was going stretch out history by 70 times seven years (i.e., 490 years). Dr. David Cooper wrote a paraphrase that I believe accurately captures the sense of the passage:

> Daniel, you have been thinking that the final restoration will be accomplished and the full covenant blessings will be realized at the close of these seventy years of exile in Babylon. On this point you are mistaken. You are not now on the eve of the fulfillment of this wonderful prediction. Instead of its being brought to pass at this time, I am sent to inform you that there is decreed upon your people and the Holy City a period of "seventy sevens" of years before they can be realized. At the conclusion of this period of 490 years the nation of Israel will be reconciled and will be reinstated into the divine favor and will enter into the enjoyment of all the covenant blessings.[7]

THE MEANING OF "WEEKS"

One of the Hebrew classes I took while a student at Dallas Theological Seminary was called "Exegesis of Old Testament Problem Passages," taught by Dr. Kenneth Barker. Dr. Barker thought that Daniel 9:24-27 had more problems for an interpreter to solve than any other passage in the entire Old Testament. By the term "problems" Dr. Barker did not mean that made the text impossible to interpret, but that the passage was difficult and required great care and skill to determine the meaning. He thought there were 14 problems an interpreter needed to solve in order to correctly understand the passage. The first one has to do with the meaning of the term "weeks" found at the beginning of verse 24.

For those acquainted with Hebrew, the Hebrew term for "weeks" appears twice at the beginning of verse 24. That word is *sâbu'îm*, meaning "seventy sevens." This Hebrew word appears first as a plural noun, followed by the participle form, functioning as an adjective. That this Hebrew phrase should be rendered as "seventy sevens" is unanimously agreed upon by representatives of all interpretative schools. There is also great consensus that the "seventy sevens" refers to years, since this is what Daniel was contemplating from Jeremiah 25:11-12 and 29:10-14, as evident in Daniel 9:2. Thus, our Lord has in mind 70 weeks of years, or 490 years.

The next Hebrew word we want to note in verse 24 is a verb translated "have been decreed." This word appears only here in the entire Old Testament. This verb has the basic meaning of "cut," "cut off," and came to mean "divide," or "determine."[8] It appears that Gabriel chose this unique word to emphasize that God was carefully choosing or determining the length of Israel's history. "Just as a wise person never cuts or snips at random, the Lord as the all-wise God does so even less. All His works are determined from eternity, and the times also are only in His hands."[9] Leon Wood adds, "The thought is that God had cut off these 490 years from the rest of history through which to accomplish the deliverances needed for Israel."[10] G. H. Lang declares: "*Decreed* means divided or severed off from the whole period of world-empire in the hands of the Gentiles, as to which Daniel was already well informed. It points to a fixed and limited period, of definite duration, forming part of a longer period the duration of which is not fixed, or at least not declared."[11]

THE AUDIENCE

For whom did God reveal this period of prophetic destiny? The text says it had been decreed "for your people and your holy city" (Daniel 9:24). This is such an obvious statement, yet too many interpreters attempt to shoehorn in a people not mentioned in the passage. In the sixth century B.C., when Daniel wrote, who were Daniel's people and holy city? Clearly it can only refer to Israel as Daniel's people and Jerusalem as Daniel's holy city. Yet many interpreters insist the words mean something more, something different than what the text actually says. For instance, H. C. Leupold says, "Here, as so often in prophecy, terms like God's 'people' and God's 'holy city' broaden out to the point where they assume a breadth of meaning like that found in the New Testament (cf. Gal. 6:16)."[12] Another non-literalist, E. J. Young, says, "It is true that the primary reference is to Israel after the flesh, and the historical

Jerusalem, but since this very verse describes the Messianic work, it also refers to the true people of God, those who will benefit because of the things herein described."[13]

Notice both allegorizers appeal to reasons that are outside of the text. They state that it refers to individuals beyond Israel simply because that's what they believe. Therefore, the text must have in mind something beyond what it actually does say. This is a clear example of reading meaning into the text from one's own belief system, which is not what the Bible wants us to do. Paul warns in 1 Corinthians 4:6 "that in us you may learn not to exceed what is written." Gabriel goes out of his way to inform Daniel that the 70 weeks of years are decreed for Israel and Jerusalem. Lang notes, "The endeavour to apply this prophecy, in general or in detail, to others than Daniel's people, Israel, and Daniel's city, Jerusalem, is an outrage upon exegesis, being forbidden in advance by the express terms used."[14] Gabriel says that God has specifically cut away those 490 years for Israel and Jerusalem, which would not include the addition of anyone else. Wood expands upon this idea and observes:

> It should be noted that Gabriel said the 490 years will be in reference to the Jewish people and the Jewish capital city, which would seem to exclude any direct concern with Gentiles. That this concern is to be with the city, as well as the people, militates against the idea that the 490 years carry reference only to Christ's first coming and not to His second. It is difficult to see how the physical city of Jerusalem was involved in the deliverance from sin which Christ then effected but it will be in the deliverance from the destructive oppression which the Antichrist will bring prior to Christ's second coming.[15]

THE SIX PURPOSE CLAUSES

As we delve more deeply into the meaning of this text, let's drop back and note a few structural observations about the passage as a whole (Daniel 9:24-27). Verse 24 is the general statement from Gabriel, while the final three verses provide a particular explanation of the general point. Thus, verses 25-27 can help us understand the main statement in verse 24.

There are six infinitives that tell us when the 70 weeks that have been decreed for Israel and Jerusalem will be fulfilled in history. These six goals are 1) to finish the transgression, 2) to make an end of sin, 3) to make atonement for iniquity, 4) to bring in everlasting righteousness, 5) to seal up vision and prophecy, and 6) to anoint the most holy place. Usually when a list appears in Scripture, it is important to see if the items should be grouped into subsets.

I believe that these six items are to be arranged into two groups of three, rather than three groups of two. The first triad has to do with sin, and interestingly, these are the exact words Daniel used in his prayer in 9:5. God is speaking to Daniel's prayer through the first three goals. The second set of three goals for the 490-year period has to do with God's righteousness. This was a matter Daniel also inquired about in his prayer (9:7). G. H. Lang agrees when he notes that "the first three are concerned with the removal of sin, and the last three with the bringing in of righteousness."[16] "The first three are negative in force, speaking of undesirable matters to be removed; and the last three are positive, giving desirable factors to be effected."[17]

The division of these six statements into two groups of three appears to be supported by a structural observation from the Hebrew text. The first three goals are all made up of two-word units in Hebrew. The second group of descriptives all use three-word phrases. This structural arrangement lends literary support to the groupings I've suggested.

Now, before we can determine when these six goals will be fulfilled, we must first ascertain their purpose. This we will now pursue as we inspect each phrase.

The First Three Clauses Stated
To Finish the Transgression

The verb "to finish" looks to bring something to its culmination. It has the idea of "to close, shut, restrain." Here it has the idea of "firmly restraining" the transgression, thus the specific idea of restraint of sin. "Examination of the use of this word shows that it means the forcible cessation of an activity. It always points to a complete stop, never to a mere hindrance."[18] In this context it is "the transgression" that is being firmly restrained. As I hope to demonstrate throughout this series, I believe that "finish" looks toward the completion of the 70 weeks at the second coming of Christ to set up His millennial kingdom.

The noun "transgression" in Hebrew is derived from the verbal root with the basic meaning of "rebel, revolt, transgress." Transgression is the idea of going beyond a specific limit or boundary. "From all the definitions given we may be certain that it emphasizes the idea of rebellion against God and disobedience to His will."[19] Gabriel has in mind, in verse 24, more than just sin in general, but a specific sin, as there's a definite article attached to this word—"*the* transgression." "The article in Hebrew, as in Greek, is very definite and points clearly to some outstanding thing or object," notes David Cooper. "Thus the expression 'the transgression' seems to indicate some specific, outstanding, national sin of the Chosen People."[20] Since the emphasis in this phrase is upon the finishing of Israel's transgression, this leads to the conclusion that it will occur at the second coming of Jesus, Israel's Messiah. Arnold Fruchtenbaum points out that "when speaking of the basis of the second coming of Christ there are two facets to this basis: first, there must be the confession of Israel's national sin (Leviticus 26:40-42; Jeremiah 3:11-18; Hos. 5:15)...."[21]

The emphasis in this first goal, then, is upon when Israel's national sin—the rejection of her Messiah—will be brought to an end. "This passage assumes, therefore," notes Cooper, "that the whole nation repents and turns to God for mercy and forgiveness. Thus this first phrase implies the conversion of the nation. But what is assumed here is stated specifically in the third phrase."[22]

To Make an End of Sin

The second goal to be completed at the end of the 70 weeks is to make an end of sin. In the Hebrew text, the word translated "to make an end of" literally means "to shut, close, seal; to hide, to reveal as a secret," and has the primary meaning of bringing a matter to a conclusion. Cooper explains: "This word was regularly used to indicate the closing of a letter or an official document. When the scribe had finished his work, the king placed his royal seal upon it, thus showing that the communication was brought to a close and at the same time giving it the official imprimatur."[23]

The Hebrew root word for "sin" is the most commonly used word for sin in the Hebrew Old Testament. Its core meaning is "to miss the mark, to be mistaken." This is illustrated in Judges 20:16, which says, "Out of all these people...each one could sling a stone at a hair and not *miss*." This word itself conveys the basic meaning of "to miss, to be mistaken." Interestingly, the only other uses of this word in Daniel occur in 9:20 (twice). Daniel speaks of "my sin and the sin of my people Israel." Since this Hebrew word is not accompanied by a definite article, as was "transgression" in the previous phrase, and since "sin" is plural, it seems to refer to the sins of the nation in general. "The sealing up of sins, consequently, signifies their restraint under safe custody."[24] "Since the cause of sin must be removed before the cure can be effected, this expression assumes that at the time here foreseen the nation will have turned to the Lord, and that by His Spirit a new heart and spirit will have been given to all the people."[25] The fulfillment of this can only take place after the second coming, which will be followed by the installation of the millennial reign of Jesus the Messiah.

To Make Atonement for Iniquity

The third infinitive, "to make atonement for iniquity," is translated from two Hebrew words. Taking the second one—iniquity—first, we see that it is one of the most common Hebrew words for sin. It has the core idea of twisting or defacing something beyond its intended purpose. While speaking of a sinful act, this word, at the same time, looks to the fact that the reason one commits iniquity is due to the perverted sinful nature inherited from Adam's fall. According to the *Oxford English Dictionary*, "iniquity" means "the quality of being unrighteous, or (more often) unrighteous action or conduct." Its core meaning is "uneven, unequal, wrong, wicked."[26] Thus, the idea of iniquity is used here to speak of that most aggressive nuance of sin flowing from human willful disobedience. This paints a picture of the worst kind of offense before God.

Such an offense requires a heroic response from God. And such a provision, in fact, is taught in the verb "to make atonement." Many are familiar with the word "atone" since it takes a prominent place in Israel's Old Testament sacrificial system. It is used in Genesis 7:14 as both a noun and a verb and carries with it the idea of covering the wood of Noah's Ark with pitch. When applied theologically to salvation, it communicates "the act functioned to cleanse, wipe away, or purify objects contaminated by sin or uncleanness or make kôper on behalf of persons. This act of purgation served to propitiate Yahweh, thus enabling Him to dwell among His people to work out His purpose through them in the world."[27]

The significance of this third phrase is noted by Cooper, who says this

> doubtless is a clear reference to the time when all Israel in genuine penitence shall acknowledge her departure from God and her national sin. At the same time each individual, of course, will acknowledge his own wrongs and all will call upon God for pardon. Then that which was foreshadowed by the annual atonement will become a reality. At that time the nation will be brought back into fellowship with God and become a blessing in the earth.[28]

The First Three Clauses Summarized

The first three of the six goals in Daniel 9:24 have to do with the sin of Daniel's people, Israel. The basis for dealing with Israel's sin was provided during the first coming of Jesus when He died on the cross and rose again from the dead to pay for the sin of the Jews and for the sins of the entire human race. However, the application of this wonderful provision for sin will not be realized for Daniel's people until the end of the 70 weeks. This will be fulfilled at the second coming of Messiah at the end of the Tribulation period, which is yet future to our day. Leon Wood gives this excellent summary of the first three goals:

The first introduces the idea of riddance, saying that the coming 490-year period would see its firm restraint. In other words, God was about to do something to alleviate this basic, serious problem. The second speaks of the degree of this restraint: sin would be put to an end. The third indicates how this would be done: by atonement. Though Christ is not mentioned in the verse, the meaning is certain, especially in view of verse twenty-six, that He would be the One making this atonement, which would serve to restrain the sin by bringing it to an end. It is clear that reference in these first three items is mainly to Christ's first coming, when sin was brought to an end in principle. The actuality of sin coming to an end for people, however, comes only when a personal appropriation of the benefit has been made. Since Gabriel was speaking primarily in reference to Jews, rather than Gentiles…this fact requires the interpretation to include also Christ's second coming, because only then does Israel as a nation turn to Christ (cf. Jeremiah 31:33, 34; Ezek. 37:23; Zechariah 13:1; Romans 11:25-27).[29]

These clauses are prophetically important, because if they are descriptive of elements that have yet to be fulfilled, then the seventy weeks of Daniel have yet to be fulfilled. This means that the final (seventieth week) has to be future to our day, since all of the purposes must be brought to completion by the end of the prescribed time period.

The Second Three Clauses Stated

As stated earlier, the second three clauses relate to God's righteousness. Let's examine them now.

To Bring in Everlasting Righteousness

The first of the three Hebrew words that compose the fourth purpose clause is the infinitive that is usually translated into English as "bring in." This is a widely used Hebrew verb that has the primary meaning of "come in, come, go in, or go."[30] Since this occurrence of the verb is in the causative Hebrew stem known as *hiphil*, it has the sense that "everlasting righteousness" will be caused to come in.

This word used to speak of the righteousness to be brought in is the same word Daniel used in his prayer in 9:7, where righteousness is said to belong exclusively to the Lord. David Cooper explains: "The English word, righteousness, primarily refers to the correct and proper motives and dealings of man with man. God's righteousness would, therefore, consist of His correct attitude and actions towards His creatures and His standards for them....It also carries that idea."[31]

Thus, the righteousness to be brought in will not be the twisted and volatile standards of human invention. Instead, God's righteousness will be a changeless measure of God's enviable code.

The Hebrew Lexicon of Brown, Driver, and Briggs (BDB) says that the Hebrew noun *holamim* has the core meaning of "long duration, antiquity, futurity."[32] The lexicon specifically says that the use in Daniel 9:24 is a plural intensive and thus renders it with the specific sense of "everlastingness, or eternity."[33] Cooper provides a literal translation of "righteousness of the ages," which captures its precise English meaning and notes that it

> signifies that there are rules or formulas of attitude and conduct that are right and will be reckoned as correct throughout all ages—past, present, and future....
>
> When, however, the 490 years are completed and the Almighty brings in His great regimé of righteousness, these eternal principles of justice and equity will be in force; therefore, Gabriel said that at this future time God will bring in the righteousness of the ages.[34]

I believe this clause is a prophecy concerning the future time we know as the kingdom or millennial reign of Christ (see Revelation 20:1-9). This means it is still future to our day. In contrast to Israel's many past failures to live up to God's righteous standards (cf. Daniel 9:3-19), this time the Lord will provide everlasting righteousness for the nation. Randall Price points out that Gabriel has

> in view a theodicial "age of righteousness" (cf. Isa. 1:26; 11:2-5; 32:17; Jeremiah 23:5-6; 33:15-18) that resolves the theological scandal (note Daniel 9:15-16) of the former age characterized by "the rebellion" (i.e., Israel's rejection of the Messiah). Therefore, this age will be vindication of God's promise to national Israel (Ezek. 36:17-23) and a reversal of her condition and fortunes with respect to Messiah, hence a "messianic age" or the messianic kingdom.[35]

To Seal Up Vision and Prophecy

This triad of Hebrew words commences with the same infinitive used above in the second clause, which was "to make an end of sin." The notion of this Hebrew word "seal up" carries the idea of completion. In this context it is rendered "seal up" because the last action taken by a writer when he completes a letter or document is to seal up the finished product. Charles Feinberg expounds that this

> refers to giving the seal of confirmation to Daniel and his vision by fulfilling his predictions. In Isaiah 8:16, this phrase meant that the prophecy was complete, and the command was given to bind it up, to roll it up like a scroll and seal it. Again, in Daniel 8:26 the thought was to seal up the prophecy and make a permanent record of it, so that when it is fulfilled the event can be compared to the prophecy to show how completely the one corresponds to the other.[36]

The dual nouns, which are singular, are literally translated "vision" and "prophet." "Prophet" is a concrete noun for the abstract thing that the prophet produces, which is prophecy. Vision is a prophetic vehicle (cf. Daniel 7), while the human instrument is the prophet who produces the prophecy. Both are collective nouns for the sum total of all vision and prophecy.

Some think this clause was fulfilled during the first coming of Jesus. Preterist Ken Gentry advocates this view: "The fifth result…has to do with the ministry of Christ on earth, which is introduced at His baptism: He comes '*to seal up vision and prophecy.*' By this is meant that Christ fulfills (and thereby confirms) the prophecy (Luke 18:31; cf. Luke 24:44; Acts 3:18)."[37]

Gentry's assertion is typical of those who advocate such a position, which lacks exegetical support. Allan MacRae rightly concludes that there "is no Scriptural warrant for saying that the functions of the Old Testament vision and prophecy came to an end at the time of Christ's first advent or that these terms do not also include visions and prophecies of the New Testament."[38] Harry Bultema declares, "'Prophecy' does not refer to Christ here but to prophecy in general. The 'vision' this verse speaks of is not a reference to this vision nor to any of the other visions Daniel received, but together with the word 'prophecy' refers to all predictions. A scroll was not complete until it was completely filled. Thus this sealing of a scroll became a symbol of fulfillment (Isa. 8:16). So also here it indicates a complete fulfillment of all prophecy."[39]

This fifth prophetic declaration, like the previous ones, can only refer to a future time when all the prophecies relating to Israel will be fulfilled. There are hundreds of prophecies relating to Israel and Jerusalem that await a future fulfillment.

To Anoint the Most Holy

The sixth and final prophetic clause begins with the Hebrew verb usually translated as "anoint" which means to pour oil on something or someone.[40]

BDB says it is used in Daniel 9:24 to mean "anoint or consecrate to religious service."[41]

This much-debated phrase, usually translated in English as "most holy," is a dual use of the same Hebrew word. It is common in Hebrew for the superlative of a noun to be intended, as is the case here. The first use of the word is singular, while the second one is plural and can literally be rendered "most holy," or "a most holy *place*." The German commentator C. F. Keil notes that the same exact phrase is used in Ezekiel 45:3 of a future temple and concludes that "the reference is to the anointing of a new sanctuary, temple, or most holy place."[42] Specific reasons for this interpretation of the sixth clause are stated well by Leon Wood:

> The phrase "holy of holies" (*qodesh qadashîm*) occurs, either with or without the article, thirty-nine times in the Old Testament, always in reference to the Tabernacle or Temple or to the holy articles used in them. When referring to the most holy place, where the Ark was kept, the article is regularly used (e.g., Exodus 26:33), but it is not when referring to the holy articles (e.g., Exodus 29:37) or to the whole Temple complex (e.g., Ezek. 43:12). In view of these matters, it is highly likely that the phrase refers to the Temple also here, which, in view of the context, must be a future Temple; and, since the phrase is used without the article, reference must be to a complex of that Temple, rather than its most holy place.[43]

Without exegeting any of the details of Daniel 9:24, Ken Gentry, like many non-literal interpreters, simply declares this clause refers to Jesus: "at His baptismal anointing…the Spirit came upon Him (Mark 1:9-11)."[44] But as Leon Wood explained, this expression is never used of a person, only of things. "So it is not a reference to the Messiah. Nor to the church, for the church is nowhere mentioned or found in the whole prophecy of Daniel," declares Harry Bultema. "It refers to Daniel's people Israel.…It refers to the state of bliss and holiness of all Israel after the Savior has come to Zion and has turned away the ungodliness from Jacob (Romans 11:26)."[45] Thus, we see that this final prophetic purpose clause also awaits a future fulfillment.

The Six Clauses Surveyed

As we survey the lessons from all six prophetic purpose clauses, we find that none of them have yet to be fulfilled in their entirety. Therefore, we know from the goals that our Lord set for His people (Israel) and for His city (Jerusalem) that there remains a time of future fulfillment. "Therefore, this twenty-fourth verse of our chapter," notes Cooper, "read in the light of the various predictions of the prophets, is obviously a forecast of the establishment of the kingdom of God upon earth in all its glory."[46]

G. H. Lang echoes Cooper's thoughts when he concludes: "We have now before us an outline of the whole prophecy. And, after considering the statement of results which are to follow God's disciplinary dealings, we cannot but conclude that the close of the Seventy Sevens must coincide with the end of the present order of things and the beginning of the Coming or Millennial Age."[47]

Even Keil, the German scholar, cannot resist the clear implications of this prophecy when he states, "From the contents of these six statements it thus appears that the termination of the seventy weeks coincides with the end of the present course of the world."[48]

THE SABBATICAL YEAR

In reaching a correct understanding of Daniel 9:24-27, it is most helpful to understand the circumstances that occasioned the giving of this revelation by God to Daniel. No one questions that the occasion relates to Israel's captivity in Babylon as a result of failing to observe the sabbath-year rest commanded by the Lord. But how does that relate to the 70-weeks prophecy?

As part of the stipulations in the Mosaic Law, Israel was to let her land lay fallow every seventh year. Scripture says,

> Speak to the sons of Israel and say to them, "When you come into the land which I shall give you, then the land shall have a sabbath to the LORD. Six years you shall sow your field, and six years you shall prune your vineyard and gather in its crop, but during the seventh year the land shall have a sabbath rest, a sabbath to the LORD; you shall not sow your field nor prune your vineyard. Your harvest's aftergrowth you shall not reap, and your grapes of untrimmed vines you shall not gather; the land shall have a sabbatical year. And all of you shall have the sabbath products of the land for food; yourself, and your male and female slaves, and your hired man and your foreign resident, those who live as aliens with you" (Leviticus 25:2-6).

Leviticus 26 also lists the sanctions God would impose upon the nation for not obeying the requirement to observe a sabbath year.

> Then the land will enjoy its sabbaths all the days of the desolation, while you are in your enemies' land; then the land will rest and enjoy its sabbaths. All the days of its desolation it will observe the rest which it did not observe on your sabbaths, while you were living on it (Leviticus 26:34-35).

> For the land shall be abandoned by them, and will make up
> for its sabbaths while it is made desolate without them. They,
> meanwhile, will be making amends for their iniquity, because
> they rejected My ordinances and their soul abhorred My statutes
> (Leviticus 26:43).

In the historical books of Samuel, Kings, and Chronicles, the Lord provided a divine commentary to the nation on how they were keeping or not keeping His Law. And in 2 Chronicles 36:20-21 He explains why Israel was sent away to Babylon for 70 years:

> Those who had escaped from the sword he carried away to
> Babylon; and they were servants to him and to his sons until the
> rule of the kingdom of Persia, to fulfill the word of the LORD by
> the mouth of Jeremiah, until the land had enjoyed its sabbaths.
> All the days of its desolation it kept sabbath until seventy years
> were complete (2 Chronicles 36:20-21).

What "word of the LORD by the month of Jeremiah" was 2 Chronicles 36:21 referring to? The following two references provide the answer:

> This whole land will be a desolation and a horror, and these
> nations will serve the king of Babylon seventy years (Jeremiah
> 25:11).

> Thus says the LORD, "When seventy years have been com
> pleted for Babylon, I will visit you and fulfill My good word to
> you, to bring you back to this place" (Jeremiah 29:10).

It is clear from the above passages that God had a specific reason behind the deportation of the Southern Kingdom (Judah) to Babylon for 70 years. Israel had violated the sabbatical year 70 times. The Jews entered the Promised Land around 1400 B.C. and were deported to Babylon around 600 B.C. This means they were in the land about 800 years before the Babylonian deportation. Had they disobeyed the sabbatical year commandment every seventh year, it would mean they should have been in captivity for about 114 years. Instead, they were held captive for 70 years, meaning that they were disobedient for only 490 of the 800 years in the land. This means there were breaks or gaps in the accumulation of the 490 years, during the 800-year period, that resulted in Israel's 70-year captivity. Why is this important? Because many of the critics of the literal interpretation of Daniel 9:24-27 insist that it is unreasonable to have gaps in that 490-year period. Of course, it is not, since there were many gaps in the 490-year period related to the Babylonian captivity.

THE 70 WEEKS

The Explanation of the 70 Weeks

Preterist Gary DeMar is one of the most outspoken critics against the view that the seventieth week of Daniel is still future. DeMar argues that there are no gaps in any of the time periods he has examined in Scripture.[49] He declares, "If we can find no gaps in the sequence of years in these examples, then how can a single exception be made with the 'seventy weeks' in Daniel 9:24-27?"[50] Interestingly, DeMar does not examine the 490-year period that took place during Israel's 800 years of occupation in the land. As I have noted, there are all kinds of gaps within this sequence. There were roughly 310 years of gaps interspersed throughout the 800-year period. This makes it directly related to the 70-weeks prophecy given to Daniel. DeMar acknowledges that Daniel's 70 weeks are related to the violation of the sabbatical year laws found in Leviticus 25 and 26, and are connected to 2 Chronicles 36 and Jeremiah 25.[51] But he fails to observe the fact that the 490 years of Daniel 9:24-27 are derived from the 490 years of Israel's violation of the sabbatical years that were prescribed by God in His covenant with the nation.

Dr. Harold Hoehner answers critics such as DeMar when he notes that "the seventy-year captivity was due to the Jews having violated seventy sabbatical years over a 490-year period and Daniel now saw seventy units of sevens decreed for another 490 years into Israel's future."[52] Hoehner has diagramed this relationship as noted in the "Units of Seventy" chart below.[53]

Units of Seventy

70 x 7 Sabbatical Years Violated (Leviticus 26:34-35, 43)	70-Year Captivity (Jeremiah 25:11; 29:10)	70 x 7 Sabbatical Years Remaining (Daniel 9:24-27)

	490 years		490 years	
PAST ◄—	—	DANIEL'S DAY	—	—► FUTURE

We also know that Daniel himself was familiar with the reason God had sent His people into the Babylonian captivity:

> In the first year of Darius the son of Ahasuerus, of Median descent, who was made king over the kingdom of the Chaldeans—in the first year of his reign, I, Daniel, observed in the books the number of the years which was revealed as the word of the LORD to Jeremiah the prophet for the completion of the desolations of Jerusalem, namely, seventy years. So I gave my

attention to the Lord God to seek Him by prayer and supplica-
tions, with fasting, sackcloth and ashes (Daniel 9:1-3).

Leon Wood explains that

> since Daniel was here thinking in terms of the seventy-year cap-
> tivity, he, as a Hebrew, could have easily moved from the idea of
> one week of years to seventy weeks of years. This follows because,
> according to 2 Chronicles 36:21, the people had been punished by
> this Exile so that their land might enjoy the sabbath rests which
> had not been observed in their prior history (cf. Leviticus 26:33-
> 35, Jeremiah 34:12-22). Knowing this, Daniel would have recog-
> nized that the seventy years of the Exile represented seventy
> sevens of years in which these violations had transpired; and he
> would have understood Gabriel to be saying, simply, that another
> period, similar in length to that which had made the Exile nec-
> essary, was coming in the experience of the people.[54]

Even though DeMar recognizes the cause for Daniel's prayer and Gabriel's
subsequent revelation of the 70-weeks prophecy to Daniel, he fails to recognize that the 70-year captivity was based upon a 490-year period that contained multiple gaps of time.[55] DeMar argues that a gap of time between the
sixty-ninth and seventieth weeks of Daniel is not justified because there are no
other examples of this in Scripture.[56] This appears to justify such a gap if an
example of another gap could be found. We have not only found an example,
but it is an example directly related to the 70-weeks prophecy of Daniel. Thus,
using DeMar's standard, he should recognize that a gap in Daniel 9:24-27 is
justifiable.

DeMar goes on to insist that it's impossible to have any kind of gap or
chronological postponement of time between the sixty-ninth and seventieth
weeks of Daniel:

> As has already been noted, the text says nothing about "a period
> between the sixty-ninth and seventieth weeks." There can be no
> "period between" any time period, whether seconds, minutes,
> hours, days, weeks, or years unless a period of time is expressly
> given. It is impossible to insert time between the end of one year
> and the beginning of another. January 1st follows December
> 31st at the stroke of midnight. There is no "period between" the
> conclusion of one year and the beginning of the next year.
> Culver, therefore, begs the question. He first must prove that a
> period of time should be placed between the sixty-ninth and
> seventieth weeks before he can maintain that there is a "period

between" the sixty-ninth and seventieth weeks. The "simple language of the text" makes no mention of a gap.[57]

I believe there *is* clear evidence why the seventieth week of Daniel is yet future and, thus, the necessity of a gap of time between the sixty-ninth and seventieth week. Daniel 9:24-27 allows for a gap of time because the advancing of God's program for His people Israel was put on hold and will be postponed until a future time. Apparently critics such as DeMar are not able to see the time gaps of the past, such as the one I demonstrated in this chapter, so it is not surprising that they do not understand how there is a gap in God's future plan for His people Israel.

The *Terminus a Quo* of the 70 Weeks

Daniel 9:25 provides the starting point for the chronological unfolding of the 70-weeks prophecy. But, at what point does the text tell us it was to begin? Because there are different views concerning the beginning point (sometimes know by the Latin phrase *terminus a quo*), we'll want to take a closer look at this verse, which reads, "So you are to know and discern that from the issuing of a decree to restore and rebuild Jerusalem until Messiah the Prince there will be seven weeks and sixty-two weeks; it will be built again, with plaza and moat, even in times of distress."

Gabriel tells Daniel that he is "to know and discern" the message that follows. The Hebrew word for "know" is a common word for knowledge or information. However, "discern" has the notion of "to gain insight," "comprehension," or "to reach understanding." Thus, Daniel was to learn "from the issuing of a decree to restore and rebuild Jerusalem" that the 70 weeks of years would begin the countdown. Why Gabriel's exhortation to Daniel? "The history of the interpretation of these verses is confirmation of the fact that this prophecy is difficult and requires spiritual discernment."[58]

A Decree to Restore and Rebuild Jerusalem

The next element of Daniel 9:25 is clear: The countdown of time will begin with "a decree to restore and rebuild Jerusalem." The Hebrew word for "decree" is the common word *dâbâr*, which means "thing," "speak," "word," or "instruction." In this context, it has the force of an urgent and assertive statement. And, the text specifically states the countdown will start with "a decree to restore and rebuild Jerusalem." The decree involves the rebuilding of the city of Jerusalem, not the Temple. This is important to note, for earlier edicts were issued in relation to the Temple (see 2 Chronicles 36:22-23; Ezra 1:1-4; 5:3-17; 6:3-5).

There are at least three different decrees that are considered in an attempt to "know and discern" the beginning of the 70 weeks of Daniel. First, there was the decree of Cyrus (Ezra 1:2-4; 6:3-5), issued in 537 B.C., which I will call decree one. Second was the decree of Artaxerxes (Ezra 7:11-26) given in 458 B.C. (decree two). Third was a second decree from Artaxerxes (Nehemiah 2:5-8,17-18) given in 444 B.C., at the time of Nehemiah's return to Jerusalem (decree three). I want to note at the outset that the third decree is the only one that literally fits the exact words of Daniel 9:25, as we shall see. Leon Wood notes that the "first stressed rebuilding the Temple; the second, the establishment and practice of the proper services at the Temple; and the third, the rebuilding of the walls, when, long before, most of the city had been rebuilt."[59]

Non-literal interpreters of the 490 years of the 70 weeks of Daniel are vague and non-precise in their overall handling of the numbers. If they try to establish a *terminus a quo*, it is rarely, if ever, the one given to Artaxerxes in Nehemiah 2:1-8. For example, DeMar is fuzzy, at best, in explaining his beginning point for the prophecy. In a lengthy quote of J. Barton Payne,[60] DeMar appears, at first, to favor the third decree when he says, "The beginning point would be indicated by the commandment to restore Jerusalem (verse 25), an event that was accomplished, a century after Daniel, in the reign of the Persian, Artaxerxes I (465– 424 B.C.), under Nehemiah (444 B.C.)."[61] He then proceeds to say that he favors the second view noted above, of Artaxerxes' first decree (Ezra 7:11-26) which was issued in 458 B.C. DeMar declares that "from 458 B.C. this brings one to A.D. 26, the very time which many would accept for the descent of the Holy Spirit upon Jesus Christ and the commencement of His incarnate ministry."[62]

Like DeMar, Gentry is vague, perhaps on purpose, as to the starting point of the 490 years. Like DeMar, Gentry also references J. Barton Payne, but without specifically stating his *terminus a quo*. Also, like DeMar, Gentry holds that the 483-year period comes to an end at the beginning of Jesus' public ministry, "sometime around A.D. 26."[63] Gentry's support for his view, however, does not come from biblical data. Instead, he says, "This interpretation is quite widely agreed upon by conservative scholars, being virtually 'universal among Christian exegetes'—excluding dispensationalists."[64] In contrast to Gentry and DeMar, I will present reasons from the biblical text for holding that the correct starting point is the decree of Artaxerxes given in 444 B.C., as recorded in Nehemiah 2:1-8.

Artaxerxes' Decree

Of all the options available, the only decree that specifically fits the statements of Daniel 9:25 is the one by Artaxerxes given in 444 B.C. Why? Because decrees one and two relate to rebuilding the Temple. Only decree three speaks specifically of Jerusalem. It is clear that Nehemiah received from King Artaxerxes a decree to "rebuild and restore Jerusalem." The passage says, "Let letters be given me" and "a letter to Asaph" (Nehemiah 2:7-8). These were letters from King Artaxerxes to Nehemiah for permission and authority to go back to Jerusalem and rebuild it. Said another way, the letters were decrees that granted Nehemiah the right to rebuild Jerusalem (Nehemiah 2:5). "The entire book of Nehemiah is proof that this godly governor built Jerusalem and its streets and walls," declares Bultema, "and that, as this prophecy says, in troublous times. According to qualified chronologists this also agrees with the needed chronology set forth in Daniel."[65]

Problems with Decrees One and Two

Further examination of the first two decrees provides us with even more objections to their being the ones that Gabriel had in mind in Daniel 9:25. Dr. Harold Hoehner, chairman of the New Testament department at Dallas Theological Seminary, has written one of the best books on the chronological aspects of the 70 weeks of Daniel, titled *Chronological Aspects of the Life of Christ*.[66] Dr. Hoehner provides the following objections against the first decree being the one that fulfills Daniel 9:25:

> First, Cyrus' edict refers to the rebuilding of the temple and not to the city....
>
> Second, a distinction should be made between the rebuilding of a city and the restoration of a city to its former state....The commencement of the rebuilding began with Cyrus' decree but the city's complete restoration was not at that time.
>
> Third, if one accepts the seventy weeks as beginning with Cyrus' decree, how does one reckon the 490 years?...the final week would be divided into two parts, the first half covering the life of Christ and going even until the destruction of the temple in A.D. 70, a period of thirty-five to seventy years (about ten to twenty years for each week), and the second half of the seventieth week would have not *terminus ad quem*....it seems that this system makes havoc of Gabriel's sayings, which were rather specific.[67]

Dr. Hoehner demonstrates that the second decree does not fare any better than the first:

> First, and foremost, is that this decree has not a word about the rebuilding of the city of Jerusalem but rather the temple in Jerusalem....
>
> Second, to have the sixty-nine weeks terminate at the commencement of Christ's ministry in A.D. 26 or 27 is untenable for two reasons: (1) The cutting off of the Messiah (Daniel 9:26) is a

very inappropriate way to refer to the descent of the Holy Spirit upon Jesus at the commencement of His ministry. (2) The date for the beginning of Jesus' ministry is not A.D. 26 or 27 but A.D. 29, as discussed previously.[68]

Third, to what does Daniel refer in 9:27 when he states he is confirming a covenant? If it refers to Christ, then what covenant was it and how did He break it?

Fourth, to say that the middle of the seventieth week refers to Christ's crucifixion in A.D. 30 is untenable on two grounds: (1) the sacrifices did not cease at Christ's crucifixion, and (2) though the date of A.D. 30 is possible the A.D. 33 date is far more plausible.[69]

Fifth, to say that the end of the seventieth week refers to Stephen's death and Paul's conversion in A.D. 33 is pure speculation. There is no hint of this in the texts of Daniel 9:27 and Acts 8-9 to denote the fulfillment of the seventieth week. Also, the dates of Paul's conversion as well as Stephen's martyrdom were more likely in A.D. 35.[70]

In conclusion, the decree of Artaxerxes to Ezra in 457 B.C. serving as the starting point of the seventy weeks is highly unlikely.[71]

The third decree, then, is clearly the beginning point for the countdown of the 70 weeks of Daniel. Dr. Hoehner provides the following arguments in support of this decree as the *terminus a quo* as recorded in Nehemiah 2:1-8:

First, there is a direct reference to the restoration of the city (2:3, 5) and of the city gates and walls (2:3, 8). Second, Artaxerxes wrote a letter to Asaph to give materials to be used specifically for the walls (2:8). Third, the book of Nehemiah and Ezra 4:7-23 indicate that certainly the restoration of the walls was done in the most distressing circumstances, as predicted by Daniel (Daniel 9:25). Fourth, no later decrees were given by the Persian kings pertaining to the rebuilding of Jerusalem.[72]

The third decree, then, is surely the starting point for the countdown of Daniel's 70 weeks. What's more, it is possible for us to pinpoint the exact date of this decree to March 5, 444 B.C. This provides us with a solid plank in developing a literal interpretation of Gabriel's great prophecy to Daniel.

Again, let's consider Daniel 9:25: "So you are to know and discern that from the issuing of a decree to restore and rebuild Jerusalem until Messiah the Prince there will be seven weeks and sixty-two weeks; it will be built again, with plaza and moat, even in times of distress."

Because there is no need to reinvent the wheel, I want to address the matter of dating this decree by presenting two of the best treatments on this subject. First, we will look at Sir Robert Anderson's masterful presentation in *The Coming Prince*.[73] Then, we will examine Dr. Harold Hoehner's insightful refinement of Anderson's basic position from his work *Chronological Aspects of the Life of Christ*.[74]

Sir Robert Anderson

Sir Robert Anderson, a British Brethren, developed a chronology that used a 360-day year which he called a "prophetic year." Anderson bases this upon the Jewish calendar and the clear implication that Daniel's prophetic timetable was derived from it as well (i.e., 42 months = 1260 days). Anderson began the 483-year countdown with Artaxerxes' decree that he said was given March 14, 445 B.C. (Nisan 1, 445 B.C.) and it culminates in Christ's triumphal entry into Jerusalem on April 6, A.D. 32 (Nisan 10, A.D. 32). Here is Anderson's explanation:

> …According to the Jewish custom, our Lord went up to Jerusalem on the 8th Nisan, which, as we know, fell that year upon a Friday. And having spent the Sabbath at Bethany, He entered the Holy City the following day, as recorded in the Gospels. The Julian date of that 10th Nisan was Sunday the 6th of April, A.D. 32. What then was the length of the period intervening between the issuing of the decree to rebuild Jerusalem and this public advent of "Messiah the Prince"—between the 14th of March, B.C. 445 and the 6th of April A.D. 32 (when He entered into Jerusalem)? THE INTERVAL WAS EXACTLY AND TO THE VERY DAY 173,880 DAYS, OR SEVEN TIMES SIXTY-NINE PROPHETIC YEARS OF 360 DAYS.
>
> From B.C. 445 to A.D. 32 is 476 years = 173,740 days (476 x 365) + 116 days for leap years. And from 14th March to 6th April, reckoned inclusively according to Jewish practice is 24 days. But 173,740 + 116 + 24 = 173,880. And 69 x 7 x 360 = 173,880.
>
> It must be borne in mind here that in reckoning years from B.C. to A.D. one year must always be omitted; for, of course, the interval between B.C. 1 and A.D. 1 is not two years but one year. In fact, B.C. 1 ought to be called B.C. 0; and it is so described by astronomers, with whom B.C. 445 is—444. And again, as the Julian year is 11 m. 10.46 s., or about the 129th part of a day, longer than the mean solar year, the Julian calendar has three leap years too many in every four centuries. This error is corrected by the Gregorian reform, which reckons three secular years out of four as common

years. For instance, 1700, 1800, and 1900 were common years, and 2000 [was] a leap year.[75]

As valuable as Anderson's work continues to be, I believe it does contain a few errors, even though his overall approach provided a major break-through in understanding this part of Daniel's prophecy. The needed corrections have been provided by Dr. Hoehner.

Harold Hoehner

Dr. Hoehner has questioned the starting and ending times put forth by Anderson, advocating that Artaxerxes' decree was given in 444 B.C. and not 445 B.C. Hoehner explains:

> The date of this decree is given in the biblical record. Nehemiah 1:1 states that Nehemiah heard of Jerusalem's desolate conditions in the month of Chislev (November/December) in Artaxerxes' twentieth year. Then later in Artaxerxes' twentieth year in the month of Nisan (March/April) Nehemiah reports that he was granted permission to restore the city and build its walls (2:1). To have Nisan later than Chislev (in the same year) may seem strange until one realizes that Nehemiah was using a Tishri-to-Tishri (September/October) dating method rather than the Persian Nisan-to-Nisan method. Nehemiah was following what was used by the kings of Judah earlier in their history.[76] This method used by Nehemiah is confirmed by the Jews in Elephantine who also used this method during the same time period as Nehemiah.[77]
>
> Next, one needs to establish the beginning of Artaxerxes' rule. His father Xerxes died shortly after December 17, 465 B.C.[78] and Artaxerxes immediately succeeded him. Since the accession-year system was used[79] the first year of Artaxerxes' reign according to the Persian Nisan-to-Nisan reckoning would be Nisan 464 to Nisan 463 and according to the Jewish Tishri-to-Tishri reckoning would be Tishri 464 to Tishri 463....
>
> In conclusion, the report to Nehemiah (1:1) occurred in Chislev (November/December) of 445 B.C. and the decree of Artaxerxes (2:1) occurred in Nisan (March/April) of 444 B.C.[80]
>
> Therefore, Nisan 444 B.C. marks the *terminus ad quo* of the seventy weeks of Daniel 9:24-27.[81]

Hoehner also objects to Anderson's use of the solar year instead of the sabbatical year, and corrects some of Anderson's calculations:

First, in the light of new evidence since Anderson's day, the 445 B.C. date is not acceptable for Artaxerxes' twentieth year; instead the decree was given in Nisan, 444 B.C. Second, the A.D. 32 date for the crucifixion is untenable. It would mean that Christ was crucified on either a Sunday or Monday.[82] In fact, Anderson realizes the dilemma and he has to do mathematical gymnastics to arrive at a Friday crucifixion. This makes one immediately suspect. Actually there is no good evidence for an A.D. 32 crucifixion date.

In previous chapters in this book it was concluded that Christ's crucifixion occurred on Friday, Nisan 14, in A.D. 33. Reckoning His death according to the Julian calendar, Christ died on Friday, April 3, A.D. 33.[83] As discussed above, the *terminus a quo* occurred in Nisan, 444 B.C. Although Nehemiah 2:1 does not specify which day of Nisan the decree to rebuild Jerusalem occurred, it cannot have occurred before Nisan 1.... it could have occurred on some other day in Nisan.[84]

"Using the calculating method Anderson used, Hoehner comes up with the 476 solar years. This is the difference between 444 B.C. and A.D. 33. By multiplying 476 by 365.24219879 days, comes to 173,855 days."[85] Hoehner states:

This leaves only 25 days to be accounted for between 444 B.C. and A.D. 33. By adding the 25 days to Nisan 1 or March 5 (of 444 B.C.), one comes to March 30 (of A.D. 33) which was Nisan 10 in A.D. 33. This is the triumphal entry of Jesus into Jerusalem.... The *terminus ad quem* of the sixty-ninth week was on the day of Christ's triumphal entry on March 30, A.D. 33.

As predicted in Zechariah 9:9, Christ presented Himself to Israel as Messiah the king for the last time and the multitude of the disciples shouted loudly by quoting from a messianic psalm: "Blessed is the king who comes in the name of the Lord" (Ps. 118:26; Matthew 21:9; Mark 11:10; Luke 19:38; John 12:13). This occurred on Monday, Nisan 10 (March 30) and only four days later on Friday, Nisan 14, April 3, A.D. 33, Jesus was cut off or crucified.

The seventieth week of Daniel's prophecy is yet to be fulfilled. When that is accomplished, Daniel's inquiry will be fully realized for Israel will be back in her homeland with her Messiah.[86]

Hoehner has put together an airtight case for his understanding of the beginning and ending of the first 69 weeks of Daniel's prophecy. Dr. John Walvoord notes, in support of Hoehner, that "the best explanation of the time when the sixty-nine sevens ended is that it occurred shortly before the death of Christ anticipated in Daniel 9:26 as following the sixty-ninth seven. Practically all expositors agree that the death of Christ occurred after the sixty-ninth seven."[87]

To date, no one has been able to challenge the work done by Hoehner. It is fully supportive of the literal interpretation of Daniel's prophecy and is the only approach that has been demonstrated, thus far, to make the numbers work out. That is why most all those who take this text literally have adopted Hoehner's view. Those taking other views, such as preterists DeMar[88] and Gentry,[89] offer vague generalities when it comes to the numbers related to the 70-weeks prophecy.

A further value of Hoehner's literal approach is that when it's applied to this prophecy, we come up with the exact time at which Israel's Messiah was predicted to show up in history. "When He approached Jerusalem, He saw the city and wept over it, saying, 'If you had known in this day, even you, the things which make for peace! But now they have been hidden from your eyes.... because you did not recognize the time of your visitation'" (Luke 19:41-42,44). How was Israel to have known the *time* of their visitation? From a literal understanding of Daniel's prophecy. In fact, this prophecy, along with Christ's fulfillment of all the other first-coming messianic prophecies, proves beyond a shadow of a doubt that Jesus was Israel's Messiah.[90] Many Jews have come to faith, over the years, as a result of being challenged by this prediction about the time of Messiah's coming. It is clear, then, that a literal interpretation of this passage is demanded by the text itself.

THE SEVEN WEEKS

As we move on in our study to verse 26, it is important to note that God, through Gabriel the archangel, divides the seventy weeks into three sections: "seven weeks," "sixty-two weeks," and "one week" (Daniel 9:25-27). What is the significance of these divisions?

The first seven weeks of years (49 years) is segmented from the whole. To what does it refer? There is not much debate about this; the general agreement is that the first seven weeks refers to the time when "it [Jerusalem] will be built again, with plaza and moat, even in times of distress" (Daniel 9:25). This modifying statement connects the first seven weeks with the distressing days of Ezra and Nehemiah. Walvoord notes:

> The best explanation seems to be that beginning with Nehemiah's decree and the building of the wall, it took a whole generation to clear out all the debris in Jerusalem and restore it as a thriving city. This might well be the fulfillment of the forty-nine

years. The specific reference to streets again addresses our attention to Nehemiah's situation where the streets were covered with debris and needed to be rebuilt. That this was accomplished in troublesome times is fully documented by the book of Nehemiah itself. [91]

The fact that this prophecy divides the 70 weeks of years into three sections will come into play later when we examine the single week mentioned in verse 27.

THE SIXTY-TWO WEEKS

The next segment of time is the 62 weeks of years that are said to follow the first seven weeks of years. The total of the two parts equals 69 weeks of years, or 483 years. The 62 weeks come *after* the first seven weeks because there are no textual indicators or historical events that would lead to any other conclusion. The 62 weeks will end with the arrival of "Messiah the Prince"—Daniel 9:25 says, "Until Messiah the Prince there will be seven weeks and sixty-two weeks." Messiah the Prince can be none other than the Jewish Messiah—Jesus the Christ. As was noted earlier, Hoehner demonstrated that the seven and 62 weeks (that is, 69 weeks) ended on the day of Christ's triumphal entry into Jerusalem.[92] This is diagrammed in the chart below, which was adapted from Hoehner's book.[93] The fulfillment of the seven and 62 weeks is recorded in Luke 19:41-42,44: "When He [Jesus] approached Jerusalem, He saw the city and wept over it, saying, 'If you had known in this day, even you, the things which make for peace! But now they have been hidden from your eyes....because you did not recognize the time of your visitation.'"

Daniel's 70 Weeks
Daniel 9:24-27

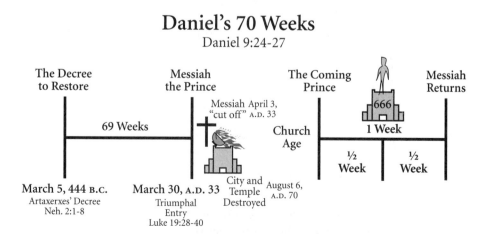

AFTER THE 62 WEEKS

We now enter the area of the greatest controversy concerning the 70-weeks prophecy. The debate is focused upon whether the seventieth week follows immediately after the first sixty-nine weeks. Futurists believe that the seventieth week is postponed until a future time we know as the Tribulation. In the rest of this chapter, we will look at whether we can support the possibility of a gap between the sixty-ninth and seventieth weeks.

In this debate there are two basic views, regardless of how an individual may handle the details. One view says all 70 weeks of years have already been fulfilled in the past, and the other says that the final, seventieth week is still future. To set the context, let's note what Daniel 9:26 says: "Then after the sixty-two weeks the Messiah will be cut off and have nothing, and the people of the prince who is to come will destroy the city and the sanctuary. And its end will come with a flood; even to the end there will be war; desolations are determined."

THE POSTPONEMENT

The Need for a Gap

Before I look at broader arguments for a gap or parenthesis, I want to point out some supports found in Daniel 9 itself. Critics of the literal, futurist understanding of this text claim there is no justification for a gap between the sixty-ninth and seventieth weeks. Perhaps no one is more shrill in his criticism of a gap than preterist DeMar, who says: "The 'gap' that has been placed between the sixty-ninth and seventieth weeks of Daniel's prophecy was created because it was needed to make the dispensational hermeneutical model work. Nothing in the text of Daniel 9:24-27 implies a 'gap.'"[94]

He later asks the following question: "Since there is no gap between the seven and sixty-two weeks, what justification is there in inserting a gap between the sixty-ninth week (seven weeks + sixty-two weeks = sixty-nine weeks) and the seventieth week?"[95]

Futurists believe there *are* textual supports for a gap of time between the sixty-ninth and seventieth weeks! Note that the text says, "Then *after* the sixty-two weeks...." Chronologically, this refers to a time *after* the seven plus 62 weeks, which equals 69 weeks of years (483 years). The Hebrew text uses a conjunction, combined with a preposition, usually translated "and after," or better, "then after." "It is the only indicator given regarding the chronological relation between the 62 weeks and the cutting off of the Anointed One. This event will occur 'after' their close, but nothing is said as to how long after."[96] Culver clearly states the implication of what this text says: "There can be no honest difference of opinion about that: the cutting off of *Messiah* is 'after' the sixty-two weeks. It is not the concluding event of the series of sixty-two weeks. Neither is it said to be the opening event of the seventieth. It is simply after the seven plus sixty-two weeks."[97]

Dr. Steven Miller, in his commentary on Daniel, summarizes developments in the passage thus far as follows: "After the reconstruction of Jerusalem in the first seven sevens (forty-nine years), another 'sixty-two sevens' (434 years) would pass. Then two momentous events would take place. First, the 'Anointed One' would come (verse 25), then he would be 'cut off.' Apparently his coming would be immediately at the end of the sixty-nine sevens....'"[98]

There is no real debate among conservative interpreters as to the meaning of the phrase "the Messiah will be cut off"—it's a reference to the crucifixion of Christ. Thus, Jesus would be crucified after the completion of the seven and 62 weeks, but before the beginning of the seventieth week. For this to happen requires a gap of time between the end of the 69 weeks and the beginning of the seventieth week. This is not the result of an *a priori* belief like dispensationalism, as claimed by some. Lang notes, "It is here that the interval in the Seventy Sevens must fall. This is not a matter of interference, but of fact."[99]

The Denial of a Gap

Interestingly, interpreters like DeMar, who advocate a continuous fulfillment view of all 70 weeks without a break, are required to put *both* the crucifixion of Christ and the destruction of Jerusalem some 40 years later into the final week of years, which is only seven years in length. Yet DeMar accuses those who see a gap between the sixty-ninth and seventieth week as exercising 'silly-putty' exegesis,"[100] of stretching out this biblical time frame in a manner not supported by the text itself. DeMar argues that Christ's death took place in the middle of the final week, which would then draw to a conclusion in A.D. 33 with the conversion of Paul (an event which in no way is even remotely alluded to in Gabriel's prophecy).[101] What DeMar fails to tell his readers is that while he argues vehemently against a gap, he is very silent about how to cram two events separated by 40 years into a seven-year period. Perhaps his approach should be called "shoehorn" exegesis!

A closer look at DeMar's problem reveals a grave contradiction in his understanding of Daniel 9:24-27 and his view of Matthew 24:15 as having been fulfilled in A.D. 70. "The abomination of desolation is mentioned in one Old Testament book (Daniel 9:27; 11:31; 12:11),"[102] declares DeMar. He then states that "there was no doubt in the minds of those who read and understood Jesus' words in Matthew 24:15 that the abomination of desolation prophecy was fulfilled in events leading up to the temple's destruction in A.D.

70."[103] Clearly DeMar links the fulfillment of the abomination of desolation in Daniel 9:27, which will occur in the middle of the week, with the Roman destruction of the temple in A.D. 70 some 40 years later. The problem is that the numbers clearly don't add up. There is absolutely no way to jam events that occurred at least 40 years apart into a mere seven years.

Price notes that "the events in verse 26: 'the cutting off of Messiah,' and of 'the people of the prince,' are stated to occur *after* the sixty-nine weeks. If this was intended to occur *in* the seventieth week, the text would have read here 'during' or 'in the midst of' (cf. Daniel's use of *hetzi*, 'in the middle of,' verse 27). This language implies that these events precede the seventieth week, but do not immediately follow the sixty-ninth. Therefore, a temporal interval separates the two."[104] Only the literal, futurist understanding of the 70 weeks of Daniel, then, can harmonize in a precise manner the interpretation of this passage.

THE EVENTS

The Messiah Will Be Cut Off

We have seen thus far that verse 26 begins with the phrase "after the sixty-two weeks." The text goes on to describe three things that will take place at the end of the sixty-ninth week of years (i.e., 483 years). They are: 1) "the Messiah will be cut off and have nothing," 2) "the people of the prince who is to come will destroy the city and the sanctuary," and 3) "its end will come with a flood; even to the end there will be war; desolations are determined."

All evangelical interpreters agree that the cutting off of Messiah refers to the death of Jesus. Since the 483 years were fulfilled to the day on March 30, A.D. 33—the date of Christ's triumphal entry (Luke 19:28-40)—and Jesus was crucified four days later on April 3, A.D. 33, then the crucifixion took place after the 483 years, but not during the final week of years. This textual point is recognized by many, including amillennialist E. B. Pusey, who says, "[N]ot *in*, but *after* those *three score and two weeks*, it said *Messiah shall be cut off*."[105] "As this relates to the chronology of the prophecy," notes Walvoord, "it makes plain that the Messiah will be living at the end of the sixty-ninth seventh and will be cut off, or die, soon after the end of it."[106] G. H. Pember further explains:

> Now, His crucifixion took place four days after His appearance as the Prince—that is, four days after the close of the Four Hundred and Eighty-third Year. Nevertheless, the prophecy does not represent this great event as occurring in the Seven Years which yet remained to be fulfilled. Here, then, is the beginning of an

interval, which separates the Four Hundred and Eighty-three Years from the final Seven.[107]

The next phrase in Daniel 9:26 is "and have nothing," which literally means "and shall have nothing." To what does this refer? Certainly Christ gained what was intended through His atoning death on the cross as far as paying for the sins of the world. What was it that He came for but did not receive, especially in relationship to Israel and Jerusalem, which is the larger context of this overall passage? It was His messianic kingdom! Indeed, it will come, but not at the time that He was cut off. Feinberg declares, "It can only mean that He did not receive the Messianic kingdom at that time. When His own people rejected him (John 1:11), He did not receive what rightly belonged to Him."[108] Before the kingdom can come, the Jews must accept Jesus as Messiah so He can establish the kingdom in Jerusalem. Also, the kingdom will arrive by the time the final week is brought to fruition. Since Israel's kingdom has not yet arrived, this means it is future to our day. That gives us yet another support affirming that the final week of years is also future to our day.

The Prince Who Is to Come

The identity of "the prince who is to come" (Daniel 8:26) is a matter of considerable debate. The full statement says, "The people of the prince who is to come will destroy the city and the sanctuary." Perhaps the best way to determine the identity of this prince is to first look at what he is prophesied to do at his arrival upon the stage of history. The people of this coming prince will destroy the city, clearly a reference to Jerusalem because of the overall context, and also the sanctuary. What sanctuary was there in Jerusalem? It could be nothing other than the Jewish Temple. Have the city and Temple been destroyed? Yes! Both were destroyed in A. D. 70 by the Romans. This cannot be a reference to a future time, since, as Walvoord notes, "there is no complete destruction of Jerusalem at the end of the age as Zechariah 14:1-3 indicates that the city is in existence although overtaken by war at the very moment that Christ comes back in power and glory. Accordingly, it is probably better to consider all of verse 26 fulfilled historically."[109]

The subject of this sentence is "the people," not "the prince who is to come." Thus, it is the *people* of the prince who is to come that destroy the city and the sanctuary. We have already identified the people as the Romans, who destroyed Jerusalem and the Temple in A.D. 70 under the leadership of Titus. Yet I believe that "the prince who is to come" is a reference to the yet-to-come Antichrist. Dr. Dwight Pentecost explains, "The ruler who will come is that final head of the Roman Empire, the little horn of 7:8. It is significant that the *people* of the ruler, not the ruler himself, will destroy

Jerusalem. Since he will be the final Roman ruler, the people of that ruler must be the Romans themselves."[110]

The coming prince cannot be a reference to Christ, since He is said to be "cut off" in the prior sentence. This prince has to be someone who comes after Christ. The only two viable possibilities are that the words are referring to a Roman prince who destroyed Jerusalem in A.D. 70, or to a future Antichrist.

Why should we not see "the prince who is to come" as a reference to Titus, who led the Roman conquest in A.D. 70? Because the emphasis of this verse is upon "the people," not the subordinate clause, "the prince who is to come." Apparently this passage is stated this way so that this prophecy would link the Roman destruction with the A.D. 70 event, but at the same time, set up the Antichrist to be linked to the final week of years to the first "he" in verse 27. He is not described as the prince coming with the people, but instead, as one who *is coming*. This suggests that the people and the prince will not arrive together in history. Miller adds, "But verse 27 makes clear that this 'ruler' will be the future persecutor of Israel during the seventieth seven. 'The people of the rule' does not mean that the people 'belong to' the ruler but rather that the ruler will come from these people."[111] Interestingly, our amillennial friends agree that this is a reference to the Antichrist, as noted by Culver: "Neither is there any difficulty with our amillennial friends over the identity of 'the coming prince,'...Keil and Leupold recognize him as the final Antichrist, said to be 'coming' because already selected for prophecy in *direct language* in chapter 7 as 'the little horn,' and in *type* in chapter 8 as 'the little horn.' Young thinks otherwise but is outweighed on his own 'team.'"[112]

The End Will Come with a Flood

Chronologically, the final sentence of verse 26 describes happenings that take place during the interval between the sixty-ninth and seventieth weeks. However, the first part, "its end will come with a flood," refers back to the destruction of Jerusalem in A.D. 70, while the final phrase, "even to the end there will be war; desolations are determined," is being fulfilled throughout the entire period (2,000 years thus far) of the interval.

"The antecedent of 'it' is obviously Jerusalem," explains Wood. 'Flood' or 'overflowing' can refer only to the degree of destruction meted out. History records that the destruction of Jerusalem was very extensive."[113] The wars and desolations that began with the destruction of Jerusalem in A.D. 70 would continue throughout the interval leading up to the seventieth week. In fact, this language appears to parallel that of Luke 21:24, which says, "they will fall by the edge of the sword, and will be led captive into all the nations; and Jerusalem will be trampled under foot by the Gentiles until the times of the

Gentiles are fulfilled." Feinberg agrees: "The final words of verse 26 sum up the history of Israel since A.D. 70: 'desolations are determined.' Surely the determined wars and desolations have come upon them (cf. Luke 21:24). Such has been the lot of Israel and the city of Jerusalem, and such will be the portion, until the 'time of the Gentiles' have been fulfilled." [114]

Pentecost adds the following: But that invasion, awesome as it was, did not end the nation's sufferings, for war, Gabriel said, would continue until the end. Even though Israel was to be set aside, she would continue to suffer until the prophecies of the 70 "sevens" were completely fulfilled. Her sufferings span the entire period from the destruction of Jerusalem in A.D. 70 to Jerusalem's deliverance from Gentile dominion at the Second Advent of Christ. [115]

Once again we see that a plain, straightforward reading of the Bible text provides a clear and convincing understanding that there is a biblical basis for halting God's clock between the sixty-ninth and seventieth weeks. Culver summarizes our findings as follows:

> All attempts to place the events of verse 26 (the cutting off of Christ and the destruction of Jerusalem) in either the period of the sixty-two weeks (Keil and Leupold) or in the seventieth week (Young and a host of writers in the past) stumble and fall on the simple language of the text itself. It seems that a more natural interpretation is the one that regards the events of verse 26 as belonging to a period between the sixty-ninth and seventieth weeks, when God has sovereignly set aside His people Israel, awaiting a time of resumption of covenant relationship in the future, after Israel has been restored to the land. [116]

Thus, with each phrase that we examine in Daniel 9:24-27, we find that complaints such as this one from Gentry end up falling silent to the ground. "Only hermeneutical gymnastics, a suspension of sound reason, and an *a priori* commitment to the dispensational system allows the importing of a massive gap into Daniel's prophecy. Such ideas interrupt the otherwise chronologically exact time-frame." [117]

To the contrary, as we have seen, the text of Daniel 9:24-27 itself demands a gap of time.

ANTICHRIST OR CHRIST?

Our study of Daniel's 70-weeks prophecy now moves to the final verse in the passage, which also deals with the final week of years: "He will make a firm covenant with the many for one week, but in the middle of the week he will put a stop to sacrifice and grain offering; and on the wing of abominations will come one who makes desolate, even until a complete destruction, one that is decreed, is poured out on the one who makes desolate" (Daniel 9:27).

As we study Daniel 9:27, we will find further evidence supporting the idea of a gap between the sixty-ninth and seventieth weeks, and we will note how the text supports the interpretation that this seven-year period is the yet-to-come Tribulation.

The first question that arises with verse 27 is this: To whom does the pronoun "he" refer? I believe that "he" must refer to "the prince who is to come" (verse 26). However, opponents of literal interpretation disagree. Gentry says, "[T]he indefinite pronoun 'he' does not refer back to 'the prince who is to come' of verse 26."[118] DeMar insists "it is Jesus who 'will make a firm covenant with the many,' not the antichrist."[119] Yet such an interpretation violates the grammar and syntax of the Hebrew text.

In Hebrew grammar, as with most languages, a pronoun refers to the nearest antecedent unless there is a contextual reason to think otherwise. In this instance, the nearest antecedent in agreement with "he" is "the prince who is to come" in verse 26. This is recognized by a majority of scholars,[120] including a number of amillennialists such as Kiel[121] and Leupold.[122] Only *a priori* theological bias could lead a trained interpreter of Scripture to any other conclusion. Culver explains the correct meaning of this text:

> The ordinary rules of grammar establish that the leading actor of this verse is the Antichrist, the great evil man of the end time....If the pronoun "he" were present in the Hebrew, a case might possibly be made for the introduction of an entirely new personality into the story at this point. However, there is no pronoun; only the third masculine singular form of the verb indicates that an antecedent is to be sought, and that of necessity in the preceding context. Usually, the last preceding noun that agrees in gender and number and agrees with the sense is the antecedent. This is unquestionably..."the coming prince" of verse 26. He is a "coming" prince, that is, one whom the reader would already know as a prince to come, because he is the same as the "little horn" on the fourth beast of chapter 7.[123]

Wood provides a list of additional reasons for accepting the word "he" in verse 27 as a reference to "the prince who is to come":

> ...the unusual manner of mention in verse twenty-six regarding that prince calls for just such a further reference as this. There is no reason for the earlier notice unless something further is to be

said regarding him, for he does nothing nor plays any part in activities there described. Third, several matters show that what is now said regarding the one in reference does not suit if that reference is to Christ. (a) This person makes a "firm covenant" with people, but Christ made no covenant. God made a Covenant of Grace with people, and Christ fulfilled requirements under it, but this is quite different from Christ's making a covenant. (b) Even if Christ had made a covenant with people during His lifetime, the idea of mentioning it only here in the overall thought of the passage would be unusual, when the subjects of His death and even the destruction of Jerusalem have already been set forth. (c) The idea of the seventieth week, here closely associated with this one, does not fit the life or ministry of Christ, as will be shown presently. (d) The idea that this one causes "sacrifice and offering to cease" does not fit in reference to Christ in this context. The amillennial view holds that these words refer to Christ's supreme sacrifice in death, which made all other sacrifices and offerings of no further use, thus making them to cease in principle. But, if so, what would be the reason for such a statement (true as it is) in view of the purpose of the overall prediction? One could understand a direct statement concerning Christ's providing atonement for sin—though its placing at this point in the general thought order of the passage would be strange—because that would be important to sin-bondaged Israelites. But why, if that is the basic thought, should it be expressed so indirectly, in terms of sacrificing and offering being made to cease?[124]

It is safe to conclude that the immediate context of this passage and the book as a whole supports the word "he" as referring to the Antichrist. This interpretation also fits the futurist understanding of verse 27.

The Making of a Covenant
Scriptural Examination

What is it that "he" will do? The Antichrist will "make a firm covenant with the many for one week"—that is, seven years. Non-literal interpreters of Daniel's 70-weeks prophecy usually say this covenant refers to Christ's covenant to save His people, usually known as the covenant of grace. "This, then, is a confirming of a covenant already extant, i.e., the covenant of God's redemptive grace that Christ confirms (Romans 15:8),"[125] says Gentry. Gentry and those advocating a similar view must resort to a non-textual, theological interpretation at this point because there was no seven-year covenant made by Christ with the Jewish people at the time of His first coming. Gentry and others must back off from the specifics of the text in verse 27 and import a theological interpretation, thus providing us with a classic example of spiritualization or allegorical interpretation.

If this is supposed to be a reference to the covenant of grace, then "it may be observed first that this would be a strange way to express such a thought,"[126] notes Wood. Christ's salvation covenant is not limited to seven years; rather, it is an eternal covenant. Daniel 9:27 says the covenant is to be made with "the many." This term always refers in some way to Israel throughout the book of Daniel (Daniel 11:33,39; 12:3). Thus it is a narrow term used in a specific context. It is not a broad term synonymous with the language of global salvation. Further, "it is evident that the covenant is subsequent to the cutting off of Messiah and the destruction of the City and the Sanctuary, in the twenty-sixth verse; therefore, it could not have been confirmed at the First Advent,"[127] says Pember. Such an interpretation does not fit this text and it does not account for the seven years during which the covenant will be in force. Wood further explains: "Since the word for 'covenant'...does not carry the article (contrary to the KJV translation), this covenant likely is made at this time for the first time (not a reaffirmation of an old one, then) and probably will concern some type of nonaggression treaty, recognizing mutual rights. Israel's interest in such a treaty is easy to understand in the light of her desire today for allies to help withstand foes such as Russia and the Arab bloc of nations."[128]

There is absolutely no historical evidence of the covenant described in verse 27 having become a reality in reference to the nation of Israel. Thus, this covenant is yet another still-to-come future event. This, then, demands a postponement of the seventieth week, with a gap of time between the sixty-ninth and seventieth weeks of years.

For One Week

This passage clearly says that the covenant "he" makes will last for one week or seven years. This could mean that the covenant will be seven years long by design, or that it will exist for only seven years. Many of those who believe that the entire 70-weeks prophecy was fulfilled around the time of Christ's first coming teach that the first half of the seventieth week was fulfilled by Christ's ministry.[129] "We know Christ's three-and-one-half-year ministry," says Gentry, "was decidedly focused on the Jews in the first half of the seventieth week (Matthew 10:5b; cf. Matthew 15:24)."[130] Pember objects, saying that:

if the Messiah could be the subject, and the time that of the First Advent, we should then be plunged into the greatest perplexity; for the Lord did none of the things that are mentioned in the twenty-seventh verse. To fulfill that part of the prophecy, He must have made a covenant with the majority of the Jewish people for seven years, neither more nor less. But there is no hint of such a covenant in the Gospels. And, indeed, one of the prophets has intimated to us, that the Lord, just before His death, suspended all His relations with the Jews, and through them with the whole of the Twelve Tribes. This exactly corresponds to the suspension of His dealings with the Jews at the close of the Four Hundred and Eighty-third Year, and to the facts of history. Still further, the very next verse of Zechariah carries us over the interval, and brings us face to face with the Prince that shall come, the Antichrist, who will make the seven years' covenant on pretence of being the Shepherd of Israel. Lastly, Christ did not cause sacrifice and offering to cease, when He suffered without the gate: the Temple-services were carried on for nearly forty years longer.[131]

Once again, the text of this passage supports a gap of time between the sixty-ninth and seventieth weeks. It is becoming increasingly obvious that the seventieth week is still future to the time in which we now live. "Israel has now been reestablished as a nation (1948), suggesting that the seventieth seven may soon begin."[132]

In the Middle of the Week

The archangel Gabriel divided his prophecy of 70 weeks of years into three sections: seven weeks, sixty-two weeks, and one week. The final week of years—seven years—is detailed in Daniel 9:27. We have already looked at the first part of verse 27, "And he will make a firm covenant with the many for one week." Now let's focus on the rest of the verse, which says, "But in the middle of the week he will put a stop to sacrifice and grain offering; and on the wing of abominations will come one who makes desolate, even until a complete destruction, one that is decreed, is poured out on the one who makes desolate." This verse tells us what will happen during the final week of years, which futurists believe to be a yet-future seven-year period often called the Tribulation.

Since the week of years is a seven-year period, the middle of a week of years would place us three-and-a-half years into the seven-year period. Interestingly, Daniel 7:25 and 12:7 both refer to a three-and-a-half year period (time, times, and half a time). The context of both passages speaks of the future time of the Antichrist or the Beast. This would support a futurist understanding of the seventieth week of Daniel 9:27. Daniel 7:25 says, "He will speak out against the Most High and wear down the saints of the Highest One, and he will intend to make alterations in times and in law; and they will be given into his hand for a time, times, and half a time." While this passage was given to Daniel before he received the revelation stated in chapter 9, it seems clear that the logic for the chronology of Daniel 7:25 is drawn from the 70-weeks prophecy of chapter 9.

In addition, Daniel 12:7 reads, "I heard the man dressed in linen, who was above the waters of the river, as he raised his right hand and his left toward heaven, and swore by Him who lives forever that it would be for a time, times, and half a time; and as soon as they finish shattering the power of the holy people, all these events will be completed." Both Daniel 9:27 and 12:7 speak of the Antichrist's rule coming to an end at the conclusion of the same three-and-a-half year period. This supports the notion that they both refer to a yet-future time that we often call the Great Tribulation. Dr. John Whitcomb notes:

> This important prophetic statement clearly refers to the same time units as previously described in the end-time activities of the Antichrist ("little horn") of Daniel 7, where "he will intend to make alterations in times and in law; and they [the saints] will be given into his hands for a time, times, and half a time" (7:25). The clarification provided here is that the three-and-one-half-year period at the beginning of which Antichrist "shall cause a covenant [with the many] to be made strong" (literal translation). Then, for some unexplained reason, "in the middle" of this final seven-year period "he will put a stop to sacrifice [*zebâh*, bloody sacrifices] and grain offering [*minhah*, non-bloody sacrifices]."[133]

Allegorical Alchemy

I once attended a conference at which Hal Lindsey spoke. He used a phrase that I believe applies to non-literal interpreters such as DeMar[134] and Gentry,[135] who do not provide a textual interpretation of Daniel 9:27. They are rightly called "allegorical alchemists," because they try to brew up interpretations from out of thin air by just stating them and then declaring them to be true. In Daniel 9:27 they attempt a topical approach, selecting a word or two from the passage and declaring that "Daniel's famous prophecy finds fulfillment in the first century of our era."[136] DeMar is even more bizarre in his alchemy when he teaches this:

As the result of the Jews' rejection of Jesus, they would lose their inheritance. This would not occur for another forty years (Matthew 21:33-46; 22:1-14). Similarly, Jesus pronounced the temple "desolate" when He walked out of it even though its destruction did not come for another forty years (23:38). In principle, it was a "done deal" when He turned His back on the temple. It is no wonder that Jesus described the temple as "*your house*" (23:38). The temple's destruction was a *consequence,* a result, of the apostate Jews' rejection of Jesus (see 2 Samuel 13:32; Job 14:15; Isa. 10:22; Lam. 2:8; Luke 22:22)....

...The sentence is determined on one day while the sentence may not be carried out until some time in the future. In similar fashion, we are told that the destruction of Jerusalem was "determined" within the seventy weeks while the sentence was not carried out until forty years later. [137]

As we saw earlier, Gentry's claim that Daniel 9:27 refers to Christ's salvation covenant runs into a problem because the text says this is a seven-year covenant, and Scripture does not state anywhere that Christ made such a covenant with Israel. Pentecost further explains:

This covenant could not have been made or confirmed by Christ at His First Advent...because : (a) His ministry did not last seven years, (b) His death did not stop sacrifices and offerings, (c) He did not set up "the abomination that causes desolation" (Matthew 24:15). Amillenarians suggest that Christ confirmed (in the sense of fulfilling) the Abrahamic Covenant but the Gospels give no indication He did that in His First Advent.[138]

What Gentry says just does not explain Daniel 9:27 in context. When an allegorical alchemist's interpretation cannot explain the details of a passage, he will take words or phrases out of context and place them into a different context so that, to some, it appears that he has explained the passage. Yet, Gentry has done nothing of the sort, and this a clear example of his interpretative sleight-of-hand. The text of verse 27 is simply not explained by Gentry's statements.

In a way, DeMar's explanation is even worse. While verse 27 clearly says the events mentioned in the verse will take place within the seven-year period, DeMar, however, says otherwise. Verse 27 says that in the middle of the seven-year period, "he will put a stop to sacrifice and grain offering." This language speaks of something that will actually take place. It does not speak of something that someone is proposing to do later, as DeMar states. The final part of verse 27 says, "And on the wing of abominations will come one who makes desolate, even until a complete destruction, one that is decreed, is poured out on the one who makes desolate." How is this just a *proposal* of what has been determined when the passage clearly says that this *will* take place within the time frame specified?

The Abomination of Desolation

Verse 27 says that in the middle of the week (three-and-a-half years), "on the wing of abominations will come one who makes desolate." Here we have a reference to the Antichrist, who will desecrate the Temple. This did not happen near the time of Christ's first coming. So when did it happen? If it happened in A.D. 70, as some might say, then it did not take place within the time span of the 70 weeks of years. Yet Jesus clearly said in Matthew 24:15, "Therefore when you see the abomination of desolation which was spoken of through Daniel the prophet, standing in the holy place (let the reader understand)...." Here we have Jesus' own interpretation concerning the event Gabriel describes to Daniel in Daniel 9:27. The event has to be future to the time of Christ, and since nothing like it corresponds to within seven years of His prediction, then we have to see this as a yet-future event. This once again supports the idea of a gap between the sixty-ninth week of years and the seventieth week. Posttribulationist Dr. Robert Gundry notes:

> ...to place the complete fulfillment of the seventieth week at A.D. 70 or before severs the obvious connection between Daniel 9, Matthew 24, and Revelation. (Compare "in the middle of the week" [Daniel 9:27], forty-two months and 1,260 days [Revelation 11:2; 12:6; 13:5], and time, times, and half a time [Daniel 12:7; 7:25; Revelation 12:14]. Under the historical view, if the relationship between Daniel and Revelation were retained, Revelation, which was written probably a quarter century after the destruction of Jerusalem, would be history instead of the prophecy it purports to be.)[139]

Daniel 9:27 closes with these words: "even until a complete destruction, one that is decreed, is poured out on the one who makes desolate." Did this happen in conjunction with Christ's first advent? It did not! Therefore, we must conclude that the Antichrist will be destroyed at the second coming of Christ, which will bring to an end the seventieth week of years sometime in the future.

DeMar sees the abomination of desolation taking place in A.D. 70, which violates the clear statements of the biblical text: "The abomination of desolation is mentioned in one Old Testament book (Daniel 9:27; 11:31; 12:11)...."

There was no doubt in the minds of those who read and understood Jesus' words in Matthew 24:15 that the abomination of desolation prophecy was fulfilled in events leading up to the temple's destruction in A.D. 70." [140]

In addition to the problem that an A.D. 70 fulfillment does not fit into anyone's scheme of the 70 weeks of years, none of the Romans, such as Titus, could be said to have been destroyed after performing the supposed deed. Price rebuts such an approach with the following:

> ...historically, no known Roman leader ever "made a covenant with the Jewish leaders...for seven years, and so this awaits future fulfillment when the seventieth week commences.
>
> ...However, if this is applied to the Romans in their crushing the Jewish Revolt in A.D. 70, then how was the Roman empire punished at this point, since the fall of the empire itself was still several hundred years away? [141]

It is obvious that the events described in Daniel 9:27 did not take place at or in conjunction with Christ's first coming in the first century A.D. A gap between the sixty-ninth and seventieth week is needed in order for the prophecy to work out historically with the exact precision that our Lord intends. It is a shame that some let their theological bias prevent them from seeing this, and many other passages, as God intended them to be seen when He revealed them to His prophets. When one takes the final week of years literally, the conclusions fully harmonize with hundreds of other verses that speak of the Tribulation period that will lead up to the defeat of Christ's enemies and the victory of our Lord.

THE CRITICISMS

Those who do not believe that the 70 weeks of Daniel 9:24-27 have a literal and chronologically precise fulfillment are opposed to the idea that the seventieth week is a yet-future time of seven years. Preterists are some of the leading critics. DeMar complains: "Placing a gap between the sixty-ninth and seventieth weeks of Daniel 9:24-27 'must be fixed' because of the system created by dispensationalists, not because the Bible mentions anything about a gap....dispensationalists force the Bible to comply to an already developed system that insists that these events cannot be describing first-century events." [142]

Gentry echoes DeMar's refrain with these words:

> An overriding concern of the prophecy, in distinction to all other Messianic prophecies is that it is specifically designed to be

> a measuring time-frame.....If there were gaps between the units, the whole idea of measurement in the "seventy weeks" would vanish. An elastic yardstick is a worthless measure. None of the other prophecies brought forward as illustrations of a gap claim to be a *measure of time.*[143]

Gentry is right about one thing: Daniel 9 is the only messianic prophecy that specifically deals with chronology or a time element. While I believe that I have shown that the passage itself requires a chronological gap between the sixty-ninth and seventieth weeks of years, this thinking is also supported by other messianic passages that are not specifically time-oriented but clearly do refer to distinct time periods. These passages have to do with Christ's first and second comings.

If anyone believes in the two comings of Christ, and both DeMar and Gentry do, then they also believe in a gap of time between the first and second comings of Christ. I want to show a clear biblical pattern related to Christ's two comings that, in turn, lends support to the notion of a gap of time in Daniel 9:24-27.

THE TWO PHASES OF CHRIST'S CAREER

The Context

If you view the ministry or career of Christ in its entirety, then it's obvious from Scripture that it is composed of two major parts or phases. The first phase encompasses the first coming of Jesus 2,000 years ago, while the second phase will consist of His second coming some time in the future. Yet many Old Testament prophecies about the coming Messiah referenced both phases in a single passage, without distinguishing them from one another.

It is commonly understood today that the Jews of the first century did not understand that these Old Testament prophecies spoke of a single Messiah who would come twice—once in humiliation, then again in glorious exaltation. We have learned that many Jews of Christ's day thought there would be two different Messiahs—Messiah ben Joseph and Messiah ben David. Messiah ben Joseph would suffer and die, and would be followed by Messiah ben David, who would reign in glory.[144] The reality of Scripture, however, is that there is but one Messiah—Jesus of Nazareth—who comes twice. This means there is a gap of time between the two comings.

Even though preterists such as DeMar and Gentry belittle a gap of time between the sixty-ninth and seventieth weeks of Daniel 9:24-27, they are driven to believe in a gap of time between Christ's two comings. DeMar and Gentry even believe in a gap, so far, of almost 2,000 years. Yet this gap is not explicitly stated in Scripture. So how can DeMar and Gentry hold to a gap of time that is not explicitly stated in Scripture? Because the only possible implication that can be deduced from the facts of Christ's two comings is that there is a gap between the two events. In like manner, such a gap must also follow from the fact that Christ has a career that is two-phased.

Why is this important to our study of the 70 weeks of Daniel? It is important because, as Gentry noted earlier, "An overriding concern of the prophecy, in distinction to all other Messianic prophecies is that it is specifically designed to be a measuring time-frame."[145] Though that is true, Gentry believes in a gap of time between the two comings of Christ even though such a gap is not specifically stated in the Bible. In the same way, I would argue that all other messianic passages that speak of the two aspects or phases of Messiah's career must also imply that they are fulfilled at His two comings with a gap of time in between. This means there are many Bible passages that speak, in a single statement, of elements that encompass both phases of Christ's career—the first and second advents. However, as Gentry has noted, only the Daniel 9:24-27 passage deals with measuring time. This explains why the Daniel passage is the only messianic text that deals specifically with a time frame. Moreover, a significant number of other messianic passages share elements in common with the prophecy in Daniel 9:24-27. They all speak of components of Christ's career that will take place in the two phases of His single career.

The Passages

This means it is legitimate to argue for a gap of time in messianic passages that also include, in a single passage, the two aspects of Christ's career. Price notes the existence of time gaps in Scripture and provides a list of passages that fit into this category:

> The revelation of a prophetic postponement in the fulfillment of the eschatological aspect of the messianic program is in harmony with numerous passages in the Old Testament that reveal the two advents of Christ (e.g. Gen. 49:10-12; Deuteronomy 18:16; 2 Samuel 7:13-16; Isa. 9:1-7; 11:1-2,11; 52:13–59:21; 61:1-11, cf. Luke 4:16-19; 7:22; Joel 2:28, cf. Acts 2:17; Zeph. 2:13–3:20; Zechariah 9:9-10; Micah 5:2-15; Ps. 2:7-8, cf. Acts 13:33; Heb. 1:5; 5:5; Ps. 22:1-32; 34:14,16; Mal. 3:1-3; 4:5-6; 53:10-11).[146]

Perhaps the most well-known example of this kind of prophecy is found in Christ's reading of Isaiah 61:1-2 as recorded in Luke 4:18-19. Isaiah 61:1-2 says, "The Spirit of the Lord GOD is upon me, because the LORD has anointed me to bring good news to the afflicted; He has sent me to bind up the broken-hearted, to proclaim liberty to captives, and freedom to prisoners; to proclaim the favorable year of the LORD and the day of vengeance of our God; to comfort all who mourn."

Tim LaHaye and I have a chart that diagrams this passage in our book called *Charting the End Times*.[147] We say concerning this passage:

> Now when Jesus read the prophecies about Himself in Isaiah 61, why did He stop at the beginning of verse 2? Because He was announcing the reasons for His first coming and because He was to "proclaim the acceptable year of Jehovah's favor" (KJV). That's a reference to the church age, often called the age of grace, a time when sinners can freely call on the name of the Lord to be saved (Romans 10:13). Jesus stopped at the words, "and the day of vengeance of our God," which speaks of the Tribulation period, mentioned by the Hebrew prophets as "the day of wrath" and "the time of Jacob's trouble," and by Jeremiah as "a day of vengeance" (46:10). That's because the purpose of His first coming was to announce the period of grace and salvation we are living in, not the time of judgment that is yet to come.[148]

Another example of what some have called "double reference" is found in Zechariah 9:9-10. Dr. Arnold Fruchtenbaum says this concerning double reference:

> This rule should not be confused with another rule often called *Double Fulfillment*. This author does not accept the validity of the principle of double fulfillment. This law states that one passage may have a near and a far view; hence, in a way, it may be fulfilled twice....This author, however, does not believe that there is such a thing as double fulfillment. A single passage can refer to one thing only, and if it is prophecy, it can have only one fulfillment unless the text itself states that it can have many fulfillments. The law of double reference differs from the law of double fulfillment in that the former states that while two events are blended into one picture, one part of the passage refers to one event and the other part of the passage to the second event. This is the case in Zechariah 9:9-10.[149]

A closer look reveals that Zechariah 9:9 refers to Christ's first coming: "Rejoice greatly, O daughter of Zion! Shout in triumph, O daughter of Jerusalem! Behold, your king is coming to you; He is just and endowed with salvation, humble, and mounted on a donkey, even on a colt, the foal of a donkey."

And verse 10 can refer only to Christ's second coming: "I will cut off the chariot from Ephraim and the horse from Jerusalem; and the bow of war will be cut off. And He will speak peace to the nations; and His dominion will be from sea to sea, and from the River to the ends of the earth."

In Zechariah 9:9-10, there has to be a gap of time between the fulfillment of verse 9 (which relates to Messiah's first coming 2,000 years ago) and verse 10 (which is still a yet-future event). Even though no time factor is explicitly stated in the text, we can know a gap of time is required because of the nature of the events described in the two verses. Verse 9 can be connected with a historical event that took place in the past, but not verse 10. Verse 10, then, must have a future fulfillment.

Thus, it's clear that Scripture does contain time gaps in certain messianic passages in the Old Testament. I believe the evidence we examined earlier makes a persuasive case for gaps. That there are two phases to Messiah's career tells us, it is not unreasonable to find a gap in the fulfillment of different parts of a messianic passage.

THE CHURCH'S VIEW

What Preterists Claim

Through the ages, what has the church believed about Daniel 9:24-27? Some say that the idea of a gap between the sixty-ninth and seventieth weeks of Daniel is a recent development in church history. But the truth of the matter is that it is the oldest known view in church history. Read on and see.

Over the last few years, I have come to expect outbursts against all aspects of the literal interpretation of Scripture from preterists who believe that Bible prophecy is a thing of the past. They respond in a predictable fashion regarding the church's historical interpretation of Daniel 9:24-27.

DeMar is perhaps the most strident when he says that "nearly all Bible scholars agree that the first sixty-nine weeks of Daniel's prophecy refer to the time up to Jesus' crucifixion, only dispensationalists believe that the entire seventieth week is yet to be fulfilled."[150] In a later edition of the same book, DeMar says that a non-gap view "has been the standard interpretation for centuries, except for minor differences in details. John Nelson Darby and others changed all this with their church-parenthesis hypothesis."[151] DeMar also footnoted a reference to an errant source on the matter, Philip Mauro, who declares the following: "Nor, so far as we are aware, was any other meaning ever put upon them until within recent years, and then only by those belonging to a particular 'school' of interpretation."[152] Of course, Mauro's recent "school" is a reference to those of us who see a future seventieth week in Daniel's prophecy. Mauro was ignorant of what was taught in the early church, as we shall shortly see.

Gentry, speaking of his non-gap interpretation, insists that "conservative scholars widely agree on such an interpretation, which is virtually 'universal among Christian exegetes'—excluding dispensationalists."[153] Later, Gentry continues his inaccurate statements by saying "that the early Fathers held to a non-eschatological interpretation of the Seventieth Week."[154] That is not true at all.

What History Confirms
The Early Church

Did the early church see a gap between the sixty-ninth and seventieth weeks of years in Daniel's 70-weeks prophecy? Interestingly, an article of note was written on this subject and published in a Reformed journal that would circulate in the general theological orbit of DeMar and Gentry. The article was written by Louis E. Knowles[155] and referenced errantly by Gentry when he said "that the early Fathers held to a non-eschatological interpretation of the Seventieth Week."[156] Gentry's statement is clearly in error when compared with the writings of the early church fathers.

The earliest extant writings of the church fathers reveal just the opposite of Gentry's claim, with the exception of *The Epistle of Barnabas* (about A. D. 90–100), which presents a short and incomplete treatment on the subject. Knowles divides the early church (Barnabas through Augustine) into two interpretive groups, "the eschatological and the historical."[157] By eschatological Knowles means those who took the seventieth week of Daniel as future prophecy leading up to Christ's return. By historical he means those who believe that Daniel's final week has already been fulfilled. Knowles concludes that *Barnabas* "envisioned the completion of all the weeks before the development of the church."[158]

When Knowles deals with the next major contributors—Irenaeus (130–200) and his disciple Hippolytus (170–236)—he describes their views as "undoubtedly the forerunners of the modern dispensational interpreters of the Seventy Weeks."[159] Knowles draws the following conclusion about Irenaeus and Hippolytus:

> ...we may say that Irenaeus presented the seed of an idea that found its full growth in the writings of Hippolytus. In the works of these fathers, we can find most of the basic concepts of the modern futuristic view of the seventieth week of Daniel ix. That they were dependent to some extent upon earlier material is no doubt true. Certainly we can see the influence of pre-Christian

Jewish exegesis at times, but, by and large, we must regard them as the founders of a school of interpretation, and in this lies their significance for the history of exegesis.[160]

Thus, it is clear "that in Irenaeus and Hippolytus we have the originators of that method of interpretation that places the seventieth week of Daniel at the time of the consummation."[161]

Although Irenaeus does not explicitly spell out a gap in his writings, there is no other way that he could have come up with his view of a future Tribulation period of at least three-and-a-half years.[162] Irenaeus speaks of how "three years and six months constitute the half-week" in his section on the prophecy of Daniel 9.[163] This is why Knowles says that in Irenaeus "we have the basic concept for a futuristic construction of the Seventy Weeks, *viz.*, the position of the last week at the end of the age."[164]

Hippolytus, Irenaeus' pupil is even clearer. Hippolytus is the first known person in the history of the church to write a commentary on any book of the Bible, and he wrote on Daniel.[165] "Hippolytus gives us the first attempt at detailed interpretation of the Seventy Weeks," observes Knowles. "He is dependent, no doubt, upon Irenaeus for the foundational proposition that the last half-week of the seventy is to be connected with the Antichrist, but the detailed development is not found in Irenaeus."[166] In fact, Hippolytus refers to a gap or, in his words, "division," multiple times.[167] He says, "For when the threescore and two weeks are fulfilled, and Christ is come, and the Gospel is preached in every place, the times being then accomplished, there will remain only one week, the last, in which Elias will appear, and Enoch, and in the midst of it the abomination of desolation will be manifested, viz., Antichrist, announcing desolation to the world."[168]

LeRoy Froom grudgingly admits that "Hippolytus...arbitrarily separates by a chronological gap from the preceding sixty-nine weeks, placing it just before the end of the world."[169] "Certainly Hippolytus's interpretation does not have the refinements of the later development, but it is the direct ancestor of it,"[170] concludes Knowles.

Other Views

There were a number of others in the early church, up till the time of Augustine (354–430), who spoke about the 70-weeks prophecy. Jerome (340–420), in his commentary on Daniel, is reluctant to set forth his own interpretation of Daniel's 70-weeks prophecy "because it is unsafe to pass judgment upon the opinions of the great teachers of the Church and to set one above another."[171] So Jerome simply records the various views up till his time. The first view he cites is that of Africanus (160–240), who does not mention a gap between the sixty-ninth and seventieth weeks, but like early gap proponents, he "definitely views this passage as eschatological and decidedly Messianic."[172] Thus, Africanus fits into the eschatological camp, placing him closer to the futurist gap position then the historical view.

Eusebius (270–340), the father of church history, teaches a historical view, but he places a gap of time between the sixty-ninth and seventieth weeks. Knowles explains: "In regards to the last week, we have some rather distinct views in Eusebius. We must recall that the last week does not follow immediately upon the sixty-ninth, but comes after the 'indeterminate space of time' in which the events of verse 26 are being fulfilled. This last week, then, covers a period of seven years that extend from three and one-half years before the crucifixion to three and one-half years after it."[173]

Knowles also speaks of a writer named Hesychius, whom Augustine considered an opponent of his historical fulfillment view. "Hesychius has questioned Augustine about the fulfillment of the Seventy Weeks, and seems to be an adherent of the futurist school of interpretation."[174] Thus, it is clear that even in the early fifth century there are still proponents of the eschatological and futurist schools of interpretation in relation to Daniel's seventieth week. "We have seen the formation of two definite schools of interpretation...." notes Knowles. "All the later developments in Christian literature will be found to fit into one of these categories."[175]

What Really Matters

In one sense, it doesn't matter what previous generations think about an issue because ultimately, the test we should follow is whether or not a teaching squares with God's Word. However, in another sense, it *does* matter what others have thought through church history. If something specific is taught in the Bible, then it may be legitimate to ask why others have not understood that particular teaching. While we can point to teachings that have been overlooked for many years before Christians have come to realize their presence in Scripture, the necessary gap of time between the sixty-ninth and seventieth weeks of Daniel is not one of those teachings. Why opponents of a future seventieth week of Daniel want to make matters worse for themselves by saying that futurists do not have ancient historical precedent is beyond me. It is obvious the futurist view was evident early and often in the early church, and didn't become scarce until premillennialism was banded from the medieval church as a result of Augustine and Jerome's influence. "But the saints shall never possess an earthly kingdom," declares Jerome, "but only a heavenly. Away, then, with the fable about a millennium!"[176] With Jerome's banishment of early premillennialism went the literal interpretation of prophecy. History would have to wait more than 1,000 years for the revival of a literal interpretation of Bible prophecy and the literal approach to understanding the seventieth week of Daniel.

THE SUMMATION

I believe a sound biblical exegesis of Daniel 9:24-27 leads to an understanding that the seventieth week is separated from the first sixty-nine weeks of years because of Israel's failure to accept Jesus as the promised Messiah. God has postponed the final week of years until the start of the seven-year Tribulation. In the meantime, the New Testament teaches that the church age will intervene during the postponement of Israel's final week of years. The church will be composed of the Jewish remnant and elect Gentiles made into a single body—the body of Christ (Acts 15:13-16; Ephesians 2–3). And the final week of years is the yet-future seven-year Tribulation that will lead to the conversion of all Israel (Roman 11:26). This will lead to a full and literal fulfillment of God's entire program for His people Israel. May it happen today!

Chapter 14

HISTORICAL PROBLEMS WITH PRETERISM'S INTERPRETATION OF EVENTS IN A.D. 70

J. RANDALL PRICE

The defining premise of preterism as an eschatological system is its placement of "many or all eschatological events in the past, especially during the destruction of Jerusalem in A.D. 70."[1] Futurists agree with preterists that the events of A.D. 70 fulfilled Jesus' prediction of judgment against national Israel for its rejection of Messiah (Luke 19:41-44), but futurists reject the conclusion that these events fulfilled any other predictions in the Olivet Discourse, such as those of the Great Tribulation, which is preceded by the sign of the abomination of desolation, and the signs that accompany the coming of Christ in glory to establish His kingdom. This is also true with respect to predictions in the Old Testament and the New Testament "fulfillments" that require a reinterpretation or replacement of Israel by the church (such as those concerning Israel's national restoration). Because such fulfillment in preterism is predicated upon the premise that the end of the age had to occur in the generation of those Jews who had rejected Jesus (the first century), the events of A.D. 70 are hard-pressed into service, particularly through the historical record of Josephus, to explain every detail of end-time prophecy, especially those that appear in the Olivet Discourse and book of Revelation. Preterists, therefore, reject any prospect of a future for ethnic Israel (apart from the church) and contend that any eschatological system (such as dispensationalism) that sees not only a future regeneration and restoration of national Israel but also a revival of her ritual institutions (Temple and priesthood) as heretical. For example, Gary DeMar states, "Does the Bible, especially the New Testament, predict that the temple will be rebuilt? It does not....To make the temple of stone a permanent structure in the light of Jesus' atoning work would be a denial of the Messiah and His redemptive mission."[2] Preterists, however, do have a temple—the church—to which they invite Jews to come to find the fulfillment of their expected restoration. Futurists agree that the church is a spiritual Temple, but it is not the rebuilt Temple that is promised national Israel as part of God's program of restoration. Futurists also agree that individual Jews should be invited to accept their Messiah, the Lord Jesus, and receive the spiritual blessings of the New Covenant mediated by Him (Hebrew 12:24). But futurists reject the notion that all the promises of restoration made to national Israel have been realized by the church.

The differences between idealism, historicism and futurism can be explained on hermeneutical and theological grounds, but only preterism differs on the grounds of historical interpretation, since its position depends on the defense of an A.D. 70 fulfillment of prophecy. Therefore, in this chapter, we will examine the preterists' use of the historical events of A.D. 70 and the effect of this usage on their eschatological interpretation. This will involve a consideration of historical concerns in the preterists' use of first-century sources and of the historical consequences of A.D. 70 for the Jewish people.

CONCERN ABOUT THE PROPHETIC SIGNIFICANCE OF A.D. 70

Preterist writers are prodigious in their use of historical sources because as historicists, they are obliged to find the fulfillment of prophetic texts within the context of the historical past. However, because their context of fulfillment is a narrow point in history, namely the events surrounding the First Jewish Revolt of A.D. 66–73, and especially the events of the year 70, they must make special use of the primary literature that documents this history and particularly the works of Josephus. Because preterist interpretations depend significantly on finding historical correlation in these sources, it is necessary to examine the use of these sources and these sources themselves to see if they support preterism, or if they complicate and even contradict the preterist position.

CONCERN ABOUT THE USE OF JOSEPHUS

Almost all the surviving Judaeo-Greek writings were preserved by the Christian rather than the Jewish tradition. The treatises of Philo, the Alexandrian Jew who introduced an allegorical interpretation of the scriptures (adopted by church fathers such as Origen), and Flavius Josephus, the Hellenistic historian and principal source for the events of A.D. 70, were regarded "by the Church as edifying tracts and [their authors] treated by some early

Christian fathers as honorary Christians."[3] The writings of Josephus, while generally considered accurate in most details, such as architectural and cultural descriptions, are famous for their Roman political bias and openly antagonistic attitude to the aspirations of Jewish nationalism. Josephus's involvement in the Great War was primarily on the side of the Romans, a fact that caused him to be regarded as a traitor by his own Jewish nation. His works, composed for a Roman imperial audience, while dignifying his own nationality, were designed to applaud the triumphs of the Roman empire. These factors influenced Josephus's reporting of historical facts, and his historiography (especially in his *Jewish War* and *Vita*) reveals a twofold polemical purpose to refute Jewish accusations (against his defection) while winning the acceptance of the Roman court. His rejection of Jewish nationalism and accommodation to the Roman empire is most evident in his recording of speeches by leading figures (e.g., Agrippa II in *Jewish War* 2.345-401 and that at Masada).

In keeping with his rejection of Jewish nationalism, Josephus scorned popular movements, especially messianic movements whose hopes included an earthly kingdom for Israel. Andrew Chester, a member of the Faculty of Divinity at Cambridge University, in his study of eschatology and messianic hope in the post-A.D. 70 period, draws the following conclusions about Josephus and prophetic interpretation:

> He deliberately defuses popular messianic hope, shifting the emphasis away from final deliverance towards acceptance of Roman rule as God-given....It is, then, a mistake to see Josephus himself as holding to popular messianic hope, with its yearning for national and earthly realization. In fact he goes in precisely the opposite direction, deliberately defusing and de-eschatologizing it, and reinterpreting it to make it apply to the Roman Emperor, seeing him as a ruler, certainly, but equally certainly not of the end time. It is completely consistent with this that... Josephus fails to use any of the prophecies of salvation in Daniel, although he makes considerable reference to Daniel otherwise. In short, Josephus has no collective, material eschatological hope; where he indicates his own eschatological views, they turn out to be of a completely individualizing, philosophical character, very much the antithesis of the messianic traditions he touches on elsewhere.[4]

This lack of eschatological hope evidently influenced Josephus to make unwarranted historical compromises and concessions. For example, despite the fact Josephus accepted the Maccabean interpretation that Antiochus IV

Epiphanes fulfilled a prophecy of Daniel concerning the "abomination of desolation" in the Temple, when he wrote his history of the Roman conquest of Jerusalem, he abridged this view to "make room" to incorporate Titus and the Romans as "also" fulfilling Daniel's prophecy. Such an abuse of the historical data, however, since it agrees with the preterists' position, is hardly scrutinized for eschatological bias. This understanding of Josephus' anti-eschatological bias must be taken into consideration when preterist R. C. Sproul says that "Josephus's account of many preliminary events reads like a chronicle of fulfilled biblical prophecy. He refers to the rise of false prophets, a massacre in Jerusalem, the slaughter of Jews in Alexandria, and the invasion of Galilee."[5] Given that Josephus denied a future national redemption for Israel, the heart of the messianic hope, and recast Jewish prophecies as being fulfilled in the first century through the Romans, is it any wonder that preterists are attracted to Josephus as a moth to a flame?

In order to defend his treason by joining the national enemy, Josephus, who was from a priestly family, portrayed Jewish nationalism (and the Temple priesthood) as revolting not only against Rome but also against God, who had used the Romans as the instrument of divine judgment. Therefore, the issue was not that the Romans had become the Jews' enemy, but that the Jews had become God's enemies. Sproul seizes upon Josephus's statements to this effect as a parallel to Jesus' condemnation of the Jews:

> In book 5 Josephus records his former pleas to his own people to repent of their sins. He saw that their fight was ultimately not against the Romans but against God: "Wherefore I cannot but suppose that God is fled out of his sanctuary, and stands on the side of those against whom you fight."... In castigating the Jews for their sins, Josephus claimed that his generation was more wicked than any generation before it, an assessment remarkably similar to that of Jesus.[6]

Sproul seems unaware that Josephus's purpose in making such statements was political, such as when Josephus himself prophesies to Vespasian that he would become the Roman emperor (*Wars* 3.8.9). Such a statement on Josephus's part was not written out of religious conviction but rather, out of political expediency in an attempt to safeguard his life and gain a position within the Roman army. This same motive controls Josephus's linkage of the Roman invasion with supernatural signs that were claimed to have appeared to the Jews in Jerusalem. Other writers also recorded that some of these signs were reported, but without the political spin offered by Josephus that these were omens of judgment interpreted falsely by the Jews as favorable signs.

This understanding is significant when one attempts, as do the preterists, to move beyond the use of Josephus for historical comparison and develop prophetic conclusions based on his accounts. R. C. Sproul, who acknowledges that Josephus's accuracy as a historian could be doubted in relation to his account of signs in the sky (such as that of a heifer about to be sacrificed giving birth to a lamb in the midst of the Temple, *Wars* 6.5.3), nevertheless defends Josephus's testimony in general because other historians mention that signs surrounded the destruction of Jerusalem.[7] These historians, however, do not include the same kind of questionable details in their reports of signs. Thus, Josephus's inclusion of them is sufficient to warn against an indiscriminate use of such testimony in making comparisons with biblical accounts. Sproul, however, disregards this problem, as does DeMar (whose interpretation of the "sign" of Halley's Comet in A.D. 66 he cites), and states, "What is remarkable about this testimony is its similarity to incidents related in the Old Testament."[8] He then proceeds to compare the sign of Halley's Comet and Josephus's report of a vision of chariots and soldiers running among the clouds with Ezekiel's account of a theophany in the Temple (Ezekiel 1:22-28; 10:15-19). The conclusion he draws from this is that "Ezekiel's vision was not of the destruction of Jerusalem in A.D. 70, but of the fall of Jerusalem to the Babylonians in 586 B.C. It is significant that this earlier destruction of the holy city was marked by this kind of vision-sign."[9]

However, it is difficult to interpret Ezekiel's theophany as a "vision-sign" because the purpose of the detailed description was primarily to reveal to Ezekiel the glory of God. In 1:22-28 this is done in order to commission him as a prophet, and in 10:15-19 this is done to recall the previous theophany (verse 15) in order to reveal the departure of God's glory from the Temple. No attempt is made by Sproul to compare other details in Ezekiel's description (such as the cherubim, colors of the expanse, fiery loins, and the rainbow), but only those that seem to fit with Josephus's "signs." Nor does Sproul consider those details which are dissimilar, such as Josephus's sign being seen in Jerusalem while Ezekiel's vision is seen in Babylon, or that God's glory was not resident in the Second Temple as it had been in the Temple of Ezekiel's day, or the fact that Ezekiel's vision is not simply one of judgment but also restoration (of the same city and Temple), which includes a return of God's glory to the Temple (using identical language in Ezekiel 43:1-7). To take this contrived comparison and then use it as support for a first-century fulfillment of "the parousia of Christ in His judgment-coming" should alarm any responsible exegete, despite his hermeneutic.

In summary—though Christians may generally agree with the premise that the Romans were used by God to judge the Jewish nation and find historical parallels to the prophetic accounts in the Gospels, it is unwarranted to accept details of Josephus's account as though they were "gospel." Josephus gave a "highly interpretive account" of the events around him, and his writings should receive the same critical scrutiny as that applied to any other ancient interpretation of history. I believe if preterists viewed Josephus's writings as critically as they do those of dispensationalists, they would be forced to rewrite many of their own books—books that depend heavily on accounts from *Wars* in support of their eschatological interpretation.

CONCERN REGARDING THE CAUSE OF THE DESTRUCTION IN A.D. 70

While there is agreement that the destruction of Jerusalem and the Temple was a divine judgment on the Jewish nation for its rejection of Jesus as Messiah, we should remember that causes other than the Roman invasion of A.D. 70 ended Jewish nationalism. What's more, while the "Roman" judgment on national Israel was in keeping with previous judgments (such as the Assyrian and Babylonian judgments), which were predicted for violations of the Land Covenant—Deuteronomy 28:49-57,64-65), it was far from the climatic judgment predicted to end the age for the cause of universal rebellion by the nations (Revelation 19:15). For example, the collapse of the Jewish political infrastructure occurred some 30 years *before* the Roman invasion of A.D. 70. Hebrew University professor of ancient history Doron Mendels states:

> The moment Agrippa (I) died in 44 C.E. and the whole of Palestine came under direct Roman rule, there was no longer any local leader who could be a unifying symbol to both strata of society (as the Ptolemies and later Roman emperors were in Egypt and elsewhere). The result was complete national disintegration in Palestine. The Jews lost even the national symbols that they had managed to retain up to that point. Their land was overrun and full of non-Jews, their king was gone, their army dispersed, and their Temple in the hands of hated high priestly houses, some of whom the population associated with the Roman authorities.[10]

This situation resulted not only in political and religious infighting between the Jewish sects and the Zealot revolt against non-Jews (which Josephus posits as causes), but also brought to surface other contributing factors, such as the socioeconomic polarity and the personal ambition of various leaders. Doron explains why this set of circumstances ultimately led to the conflict of A.D. 70:

> Thus the gap, or "schizophrenia," between non-Jews and Jews (and within Jewish society itself) in terms of their attitudes about religio-political nationalism in Palestine during and after Herod the Great's reign was a major cause of the Great War. This state of affairs explains why so many Jews participated at the start, in other words, why people like Josephus and other Jews viewed the war against Rome as the final battle against the split national personality in the land of Israel. They went to war because they wished to get rid of the disturbing and disruptive "half" that was strongly associated with Rome. By the same token, the non-Jews in the land became free to act against the Jews at the very moment that the Jewish or half-Jewish authority, with all of its nationalistic overtones, ceased to exist. It also becomes easier to explain why, of all the nations of the ancient Near East, only the Jewish people revolted. The nationalistic situation…cannot be found to such an extent elsewhere in the region [where] the indigenous populations could in most instances adjust to transformed symbols of nationalism… that did not contradict the very essence of Roman imperialism. Although scholars at times followed Josephus in attributing the cause of the war to gentile-Jewish fights, they failed to see it in this wider perspective, which makes it more plausible.[11]

It should also be noted that unlike the preterists, who view Israel's apostasy as the reason for the Roman invasion, Josephus singles out a more specific Jewish cause. According to Frederick Murphy, "Josephus blames God's abandonment of the second temple not on the Jews as a whole but on the insurgents, especially the Zealots, who defiled the holy city."[12] In addition, we may point to Roman factors wholly apart from Jewish causes. As Martin Goodman, professor of Hebrew Studies at Oxford, notes: "The rapid siege and capture of Jerusalem may have been brought about almost entirely by the need of the new emperor Vespasian to justify to the Roman people his seizure of the purple by military force despite his humble origins; victory over foreign enemies was the surest route to prestige in Roman society."[13] In like manner, it is believed that Vespasian wanted to preserve the Temple so that he could return it to the Jews as an act of clemency once they were properly subjugated. Yet the Temple was destroyed by the Romans under command of Vespasian's son, Titus. According to Josephus's account, Titus supposedly followed Vespasian's orders, but the Temple was accidentally set on fire by the enraged

Roman soldiers (*Wars* 6.220-270). However, a fourth-century writer, Sulpicius Severus (whose source is thought to be the Roman historian Tacitus), contradicts Josephus and states that Titus personally ordered the Temple's destruction. While we cannot know the facts—especially in light of Josephus's political bias—it is more probable that Josephus invented the cover story to protect his friend Titus than to suppose that Severus (or Tacitus) was slandering Titus.

While we may ultimately accept these socio-economic and religio-political causes, as well as Roman political ambition, as part of the divine discipline that culminated in the crisis of A.D. 70, these causes do not merit comparison with, much less an identity as, the unparalleled cataclysmic events that are described for the Great Tribulation. The Tribulation events are declared to have "not occurred since the beginning of the creation which God created until now, and never will" (Mark 13:19; cf. Matthew 24:21). The destruction of Jerusalem and the Temple and subsequent Jewish exile were events that had occurred previously (in 722, 605, 589, and 586 B.C.) and greater disasters have befallen the Jewish people since A.D. 70 (e.g., six million Jews murdered in the Holocaust). Furthermore, the events of A.D. 70 were localized and do not approximate the global scale of the Tribulation judgments described by Jesus (Matthew 24:22,27,30-31; Mark 13:20,27; Luke 21:25-26). The events of A.D. 70 may be evidence of political upheaval and loss of national sovereignty, but cannot be considered evidence of the direct intervention of God's wrath through supernatural cosmic and terrestrial disasters as are expected in the Tribulation (Revelation 6–19). Furthermore, as demonstrated above, the historical details of A.D. 70 included some quite human causes, that, while subsumed within the divine plan, cannot compare with the eschatological accounts of strictly divine judgment recorded in Scripture (Zechariah 12:4,8-9; 14:3-5,12-15; Matthew 24:27-30,37-41; 2 Thessalonians 1:7-9; 2:8; Revelation 19:11-21). For this reason, preterists must either disregard the contradictions in such comparisons or else attribute the description of the Great Tribulation to hyperbole.

CONCERNS ABOUT THE CONSEQUENCES
OF THE DESTRUCTION IN A.D. 70

Despite the "world-changing" religious and political consequences of the destruction of Jerusalem and the Temple for Jewish nationalism and ritual Judaism, the preterists' scheme of a final judgment on the Jews fails in light of the ongoing survival of the Jewish people, the preservation of their religion through rabbinic Judaism, their reemergence as a national force and return to independence in the Bar-Kokhba Revolt, their continued eschatological hope of restoration, their 20 centuries of unbroken habitation in the land of Israel, and the modern revival of Jewish national sovereignty in the State of Israel and over the city of Jerusalem. Let us consider each of these historical realities.

First, Jewish survival was never threatened, since large Jewish communities had been thriving in Egypt and Persia for half a millennia, as well as throughout the Roman world (including Rome itself). These Diaspora communities were certainly affected by the loss of the central sanctuary in Jerusalem that had regulated much of their lives, yet their existence argues against a *final* act of divine judgment against the Jewish nation, as preterists interpret the consequences of A.D. 70, and even made possible a future reversal of the desolation and return to Jerusalem (as some in these communities attempted during the Roman era). Now, some might wonder why Diaspora Jewry did not join in the fight against the Romans in A.D. 70. The answer to this reveals that the events of A.D. 70 did not appear as "end of the age" as preterism demands. As Martin Goodman explains,

> The considerable aid that these Jews could have provided to the rebels was not forthcoming: they singularly failed to flood to the rescue of Jerusalem as optimistic Judaeans might have hoped. The cause of such inactivity was not, I suspect, indifference so much as over-confidence. Until the very last months of the war, from the spring of A.D. 70, the risk of the fall of Jerusalem, let alone the destruction of the Temple, must have seemed minimal. After all, no Roman forces came near to the walls of the city for more than three years after the resounding defeat of Cestius Gallus in October A.D. 66.[14]

Second, a new religio-cultural synthesis emerged early in the post-70 period as formative Judaism, helping to consolidate, organize, and obtain a structure on the program of the pharisaic system that could be applied universally to all Jews. This continuation of Judaism led to the council of Yavneh (Jamnia), a Roman center west of Jerusalem near the Mediterranean coast, where, around A.D. 90, some rabbis, as an authoritative body, established rabbinic Judaism as the normative form of Judaism. According to J. Andrew Overman, professor of Religion and Classics at the University of Rochester, "The aim of Yavneh…was the end of sectarianism and the forging of a unified coalition within Judaism. Yavneh reflects the *beginning* of the task of social reconstruction in the wake of the destruction of Jerusalem. The traditions about Yavneh focus on Johanan, the sanction of Rome upon Johanan and his successors, and the founding of a school where the teachers of formative Judaism could instruct and interpret Torah for the people."[15] Interestingly, the rabbinic academy of sages at Yavneh preserved the Jewish religion, keeping alive (from the viewpoint of preterism) the idolatry that had brought God's judgment—and with the support of the same Roman emperor who destroyed Jerusalem and the Temple! If preterists interpret Vespasian's army to have embodied Christ's coming visibly in judgment, how do they interpret Vespasian's help toward restoring the Judaism he and his army were supposedly sent by God to destroy? Rabbi Eliyahu Dessler makes this point when he writes concerning the contrast between the Romans and the rabbis:

> Nearly 2,000 years have passed since Rabban Yochanan ben Zakkai stood before the Roman emperor and asked of him, not the preservation of the state, because it was no longer a state of the Torah, and not the preservation of the Holy Temple, because Herod's name was associated with it—but the preservation of the Oral Law of the Torah, which depended on Yavneh and its Sages. He knew that if there was the Oral law of the Torah, there would be a people of the Torah; and if there was a people of the Torah, there would be a land of the Torah; and in the future—a state of the Torah. With Yavneh and its Sages, he saved everything. Now this emperor, his people, and his empire—Rome, the world power: where are they now? But the people of the Torah, the people of Yavneh and its Sages are alive and vigorous, every day awaiting the coming of the righteous Mashiach and the establishment of the state of the Torah in the land of the Torah.[16]

Third, preterists say that the Roman judgment of A.D. 70 ended Jewish rule forever and began the dominion of the church. Titus, whom preterists view as "the little horn" predicted by Daniel, would "wear down the saints of the Highest One" until "judgment was passed in favor of the saints," he is "annihilated and destroyed," and "the dominion will be given to the saints" (Daniel 7:25-27). In fact, a very different history resulted. Some Romans felt themselves as conquered rather than as conquerors. As authors Gerard Israel and Jacques Lebar record, "The Gentiles, who worshipped stone gods, considered the Jews' endless struggle against Roman might—in the name of a unique and invisible God and following on the violation of the Temple—an amazing act of courage which never ceased to astonish them. Some actually became Jews...."[17] As far as Titus was concerned, he died of natural causes in A.D. 81 while the church ("the saints"), instead of receiving dominion, was brutally persecuted for the next 300 years. By contrast, the Jews, whose dominion was supposedly ended (according to preterism), continued to assert themselves politically. From A.D. 115–117, the Levantine Jews revolted against Emperor Trajan.

The earliest movement among Jews in the land to rebuild the Temple occurred only 60 years after the Temple's destruction. Although the Temple Mount and much of the city of Jerusalem had remained in ruins during this time, there was no ban on Jewish settlement in the city. Consequently, 75 Jewish communities had been established in Judea and seven synagogues were built at the foot of Mount Zion. Although the political means did not exist to rebuild the Temple, a fervent religious desire for its restoration continued. These hopes were excited when the Roman emperor Publius Aelius Hadrian began his reign in A.D. 117. According to all indications, Hadrian did not initially entertain any hostility toward the Jews, leading them to believe their situation would improve. This belief may appear in the *Sibylline Oracles*, a Jewish pseudepigraphal writing that states, "After him another will reign, a silver-headed man. He will have the name of a sea. He will also be a most excellent man and he will consider everything…" (*Sibylline Oracles* 5:46-50). This poetic description may refer to Hadrian because his name was like that of a sea (Hadrian–Adriatic), and implies that he would act favorably toward the Jews. The Jewish Midrash also indicates that, under Hadrian, official contacts between Judean Jews and the Roman government led the Jews in Jerusalem to believe that the emperor was even willing to grant permission for the rebuilding the Temple (*Genesis Rabbah* 64:10). Early Christian sources also seem to confirm this by recording that the Jews attempted to raise funds for the project.

In A.D. 130 when Emperor Hadrian banned circumcision, the Jewish leader Simon Bar Kokhba led a second revolt against the Romans, defeating their forces, recapturing Jerusalem, and re-establishing Jewish rule over the city and country until A.D. 136. The Bar Kokhba kingdom was also dubbed a messianic one, and it is believed that as king, Bar Kokhba reinstituted the priesthood and began rebuilding the Temple. William Horbury has noted that some Christians were attracted to nationalistic Jewish hopes because they seemed close to fulfillment at the time of the Bar Kokhba revolt.[18] In light of the preterist contention that the church has replaced Israel, why would Christians, who had received the promised kingdom and all the blessings promised to Israel, be attracted to a Jewish nationalism that might fulfill prophecy? The implication is that these early second-century Christians had never heard preterist doctrine. Evidentially the reason for this was that preterism was unknown in the church at this time.

Moreover, if the early church had really understood the Roman response to the Jewish revolt (and particularly the destruction of the center of Jewish political and religious authority at Jerusalem in A.D. 70) as the coming of Christ in judgment, Christian apologists would have surely used this interpretation to their advantage with the Roman rulers. As a new religion, Christianity was regarded by the Romans as more odious than the older religion of Judaism that the Romans had attacked. The Christian community might have avoided much of Roman persecution had it argued that the Roman army had been sent by God to defeat the Jewish nation, the mutual enemy of Christianity and the empire. The fact, however, is this: No one in church history (or secular history) ever recorded that Jesus returned (spiritually or physically) in A.D. 70.

Though the Romans later asserted their dominion again and a Hadrianic edict exiled Jews from Jerusalem, sizeable Jewish populations remained throughout the land. Israeli archaeologist Dan Bahat, who has edited a century-by-century account of Jewish life in Israel from the first century to the twentieth century,[19] has demonstrated that Jews exercised a degree of independence to a lesser or greater extent for most of this period, under Roman, Christian, and Islamic rule. For example, during the early centuries under the Roman empire, Judaism again flourished in Israel and established itself religiously alongside Christianity. According to Goodman, "by the fourth century A.D. the rabbinic patriarch in Galilee had established semi-formal control over many, eventually perhaps all, Jewish communities in the Diaspora ruled by Rome, and the patriarch's *apostoloi* collected contributions on his behalf which by the 390s A.D., if not before, enjoyed the official sanction of the Roman government."[20] In addition, archaeological evidence from the Galilee during the fourth century indicates that synagogues and churches were built next to one another. Eusebius, the bishop of Caesarea and a church historian, even complained that some Christians were attending both synagogue and church services. Even though Hadrian had built a temple of Jupiter over the ruins of the Jewish Temple and later a Byzantine church was built on the Temple Mount, the Jews never abandoned their attempts to rebuild their Temple. One account tells of an attempt that occurred during the reign of the Roman emperor Julian in A.D. 363; Julian rescinded anti-Jewish laws and granted the Jews permission to rebuild the Temple. While additional examples could be cited, these are sufficient to show that the events of A.D. 70 were far from a final and complete destruction of Israel and bear no comparison to the everlasting dominion of the saints as predicted by Daniel.

Fourth, the continued Jewish hope for eschatological restoration argues that the consequences of the Great War, did not crush false Jewish messianic hopes (as Josephus called them), but rather, further excited them. As Chester notes: "So then, it is clear that the yearning for God to intervene and bring about his kingdom on earth in the immediate future persisted among the ordinary Jewish people; and we have various indications, which should not surprise us, that concern for the restoration of Jerusalem and the Temple was often bound up with this. Fervent messianic and eschatological hopes survive the catastrophe of 66–70."[21] This verdict is confirmed by comparing other Jewish accounts of the events of A.D. 70 to that of Josephus. Two of these accounts were written by the authors of the pseudepigraphical works 4 Ezra and 2 Baruch. These apocalypses represent a religious response to the loss of Jerusalem and the Temple, but they also reveal a more fundamental fact, as James VanderKam explains: "The very existence of these books shows that the apocalyptic mentality which may well have played a role in fanning enthusiasm for the revolt did not perish with the flames of 70 C.E...."[22] These works were so influential that they were referenced by early second-century Christian writers such as Pseudo-Barnabas and cited in support of their position by Christian chiliasts such as Commodianus and Lactantius.[23]

According to preterists, however, the terminal judgment of Judaism should have decisively ended any further Jewish messianic hope. After all, the Jewish Messiah Himself had come to destroy the Jews and end such false hope forever. But, the pseudepigraphical Jewish apocalypses advance the confident belief that just as God punished Israel for its sins by the destruction of Jerusalem and the Temple, so will He restore both the city and Temple in fulfillment of His prophetic promise. Chester affirms this from the history of the period:

> Obviously, the catastrophe of 70 dampened the messianic and eschatological fervor of many Jews in Palestine, at least in the form of militant expression and organized revolution against Rome. Yet the hopes for deliverance by God, or by his Messiah, from Roman oppression and (in the changed circumstances after 70) for the rebuilding of the temple certainly did not die out; they were constantly sustained and reinforced, not least by prayers and liturgical pieces....Nevertheless, we do at least know from Josephus that there were large popular movements in the first century prior to 70, attracted by a message of eschatological deliverance or by a leader claiming messianic status. Thus, the large-scale attraction of a messianic and eschatological movement looking apparently to liberate the people is a

further indication that these movements would scarcely simply die out post-70, even if they were subdued or even suppressed. And there are, of course, more tangible signs of it continuing… for the Diaspora setting, the fact that the messianic hope of Sibylline 5 is entirely compatible with the little we know of the massive outbreak of messianic revolt amongst Jews in Egypt, Cyprus and Cilicia.[24]

In like manner, E. P. Sanders, after a careful consideration of the extant Jewish literature of this period, concluded that "the hope that seems to have been most often repeated was that of the restoration of the people of Israel."[25] Such a hope of restoration was voiced by Rabbi Yochanan, who founded the rabbinical academy at Yavneh. Because of, rather than in spite of, Yochanan considered the ruined condition of the City and Temple and taught that "the Son of David will not come until the Jews have despaired of redemption." Such an affirmation accords with Jesus' statement in Luke 21:28 ("But when these things take place [events of Tribulation], straighten up and lift up your heads, because your redemption [with the coming of Messiah] is drawing near") and reminds us that an essential element of the messianic hope is a rescue of the Jews in a time of distress. For this reason the events of A.D. 70, which produced *opposite* results, could not (as preterists contend) have fulfilled the expected coming of Christ.

It should also be noted that various Jewish groups did not view the destruction in A.D. 70 as a judgment on their own beliefs and actions, but rather on those whom they deemed had departed from the true way of God. They believed their suffering would lead to redemption and restoration based on their faithfulness to God's covenant. From the Qumran covenanters to the apocalyptic sages of post-A.D. 70 this conviction is clearly displayed. Overman succinctly presents this viewpoint when he writes:

> The sectarian communities interpreted the significant political events of their history as divine vindication of their position and as God's rejection of their opponents. Whether it was the corrupt Jerusalem priesthood and the hellenized Hasmonean rulers or the invasion and destruction of Jerusalem by Pompey or the destruction of the Jerusalem temple in 70, these events were interpreted as confirmations of the beliefs of the community concerning God's rejection of the parent group. What then is the future of God's covenant people? The Damascus Document begins by stating that despite Israel's lack of faith and its having forsaken God, God will remember the covenant made with Israel and leave a remnant. This remnant was not delivered up

to be destroyed (CD 1:2ff.). [Those at Qumran] are "the remnant of God's name" (1QM 14). The community believed that the day would come when God would drive out the unrighteous and corrupt and restore the true people of God to their rightful place. The *Psalms of Solomon* also reflect the belief that God will remember the covenant made with Israel. God is faithful to those who themselves remain faithful amid the suffering and persecution the community is experiencing. "God remembers those who live in the righteousness of his commands" (Pss. Sol. 14:1-2). The people of this community of the mid-first century B.C.E. believed that in time God would gather a holy people. The righteous will endure forever because the Lord has remembered them. 2 Baruch and 4 Ezra also maintain that God will have mercy and remember Israel. The true Israelites will find consolation for their suffering. God will punish their enemies (2 Bar. 82:1-2). The true covenant people are a faithful remnant who will finally be vindicated. Those who live according to the law will be gathered together. They shall partake in the resurrection. 4 Baruch proclaims this hope, saying, "God has not left us desolate and outraged. For this reason the Lord has taken pity on our tears and remembered the covenant that he established with our fathers" (4 Bar. 6:21).[26]

Where did these Jewish groups get such ideas? The only possible source was their scriptures—the same source Jesus employed when He answered His disciples' questions on the Mount of Olives. Just as these Jews read the prophetic promises to mean there would come a literal restoration of their land and national existence, so did Jesus. Just as these Jewish groups could not have understood their scriptures to predict an ultimate judgment on their nation by Messiah and a transfer of their promised restoration to the church, so neither could have Jesus. It is often thought that Jesus' teachings about Jerusalem's desolation and the destruction of the Temple were unique and unclear to the Jewish people. But this is a mistaken notion, for many Jewish groups shared with Jesus the belief that the Temple would be (or even should be) destroyed. Because the Second Temple was not the Restoration Temple, they believed the prophetic oracles warning of judgment still applied to it. It was these oracles Jesus used to explain both the coming Roman destruction of the Temple and the anticipated rebuilt Temple that would exist at the time of the eschaton and be delivered and restored in fulfillment of the eschatological predictions. This was the perspective of a fairly large percentage of Jews in Jesus' day, as has been argued by Markus Bockmuehl with substantial evidence from historical sources.[27] In his article, he cites examples from Josephus, Tacitus, and early rabbinic literature that indicate there was a flourishing hermeneutical tradition before A.D. 70 that predicted the Temple's destruction. He gives a twofold reason for the development of this school of interpretation: theological and socio-political.

Theologically, the restoration promises of the biblical prophets had not been fulfilled. Prophecies about the exile and subsequent return to the land under ideal conditions had obviously not been fulfilled. Confirmation of this awareness is found in the pre-Maccabean book of Tobit (13:16-18; 14:5) as well as in Daniel 9:17,26-27. The corruption and decline of the Hasmonean dynasty and subsequent occupation by Roman forces exacerbated doubts that a full restoration, much less a liberation, of the Jewish nation would take place. In addition, there were doubts, among groups such as the Essenes, and among those who frequented the Jewish Temple at Leontopolis, that the Maccabees had effected a complete cleansing of the Temple. If despite its Herodian-restored splendor it was not the eschatological Temple, and if the purity of the Zadokite priestly line was at all a matter of concern, then the only logical conclusion was that the present corrupt system would need to give way to a new one.

Socially and politically, the degeneration of the priestly aristocracy invited comparison with the earlier prophetic oracles of judgment and destruction (the desecration motif). Of the 28 high priests between 37 B.C. and A.D. 70, all but two came from illegitimate non-Zadokite families.[28] It became increasingly clear to most Jews that the cultic center that regulated all of Jewish life was in the hands of a vast network of economic and religious oppression. The legitimate and necessary operation of the Temple was supported by a maze of intrigue, nepotism, and graft (Mishnah *Keritot* 1.7) at the hands of certain priestly families, such as the house of Kathros (cf. *Baraita*, TB *Pesahim* 57a). Such social and political factors prompted many Jews to believe God would judge the present order and restore it to His divine ideal. This can be seen especially in the sectarian writings among the Dead Sea Scrolls, as stated by Overman:

> Even though they expected the Temple to be destroyed, they also expected (on the basis of the same prophecies) that it would be rebuilt. According to those Jews established at Qumran, "Israel has forsaken God and has been unfaithful. God has deserted the sanctuary. The priests profane the temple and fail to observe the distinction between clean and unclean. The leaders who misguide the people are "teachers of lies" and "false prophets." They are seers of falsehood who have wickedly schemed to cause the people to exchange the law engraved on their hearts for the

"smooth things" which they speak. The *War Scroll,* which describes the final battle of the community with the Kittim, reveals the belief on the part of the community that they, following the victory, will reorganize and reconstitute the temple in its pure and true form." [29]

The anticipation of restoration expressed at Qumran was not simply a sectarian tenet but an apocalyptic tradition that had developed from the biblical prophets. For this reason this anticipation did not end with the Roman destruction of the Qumran community in A.D. 68, but was preserved by the rabbis with other tenets of Judaism. University of Oxford professor Christopher Rowland clarifies this in the eschatological outlook of post-A.D. 70 Judaism:

> It has been widely accepted that there was a connection between the apocalyptic tradition of early rabbinic Judaism and strands within Second Temple Judaism. Emerging rabbinic Judaism would have been faced with the issue of controlling a lively apocalyptic tradition after A.D. 70...[and it] may well have been a more influential force in nascent rabbinic Judaism than has often been allowed.... In Syriac Baruch there is a more obvious concern with the destruction of Jerusalem. The reader is left in little doubt that this destruction is not only ordained by God, but also carried out with God's active participation. Israel is culpable and entirely deserves judgment at God's hand. Zion's destruction is not a total disaster. However, as it paves the way for God's eschatological act, which is near at hand when the nations are to be judged.... The issues which are raised are what we would have expected Jews to have struggled with after the traumatic experience of 70 C.E. There would be an inevitable reappraisal of attitudes with needs for more precise definition of what was required of the people of God and an emphasis on the centrality of the Law. What is also significant is the continuing pervasiveness of eschatological interest and the clear belief that the consummation of all things is near. Thus the debacle of 70 does not appear to have lessened the impact of these beliefs, and there is evidence to suppose that the years between the two revolts continued to be full of eschatological hope.[30]

This eschatological hope may be seen in the fact that while the events of A.D. 70 forced rabbinic Judaism to adopt a spiritualized interpretation of some of the 613 commandments, such as those related to the institution of the

Temple (since these could no longer be observed), this was not the kind of "replacement" that took place within Christianity (as preterists say). For example, Rabbi Yohanan ben Zakk'ai had maintained the memory of the Temple as the major sanctuary by transferring its rites and ceremonies to the synagogue as a "minor sanctuary" (see *Ro'sh ha-Shanah* 4.1-3; *Sukkah* 3.12). This deliberate act served to preserve the Temple's function for the future. Therefore, ceremonies such as the morning and evening synagogue services, which replaced the Temple's daily sacrifices, and the Musaf service, which commemorated the additional sacrifices on the days on which these used to be offered, reminded worshipers that a semblance of the past Temple service was still present while encouraging hope for its complete restoration in the future. This is evident in that the biblical verses that pertained to the sacrifices were combined, in the synagogue, with prayers for the restoration of Israel to the land and the rebuilding of the Temple. This can also be seen in the development of the *Shemoneh Esreh*, the "Eighteen Benedictions," which the Mishnah (Berekoth 4:1) required every Jew to pray three times daily. Benediction 14, in particular, is a prayer for the restoration of Jerusalem and the rebuilding of the Temple: "Be merciful, O Lord our God, in Thy great mercy, towards Israel Thy people, and towards Jerusalem Thy city, and towards Zion the abiding place of Thy glory, and towards the Temple and Thy habitation, and towards the kingdom of the house of David, Thy righteous anointed one. Blessed art Thou, O Lord God of David, the builder of Jerusalem." In this manner, a "Temple consciousness" was maintained throughout the period of exile. Such a consciousness provides evidence that rabbinic Judaism could not recast the hope of a literal restoration of national Israel. This is seen even among those who adopted an allegorical hermeneutic. As David Lowery notes, "even Philo, despite his inclination to allegorize aspects of Jewish belief, shared this hope and looked forward to the day when 'the cities which now lay in ruins will be cities once more,' indicating as well that he conceived of the kingdom in what might be called 'this-worldly' terms."[31]

Perhaps one of the most popular examples of this literal hope of restoration is the account of Rabbi Akiva and his students on the Temple Mount. As the story goes, Rabbi Akiva and his students were walking near the destroyed remains of the Temple Mount (A.D. 70) when they saw a fox run into its lair nestled among the ruins. Immediately the students recalled Jeremiah's statement concerning the judgment on the First Temple. "Because of Mount Zion which lies desolate, foxes prowl in it" (Lamentations 5:18), and began to rend their garments and mourn (as custom demanded). To the surprise of the students, instead of crying, the rabbi laughed. Startled by this contrary action, they asked him why he was not mourning. To this he replied, "Because if the prophecies of the Temple's destruction have come to pass, we are certain to see the prophecies of its restoration fulfilled!" Therefore, the historical events of A.D. 70, far from forcing the Jews to reinterpret the prophecies of restoration, further stimulated the literal hope that because of these events (viewed by many, such as Rabbi Akiva, as a literal fulfillment of prophecy) the greater event of national restoration would be realized. The existence of this viewpoint, held by both Jews and Christians, argues against the preterists' claim that the events of A.D. 70 demand the opposite conclusion.

Fifth, the political revival of Jewish nationalism (Zionism), the regathering of some six million Jews to the land of Israel, and rebirth of the Jewish nation in that land and its exercise of sovereignty over Jerusalem and the Temple Mount appear quite opposite the conditions that resulted from the events of A.D. 70. As one Jewish historian observed:

> True, Judea was defeated by Rome, but the Jewish people were not. Just as the words of the prophecy, "And I will scatter you among the nations" (Leviticus 26:33), came true against the Jews, so did the words of consolation: "And I will remember my covenant with Isaac and also My covenant with Abraham will I remember; and I will remember the Land" (Leviticus 26:42). The Roman Empire was destroyed by wild and primitive tribes and disappeared from the stage of human affairs. Only history books remind us of her former existence and power. But the Jewish people live on.[32]

In like manner, the first prime minister of Israel, David Ben-Gurion, declared at his inauguration that Israel was "a nation fulfilling prophecy." A similar thought is present in the words of Gerard Israel and Jacques Lebar, authors of *When Jerusalem Burned:*

> When Jewish nationality as such dissolved in the wake of the Roman victory, the religious element in Judaism took priority. The Temple at Jerusalem was the only place where ritual sacrifice might be made, but it had been destroyed. Nevertheless, the Jews of the Diaspora were determined to preserve their identity, and adapted themselves to the changed conditions. Since the One Temple had ceased to exist, they created other fortresses in which to entrench themselves. These were the synagogues and places of study—all of which kept the flame burning in myriad Jewish communities. Priests and aristocrats were succeeded by scholars and rabbis, the tireless dispensers of traditional teaching. Henceforth it was the study of the Law which

prevailed, and which preserved the supranational links among the Jews who were scattered throughout Christian or Islamic societies. It was almost nineteen hundred years before the wounds began to heal, wounds inflicted on the descendants of the defenders of the Temple, who lived among other nations and experienced the terrible sufferings that occurred in the Diaspora. Then, in 1948, with the resurrection of the Jewish state, a new fusion of nationhood and religion suddenly became possible. Was the creation of the new state an extraordinary and rather late revenge on the Roman Empire, whose power and whose gods had now disappeared for ever? Had the nineteen hundred years since 70 been only a very long period in the wilderness, an agonized interlude in Jewish continuity?...Unlike other great events in Antiquity, and even in times nearer to our own, all the consequences of the battle and fall of Jerusalem have not yet run their course.... [Yet] for the first time in almost nineteen hundred years the people of Israel organized as a state responsible for its own destiny, extended its sovereignty over the Temple in Jerusalem. It was not the prayer of various individuals that went up to heaven, but that of a people descended from the kings and prophets of Israel, whose thanksgiving was no longer a concession from a controlling authority. Israel and its prayer were free. [33]

CONCERNS FOR CAREFULLY EVALUATING THE EVIDENCE

For Israel, the historical consequences of the aftermath of A.D. 70 were indeed critical. Yet not only did the Jewish people and Jewish nationalism survive, but the hope for a future restoration increased. Moreover, the "Temple consciousness" perpetuated through a spiritual transference to the synagogue by rabbinic Judaism also expressed itself in tangible ways. Whenever circumstances favored the rebuilding of the Temple there existed an activist movement among the Jewish people, who would return to Jerusalem to attempt this effort. Today, the Roman Empire is long vanished and the Jewish people are again in the Promised Land, in control of the Holy City and its Temple Mount, and making plans to rebuild the Temple. Is it reasonable, then, to accept the events of A.D. 70 as a fulfillment of God's program for the Jews but not accept the events that followed as also part of His ongoing divine plan? Preterists recognize the historical existence of the Jewish state and even the possibility that the Jews could one day rebuild their Temple, but to them this is meaningless because, in their scheme, all such prophecy has already been fulfilled. As DeMar says, "But what if the Jews were able to rebuild the temple? Such a temple would have nothing to do with the fulfillment of any part of this prophecy."[34] Preterists deny any hope for a future fulfillment (after A.D. 70) for national Israel based on their belief that the events of A.D. 70 fulfilled all that the Hebrew prophets, Jesus, and the apostles predicted.

However, based on the continued history of Israel—including the present-day regathering and the political restoration of the Jews—it is likely that the events of A.D. 70 are part of the divine program of preparation for future fulfillment. This is what futurism advocates rather convincingly, for it has the support of a larger and longer historical context than does preterism. And, as explained earlier, preterists cannot argue for a first-century fulfillment of certain biblical prophecies by the indiscriminate use of primary sources (such as Josephus) or by disregarding as relevant any restorative consequences for the Jews (especially national ones) that have occurred since that time.

Chapter 15

HISTORICAL PROBLEMS WITH A FIRST-CENTURY FULFILLMENT OF THE OLIVET DISCOURSE

J. RANDALL PRICE

Jesus' prediction of the destruction of Jerusalem and the Temple and the events He described to His disciples in the Olivet Discourse has produced a tremendous volume of scholarly interpretations, most of which fall into the historicist camp and interpret Jesus' words as a threat or curse on the sacrificial institution represented by the Temple.[1] Most of these interpreters assume that Jesus' statements of destruction are pronouncements, as though He Himself were judging and condemning the city and sanctuary. This is generally because they view the Temple's removal as marking the end of the Jewish age and symbolizing the removal of Israel as God's chosen people.

Preterism, as a subset of historicism, agrees with this interpretation. However, in order to prove a first-century fulfillment of Jesus' prophecies, preterists must find a historical correlation between actual events in the first century, principally the events of the First Jewish Revolt (A.D. 66–70), and the text of the Olivet Discourse.

The problem, however, is that much of what happened at that time does not fit with the descriptions in the biblical text. For example, such a detail as the direction of Christ's advent to Jerusalem, is compared with lightning flashing from *east to west* (Matthew 24:27), whereas the Roman army, which preterists interpret as fulfilling this prophecy, advanced on Jerusalem from *the west to the east*. Even if we take Matthew 24:27 simply to mean the Roman army advanced like lightning (i.e., quickly), the historical record reveals a very slow assault on Jerusalem, the war lasting for several years before Jerusalem was even besieged!

For this reason, most attempts to make "correlations" can only be made through an eschatologically biased interpretation of Josephus's writings (such as associating divine signs with the Roman army's impending conquest), reinterpreting the biblical text to fit the preferred historical data (such as taking "the clouds of heaven" as the dust kicked up by the Roman army's advance), or by taking statements that do not fit the historical events of the great Jewish revolt as hyperbole (such as the unprecedented and unsurpassed nature of the Tribulation), in order to claim first-century fulfillment. In this chapter, building on the work of the previous chapter, which considered the preterists' misuse of the historical sources, we will examine how the historical data affects the preterists' interpretation of the Olivet Discourse.

THE CONTEXT OF THE OLIVET DISCOURSE

When interpreting the Olivet Discourse, it is important to remember the disciples asked Jesus three questions: 1) "when will these things [i.e. the destruction of the Second Temple] happen?" 2) "what will be the sign of Your coming?" and 3) "[what will be the sign] of the end of the age?" Preterists interpret Jesus' answer to the disciples as having a *single* temporal reference—the end of "this generation," which they define as the generation that crucified Jesus and "the present [Jewish] age," which they understand to have terminated in A.D. 70. However, we need to recognize that Jesus was asked three questions, and He gave three answers. The disciples' desire for a discernible timetable of events evoked their questions, and the content of their questions indicates they understood the prophetic program (particularly as outlined by Zechariah) that connected an end-time attack on Jerusalem by Gentile armies with the coming of the Messiah to rescue Israel and reign as universal King (Zechariah 14:2-9). The disciples were probably thinking that if Jesus had just announced the destruction of the Temple, it must mean that the end of the age was at hand and that it was the time for Him to be revealed in Jerusalem as the messianic King. If these events were indeed imminent, then they wanted to know when they would occur and how Jesus' messianic appearance would be announced to the Jewish nation.

Jesus, however, knew that the immediate rejection of His messiahship would result in the nation being judged according to the disciplinary provisions of the Mosaic Covenant (Deuteronomy 28:15-68). The means of this judgment was to be invasion and exile by a foreign power, and Jesus understood that the Romans would carry out the divine sentence and that it would be enacted on Jerusalem and the Temple in accordance with the discipline enacted in 586 B.C. Jesus also understood that Daniel 9:24-26 prophesied His death and soon afterward the destruction of the city and sanctuary. Jesus also saw in the near political events of the Roman invasion the type of scenario that would again be present in the end-time at His return—namely, a geographical setting in Jerusalem and an attack from Gentile armies. Jesus used the similarities in both the coming and distant conflicts to answer both the disciples' immediate concerns about Jerusalem and the Temple and to instruct them concerning the events that would occur at the end of the age.

THE PURPOSE OF THE OLIVET DISCOURSE

The purpose of the Olivet Discourse, as interpreted by the schools of Historicism[2] and Preterism,[3] is exclusively as a judgment text in which Jesus' denunciations of the Temple find their final fulfillment in the Temple's destruction by the Romans in A.D. 70. As with the previous passage, this text has been understood to have had a past fulfillment resulting in an irreversible abandonment (by God) of the Jewish people, Jerusalem, and the Temple. For preterism in particular, the basis for this interpretation rests upon understanding the phrase "this generation" as only and always having reference to the first-century people to whom Jesus spoke.

Futurism, by contrast, accepts some uses of "this generation" as referring to those to whom Jesus spoke and other uses as having reference to those about whom Jesus spoke, with context being the determining factor. For example, the use of "this generation" in Matthew 23:36 is applied as an indictment (in context) to the generation of the "scribes and Pharisees" (Matthew 23:29), whose actions against Jesus demonstrate their affinity with those who persecuted the prophets of the past (verses 30-35). Jesus then proclaims that "all these things shall come upon this generation." The phrase "these things" must also be interpreted in its context. In this case, the next verse (verse 37) describes "these things" as the future experience of Temple desolation. It is important to observe here that even though this event is now historically past, the phrase "this generation," in its context, referred to a *future* generation at the time it was spoken by Jesus and then recorded by Matthew. It was future from the perspective of the sins "this generation" (in context) would yet commit (complicity in the crucifixion) and the judgment they would receive (the Roman destruction in A.D. 70; see Luke 21:20-24).

The future sense of "this generation" in a judgment context sets a precedence for its interpretation in contexts that are both judicial and eschatological. If the desolation experienced by "this generation" in Matthew 23:36 can be understood as a future fulfillment that came some 40 years later, it should not be a problem to understand the Tribulation judgment as a future fulfillment that will come on the generation that will experience it at the end of the age. However, the difference is not simply a span of time, but the nature of that time as eschatological. For the "this generation" of Matthew 24:34, Mark 13:30, and Luke 21:32, "all these things" (Matthew 24:34; Mark 13:30; Luke 21:28) must refer contextually to the events of the "great tribulation," the conclusion of "the times of the Gentiles," the coming of Christ in glory, and the regathering and redemption of Israel, all of which are not only declared to be future by Jesus at the time of His proclamation (Mark 13:23), but are also cast in typical eschatological language (for example, "end of the age," "such as has not occurred since the beginning of the world until now, *nor ever shall,*" "powers of the heavens will be shaken").

Even though in context Jesus may refer to the future "this generation" as "you," this is a conventional usage of language with respect to reference and does not have to apply to a present audience.[4] In the prophetic passages of the Old Testament, it is common to find such language. For instance, Moses used language similar to Jesus' when he said, "So it will be when *all of these things* have come upon *you...*" (Deuteronomy 30:1). Even though he is speaking to the present generation ("you"), it is evident from the context that His words speak about a future generation that will live thousands of years later and into the eschatological period. The people of this "generation" (the "you") are those who will have already suffered the judgment of exile (verse 1), captivity (verse 3), been regathered and restored (verses 4-5), and received spiritual regeneration ("circumcision of heart," verse 6).

However, as an examination of the prophecy will reveal, Jesus' statements were not driven by thoughts of God's vengeance on Israel or a prophetic compulsion to denounce the Temple, but arose in response to specific questions asked by the disciples, who wanted to better understand Jesus' words concerning the Temple's future. While Matthew and Mark present generally parallel accounts, Luke's account has significant differences. These differences relate to the three questions posed by the disciples: 1) "Tell us when these things [destruction of the Temple] will happen?" 2) "What will be the sign of Your [Messiah's] coming?" 3) "[What will be the sign] of the end of the [Gentile] age?" From the futurists' perspective, it should be observed that while all three questions are asked in Matthew 24:3 and Mark 13:4, Jesus answers only questions two and three in these contexts. Luke may have only recorded the first question (Luke 21:6-7), which explains Jesus' answer concerning Jerusalem's desolation being included only here (verses 20-24). However, there are also exegetical reasons for supposing that Luke alone deals with the nearer destruction of Jerusalem and the Temple by Titus in A.D. 70.[5]

What is common to the questions in each account is that they come in response to Jesus' unsolicited statement concerning the Temple that "not one stone here will be left upon another, which will not be torn down" (Matthew

24:2; see also Mark 13:2; Luke 21:6). Whether or not we accept the preceding interpretation of the differences between these accounts, each contains Jesus' *predictions* concerning the desecration of the Temple (either in A.D. 70 or at the end of the age).[6] In every question and every account, it is the *future* that concerns the disciples, both immediate and especially in terms of the Old Testament prophecies. Matthew in particular reveals that Jesus' preview of the future was intended to answer His disciples' questions concerning His [second] coming, and the end of the age (Matthew 24:3). Jesus here explains why His coming is necessary (for divine intervention and national repentance, verses 27-31; cf. Zechariah 12:9-10) and when it will occur: "*after* the tribulation of those days" (verse 29). According to Matthew,[7] the events described in this period prior to the Messianic advent could not have been fulfilled in A.D. 70 with the destruction of Jerusalem, since these events usher in and terminate with the coming of Messiah.[8]

Moreover, the Olivet Discourse predicts a victorious outcome for Israel and a fulfillment of restoration, rather than a defeat that ends its prophetic hopes. This is seen in the provisions of "protection" (Matthew 24:16-17,22; Mark 13:15-16,20) and the promises of "regathering" (Matthew 24:31; Mark 13:27) and "redemption" (Luke 21:28) at the return of Messiah. These are in harmony with the other positive expectations of Israel attending Messiah's coming (see Acts 1:6; 3:20-21; Romans 11:26-27). To interpret these positive references as something else or for someone else requires the text to be read in a nonliteral way. For preterists, whose case is argued on the basis of a literal historical fulfillment (in and around the events of A.D. 70), such an approach is inconsistent and fails to reckon with Jesus' eschatological method of interpretation, which is consistently literal and Jewish in character.[9]

THE PRONOUNCEMENTS OF THE OLIVET DISCOURSE

Was the Roman Destruction in A.D. 70 a Final Judgment of Israel?

Preterist Gary DeMar cites P. W. L. Walker in support of his view that the destruction of the Temple in A.D. 70 symbolized a final judgment of Israel in Matthew: "There is nothing in Jesus' teaching in this Gospel which suggests that after this period of judgment there will be a restoration; the 'seven evil spirits enter and live there' (Matthew 12:45), 'the vineyard is leased to others' (21:41), the city is 'burnt' (22:7), the Temple is 'abandoned' (23:38); the Apocalyptic Discourse (ch. 24) moves away from Jerusalem to focus on the coming of the Son of Man."[10] However, it would be incongruous for Matthew to begin his gospel ("good news") by announcing that the purpose of Jesus' coming was to "*save* His people from their sins" (1:21) only to conclude by predicting

that Jesus was coming at the end of that generation to *destroy* them perme-
nantly because of their sins.

One cannot escape this difficulty by interpreting "His people" as any
"people" other than the Jews, for this term is uniformly used in Matthew (13
times) for ethnic Israel. Indeed, the very focus of Jesus' mission is identified
with Israel (Matthew 2:6; 10:6; 15:24). It is generally conceded that Matthew's
gospel was written by a Jew to a largely Jewish audience with the intent of
proving Jesus is Israel's messianic king. This appeal to a Jewish audience
indicates that Matthew did not interpret Jesus' Olivet Discourse preteristi-
cally, otherwise his purpose would have been to prove the rejection of Israel
and that Jesus was the Savior of the church. On the contrary, while Matthew
certainly condemns the religious hypocrisy and apostasy within Judaism, he
nowhere condemns the biblical Judaism that had preserved and practiced
God's commandments. As David Lowery has observed, "Matthew's...and his
community's...relationship to Judaism [reveals that they] were unwilling to
dissociate themselves completely from Judaism and some of its practices
(such as the Temple tax). This is a further indication that Matthew does not
regard Israel's present plight as irreversible or irredeemable. In part this is
related to his conviction that the promises of the OT made to Israel by God
have not been rendered (nor will they become) null and void."[11]

Moreover, the conclusion that the purpose of Jesus "at the end of the age"
is to destroy Israel contradicts the repeated call in Matthew's gospel of a
salvific mission to Israel (10:5-6; 23:34), a mission never rescinded, but said to
continue until the coming of the Son of Man (10:23). By contrast, preterists
interpret Matthew 10:23 to mean Christianity no longer has a mission to
Israel, since this was to last only "until the coming of the Son of Man," which
they say occurred in A.D. 70. Yet how can the mission to Israel be separated
from the universal commission to "all nations" (28:19)? Where does Matthew
imply that one would continue and the other would be discontinued? If
Jesus' intention had been to destroy Israel in A.D. 70, why would He bother to
send His disciples to it up until this time? Why not simply abandon this mission in light of the national rejection of Jesus (as some interpret Matthew
21:43) that was to soon culminate with the punishment for this rejection in
A.D. 70? If one argues that it was to confirm their rejection and further justify
their condemnation in A.D. 70, then the purpose seems deceptive and dishar-
monious with the general commission. However, such a conclusion flies in
the face of the Gospel's purpose to authenticate Jesus' messianic credentials to
Israel. If Jesus came "only to the lost sheep of the house of Israel" (15:24), and
His intent was to "shepherd My people, Israel" (2:6), then the lack of fulfillment of this purpose presents a problem to the prophetic proof of His mes-

siahship. Further, the lack of correlation between the historical events surrounding the Roman invasion of A.D. 70 and the text of the Olivet Discourse poses a significant problem for preterism, as well.

Does History Back Up the Preterist Claims?

Preterists claim that the historical context for the fulfillment of the Olivet Discourse is exclusively the destruction of Jerusalem and the Temple in A.D. 70. If this is so, then why don't the accounts in Matthew 24 and Mark 13 unambiguously reveal this setting? Preterists insist that these Gospels do reveal this, but only by first comparing their accounts with that of Luke 21:20-24 and then arguing that all three are reporting exactly the same chronological event. However, if we look at Matthew and Mark as independent accounts (and indeed they circulated within the first-century church as such), then we are forced to conclude that neither one mentions the destruction of Jerusalem or the Temple. This has been the very objection argued by conservative evangelicals against the liberal critics of predictive prophecy, who claim an A.D. 70 fulfillment as evidence of *vaticinia ex eventu* ("prophecy after the event"). Robert Gundry addresses this usage in his futurist defense of the prophecy:

> From the disparity between destruction in the disciples' question and profanation in Jesus' answer, many have concluded to a prophecy after the event….On the contrary, such a prophecy would have reiterated the destruction initially predicted in v 2 and would have set out the chronology and sign for which the disciples asked; for the chronology and precursive events would have been available to a historian posing as a prophet. The failure of this discourse to return to the destruction of the temple after the preceding, brief prediction in v 2, the failure of it to answer the four disciples' questions in v 3 concerning the time and sign of the destruction, and the failure even of v 2 to say anything about the destruction of Jerusalem all make it unlikely that the discourse reflects the destruction of Jerusalem and the temple in 70 C.E.…. [12]

One example of a lack of historical correlation is the lack of description concerning the distinct nature of the Temple's destruction. The first-century historian Josephus especially emphasizes this destruction as a fiery conflagration, which engulfed the Temple: "You would indeed have thought that the Temple Mount was boiling over from its base, being everywhere one mass of flame" (*Wars* 6.5.1 §275). Yet, nothing about fire is even implied in Jesus' prediction concerning the Temple in Matthew 24:15 or Mark 13:15. In fact, fire is also missing from Daniel's citation of the "abomination of desolation," which was implicitly referenced by Jesus as a chronological marker and explanation of the event. Whether one contends that the closest citation is from Daniel 11:31, where the historical background is of Antiochus IV Epiphanes' invasion of the Temple, or Daniel 9:26-27, in which context the city and Temple are said to be destroyed, or Daniel 12:11, there is still no allusion made to fire as the means of destruction. However, in Daniel 9 it is verse 27 that contains the reference to the "abomination," and as Thomas Ice has argued in chapters 7 and 12, it may best be understood as chronologically distinct and eschatological. Daniel 12:11 is entirely eschatological, as verses 9-10 and the eschatological time-marker "end time" attests. The omission of fire from Matthew and Mark is strange in light of the fact that other verses about the second advent speak of Jesus' being revealed "in flaming fire" (2 Thessalonians 1:7; 2; cf. Hebrews 12:29), with "eyes aflame of fire" (Revelation 19:12), with the earth "burned up" (2 Peter 3:10). This is also exceptional given the mention of fire in the near context of Matthew in relation to Jesus' judgment (Matthew 25:41; cf. 1 Corinthians 3:13). If Jesus wanted readers to "understand" (as He says He does in Matthew 24:13; Mark 13:14) and connect His second advent as a "judgment-coming" with the event of A.D. 70, He could have done so by making a reference to fiery destruction. That He did not do so argues for His differentiating the destruction of the Temple in A.D. 70 from the desolation of the Temple during the future Tribulation, at which time His judgment will be centered not on the Jewish Temple but on the Gentile nations.

Another lack of correlation between the events of A.D. 66–70 and the description in the Olivet Discourse (in all three gospels) is that the discourse is missing key details related to the destruction of Jerusalem and the Temple. Josephus reported cannibalism, pestilence, internecine conflict, and supernatural events (see *Wars* 5.1.1-5 §§1-38; 5.10.2-5 §§424-45; 5.13.1 §§527-33; 6.3.1-6.5.3 §§177-309; 7.1.1 §1). Why would the gospel writers have omitted these details when they were so explicit about other specifics regarding the end times, such as false christs, false prophets, widespread warfare, persecution, and the desecration of the Temple?

Interpreting the Abomination of Desolation

Further problems in correlation result from preterists attempting to make historical events from the first century fit the Olivet Discourse. For example, the Zealot-led revolt against the Romans scarcely fits the passage "many will come in My name, saying 'I am the Christ' and will mislead many" (Matthew 24:5; see also Mark 13:6). True, the Zealots occupied the Temple precincts and used it as a military fortress, positioned their own high priest, desecrated the minor vessels, and plundered the resources of the Temple (wine, oil, etc.), interrupted the sacrificial service, and even shed blood in the Temple (*Wars*

4.3.7-10 §151-192; 5.13.6 §§562-66; 6.2.1 §§93-110). But as Gundry properly observes, "none of these crimes against the temple caused it to be deserted,"[13] for the sacrificial services continued to the end and the Jews demonstrated zealous devotion to the Temple, defending it even with their lives (see *Wars* 4.3.11-14 §§193-223). However, it is possible, as we have seen and Martin Hengel has proposed, that Josephus falsely accused the Zealots in his account because of his anti-nationalistic bias.[14] Preterist Kenneth Gentry, likewise interprets the "abomination of desolation" in light of the Jewish Zealots' actions in the war:

> The A.D. 70 stone-by-stone dismantling of the temple surely involves its "desolation." And…it includes abominable acts.…Well then, what *is* this "abomination of desolation" that befalls the city and temple? The holy city *and* the temple are both desecrated and desolated in the Jewish War. During the Roman siege, the Zealots hole up in Jerusalem, and stir up factional infighting between the parties.…Even while Jerusalem's mighty walls resist the Romans, this internal strife brings war into the holy temple itself.… As Titus begins his final march toward Jerusalem in A.D. 70, the Zealots "seize upon the inner court of the temple…so that the temple was defiled everywhere with murders" (*Wars* 5:12).[15]

Gentry also explains the "abomination of desolation" in light of the invading Roman army's actions. He views the presence of these attacking soldiers—who possessed military regalia carrying standards that bore images of Tiberias Caesar and brought these images into Jerusalem and the Temple precincts—as "an abomination leading to desolation."[16] However, the problem with proposing such an explanation is that any one of a number of similar events could also fit the historical fulfillment. Examples would include Pontius Pilate's orders for soldiers to march with their standards into Jerusalem, Gaius Caligula's order to place his statue in the Jewish Temple, the illegitimate service of the Zealot-sponsored high priest Phanni in the Temple, Titus and his general's entrance into the Holy Place of the Temple, and the erection of Roman standards in the Temple court and Roman sacrifices proclaiming Titus as imperator. All of these acts could qualify as "abominations of desolation." But, the problem with a nonspecific reference of Temple desecration is that Jesus' hearers would have been left to choose from an assortment of possible desecration scenarios, each of which has been argued as fulfilling Jesus' prophecy of the "abomination of desolation" by modern preteristic commentators.[17] Yet most of these aforementioned "abominations" leading to "desolation" never even occurred or have been seriously misrepresented! As Craig Evans explains:

> None of these events, however, fits well the context of Jesus' warning in [Mark 13] v 14. Pilate's attempted sacrilege did not take place. The temple was not in any way desecrated or left desolate. Caligula's order to erect his statue was never carried out, so again there was no abomination and the temple was not left desolate. Josephus's discussion of Phanni's appointment as high priest reflects Josephus's own bias against the Zealots, as well as his bias in favor of the non-Zadokite priestly aristocracy. It is very probable that many Jews, including Christians, would not have viewed Phanni's appointment as an outrage and certainly not as "the abomination that makes desolate" (note well *J. W.* 4.3.9 §160, where according to Josephus, the priestly aristocracy found it necessary to upbraid the people for their apathy against the Zealots!). And finally, Titus' stroll through the sanctuary occurred after the temple had already been seriously damaged and was in fact in flames, and after Jewish sacrifices had ceased. Moreover, the "abomination of desolation" of which Daniel speaks and to which Jesus alludes envisioned the cessation of sacrifice in the Jerusalem temple, not its destruction (Gundry, 741). Thus, none of the four events often cited as an explanation actually offers a parallel to v 14.[18]

In order for Jesus' warning to flee because of the sign of the "abomination of desolation" to be viable, only *one* clearly identifiable desecration must be understood. Otherwise, Jesus' first-century audience might have taken flight at every rumor of attempted desecration. And, unless Jesus' interpretation is unique, the Jews of His time apparently held a futurist rather than a preterist view of the fulfillment of the "abomination of desolation." How is this evident? Consider that the prediction in Daniel 11:21-35 had already been fulfilled 200 years previously (in 167 B.C.) when the Syrian-Greek ruler Antiochus IV Epiphanes placed a statue of Zeus Olympias next to the Great Altar of the Temple and forced the Jewish priests to offer sacrifices to pagan gods. Despite this well-known historical fulfillment, one which Jesus probably commemorated (see John 10:22), He still cited Daniel with an understanding that the *fulfillment* was *yet future*. From this it is clear that Jesus could have understood the phrase only in light of the event of 167 B.C.—a literal desecration by idols and pagan worship in the Temple. However, just as He sees the Tribulation (a term also found in Daniel 12:1-2) as future and unprecedented, so also does He see this "abomination of desolation" as future and unprecedented. Israel had experienced many past "tribulations," but it had not yet experienced "the Great Tribulation." In like manner, Jerusalem and the Temple had seen (and would see) "abominations" that led to "desolation," but they had yet to see Daniel's "abomination of desolation" which served to signal the advent of this greatest of all tribulations.

The Meaning of "Abomination of Desolation"

In my own study of the phrase "abomination of desolation" in the context of Temple desecration I discovered the phrase served as a technical reference to the introduction of an idolatrous image or an act of pagan sacrilege within the sanctuary that produces the highest level of ceremonial impurity, Temple profanation.[19] With respect to the term "abomination," two Hebrew nouns (*sheqetz* and *shiqqutz*) are derived from the Hebrew root *shaqatz*, the first always related to unclean animals (for dietary purposes), especially loathsome creatures such as "swarming things" (Leviticus 11:10) and "creeping things" (Isaiah 66:17),[20] and the second referred to idols as "detestable things" and the idolatrous practices associated with them[21] (Deuteronomy 29:17; 1 Kings 11:5,7; 2 Kings 23:13,24; 2 Chronicles 15:8; Isaiah 66:3; Jeremiah 4:1; 7:30; 13:27; 16:18; 32:34; Ezekiel 5:11; 7:20; 11:18,21; 20:7-8,30; 37:23; Nahum 3:6; Zechariah 9:7). The root *shaqatz* appears 45 times in the Old Testament, primarily as a technical term to denote animals and other things that rendered the Israelite "unclean." The term is used of any detestable thing (Hosea 9:10; Nahum 3:6; Zechariah 9:7), but predominately in connection with idolatrous practices. In Jeremiah 7:30-32 the prophet decries the desecration of the Temple by the erection of "abominations" (*shiqutzim*) in the Holy Place. Here the reference must be to the images of idols, referred to by hypocatasasis as "detestable, or horrible things." In its verbal form (occurring only in the Pi'el as *shiqqetz*) it appears seven times (Leviticus 7:18; 19:7; Isaiah 65:4; Ezekiel 4:14) with the factitive meaning of "abhor, detest," but since what is detested is that which defiles, it has a causative connotation of "contaminate" or "make abominable."[22] The phrase "abomination of desolation" or "desolating abomination" (Hebrew, *shiqqutz m^eshomem*) occurs in Hebrew only in Daniel (9:27; 11:31; 12:11). The form of the Hebrew term for "desolation" in this phrase is the *Pol'el* participle *shomem* or *m^eshomem*, which has a range of verbal meanings: "devastate, desolate, desert," and "appall," with nominal derivatives: "waste, horror, devastation, appallment." Hermann Austel, in his study of this term, says that "basic to the idea of the root is the desolation caused by some great disaster, usually as a result of divine judgment."[23] Perhaps for this reason it has also been used to describe an attitude of appalling horror due to criminal and barbaric acts of idolatry.[24] The *Pol'el* here has a causative (or better, factitive) force similar to the use of the *Hiphil*, except that the *Hiphil* generally involves a physical devastation, while the *Pol'el* seems to put more stress on the fact that someone has caused (active) the sanctuary or altar to be desecrated, thus rendering it unfit for the worship and service of God. In Daniel, two nuances of the term, "desolation due to war" and "desolation due to idolatry," are combined in Daniel 8:13, which describes the condition of Jerusalem under foreign domination: "How long will be the vision concerning the daily sacrifice, and the transgression *that causes desolation* so as to permit both the Sanctuary and its vessels *to be trampled?*" [25] This is very similar to the description of Jerusalem in Daniel 12:11, where a foreign invader has both abolished the regular sacrifice and substituted "an abomination that causes desolation." When combined with the Hebrew term for "abomination" (*shiqqutz*), the idea of the forcible intrusion of idolatry into a place of sanctity in order to defile is significantly intensified.

In the New Testament, the expression appears in Greek as *bdelugma tes eremoseos* (Matthew 24:15; Mark 13:14; Luke 21:20). The first part of this phrase, the word *bdelugma* ("abomination"), is used by the New Testament four times (Luke 16:15; Revelation 7:4-5; 21:27), and by the Septuagint (Greek translation of the Old Testament) 17 times, to translate the Hebrew *shiqqutz*. [26] The term *bdelugma* comes from a root with meanings "to make foul" and "to stink." Thus it has the basic idea of something that makes one feel nauseous, and by transference, psychologically or morally abhorrent and detestable. As with the Hebrew meaning in the Old Testament, the Greek term is applied particularly to idols or is associated with idolatrous practices, [27] and in the Septuagint in the writing prophets some usages are paralleled by the word "lawlessness" (Greek, *anomia*). This supports the allusion to the "abomination of desolation" in 2 Thessalonians 2:3, which describes the same figure by the phrase "man of lawlessness." [28] In this regard, *bdelugma* appears as an expression of antithesis between the divine and human wills, as well as denoting the repugnance of the ungodly to the will of God [29] and is used in Luke 16:15 of the repugnance of God to human pride (i.e., to things highly esteemed by men, which is tantamount to idolatry). [30] The second member of our expression "desolation" (Greek, *eremoseos*) is the genitive feminine singular of a root that signifies "to lay waste, make desolate, bring to ruin" (see Matthew 12:25; Luke 11:17; Revelation 17:16; 18:17,19). It is used most commonly in the Septuagint for *meshomem* or its cognates (cf. Leviticus 26:34-35; Psalm 73:19; 2 Chronicles 30:7; 36:21; Jeremiah 4:7), generally in reference to the condition of desolation of the land as a result of desecration and exile. It is this sense that is most likely in the background of Daniel 9:27 in the Septuagint.

Preterism's Perspective of the Abomination of Desolation

Kenneth Gentry in a later book,[31] recognizes the technical distinction of the phrase "abomination of desolation" but continues to accept its fulfillment according to Luke's more general prediction of a "desolation" resulting from the Roman army surrounding Jerusalem (Luke 21:20). However, such a general event does not meet the specific criteria for the full phrase, especially the requirement of an intrusion into the "holy place" (Matthew 24:15), "the place where it must not" (Mark 13:14). For this reason Gentry must try to prove that "the holy place" is a "reference [that] is broader, speaking of both the city and the temple."[32] But, as already recognized by Gentry, the phrase is technical and therefore cannot be broadened to include the city, since its original usage in Daniel is limited to the Temple and does not mention the city's or the Temple's *destruction* but only a desecration that interrupts the ceremonial service.

Any serious study of the term "Holy Place" in Scripture will yield the conclusion that it primarily refers to the most sanctified areas of the Temple, which include the *Hekal* ("the Holy Place") and the *Devir* ("the Most Holy Place"). Furthermore, as Craig observes, "the masculine gender of the participle *ejsthkovta*, "standing" (in contrast to the neuter *bdevlugma*, "abomination"), may suggest that the abomination is a statue or image of a pagan deity or deified man. Probably related to this tradition is the Pauline prediction in 2 Thessalonians 2:3-4: "for that day will not come, unless…the man of lawlessness is revealed…so that he takes his seat in the temple of God, proclaiming himself to be God."[33] Thus, the grammar itself further limits the interpretation of the "abomination of desolation," precluding its broader reference to the city. In addition, preterists cannot associate Paul's prophecy in 2 Thessalonians 2:3-4 with the prophecy of the "abomination of desolation" in the Olivet Discourse since Nero, whom they identify as the "man of lawlessness" who was being "restrained" by Claudius, never set up anything in the Jerusalem Temple! Moreover, when 2 Thessalonians was written (A.D. 51), Nero was only 14 years old and was hardly being "restrained" by the emperor from getting his hands on the Jewish Temple. Further, Nero certainly never performed the supernatural "signs and wonders" ascribed to the beast of Revelation (Revelation 13:11-15), as preterists contend, despite the Nero *redivivus* tradition recorded by his Roman historian Suetonius (*Nero* 6.57).

The Temple and the Abomination of Desolation

An objection preterists frequently voice against the futurist interpretation of the "abomination of desolation" is that the Temple spoken of by Jesus, in this context, could not have referred to anything other than the Second (Herodian) Temple known by the disciples. After all, it was Jesus' prediction of this Temple's destruction that originally provoked the disciples' questions. However, futurists do not doubt that the disciples understood Jesus to be speaking about the Second Temple. This understanding was appropriate as Jesus indeed addressed their concern for the Second Temple, a fact that Luke records (21:20-24). However, if Luke's straightforward description of the A.D. 70 "desolation of Jerusalem" was in fact Jesus' signal warning about the "abomination of desolation" and the Tribulation events following it at "the end of the age," why was it not linked to Daniel's prophecy, as in Matthew and Mark? How could Luke omit this crucial reference to Daniel's prophecy that Jesus stated was essential to understanding its interpretation and identification? Likewise, how would Luke exclude from his statement of the "desolation" the mention of the "Great Tribulation" as the unsurpassed event that would conclude the age? Such an inclusion would have removed any doubt of an A.D. 70 fulfillment for the prophecy. Conversely, how could Matthew and Mark fail to include the language of Luke's description of Jerusalem's desolation if they understood that the events they were describing were one and the same?

Now, it was not necessary that the disciples immediately grasp the full eschatological scope of Jesus' prophecy concerning the Temple. It was sufficient for them to understand that the prophecies would be fulfilled when a Jerusalem Temple was standing (now or in the future, whenever the respective fulfillment was to occur), as the former and latter prophets had proclaimed. In addition, it *is* possible that perceptive disciples did recognize a distinction, since Daniel, in the context of his prophecy of the "abomination of desolation," had promised "those with insight would understand" (Daniel 12:11), and the prophecies concerning Jerusalem and the Temple predicted that "in the Last Days" the Temple Mount would "be raised above all the other mountains" (Isaiah 2:2-3) and that a "greater Temple" (than the Second Temple) would exist at the time of the end (Haggai 2:6-9). Jesus directed the disciples to this eschatological interpretation by linking the events of the Great Tribulation and the subsequent revelation of the Son of Man to the signal event of Daniel's "abomination of desolation." By doing so, He guided them (or those who would later seek the interpretation) to interpret the event within the eschatological context of the end time (Daniel 12:4,9,13), and to use this understanding as a guide for their interpretation of the rest of the Olivet prophecy.

This also implies that Jesus did not intend His prophecy to be exclusive to a first-century "generation" but for generations after the destruction of A.D. 70, who would consider that event in light of Jesus' instruction concerning wars "that must take place, but [that are] not yet the end" (Matthew 24:6;

Mark 13:7). Such interpreters would then expect the future fulfillment of the "abomination of desolation" within a future (rebuilt) Temple as "naturally" as the disciples may have expected a fulfillment within the Second Temple before A.D. 70. If one should further ask why Jesus did not simply say it was a future Temple, the answer would be for the same reason He did not explain any of the other eschatological references in His prophecy (such as famines, earthquakes, false christs, false prophets, lightning, darkened sun and moon, falling stars, etc.). Such an explanation was unnecessary because a first-century reference to these things was sufficient for comprehension of the prophecy itself (a phenomenon typical of accommodation in prophecy).

In addition, the events that would come in A.D. 70 (like those that came in 167 B.C.) followed a template of divine discipline that could be employed for both a near and far fulfillment. From the time God predicted Jerusalem would be the site of the central sanctuary (Deuteronomy 12:11-32), its role as the symbol of both divine judgment and restoration was assured. Once the Temple was built, every violation of the national covenant that called for divine discipline would thereafter be carried out on the visible symbol of God's relationship with Israel, the Temple, in the chosen city of the divine presence, Jerusalem. Jesus' prediction of the Second Temple's destruction followed the established pattern of judgment pronounced and executed on the First Temple. And as Josephus and the rabbis point out, the proof of this pattern was the destruction and burning of the Second Temple on the Ninth of Av (August 10) A.D. 70, the exact same day and month on which the First Temple had been burnt by the king of Babylon (*Antiquities* 20.100.11 §8).

In addition, Jesus' own statements concerning ritual abuses in the Temple precincts were based on those of the prophet Jeremiah, who had made similar accusations in regard to the Temple's destruction (Jeremiah 7:1–8:3). Therefore, Jesus' pronouncement on the Temple no more required a fulfillment of the end of the age than did that of Jeremiah, for the Temple stands as the focal point of national judgment in any age in which Israel exists within a covenantal structure. Given this pattern, each event of judgment serves as a preview of the end of the age and as a pledge that the final judgment will be effected in the eschatological program. Darrel Bock recognizes this as how we're to understand Luke, who focused on the Jerusalem destruction in A.D. 70 as a picture of the end-time Tribulation:

> The different emphases are most clearly indicated by what Luke lacks: he does not mention that the Tribulation in this period is the most intense ever to fall on humans; he does not mention that no human would have survived if the Lord had not cut short these days; he does not note that the time should not be in

winter; and he does not discuss the "abomination of desolation," only "its desolation." Conversely, Luke alone mentions "the time of the Gentiles." What do these differences mean? They indicate that Luke emphasizes a different element in Jesus' teaching at this point. He focuses on the nearer fulfillment in the judgment pattern described here, the fall of Jerusalem in A.D. 70, rather than the end (which he will introduce in 21:25). The end is directly alluded to by the language of 21:23-24, which shows Luke's linkage and concern. It would seem that Luke sees in Jerusalem's collapse a preview, but with less intensity, of what the end will be like. So the instructions he offers here are like those that appear in the description of the end in 17:23, 31. He wants to make clear that when Jerusalem falls the first time, it is not yet the end. Nonetheless, the two falls are related and the presence of one pictures what the ultimate siege will be like. Both are eschatological events in God's plan, with the fall of Jerusalem being the down payment and guarantee of the end-time.[34]

Even if we allow for Luke's language to have a dual role encompassing both the near-historical and the far-eschatological fulfillment, it must be recognized that the *differences* between the gospel accounts of Matthew, Mark, and Luke can only be explained by their *distinct* presentations of A.D. 70 and end-time fulfillments. This must also be observed when preterists attempt a comparison between the Olivet Discourse and prophetic Old Testament texts, such as Zechariah 12–14, that describe an end-time attack on Jerusalem. For example, Zechariah's prophecy states that half of the population of Jerusalem remains in the city after the attack to await the Lord's rescue (Zechariah 14:2), whereas Josephus plainly states that Titus completely destroyed the city (except for the towers) and that the Jews were all killed or deported from the city (*Wars* 7.1.1). For additional discrepancies between Zechariah 12–14 and the Olivet Discourse, see my chart in chapter 7 and for further problems between the historical account of A.D. 70 and the prophecy of Zechariah 12–14 see chapter 11.

Preterist Problems with the Abomination of Desolation
Understanding A Key Distinction

An additional problem for Gentry's interpretation is that he identifies the "abomination" of the Roman army's presence in the holy city as the "desolation." However, does Jesus mean that the "abomination" *is* the "desolation" or a *part* of the desolation, or that the "abomination" *causes* the "desolation?" The word "abomination," in Jesus' usage, is singular (Greek *bdelugma*), and follows Daniel's two singular Hebrew uses of *shiqqutz* ("abomination") in association with *mᵉshomem* ("desolation") in Daniel 11:31 and 12:11, both of which have the "abomination" *causing* the "desolation." In Daniel 9:27 the plural (*shiqqutzim*) is used; however, this is cryptic grammatical construction and has been explained by Daniel's desire to pattern the association of the terms "abominations" (*shiqqutzim*) and "desolation" (*shomem*) in Jeremiah and Ezekiel, well-known texts that decry covenantal violations (such as Jeremiah 44:22 and Ezekiel 33:29) that state that "abominations" (plural) by the Jewish nation will *cause* "desolation" to the land of Israel.[35] If this is so, then Daniel may be attempting to load a theological summation of desecration into this expression to convey in a single thought the entire corpus of prophetic doctrine touching on any future events earmarked by this phrase. This may be helpful in explaining why Jesus, in the Olivet Discourse (Matthew 24:15; Mark 13:14a), used this expression to denote the signal event that would serve as a warning of the arrival of prophetic fulfillment (Matthew 24:16-31; Mark 13:14-27). One significance of this for the interpretation of the Olivet Discourse is that Daniel's prophecy must be interpreted within the context of his contemporaries, who envisioned fulfillment in eschatological terms (see Jeremiah 31:27-37; Ezekiel 37:23-28).[36] At any rate, Daniel 9:27 can be added as a further example.

The application of this understanding in the immediate discussion is that the Lord makes the land desolate because of the abominations of His covenant people. For a foreigner to be able to cause the land to be desolated, a majority of the people of the land would have to support the desolator in some way. In the futurist interpretation of prophecy, it is the false covenant between the Jewish leaders (who represent the people) and the "prince that shall come" (the Antichrist, Daniel 9:27), that allows for the introduction of the "abomination that makes desolate." However, in the preterist interpretation of A.D. 70, the Jewish nation did not support Titus, but fought against him to their deaths. Therefore, the preterist interpretation of the "abomination" as a "desolating" event (the Roman invasion) does not meet the criteria of causation nor fit with the covenantal violation texts, which require complicity with the desecrator for fulfillment.

Understanding the Warning to Flee

Preterists also attempt to find a first-century fulfillment in the flight of those who correctly identified and heeded the sign of the "abomination of desolation"(Matthew 24:16-20; Mark 13:14-18)—in agreement with Luke 21:21—in the event of the Jewish-Christian flight to Pella (Eusebius, *Ecclesiastical History* 3.5.2-3; Epiphanius, *De mensuris et ponderibus* 15). Yet the historicity of the Pella tradition is questioned by many ancient and modern scholars, significantly compromising its authority as a source for comparison with Scripture. However, even if we accept its historicity, fatal problems present themselves for any attempt at correlation. According to the fourth-century church historian Eusebius, Christians fled to Pella in A.D. 61–62, which was several years before the beginning of the Jewish Revolt in A.D. 66, and many more years before the "abomination of desolation" (according to the preterists' interpretation) occurred with the Roman army surrounding Jerusalem or entering the Temple precincts in A.D. 70. To this problem should be added the fact that the Romans controlled the Judean countryside (to which Jerusalem belonged) as well as its immediate environs for some time prior to their siege of the city, which would have made it practically impossible for either Jerusalemites or those in fields outside the city to make an escape. Neither could Jesus have meant that a flight should take place once the siege began, for any escaping at this time would have had the Jewish people running into the hands of the enemy! Moreover, as many commentators have observed, the biblical command to "flee to the *mountains*" (Matthew 24:16; Mark 13:14; cf. Luke 21:21) hardly agrees with the geographical setting of Pella in the low-lying foothills of the Transjordan valley on the other side of the River Jordan. Since Jerusalem is called "the holy mountain" (Psalm 48:1; cf. 87:1-2), "Mount Zion" (Psalm 74:2; 78:68-69), and is situated and surrounded by "mountains" (Psalm 125:1-2; cf. 48:2), "fleeing to the mountains" could not be interpreted as descending to a lower elevation. It is far more reasonable that "the mountains" would be those that immediately surrounded the city (i.e., the Judean hills, cf. Ezekiel 7:15-16), since Jesus' command was not to flee *from* Judea, but *within* it.

In like manner, Jesus' unrestricted warning "to all who are in Judea" to quickly escape once the sign of the "abomination of desolation" was "observed" extended even to the extreme of leaving behind possessions in order to flee in haste (Matthew 24:17-18; Mark 13:15-17). The urgency of an immediate departure (and of the threat of danger if the escapees delayed) does not accord with the prolonged Roman war, especially before the siege (three years), which would have offered ample opportunity to make a well-prepared escape. This same objection applies to the admonition to pray that the "flight might not be in winter or on a Sabbath" (Matthew 24:20; cf. Mark 13:18). In the winter (especially in Jerusalem, where temperatures are 10 percent colder than the rest of the country) stormy weather comes with torrential rains that make crossing wadis in the Judean hills treacherous, and Jesus' warning seems superfluous (or ill-informed) if the prophetic fulfillment actually took place during the spring-to-summer siege and assault on the city and Temple in A.D. 70. Why would Jesus say the Jewish people should pray for something He knew would not happen? What's more, why would Jesus mention concern about the possibility of travel on the Sabbath, where rabbinic law prohibited going more than a Sabbath day's journey (i.e., beyond the immediate vicinity of the city), when the prolonged war with Rome gave plenty of opportunity for escape on days other than the Sabbath?

Jesus was predicting conditions very different than those that existed during the conflict that culminated in A.D. 70. More problematic for preterists is Jesus' statement that "unless those days had been shortened, no life would have been saved" (Matthew 24:22; Mark 13:20). According to preterists, the purpose of "those days" was to effect a final judgment on the Jewish people in fulfillment of Christ's judgment-coming. Why, then, should any life be saved? The satisfaction of divine justice should require a complete accounting (although thousands of Jews did, in fact, survive the war).

If the reason is to spare "the elect," one must wonder: Who are these "elect"? Preterists would not identify them as the Jews, for the reason just stated. But if the elect are identified as "Christians," why had they not believed Jesus' prophecy and fled to Pella with the rest of their brethren? Moreover, the language here cannot be restricted to a local population, but rather, applies to the whole of the human race, as the Greek *ouk an esôthê pasa sarx* ("*all flesh* would not be saved") reveals. Only an end-time conflict of global proportions could adequately satisfy the language of this unprecedented warning (in keeping with the nature of the Great Tribulation, mentioned in the previous verse). Preterism can explain this verse only by hyperbole or minimizing the application of the term *sarx* ("flesh").

The same problem applies to the preterists' interpretation of the eschatological language in the climax of the Olivet Discourse, as we'll see next.

Why Are Preterists Inconsistent in Interpreting Scripture?

As we approach the climax of the Olivet Discourse, it is evident that Jesus' eschatological (not apocalyptic) warning is of a judgment preceding His glorious advent and the establishment of His kingdom. This order is inescapable in light of Matthew 25:31: "When the Son of Man comes in His glory, and all the angels with Him, then He shall sit on His glorious throne. All the nations will be gathered before Him...." Based on this verse, Christ's kingdom will replace earthly governments. It follows, then, that judgment should be expected upon those nations that oppose its inauguration. This is what the verse confirms when it speaks of the judgment of the nations by Christ, and indeed, Jesus' messianic claim was a political threat to the Roman authorities (see John 11:48; 18:36; 19:12,15). Thus, if this passage had been prophetically fulfilled, the judgment of God should have fallen on *both* the Roman empire for its first-century opposition to Christ and the first-century Jewish nation—not just the Jews alone, as preterists inconsistently argue. If it is contended that Rome was also finally judged, then the argument for a first-century fulfillment again breaks down, for why should God's judgment fall on the Jews in the first century "at Christ's parousia," but wait many centuries to fall on the Romans after "Christ's kingdom has come" and especially long after that empire had adopted Christianity as its official religion?

Another inconsistency is the preterists' use of the prophecy of the 70 weeks in Daniel 9:24-27 to support a first-century fulfillment for the Olivet Discourse and the book of Revelation. Most Christian commentators would agree that the prediction of a coming Messiah (verse 25) that is "cut off" and of a city and sanctuary (Jerusalem and the Temple) that are destroyed (verse 26) were fulfilled with the death of Jesus and the Roman conquest 40 years later, which Preterists see as the time of the "judgment-coming" of Christ. The problem in using Daniel 9 as a first-century fulfillment of this event is that it predicts the Temple will be destroyed *after* the Messiah has come, while in the Olivet Discourse and Revelation, the Temple is "desolated" *before* the coming of the Messiah. Although Luke 21:20 accords with Daniel's chronology at this point, as it has been pointed out, this verse is part of Jesus' answer as to "when these things shall be" (i.e., the destruction of the Temple), and not part of His answer concerning His second coming.

Finally, there is remarkable inconsistency amongst preterists when they interpret prophetic texts that speak of national Israel and the Temple's "desolation." When they reference such texts, they interpret them literally—that is, as having a historical fulfillment without replacement of the object. But when they deal with texts that speak of Israel or the Temple's restoration, these are interpreted figuratively and applied by replacement to the church. However, since the disciples asked pointed questions and Jesus answered them directly, can we doubt that if the disciples had not clearly understood any aspect of Jesus' teaching that they would not have simply asked additional questions and received clarification? How is it, then, that these disciples still believed Jesus was "the restorer of Israel" at the time of His ascension (Acts 1:6)? It is true that the disciples did not understand the prophecies concerning Jesus' death and resurrection before these events occurred (John 20:9), but the statement in Acts 1:6 is post-resurrection and after the disciples had received an enablement from the Holy Spirit (John 20:22). Moreover, after receiving the permanent and promised bestowal of the Spirit at Pentecost, who would "teach you all things" (John 14:26), Peter declared in Acts 3:18-21 concerning the coming of "the Christ appointed for you" (verse 20—national Israel, not individual Jews) that His coming was predicated upon collective (national) Jewish repentance. This indeed appears to be enlightened comprehension of the Old Testament prophecies (as stated), but may also reflect the apostolic understanding of Jesus' Olivet Discourse. At any rate, it repeats the conviction that Jesus is promised as Israel's "restorer."

If Peter had understood a preteristic interpretation of the Olivet Discourse, his declaration to that generation of Jews who were destined for final judgment in A.D. 70 would have been deceptive. Rather, these apostles, as well as the apostle Paul, understood that repentance was a part of the divine plan and would be effected after "the fullness of the Gentiles has come in" (Romans 11:25)—a text which also seems to understand Luke's statement concerning the duration of Jerusalem's desolation "until the times of the Gentiles are fulfilled" (Luke 21:24), and the promise of rescue from God's wrath to redemption at Christ's revelation (Luke 21:28). The phrase "until the times of the Gentiles are fulfilled," when associated with the fall of the city of Jerusalem, at least implies that the fall is of limited duration. And, as Bock notes, a contrast between Israel and the Gentile nations here is also implicit.[37] How, then, can preterism adopt the interpretation that Christ came in A.D. 70 through the Gentile Roman army in a final (and irreversible) judgment against the Jewish nation when, in this explicit context Jesus himself consoles the persecuted Jewish remnant with the words, "But when these things begin to take place [to] straighten up and lift up your heads, because your redemption is drawing near"? According to preterism, this verse should read, "But when these things begin to take place, bend low and bow your heads [in shame and sorrow], because your destruction is drawing near."

In like manner, because the geographical context for the Olivet Discourse was Jerusalem, this city would logically be the geographical referent for the discourse's predictions. This, of course is implied by reference to the Temple in Matthew and Mark, or explicitly stated, as in Luke 21:20-24. Preterists, therefore, make much of Jerusalem as the object of the Roman wrath, since they can use this to "prove" a historical fulfillment of prophetic judgment texts. However, they are inconsistent in their interpretation of statements of prophetic restoration in the *same* geographical context. For example, Jews are told to flee from Judea (Matthew 24:15-16), but then promised that God would gather them from one end of heaven to the other (verse 31). If their exile was from the land of Israel, and particularly Judea, where else would their return (i.e., their regathering) be than to that same place? When "the Son of Man comes [to Jerusalem] in power and great glory" (Luke 21:27), those who are to "lift up their heads, because [their] redemption is drawing near" (verse 28) must also be in the city. In like manner, Jesus cried out, "Jerusalem, Jerusalem" with reference to those Jews whose "house is being left desolate" (Matthew 23:37-38), and then added that they "will not see [Him] until [they] say, 'Blessed is He who comes in the name of the Lord'" (verse 39). How else can we understand the place where these future repentant Jews will see Him as the "Blessed One" but the city of Jerusalem? And again, when the disciples on the Mount of Olives ask the risen Christ about the timing of the restoration of the kingdom to Israel, the place assumed (and never corrected) for this restoration is Jerusalem. If the apostolic attitude toward a recalcitrant national Israel *before* A.D. 70 was not one of rejection without restoration, the theological position of the Christian community (of which they were the foundation) *after* the destruction of Jerusalem should not have been fundamentally different (see Romans 11:28-29). Whether or not the early church consistently adopted the attitude of the apostles, we can find no evidence in the early history of the church to support the preterist interpretation of eschatological fulfillment in the first century.

THE VERDICT REGARDING THE OLIVET DISCOURSE

We can only agree with Gundry's conclusion concerning the preterists' interpretation of a first-century fulfillment of the Olivet Discourse: "Whether writing just before, or right after 70 C.E., Mark [or any of the other gospel writers] is not liable to have suffered from very much ignorance of what went on. From beginning to end, then, the events and circumstances of the Jewish war disagree with the text of Mark [and also Matthew and in part, Luke] too widely to allow that text to reflect those events and circumstances."[38] If, then, the attempt to correlate the historical events of A.D. 70 with the Olivet Discourse fails, and preterism depends on such a correlation for the maintenance of its eschatological system, then preterism itself fails as a viable eschatological interpretation.

Chapter 16

WHY FUTURISM?

THOMAS ICE

I believe it is important for Christians to know whether the key Bible prophecies we have been discussing in this book are past or future. This issue is not just an academic exercise; if the Tribulation and coming of Christ are past events, then there are many practical implications that should follow. If these events are really past, then the rapture of the church is impossible, premillennialism cannot be true, Israel does not have a future national blessing, the current nation of Israel is not prophetically significant, our current state of existence would have to be the millennial kingdom or new heavens and new earth, there will be no future Antichrist and false prophet, and none of the Tribulation events should be of concern to us or future generations. In short, the present perspective of Christianity for millions of believers would be very different because our view of the future would change significantly.

A FUTURIST OVERVIEW

I do not believe the Bible teaches that the disputed prophetic events are in any way *past*. Instead, Scripture tells us they are yet *future* events that could commence very soon. I believe the correct teaching of Scripture includes a future Tribulation period of seven years in length, which will commence with the signing of a covenant between the nation Israel and the European Antichrist, who will have reconstituted his version of a revived Roman Empire. At the midpoint of the seven years, the Antichrist (also known as the Beast) will defile a rebuilt Jewish Temple in Jerusalem and set himself up as god, demanding that all the world show allegiance to him by receiving his mark (666) on their right hand or forehead. At this point, the Antichrist will turn against the Jews and those in Jerusalem will flee to the wilderness, where they will experience divine protection for the second three-and-a-half years of the Tribulation. Toward the end of the Tribulation the Antichrist will gather the armies of the world against Jerusalem in an effort to destroy the Jews. This will lead to the conversion of all Israel to Jesus as their Messiah. Once converted, the Jews will plead for their Savior to rescue them from sure destruction. Jesus will hear their plea and return from heaven to earth with His entourage of angles and saints to rescue now-submissive Israel. Upon His return, Jesus will prepare the world for His 1,000-year reign on earth from Jerusalem.

Does the scenario described above have a basis in future reality, or is it just the product of an overactive imagination? Is it based on Scripture, or better suited for novels and science fiction movies? Are the Tribulation and Christ's coming still future, or did they occur symbolically in the destruction of Jerusalem in A.D. 70?

I believe we *can* know from Scripture that the Tribulation has not yet occurred on the stage of history.

The Old Testament

The ancient philosopher Archimedes said, "Give me a place to stand and I can move the universe." Applied philosophically, if the starting point of one's position can be established, then it provides a base upon which to develop further thought. The starting point for any Christian should be God's revelation as found in the Bible. But how do we go about establishing an Archimedean starting point in order to resolve an interpretive difference over whether certain prophetic events are past or future? In the upcoming pages I will explain the various reasons why these prophetic events—as revealed by God in the Bible—are future events. Once we've established a biblical place upon which we can stand, we will see that these prophetic events have not yet taken place. This is important because God's reputation—in the areas of clearness of speech and His veracity—is at stake.

The Pentateuch: Prophetic Pacts
Covenantal Arrangements
The Abrahamic Covenant

Instead of starting with the Olivet Discourse, where preterists like to begin, we will begin in Genesis, where the Bible begins. Following the dictum that "Scripture interprets Scripture," we need to also let the Bible itself teach us God's plan for history. The Bible *does* provide an Old Testament framework for the Tribulation, and it makes sense to put the Tribulation and other future events within the time frame God intended rather than one that is superimposed upon the biblical text, as preterists do.

In relation to Matthew 24:29 and the Tribulation, preterist Greg Bahnsen said, "The difficulty, however, is that dispensational and modern interpreters have come to these words without an appreciation for, in many cases, even a knowledge of the literature of the Old Testament. Scripture is its own best interpreter...." [1]

In pursuit of letting Scripture provide the questions as well as the answers, we will start in the Old Testament with the fountainhead of Bible prophecy— the Abrahamic Covenant (Genesis 12:1-3,7; 13:14-17; 15:1-21; 17:1-21; 22:15-18). This agreement is the "mother of all redemptive covenants" and God's blessings spring forth from it and extend to all mankind and planet earth.

The Abrahamic Covenant is an unconditional agreement or pact in which God's sovereign election of Abraham and his descendants are revealed and God's decrees for them are declared. Arnold Fruchtenbaum explains,

> An unconditional covenant can be defined as a sovereign act of God whereby God unconditionally obligates Himself to bring to pass definite promises, blessings, and conditions for the covenanted people. It is a unilateral covenant. This type of covenant is characterized by the formula I will which declares God's determination to do exactly as He promised. The blessings are secured by the grace of God. [2]

The unconditional nature of the Abrahamic Covenant is reinforced by understanding the covenant or treaty formats of the second millennium B.C. within which biblical covenants were cast. There are three kinds of covenants in the Bible: 1) the Royal Grant Treaty, 2) the Suzerain–Vassal Treaty, and 3) the Parity Treaty. They may be described as follows:

- The Royal Grant Treaty (*unconditional*)—a promissory covenant that arose out of a king's desire to reward a loyal servant.
  Examples:
  The Abrahamic Covenant
  The Davidic Covenant
  The Palestinian Covenant

- The Suzerain–Vassal Treaty (*conditional*)—bound an inferior vassal to a superior suzerain and was binding only on the one who swore.
  Examples:
  The Adamic Covenant
  The Noahic Covenant

> Chedorlaomer (Genesis 14)
> The Mosaic Covenant (book of Deuteronomy)
> Jabesh-Gilead serving Nahash (1 Samuel 11:1)

- The Parity Treaty—bound two equal parties in a relationship and provided conditions as stipulated by the participants.
  Examples:
  > Abraham and Abimelech (Genesis 21:25-32)
  > Jacob and Laban (Genesis 31:44-50)
  > David and Jonathan (1 Samuel 18:1-4; cf. 2 Samuel 9:1-13)

The Abrahamic Covenant is classified as a Royal Grant Treaty, thus underscoring its *unconditional* nature. The confirmation of the covenant is given in Genesis 15, when God sealed the treaty through a unique procedure whereby He put Abram into a deep sleep and bound Himself to keep the covenant regardless of Abraham's response. Because God is the only one who swore to keep the covenant, then it is clearly an unconditional covenant, based solely on what God does alone. Thus, we can be absolutely confident that He will keep it and bring to pass in history every stipulation of the agreement.

There are three major provisions of the Abrahamic Covenant (Genesis 12:1-3). They are usually summarized as 1) a *land* to Abram and Israel, 2) a *seed*, and 3) a worldwide *blessing*. A more complete breakdown of the covenant can be seen in its 14 provisions gleaned from the five major passages that mention the treaty and its reconfirmations. Fruchtenbaum lists them as follows:

a. A great nation was to come out of Abraham, namely, the nation of Israel (12:2; 13:16; 15:5; 17:1-2,7; 22:17b).

b. He was promised a land, specifically, the Land of Canaan (12:1,7; 13:14-15,17; 15:17-21; 17:18).

c. Abraham himself was to be greatly blessed (12:2b; 15:6; 22:15-17a).

d. Abraham's name would be great (12:2c).

e. Abraham will be a blessing to others (12:2d).

f. Those who bless will be blessed (12:3a).

g. Those who curse will be cursed (12:3b).

h. In Abraham all will ultimately be blessed, a promise of Gentile blessing (12:3c; 22:18).

i. Abraham would receive a son through his wife Sarah (15:1-4; 17:16-21).

j. His descendants would undergo the Egyptian bondage (15:13-14).

k. Other nations as well as Israel would come forth from Abraham (17:3-4,6; the Arab states are some of these nations).

l. His name would be changed from Abram to Abraham (17:5).

m. Sarai's name was to be changed to Sarah (17:15).

n. There was to be a token of the covenant—circumcision (17:9-14) and so according to the Abrahamic covenant, circumcision was a sign of Jewishness.[3]

This breakdown of the Abrahamic Covenant exhibits a wide variety of promises that will prove to give direction to an interesting history for Israel and the world.

Fruchtenbaum notes that the fulfillment of these 14 promises are distributed and fulfilled among the following three parties (the letters given below are based on the preceding list):

a. Abraham—The following promises were made to Abraham: a, b, c, d, e, f, i, k, l, m.

b. Israel, the Seed—The following promises were made to Israel: a, b, e, f, g, j, n.

c. Gentiles—The following promises include the Gentiles: f, g, h, k.[4]

John F. Walvoord summarizes the importance of the Abrahamic Covenant as foundational to the study of Bible prophecy:

> The Abrahamic covenant contributes to the eschatology of Israel by detailing the broad program of God as it affects Abraham's seed....It is not too much to say that the exegesis of the Abrahamic covenant and its resulting interpretation is the foundation for the study of prophecy as a whole, not only as relating to Israel, but also for the Gentiles and the church. It is here that the true basis for premillennial interpretation of the Scriptures are found.[5]

The Abrahamic Covenant is important to a discussion of prophecy for it expresses many unconditional decrees that will be expanded upon in subsequent revelation and thus surely fulfilled in history. This expansion of a biblical theme in the later revelation of Scripture has been called "progressive revelation." Progressive revelation is clearly at work in relation to the Tribulation. As we make our way forward through the pages of Holy Writ, we can see more and more details about God's program for the Tribulation and future events.

The Mosaic Covenant

The Mosaic or Sinaitic Covenant is in the form of a Suzerain–Vassal treaty from the second millennium B.C. The book of Deuteronomy is generally recognized to have been set within the following structure of a Suzerain–Vassal treaty:[6]

> Suzerain–Vassal Treaty Format of Deuteronomy
> • Preamble (1:1-5)
> • Historical Prologue (1:6–4:49)
> • Main Provisions (5:1–26:19)
> • Blessing and Curses (27:1–30:20)
> • Covenant Continuity (31:1–33:29)

Suzerain–Vassal Treaties or covenants are conditional. This is important because it is within this framework that the Tribulation is first mentioned in the Bible as an event in Israel's history that will occur in "the latter days" and will lead to their repentance and conversion to Jesus as their Messiah (Deuteronomy 4:30). An interesting aspect of Deuteronomy is that its covenantal structure provides the framework for Israel's history, both past and future. In the historical prologue section (1:6–4:49), the Lord does not merely provide the customary history of the two contractual parties' dealings up to the time of the treaty, but He goes one step further and provides a prophetic overview of Israel's entire future history. This is a significant observation for determining when the Tribulation will occur, for Deuteronomy provides a prophetic road map of Israel's history.

Covenantal Relationships

Perhaps it would be helpful at this point to stop and contemplate the relationship of an unconditional covenant, such as the Abrahamic Covenant, to that of a conditional covenant, such as the Mosaic Covenant. The unconditional covenants provide humanity with God's sovereign decrees of where He is taking history, while the conditional covenants provide us with the means He will use to get us there. God has said in the Abrahamic Covenant that he will do certain things for the seed of Abraham, and the Mosaic Covenant provides conditional stipulations that must be met before a decree from the Abrahamic Covenant can take place. God decreed that Israel would receive certain blessings within the land of Israel, but said the people would enjoy them only if they were obedient. When the Israelites disobeyed, they would be cursed. That cursing would eventually lead them back to obedience and finally result in the ultimate blessing promised in the Abrahamic Covenant.

"The primary purpose of the Sinaitic covenant," explains George Harton, "was to instruct the newly redeemed nation how they were to live for YHWH."[7] Harton then concludes:

> The covenant program revealed in the Pentateuch rests squarely on the twin pillars of the Abrahamic and Sinaitic covenants. This covenant program contains unconditional elements which reveal some things that God has bound himself to do for the nation Israel. It also contains some conditional elements which define the conditions upon which any individual Israelite may receive the benefits of the covenant. The Jews in Christ's day felt that the unconditional covenant guaranteed their participation in the promised kingdom. They had forgotten that an unconditional covenant may have conditional blessings. The Sinaitic covenant is essentially an amplification of these promises and covenant on which they rested.[8]

Just such a covenantal relationship is displayed in Deuteronomy, providing a masterful interplay between the certainty of Israel's destiny while at the same time insisting the people will get to their blessing by traveling God's road and not one of their own choice. Thus, Deuteronomy provides a prophetic road map covering the whole of the history of Israel before the nation started down the road. This map includes a stop in the Tribulation, as well as other judgments along the way.

Deuteronomy: A Prophetic Road Map

As the nation of Israel sat perched on the banks of the Jordan River, before she ever set one foot upon the Promised Land, the Lord gave an outline of her entire history through Moses, His mouthpiece. Deuteronomy is this revelation, and it is like a road map for where history is headed before the trip got underway. Disclosure of an event called the Tribulation was included by God as part of the original itinerary. While different segments of the historical journey have been updated, with more details being added along the way, not a single adjustment from the earlier course has ever been made. Part of that journey includes the Tribulation.

Before we look at God's prophetic road map, it is important that we see the purpose of all the books in the Pentateuch. This will help us to better understand the contribution that Deuteronomy makes in understanding the Tribulation's place in history. Harton will prove helpful once again by providing the following overviews:

The purpose of Genesis is to reveal to Israel at the time of the exodus her place as God's chosen instrument of ministering to His fallen world...."[9]

The purpose of Exodus is the revelation of the deliverance of Israel to independent status as a nation...."[10]

The purpose of Leviticus is to show how Israel could maintain fellowship with their holy Redeemer...."[11]

The purpose of Numbers is to reveal God's response to Israel's disobedience...."[12]

...Numbers reveals God's response to Israel's disobedience by removing from them conditional blessings and by reassuring them of His unconditional promise...."[13]

The purpose of Deuteronomy is to call for new commitment to the covenants by new generations in Israel....The point of the book is not primarily legal (to recite a corpus of law), nor historical (to recount a series of events), but it is hortatory (to preach so as to move Israel to faith and obedience).[14]

As Moses exhorts the nation of Israel, he provides in Deuteronomy 4:25-31 an outline of what will happen once this elect nation crosses over the Jordan River and settles the land:

"When you become the father of children and children's children and *have remained long in the land, and act corruptly,* and make an idol in the form of anything, and do that which is evil in the sight of the LORD your God so as to provoke Him to anger, I call heaven and earth to witness against you today, that you *will surely perish quickly from the land* where you are going over the Jordan to possess it. You shall not live long on it, but will be utterly destroyed. *The LORD will scatter you among the peoples,* and you will be left few in number among the nations where the LORD drives you. There you will serve gods, the work of man's hands, wood and stone, which neither see nor hear nor eat nor smell. *But from there you will seek the LORD your God,* and you will find Him if you search for Him with all your heart and all your soul. *When you are in distress and all these things have come upon you, in the latter days, you will return to the LORD your God and listen to His voice.* For the LORD your God is a compassionate God; He will not fail you nor destroy you nor forget the covenant with your fathers which He swore to them.

The phrases in italicized type help to highlight those major events that are key in the history of Israel. Here's a summary of these events:

1. Israel and her descendants would remain long in the land.

2. Israel would act corruptly and slip into idolatry.

3. Israel would be kicked out of the land.

4. The Lord would scatter the people among the nations.

5. Israel would be given over to idolatry during their wanderings.

6. While dispersed among the nations, Israel would seek and find the Lord when they search for Him with all their heart.

7. There would come a time of *tribulation,* said to occur in the latter days, during which time they would turn to the Lord.

8. "For the LORD your God is a compassionate God; He will not fail you nor destroy you nor forget the covenant with your fathers which He swore to them" (Deuteronomy 4:31).

If the first five events have happened to Israel—and no one would deny that they have—then it is clear from the text that the final events will also occur to the same people in the same way. This is most clear from the context. The Bible does not "change horses in midstream" so that suddenly Israel, who has received the curses, is dropped out of the picture and the church takes over and receives the blessings. Despite various systems of theology, the Bible simply does not teach that God has forsaken Israel. Any reader of the text will have to admit that the identity of the people referred to throughout the whole of the passage under examination is the same. If it is true that the same Israel is meant throughout the text, then the last three events have yet to be fulfilled for Israel in the same historical way in which the first five events are recognized by all to have taken place. Thus, a fulfillment of the final three events in the life of Israel will have to happen in the future. Israel was not rescued as a result of tribulation in A.D. 70; instead, she was judged. Deuteronomy 4 pictures a return to the Lord after tribulation, not judgment. This means that a futurist view of the Tribulation is supported from this early passage.

As significant as Deuteronomy 4 is in establishing the Tribulation and its purpose, an expanded narrative of Israel's future history is provided in Deuteronomy 28–32. "The last seven chapters of Deuteronomy (28–34)," says David Larsen, "are really the matrix out of which the great prophecies of the Old Testament regarding Israel emerge."[15] Larsen provides the following breakdown of Israel's future history:

26:3-13; 28:1-14	The conditions of blessing to follow obedience
31:16-21	The coming apostasy
28:15-60	The affliction that God would bring upon Israel, while still in the land, because of her apostasy
28:32-39, 48-57	Israel will be taken captive
27; 32	The enemies of Israel will possess her land for a time
28:38-42; 29:23	The land itself will remain desolate
28:63-67; 32:26	Israel will be scattered among the nations
28:62	The time will come when Israel will be "few in number"
28:44-45	Though punished, Israel will not be destroyed if she repents
28:40-41; 30:1-2	Israel will repent in her tribulation
30:3-10	Israel will be gathered from the nations and brought back to her divinely given land[16]

Exodus 23 and Leviticus 26 present similar material as that found above. Leviticus 26 evidences a striking similarity with that of Deuteronomy 28–30, except Leviticus 26 presents the cursings (26:14-39) within the framework of five progressive stages to the covenantal curse. Each stage was to increase by a factor of seven (26:18,21,24,28), resulting in the fifth stage, which would be devastation and deportation from the land. However, the chapter ends with hope that if the people repented of their sin while in exile, they would be returned to the land and receive blessing (26:40-46). There are many significant parallels between Leviticus 26 and Deuteronomy 28–30.

Within Deuteronomy 28–30 we see a specific reference to the Tribulation: "The LORD your God will inflict all these curses [chap. 28] on your enemies and on those who hate you, who persecuted you" (Deuteronomy 30:7). Moses tells us that the time of tribulation will include among its purposes a time of retribution to the Gentiles for their ill treatment of the Jews. This certainly did not take place at all during either the A.D. 70 destruction of Jerusalem or at any time in history up to today. Thus we are beginning to find that the Bible does not regard the Tribulation as a time of punishment for the Jews, as preterists insist. Instead, it is a time of preparation for the Jews leading to their conversion and deliverance. This time will include the purging of non-elect Israel: "I will bring you into the bond of the covenant; and I will purge from you the rebels and those who transgress against Me" (Ezekiel 20:37-38). But elect Israel will be protected and delivered through the Tribulation (cf. Zechariah 13:8-9; Matthew 24:31; Romans 10:13-15).

It appears to be shaping up that while the A.D. 70 incident was indeed a prophesied event, it is not the same as the Tribulation. Harton concludes, "Inasmuch as Deuteronomy 28–30 is merely a restatement and amplification of this same promise in Deuteronomy 4, it may be concluded that Deuteronomy 28:15-68 will have an eschatological fulfillment."[17]

After enumerating the relatively short list of blessings that God would bestow upon Israel in the land (Deuteronomy 28:1-14), Moses commences to enumerate the much longer list of curses God would inflict upon His people should they disobey (Deuteronomy 28:15-68). The Lord would start inflicting the nation with mild curses at the inception of disobedience and gradually turn up the heat as insubordination persisted. The most severe chastisement the Lord would inflict upon His wayward people would be expulsion from their land, mediated through the agency of a foreign invader (Deuteronomy 28:49-68). The Lord's logic is something along the line that if Israel did not want to obediently serve Him in their own land, then they could go and serve other gods outside the land (Deuteronomy 28:47-48).

Interestingly Deuteronomy 28:49-68 mentions two specific instances of removal from the land. The first reference is clearly to the Babylonian captivity, which takes place in the sixth century B.C. (Deuteronomy 28:49-57). For example, verse 49 speaks of "a nation" that the Lord would bring against Israel in judgment. This is followed by a second statement of dispersion (verse 64), which says, "Moreover, the LORD will scatter you among all peoples, from one end of the earth to the other end of the earth." This was undoubtedly fulfilled by the Romans when they destroyed Jerusalem in A.D. 70. Luke 21:24, which speaks of the A.D. 70 Roman destruction of Jerusalem, says that the Jewish people "will be led captive into all the nations," a statement that reflects the language of Deuteronomy 28:64. Thus we see two different instances of the judgment of God's covenantal curse being worked out in history. But neither of them is the Tribulation.

We have seen thus far, from our prophetic road map, that Deuteronomy 28 has predicted two different instances when the ultimate covenant curse of expulsion from the land will be applied to national Israel. However, we have also noted that Deuteronomy 28–30 indicates that the Tribulation will come after Israel has been regathered back into the land and Jerusalem; then God will bring to pass the Tribulation. Thus, because the second covenantal dispersion in A.D. 70 by the Romans led to Israel's scattering among the nations, that could not have been the Tribulation, which is to take place *after* a worldwide regathering. This makes the Tribulation a future event and supports the futurist interpretation of prophecy in general.

The Prophets: A Continuing Pattern

As we move progressively through the Bible, from the Pentateuch to the prophets, we find that the role of the prophets is similar to modern ambassadors who represent their government's positions and policy. The prophets provide divine commentary and rebuke to the nation on behalf of God, but always in terms of how the people measure up to their Mosaic covenantal responsibilities. For example, Isaiah the prophet is called up to the throne room of God for commissioning and consultations before he brings God's indictment against the nation for her disobedience (Isaiah 6). Following the template of the Lord's preordained pattern for Israel's history (as stated in Deuteronomy), the prophets speak about covenantal disobedience (which they document with many specific examples) and the resulting curse (ultimately involving expulsion from the land). But then they always include a future hope. This is often preceded with the Deuteronomic tribulation, which gives rise to Israel's obedience and results in her ultimate blessing.

The Scenario

By the time of the exilic and post-exilic prophets, all hope that the nation will accomplish her destiny through corporate obedience has been abandoned. The hope for the nation, as well as for the entire Gentile world, is focused on the performance of a single individual—the *Messiah*. This prophetically prepares the nation for the first appearance of Messiah in the person of Jesus of Nazareth, whom the nation rejected, as she had the prophets who had come before. Thus, Jesus and the New Testament writers follow the Mosaic and prophetic pattern of documenting specific violations of Israel's covenant (see, for example, Matthew 21–23), and this provides the basis not for the Tribulation, but for expulsion from the land and scattering among the nations. Thus, the ultimate rejection of God's Son Himself led to a more severe application of the ultimate curse upon the nation than she had experienced during her first expulsion in the sixth century B.C. under the Babylonians.

Just as Israel was regathered after the Babylonian captivity and returned to the land, so will she be regathered from her A.D. 70 Diaspora among the nations. However, this time she will be regathered in preparation for a seven-year period we know as the Tribulation, which will serve to prepare her for conversion and ultimate covenantal blessing. Such a scenario is supported by an examination of passages from the Old Testament prophets that expand upon—but do not contradict—the Mosaic prophecy of the Tribulation.

The Terms

The Bible uses different terminology when speaking of the Tribulation. Various descriptions are needed because there are a multiplicity of aspects and purposes for the Tribulation. J. Randall Price has identified 22 terms and expressions used by the Old Testament writers to describe the Tribulation, as noted in the chart on the following page.[18]

With this data as our guide, let's examine the major terms and passages relating to the Tribulation so we can gather a composite of what the Old Testament writers expected the Tribulation to be like. This profile will also provide a framework for examining the New Testament passages, which often are the basis for debate over the timing of the Tribulation.

"Tribulation" or "Trouble"

The prophets build up the Mosaic introduction of the concept of "tribulation" from Deuteronomy 4:30. They use this term to refer to the future time of great distress at least four times in three passages. If we take these passages chronologically, the first one is Jeremiah 30:7, which deals with the well-known "time of Jacob's trouble" (KJV). Notice the following observations from verses 1-11 about the "Day of Jacob's Trouble":

- It will be a time of restored fortunes for Israel and Judah (30:3)

- It will be a time when Israel and Judah will be brought back into their land in order to possess it (30:3)

- It will be a time of distress for Jacob (i.e., national Israel) from which she will be delivered (30:7)

- It will be a unique time in history (30:8)

- It will be a time when Israel's national slavery is ended (30:8)

- It will lead to a time when Israel will serve the Lord and David their king (30:9)

- It will lead to a time when Israel will be regathered from afar and dwell in the land in quiet and ease with no one making her afraid (30:10)

- It will be a time when the nations where Israel was scattered will be destroyed (30:11)

- It will be a time when God will punish Jacob justly and destroy part of her (30:11)

The composite in this passage does not fit any past time of judgment upon Israel, but does fit the prophetic pattern of a future time when God's people will be returned from the nations to her land, put through the testings

Old Testament Tribulation Terms and Expressions	
Tribulation Term	**Old Testament Reference**
1. Day of the Lord	Isaiah 2:12; 13:6,9; Ezekiel 13:5; 30:3; Joel 1:15; 2:1,11,31; 3:14; Amos 5:18,20; Obadiah 15; Zephaniah 1:7,14; Zechariah 14:1
2. Great and terrible day of the Lord	Malachi 4:5
3. Trouble, tribulation	Deuteronomy 4:30; Zephaniah 1:16
4. Time/Day of trouble	Daniel 12:1; Zephaniah 1:15
5. Day of Jacob's trouble	Jeremiah 30:7
6. Birth pangs	Isaiah 21:3; 26:17-18; 66:7; Jeremiah 4:31; Micah 4:10 (cf. Jeremiah 30:6)
7. The day of calamity	Deuteronomy 32:35; Obadiah 12–14
8. Indignation	Isaiah 26:20; Daniel 11:36
9. The [Lord's] strange work	Isaiah 28:21
10. Overflowing scourge	Isaiah 28:15,18
11. Day of vengeance	Isaiah 34:8a; 35:4a; 61:2b; 63:4a
12. Day of wrath	Zephaniah 1:15
13. Day of the Lord's wrath	Zephaniah 1:18
14. Day of distress	Zephaniah 1:15
15. Day of destruction	Zephaniah 1:15
16. Day of desolation	Zephaniah 1:15
17. Day of darkness and gloom	Joel 2:2; Amos 5:18,20; Zephaniah 1:15
18. Day of clouds and thick darkness	Joel 2:2; Zephaniah 1:15
19. Day of trumpet and alarm	Zephaniah 1:16
20. Day of the Lord's anger	Zephaniah 2:2-3
21. [Day of] destruction, ruin, from the Almighty	Joel 1:15
22. The fire of His jealousy	Zephaniah 1:18

of the Tribulation, and rescued from that time of distress as the Lord judges the nations. This then leads to the Israelites' time of national obedience and blessing. This scenario describes the Tribulation, and thus it is yet future.

Daniel 12:1-2 provides us with another important Tribulation passage. It reads as follows:

> Now at that time Michael, the great prince who stands guard over the sons of your people, will arise. And there will be a time of distress such as never occurred since there was a nation until that time; and at that time your people, everyone who is found written in the book, will be rescued. Many of those who sleep in the dust of the ground will awake, these to everlasting life, but the others to disgrace and everlasting contempt.

This Tribulation passage includes the following elements:

- "Now at that time" refers back to the previous section (11:36-45), which is descriptive of many of Antichrist's activities during the Tribulation (12:1)
- It will be a time when the archangel Michael "will arise," indicating that he will defend Israel against her enemies (12:1)
- It will be a time of distress such as has never occurred in national history up to that point (verse 1)
- It will be a time in which all elect Israelites will be rescued (verse 1)
- It will be a time followed by the resurrection of saved and unsaved Israelites (verse 2)

Once again, we have a picture of national Israel during the time of greatest distress and persecution from her enemies. During this yet unfulfilled time period, God (through angelic intervention) will intervene and rescue His elect nation (Matthew 24:31). This fits the pattern of a future tribulation and does not correlate with the A.D. 70 judgment of Israel.

Zephaniah 1:14-18, the final Old Testament passage we want to examine, heaps together just about every term in the Bible that is used to describe and designate the Tribulation. More than half of the Old Testament Tribulation terms noted in the chart on page 412 are found in Zephaniah 1:14-18. Interestingly, the emphasis in this passage is upon the Lord's judgment of the nations, when "all the earth will be devoured...all the inhabitants of the earth" (verse 18). This passage teaches us that during the Tribulation the Lord will judge the nations.

"Day of the Lord"

The "day of the Lord" is the most widely used term in the Old Testament describing the time we call the Tribulation. Paul Benware summarizes the activities of the "day of the Lord" as a time when "the Lord will intervene in human history to judge the nations, discipline Israel, and establish His rule in the Messianic kingdom."[19] Once again we see a recurring feature in the day of the Lord that we have seen in other Tribulation descriptions—namely, the Lord's defense of Israel against the nations. This is especially clear in Zechariah 14:1-8. "I will gather all the nations against Jerusalem to battle" (verse 2). "Then the LORD will go forth and fight against those nations, as when He fights on a day of battle" (verse 3). This hardly fits the A.D. 70 event or any historical possibility. Rather, it awaits future fulfillment.

Daniel: The Seventieth Week

Daniel's 70 weeks (prophesied in Daniel 9:24-27) provides the framework within which the Tribulation (or the seventieth week) occurs.[20] And the seven-year period of Daniel's seventieth week provides the time span or length of the Tribulation. A graphic presentation of the 70 weeks assists greatly in helping us to understand this intricate prophecy (see chart on page 321 in chapter 13).

The seventieth week of Daniel is the basis for our understanding that the future Tribulation will be seven years in length. The length of this period is confirmed in Revelation, where we find references to two three-and-one-half-year periods. The ministry of the two witnesses occurs during the first three-and-a-half years (Revelation 11:3), while other Tribulation events are said to occur during the second half of the seven years (Revelation 12:6; 13:5). Since the first 69 weeks were fulfilled literally in history, it follows that the final week must be fulfilled in the same way. Any attempt to find a literal fulfillment of the final seven years of Daniel's prophecy requires a gap of time between the sixty-ninth and seventieth weeks. This provides the basis for the final week of Daniel's prophecy to be fulfilled literally in the future (as explained in chapter 12).

Zechariah: Pointing to the Future

Zechariah was one of the final contributions to the Old Testament canon. This book should prove especially helpful in determining the timing of the Tribulation because it focuses not only on the nation of Israel, but also provides a prophetic focus on Jerusalem. Chapters 12–14 include details that I believe are descriptive of a future time of tribulation, while preterists believe these details were fulfilled in the A.D. 70 destruction of Jerusalem. Support for the futurist understanding of Zechariah 12–14 is explained in chapter 11 in this book.

Zechariah 14 describes a picture consistent with a futurist interpretation of these events: 1) The Tribulation ends with the second coming of Jesus to Jerusalem to rescue his repentant people Israel; 2) the coming of the Lord does not result in judgment upon Israel through the surrounding armies; rather, it leads to a divine judgment of the nations and rescue of Israel. This is just the opposite of what happened in the first century; 3) after the second coming, the millennium begins, during which Israel is blessed nationally; and 4) Israel's reception of Jesus as her Messiah results in worldwide blessings to all the nations of the world.

Despite the above facts, preterist Ken Gentry insists, "The siege of Jerusalem described in Zechariah 14:1-2 has to do with the A.D. 70 devastation of Jerusalem....Yet the Lord defends those who are truly His people, insuring their escape from the besieged city (vv. 3-4)." [21] While it is certainly true that the Lord defends His people in this passage, the point of Zechariah 14 is that the whole nation has become His people, not just a minority, as in A.D. 70. The text in Zechariah 14:3 makes it clear the Lord is not only defending His people, but that "the LORD will go forth and fight against those nations, as when He fights on a day of battle." When did the Lord fight against and defeat the Roman army in A.D. 70? Preterists teach rightly that the A.D. 70 event was a time when God used the Romans, as He had done previously with the Babylonians, to bring judgment upon national Israel. However, Gentry's tortured interpretation of Zechariah 14:1-2, does not fit the broad features of the passage, let alone the details. Note further what Zechariah 14:12,14 prophesizes:

> Now this will be the plague with which the LORD will strike all the peoples who have gone to war against Jerusalem; their flesh will rot while they stand on their feet, and their eyes will rot in their sockets, and their tongue will rot in their mouth....Judah also will fight at Jerusalem; and the wealth of all the surrounding nations will be gathered, gold and silver and garments in great abundance.

When in A.D. 70 did the Romans have their flesh rot while they stood on their feet, and their eyes rot in their sockets, and their tongue rot in their mouth? Did Josephus describe such an event? When, as a result of the siege in A.D. 70, did the wealth of all the surrounding nations stream into Jerusalem in great abundance? Of course, the obvious answer is that it *did not happen.* This further shows that if we are to fit the A.D. 70 destruction of Jerusalem into biblical prophecy—and we must—then it fits as the second prophesied dispersion of the Jewish people for disobedience to the Mosaic Covenant and their rejection of the Messiahship of Jesus as predicted in Deuteronomy 28:64-68 and reiterated by Jesus in the New Testament (Matthew 23:37-39; Luke 21:24). But the A.D. 70 event was not the Tribulation predicted early and often throughout the Old Testament. The Tribulation awaits a future time of fulfillment.

The New Testament

The New Testament does not contradict the prophetic road map present in the Old Testament. Instead, it develops and advances the notion that the Tribulation and other prophetic events are still future to our day. The New Testament expands upon the two major events that were prophesied in the Old Testament, which are the Tribulation and the A.D. 70 judgment of God upon Israel for disobedience and rejection of the messiahship of Jesus. Preterists want to see the two prophecies as a single event, yet this is impossible because there is a major difference between them. That difference consists of the fact that it is impossible for God to be both judging and rescuing the nation of Israel at the same time. He clearly judged in the first century (Luke 21:20-24) and will rescue His repentant people in the future (Matthew 24:31; Luke 21:28).

Preterists are right to note that the Roman siege and eventual destruction of Jerusalem and the Second Temple in A.D. 70 was a major event in biblical history. However, it was neither the second coming of Christ nor a coming of Christ. It was an event that can be paralleled with the Babylonian destruction of Jerusalem in 586 B.C.

The ministry of Christ, leading up to His crucifixion, is similar to that of many Old Testament prophets. Jesus documents the offenses of national Israel that would lead to the A.D. 70 judgment and dispersion at the hand of the Romans. Jesus' teaching in Matthew 21–23, in many senses, sounds like proclamations from Isaiah and Jeremiah because in Matthew, our Lord demonstrates Israel's violation of specific stipulations found in the governing Mosaic Covenant. Thus, Israel's ultimate violation—the rejection of the messiahship of Jesus—was met with the covenantal curse of Leviticus 26:27-39 and, specifically, Deuteronomy 28:64-68. Israel was under the curse because of her failure to "recognize the time of [her] visitation" (Luke 19:44) from Jesus the Messiah.

In a style similar to Jeremiah in Lamentations, Jesus weeps over the impending judgment (A.D. 70) destined for Jerusalem in Matthew 23:37-39: "Jerusalem, Jerusalem, who kills the prophets and stones those who are sent to her! How often I wanted to gather your children together, the way a hen gathers her chicks under her wings, and you were unwilling. Behold, your house is being left to you desolate! For I say to you, from now on you will not see Me until you say, 'Blessed is He who comes in the name of the Lord!' "

Also, in characteristically Old Testament prophetic style, Jesus does not pronounce an impending judgment without at the same time holding forth an ultimate hope for the people of Israel. The little word "until" breaks the pessimism of judgment and holds forth the assurance that one day Israel will bless the presence of Jesus. This is not stated as a mere theoretical possibility, but is just as certain to take place as was the nation's impending judgment that came to pass in A.D. 70. Thus, once again we see the recurring theme of judgment followed by restoration—an ultimate restoration related to the end times.

J. Randall Price has argued that God expresses His cursing for disobedience and blessing for obedience in relation to His people Israel within a pattern of "desecration/restoration," especially in relation to the Temple, God's visible symbol of His dwelling in favor with His people.[22] Thus, the A.D. 70 desecration is certainly an important event in the flow of history, but this will be followed by an eventual restoration of Israel to a future place of blessing. This explains the important transitional role of the word "until" at the end of a major judgment passage.

Further, the book of Hebrews is to be understood as containing warnings to Israel upon the eve of God's judgment in the first century. This is an epistle in the New Testament canon that revolves around the judgment of A.D. 70, yet preterists do not deal with this portion of Scripture often in their presentations. Hebrews 10:25, for example, which tells the recipients of Hebrews to be, "not forsaking our own assembling together, as is the habit of some, but encouraging one another; and all the more as you see the day drawing near." That is a reference to the A.D. 70 destruction of the Temple.

A FUTURIST CONCLUSION

A futurist understanding of the Tribulation and Bible prophecy in general is also the only view that makes sense of the Old Testament pattern of Bible prophecy. This pattern is reinforced in the New Testament by a literal—and thus futurist—interpretation. The future conversion of the Jewish people and God's rescue of them did not take place in A.D. 70, thus requiring both to be future events. The fact that Israel became a state in 1948 is historical verification that God is preparing the world for the coming Tribulation. This is the kind of development that, for almost 2,000 years, futurists have taught would precede the beginning of the seven-year Tribulation. The stage is set, and soon our Lord will bring to pass in history the events of a literal

Tribulation that will no doubt lay to rest forever the notion that the Tribulation is past. John Walvoord says, "Of the many peculiar phenomena which characterize the present generation, few events can claim equal significance as far as Biblical prophecy is concerned with that of the return of Israel to their land. It constitutes a preparation for the end of the age, the setting for the coming of the Lord for His church, and the fulfillment of Israel's prophetic destiny." [23]

Chapter 17

SOME PRACTICAL DANGERS OF PRETERISM

THOMAS ICE

The heart and soul of preterism is built around the belief that the Tribulation has already occurred in the past through events surrounding the Roman conquest and destruction of Jerusalem in A.D. 70. No doubt this was a pivotal event of great importance to a proper understanding of the Bible, which all too many believers today underestimate. All doctrinal teachings have practical implications on our lives, and the doctrine of preterism can have a tremendous impact upon how one should live. For example, many preterists teach we are now living in the new heavens and new earth of Revelation 21–22, which tells us that in that setting, there are no more tears and no more pain. But as we know, that's not descriptive of what is happening around us today. Also, while the main focus of preterism is their interpretation of prophecies concerning the Tribulation, their deviant perspective has a ripple effect that distorts their prespective of other time periods as well, not just the Tribulation period.

DANGERS OF DOCTRINAL ERROR

All doctrine has practical implications. What are the practical implications of those who hold to the view that most (in some cases, all) Bible prophecy has already been fulfilled? This is the question we will explore now.

When a person teaches false doctrine, at least two things occur. First, when someone presents false doctrine, he is advocating something the Bible does not teach. Preterism teaches that Christ returned in A.D. 70, which, of course, He did not. Second, the truth of a misinterpreted text ends up not being understood. Preterism either teaches no future second coming, or it shrinks to near extinction the truth of our blessed hope (see Titus 2:13). Even if there were not practical implications—there are in the case of preterism—the doctrinal error is great. Preterism greatly distorts the culmination of God's plan for history.

The Bible teaches in protology that history began in a garden (Genesis), and through eschatology that it comes to an end in a city (Revelation). If preterism is true—especially full preterism—then we are already at the end of history and don't really know where it is headed. In fact, even partial preterist Kenneth Gentry says of Revelation 21–22 that "the new creation begins in the first century," and that "my understanding of this antithesis is that the new Jerusalem is replacing the old Jerusalem. The coming of the new Jerusalem down from heaven (chaps. 21–22) logically should follow soon upon the destruction of the old Jerusalem on the earth (Revelation 6–11, 14–19), rather than waiting thousands of years."[1]

Thus, Gentry actually believes we are in some way in the new heavens and new earth of Revelation 21–22. If this is true, then we all must be living in the ghetto side of the New Jerusalem. But there is no ghetto in the New Jerusalem. Such a false teaching reminds one of the Hindu belief that says that current reality is "Maya"—a mere illusion—especially the current existence of evil.[2] The logic of the preterist position leads one to delusional views of present reality.

Fortunately, most preterists do not follow the logic of their position, and they do act as if evil is still present in this world. However, in the nineteenth century there was a preterist named John Humphrey Noyes (1811–86) who founded a perfectionist society called the Oneida Community in the state of New York. This was a group of people where everyone was married to everyone else in the community, in a "complex marriage."[3] While there were a number of perfectionist communities in the early nineteenth century, Noyes was unique as to why he believed in sinless perfection. His views were based on his preterist beliefs, and "in 1839 he proclaimed that Jesus had returned to earth in A.D. 70."[4] Richard Kyle notes: "The basis of Noyes's perfectionism resided in his postulation that Christ's second coming had occurred in A.D. 70. When the Romans destroyed the temple in Jerusalem, Christ had appeared spiritually to his apostles. Thus, liberation or redemption from sin was an accomplished fact for the followers of Jesus, who were potentially perfect beings."[5]

Many bizarre possibilities become viable when people begin to believe and think through the implications of preterism. This potential has already surfaced in the past through deviant groups like the Oneida Community.

RESULTS OF PRETERIST THINKING

Regarding the New Heavens and New Earth

"The overwhelming majority of the eschatological events prophesied in the Book of Revelation have already been fulfilled," declares preterist Gary North.[6] Since subjects relating to prophecy dominate virtually every page of the New Testament, this would logically mean, for the preterist, that most of the New Testament does not refer directly to the church today. Most of the New Testament was written to tell believers how to live between the two comings of Christ, so it makes a huge difference if one interprets Christ's coming as a past or future event. If preterism is true, then the New Testament was written primarily to believers who lived during the 40-year period between the death of Christ and the destruction of Jerusalem in A.D. 70. Therefore, virtually no part of the New Testament applies to believers today, according to preterist logic. There is no canon that applies directly to believers during the current church age.

Not only does Gentry believe that the Tribulation is a past event, he actually believes that current history is identified as the new heavens and new earth of Revelation 21–22 and 2 Peter 3:10-13.[7] This is a common preterist viewpoint. Talk about lowering one's expectations! Gentry provides four major reasons why "the new creation begins in the first century."[8] It stretches credulity to think of the implications of such a conclusion. If we are currently living in any way in the new heavens and new earth, then this means the following:

- The 1,000 years and the new heavens and earth must be equated (cf. Revelation 20:1-9 with 21–22)

- Satan has been removed from any more influence in history (20:10)

- There is no longer any sea (21:1)

- There is no longer any death, crying, or pain (21:4)

- All things have been made new (21:1)

- There is no longer any need for the sun or the moon (21:23)

- There is no longer any night (21:25)

- There is no longer any thing unclean, nor anyone practicing abomination and lying (21:27)

- There is no longer any curse (22:3)

- Believers are now able to see the Father's face (22:4)

- There is no longer any sun (22:5)

If Revelation 21–22 is a description of the state in which we are now living, then it also renders most of the New Testament obsolete and impractical because it relates to believers and how they should live between Christ's two comings. The logic of the preterist position leads to this conclusion, even though many preterists do not think this way in practice. They don't, but according to their theology, they should! They must seperate preterist theory from practice, since they cannot implement in practice preterist theory.

Regarding Commands in the Epistles

Many preterists believe that passages such as Titus 2:13 refer to the coming of Christ in A.D. 70.[9] This means that the hope of the second coming applied only to those Christians living between the time the epistle was written and the destruction of Jerusalem, namely, A.D. 65–70. It's interesting to note that just one verse earlier—in Titus 2:12—Paul said that Christ's first coming (mentioned in verse 11) has instructed us "to deny ungodliness and worldly desires and to live sensibly, righteously and godly in the present age." And as we live through "this present age," we are to be "looking for the blessed hope and the appearing of the glory of our great God and Savior, Christ Jesus" (Titus 2:13).

If Titus 2:13 was fulfilled in A.D. 70 with Christ's return, then the "present age" in verse 12 would have ended when verse 13 was fulfilled. Therefore, the entire admonition in verse 12 was applicable only to Christians up until A.D. 70. This means the instruction "to deny ungodliness and worldly desires and to live sensibly, righteously and godly in the present age" does not apply to our current age, but to the past age that ended in A.D. 70 when "the appearing of the glory of our great God and Savior, Christ Jesus" was manifested in the destruction of Jerusalem. This (sadly) is one of the practical implications of the preterist view, as applied to this passage and to most of the imperatives relating to the Christian life as found in the New Testament.

The preterist viewpoint affects the practical application of the Christian life in two major ways, depending on whether Titus 2:13 is a fulfilled prophecy or a future event. First, if this is a fulfilled prophecy, the *motivation* of the blessed hope as it relates to living a godly life in "the present age " (2:12) would not apply to believers today. Second, the *ethical* admonitions of 2:12 would not apply to believers today, for the basis for compliance would have been fulfilled in A.D. 70.

The clear implication of preterist thinking is that the teachings in Titus no longer relate to the age in which we live. Instead, they were relevant for only three or four years, as Paul wrote Titus around A.D. 65. There is no way that a preterist can use this or similar passages as doctrine, reproof, correction, and training in righteousness for believers, who are said to be living in the new heavens and new earth. Yet, hypocritically, preterists regularly use and apply these passages in a way that practically denies their theoretical belief that Jesus returned in A.D. 70.

The story of Pandora's box is an apt illustration of how one act can have a widespread and multiplying effect upon many other issues. The belief that there "are no major eschatological discontinuities ahead of us except the conversion of the Jews (Rom. 11) and the final judgment (Revelation 20)"[10] has great impact upon New Testament prophecy, especially as found in the epistles. It is clear that adhering to the preterist interpretation of prophecy virtually wipes out the *direct* application of the teaching of the epistles to our current age. Just as the Law of Moses was given by God to Israel to be the focus of their dispensation, so the New Testament epistles are our focus, giving vision and direction to the church during "this present age."

Regarding the Work of Satan

The preterist view relating to the current work of Satan and his demons should reflect their theology on the subject. According to the preterist view, Satan is currently bound (Revelation 20:2-3) and crushed (Romans 16:20). The enemy was not just defeated *de jure* (legally) at the cross, but has been crushed *de facto* (in fact). Therefore, there is no external spiritual roadblock prohibiting Christians from reigning and ruling now.

On the other hand, if the binding and crushing of Satan and his company are still future, then certain commands in the epistles make sense in this present age—commands such as: "Resist the devil and he will flee from you" (James 4:7). "Be of sober spirit, be on the alert. Your adversary, the devil, prowls about like a roaring lion, seeking someone to devour. But resist him, firm in your faith, knowing that the same experiences of suffering are being accomplished by your brethren who are in the world" (1 Peter 5:8-9). "Be angry, and yet do not sin; do not let the sun go down on your anger, and do not give the devil an opportunity" (Ephesians 4:26-27). "Our struggle is not against flesh and blood, but against the rulers, against the powers, against the world forces of this darkness, against the spiritual forces of wickedness in the heavenly places" (Ephesians 6:12).

These instructions are clearly intended for our age, for we are not yet in the new heavens and new earth. If Satan has been bound and crushed (as the preterist interpretation insists), then advocates of this view are unfaithful to their understanding of Scripture when (as they often do) they just cite the above passages to the Christian life and apply them to today. A crushed and bound enemy does not prowl or wage war. This becomes crystal clear when one realizes that Satan resumes his war with God only after he has been "released from his prison" (Revelation 20:7).

If preterism is true, then it should alter much of what we understand the Bible to be saying about the Christian life. Just think: No more suffering! If there is no more suffering, then there is no need for endurance. There is also no need for the sanctification process, which involves more suffering, endurance, faith, and hope. There's also no hope, for Christ has already returned in A.D. 70 and ushered in a new day. We no longer need to be concerned about the apostasy of the church, as well as pain, suffering, or death. But because all these things are still with us, preterism must be incorrect.

Regarding the Sufferings of This Present Time

According to the Bible, the new heavens and new earth are to be marked by peace and rest for God's people, and the era preceding this time will be one of suffering and struggle. Again, if the preterist interpretation is correct, then the New Testament instructions related to suffering had relevance to believers only until A.D. 70, as once Christ returned, He would usher in a time of peace.

Gary DeMar argues that the phrase "end of the age" is "a covenantal phrase."[11] Fellow preterist David Chilton agrees and says, "The fact is that *every* time Scripture uses the term 'last days' (and similar expressions) it means, not the end of the physical universe, but the period from A.D. 30 to A.D. 70—the period during which the Apostles were preaching and writing, the 'last days' of Old Covenant Israel."[12]

Continuing the logic of DeMar and Chilton, that "the expression 'end of the age' refers to the end of the 'Jewish age,'"[13] would mean that this New Testament expression was fulfilled in A.D. 70. Keep in mind that in Matthew 28:20, Christ said, "I am with you always, even to the end of the age." Thus, according to preterist logic, the "end of the age" of which Christ spoke in His Great Commission was culminated in A.D. 70. The practical implication, then, is that Christ is no longer with us as we carry out His commission. Even though DeMar does not comment on this implication in his writing, nevertheless, that is the implication of his position. This illustrates my point that preterists are not able to live out in practice what their position teaches in theory. Interestingly, even though partial preterist DeMar ignores this implication, full preterists such as J. Stuart Russell and Don Preston recognize an A.D. 70 fulfillment for Jesus' "end of the age" statement in Matthew 28:20.[14]

The reality that Christians will have to endure through unjust suffering is a major theme in the epistles, and God uses this suffering to produce Christlike character in us (Hebrews 12:1-17). Peter notes, "For this [unjust suffering] finds favor, if for the sake of conscience toward God a person bears up under sorrows when suffering unjustly....But if when you do what is right and suffer for it you patiently endure it, this finds favor with God" (1 Peter 2:19-

20). Revelation 3:21 promises a future reward of co-rulership with Christ to believers who have remained faithful and loyal to Christ during this present age of humiliation (see also 2:25-28). Not only does Revelation 3:21 promise a future rule with Christ, but it also makes a distinction between Christ's future kingdom and the Father's current rule: "He who overcomes, I will grant to him to sit down with Me on My throne, as I also overcame and sat down with My Father on His throne." These passages do not make sense and certainly does not apply to today if we are in the new heavens and new earth.

Regarding Apostasy

"If preterism is true," says Gary North, "then most of the prophesied negative sanctions in history are over."[15] "Negative sanctions," in North's vocabulary, means apostasy. While preterists say apostasy is behind us, futurists say apostasy lies ahead, with the church age becoming increasingly apostate, culminating with "the Great Apostasy" during the Tribulation. Chilton says, "The 'Great Apostasy' happened in the first century. We therefore have no Biblical warrant to expect increasing apostasy as history progresses; instead, we should expect the increasing Christianization of the world."[16]

If preterists are right, then once again Christians in general have understood the Bible wrong for the last couple thousand years. For example, consider Paul's warning that "in the last days difficult times will come" (2 Timothy 3:1). The "last days" likely refers to either the whole current church age, or to the final portion of the current church age. Either way, it is a reference to the period of time before the final phase of history, which preterists say we are not in. Paul goes on to describe how "the last days" will be characterized by men who "will be lovers of self...rather than lovers of God" (3:2,4). The general course of "the last days" is described as a time when "all who desire to live godly in Christ Jesus will be persecuted. But evil men and impostors will proceed from bad to worse, deceiving and being deceived" (3:12-13). Therefore, if "the last days" have already come and gone, we should expect that the persecution of the godly should be absent and "evil men and impostors" should not "proceed from bad to worse." According to preterism, that may have happened in the days leading up to A.D. 70, but not after that time.

In reality, the evidence around us points to increasing apostasy, not decreasing. Doctrinal error is as prevalent as it has ever been. It is clear, then, that the preterist interpretation of New Testament prophecy is far removed from what the Bible teaches because it is impossible to apply the implications of their teachings in our current age. In fact, given the condition of this world, preterists have to function as futurists. They have to act as though

Satan is not bound and as if apostasy is still a serious problem within the church. They are operational futurists.

Regarding the Possibility of Heterodoxy

An even more serious problem is that more and more partial preterists have come to believe that all Bible prophecies have already been fulfilled. For instance, extreme preterists believe all last-days prophecies were fulfilled in A.D. 70 and that there is no future coming of Christ. Allegedly, Christ's second coming occurred sometime in A.D. 70.

Such a position not only denies the hope of the second advent, but also rules out any future resurrection of the saints. Extreme preterists believe that whatever the resurrection was, it occurred in the first century. Such a view is heretical. Even partial preterist Gentry admits that, "hyper-preterism is heterodox. It is outside of the creedal orthodoxy of Christianity. No creed allows any Second Advent in A.D. 70. No creed allows any other type of resurrection than a bodily one."[17] R. C. Sproul adds, "I share Gentry's concerns about full preterism, particularly on such issues as the consummation of the kingdom and the resurrection of the dead."[18]

Yet it seems that more and more preterists are becoming hyperpreterists. Gentry's moderate preterism may satisfy him and others in terms of having a systematic answer to dispensational futurism, but their views open the door for people to move into the heretical position of hyper-preterism. Within Gentry's own reconstructionist circle we have already seen the late David Chilton take this route.[19] Walt Hibbard, the former owner of Great Christian Books (previously known as Puritan and Reformed Book Company), once a reconstructionist, moved from partial to full preterism.[20] More are following in their footsteps. Sproul says, "Gentry has been debating on two fronts. On the one side he is engaging Dispensationalism with its futurism. Against them he argues for a limited preterism with reference to specific prophecies that he believes were fulfilled in A.D. 70. On the other side he is engaging full preterists. Against them Gentry stresses events that he believes have not been fulfilled."[21]

Once a person accepts the basic tenets of preterism, it is hard to stop and resist the appeal to preterize all Bible prophecy. Preterism tends to start with its different interpretation of the phrase "this generation" in Matthew 24:34, but usually does not rest until one's perspective of the entire Bible has been infected.

What's more, there is no such thing as extreme futurism. Applied futurism does not lead to heresy. Yet the same cannot be said of preterism. Partial preterists warn about the dangers of taking their system too far, as noted earlier. That alone should serve as a warning to us about the dangers of interpreting the Bible as preterists do.

Regarding No Future for National Israel

Preterists advocate the replacement of Old Testament Israel with the church often called the "New Israel." This sytem of theology is known as replacement theology. Preterists believe Israel does not have a future different than that of any other nation. "Although Israel will someday be restored to the true faith, the Bible does not tell of any future plan for Israel as a special nation,"[22] insists Chilton. He adds that "ethnic Israel was excommunicated for its apostasy and will never again be God's Kingdom."[23] Preterists believe that Christ already destroyed the Jewish state and that the church is the new nation that has replaced Israel. Gary DeMar and Peter Leithart say that, "in destroying Israel, Christ transferred the blessings of the kingdom from Israel to a new people, the church."[24] Ray Sutton, also a preterist, teaches that God permanently divorced Israel.[25] In the course of explaining the parables of Matthew 21 and 22, he says, "For the next several chapters, one section after another pronounces judgment and total discontinuity between God and Israel…total disinheritance."[26]

Gentry also follows lockstep in the preterist chant that Israel has no national future. In fact, Gentry teaches that the seven-sealed scroll of Revelation 6 "is God's divorce decree against his Old Testament wife for her spiritual adultery."[27] Gentry clearly teaches replacement theology when he says, "In his divorce of Israel God disestablishes her."[28] In fact, Gentry is so enamored with his divorce thesis that he says the title of his forthcoming commentary on Revelation will be *The Divorce of Israel: A Commentary on Revelation.*[29] But in the Bible, not only did God threaten to divorce Israel, He also made it is quite clear that He will remarry her in the future (Hosea 2:21–3:5; Zechariah 13:9).

There are many passages in the Bible that teach a national future for ethnic Israel as a result of the people's conversion to Jesus as Israel's Messiah. They include Leviticus 26:40-45; Deuteronomy 4:27-31; 30:1-6; Isaiah 2:2-3; 14:1-3; Jeremiah 23:5-6; 32:37-42; Ezekiel 36:10-11; 36:22-32; 39:25-29; Hosea 3:4-5; Amos 9:11-15; Micah 4:6-7; Zephaniah 3:14-15; Zechariah 8:2-3,7-8,13-15; 12:10; Romans 11:15,25-27. Notice what Isaiah 14:1-3 says about the future of national Israel—a passage that all must agree has not yet been literally fulfilled on behalf of the Jewish nation.

> When the LORD will have compassion on Jacob and again choose Israel, and settle them in their own land, then strangers will join them and attach themselves to the house of Jacob. The

peoples will take them along and bring them to their place, and the house of Israel will possess them as an inheritance in the land of the LORD as male servants and female servants; and they will take their captors captive and will rule over their oppressors. And it will be in the day when the LORD gives you rest from your pain and turmoil and harsh service in which you have been enslaved.

Preterists miss the fact that Israel's national unbelief is temporary, not permanent. They want to rush the program of God and usher us into the final phases of history before God is ready. Their impatience leads to a major distortion of what Scripture has to say.

Acts 15:16 quotes God's Old Testament promise concerning the restoration of national Israel: "After these things I will return, and I will rebuild the tabernacle of David which has fallen, and I will rebuild its ruins, and I will restore it." This language fits the futurist expectation of God returning to deal with Israel after the church age is completed. It is during the Tribulation period and the millennium that Acts 15:16 will be fulfilled. God's unconditional promises to Abraham and Israel will yet be fulfilled to Israel in the future, after the current church age is completed.

This is also the picture painted by Paul in Romans 11. He teaches that Israel's rejection of the Messiah led to the proclamation of the gospel to the Gentiles, even though God still maintains a remnant of elect Israel during this present age. God will restore Israel to a place of blessing after the church age is completed, and Romans 11 teaches that the salvation of Israel (the rebuilding of the Tabernacle of David) will result in even greater gospel blessing for the whole world: "Now if their [Israel's] transgression is riches for the world and their failure is riches for the Gentiles, how much more will their fulfillment be!" (Romans 11:12).

This is the point: Once Israel is restored to the place of blessing (called by James the rebuilding of the tabernacle of David), then the next phase of God's plan will unfold. That phase is the millennium, the time in which the nations will indeed be converted and ruled over by Christ. If Israel's disobedience led to the calling out of many Gentiles to be part of the Bride of Christ, think of what will happen when *Israel* is converted! That, in turn, will lead to mass conversion of the Gentile nations " 'so that the rest of mankind may seek the Lord, and all the Gentiles who are called by My name,' says the Lord, who makes these things known from of old" (Acts 15:17-18). As Romans 11:32 declares, "God has shut up all in disobedience so that He may show mercy to all." Preterists do not need to dismiss a future for national Israel.

BACK TO THE FUTURE

When Bible prophecy is taken literally, it leads to a proper understanding of God's plan for history and the individual believer. Such an understanding provides a great hope—indeed, a "blessed hope," that Christ's prophetic program for the church and Israel will yet provide a future we can look forward to with great anticipation. A futurist eschatology provides a fitting climax for history that began in a garden and concludes in a city—the New Jerusalem. Christ's church will be raptured before the Tribulation so that our Lord can complete His plan for His ancient people Israel. In fact, the modern restoration of national Israel is preparing the stage for the Tribulation, a time in which God will not judge, but rescue the Jews so that "all Israel will be saved" (Romans 11:26). No, the Tribulation and much of Bible prophecy is not past; rather, it is future. If it was fulfilled in the past, then we have no future.

BIBLIOGRAPHY

* Denotes preterist perspective

* Adams, Jay. *The Time Is at Hand*. Phillipsburg, NJ: Presbyterian and Reformed, 1966.

Allen, James. *Revelation: What the Bible Teaches*. Kilmarnock, Scotland: John Ritchie, LTD, 1997.

Armerding, Carl. *The Olivet Discourse of Matthew 24–25 and Other Studies*. Findlay, OH: Dunham Publishing Company, n.d.

* Bahnsen, Greg L. and Gentry, Kenneth L. *House Divided: The Break-Up of Dispensational Theology*. Tyler, TX: Institute for Christian Economics, 1989.

* Balyeat, Joseph R. *Babylon, The Great City of Revelation*. Servierville, TN: Onward Press, 1991.

Barker, S. Barker & Godfrey, W. Robert. *Theonomy: A Reformed Critique*. Grand Rapids, MI: Zondervan, 1990.

Beale, G. K. *The Book of Revelation*. Grand Rapids, MI: Eerdmans, 1999.

Beasley-Murray, G. R. *The Book of Revelation*. Grand Rapids, MI: Eerdmans, (1974), 1978.

* Beckwith, Isbon T. *The Apocalypse of John*. Grand Rapids, MI: Baker, (1919), 1979.

Blomberg, Craig L. *Matthew: The New American Commentary*. Nashville, TN: Broadman Press, 1992.

* Bray, John L. *Matthew 24 Fulfilled*. Lakeland, FL: John L. Bray Ministry, 1996.

Buck, D. D. *Our Lord's Great Prophecy, and Its Parallels Throughout the Bible, Harmonized and Expounded: Comprising a Review of the Common Figurative Theories of Interpretation, with a Particular Examination of the Principal Passages Relating to the Second Coming, Etc.* Nashville, TN: South Western Publishing House, 1857.

Bullinger, E. W. *Commentary on Revelation*. Grand Rapids, MI: Kregel, (1935), 1984.

Caird, G. B. *The Revelation of St. John the Divine*. New York: Harper & Row, 1966.

* Campbell, Roderick. *Israel and the New Covenant*. Philadelphia, PA: Presbyterian and Reformed, 1954.

Carson, D. A. "Matthew," in *The Expositor's Bible Commentary*, vol. 8. Edited by Grank E. Gaebelein. Grand Rapids, MI: Zondervan, 1984.

Case, Shirley Jackson. *The Revelation of John*. Chicago, IL: The University of Chicago Press, 1910.

* Charles, R. H. *A Critical and Exegetical Commentary on the Revelation of St. John*, 2 vols. Edinburgh: T. & T. Clark, 1920.

* ——— . *Lectures on the Apocalypse*. London: Oxford University Press, 1923.

* ——— . *Studies in the Apocalypse*. Edinburgh: T. & T. Clark, 1913.

* Chilton, David. *Paradise Restored: An Eschatology of Dominion*. Tyler, TX: Reconstruction Press, 1985.

* ——— . *The Days of Vengeance: An Exposition of the Book of Revelation*. Ft. Worth, TX: Dominion Press, 1987.

* ——— . *The Great Tribulation*. Ft. Worth, TX: Dominion Press, 1987.

* Clark, David S. *The Message from Patmos: A Postmillennial Commentary on the Book of Revelation*. Grand Rapids, MI: Baker, 1989.

Cohen, Gary G. *Understanding Revelation: A Chronology of the Apocalypse*. Collingswood, NJ: Christian Beacon Press, 1968.

Collins, Adela Yarbro. *Crisis and Catharisis: The Power of the Apocalypse*. Philadelphia, PA: The Westminster Press, 1984.

Collins, John J., McGinn, Bernard, and Stein, Stephen J., editors. *The Encyclopedia of Apocalypticism*, 3 vols. New York: Continuum, 2000.

Cooper, David L. *Future Events Revealed According to Matthew 24 and 25*. Los Angeles, CA: published by author, 1935.

——— . *An Exposition of the Book of Revelation*. Los Angeles, CA: Biblical Research Society, 1972.

Corsini, Eugenio. *The Apocalypse: The Perennial Revelation of Jesus Christ*. Translated and edited by Francis J. Moloney. Wilmington, DE: Michael Glazier, Inc., 1983.

Couch, Mal. *A Bible Handbook to Revelation*. Grand Rapids, MI: Kregel, 2001.

* DeMar, Gary. *The Debate over Christian Reconstruction*. Ft. Worth, TX: Dominion Press, 1988.

* ———. *Last Days Madness: The Folly of Trying to Predict When Christ Will Return*, 4th ed. Powder Springs, GA: American Vision, 1999.

* ———. *"You've Heard It Said": 15 Biblical Misconceptions That Render Christians Powerless*. Brentwood, TN: Wolgemuth & Hyatt, Publishers, 1991.

* ———. *End Times Fiction: A Biblical Consideration of The* Left Behind *Theology*. Nashville, TN: Thomas Nelson Publishers, 2001.

* DeMar, Gary & Leithart, Peter. *The Reduction of Christianity: Dave Hunt's Theology of Cultural Surrender*. Ft. Worth, TX: Dominion Press, 1988.

De Young, James Calvin. *Jerusalem in the New Testament: The Significance of the City in the History of Redemption and in Eschatology*. Amsterdam, H. H. Kok N.V. Kampen, 1960.

Easley, Kendell H. *Revelation*. Nashville, TN: Holman Reference, 1998.

Elliott, E. B. *Horae Apocalypticae; or A Commentary on the Apocalypse, Critical and Historical*. 4th ed., 4 vols., London: Seeleys, 1851.

Eusebius. *The Ecclesiastical History*. Translated by Frederick Cruse. Grand Rapids, MI: Baker, n.d.

———. *The Proof of the Gospel*. Edited and translated by W. J. Ferrar. Grand Rapids, MI: Baker, (1920), 1981.

* Farrar, F. W. *The Early Days of Christianity*. New York: Belford, Clarke & Company, 1882.

* Farrer, Austin. *A Rebirth of Images: The Making of St. John's Apocalypse*. Glasgow: University Press, 1949.

* ———. *The Revelation of St. John the Divine*. Oxford: At the Clarendon Press, 1964.

Fiorenza, Elisabeth Schüssler. *The Book of Revelation: Justice and Judgment*. Philadelphia, PA: Fortress Press, 1985.

Ford, J. Massyngberde. *Revelation: Introduction, Translation, and Commentary*. New York: Doubleday, 1975.

* France, R.T. *Matthew: The Tyndale New Testament Commentaries*. Grand Rapids, MI: Eerdmans, 1985.

Froom, LeRoy Edwin. *The Prophetic Faith of Our Fathers*, 4 vols. Washington, DC: Review and Herald, 1950.

Frost, Henry W. *Matthew Twenty-Four and the Revelation: An Analysis, Literal Translation and Exposition of Each*. New York: Oxford University Press, 1924.

* Frost, Samuel. M. *Misplaced Hope: The Origins of First and Second Century Eschatology*. Colorado Springs, CO: Bimillennial Press, 2002.

Fruchtenbaum, Arnold. *The Footsteps of the Messiah: A Study of the Sequence of Prophetic Events*. San Antonio, TX: Ariel Press, 1982.

———. *Israelology: The Missing Link in Systematic Theology*, rev. ed. Tustin, CA: Ariel Press, (1989), 1992.

Gaebelein, Arno C. *The Gospel of Matthew: An Exposition*. Neptune, NJ: Loizeaux Brothers, (1910), 1961.

Gaston, Lloyd. *No Stone on Another: Studies in the Significance of the Fall of Jerusalem in the Synoptic Gospels*. Leiden: E. J. Brill, 1970.

* Gentry, Kenneth, L. *The Beast of Revelation*. Powder Springs, GA: American Vision, (1989), 2002.

* ———. *Before Jerusalem Fell: Dating the Book of Revelation*. Atlanta, GA: American Vision, (1989), 1998.

* ———. *He Shall Have Dominion: A Postmillennial Eschatology*. Tyler, TX: Institute for Christian Economics, 1992.

* ———. *Perilous Times: A Study in Eschatological Evil*. Texarkana, AR: Covenant Media Press, 1999.

Govett, Robert. *How to Interpret the Apocalypse?* Miami Springs, FL: Conley & Schoettle, (1879), 1985.

———. *The Prophecy on Olivet*. Miami Springs, FL: Conley & Schoettle, (1881), 1985.

Grant, F. W. *The Revelation of John*. London: Hodder and Stoughton, 1889.

Gray, James R. *Prophecy on the Mount*. Chandler, AZ: Berean Advocate Ministries, 1991.

* Gregg, Steve. *Revelation, Four Views: A Parallel Commentary*. Nashville, TN: Thomas Nelson, 1997.

* Groh, Ivan. *Jesus Has Returned to Planet Earth*. Peterborough, NH: Inspirational Publications, 1984.

Gundry, Robert H. *Matthew: A Commentary on His Literary and Theological Art*. Grand Rapids, MI: Eerdmans, 1982.

Hemer, Colin J. *The Letters to the Seven Churches of Asia in Their Local Setting*. Sheffield, England: JSOT Press, 1986.

Hindson, Edward. *Revelation: Unlocking the Future*. Chattanooga, TN: AMG Publishers, 2002.

Hoehner, Harold W. *Chronological Aspects of the Life of Christ*. Grand Rapids, MI: Zondervan, 1977.

Hopkins, Keith. "Divine Emperors or the Symbolic Unity of the Roman Empire," in *Conquerors and Slaves*. Cambridge: The University Press, 1978.

House, H. Wayne and Ice, Thomas. *Dominion Theology: Blessing or Curse? An Analysis of Christian Reconstructionism*. Portland, OR: Multnomah, 1988.

Hughes, Philip E. *The Book of the Revelation*. Grand Rapids, MI: Eerdmans, 1990.

Ice, Thomas and Demy, Timothy, eds. *When the Trumpet Sounds: Today's Foremost Authorities Speak Out on End-Time Controversies.* Eugene, OR: Harvest House Publishers, 1995.

Ice, Thomas and Demy, Timothy. *Fast Facts on Bible Prophecy.* Eugene, OR: Harvest House Publishers, 1997.

* Ice, Thomas and Gentry, Kenneth, L. *The Great Tribulation: Past or Future?* Grand Rapids, MI: Kregel, 1999.

Ice, Thomas and House, H. Wayne. *Dominion Theology: Blessing or Curse? An Analysis of Christian Reconstructionism.* Portland, OR: Multnomah Press, 1988.

Ice, Thomas and Price, Randall. *Ready to Rebuild: The Imminent Plan to Rebuild the Last Days Temple.* Eugene, OR: Harvest House Publishers, 1992.

* James, Timothy A. *The Messiah's Return: Delayed?, Fulfilled?, or Double Fulfillment?* Bradford, PA: Kingdom Publications, 1991.

Jeffrey, Grant R. *Triumphant Return: The Coming Kingdom of God.* Toronto: Frontier Research Publications, 2001.

Johnson, Alan F. "Revelation," in *The Expositor's Bible Commentary,* vol. 12. Edited by Grank E. Gaebelein. Grand Rapids, MI: Zondervan, 1981.

Johnson, Andrew, & Pickett, L. L. *Postmillennialism and the Higher Critics.* Chicago, IL: Glad Tidings Publishing Company, 1923.

Josephus. *Complete Works.* Translated by William Whiston. Grand Rapids, MI: Kregel, (1867), 1960.

Keith, Alexander. *Evidence of the Truth of the Christian Religion Derived from the Literal Fulfillment of Prophecy; Particularly as Illustrated by the History of the Jews, and by the Discoveries of Recent Ravellers.* Philadelphia, PA: Presbyterian Board of Publication, n.d.

———. *The Harmony of Prophecy; Or, Scriptural Illustrations of the Apocalypse.* New York: Harper & Brothers, Publishers, 1851.

Kelly, William. *Lectures on the Gospel of Matthew.* Sunbury, PA: Believers Bookshelf, (1868), 1971.

Kiddle, Martin. *The Revelation of St. John.* London: Hodder and Stoughton, 1940.

* Kik, J. Marcellus. *An Eschatology of Victory.* Phillipsburg, NJ: Presbyterian and Reformed, 1971.

* Kimball, William R. *What the Bible Says About the Great Tribulation.* Grand Rapids, MI: Baker, 1983.

* King, Max R. *The Cross and the Parousia of Christ: The Two Dimensions of One Age-Changing Eschaton.* Warren, OH: by the author, 1987.

* ———. *Old Testament Israel and New Testament Salvation.* Warren, Ohio: Eschatology Publications, 1990.

* ———. *The Spirit of Prophecy.* Warren, OH: by the author, 1971.

Kistemaker, Simon J. *Revelation.* Grand Rapids, MI: Baker Books, 2001.

Kyle, Richard. *The Last Days Are Here Again: A History of the End Times.* Grand Rapids, MI: Baker Book House, 1998.

Ladd, George Eldon. *A Commentary on the Revelation of John.* Grand Rapids, MI: Eerdmans, 1972.

LaHaye, Tim. *Revelation Unveiled.* Grand Rapids, MI: Zondervan, 1999.

———. *Tim LaHaye Prophecy Study Bible.* Chattanooga, TN: AMG Publishers, 2000.

———. *Understanding Bible Prophecy for Yourself.* Eugene, OR: Harvest House Publishers, 2001.

LaHaye, Tim and Ice, Thomas. *Charting the End Times: A Visual Guide to Understanding Bible Prophecy.* Eugene, OR: Harvest House Publishers, 2001.

Lang, G. H. *The Revelation of Jesus Christ.* Miami Springs, FL: Conley & Schoettle, (1945), 1985.

Lange, John Peter. *The Revelation of John,* vol. 12. Translated from the German by Evelina Moore. Enlarged and edited by E. R. Craven. Grand Rapids, MI: Zondervan, (1871), 1960.

* Leonard, J. E. *Come Out of Her, My People: A Study of the Revelation to John.* Chicago, IL: Laudemont Press, 1991.

* Lightfoot, John. *A Commentary on the New Testament from the Talmud and Hebraica,* 4 vols. Grand Rapids, MI: Baker Book House, (1859) 1979.

Lindsey, Hal. *The Road to Holocaust.* New York: Bantam, 1989.

* Lockman, Vic. *The Book of Revelation: A Cartoon Illustrated Commentary.* Ramona, CA: by the author, 1993.

MacArthur, John, Jr. *Matthew 24–28.* Chicago, IL: Moody Press, 1989.

———. *Revelation 1–11.* Chicago: Moody Press, 1999.

———. *Revelation 12–22.* Chicago: Moody Press, 2000.

———. *The Second Coming: Signs of Christ's Return and the End of the Age.* Wheaton, IL: Crossway Books, 1999.

* Mattill, A. J., Jr. *Luke and the Last Things: A Perspective for the Understanding of Lukan Thought.* Dillsboro, NC: Western North Carolina Press, 1979.

McClain, Alva J. *The Greatness of the Kingdom.* Winona Lake, IN: BMH Books, 1959.

* McRay, Ron. *The Last Days?* Bradford, PA: Kingdom Press, 1990.

* Miladin, George C. *Is This Really the End? A Reformed Analysis of the Late Great Planet Earth.* Cherry Hill, NJ: Mack Publishing Co., 1972.

Milligan, William. *Discussions on the Apocalypse.* New York: Macmillan and Company, 1893.

Moffatt, James. *The Revelation of St. John the Divine,* in *The Expositor's Greek Testament,* 5 vols. Grand Rapids, MI: Eerdmans, n.d.

Morris, Leon. *The Revelation of St. John.* Grand Rapids, MI: Eerdmans, 1969.

———. *The Gospel According to Matthew.* Grand Rapids, MI: Eerdmans, 1992.

Mounce, Robert H. *The Book of Revelation.* Grand Rapids, MI: Eerdmans, 1977.

———. *Matthew: New International Bible Commentary.* Peabody, MA: Hendrickson Publishers, (1985), 1991.

Newport, John P. *The Lion and the Lamb: A Commentary on the Book of Revelation for Today.* Nashville, TN: Broadman Press, 1986.

Newton, Bishop Thomas. *The Prophecy of Matthew 24.* Lakeland, FL: John L. Bray Ministry, (1754) 1991.

———. *Dissertations on the Prophecies, Which Have Remarkably Been Fulfilled and at This Time Are Fulfilling in the World.* Philadelphia, PA: J. J. Woodward, 1835.

* Nisbett, N. *The Prophecy of the Destruction of Jerusalem.* Lakeland, FL: John L. Bray Ministry, (1787), 1992.

* Noe, John. *Beyond the End Times: The Rest of…the Greatest Story Ever Told.* Bradford, PA: Preterist Resources, 1999.

* North, Gary and DeMar, Gary. *Christian Reconstruction: What It Is, What It Isn't.* Tyler, TX.: Institute for Christian Economics, 1991.

* Ogden, Arthur M. *The Avenging of the Apostles and Prophets: Commentary on Revelation.* Somerset, KY: Ogden Publications, 1985, 1991.

———. *The Development of the New Testament.* Somerset, KY: Ogden Publications, 1992.

* Paher, Stanley W. *If Thou Hadst Known.* Las Vegas, NV: Nevada Publications, 1978.

* Pate, C. Marvin, ed. *Four Views on the Book of Revelation.* Grand Rapids, MI: Zondervan, 1998.

Pentecost, J. Dwight. *Things to Come: A Study in Biblical Eschatology.* Grand Rapids, MI: Zondervan, 1958.

———. *Thy Kingdom Come.* Wheaton, IL: Victor Books, 1990.

Peters, George N. H. *The Theocratic Kingdom,* 3 vols. Grand Rapids, MI: Kregel, (1884), 1972.

Poellot, Luther. *Revelation.* St. Louis, MO: Concordia Publishing House, 1962.

* Preston, Don K. *II Peter 3: The Late Great Kingdom.* Ardmore, OK: by the author, 1990.

* ———. *Have Heaven & Earth Passed Away? A Study of Matthew 5:17-18.* Ardmore, OK: by the author, 1993.

* ———. *How Is This Possible? A Study of the Coming of the Lord.* Ardmore, OK: by the author, 1991.

* ———. *Seal Up Vision & Prophecy: A Study of the 70 Weeks of Daniel 9.* Ardmore, OK: by the author, 1991.

Price, Walter K. *Jesus' Prophetic Sermon: The Olivet Key to Israel, the Church, and the Nations.* Chicago, IL: Moody Press, 1972.

Ramsay, William. *The Letters to the Seven Churches of Asia and Their Place in the Plan of the Apocalypse.* Minneapolis, MN: James Family Publishing Company, (1904), 1978.

Richards, Hubert J. *What the Spirit Says to the Churches.* New York: P. J. Kennedy & Sons, 1967.

Roberts, Alexander, & Donaldson, James. *The Ante-Nicene Fathers,* vol. I. Grand Rapids, MI: Eerdmans, n.d.

* Robinson, John A. T. *Redating the New Testament.* Philadelphia, PA: Westminster, 1976.

Roloff, Jurgen. *The Revelation of John.* Minneapolis, MN: Fortress Press, 1993.

* Russell, J. Stuart. *The Parousia: A Study of the New Testament Doctrine of Our Lord's Second Coming.* Grand Rapids, MI: Baker, (1887), 1983.

Ryle, J. C. *Matthew: Expository Thoughts on the Gospels.* Wheaton, IL: Crossway Books, (1860), 1993.

* Schaff, Philip. *History of the Christian Church,* 8 vols. Grand Rapids, MI: Eerdmans, (1910), 1971.

Scroggie, W. Graham. *The Great Unveiling: An Analytical study of Revelation.* Grand Rapids, MI: Zondervan, 1979.

Seiss, J. A. *The Apocalypse: Lectures on the Book of Revelation.* Grand Rapids, MI: Zondervan, (1900), 1977.

* Seraiah, C. Jonathin. *The End of All Things: A Defense of the Future.* Moscow, ID: Canon Press, 1999.

Shimeall, Richard Cunningham. *Christ's Second Coming: Is it Pre-Millennial or Post-Millennial?* New York: by the author, 1865.

Silver, Jesse Forrest. *The Lord's Return: Seen in History and in Scripture as Pre-Millennial and Imminent.* New York: Revell, 1914.

Smith, J. B. *A Commentary on the Book of Revelation.* Scottsdale, PA: Herald Press, 1961.

* Sproul, R. C. *The Last Days According to Jesus: When Did Jesus Say He Would Return?* Grand Rapids, MI: Baker Books, 1998.

* Stevens, Edward E. *What Happened in A.D. 70?* 5th ed. Bradford, PA: Kingdom Publications, 1997.

Stonehouse, Ned Bernard. *The Apocalypse in the Ancient Church.* Goes, Holland: Oosterbaan & Le Cointre, 1929.

* Stuart, Moses. *A Commentary on the Apocalypse.* 2 vols. (Eugene, OR: Wipf and Stock Publishers, (1845) 2001.

* Summers, Ray. *Worthy Is the Lamb.* Nashville, TN: Broadman Press, 1951.

Sweet, J. P. M. *Revelation*. Philadelphia, PA: Westminster, Pelican, 1979.

* Swete, Henry Barclay. *Commentary on Revelation*. Grand Rapids, MI: Kregel Publications, (1911), 1977.

Tenney, Merrill C. *Interpreting Revelation*. Grand Rapids, MI: Eerdmans, 1957.

* Terry, Milton S. *Biblical Apocalyptics: A Study of the Most Notable Revelation of God and of Christ*. Grand Rapids, MI: Baker, (1898), 1988.

Thomas, Robert L. *Revelation: An Exegetical Commentary*, 2 vols. Chicago, IL: Moody Press, 1992, 1995.

Toussaint, Stanley D. *Behold the King: A Study of Matthew*. Portland, OR: Multnomah Press, 1980.

Trench, Richard Chenevix. *Commentary on the Epistles to the Seven Churches in Asia*. Minneapolis, MN: Klock & Klock Christian Publishers, (1897), 1978.

* Vanderwaal, Cornelis. *Hal Lindsey and Biblical Prophecy*. St. Catharine, Canada: Paideia Press, 1978.

Wainwright, Arthur W. *Mysterious Apocalypse: Interpreting the Book of Revelation*. Nashville, TN: Abingdon Press, 1993.

* Wallace, Foy. *The Book of Revelation*. Nashville, TN: by the author, 1966.

Walvoord, John F. *Matthew: Thy Kingdom Come*. Chicago, IL: Moody Press, 1974.

————. *The Revelation of Jesus Christ*. Chicago, IL: Moody Press, 1966.

Walvoord, John F. & Zuck, Roy B. *The Bible Knowledge Commentary: An Exposition of the Scriptures by Dallas Seminary Faculty*, New Testament. Wheaton, IL: Victor Books, 1983.

Wenham, David. *Gospel Perspectives: The Rediscovery of Jesus' Eschatological Discourse*, vol. 4. Sheffield, England: JSOT Press, 1984.

West, Nathaniel. *The Thousand Years in Both Testaments*. New York: Revell, 1889.

Willis, Wesley R. & Master, John R., eds., with Ryrie, Charles C., consulting editor. *Issues in Dispensationalism*. Chicago, IL: Moody, 1994.

* Woodrow, Ralph. *His Truth Is Marching On*. Riverside, CA: Ralph Woodrow Evangelistic Association, 1977.

Yeager, Randolph O. *The Renaissance New Testament*, 18 vols. Bowling Green, KY: Renaissance Press, 1978.

NOTES

Introduction—Has Jesus Already Come?

1. R. C. Sproul, *The Last Days According to Jesus* (Grand Rapids, MI: Baker Books, 1998) p. 155.

2. Sproul, *The Last Days*, p. 156.

3. Sproul, *The Last Days*, p. 156.

Chapter 1—What Is Preterism?

1. David Chilton, *Paradise Restored: An Eschatology of Dominion* (Tyler, TX: Reconstruction Press, 1985), p. 224.

2. David Chilton, *The Days of Vengeance* (Ft. Worth, TX: Dominion Press, 1987), p. 43.

3. Kenneth L. Gentry, Jr. *He Shall Have Dominion: A Post-millennial Eschatology* (Tyler, TX: Institute for Christian Economics, 1992), p. 159.

4. Gary DeMar, *Last Days Madness: Obsession of the Modern Church* (Powder Springs, GA: American Vision, 1999), p. viii.

5. Merrill G. Tenney, *Interpreting Revelation* (Grand Rapids, MI: Eerdmans, 1957), p. 137.

6. Albert Barnes, *Revelation*, pp. lvi-lxii; cited in Gary G. Cohen, *Understanding Revelation* (Chicago, IL: Moody Press, 1978), pp. 28-29.

7. Tenney, *Interpreting Revelation*, p. 138.

8. G. K. Beale, *The Book of Revelation* (Grand Rapids, MI: Eerdmans, 1999), p. 177.

9. Raymond Calkins, *The Social Message of the Book of Revelation* (New York: The Woman's Press, 1920), pp. 3-9; cited in Tenney, *Interpreting Revelation*, p. 143.

10. Tenney, *Interpreting Revelation*, pp. 142-43.

11. Tenney, *Interpreting Revelation*, p. 136.

12. Tenney, *Interpreting Revelation*, p. 136.

13. LeRoy Froom, *The Prophetic Faith of Our Fathers*, vol. II (Washington, DC: Review and Herald, 1948), p. 509.

14. Froom, *The Prophetic Faith*, vol. II, p. 509.

15. Froom, *The Prophetic Faith*, vol. II, pp. 506-07.

16. Moses Stuart, *A Commentary on the Apocalypse*, 2 vols. (Eugene, OR: Wipf and Stock Publishers, [1845] 2001).

17. R. H. Charles, *The Revelation of St. John*, 2 vols. (Edinburgh: T. & T. Clark, 1920).

18. Henry Barclay Swete, *Commentary on Revelation* (Grand Rapids, MI: Kregel Publications, 1977 [1911]).

19. Isbon T. Beckwith, *The Apocalypse of John* (Grand Rapids, MI: Baker Book House, 1979 [1919]).

20. R. C. Sproul, *The Last Days According To Jesus* (Grand Rapids, MI: Baker, 1998), p. 158.

21. Kenneth L. Gentry, Jr. *The Beast of Revelation*, rev. ed. (Powder Springs, GA: American Vision, 2002); *He Shall Have Dominion: A Postmillennial Eschatology* (Tyler, TX: Institute for Christian Economics, 1992); "A Preterist View of Revelation" in C. Marvin Pate, ed., *Four Views on the Book of Revelation* (Grand Rapids, MI: Zondervan, 1998); *Before Jerusalem Fell: Dating the Book of Revelation* rev. ed. (Atlanta, GA: American Vision, 1998); *Perilous Times: A Study in Eschatological Evil* (Texarkana, AR: Covenant Media Press, 1999); Greg L. Bahnsen and Kenneth L. Gentry, Jr., *House Divided: The Break-up of Dispensational Theology* (Tyler, TX: Institute for Christian Economics, 1989); Thomas Ice and Kenneth L. Gentry, Jr., *The Great Tribulation: Past or Future?* Grand Rapids, MI: Kregel, 1999).

22. Gary DeMar, *Last Days Madness: Obsession of the Modern Church* (Powder Springs, GA: American Vision, 1999); *End Times Fiction: A Biblical Consideration of the* Left Behind *Theology* (Nashville, TN: Thomas Nelson Publishers, 2001).

23. Chilton, *Paradise Restored; The Great Tribulation* (Ft. Worth, TX: Dominion Press, 1987); *The Days of Vengeance*, 1987.

24. Edward Stevens, *What Happened in A.D. 70? A Study in Bible Prophecy* (Bradford, PA: by the author, 1988), p. 22.

25. J. Stuart Russell, *The Parousia: A Study of the New Testament Doctrine of Our Lord's Second Coming*, second edition, (Grand Rapids, MI: Baker Book House, [1887], 1985).

26. Russell, *The Parousia*, "Preface to the New Edition," no page numbers, but it is on the fifth page; see also pp. 165-69.

27. Max R. King, *The Spirit of Prophecy* (Warren, OH: Parkman Road Church of Christ, 1971); *The Cross and the Parousia of Christ* (Warren, OH: Writing and Research Ministry, 1987); *Old Testament Israel and New Testament Salvation* (Warren, OH: Eschatology Publications, 1990).

28. This is a well-known fact that has been documented on the following web site at "ourworld-top.cs.com/preter-istabcs/ id88.htm. See also Edward E. Stevens, "Tribute to David Chilton" in *Kingdom Counsel* (vol. 8, #2 and vol. 9; Oct. 1996–Dec. 1997), pp. 17-18.

29. Edward E. Stevens, *What Happened in A.D. 70?* 5th ed. (Bradford, PA: Kingdom Publications, 1997).

30. Don K. Preston, *Who Is This Babylon?* (no publishing information, 1999).

31. John Noe, *Beyond the End Times: The Rest of…the Greatest Story Every Told* (Bradford, PA: Preterist Resources, 1999).

32. John L. Bray, *Matthew 24 Fulfilled* (Lakeland, FL: John L. Bray Ministry, 1996).

33. See Sproul, *Last Days*, pp. 153-70.

34. Sproul, *Last Days*, p. 166.

35. Kenneth L. Gentry, Jr., "A Brief Theological Analysis of Hyper-Preterism," in *The Counsel of Chalcedon*; vol. XVII, no. 1, p. 20. March 1995; It can also be found on the Internet at http://www.preteristarchive.com/CriticalArticles/gentry-ken_ca_02.html.

36. Gentry, "Analysis of Hyper-Preterism," p. 2.

37. Gentry, "Analysis of Hyper-Preterism," p. 3.

38. Chilton, *Paradise Restored*, p. 224.

39. Chilton, *Paradise Restored*, p. 225.

40. Chilton, *Paradise Restored*, p. 225.

41. Chilton, *Paradise Restored*, p. 224.

42. Chilton, *Paradise Restored*, p. 148.

43. Chilton, *Paradise Restored*, p. 148.

44. Chilton, *Paradise Restored*, p. 225.

45. Chilton, *Paradise Restored*, p. 183.

46. Chilton, *Paradise Restored*, pp. 188, 225.

47. Chilton, *Paradise Restored*, pp. 225, 195.

48. Gary DeMar & Peter Leithart, *The Reduction of Christianity* (Fort Worth, TX: Dominion Press, 1988), pp. 41-42.

49. Chilton, *Paradise Restored*, p. 225.

50. Chilton, *Days of Vengeance*, pp. 506-07.

51. Chilton, *Paradise Restored*, p. 226.

52. Chilton, *Paradise Restored*, p. 224.

53. Chilton, *Paradise Restored*, p. 224.

54. DeMar and Leithart, *Reduction of Christianity*, p. 213.

55. Chilton, *Paradise Restored*, p. 224.

56. Chilton, *Days of Vengeance*, p. 519.

57. Chilton, *Days of Vengeance*, p. 526.

58. Chilton, *The Great Tribulation*, pp. 144, 142.

59. Sproul, *Last Days*, p. 13.

60. DeMar, *Last Days Madness*, p. 37.

61. DeMar, *Last Days Madness*, pp. 37-38.

62. Gentry, *He Shall Have Dominion*, pp. 160, 163.

63. Gary DeMar, *Last Days Madness: The Folly of Trying to Predict When Christ Will Return*, (Brentwood, TN: Wolgemuth & Hyatt, 1991), p. 25.

64. Kenneth Gentry, "Context! Context! Context!," *Dispensationalism in Transition* (vol. IV, no. 5; May 1991), p. 1.

65. Kenneth Gentry, "When I Survey the Wondrous Discourse," *Dispensationalism in Transition* (vol. IV, no. 7; July 1991), p. 2.

66. Gentry, "When I Survey," p. 2.

67. Kenneth Gentry, "The End Is Not Yet," *Dispensationalism in Transition* (vol. IV, no. 8; August 1991), p. 1.

68. Gentry, "End Is Not Yet," pp. 1-2.

69. Kenneth Gentry, "The Gospel of the Kingdom in All the World," *Dispensationalism in Transition* (vol. IV, no. 9; September 1991), p. 1.

70. Gentry, "Gospel of the Kingdom," p. 1.

71. Gentry, "Gospel of the Kingdom," pp. 1-2.

72. Kenneth Gentry, "The Abomination of Desolation," *Dispensationalism in Transition* (vol. IV, no. 10; October 1991), p. 2.

73. Kenneth Gentry, "The Greatness of the Great Tribulation," *Dispensationalism in Transition* (vol. IV, no. 11; November 1991), pp. 1-2.

74. Kenneth Gentry, "Lightning, Eagles, and Jerusalem," *Dispensationalism in Transition* (vol. V, no. 1; January 1992), pp. 1-2.

75. Gentry, "Abomination of Desolation," p. 2.

76. Kenneth Gentry, "The Collapse of the Universe; or the Collapse of Dispensationalism?," *Dispensationalism in Transition* (vol. V, no. 2; February 1992), pp. 1-2.

77. Kenneth Gentry, "Then Shall Appear the Sign," *Dispensationalism in Transition* (vol. V, no. 3; March 1992), pp. 1-2.

78. Gentry, *He Shall Have Dominion*, p. 349.

79. Kenneth Gentry, "Dispensationalism As a Non-Prophet Movement," *Dispensationalism in Transition* (vol. V, no. 5; May 1992), p. 1.

80. Gentry, "A Preterist View of Revelation," p. 37.

81. Sproul, *Last Days*, pp. 131-49; 179-89; 200-03.

82. Chilton, *Days of Vengeance*, p. 43.

83. Gentry, *Before Jerusalem Fell*, p. 130.

84. Gentry, *Before Jerusalem Fell*, p. 131.

85. Gentry, *Before Jerusalem Fell*, p. 133.

86. DeMar, *Last Days Madness*, p. 358. Numbers and Greek transliteration added by T. D. I.

Chapter 2—The History of Preterism

1. David Chilton, *The Days of Vengeance: An Exposition of the Book of Revelation* (Ft. Worth, TX: Dominion Press, 1987), p. 40.

2. Chilton, *Days of Vengeance*, p. 41.

3. Kenneth L. Gentry, Jr., *He Shall Have Dominion: A Postmillennial Eschatology* (Tyler, TX: Institute for Christian Economics, 1992), p. 396.

4. Gentry, *He Shall Have Dominion*, p. 397.

5. Moses Stuart, *A Commentary on the Apocalypse*, vol. 1 (Eugene, OR: Wipf and Stock Publishers, [1845] 2001), p. iv.

6. Stuart, *Apocalypse*, vol. 1, p. 450.

7. E. B. Elliott, *Horae Apocalypticae*, rev. ed., vol. IV (London: Seeleys, 1851), p. 535.

8. Stuart, *Apocalypse*, vol. 1, p. 451.

9. Edward E. Stevens, "Silence Demands a Rapture," privately printed paper by the International Preterist Association, p. 3. It can be obtained from the website www.preterist.org.

10. R. H. Charles, *Studies in the Apocalypse* (Eugene, OR: Wipf and Stock Publishers, [1913] 1996), p. 8.

11. Chrysostom, *Homilies on the Gospel of Saint Matthew*, Homily 76.1.

12. Chrysostom, *Matthew*, Homily 76.3.

13. D. A. Carson notes concerning an interpretative approach to the Olivet Discourse, "the most common approach—and that of most evangelicals today—is exemplified by Broadus and Lane (Mark). Broadus holds that vv 15-21, 34 foretell the destruction of Jerusalem, and at least vv 29-31 foretell the Lord's return." D. A. Carson, "Matthew," *The Expositor's Bible Commentary*, vol. 8, gen. ed. Frank E. Gaebelein (Grand Rapids, MI: Zondervan, 1984), pp. 491-92. Even dispensationalist David Turner takes a mixed approach. David L. Turner, "The Structure and Sequence of Matthew 24:1-41: Interaction with Evangelical Treatments," *Grace Theological Journal*, vol. 10, no. 1 (Spring, 1989), pp. 3-27.

14. Samuel M. Frost, *Misplaced Hope: The Origins of First and Second Century Eschatology* (Colorado Springs: Bimillennial Press, 2002), p. 210.

15. Stevens, "Silence," p. 16. "Christ came in A.D. 66 to begin that judgment. He resurrected the dead out of Hades (in the unseen realm) and 'snatched away' his living and remaining true saints to him in the heavenly realm."

16. Stevens, "Silence," p. 2. See also J. Stuart Russell, *The Parousia: A Study of the New Testament Doctrine of Our Lord's Second Coming* (Grand Rapids, MI: Baker Book House, [1887] 1985), "Preface to the New Edition," No page numbers, but it is on the fifth page; pp. 165-69.

17. Stevens, "Silence," p. 19.

18. Stevens, "Silence," p. 15.

19. Stevens, "Silence," pp. 11-13.

20. For a rebuttal of Steven's claim that the Apostle John did live into the A.D. 90s, see Mark Hitchcock's chapter in this book.

21. C. Jonathin Seraiah, *The End of All Things: A Defense of the Future* (Moscow, ID: Canon Press, 1999), p. 19.

22. Kenneth L. Gentry, Jr., *Before Jerusalem Fell: Dating the Book of Revelation* (Atlanta, GA: American Vision, [1989], 1998), pp. 41-109.

23. Steve Gregg, *Revelation, Four Views: A Parallel Commentary* (Nashville, TN: Thomas Nelson, 1997), p. 39.

24. Eusebius, *Ecclesiastical History*, 2 vols., translated by Kirsopp Lake, *Loeb Classical Library* (Cambridge, MA: Harvard University Press, 1926), book III, chapter VII, vol. 1, p. 215.

25. Eusebius, *The Proof of the Gospel*, edited and translated by W. J. Ferrar (Grand Rapids, MI: Baker Book House, [1920] 1981).

26. Ferrar thinks that *The Proof of the Gospel* was "written between A.D. 124 and A.D. 318." "Introduction," p. xiii. Lake believes that the earliest editions of *Ecclesiastical History* were written around A.D. 313 "Introduction," p. xxii.

27. Greg L. Bahnsen and Kenneth L. Gentry, Jr., *House Divided: The Break-up of Dispensational Theology* (Tyler, TX: Institute for Christian Economics, 1989), p. 276.

28. Bahnsen and Gentry, *House Divided*, pp. 277-78.

29. Bahnsen and Gentry, *House Divided*, p. 278.

30. Clementine is said to employ a "loose method of Scripture citation...Sometimes the meaning is perverted," says M. B. Riddle, editor of Clementine literature in Alexander Roberts and James Donaldson, editors, *The Ante-Nicene Fathers*, vol. VIII (Grand Rapids, MI: Eerdmans, 1986), p. 215, fn. 3.

31. Bahnsen and Gentry, *House Divided*, p. 278.

32. Cyprian, *Treatises*, 12:1:6, 15. Gentry says, "See especially Roberts and Donaldson, *Ante-Nicene Fathers*, vol. 5, pp. 507-11."

33. Cyprian, *Treatises*, 12:1:6.

34. Cyprian, *Treatises*, 12:1:15.

35. Cyprian, *Treatises*, 11:11.

36. Bahnsen and Gentry, *House Divided*, p. 279.

37. See the historical section on the 70 weeks of Daniel in this book for a clarification of what the early church believed on this matter.

38. Kenneth L. Gentry, Jr., *Perilous Times: A Study in Eschatological Evil* (Texarkana, AR: Covenant Media Press, 1999), pp. 16, 19-20, 24, 31.

39. Gentry, *Before Jerusalem Fell*, p. 106.

40. Gentry, *Before Jerusalem Fell*, pp. 106-07.

41. Bahnsen and Gentry, *House Divided*, p. 279. See also Gentry, *Before Jerusalem Fell*, p. 107.

42. Stuart, *Apocalypse*, vol. 1, p. 267.

43. Gregg, *Revelation*, pp. 39, 48, fn. 76.

44. Stuart, *Apocalypse*, vol. 1, p. 267; Bahnsen and Gentry, *House Divided*, p. 279; Gentry, *Before Jerusalem Fell*, p. 107.

45. Stuart, *Apocalypse*, vol. 1, p. 268.

46. Gentry, *Before Jerusalem Fell*, p. 107.

47. Bahnsen and Gentry, *House Divided*, p. 279.

48. Dr. Gentry withholds Dr. Stuart's information noted on the text in both *House Divided*, p. 279 and in *Before Jerusalem Fell*, pp. 107-08.

49. See Stuart, *Apocalypse*, vol. 1, p. 268.

50. Stuart, *Apocalypse*, vol. 1, p. 268.

51. Stuart, *Apocalypse*, vol. 1, p. 268.

52. LeRoy Froom, *The Prophetic Faith of Our Fathers: The Historical Development of Prophetic Interpretation*, vol. I (Washington, DC: Review and Herald, 1950), p. 572.

53. Stuart, *Apocalypse*, vol. 1, p. 457.

54. Stuart, *Apocalypse*, vol. 1, p. 268.

55. Elliott, *Horae Apocalypticae*, vol. IV, p. 361.

56. Henry Alford, *Alford's Greek Testament: An Exegetical and Critical Commentary*, vol. IV, part I (Grand Rapids, MI: Guardian Press, [1875] 1976), p. 245.

57. See Marjorie Reeves, *The Influence of Prophecy in the Later Middle Ages* (London: Oxford University Press, 1969).

58. Froom, *Prophetic Faith*, vol. II, p. 214.

59. Froom, *Prophetic Faith*, vol. II, p. 214.

60. Stuart, *Apocalypse*, vol. 1, p. 458.

61. Stuart, *Apocalypse*, vol. 1, p. 461.

62. Jean-Robert Armogathe, "Interpretations of the Revelation of John: 1500–1800," in John J. Collins, Bernard McGinn, and Stephen J. Stein, ed. *The Encyclopedia of Apocalypticism*, vol. 2 (New York: Continuum, 2000), p. 191.

63. Alford, *Greek Testament*, vol. IV, part I, p. 245.

64. Froom, *Prophetic Faith*, vol. II, p. 507.

65. Froom, *Prophetic Faith*, vol. II, p. 509.

66. Stuart, *Apocalypse*, vol. 1, pp. 463-64.

67. Froom, *Prophetic Faith*, vol. II, pp. 506-07.

68. Froom, *Prophetic Faith*, vol. II, p. 507.

69. Isbon T. Beckwith, *The Apocalypse of John* (Grand Rapids, MI: Baker Book House, 1979), p. 332.

70. Elliott, *Horae Apocalypticae*, vol. IV, p. 469.

71. Armogathe, "Interpretations of the Revelation," vol. 2, p. 189.

72. Armogathe, "Interpretations of the Revelation," vol. 2, p. 193.

73. Armogathe, "Interpretations of the Revelation," vol. 2, p. 193.

74. Froom, *Prophetic Faith*, vol. II, p. 503.

75. Froom, *Prophetic Faith*, vol. II, pp. 486-88.

76. Froom, *Prophetic Faith*, vol. II, p. 506.

77. Froom, *Prophetic Faith*, vol. II, p. 521.

78. See Walter A. Elwell, ed. *Evangelical Dictionary of Theology* (Grand Rapids, MI: Baker Book House, 1984), pp. 102, 489.

79. Froom, *Prophetic Faith*, vol. II, p. 521.

80. Elwell, *Dictionary of Theology*, p. 489.

81. Froom, *Prophetic Faith*, vol. II, pp. 522-23.

82. Froom, *Prophetic Faith*, vol. II, pp. 522-23.

83. Froom, *Prophetic Faith*, vol. II, p. 524.

84. David Brady, *The Contribution of British Writers between 1560 and 1830 to the Interpretation of Revelation* 13:16-18 (Tubingen: J. C. B. Mohr, 1983), p. 158.

85. Brady, *Contribution of British Writers*, p. 158. Contra Froom, whom mistakenly says that Hammond did not refer to Grotius. See Froom, *Prophetic Faith*, vol. II, p. 525.

86. Brady, *Contribution of British Writers*, p. 160.

87. Froom, *Prophetic Faith*, vol. II, p. 525.

88. Brady, *Contribution of British Writers*, p. 168.

89. Brady, *Contribution of British Writers*, p. 159.

90. Brady, *Contribution of British Writers*, p. 164.

91. Brady, *Contribution of British Writers*, p. 164.

92. Armogathe, "Interpretations of the Revelation," vol. 2, p. 195.

93. Armogathe, "Interpretations of the Revelation," vol. 2, p. 196.

94. Bernard McGinn, *Anti-Christ: Two Thousand Years of the Human Fascination with Evil* (San Francisco: HarperCollins, 1994), p. 228.

95. Elliott, *Horae Apocalypticae*, vol. IV, p. 480.

96. Froom, *Prophetic Faith*, vol. II, pp. 636-37.

97. Armogathe, "Interpretations of the Revelation," vol. 2, p. 198.

98. Brady, *Contribution of British Writers*, pp. 164, 166.

99. James West Davidson, *The Logic of Millennial Thought: Eighteenth-Century New England* (New Haven: Yale University Press, 1977), p. 41.

100. Reiner Smolinski, "Apocalypticism in Colonial North America," in John J. Collins, Bernard McGinn, and Stephen J. Stein, ed. *The Encyclopedia of Apocalypticism*, vol. 3 (New York: Continuum, 2000), pp. 51-55.

101. Smolinski, "Apocalypticism in Colonial North America," vol. 3, p. 53.

102. Smolinski, "Apocalypticism in Colonial North America," vol. 3, p. 51.

103. Smolinski, "Apocalypticism in Colonial North America," vol. 3, p. 54.

104. Froom, *Prophetic Faith*, vol. III, p. 251.

105. F. L. Cross and E. A. Livingstone, ed. *The Oxford Dictionary of the Christian Church*, 2nd ed. (Oxford: Oxford University Press, 1974), p. 823.

106. John Lightfoot, *A Commentary on the New Testament from the Talmud and Hebraica*, 4 vols., (Grand Rapids, MI: Baker Book House, [1859], 1979).

107. R. Laird Harris, "Introduction" in Lightfoot, *A Commentary*, vol. 1, p. iv, fn. 3.

108. Lightfoot, *A Commentary*, vol. 2, p. 320.

109. Lightfoot, *A Commentary*, vol. 2, p. 442.

110. Lightfoot, *A Commentary*, vol. 3, p. 199.

111. Brady, *Contribution of British Writers*, p. 170.

112. Froom, *Prophetic Faith*, vol. II, pp. 510.

113. Elliott, *Horae Apocalypticae*, vol. IV, p. 501.

114. Merrill C. Tenney, *Interpreting Revelation* (Grand Rapids, MI: Eerdmans, 1957), p. 136.

115. Froom, *Prophetic Faith*, vol. III, p. 596.

116. Froom, *Prophetic Faith*, vol. II, p. 706.

117. James H. Moorhead, "Apocalypticism in Mainstream Protestantism, 1800 to the Present," in John J. Collins, Bernard McGinn, and Stephen J. Stein, ed. *The Encyclopedia of Apocalypticism*, vol. 3 (New York: Continuum, 2000), pp. 87-88.

118. Charles, *Studies in the Apocalypse*, pp. 44-45.

119. Stuart, *Apocalypse*, vol. 1, p. 470.

120. Froom, *Prophetic Faith*, vol. II, p. 706.

121. Froom, *Prophetic Faith*, vol. II, p. 706.

122. Stuart, *Apocalypse*, vol. 1, p. 443.

123. Stuart, *Apocalypse*, vol. 1, p. 470.

124. Froom, *Prophetic Faith*, vol. II, p. 708.

125. Stuart, *Apocalypse*, vol. 1, p. 471.

126. Stuart, *Apocalypse*, vol. 1, p. 471.

127. Stuart, *Apocalypse*, vol. 1, p. 472.

128. Stuart, *Apocalypse*, vol. 1, p. 473.

129. Froom, *Prophetic Faith*, vol. II, p. 805.

130. Froom, *Prophetic Faith*, vol. III, p. 282.

131. Brady, *Contribution of British Writers*, p. 169, fn. 60.

132. Froom, *Prophetic Faith*, vol. III, p. 596.

133. Brady, *Contribution of British Writers*, p. 169, fn. 60.

134. Froom, *Prophetic Faith*, vol. III, pp. 596-97.

135. Information taken from the back cover of Russell, *The Parousia*.

136. R. C. Sproul, *The Last Days According to Jesus: When Did Jesus Say He Would Return?* (Grand Rapids, MI: Baker Book House, 1998), p. 33.

137. See Sproul, *Last Days*, pp. 33, 25.

138. Russell, *The Parousia*, pp. 548-49.

139. Russell, *The Parousia*, p. 1.

140. Russell, *The Parousia*, Preface to the new edition.

141. Froom, *Prophetic Faith*, vol. II, p. 510.

142. See Moses Stuart, *A Commentary on the Apocalypse*, 2 vols. (Eugene, OR: Wipf and Stock Publishers, [1845], 2001).

143. Stuart, *Apocalypse*, vol. 1, p. 162.

144. Stuart, *Apocalypse*, vol. 1, p. 161.

145. Stuart, *Apocalypse*, vol. 2, p. 5.

146. Enoch Pond, "Review of Professor Stuart on the Apocalypse," at the following Internet address: www.covenanter.org/Postmil/AntiPreterist/Pondreview.htm.

147. Stuart, *Apocalypse*, vol. 1, pp. 472-75.

148. Emphasis added, Stuart, *Apocalypse*, vol. 1, p. 475.

149. See Stuart, *Apocalypse*, vol. 1, pp. 40-74, 87-107, 495-504. Also in his first volume Stuart cites the importance of extrabiblical material for interpreting the Apocalypse, pp. 36-127.

150. Jay Adams, *The Time Is at Hand* (Greenville, SC: A Press, 1966).

151. J. Marcellus Kik, *An Eschatology of Victory* (Phillipsburg, NJ: Presbyterian and Reformed Publishing Company, 1971).

152. See Gary North and Gary DeMar, *Christian Reconstruction: What It Is, What It Isn't* (Tyler TX: Institute for Christian Economics, 1991). For a critique of this movement see H. Wayne House and Thomas Ice, *Dominion*

Theology: Blessing or Curse? An Analysis of Christian Reconstructionism (Portland, OR: Multnomah, 1988).

153. Max R. King, *The Spirit of Prophecy* (Warren, OH: Parkman Road Church of Christ, 1971).

154. King, *Spirit of Prophecy*, p. 392.

155. King, *Spirit of Prophecy*, pp. 1-8.

156. Max R. King, *The Cross and the Parousia of Christ* (Warren, OH: Writing and Research Ministry, 1987).

157. Max R. King, *Old Testament Israel and New Testament Salvation* (Warren, OH: Eschatology Publications, 1990).

158. See their web site www.livingpresence.org.

159. Kenneth Gentry says that Bahnsen's influence upon his eschatology came as a result of a course called "History and Eschatology" which was taught by Dr. Bahnsen. See Bahnsen and Gentry, *House Divided*, p. xlviii. See also David L. Bahnsen, "The Life of Dr. Greg L. Bahnsen," in Steven M. Schlissel, ed., *The Standard Bearer: A Festschrift for Greg L. Bahnsen* (Nacogdoches, TX: Covenant Media Press, 2002), pp. 15-16.

160. Bahnsen's tapes on Revelation are available from Matthew Olive Tape Library, p. O. Box 422, Matthew Olive, MS 39119.

161. "The first 35 verses of Matthew 24 relate to the destruction of Jerusalem and the events preceding that destruction. With verse 36 a new subject is introduced, namely, the second coming of Christ and the attendant final judgment." Kik, *Eschatology of Victory*, p. 158.

162. Greg L. Bahnsen, *Victory in Jesus: The Bright Hope of Postmillennialism*, ed. by Robert R. Booth (Texarkana, AR: Covenant Media Press, 1999), p. 65, fn. 27.

163. Bahnsen, *Victory in Jesus*, pp. 16-17.

164. David Chilton, *Paradise Restored: An Eschatology of Dominion* (Tyler, TX: Reconstruction Press, 1987).

165. David Chilton, *The Days of Vengeance: An Exposition of the Book of Revelation* (Fort Worth, TX: Reconstruction Press, 1985), pp. 149-226.

166. David Chilton, *The Great Tribulation* (Fort Worth, TX: Dominion Press, 1987).

167. Chilton, *Paradise Restored*, p. 224.

168. Chilton, *Days of Vengeance*, p. 43.

169. Greg L. Bahnsen, cited by Joseph C. Morecraft, III in his editorial in *The Counsel of Chalcedon* (vol. X, no. 5; July, 1988), p. 3.

170. This is a well-known fact that has been documented on the web site ourworld-top.cs.com/preteristabcs/id88.htm. See also Edward E. Stevens, "Tribute To David Chilton" in *Kingdom Counsel* (vol. 8, #2 and vol. 9; Oct. 1996–Dec. 1997), pp. 17-18.

171. Kenneth L. Gentry, Jr., *Before Jerusalem Fell: Dating the Book of Revelation* (Tyler, TX: Institute for Christian Economics, 1989). It is currently in a second edition. Kenneth L. Gentry, Jr., *Before Jerusalem Fell: Dating the Book of Revelation* (Atlanta, GA: American Vision, 1998).

172. Kenneth L. Gentry, Jr., *The Beast of Revelation* (Fort Worth, TX: Dominion Press, 1989). A second edition has just been released. Kenneth L. Gentry, Jr., *The Beast of Revelation* (Powder Springs, GA: American Vision, 2002).

173. Greg L. Bahnsen and Kenneth L. Gentry, Jr., *House Divided: The Break-up of Dispensational Theology* (Tyler, TX: Institute for Christian Economics, 1989).

174. Kenneth L. Gentry, Jr., *He Shall Have Dominion: A Postmillennial Eschatology* (Tyler, TX: Institute for Christian Economics, 1992). Kenneth L. Gentry, Jr., "A Preterist View of Revelation" in C. Marvin Pate, ed., *Four Views on the Book of Revelation* (Grand Rapids, MI: Zondervan, 1998). Kenneth L. Gentry, Jr., *Perilous Times: A Study in Eschatological Evil* (Texarkana, AR: Covenant Media Press, 1999).

175. Thomas Ice and Kenneth L. Gentry, Jr., *The Great Tribulation: Past or Future?* (Grand Rapids, MI: Kregel, 1999).

176. Gentry, *Perilous Times*, pp. 89-93.

177. Kenneth L. Gentry, Jr., "Introduction to the 1990 Edition" in David Brown, *Christ's Second Coming: Will It Be Premillennial?* (Edmonton, Canada: Still Waters Revival Books, 1990 [1882]), p. v.

178. Gentry, *Perilous Times*, p. 141, fn. 12.

179. Gary DeMar, *Last Days Madness: Obsession of the Modern Church*, 4th ed. (Powder Springs, GA: American Vision, Inc., 4th ed., 1999), pp. 355-59.

180. Gary DeMar, *Last Days Madness: Obsession of the Modern Church* (Powder Springs, GA: American Vision, Inc., 4th ed., 1999 [1991, 1994, 1997]).

181. Gary DeMar, *End Times Fiction: A Biblical Consideration of The Left Behind Theology* (Nashville, TN: Thomas Nelson Publishers, 2001).

182. DeMar, *Last Days Madness*, p. 71.

183. See for example the following preterist Internet sites: Planet Preterist (planetpreterist.com); The Preterist Archive (preteristarchive.com); The American Preterist Society (theamericanpreteristsociety.com); The International Preterist Association (preterist.org/index.html), to cite just a few.

184. Edward E. Stevens, *What Happened in A.D. 70?* 5th ed. (Bradford, PA: Kingdom Publications, 1997).

185. Don K. Preston, *Who Is This Babylon?* (no publishing information, 1999).

186. John Noe, *Beyond the End Times: The Rest of...the Greatest Story Every Told* (Bradford, PA: Preterist Resources, 1999).

187. John L. Bray, *Matthew 24 Fulfilled* (Lakeland, FL: John L. Bray Ministry, 1996).

188. R. C. Sproul, *The Last Days According to Jesus: When Did Jesus Say He Would Return?* (Grand Rapids, MI: Baker Books, 1998).

189. D. H. Kromminga, *The Millennium in the Church* (Grand Rapids, MI: Eerdmans, 1945), p. 295.

190. Gentry, *Before Jerusalem Fell*, p. 26.

191. Gentry, *Before Jerusalem Fell*, p. 145.

192. Charles Hodge, "Introduction" in James B. Ramsey, *The Spiritual Kingdom: An Exposition of the First Eleven Chapters of the Book of the Revelation* (Richmond, VA: Presbyterian Committee of Publication, 1873), p. xxxiii.

193. See for example DeMar, *End Times Fiction*, pp. xi-xxiv; Gentry, *Perilous Times*, pp. 1-9; Seraiah, *End of All Things*, pp. 11-15.

194. R. C. Sproul, Jr., "Foreword" in Seraiah, *End of All Things*, p. 9.

195. Gentry, "Introduction" in Brown, *Christ's Second Coming*, p. v.

196. Walter C. Kaiser, Jr., "Evangelical Hermeneutics: Restatement, Advance or Retreat from the Reformation?" *Concordia Theological Quarterly* 46 (1982), p. 167.

197. Kaiser, "Evangelical Hermeneutics," p. 167.

198. Kaiser, "Evangelical Hermeneutics," p. 167.

199. Kaiser, "Evangelical Hermeneutics," p. 167.

200. Walter C. Kaiser, Jr., "An Evangelical Response," in Craig A. Blaising and Darrell L. Bock, eds., *Dispensationalism, Israel, and the Church: The Search for Definition* (Grand Rapids, MI: Zondervan, 1992), p. 376.

201. For a critique of this movement see H. Wayne House and Thomas Ice, *Dominion Theology: Blessing or Curse? An Analysis of Christian Reconstructionism* (Portland, OR: Multnomah, 1988).

202. Elliott, *Horae Apocalypticae*, vol. iv, pp. 531-32.

Chapter 3—Hermeneutics and Bible Prophecy

1. Charles C. Ryrie, *Dispensationalism Today* (Chicago, IL: Moody, 1965), p. 46.

2. Ryrie, *Dispensationalism Today*, p. 47.

3. Earl D. Radmacher, "The Current Status of Dispensationalism and Its Eschatology," in *Perspectives on Evangelical Theology*, Kenneth S. Kantzer and Stanley N. Gundry, eds. (Grand Rapids, MI: Baker, 1979), p. 171.

4. O. Palmer Robertson, "Hermeneutics of Continuity," in *Continuity and Discontinuity: Perspectives on the Relationship Between the Old and New Testaments*, John S. Feinberg, ed. (Westchester, IL: Crossway, 1988), p. 107.

5. Kenneth L. Gentry, Jr., He Shall Have Dominion: A Postmillennial Eschatology (Tyler, TX: 1992), pp. 148, 146.

6. Bernard Ramm, *Protestant Biblical Interpretation* (Boston, MA: Wilde, 1956), pp. 89-92.

7. Ryrie, *Dispensationalism Today*, pp. 86-87.

8. E. R. Craven and J. p. Lange, eds., *Commentary on the Holy Scriptures: Revelation* (New York: Scribner, 1872), p. 98 (cited in Ryrie, *Dispensationalism Today*, p. 87).

9. Vern S. Poythress, *Understanding Dispensationalists* (Grand Rapids, MI: Zondervan, 1987), pp. 7, 8-96.

10. Poythress, *Understanding Dispensationalists*, p. 78.

11. Poythress, *Understanding Dispensationalists*, pp. 82-83.

12. Poythress, *Understanding Dispensationalists*, pp. 83-84. Poythress (Review of Books, *Westminster Theological Journal* 55, no. I [Spring 1993], p. 165) dismisses Robert L. Thomas's *Revelation 1–7: An Exegetical Commentary* (Chicago, IL: Moody, 1992) as one that "cannot be recommended" because "the over-all impact is dominated by the initial decision in favor of literalism." "This principle of 'literal if possible,'" contends Poythress, is nothing more than a "stringent idea of 'literalism,'" wildly underestimating the pervasiveness of symbolism."

13. Poythress, *Understanding Dispensationalists*, pp. 84-85.

14. Poythress, *Understanding Dispensationalists*, pp. 85-86.

15. Poythress, *Understanding Dispensationalists*, p. 96.

16. *Webster's New Twentieth Century Dictionary*, Unabridged, 2nd ed. (New York: William Collins Publishers, 1979), p. 1055.

17. Paul Lee Tan, *The Interpretation of Prophecy* (Winona Lake, IN: Assurance Publishers, 1974), p. 29.

18. Elliott E. Johnson, *Expository Hermeneutics: An Introduction* (Grand Rapids, MI: Zondervan, 1990), p. 9.

19. Radmacher, "Current Status of Dispensationalism," p. 167.

20. For excellent insight into how John Calvin pioneered the grammatical-historical approach to exegesis, with an emphasis upon the historical, see David L. Puckett, *John Calvin's Exegesis of the Old Testament* (Louisville, KY: Westminster John Knox Press, 1995).

21. Ramm, *Protestant Biblical Interpretation*, p. 141 (cited in Radmacher, "Current Status of Dispensationalism," p. 167).

22. Gentry, *He Shall Have Dominion*, p. 148.

23. For examples of his approach, see Gentry, *He Shall Have Dominion*, pp. 153-58.

24. Gentry, *He Shall Have Dominion*, p. 153.

25. Augustine, *The City of God*, 20, 7, 1.

26. Irenaeus, *Against Heresies*, 5, 35, 1.

27. Gentry, *He Shall Have Dominion*, p. 148.

28. See Gentry, *He Shall Have Dominion*, pp. 1164-72. For an exegetical and theological statement and defense of the dispensational position see Arnold G. Fruchtenbaum, "Israel and the Church" in Wesley R. Willis and John R. Master, gen. ed. *Issues in Dispensationalism* (Chicago, IL: Moody Press, 1994), pp. 112-30.

29. Poythress, *Understanding Dispensationalists*, p. 53.

30. Gentry, *He Shall Have Dominion*, p. 147.

31. For a recent presentation of a dispensational and literal hermeneutic, complete with hundreds of specific examples illustrating various principles of interpretation, see Roy B. Zuck, *Basic Bible Interpretation* (Wheaton, IL: Victor, 1991).

32. I have heard these charges in a number of personal conversations with those opposed to consistent literal interpretation.

33. David L. Cooper, *The World's Greatest Library Graphically Illustrated* (Los Angeles, CA: Biblical Research Society, 1970), p. 11.

34. Gentry, *He Shall Have Dominion*, p. 147.

35. Greg L. Bahnsen and Kenneth L. Gentry, Jr., *House Divided: The Break-Up of Dispensational Theology* (Tyler, TX: Institute for Christian Economics, 1989), p. 265.

36. Bahnsen and Gentry, *House Divided*, p. 44 n.

37. For an article-length discussion of how a literalist relates to the analogy of faith, see Elliott E. Johnson, "What I Mean By Historical-Grammatical Interpretation and How That Differs from Spiritual Interpretation," *Grace Theological Journal* (vol. 11, no. 2, Fall 1990), pp. 157-69.

38. Gentry, *He Shall Have Dominion*, p. 147.

39. Gentry, *He Shall Have Dominion*, pp. 147-49.

40. Ethelbert W. Bullinger, *Figures of Speech Used in the Bible: Explained and Illustrated* (Grand Rapids, MI: Baker, 1968), inside flap on dust jacket.

41. Tan, *Interpretation of Prophecy*, p. 31.

42. Tan, *Interpretation of Prophecy*, pp. 140-42. Roy Zuck provides an even more extensive list in Zuck, *Basic Bible Interpretation*, pp. 148-61.

43. Tan, *Interpretation of Prophecy*, pp. 141-42, fn. 1.

44. Richard Cunningham Shimeall, *Christ's Second Coming: Is It Pre-Millennial or Post-Millennial?* (New York: published by the author, 1866), p.127.

45. Shimeall, *Christ's Second Coming*, p. 128.

46. Gary DeMar, *Last Days Madness: Obsession of the Modern Church*, (Powder Springs, GA: American Vision, 1999), p. 159.

47. For a discussion on how "sense and reference" are involved in philosophy of language and its relation to hermeneutics, see John S. Feinberg, "Truth: Relationship of Theories of Truth to Hermeneutics," in *Hermeneutics, Inerrancy, and the Bible*, Earl D. Rad-

macher and Robert D. Preus, eds. (Grand Rapids, MI: Zondervan, 1984), pp. 28-30. See also Paul D. Feinberg, "Hermeneutics of Discontinuity," in *Continuity and Discontinuity: Perspectives on the Relationship Between the Old and New Testaments*, John S. Feinberg, ed. (Westchester, IL: Crossway, 1988), pp. 117-20.

48. Gentry, *He Shall Have Dominion*, p. 274.

49. Gary DeMar, *Last Days Madness: The Folly of Trying to Predict When Christ Will Return* (Brentwood, TN: Wolgemuth & Hyatt, 1991), p. 98.

50. Gentry, *He Shall Have Dominion*, p. 273.

51. Gentry, *He Shall Have Dominion*, pp. 273-74.

52. Gentry, *He Shall Have Dominion*, pp. 273-74.

53. For more interaction with the preterist viewpoint, see H. Wayne House and Thomas Ice, *Dominion Theology: Blessing or Curse? An Analysis of Christian Reconstructionism* (Portland, OR: Multnomah, 1988), pp. 285-334.

54. Gentry, *He Shall Have Dominion*, pp. 275-76, 279.

55. Gentry, *He Shall Have Dominion*, pp. 253-54, 386, 418.

56. Paul S. Karleen, "Understanding Covenant Theologians: A Study in Presuppositions," *Grace Theological Journal* (vol. 10, no. 2, Fall 1989), p. 134.

57. Walter C. Kaiser, Jr., "An Evangelical Response," in *Dispensationalism, Israel and the Church: The Search for Definition*, Craig A. Blaising and Darrell L. Bock, eds. (Grand Rapids, MI: Zondervan, 1992), p. 376.

Chapter 4—Preterist "Time Texts"

1. R. C. Sproul, *The Last Days According to Jesus* (Grand Rapids, MI: Baker, 1998), pp. 15-17, 51-68, 137-41; Gary DeMar, *Last Days Madness: Obsession of the Modern Church* (Powder Springs, GA: American Vision, 4th ed. 1999), pp. 35-42, 51-64.

2. Sproul, *Last Days*, p. 56.

3. J. Stuart Russell, *The Parousia: A Critical Inquiry into the New Testament Doctrine of Our Lord's Second Coming*, new ed. (1887; reprint, Grand Rapids, MI: Baker, 1984), pp. 28-29.

4. Russell, *The Parousia*, p. 27.

5. Russell, *The Parousia*, p. 27.

6. I used Kurt Aland, *Synopsis of the Four Gospels*, 7th ed. (Stuttgart, Germany: German Bible Society, 1984), pp. 92-94.

7. *New Geneva Study Bible*, (Nashville, TN: Thomas Nelson, 1995), p. 1521.

8. Russell, *Parousia*, p. 27.

9. William Hendriksen, *The Gospel of Matthew* (Grand Rapids, MI: Baker, 1973), pp. 466-67.

10. George N. H. Peters, *The Theocratic Kingdom*, vol. 2 (Grand Rapids, MI: Kregel, [1884], 1978), p. 563.

11. John Calvin, *Commentary on a Harmony of the Evangelists, Matthew, Mark, and Luke*, vol. I (Grand Rapids, MI: Baker, reprinted 1979), p. 458.

12. Randolph O. Yeager, *The Renaissance New Testament*, vol. 2 (Bowling Green, KY: Renaissance Press, 1977), p. 160.

13. Stanley D. Toussaint, *Behold the King: A Study of Matthew* (Portland, OR: Multnomah Press, 1980), pp. 141-42.

14. Sproul, *Last Days*, pp. 53-55.

15. *The Nelson Study Bible* (Nashville, TN: Thomas Nelson, 1997), p. 1659.

16. Toussaint, *Behold the King*, p. 209.

17. DeMar, *Last Days Madness*, p. 34.

18. William L. Lane, *Commentary on the Gospel of Mark* (Grand Rapids, MI: Eerdmans, 1974), p. 313.

19. Kenneth L. Gentry, Jr., *He Shall Have Dominion: A Postmillennial Eschatology* (Tyler, TX: 1992), p. 216.

20. Peters, *Theocratic Kingdom*, vol. 2, p. 555.

21. Yeager, *Renaissance New Testament*, vol. 2, p. 569.

22. Peters, *Theocratic Kingdom*, vol. 2, p. 562.

23. Alva J. McClain, *The Greatness of the Kingdom* (Winona Lake, IN: BMH Books, 1959), p. 336.

24. Darrell L. Bock, *Luke 1:1–9:50 (Grand Rapids, MI: Baker, 1994)*, p. 859-60.

25. *Peters*, Theocratic Kingdom, vol. 2, p. 560.

26. Lane, *Mark*, p. 314.

27. Lane, *Mark*, pp. 313-14.

28. Sproul, *Last Days*, p. 158.

29. Thomas Ice and Kenneth L. Gentry, Jr., *The Great Tribulation: Past or Future?* Grand Rapids, MI: Kregel, 1999), pp. 26-27.

30. DeMar, *Last Days Madness*, 4th ed. p. 59.

31. Gary DeMar, *End Times Fiction: A Biblical Consideration of the* Left Behind *Theology* (Nashville, TN: Thomas Nelson Publishers, 2001), p. 68.

32. DeMar, *Last Days Madness*, 4th ed. p. 56.

33. Sproul, *Last Days*, p. 66.

34. See D. A. Carson, *Exegetical Fallacies* (Grand Rapids, MI: Baker, 1984), p. 65.

35. See Roy B. Zuck, *Basic Bible Interpretation: A Practical Guide to Discovering Biblical Truth* (Wheaton, IL: Victor Books, 1991), pp. 106-09.

36. Bock, *Luke 9:51–24:53*, pp. 1691-92.

37. DeMar, *Last Days Madness*, 4th ed. p. 55.

38. Ice and Gentry, *Great Tribulation*, p. 23.

39. Merrill C. Tenney, ed., *The Zondervan Pictorial Encyclopedia of the Bible*, vol. 3 (Grand Rapids, MI: Zondervan, 1975), p. 486.

40. Kenneth L. Gentry, Jr., *Perilous Times: A Study in Eschatological Evil* (Texarkana, AR: Covenant Media Press, 1999), p. 77.

41. Gentry, *Perilous Times*, p. 79.

42. A. T. Robertson, *Word Pictures in the New Testament*, vol. I (Nashville, TN: Broadman Press, 1930), p. 183.

43. Gentry, *Perilous Times*, p. 83.

44. Arnold Fruchtenbaum, *The Footsteps of the Messiah: A Study of the Sequence of Prophetic Events* (San Antonio, TX: Ariel Press, 1982), p. 446.

45. G. K. Beale, *The Book of Revelation* (Grand Rapids, MI: Eerdmans, 1999), pp. 196-97.

46. Gentry, *He Shall Have Dominion*, p. 273.

47. Gentry, *He Shall Have Dominion*, p. 273.

48. Gentry, *He Shall Have Dominion*, p. 274.

49. Robert L. Thomas, "A Classical Dispensationalist View of Revelation" in C. Marvin Pate, ed., *Four Views on the Book of Revelation* (Grand Rapids, MI: Zondervan, 1998), p. 225.

50. Philip Edgcumbe Hughes, *The Book of The Revelation* (Grand Rapids, MI: Eerdmans, 1990), pp. 20-21.

51. Thomas, "View of Revelation" p. 225.

52. Thomas, "View of Revelation" p. 186.

53. Gentry, *Before Jerusalem Fell: Dating the Book of Revelation* (Atlanta, GA: American Vision, 1998 [1989]), p. 133.

54. John F. Walvoord, *The Revelation of Jesus Christ* (Chicago, IL: Moody Press, 1966), p. 35.

55. Gentry, *Before Jerusalem Fell*, p. 138.

56. Walter Bauer, *A Greek-English Lexicon of the New Testament and Other Early Christian Literature*, a translation and adaptation by William F. Arndt & F. Wilbur Gingrich (Chicago, IL: The University of Chicago Press, 1957).

57. Spiros Zodhiates, *The Complete Word Study Dictionary New Testament* (Chattanooga, TN: AMG Publishers, 1992), s.v. 5034, p. 1369.

58. G. H. Lang, *The Revelation of Jesus Christ: Selected Studies* (Miami Springs, FL: Conley & Schoettle Publishing Co., 1945, 1985), pp. 387-88.

59. F. Blass and A. Debrunner, *A Greek Grammar of the New Testament and Other Early Christian Literature*, translated and revised by Robert W. Funk (Chicago: The University of Chicago Press, 1961).

60. Nigel Turner, *A Grammar of New Testament Greek*, ed. by James H. Moulton, vol. III, *Syntax* (Edinburgh: T. & T. Clark, 1963), p. 252.

61. Mal Couch, gen. ed., *A Bible Handbook to Revelation* (Grand Rapids, MI: Kregel Publications, 2001), p. 200.

62. Gentry, *He Shall Have Dominion*, pp. 254; 276; 418.

63. Gentry, *Before Jerusalem Fell*, p. 141.

64. Philip Edgcumbe Hughes, *The Book of the Revelation* (Grand Rapids, MI: Wm. B. Eerdmans, 1990), p. 237.

65. William R. Newell, *Revelation: A Complete Commentary* (Grand Rapids, MI: Baker Book House, 1935, 1987), p. 362.

66. F. C. Jennings, *Studies in Revelation* (New York: Publication Office "Our Hope," n.d.), p. 22.

67. Walvoord, *Revelation*, pp. 37, 334.

68. Robert L. Thomas, "Theonomy and the Dating of Revelation," *The Master's Seminary Journal*, vol. 5 (Fall 1994), pp. 186-88.

69. Thomas, "Dating of Revelation," p. 187.

Chapter 5—Signs in the Sky

1. Revelation 6:12-17 and 8:6-12 describe the same cosmic phenomena.

2. Gary DeMar, "The Passing Away of Heaven and Earth" (http://www.preteristarchive.com./PartialPreterismppmt2425.html).

3. Several leading preterists have openly and forcefully condemned hyper-preterism as serious heresy.

4. At a February 1999 Ligonier conference on eschatology in Orlando, the preterist view was strongly promoted by a series of speakers. During the conference, Kenneth Gentry stated that Matthew 24:29-31—including the cosmic signs and Jesus' return in glory in the clouds—was already fulfilled in A.D. 70. Gentry, a preterist whose opposition to hyper-preterism is well known, hastened to add that he does not mean to deny that there will be any future literal bodily return of Christ to earth. But he also clearly believes Matthew 24 is not the place where a literal second coming is taught. A hyper-preterist critic in attendance noted that Gentry did not offer any *other* Scripture references to show where a future second coming is taught. Todd D. Dennis, "The Impact of

Preterism: Victory in Orlando" (http://www.preteristarchive.com/ MinistryUpdate/vr-0299.html).

Indeed, Gentry's own interpretation of Matthew 24:29-31 effectively eliminates all the major biblical objections to hyper-preterism. If the promise of Christ's return on the clouds in the Olivet Discourse pertains to a spiritual event already past, why not interpret all the New Testament references to His return the same way? If Matthew 24:30 is merely a metaphor describing something that took place during the destruction of Jerusalem, doesn't it make perfect sense to interpret every biblical mention of Christ's return as a reference to that same already-past event? The obvious dilemma of Gentry's position was not lost on the hyper-preterist critic, who pointed out "that this loudest second coming passage in the New Testament is applied [by Gentry] to A.D. 70, with no equal passage being given to assert a post-A.D. 70 coming" (ibid.). Plainly, preterists who allow an allegorical and symbolic interpretation of Christ's most significant second-coming prophecy have no credible answer for hyper-preterists who claim all the New Testament second-coming prophecies are allegorical.

The writer of the above-cited article derided Gentry's conviction that Christ will nonetheless return visibly someday: "Unfortunately, [Gentry] didn't supply any passages which spoke of a third coming" (ibid.). Thus hyper-preterism precisely echoes the scoffers' taunt: "Where is the promise of His coming?" (2 Peter 3:4)—and preterism's hermeneutical method simply stokes the skepticism that provokes such scorn.

5. Eusebius, *Church History*, 3:25.

6. Ironically, Kenneth Gentry argues against hyper-preterism by citing Clement of Rome's belief in a future resurrection. "Clement of Rome lived through A.D. 70 and had no idea he was resurrected! He continued to look for a physical resurrection (Clement 50:3 [sic; see rather 24:1-2; 26:1])." If Clement's looking for a future resurrection is so significant to Gentry, why does he not also think it significant that from the first-century church, through the time of the church fathers, through the Protestant Reformation, and all the way up to the present day, the overwhelming mass of believers have looked for a future fulfillment of the Olivet Discourse prophecy?

7. This prophecy seems to have had an immediate application to the judgment and destruction of Babylon (verses 1, 17; cf. Daniel 5:30-31). Yet the full meaning of the prophecy clearly looks beyond Babylon to a yet-future eschatological fulfillment, as evidenced by two things: 1) the cosmic and worldwide catastrophes spoken of in the prophecy itself (verses 10-13), and 2) Isaiah's reference to the Day of the Lord (verse 6), which is still spoken of as a yet-future reality long after the judgment of Babylon (cf. 2 Pet. 3:10). The only reasonable conclusion is that Isaiah 13 is like many passages of Scripture that deal with both near and far events. And in this case, the near event—the judgment of Babylon—was a kind of microcosm of the final Day-of-the-Lord judgments.

8. I'm aware, of course, that Peter cited this very passage in his Pentecost sermon and implied that verse 28 ("I will pour out My Spirit on all mankind; and your sons and daughters will prophesy, your old men will dream dreams, your young men will see visions") was fulfilled in some sense by the events at Pentecost. Looking at the broad context of Joel, it is clear that Joel is prophesying about the catastrophes associated with the Day of the Lord (2:1). It is equally clear that the apostle Peter

regarded the Day of the Lord as something yet future (2 Peter 3:10). So Peter could not have been declaring every aspect of Joel's prophecy fulfilled. When he cited this passage at Pentecost, he was obviously making reference to the outpouring of the Spirit in particular, and he probably meant merely that Pentecost was a preview of the Day-of-the-Lord outpouring.

9. This will include Gentile believers as well as Jewish ones. Zechariah 8:23 says, "In those days ten men from all nations will grasp the garment of a Jew saying, 'Let us go with you, for we have heard that God is with you.'"

Chapter 6—The Stake in the Heart—The A.D. 95 Date of Revelation

1. Kenneth L. Gentry, Jr. "The Days of Vengeance: A Review Article," *The Council of Chalcedon* (June 1987), p. 11. I would strengthen Gentry's point by adding that if it could be proven that Revelation was written just one year after A.D. 67 then preterism would go up in smoke. This point is made later in the chapter.

2. R. C. Sproul, *The Last Days According to Jesus* (Grand Rapids, MI: Baker Books, 1998), p. 140.

3. E. B. Elliot, *Horae Apocalypticae*, vol. IV (London: Seeleys, 1846), p. 503.

4. Howard Winters, *Commentary on Revelation* (Greenville, SC: Carolina Christian, 1989), p. 15.

5. Sproul, *Last Days*, p. 140.

6. Kenneth Gentry, *The Beast of Revelation* (Tyler, TX: Institute for Christian Economics, 1989), pp. 83-84; Kenneth L. Gentry, Jr., *Before Jerusalem Fell*, rev. ed. (Atlanta, GA: American Vision, 1998), pp. 30-38.

7. Gentry, *The Beast of Revelation*, p. 83.

8. Gentry, *The Beast of Revelation*, p. 188.

9. Gentry, *The Beast of Revelation*, p. 188; Chilton holds that Revelation must have been written during Nero's life, which ended on June 9, 68—David Chilton, *The Days of Vengeance* (Tyler, TX: Dominion Press, 1987), p. 4.

10. Here are two representative examples of some of Gentry's early-date advocates who date the book after spring 67: John A. T. Robinson, *Redating the New Testament* (Philadelphia, PA: Westminster Press, 1976); Philip Schaff, *History of the Christian Church*, vol. 1 (Grand Rapids, MI: Eerdmans, 1950).

11. J. Christian Wilson, "The Problem of the Domitianic Date of Revelation," *New Testament Studies* 39 (October 1993), 587. Paton J. Gloag, *Introduction to the Johannine Writings* (London: James Nisbet & Co., 1891), p. 316.

12. Sproul, *Last Days*, p. 140.

13. Eusebius, *Ecclesiastical History* 3.19-20.

14. Eusebius, *Ecclesiastical History* 3.18.

15. Hugh Jackson Lawlor, *Eusebiana: Essays on the Ecclesiastical History of Eusebius Bishop of Caesarea* (Oxford: Clarendon Press, 1912), p. 52.

16. Lawlor, *Eusebiana*, p. 53.

17. Eusebius *Ecclesiastical History* 3.20.

18. Lawlor, *Eusebiana*, p. 95.

19. Philip Schaff strongly supports the reliability and trustworthiness of Irenaeus. Schaff, *History of the Christian Church*, vol. II, pp. 750-51.

20. Irenaeus, *Against Heresies* 5.30.3. The Greek version of Irenaeus's statement is preserved in two places in Eusebius's *Ecclesiastical History* 3.18.3; 5.8.6.

21. G. K. Beale, *The Book of Revelation*, The New International Greek Testament Commentary, eds. I. Howard Marshall and Donald A. Hagner (Grand Rapids, MI: Eerdmans, 1999), p. 20.

22. David E. Aune, *Revelation 1–5*, Word Biblical Commentary, ed. Ralph p. Martin, vol. 52a (Dallas, TX: Word Books, 1997), p. lix.

23. BAGD, p. 92. See fn. information from chapter 4, fn. 58.

24. H. Wayne House and Thomas Ice, *Dominion Theology: Blessing or Curse?* (Portland, OR: Multnomah Press, 1988), pp. 251-52. In his critique of House and Ice, Gentry (*Before Jerusalem Fell*, p. 346) says that only the word *apokalupsis* occurs in Irenaeus's statement, not "apocalyptic vision" as it is often translated into English. However, *BAGD* (p. 92) says that in Revelation 1:1 *apokalupsis* refers to "revelations of a particular kind, through visions." So it is fitting to translate the word *apokalupsis* in Irenaeus's statement as "apocalyptic vision" or something that John saw.

25. Irenaeus, *Against Heresies* 2.22.5; 3.3.4. Both of these passages are quoted in Eusebius's *Ecclesiastical History* 3.23.3-4.

26. Beale, *Revelation*, p. 20; G. B. Caird, *The Revelation of St. John the Divine*, Black's New Testament Commentary, gen. ed. Henry Chadwick (Peabody, MA: Hendrickson Publishers, 1966), p. 6.

27. Robinson, *Redating History*, pp. 221-22.

28. Schaff, *History of the Christian Church*, vol. I, p. 834.

29. J. Ritchie Smith, "The Date of the Apocalypse," *Bibliotheca Sacra* 45 (April 1888), p. 299.

30. Deane James Woods, "Statius' *Silvae* and John's Apocalypse: Some Parallel and Contrastive Motifs," Ph.D. dissertation, Dallas Theological Seminary, 1990.

31. Woods, *Statius' Silvae*, p. i.

32. Woods, *Statius' Silvae*, p. 329.

33. Eusebius, *Ecclesiastical History* 3.23.5-19.

34. Clement of Alexandria, *Who Is the Rich Man That Shall Be Saved?* p. 42.

35. Gentry, *Before Jerusalem Fell*, pp. 83-84; Gentry, *The Beast of Revelation*, pp. 161-62.

36. BAGD, p. 157.

37. Jerome *Against Jovinianum* 1.26.

38. Eusebius, *Ecclesiastical History* 3.20.7-8; 3.32.1. Eusebius quotes from Tertullian's *Apology* 5, which was written in A.D. 197.

39. Tertullian, *Apology*, p. 5.

40. Elliott, *Horae Apocalypticae*, vol. 1, p. 37, n. 1.

41. Tertullian, *Exclusion of Heretics*, p. 36.

42. Gentry, *Before Jerusalem Fell*, p. 95. Jerome *Against Jovinium* 1.26 cites Tertullian and the story about the boiling oil and then immediately follows the story with a statement that John wrote the Apocalypse on Patmos, where he had been banished by Domitian. Clearly, Jerome made no chronological connection between the martyrdom of Peter and Paul and the banishment of John.

43. Smith, "Date" p. 301.

44. Gentry, *Before Jerusalem Fell*, p. 94.

45. Gentry, *Before Jerusalem Fell*, p. 94.

46. Donald Guthrie, *New Testament Introduction*, 3rd ed. (Downers Grove, IL: InterVarsity Press, 1970), pp. 535-36.

47. Smith, "Date" p. 302.

48. Origen, *Matthew* 16:6.

49. Smith, "Date" p. 302.

50. Simcox, an early-date proponent, says, "But, if Origen knew a tradition on this subject, he does not give it: and in default of evidence to the contrary, it is presumable that the tradition was the usual or Irenaean one—that if it named anybody it named Domitian." William Henry Simcox, *The Revelation of St. John the Divine*, The Cambridge Bible for Schools and Colleges, gen. ed. J. J. S. Perowne (Cambridge: University Press, 1902), p. xxxvi.

51. R. H. Charles, *A Critical and Exegetical Commentary on the Revelation of St. John*, The International Critical Commentary, vol. 1 (Edinburgh: T. & T. Clark, 1920), p. xciii.

52. Dio Cassius, *Roman History* 68.1.2.

53. Victorinus, *Apocalypse* 10:11.

54. Victorinus, *Apocalypse* 17:10.

55. Eusebius, *Ecclesiastical History* 3.18.1.

56. Eusebius, *Ecclesiastical History* 3.20.10.

57. Eusebius, *Ecclesiastical History* 3.23.1-2.

58. Eusebius *Chronicle* PG XIX, pp. 551-52.

59. Gentry, *Before Jerusalem Fell*, pp. 103-04.

60. Jerome, *Against Jovinianum* 1:26.

61. Jerome, *Lives of Illustrious Men* 9.6.

62. Sulpicius Severus, *Sacred History* 2.31.

63. Paulus Orosius, *The Seven Books of History Against the Pagans* 7.10, trans. Roy J. Deferrari; in *The Fathers of the Church*, vol. 50 (Washington, DC: The Catholic University of America Press, Inc., 1964), pp. 304-05.

64. Alexander Roberts and James Dobson, eds., *The Ante-Nicene Fathers* (ANF), (Grand Rapids, MI: Eerdmans, 1975), vol. 8, pp. 560-62.

65. Bede the Venerable, "Homily 1.9 on the Gospels," in *Homilies on the Gospels*, Cistercian Studies Series: Number One Hundred Ten, trans. Lawrence T. Martin (Kalamazoo, MI: Cistercian Publications, 1991), pp. 89-90.

66. Bede, *Homily on St. John the Evangelist*, works of N. Lardner, vol. 5, p. 314.

67. It should be noted at this point that Epiphanius, Bishop of Salamis, Cyprus in 367, twice asserts that John was banished under Claudius, who ruled from 41–54 (*Heresies* 51.13.33; PG XLI.909-10, pp. 949-50). He also states that John was 90 years old when he wrote his Gospel. Epiphanius was notoriously inaccurate, and his statement about John's banishment has found scant acceptance. In an attempt to find external support for his view, Gentry tries to make the case that Epiphanius really meant Nero when he wrote Claudius (*Before Jerusalem Fell*, p. 104).

68. Gentry, *Before Jerusalem Fell*, p. 108.

69. Gentry, *Before Jerusalem Fell*, p. 344.

70. Schaff, *History*, vol. I, p. 427.

71. Gloag, *Introduction*, p. 317.

72. Beale, *Revelation*, p. 27.

73. William Hendricksen, *More Than Conquerors* (Grand Rapids, MI: Baker, 1983), p. 14.

74. Charles, pp. xcii, xciv.

75. Arthur S. Peake, *The Revelation of John* (London: Holborn Publishing House, 1922), p. 96.

76. Barclay Newman, "The Fallacy of the Domitian Hypothesis," *New Testament Studies* 10 (October 1963), p. 135.

77. F. J. A. Hort, *The Apocalypse of St. John: I–III* (London: Macmillan and Co., Limited, 1908), p. xx.

78. Revelation contains more Old Testament references than any other New Testament book. In terms of actual allusions Isaiah is first, followed by Daniel, Ezekiel, and Psalms, although exact statistical counts vary. However, Daniel is generally considered to be the most influential Old Testament book on Revelation. G. K. Beale, *The Use of Daniel in Jewish Apocalyptic Literature and in the Revelation of St. John* (Lanham, MD: University Press of America, 1984); Beale, *The Book of Revelation*, p. 77. Revelation contains 53 allusions to Daniel and 43 to Ezekiel. Ferrell Jenkins, *The Old Testament in the Book of Revelation* (Marion, IN: Cogdill Foundation Publications, 1972), p. 24.

79. Beale, *Revelation*, p. 559.

80. Chris Schlect, "A Reasonable Look at Revelation," in *And It Came to Pass: A Symposium on Preterism* (Moscow, ID: Canon Press, 1993), fn. 40, pp. 102-03.

81. Most scholars date 1 *Clement* c. 95–97. M. W. Holmes, "Clement of Rome," in *Dictionary of the Later New Testament and Its Developments*, eds. Ralph p. Martin and Peter H. Davids (Downers Grove, IL: InterVarsity Press, 1997), p. 234.

82. Gematria ("mathematical") is the rabbinic Hebrew term for cryptogrammic riddles where the numerical value of letters in a proper name are added up to arrive at a numerical value for the name. These cryptograms were widely recognized in Greek and Hebrew literature. Gentry provides an excellent discussion of the meaning and ancient use of gematria in, *Before Jerusalem Fell*, pp. 193-97.

83. Gentry, *Before Jerusalem Fell*, pp. 203-12.

84. Beale, *Revelation*, p. 719.

85. Preterists make a great deal out of the fact that there is a textual variant in Revelation 13:18 that reads 616. Since 616 is the gematria value of Nero Caesar when the name is transcribed into Hebrew from Latin, they claim that the variant is intentional to make the identity of the Beast more readily discernible to a non-Hebrew mind (Gentry, *Before Jerusalem Fell*, pp. 202-03). It is much more likely that the variant resulted from a confusion of two Greek letters that would change the sum from 666 to 616. There is one good manuscript (2344) that has 665, which also could have resulted from a scribal error (Beale, *Revelation*, p, 719). O. Ruhle believes that the 616 variant is best explained by an intentional attempt to identify the cruel Roman emperor Caligula with the Beast. Caligula's title "Gaius Caesar" equals 616 (O Ruhle, *Theological Dictionary of the New Testament*, ed. Gerhard Kittel, trans. and ed. Geoffrey W. Bromiley, vol. 1 [Grand Rapids, MI: Eerdmans, 1964], p. 463.) If the final *n* is dropped from Teitan (Titus), the value of Teita is 616 (Milligan, *Discussions on the Apocalypse*, (New York: Macmillan, 1893), p. 117.

86. In the scroll fragment *Scroll from Murabba'at*, some argue that the spelling of Caesar in Hebrew without the *yodh* is present (D. R. Hillers, "Scroll from Murabba'at," *Bulletin of the American Schools of Oriental Research* 170 [April 1963], p. 65. However, in the scroll fragment the part of the word where the *yodh* should be located is missing—Beale, p. 719). Only the spelling with the *yodh* is found in a concordance search of the Talmuds, the Mishnah, the Tosephta, and the Tannaitic Midrashim

(G. W. Buchanan, *The Book of Revelation: Its Introduction and Prophecy*, Mellon Biblical Commentary, New Testament Series [Lewiston: Mellon, 1993], pp. 345-46.)

87. Robert H Mounce, *The Book of Revelation*, The New International Commentary on the New Testament, gen. ed. F. F. Bruce (Grand Rapids, MI: Eerdmans, Publishing Company, 1977), p. 264.

88. G. Salmon, *An Historical Introduction to the Study of the Books of the New Testament* (London: Murray, 1904), pp. 230-31.

89. Irenaeus, *Against Heresies* 5.30.1. Gentry (*Before Jerusalem Fell*, p. 207) states that Irenaeus may not have recorded the Nero theory because of his predisposition to a futuristic interpretation in keeping with his premillennialism. However, this is mere conjecture. Gentry presents no evidence to substantiate this claim. One could just as easily turn the argument around and say that Gentry holds the Nero theory because of his preterist predisposition.

90. Gentry (*Before Jerusalem Fell*, p. 206) argues that *Lateinos* signifies the Roman Empire and could be a reference to the empire's head, which could be Nero if the book was written during Nero's reign. He also maintains that *Teitan* is a reference to the sun god and that Nero adopted the attributes of the sun deity as his own. Kistemaker believes that *Teitan* is a reference to Titus, who destroyed Jerusalem (Simon J. Kistemaker, *Exposition of the Book of Revelation*, New Testament Commentary [Grand Rapids, MI: Baker Books, 2001], p. 31.) While these connections to Nero are possible, they seem to be a strained way to refer to Nero. If Irenaeus believed that others had identified Nero as the Beast, why wouldn't he just have said so by naming him specifically?

91. Irenaeus, *Against Heresies* 5.30.3.

92. O. F. Fritsche (1831); Ferdinandus Benary (1836); Ferdinand Hitzig and Eduard Reuss (1837). See David Brady, *The Contribution of British Writers Between 1560 and 1830 to the Interpretation of Revelation 13.16-18 (The Number of the Beast)* (Tubingen: J.C.B. Mohr, 1983), 291-93; Milligan, *Discussions on the Apocalypse*, p. 110.

93. Robert H. Gundry, *A Survey of the New Testament*, 3rd ed. (Grand Rapids, MI: Zondervan Publishing House, 1994), p. 459.

94. According to Revelation 13:3, one of the Beast's heads receives a mortal blow delivered by someone else; whereas, Nero committed suicide (Kistemaker, *Revelation*, p. 31).

95. Gentry (*The Beast of Revelation*, pp. 57-67) goes to great lengths to prove that Nero was worshiped as God and that a statue of Nero was set up in the temple of Mars in A.D. 55, but this hardly fulfills the worldwide scope of worship described in Revelation 13 or the other details in Revelation 13 that preterists simply cannot account for. Sherrer discusses the use of contrived religious wonders in the imperial cult which he believes fulfills what is stated in Revelation 13:13-15. However, he seems to miss the point that in Revelation 13 these are real signs and wonders and not tricks, manipulation, or sleight of hand (cf. Matthew 24:24; 2 Thessalonians 2:9). Steven J. Scherrer, "Signs and Wonders in the Imperial Cult: A New Look at a Roman Religious Institution in the Light of Rev. 13:13-15," *Journal of Biblical Literature* 103/4 (December 1984), pp. 599-610.

96. David E. Aune, *Revelation 17–22*. Word Biblical Commentary, ed. Ralph p. Martin, vol. 52c (Dallas, TX: Word Books, 1998), p. 947.

97. Beale, *Revelation*, p. 874.

98. J. Ramsey Michaels, *Interpreting the Book of Revelation*, Guide to New Testament Exegesis, gen. ed. Scot McKnight (Grand Rapids, MI: Baker Books, 1992), pp. 44-45; A. Yarbro Collins, "Dating the Apocalypse of John," *Biblical Research* 26 (1981), pp. 35-36.

99. Robert L. Thomas, *Revelation 8–22* (Chicago, IL: Moody Press, 1995), p. 297.

100. Mounce, *Revelation*, p. 315.

101. Hendriksen, *Revelation*, p. 204; George Eldon Ladd, *A Commentary on the Revelation of John* (Grand Rapids, MI: Eerdmans, 1972), p. 229; Thomas, *Revelation 8–22*, p. 297; John F. Walvoord, *The Revelation of Jesus Christ* (Chicago, IL: Moody Press, 1966), pp. 251-54.

102. The reference to the beast like a leopard, bear, and lion in Revelation 13:2 is an unmistakable allusion to Daniel 7, as are the ten horns of the beast in Revelation 13:1; 17:3,7,12. Gregory K. Beale, "The Danielic Background for Revelation 13:18 and 17:9," *Tyndale Bulletin* 31 (1980), pp. 163-70.

103. Beale, *Revelation*, p. 868.

104. *BAGD*, p. 660.

105. One argument commonly used to support the Domitianic date is the symbolic use of the word "Babylon" for Rome in Revelation 14 and 17–18 because Rome was the second destroyer of Jerusalem and the Temple. It is argued that since Rome is called Babylon, she must have already destroyed the Temple; therefore, Revelation must have been written after A.D. 70. A. Yarbro Collins, "Dating," pp. 35, 42. However, if "Babylon" refers to a literal, rebuilt Babylon on the Euphrates then this point disappears—see Charles H. Dyer, "The Identity of Babylon in Revelation 17–18 (part 1)" *Bibliotheca Sacra* 144 (July-September 1987), pp. 305-16; Charles H. Dyer, "The Identity of Babylon in Revelation 17–18 (part 2)" *Bibliotheca Sacra* 144 (October-December 1987) pp. 433-49; Thomas, *Revelation 8–22*, p. 307.

106. Craig S. Keener, *Revelation*, The NIV Application Commentary, gen. ed. Terry Muck (Grand Rapids, MI: Zondervan, 2000), p. 26.

107. I. T. Beckwith, *The Apocalypse of John* (New York: Macmillan, 1919; reprint, Grand Rapids, MI: Baker Books, 1979), p. 207.

108. *The Letter of Polycarp to the Philippians* 11.3.

109. Charles, *Revelation*, vol. 1, p. xciv. Donald Guthrie (pp. 954-55) supports Charles's argument.

110. Gentry, *Before Jerusalem Fell*, p. 324-35.

111. Homer Hailey, *Revelation: An Introduction and Commentary* (Grand Rapids, MI: Baker Book House, 1979), p. 34.

112. Tacitus *Annals* 14.27.

113. Colin J. Hemer, *The Letters to the Seven Churches of Asia in Their Local Setting* (Sheffield, England: The University of Sheffield, 1989), p. 194.

114. Hemer, *Letters*, pp. 194-95. The *Sibylline Oracles* 4.108 (A.D. 80) refer to the earthquake and the rebuilding of Laodicea.

115. Hemer, *Letters*, p. 195.

116. Based upon his thorough study of the seven churches in their local setting, Hemer (pp. 2-12) concludes that Revelation was written during the reign of Domitian.

117. Dio Cassius (67.14.1-3) relates how Domitilla, the niece of Domitian and wife of a senator named Flavius Clemens, was banished to Pandateria by Domitian for being a Christian. Her husband, Flavius Clemens, who

was Domitian's cousin, was executed (cf. Suetonius, *The Lives of the Caesars* 15.1). Dio Cassius (67.12.2-3) also refers to Domitian's banishment of Mettius Pompusianus to Corsica, although Domitian later had him executed.

118. J. Ramsey Michaels, p. 45.

119. James H Charlesworth, ed., *The Old Testament Pseudepigrapha*, vol. 1 (New York: Doubleday, 1983), pp. 544-47.

Chapter 7—The Olivet Discourse

1. Tim LaHaye and Thomas Ice, *Charting the End Times: A Visual Guide to Understanding Bible Prophecy* (Eugene, OR: Harvest House, 2001), p. 35.

2. Stanley D. Toussaint, *Behold the King: A Study of Matthew* (Portland, OR: Multnomah Press, 1980), pp. 264-65.

3. Alfred Edersheim, *The Life and Times of Jesus the Messiah*, vol. 2 (Grand Rapids, MI: Eerdmans, 1974 [1883]), p. 414.

4. Arnold Fruchtenbaum, *The Footsteps of the Messiah: A Study of the Sequence of Prophetic Events* (San Antonio, TX: Ariel Press, 1982), pp. 212-15.

5. Fruchtenbaum, *Footsteps*, p. 215.

6. David L. Cooper, *Messiah: His Final Call to Israel* (Los Angeles, CA: Biblical Research Society, 1962), p. 47.

7. Craig L. Blomberg, *Matthew, The New American Commentary* vol. 22 (Nashville, TN: Broadman Press, 1992), p. 353, fn. 37.

8. Toussaint, *Behold the King*, p. 269.

9. See the following passages for examples of Christ correcting the disciples beliefs: Matthew 5–7; 9:1-8; 12:1-8, 46-50; 13:10-23; 15:1-20; 16:13-26; 17:1-9; 18:1-6, 21-35; 19:3-12, 13-15, 27-30; 20:20-28; 21:33-46.

10. J. Dwight Pentecost, *The Words and Works of Jesus Christ: A Study of the Life of Christ* (Grand Rapids, MI: Zondervan, 1981), p. 398.

11. Alexander Balmain Bruce, "The Synoptic Gospels" in W. Robertson Nicoll, ed. *The Expositor's Greek Testament*, vol. 1 (Grand Rapids, MI: Eerdmans, 1976), p. 289.

12. Toussaint, *Behold the King*, pp. 269-70.

13. Kenneth L. Gentry, Jr., *Before Jerusalem Fell: Dating the Book of Revelation* (Tyler, TX: Institute for Christian Economics, 1989), p. 176.

14. Randall Price, *Jerusalem in Prophecy: God's Stage for the Final Drama* (Eugene, OR.: Harvest House, 1998), pp. 251-55

15. Gentry, *Before Jerusalem Fell*, p. 176.

16. Gary DeMar, *Last Days Madness: Obsession of the Modern Church* (Powder Springs, GA: American Vision, 1999), p. 72.

17. Kenneth L. Gentry, Jr., *He Shall Have Dominion: A Postmillennial Eschatology* (Tyler, TX: Institute for Christian Economics, 1992), p. 206.

18. J. C. Ryle, *Expository Thoughts on the Gospels: Luke*, vol. 2 (Cambridge: James Clarke & Co., [1858] n. d.), p. 374.

19. William Kelly, *An Exposition of the Gospel of Luke* (Oak Park, IL: Bible Truth Publishers, 1971), pp. 332-333.

20. John F. Walvoord, *Matthew: Thy Kingdom Come* (Chicago, IL: Moody Press, 1974), p. 183.

21. Walvoord, *Matthew*, p. 183.

22. Fruchtenbaum, *The Footsteps of the Messiah*, pp. 439-40. For the most exhaustive presentation of this view that I have found so far, see David L. Cooper, *Future Events Revealed: According to Matthew 24 and 25* (Los Angeles, CA: David L. Cooper, 1935).

23. Arno C. Gaebelein, *The Gospel of Matthew: An Exposition* (Neptune, NJ: Loizeaux Brothers, [1910], 1961), p. 476.

24. Gaebelein, *Matthew*, p. 481.

25. John McLean, "Chronology and Sequential Structure of John's Revelation," in Thomas Ice & Timothy Demy, *When the Trumpet Sounds: Today's Foremost Authorities Speak Out on End-Time Controversies* (Eugene, OR: Harvest House, 1995), p. 323.

26. McLean, "Chronology and Sequential Structure," p. 326.

27. Joseph Henry Thayer, *A Greek-English Lexicon of the New Testament* (New York: American Book Company, 1889), p. 679.

28. William F. Arndt and F. W. Gingrich, *A Greek-English Lexicon of the New Testament* (Chicago, IL: University of Chicago Press, 1957), p. 904.

29. J. Randall Price, "Old Testament Tribulation Terms," in Thomas Ice & Timothy Demy, *When the Trumpet Sounds: Today's Foremost Authorities Speak Out on End-Time Controversies* (Eugene, OR: Harvest House, 1995), p. 72.

30. Raphael Patai, *The Messiah Texts: Jewish Legends of Three Thousand Years* (Detroit, MI: Wayne State University Press, 1979), pp. 95-103.

31. Patai, *Messiah Texts*, pp. 95-96.

32. Price, "Tribulation Terms," p. 450, fn. 56.

33. William Kelly, *Lectures on the Gospel of Matthew* (Sunbury, PA: Believers Bookshelf, 1971), p. 479.

34. Kelly, *Matthew*, p. 479.

35. Ed Glasscock, *Matthew: Moody Gospel Commentary* (Chicago, IL: Moody Press, 1997), p. 464.

36. Toussaint, *Behold the King*, p. 270.

37. Alan Hugh M'Neile, *The Gospel According to St. Matthew* (London: Macmillan, 1915), p. 345.

38. Roman historian "Dio Cassius relates that the Romans demolished 50 fortresses, destroyed 985 villages, and killed 580,000 people in addition to those who died of hunger, disease, and fire." *Encyclopaedia Judaica*, vol. 4 (Jerusalem: Keter Publishing House, n.d.), p. 233.

39. Robert H. Gundry, *Matthew: A Commentary on His Handbook for a Mixed Church Under Persecution*, 2nd ed. (Grand Rapids, MI: Eerdmans, 1994), p. 477.

40. James R. Gray, *Prophecy on The Mount: A Dispensational Study of the Olivet Discourse* (Chandler, AZ: Berean Advocate Ministries, 1991), p. 29.

41. DeMar, *Last Days Madness*, p. 73.

42. Kenneth L. Gentry, Jr., *Perilous Times: A Study in Eschatological Evil* (Texarkana, AR: Covenant Media Press, 1999), p. 46.

43. Gentry, *Perilous Times*, pp. 46-47.

44. DeMar, *Last Days Madness*, p. 74.

45. Heinrich August Wilhelm Meyer, *Critical and Exegetical Handbook to the Gospel of Matthew*, vol. 2 (Edinburgh: T. & T. Clark, 1879), p. 128.

46. W. D. Davies and Dale C. Allison, Jr., *A Critical and Exegetical Commentary on the Gospel According to Saint Matthew*, vol. 3 (Edinburgh: T. & T. Clark, 1997), pp. 338-39.

47. Leon Morris, *The Gospel According to Matthew* (Grand Rapids, MI: Eerdmans, 1992), p. 597.

48. Donald A. Hagner, *Word Biblical Commentary: Matthew 14–28*, vol. 33B (Dallas, TX: Word Books, 1995), p. 690.

49. Thomas O. Figart, *The King of the Kingdom of Heaven: A Verse by Verse Commentary on the Gospel of Matthew* (Lancaster, PA: Eden Press, 1999), p. 438.

50. Gaebelein, *Matthew*, pp. 481-82.

51. Randolph O. Yeager, *The Renaissance New Testament*, vol. 3 (Bowling Green, KY: Renaissance Press, 1978), p. 277.

52. Richard C. Trench, *Synonyms of the New Testament* (Grand Rapids, MI: Eerdmans, [1880], 1953), p. 322.

53. Meyer, *Matthew*, vol. 2, p. 129.

54. Kelly, *Matthew*, p. 482.

55. Kelly, *Matthew*, p. 483.

56. M'Neile, *Matthew*, p. 346.

57. A. T. Robertson, *Word Pictures in the New Testament*, vol. 1 (Nashville, TN: Broadman Press, 1930), p. 189.

58. Meyer, *Matthew*, vol. 2, p. 129.

59. Davies and Allison, *Matthew*, vol. 3, p. 349, fn. 81.

60. Morris, *Matthew*, p.598.

61. Gray, *Prophecy on The Mount*, pp. 29-30.

62. DeMar, *Last Days Madness*, p. 88.

63. Gary DeMar, *End Times Fiction: A Biblical Consideration of the* Left Behind *Theology* (Nashville, TN: Thomas Nelson Publishers, 201), pp. 82-83.

64. DeMar, *Last Days Madness*, pp. 87-89; DeMar, *End Times Fiction*, p. 83.

65. Arndt and Gingrich, *Greek-English Lexicon*, p. 563.

66. Horst Balz and Gerhard Schneider, editors, *Exegetical Dictionary of the New Testament*, vol. 2 (Grand Rapids, MI: Eerdmans, 1991), p. 503.

67. Gary DeMar, "Will the Real Anti-Prophets Please Stand Up?" from the Internet site http://www.preteristarchive.com/CriticalArticles/demar-gary_da_01.html.

68. Gerhard Kittel and Gerhard Friedrich, eds., *Theological Dictionary of the New Testament*, vol. V (Grand Rapids, MI, Eerdmans, 1967), p. 859.

69. Colin Brown, ed., *Dictionary of New Testament Theology*, vol. 2 (Grand Rapids, MI: Zondervan, 1986), p. 899.

70. R. C. H. Lenski, *The Interpretation of St. Paul's Epistles to the Colossians…*(Minneapolis, MN: Augsburg, 1946), p. 26.

71. Ernest R. Campbell, *A Commentary of Colossians & Philemon* (Silverton, OR: Canyonview Press, 1982), p. 66.

72. J. B. Lightfoot, *Saint Paul's Epistles to the Colossians and to Philemon* (Grand Rapids, MI: Zondervan, [1879], 1959) p. 163.

73. Gray, *Prophecy on the Mount*, p. 62.

74. DeMar, "Anti-Prophets."

75. DeMar, *End Times Fiction*, p. 83.

76. Leon Morris, *The Epistle to the Romans* (Grand Rapids, MI: Eerdmans, 1988), p. 547, fn. 85.

77. H. p. Liddon, *Explanatory Analysis of St. Paul's Epistle to the Romans* (Minneapolis, MN: James and Klock, [1899], 1977), p. 307.

78. Randolph O. Yeager, *The Renaissance New Testament*, vol. 12 (Gretna, LA: Pelican, 1983), p. 282.

79. DeMar, *End Times Fiction*, pp. 74-75.

80. Don K. Preston, *Into All the World: Then Comes the End!* (no publishing information, 1996).

81. Gentry, *Perilous Times*, pp. 22-26.

82. John F. Walvoord, "Christ's Olivet Discourse on the Time of the End: Signs of the End of the Age," *Bibliotheca Sacra* (vol. 128, num. 512, Oct.-Dec., 1971), pp. 318-19.

83. Walvoord., "Olivet Discourse," p. 319.

84. Walvoord., "Olivet Discourse," p. 319.

85. Gentry in Thomas Ice and Kenneth L. Gentry, Jr., *The Great Tribulation: Past or Future?* Grand Rapids, MI: Kregel, 1999), pp. 47-48.

86. Gentry in Ice and Gentry, *Great Tribulation*, p. 47.

87. D. A. Carson, "Matthew," *The Expositor's Bible Commentary*, vol. 8 (Grand Rapids, MI: Zondervan Publishing House, 1984), p. 500.

88. See David Chilton, *Paradise Restored: An Eschatology of Dominion* (Tyler, TX: Reconstruction Press, 1985), pp. 274-6.

89. Stanley D. Toussaint, "A Critique of the Preterist View of the Olivet Discourse," an unpublished paper presented to the Pre-Trib Study Group, Dallas, TX, 1996, n.p.

90. Walvoord., "Olivet Discourse," p. 317.

91. Gentry in Ice and Gentry, *Great Tribulation*, pp. 48-50.

92. Randall Price, *Charting the Future* (San Marcos, TX: privately published charts, n.d.), n.p.

93. Gentry in Ice and Gentry, *Great Tribulation*, p. 51.

94. Gentry in Ice and Gentry, *Great Tribulation*, p. 51.

95. Gentry in Ice and Gentry, *Great Tribulation*, p. 53.

96. Gentry in Ice and Gentry, *Great Tribulation*, p. 53.

97. Gentry in Ice and Gentry, *Great Tribulation*, pp. 52-53.

98. Gentry in Ice and Gentry, *Great Tribulation*, p. 52.

99. Arnold Fruchtenbaum, personal letter to Thomas Ice, dated September 16, 1994.

100. Toussaint, "Critique," n.p.

101. Gentry in Ice and Gentry, *Great Tribulation*, p. 53.

102. Gentry in Ice and Gentry, *Great Tribulation*, p. 54.

103. Gentry in Ice and Gentry, *Great Tribulation*, p. 53.

104. Gentry in Ice and Gentry, *Great Tribulation*, p. 53.

105. Arndt and Gingrich, *A Greek-English Lexicon*, p. 635.

106. Gerhard Kittel and Gerhard Friedrich, eds., *Theological Dictionary of the New Testament*, vol. V (Grand Rapids, MI: Eerdmans, 1967), p. 859.

107. Kittel and Friedrich, *Theological Dictionary*, vol. V, p. 865.

108. Toussaint, "Critique," n.p.

109. Gentry in Ice and Gentry, *Great Tribulation*, p. 54.

110. Toussaint, "Critique," n.p.

111. Gentry in Ice and Gentry, *Great Tribulation*, p. 55.

112. Gentry in Ice and Gentry, *Great Tribulation*, p. 55.

113. Gentry in Ice and Gentry, *Great Tribulation*, p. 56.

114. D. D. Buck, *Our Lord's Great Prophecy* (Nashville, TN: South-Western Publishing House, 1857), p. 229.

115. Richard Cunningham Shimeall, *Christ's Second Coming: Is It Pre-Millennial or Post-Millennial?* (New York: John F. Trow and Richard Brinkerhoff, 1866), pp. 157-59.

116. Henry George Liddell and Robert Scott, *A Greek-English Lexicon* (Oxford England: Oxford Press, 1968), s.verse "aster", p. 261.

117. Gundry, *Matthew*, p. 487.

118. Randolph O. Yeager, *The Renaissance New Testament*, vol. 3 (Bowling Green, KY: Renaissance Press, 1978), p. 312.

119. Gentry in Ice and Gentry, *Great Tribulation*, p. 58.

120. Gentry in Ice and Gentry, *Great Tribulation*, p. 58.

121. Nigel Turner, *A Grammar of New Testament Greek*, vol. III, *Syntax* (Edinburgh: T. & T. Clark, 1963), p. 214.

122. Arndt and Gingrich, *A Greek-English Lexicon*, pp. 598-600.

123. Arndt and Gingrich, *A Greek-English Lexicon*, p. 599.

124. Buck, *Our Lord's Great Prophecy*, p. 292.

125. Gentry in Ice and Gentry, *Great Tribulation*, p. 60.

126. Shimeall, *Christ's Second Coming*, pp. 159-60.

127. For a biblical overview of the Shechinah glory see Thomas Ice and Timothy Demy, *Fast Facts on Bible Prophecy* (Eugene, OR: Harvest House, 1997), pp. 193-96.

128. Fruchtenbaum, *Footsteps*, p. 443.

129. Gentry in Ice and Gentry, *Great Tribulation*, pp. 66-67.

130. Gentry in Ice and Gentry, *Great Tribulation*, p. 67.

131. Gentry, *He Shall Have Dominion*, p. 275.

132. C. F. Keil and F. Delitzsch, *Commentary on the Book of Daniel* (Grand Rapids, MI: Eerdmans, 1975), pp. 235-36.

133. Toussaint, "Critique," n.p.

134. Gentry in Ice and Gentry, *Great Tribulation*, p. 61.

135. Gentry in Ice and Gentry, *Great Tribulation*, p. 64.

136. Gentry in Ice and Gentry, *Great Tribulation*, p. 61.

137. Gentry in Ice and Gentry, *Great Tribulation*, p. 63.

138. Gentry in Ice and Gentry, *Great Tribulation*, pp. 61-65.

139. James Barr, *The Semantics of Biblical Languages* (London: Oxford University Press, 1961), p. 218.

140. Arnold Fruchtenbaum, *Israaelology: The Missing Link in Systematic Theology*, rev. ed. (Tustin, CA: Ariel Ministries Press, 1992), pp. 798-99.

Chapter 8—How Preterists Misuse History to Advance Their View of Prophecy

1. R. C. Sproul, *The Last Days According to Jesus: When Did Jesus Say He Would Return?* (Grand Rapids, MI: Baker Books, 1998), p. 127.

2. Thomas Ice and Kenneth L. Gentry, Jr., *The Great Tribulation: Past or Future?—Two Evangelicals Debate the Question* (Grand Rapids, MI: Kregel Publications, 1999), p. 13.

3. Ice and Gentry, *The Great Tribulation*, p. 38.

4. Gary DeMar, *Last Days Madness: Obsession of the Modern Church* (Atlanta, GA: American Vision, 1997), p. 120.

5. *Josephus: Essential Works, A Condensation of Jewish Antiquities and the Jewish War*, trans. and ed. Paul L. Maier (Grand Rapids, MI: Kregel Publications, 1988), p. 356.

6. *Josephus: Essential Works*, p. 11.

7. *Josephus: Essential Works*, pp. 341-42.

8. *Josephus: Essential Works*, p. 343.

9. *Josephus: Essential Works*, p. 355, n. 3

10. *Josephus: Essential Works*, p. 355.

11. *Josephus: Essential Works*, p. 356.

12. Kenneth L. Gentry, Jr., *The Beast of Revelation* (Tyler, TX: Institute for Christian Economics, 1989), p. 40.

13. Gentry, *Beast of Revelation*, p. 41.

14. Kenneth L. Gentry, Jr., *Before Jerusalem Fell: Dating the Book of Revelation—An Exegetical and Historical Argu-

ment for a Pre-A.D. 70 Composition* (Tyler, TX: Institute for Christian Economics, 1989), p. 213.

15. Gentry, *Before Jerusalem Fell*, p. 218.

16. Gentry, *Before Jerusalem Fell*, p. 215.

17. Gentry, *Before Jerusalem Fell*, p. 215.

18. Gentry, *Before Jerusalem Fell*, p. 215.

19. Fritz Redlich, M.D., *Hitler: Diagnosis of a Destructive Prophet* (New York: Oxford University Press, 1999), p. 274.

20. Gentry, *Before Jerusalem Fell*, p. 248.

21. Gentry, *Before Jerusalem Fell*, p. 248.

22. Gentry, *Before Jerusalem Fell*, pp. 248-49.

23. Gentry, *Before Jerusalem Fell*, p. 249.

24. Jay E. Adams, *The Christian Counselor's Manual* (Philadelphia, PA: Presbyterian and Reformed Publishing Co., 1973), pp. 127-28.

25. *Josephus: Essential Works*, p. 369.

26. Paul L. Maier, *Eusebius: The Church History, A New Translation with Commentary* (Grand Rapids, MI: Kregel Publications, 1999), pp. 137-38.

27. Randall Price, *The Coming Last Days Temple* (Eugene, OR: Harvest House, 1999), p. 90.

28. Iris Chang, *The Rape of Nanking: The Forgotten Holocaust of WW II* (New York: Basic Books, 1997), p. 216.

29. Gentry, *Before Jerusalem Fell*, p. 250.

30. Gentry, *Before Jerusalem Fell*, pp. 250-53.

31. *Josephus: Essential Works*, p. 289.

32. *Josephus: Essential Works*, pp. 289-90.

33. Gentry, *Before Jerusalem Fell*, p. 252.

34. Steve Gregg, ed., *Revelation: Four Views. A Parallel Commentary* (Nashville, TN: Thomas Nelson, 1997), p. 226.

35. Gregg, *Revelation: Four Views*, p. 232.

36. Gentry, *Beast of Revelation*, p. 99.

37. Gentry, *Before Jerusalem Fell*, p. 244.

38. Gentry, *Beast of Revelation*, p. 99.

39. Gentry, *Before Jerusalem Fell*, p. 246.

40. Gordon Franz, *The Preterist View of Jerusalem: Are the "Fulfillments" Historically Accurate?* A paper presented at the Pre-Trib Study Group conference, Dallas, TX, Dec. 1999, p. 12.

41. Kenneth L. Gentry, Jr., *He Shall Have Dominion: A Postmillennial Eschatology* (Tyler, TX: Institute for Christian Economics, 1992), p. 160.

42. Flavius Josephus, *The Wars of the Jews*, book V, chapter VI, paragraph 3.

43. Charles Clough, "God's Pattern of Judgment," in the *Tim LaHaye Prophecy Study Bible*, NKJV (Chattanooga, TN: AMG Publishers, 2001), p. 1470.

44. John Calvin, *Calvin's Commentaries*, vol. IV (Grand Rapids, MI: Baker, 1979), pp. 151-52.

45. E. W. Bullinger, *Commentary on Revelation* (Grand Rapids, MI: Kregel, [1935], 1984), p. 493.

46. Bullinger, *Revelation*, p. 492.

47. Gentry, *Before Jerusalem Fell*, p. 246.

48. Henry M. Morris, *The Revelation Record* (Wheaton, IL: Tyndale, 1983), p. 322.

49. Robert L. Thomas, *Revelation 8–22: An Exegetical Commentary* (Chicago, IL: Moody Press, 1995), p. 277.

50. Thomas, *Revelation 8–22*, p. 277.

51. Clough, "God's Pattern of Judgment," p. 1470.

52. DeMar, *Last Days Madness*, p. 93.

Chapter 9—Was "Babylon" Destroyed When Jerusalem Fell in A.D. 70?

1. Gary DeMar, *End Time Fiction* (Nashville, TN: Thomas Nelson, 2001), pp. 115-30.

2. Kenneth Gentry, *Before Jerusalem Fell*. (Atlanta, GA: American Vision, 1998), fn. 26.

3. Gentry, *Before Jerusalem Fell*, pp. liv-lxvi.

4. J. Massyngberde Ford, *Revelation*, The Anchor Bible (Garden City, NY: Doubleday, 1975); Balyeat, *Babylon*; D. Preston, *Who Is This Babylon?* (self-published); Kenneth Davies, *Babylon the Harlot City* (Bradford, PA: International Preterist Association, 2000); G. Holford, *The Destruction of Jerusalem* (Nacogdoches, TX: Covenant Media, 2001).

5. Robert Thomas, "Theonomy and the Dating of Revelation," *The Master's Seminary Journal* (vol. 5, no. 2, 1994).

6. Gentry, *Before Jerusalem Fell*, p. 100.

7. *Acts of the Holy Apostle and Evangelist John the Theologian* (Peabody, MA: Hendrickson, 1994) vol. 8, pp. 560-62.

8. David Chilton, *The Days of Vengeance* (Ft. Worth, TX: Dominion, 1987), pp. 75-76.

9. John Jones, *A Dictionary of Ancient Roman Coins* (London: Seaby, 1990), p. 297.

10. Gordon Franz, "The King and I: The Apostle John and Emperor Domitian" *Bible and Spade* (vol. 12, no. 2, 1999), pp. 47-49; E. Janzen, "The Jesus of the Apocalypse Wears the Emperor's Cloth," *SBL 1994 Seminar Papers* (Atlanta, GA: Scholars, 1994): pp. 644-47.

11. Andrew Burnett, Michel Amandry, and Pere Pau Ripolles, *Roman Provincial Coinage*, vol. 1, part 2 (London: British Museum; Paris: Bibliotheque Nationale de France, 1992), Plates 54 and 55, coins pp. 963-970, 974, 975.

12. Andrew Burnett, Michel Amandry, and Pere Pau Ripolles, *Roman Provincial Coinage*, vol. 1, part 1 (London: British Museum; Paris: Bibliotheque Nationale de France, 1992), p. 230.

13. Burnett, Amandry, and Ripolles, *Roman Provincial Coinage*, vol. 1, part 1, p. 231.

14. C. H. V. Sutherland, *The Roman Imperial Coinage*, vol. 1 (London: Spink and Son, 1984), p. 211, no. 95.

15. Sutherland, *Roman Imperial Coinage*, p. 200.

16. Harold Mattingly and Edward Sydenham, *Roman Imperial Coinage*, vol. 2 (London: Spink and Son, 1926), p. 179, no. 209A, plate V:86.

17. Mattingly and Sydenham, *Roman Imperial Coinage*, p. 307, no. 785.

18. Mattingly and Sydenham, *Roman Imperial Coinage*, p. 362, no. 202; p. 381, no. 358; p. 434, no. 731.

19. Mattingly and Sydenham, *Roman Imperial Coinage*, p. 324.

20. Gentry, *Before Jerusalem Fell*, p. 239.

21. Gentry, *Before Jerusalem Fell*, p. 239.

22. Josephus, *Life* 1,2; Loeb Classical Library 1:3.

23. Josephus, *Life* 422,423; Loeb Classical Library 1:155.

24. Harold Buckwalter and Mary Shoaff, *Guide to the Reference System for the Works of Flavius Josephus* (Winona Lake, IN: Eisenbrauns, 1995).

25. Gentry, *Before Jerusalem Fell* p. 243; Chilton, *Days of Vengeance*, pp. 189-91.

26. Ford, *Revelation*, p. 107.

27. Gentry, *Before Jerusalem Fell*, p. 243, fn. 33.

28. Nogah Hareuveni, *The Emblem of the State of Israel* (Kiryat Ono: Neot Kedumim, 1988), p. 25.

29. Oded Borowski, *Agriculture in Iron Age Israel* (Winona Lake, IN: Eisenbrauns, 1987), pp. 158-60.

30. Gordon Franz, "The King and I: Opening the Third Seal." *Bible and Spade* (vol. 13, no. 1, 2000), pp. 9-11.

31. Chilton, *Days of Vengeance*, p. 236.

32. Chilton, *Days of Vengeance*, pp. 417-18.

33. Chilton, *Days of Vengeance*, p. 237.

34. Josephus, *Wars* 6:5; Loeb Classical Library 3:379.

35. Josephus, *Wars* 5:263, 264; Loeb Classical Library 3:283.

36. Josephus, *Wars* 5:522, 523; Loeb Classical Library 3:363.

37. Chilton, *Days of Vengeance*, p. 238.

38. J. Bent, "What St. John Saw on Patmos." *The Nineteenth Century* 24 (1888), pp. 813-21.

39. Chilton, *Days of Vengeance*, p. 251.

40. Chilton, *Days of Vengeance*, p. 252.

41. Josephus, *Wars* 2:499-545; Loeb Classical Library 2:517-535.

42. M. Gichon, "Cestius Gallus's Campaign in Judaea," *Palestine Exploration Quarterly* 113 (1981), pp. 39-62.

43. Pliny the Elder Places the Euphrates River 175 Roman Miles from Antioch, *Natural History* 5:67; 6:126; Loeb Classical Library 2:269, 433.

44. For the use of the word "Palestine" before A.D. 135; D. Jacobson, "Palestine and Israel," *Bulletin of the American Schools of Oriental Research* 313 (1999): pp. 65-74.

45. I am not able to determine how many four squadrons are.

46. Josephus, *Wars* 2:500-502; Loeb Classical Library 2:517, 519.

47. Josephus, *Wars* 2:555; Loeb Classical Library 2:537.

48. Josephus, *Wars* 2:519; Loeb Classical Library 2:525.

49. Josephus, *Wars* 2:555; Loeb Classical Library 2:537.

50. Chilton, *Days of Vengeance*, p. 258.

51. Chilton, *Days of Vengeance*, p. 196.

52. Foy Wallace, *The Book of Revelation* (Fort Smith, AR: Foy E. Wallace, Jr. Publications, 1997), p. 153.

53. Chilton, *Days of Vengeance*, pp. 231-35.

54. Chilton, *Days of Vengeance*, p. 285.

55. Chilton, *Days of Vengeance*, p. 413.

56. A. Ogden, *The Avenging of the Apostles and Prophets, a Commentary on Revelation* (Somerset, KY: Ogden Publications, 1996), pp. 320-21.

57. D. Amiran, E. Arieh, and T. Turcotte, "Earthquakes in Israel and Adjacent Areas: Macroseismic Observations Since 100 B.C.E.", *Israel Exploration Journal* (vol. 44, no. 3-4, 1994), p. 265.

58. Pliny, *Natural History* 2:86:200; Loeb Classical Library 2:331.viii.

59. Tacitus, *Annals* 2:47; Loeb Classical Library 2:459.

60. Chilton, *Days of Vengeance*, p. 416. Cf. Josephus, *Wars* 5:184-221; Loeb Classical Library 3:255-267.

61. Chilton, *Days of Vengeance*, p. 417.

62. Chilton, *Days of Vengeance*, pp. 417-18; Gentry, *Before Jerusalem Fell*, pp. 245-46; James Russell, *The Parousia: A Critical Inquiry into the New Testament Doctrine of Our Lord's Second Coming* (Bradford, PA: Kingdom Publications, 1996), 480-81; Ogden, *Avenging*, pp. 322-23.

63. Josephus, *Wars* 5:269-70; Loeb Classical Library 3:285.

64. Josephus, *Wars* 3:166-68; Loeb Classical Library 2:627.

65. "Weights and Measures" by M. Powell. *Anchor Bible Dictionary* (New York: Doubleday, 1992).

66. R. Siven and Giora Solar, "Excavations in the Jerusalem, Citadel. 1980–1988," *Ancient Jerusalem Revealed* (Jerusalem: Israel Exploration Society, 1994), p. 174. A photograph of the ballista stones can be seen on page 173.

67. Russell, *Parousia*, pp. 181-82.

68. John Bray, *The Man of Sin of II Thessalonians* 2 (Lakeland, FL: John L. Bray Ministry, 1999).

69. John Noe, *Beyond the End Times* (Bradford, PA: Preterist Resources, 2000), pp. 206-12.

70. Noe, *Beyond the End Times*, p. 296, fn. 2.

Chapter 10—Revelation 13 and the First Beast

1. Kenneth L. Gentry, *The Beast of Revelation*, rev. ed. (Powder Springs, GA: American Vision, 2002).

2. Gentry, *Beast of Revelation*, pp. 51-57.

3. Gentry, *Beast of Revelation*, pp. 51-52.

4. Gentry, *Beast of Revelation*, p. 51.

5. Thomas L. Constable, "Notes on Revelation," online: www.soniclight.com, accessed March 12, 2001, pp. 124-25.

6. Constable, "Notes on Revelation," pp. 124-25.

7. John F. Walvoord, *Daniel: The Key to Prophetic Revelation* (Chicago IL: Moody Press, 1971), p. 175.

8. Walvoord, *Daniel*, p. 175.

9. E. W. Bullinger, *The Apocalypse or "The Day of the Lord"* (London: Samuel Bagster & Sons, Ltd, 1902; reprint, 1972), p. 422; John F. Walvoord, *Daniel: The Key to Prophetic Revelation*, pp. 174-75.

10. Gentry, *The Beast of Revelation*, pp. 89-90; Kenneth L. Gentry, *Before Jerusalem Fell* (Tyler, TX: Institute for Christian Economics, 1989), pp. 139-40.

11. Robert H. Mounce, *The Book of Revelation*, New International Commentary on the New Testament (Grand Rapids, MI: Eerdmans Publishing Co., 1983), p. 34.

12. Steve Gregg, ed., *Revelation: Four Views* (Nashville, TN: Thomas Nelson Publishers, 1997), p. 16.

13. Robert L. Thomas, *Revelation 8–22: An Exegetical Commentary* (Chicago, IL: Moody Press, 1992), p. 166; Bullinger, *The Apocalypse or "The Day of the Lord,"* p. 430.

14. John F. Walvoord, *The Revelation of Jesus Christ* (Chicago, IL: Moody Press, 1966), pp. 203-04.

15. David Chilton, *Days of Vengeance: An Exposition of the Book of Revelation* (Fort Worth, TX: Dominion Press, 1987), p. 331.

16. Thomas, *Revelation 8–22*, p. 159; Isbon Beckwith, *The Apocalypse of John* (New York: Macmillan, 1919), p. 636.

17. J. Stuart Russell, *The Parousia: The New Testament Doctrine of Our Lord's Second Coming* (London: T. Fisher Unwin, 1887; reprint, Grand Rapids, MI: Baker Books, 1983), p. 462.

18. Cornelius Tacitus, *Histories*, trans. Clifford H. Moore, Loeb Classical Library (Cambridge, MA: Harvard University Press, 1970–1981), 1:2; 2:8,9; Frederic W. Farrar, *The Early Days of Christianity*, popular ed. (London: Cassell, 1894), p. 467.

19. Beasley-Murray, George Raymond, *The Book of Revelation*, New Century Bible Commentary Series, rev. ed. (London: Morgan & Scott, 1974; reprint, Grand Rapids, MI: Eerdmans, and London: Marshall, Morgan & Scott, 1983), pp. 210-11; Mounce, *The Book of Revelation*, pp. 252-53, Gregg, *Revelation: Four Views*, p. 282.

20. Eusebius, "The Church History of Eusebius," 5:20:4-7, online: http://www.ccel.org/fathers2/NPNF2-01/TOC. htm, accessed April 22, 2002.

21. Thomas, *Revelation 8–22*, p. 158.

22. R. Lenski, *The Interpretation of St. John's Revelation* (Minneapolis, MN: Augsburg Publishing House, 1943), p. 394.

23. J. Ritchie Smith, "The Date of the Apocalypse," *Bibliotheca Sacra* 45 (April-June 1888), p. 311.

24. Gentry, *Before Jerusalem Fell*, pp. 308-09.

25. Gentry, *Before Jerusalem Fell*, p. 309.

26. Gentry, *Beast of Revelation*, pp. 90-98.

27. Thomas, *Revelation 8–22*, p. 158; R. H. Charles, *A Critical and Exegetical Commentary on the Revelation of St. John*, The International Critical Commentary, vol. 1 (Edinburgh: T. & T. Clarke, 1920), vol. 1, p. 349.

28. Gentry, *Beast of Revelation*, pp. 71-84.

29. Thomas, *Revelation 8–22*, p. 164.

30. James Barr, *The Semantics of Biblical Languages* (London: Oxford University Press, 1961), pp. 217-18.

31. Gary North, "Publishers Preface" in Kenneth L. Gentry, *Before Jerusalem Fell* (Tyler, TX: Institute for Christian Economics, 1989), p. xii; Kenneth L. Gentry, Jr., *He Shall Have Dominion: A Postmillennial Eschatology*, 2nd ed. (Tyler, TX: Institute for Christian Economics, 1997), p. 164.

32. Gentry, *Beast of Revelation*, pp. 82-83.

33. James Moffatt, "The Revelation of St. John the Divine," 5:433.

34. Thomas, *Revelation 8–22*, p. 178.

35. John F. Walvoord, "Christ's Olivet Discourse on the Time of the End: Signs of the End of the Age," *Bibliotheca Sacra*, (vol. 128, no. 512, Oct.-Dec., 1971), pp. 318-19.

36. Walvoord, "Christ's Olivet Discourse," p. 320.

37. North, "Publishers Preface," p. xii; Gentry, *He Shall Have Dominion: A Postmillennial Eschatology*, p. 164.

38. J. B. Smith, *A Revelation of Jesus Christ* (Scottsdale, AZ: Herald, 1961), p. 204.

39. Gentry, *Beast of Revelation*, pp. 67-68.

40. Walvoord, *The Revelation of Jesus Christ*, p. 28.

41. Gentry, *Before Jerusalem Fell*, p. 224.

42. Chilton, *Days of Vengeance*, p. 206.

43. Chilton, *Days of Vengeance*, p. 507.

44. Chilton, *Days of Vengeance*, p. 507; Milton S. Terry, *Biblical Apocalyptics: A Study of the Most Notable Revelations of God and of Christ in the Canonical Scriptures* (New York: Eaton and Mains, 1898; reprint, Grand Rapids, MI: Baker Book House, 1988), p. 451.

45. Gentry, *Before Jerusalem Fell*, pp. 162-63; Gentry, *Beast of Revelation*, p. 181.

46. Gentry, *He Shall Have Dominion: A Postmillennial Eschatology*, p. 421.

47. Gentry, *Beast of Revelation*, p. 68.

48. J. Stuart Russell, *The Parousia: The New Testament Doctrine of Our Lord's Second Coming* (London: T. Fisher

Unwin, 1887; reprint, Grand Rapids, MI: Baker Books, 1983), p. 460.

49. John F. Walvoord, *Every Prophecy of the Bible* (Colorado Springs, CO: Chariot Victor Publishing, 1999), pp. 7-18.

50. Harold W. Hoehner, *Chronological Aspects of the Life of Christ* (Grand Rapids, MI: Zondervan, 1977), pp. 115-39; Alva J. McClain, *Daniel's Prophecy of the 70 Weeks* (Grand Rapids, MI: Zondervan, 1940; reprint, Grand Rapids, MI: Zondervan, 1969), pp. 25-27; Robert Anderson, *The Coming Prince* (London: Hodder and Stoughton, 1909; reprint, Grand Rapids, MI: Kregel, 1957), pp. 119-29.

51. McClain, *Daniel's Prophecy of the 70 Weeks*, p. 22.

52. Mounce, *The Book of Revelation*, p. 625.

53. Leon Morris, *The Revelation of St. John: An Introduction and a Commentary*, Tyndale New Testament Commentaries (Grand Rapids, MI: Eerdmans, 1969), p. 164.

54. Thomas, *Revelation 8–22*, p. 163.

55. Gentry, *The Beast of Revelation*, pp. 37-47.

56. Morris, *The Revelation of St. John*, p. 169; Mounce, *The Book of Revelation*, pp. 264-65; George Eldon Ladd, *A Commentary on the Revelation of John* (Grand Rapids, MI: Eerdmans, 1972; reprint, 1979), p. 186.

57. Gentry, *Before Jerusalem Fell*, pp. 209-12.

58. Smith, "The Date of the Apocalypse," p. 317.

59. Craig S. Keener, *The IVP Bible Background Commentary: New Testament* (Downers Grove, IL: InterVarsity Press, 1993), pp. 799-800.

60. Smith, "The Date of the Apocalypse," p. 317.

61. G. K. Beale, *The Book of Revelation*, eds. I. Howard Marshall and Donald A. Hagner, *The New International Greek Testament Commentary* (Grand Rapids, MI: Eerdmans, 1999), p. 719.

62. Beale, *Revelation*, p. 719; Mounce, *The Book of Revelation*, p. 264, fn. 61; Theodor Zahn, *Introduction to the New Testament*, trans. John Moore Trout and others under the direction and supervision of Melancthon Williams Jacobus, assisted by Charles Snow Thayer, vol. 3 (Grand Rapids, MI: Kregel Publications, 1953), p. 447, fn. 4.

63. Beale, *Revelation*, p. 720.

64. Mounce, *The Book of Revelation*, p. 265.

65. Mounce, *The Book of Revelation*, p. 35.

66. Smith, "The Date of the Apocalypse," p. 318.

67. Zahn, *New Testament Introduction*, vol. 3, p. 447, fn. 4; Mounce, *The Book of Revelation*, p. 35; Guthrie, *New Testament Introduction*, p. 959, fn. 4.

68. Smith, "The Date of the Apocalypse," p. 318.

69. Ladd, *A Commentary on the Revelation of John*, p. 187.

70. Mounce, *The Book of Revelation*, p. 264; Beale, *The Book of Revelation*, p. 720.

71. Alan Johnson, "Revelation," in Frank E. Gaebelein, gen. ed., *Hebrews-Revelation of Expositor's Bible Commentary* (Grand Rapids, MI: Zondervan, 1981), p. 534.

72. Thomas, *Revelation 8-22*, pp. 182-85.

73. Ladd, *A Commentary on Revelation*, p. 187; William R. Newell, *The Book of Revelation* (Chicago, IL: Moody Press, 1935), p. 205.

74. Jay Adams, *The Time Is at Hand* (Nutley, NJ: Presbyterian and Reformed Publishing Co., 1977), p. 73.

75. Mounce, *The Book of Revelation*, p. 259, fn. 31.

76. Thomas, *Revelation 8–22*, p. 174; Bullinger, *The Apocalypse or "The Day of the Lord,"* p. 434.

77. Mounce, *The Book of Revelation*, p. 260.

78. Mounce, *The Book of Revelation*, p. 261.

79. Constable, "Notes on Revelation," p. 126.

80. Thomas, *Revelation 8–22*, pp. 179-80.

81. Beckwith, *The Apocalypse of John*, p. 641.

82. North, "Publishers Preface," p. xii; Gentry, *He Shall Have Dominion: A Postmillennial Eschatology*, p. 164.

83. Thomas, *Revelation 8–22*, p. 172.

84. J. Seiss, *The Apocalypse: Lectures on the Book of Revelation* (New York: Charles C. Cook, 1909; reprint, Grand Rapids, MI: Zondervan, 1977), p. 334.

85. Thomas, *Revelation 8–22*, p. 175.

86. Seiss, *The Apocalypse*, p. 343.

87. Walvoord, *The Revelation of Jesus Christ*, p. 207.

88. Thomas, *Revelation 8–22*, pp. 180-81.

Chapter 11—The Little Apocalypse of Zechariah

1. Quoted by Charles Lee Feinberg, *God Remembers: A Study of the Book of Zechariah* (New York: American Board of Missions to the Jews, 1965), p. 215.

2. Feinberg, *God Remembers*, p. 227.

3. Feinberg, *God Remembers*, pp. 227-228.

4. Whether the massive judgments of the Tribulation will force nations to return to older methods of warfare, or whether these terms are used to represent any method of warfare, ancient or modern, remains to be seen. The point remains the same. God will neutralize whatever weapons the enemy attempts to use against Jerusalem.

5. This change of pronoun without change of person is rather common in the Hebrew Bible, especially in poetic and prophetic literature.

6. David Baron, *Visions and Prophecies of Zechariah* (Grand Rapids, MI: Kregel, 1975), pp. 489-91. This is a reprint of a work first published in 1918.

7. Baron, *Zechariah*, p. 504.

8. Feinberg, *God Remembers*, pp. 250-51.

9. James Montgomery Boice, *The Minor Prophets* (Grand Rapids, MI: Kregel Publications, 1986), p. 221. The quote is from H. C. Leupold, *Exposition of Zechariah* (Grand Rapids, MI: Baker, 1978), p. 259.

10. Boice, *Minor Prophets*, pp. 221-22.

11. Boice, *Minor Prophets*, pp. 221-23. The quote is from Thomas V. Moore, *A Commentary of Haggai, Zechariah, and Malachi* (Edinburgh & Carlisle, PA: Banner of Truth, 1979), p. 307. This is a reprint of the 1856 edition.

12. Gary DeMar, "Zechariah 14 and the Coming of Christ," American Vision's *Biblical Worldview*, July, 1999.

13. DeMar, "Zechariah 14," p. 1.

14. DeMar, "Zechariah 14," p. 1.

15. Golden Rule of Interpretation: When the plain sense of Scripture makes common sense, seek no other sense; therefore, take every word at its primary, ordinary, usual, literal meaning unless the facts of the immediate context, studied in the light of related passages and axiomatic and fundamental truths, indicate clearly otherwise. David L. Cooper, *The World's Greatest Library Graphically Illustrated* (Los Angeles, CA: Biblical Research Society, 1942, 1970), p. 11.

16. DeMar, "Zechariah 14," p. 2.

17. Kenneth L. Gentry, Jr., *Before Jerusalem Fell: Dating the Book of Revelation,* (Atlanta, GA: American Vision, 1998), p. 129.

18. Kenneth L. Gentry, Jr., *He Shall Have Dominion: A Post-millennial Eschatology*, (Tyler, TX: Incentive for Christian Economics, 1992), pp. 469-70.

19. Gentry, *He Shall Have Dominion*, p. 471.

20. Greg L. Bahnsen and Kenneth L. Gentry, Jr., *House Divided: The Breakup of Dispensational Theology* (Tyler, TX: Incentive For Christian Economics, 1989), p. 273.

21. David Chilton, *The Days of Vengeance: An Exposition of the Book of Revelation* (Fort Worth, TX: Dominion Press, 1987), p. 66.

22. Chilton, *Days of Vengeance*, pp. 411-12.

23. Thomas Ice, "Preterism and Zechariah 12–14," *Pre-Trib Perspectives* (vol. V, no. 4, July 2000), p. 3. Quotations are from G. K. Beale, *The Book of Revelation: A Commentary on the Greek Text* (Grand Rapids, MI: Eerdmans, 1999), pp. 26, 45.

24. Ice, "Preterism and Zechariah 12–14," p. 4. The quote is from Gary DeMar, *Last Day Madness: Obsession of the Modern Church* (Atlanta, GA: American Vision, 1999), p. 437.

Chapter 12—The War Over Words

1. Bertrand Russell, *Why I Am Not a Christian: And Other Essays on Religion and Related Subjects*, ed. Paul Edwards (New York: Simon & Schuster, 1957), p. 16.

2. R. C. Sproul, *The Last Days According to Jesus* (Grand Rapids, MI: Baker, 1998), pp. 20-21.

3. Sproul, *Last Days*, p. 15.

4. John Noe, *Dead in Their Tracks* (Bradford, PA: International Preterist Association, 2001), p. ix.

5. Noe, *Dead in Their Tracks*, p. 7.

6. Noe, *Dead in Their Tracks*, p. 8.

7. David Chilton, *Paradise Restored* (Tyler, TX: Reconstruction Press, 1985), p. 3.

8. Chilton, *Paradise Restored*, p. 166.

9. Gary DeMar, *Last Days Madness* (Powder Springs, GA: American Vision, 1999), p. 390.

10. Thomas Ice, "Has Biblical Prophecy Already Been Fulfilled?" in *The Conservative Theological Journal*, (Ft. Worth, TX: Tyndale Theological Seminary, Dec. 2000, vol. 4, No. 13), p. 294.

11. *Engys*=adverb; *engizo*=verb.

12. Horst Balz and Gerhard Schneider, *Exegetical Dictionary of the New Testament*, vol. 1 (Grand Rapids, MI: Eerdmans, 1994), p. 371.

13. T. Wilson & K. Stapley, gen. eds., *What the Bible Teaches, Matthew, Mark* (Kilmarnock, Scotland: John Ritchie, Ltd., 1984), p. 333.

14. Leon Morris, *The Gospel According to Matthew* (Grand Rapids, MI: Eerdmans, 1992), p. 611.

15. Charles John Ellicott, ed., *Commentary on the Whole Bible*, vol. 6 (Grand Rapids, MI: Zondervan, 1959), vol. 6, p. 150.

16. W. Sunderland Lewis and Henry M. Booth, *Commentary on the Gospel According to St. Matthew*, The Preacher's Homiletic Commentary, vol. 2 (Grand Rapids, MI: Baker, n.d.), pp. 562-63.

17. R. C. H. Lenski, *The Interpretation of St. Matthew's Gospel* (Minneapolis, MN: Augsburg, 1964), p. 952.

18. Jay p. Green and George V. Wigram, *The New Englishman's Greek Concordance and Lexicon* (Peabody, MS: Hendrickson, 1982), p. 198.

19. H. E. Dana and Julius R. Mantey, *A Manual Grammar of the Greek New Testament* (New York: MacMillan, 1958), p. 200.

20. Dana and Mantey, *Grammar*, p. 200.

21. Dana and Mantey, *Grammar*, p. 202.

22. Colin Brown, ed., *The New International Dictionary of New Testament Theology*, vol. 3 (Grand Rapids, MI: Zondervan, 1977), p. 54.

23. Lenski, *Matthew's Gospel*, p. 90.

24. Lenski, *Matthew's Gospel*, p. 93.

25. John A. Broadus, *Commentary on Matthew* (Grand Rapids, MI: Kregel, 1990), p. 36.

26. Walter L. Liefeld, "Luke," Frank E. Gaebelein, gen. ed., *The Expositor's Bible Commentary*, vol. 8 (Grand Rapids, MI: Zondervan, 1984), p. 1023.

27. J. A. Alexander, *Commentary on the Gospel of Mark* (Minneapolis, MN: Klock & Klock, 1980), p. 14.

28. Alexander, *Mark*, p. 15.

29. J. Dwight Pentecost, *Things to Come* (Findley, OH: Dunham, 1958), pp. 449-50.

30. Louis Barbieri, *Moody Gospel Commentary MARK* (Chicago, IL: Moody, 1995), p. 44.

31. Barbieri, *MARK*, p. 44.

32. Ellicott, *Commentary*. vol. 7, p. 257.

33. A. T. Robertson, *Word Pictures of the New Testament*, vol. 6 (Nashville, TN: Broadman Press, 1933), p. 124.

34. Ellicott, *Commentary*, vol. 8, p. 459.

35. DeMar, *Last Days Madness*, p. 393.

36. DeMar, *Last Days Madness*, p. 388.

37. Robertson, *Word Pictures*, vol. 6, p. 285.

38. Joseph A. Seiss, *The Apocalypse* (Grand Rapids, MI: Kregel, 1987), p. 24.

39. R. C. H. Lenski, *The Interpretation of St. John's Revelation* (Minneapolis, MN: Augsburg Publishing House, 1963), p. 34.

40. T. Wilson and K. Stapley, gen. eds., *What the Bible Teaches*, vol. 10 (Kilmarnock, Scotland: John Ritchie LTD, 1997), pp. 27-28.

41. Albert Barnes, *Notes on the New Testament*, vol. 14 (Grand Rapids, MI: Baker, 1983), p. 35.

42. Barnes, *Notes*, vol. 14, p. 39.

43. Wilson and Stapley, *What the Bible Teaches*, vol. 10, p. 28.

44. Lenski, *Revelation*, pp. 192-93.

45. Green and Wigram, *Concordance and Lexicon*, p. 829.

46. Chilton, *Paradise Restored*, p. 166.

47. DeMar, *Last Days Madness*, p. 389.

48. H. G. Liddell and R. Scott, *Greek-English Lexicon* (London: Oxford University Press, 1940), pp. 1762-63.

49. Balz and Schneider, *Exegetical Dictionary* vol. 3, p. 338.

50. Walter Bauer, *A Greek-English Lexicon of the New Testament and Other Early Christian Literature*, a translation and adaptation by William F. Arndt & F. Wilbur Gingrich (Chicago, IL: University of Chicago Press, 1957), p. 814.

51. Robertson, *Word Pictures*, vol. 6, p. 283.

52. Seiss, *The Apocalypse*, p. 15.

53. Henry Alford, *The Greek Testament*, vol. 4 (Chicago: Moody, 1958), p. 546.

54. John Peter Lange, *Revelation* (Grand Rapids, MI: Zondervan, n.d.), p. 89.

55. Wilson and Stapley, *What the Bible Teaches*, vol. 10, p. 23.

56. *Didache*, 10.6.

57. Alan F. Johnson, "Revelation" in Frank E. Gaebelein, ed., *The Expositor's Bible Commentary*, vol. 12 (Grand Rapids, MI: Zondervan, 1981), vol. 12, p. 417.

58. Bauer, *Greek-English Lexicon*, p. 502.

59. Liddell and Scott, *Greek-English Lexicon*, p. 1099.

60. Joseph Henry Thayer, *A Greek-English Lexicon of the New Testament* (Grand Rapids, MI: Baker, 1992), p. 397.

61. Balz and Schneider, *Exegetical Dictionary*, vol. 2, p. 404.

62. Balz and Schneider, *Exegetical Dictionary*, vol. 2, p. 404.

63. Broadus, *Matthew*, p. 367.

64. Thayer, *Greek-English Lexicon*, p. 397.

65. Thayer, *Greek-English Lexicon*, p. 397.

66. This is volume eight of *The World History of the Jewish People*, eds. Michael Avi-Yonah and Zvi Baras (Jerusalem: Massada Publishing, 1977).

67. Raphael Patai, *The Messiah Texts*, (Detroit, MI: Wayne State University Press, 1979).

68. Patai, *Messiah Texts*, p. xxix.

69. Avi-Yonah and Baras, *World History*, p. 260.

70. Avi-Yonah and Baras, *World History*, p. 212.

71. Avi-Yonah and Baras, *World History*, p. 210.

72. Patai, *Messiah Texts*, pp. 95-96.

73. William L. Holladay, *A Concise Hebrew and Aramaic Lexicon of the Old Testament* (Grand Rapids, MI: Eerdmans, 1974), p. 286.

74. Holladay, Hebrew and Aramaic Lexicon, p. 286.

75. A. Cohen, ed., *Soncino Books of the Bible*, Isaiah, I. W. Slotki (London: Soncino, 1972), p. 297.

76. Merrill F. Unger, *Unger's Commentary on the Old Testament*, vol. 2 (Chicago: Moody, 1981), p. 1321.

77. John Gill, *Gill's Commentary*, vol. 3 (Grand Rapids, MI: Baker, 1980), p. 1017.

78. Joseph Addison Alexander, *Commentary on the Prophecies of Isaiah* (Grand Rapids, MI: Zondervan, 1953), p. 396.

79. Harry Bultema, *Commentary on Isaiah* (Grand Rapids, MI: Kregel, 1981), p. 590.

80. John N. Oswalt, *The Book of Isaiah Chapters 40–66*, in Robert L. Hubbard, Jr., ed., *The New International Commentary on the Old Testament* (Grand Rapids, MI: Eerdmans, 1998), p. 561.

Chapter 13—The 70 Weeks of Daniel

1. Robert Culver, *Daniel and the Latter Days* (Chicago, IL: Moody Press, 1977), p. 149.

2. George N. H. Peters, *The Theocratic Kingdom*, vol. 2 (Grand Rapids, MI: Kregel, [1884], 1978), p. 659.

3. Gary DeMar, *Last Days Madness: Obsession of the Modern Church*, (Powder Springs, GA: American Vision, 1999), p. 324.

4. C. F. Keil and F. Delitzsch, *Commentary on the Book of Daniel* (Grand Rapids, MI: William B. Eerdmans Publishing Company, 1975), p. 399.

5. Harry Bultema, *Commentary on Daniel* (Grand Rapids, MI: Kregel, 1988), pp. 279-80.

6. Leon Wood, *A Commentary on Daniel* (Grand Rapids, MI: Zondervan, 1973), p. 247.

7. David L. Cooper, *Messiah: His First Coming Scheduled* (Los Angeles, CA: Biblical Research Society, 1939), p. 369.

8. See Francis Brown, S. R. Driver, and C. A. Briggs, *Hebrew and English Lexicon of the Old Testament* (London: Oxford, 1907), p. 367.

9. Bultema, *Daniel*, p. 282.

10. Wood, *Daniel*, p. 248.

11. G. H. Lang, *The Histories and Prophecies of Daniel* (Miami Springs, FL: Conley & Schoettle Publishing Co., 1985), p. 127.

12. H. C. Leupold, *Exposition of Daniel* (Grand Rapids, MI: Baker Book House, 1949), p. 411.

13. Edward J. Young, *A Commentary on Daniel* (Carlisle, PA: The Banner of Truth Trust, 1949), p. 197.

14. Lang, *Daniel*, p. 130.

15. Wood, *Daniel*, p. 248.

16. Lang, *Daniel*, p. 131.

17. Wood, *Daniel*, p. 248.

18. Allan A. MacRae, *The Prophecies of Daniel* (Singapore: Christian Life Publishers, 1991), p. 181.

19. Cooper, *Messiah*, p. 371.

20. Cooper, *Messiah*, p. 371.

21. Arnold Fruchtenbaum, *Israelology: The Missing Link in Systematic Theology* (Tustin, CA: Ariel Ministries Press, [1989, 1992], 1993), p. 784.

22. Cooper, *Messiah*, p. 374.

23. Cooper, *Messiah*, p. 374.

24. Lang, *Daniel*, p. 131.

25. Cooper, *Messiah*, p. 375.

26. *The Compact Edition of the Oxford English Dictionary* (Oxford, England: Oxford University Press, 1971), s.v. "Iniquity."

27. Jerry M. Hullinger, "A Proposed Solution to the Problem of Animal Sacrifices in Ezekiel 40–48," (Th.D. dissertation, Dallas Theological Seminary, 1993), p. 53.

28. Cooper, *Messiah*, p. 376.

29. Wood, *Daniel*, p. 249.

30. Brown, Driver, and Briggs, *Hebrew Lexicon*, p. 97.

31. Cooper, *Messiah*, pp. 376-77.

32. Brown, Driver, and Briggs, *Hebrew Lexicon*, p. 761.

33. Brown, Driver, and Briggs, *Hebrew Lexicon*, p. 762.

34. Cooper, *Messiah*, p. 377.

35. J. Randall Price, "Prophetic Postponement in Daniel 9 and Other Texts," in Wesley R. Willis, John R. Master, and Charles C. Ryrie, eds., *Issues in Dispensationalism* (Chicago, IL: Moody Press, 1994), p. 150.

36. Charles Lee Feinberg, *Daniel: The Man and His Visions* (Chappaqua, NY: Christian Herald Books, 1981), p. 128.

37. Kenneth L. Gentry, Jr., *He Shall Have Dominion: A Postmillennial Eschatology* (Tyler, TX: Institute for Christian Economics, 1992), p. 316.

38. MacRae, *Daniel*, p. 188.

39. Bultema, *Daniel*, p. 283.

40. MacRae, *Daniel*, p. 190.

41. Brown, Driver, and Briggs, *Hebrew Lexicon*, p. 603.

42. Keil and Delitzsch, *Daniel*, p. 348.

43. Wood, *Daniel*, p. 250.

44. Gentry, *He Shall Have Dominion*, p. 316.

45. Bultema, *Daniel*, p. 284.

46. Cooper, *Messiah*, p. 379.

47. Lang, *Daniel*, p. 133.

48. Keil and Delitzsch, *Daniel*, p. 349.

49. DeMar, *Last Days Madness*, pp. 229-331.

50. DeMar, *Last Days Madness*, p. 331.

51. DeMar, *Last Days Madness*, p. 330.

52. Harold W. Hoehner, *Chronological Aspects of the Life of Christ* (Grand Rapids, MI: Zondervan, 1977), p. 118.

53. Hoehner, *Chronological*, p. 118.

54. Wood, *Daniel*, p. 247.

55. DeMar, *Last Days Madness*, p. 330.

56. DeMar, *Last Days Madness*, pp. 329-331.

57. DeMar, *Last Days Madness*, p. 332.

58. John F. Walvoord, *Daniel: The Key to Prophetic Revelation* (Chicago, IL: Moody Press, 1971), p. 224.

59. Wood, *Daniel*, p. 252.

60. J. Barton Payne, *The Imminent Appearing of Christ* (Grand Rapids, MI: Eerdmans, 1962), pp. 148-49.

61. DeMar, *Last Days Madness*, p. 327.

62. DeMar, *Last Days Madness*, p. 327.

63. Gentry, *He Shall Have Dominion*, p. 313.

64. Gentry, *He Shall Have Dominion*, p. 313.

65. Bultema, *Daniel*, p. 285.

66. Hoehner, *Chronological*, pp. 115-39.

67. Hoehner, *Chronological*, pp. 122-24.

68. See Hoehner, *Chronological*, pp. 29-44.

69. See Hoehner, *Chronological*, pp. 95-114.

70. See Harold Hoehner, "Chronology of the Apostolic Age" (unpublished Th.D. dissertation, Dallas Theological Seminary, 1965), pp. 200-04; George Ogg, *The Odyssey of Paul* (Old Tappan, NJ, Fleming H. Revell, 1968), pp. 24-30.

71. Hoehner, *Chronological*, pp. 125-26.

72. Hoehner, *Chronological*, p. 126.

73. Sir Robert Anderson, *The Coming Prince*, 10th ed. (Grand Rapids, MI: Kregel, 1957).

74. Hoehner, *Chronological*.

75. Sir Robert Anderson, *The Coming Prince*, 14th ed. (Grand Rapids, MI: Kregel, 1954), pp. 128-30, as cited in Michael Kalafian, *The Prophecy of the Seventy Weeks of The Book of Daniel* (Lanham, MD: University Press of America, 1991), p. 87. I have been greatly aided by Dr. Kalafian in his outlay of the material concerning this matter.

76. Edwin R. Thiele, *The Mysterious Numbers of the Hebrew Kings* rev. ed. (Grand Rapids, MI: 1965), pp. 28-30, 161.

77. S. H. Horn and L. H. Wood, "The Fifth-Century Jewish Calendar at Elephantine," *Journal of Near Eastern Studies*, XIII (January 1954), pp. 4, 20.

78. Horn and Wood, "Fifth-Century Jewish Calendar," p. 9.

79. Horn and Wood, "Fifth-Century Jewish Calendar," p. 4.

80. Richard A. Parker and Waldo H. Dubberstein, *Babylonian Chronology 626 B.C.–A.D. 75*, 2nd ed. (Providence, RI: 1956), p. 32; Herman H. Goldstine, *New and Full Moons, 1001 B.C. to A.D. 1651* (Philadelphia, 1973), p. 47

81. Hoehner, *Chronological*, pp. 127-28.

82. J. K. Fotheringham, "The Evidence of Astronomy and Technical Chronology for the Date of the Crucifixion,"

The Journal of Theological Studies, XXXV (April 1934), p. 162.

83. See Goldstine, p. 87; Parker and Dubberstein, p. 46; Fotheringham, *The Journal of Theological Studies*, XXXV, pp. 142-62; Joachim Jeremias, *The Eucharistic Words of Jesus*, trans. Norman Perrin (3rd ed.; London: SCM Press, 1966), p. 38.

84. Hoehner, *Chronological*, pp. 137-38.

85. Kalafian, *Prophecy of the Seventy Weeks*, p. 89.

86. Hoehner, *Chronological*, pp. 138-39.

87. Walvoord, *Daniel*, p. 228.

88. DeMar, *Last Days Madness*.

89. Kenneth L. Gentry, Jr., *He Shall Have Dominion: A Postmillennial Eschatology* (Tyler, TX: Institute for Christian Economics, 1992).

90. For an explanation of the hundreds of prophecies fulfilled by Jesus at His first coming see Tim LaHaye, *Jesus: Who is He?* (Sisters, OR: Multnomah Press, 1996); and Josh McDowell, *The New Evidence That Demands a Verdict* (Nashville, TN: Thomas Nelson, 1999).

91. Walvoord, *Daniel*, p. 227.

92. Hoehner, *Chronological*.

93. Adapted from Hoehner, *Chronological*, p. 139.

94. DeMar, *Last Days Madness*, p. 325.

95. DeMar, *Last Days Madness*, p. 331.

96. Wood, *Daniel*, p. 255.

97. Culver, *Daniel*, p. 157.

98. Steven R. Miller, *Daniel*, The New American Commentary (Nashville, TN: Broadman and Holman, 1994), p. 267.

99. Lang, *Daniel*, p. 135.

100. DeMar, *Last Days Madness*, pp. 332-33.

101. DeMar, *Last Days Madness*, p. 327.

102. DeMar, *Last Days Madness*, p. 101.

103. DeMar, *Last Days Madness*, p. 101.

104. Randall Price, *Prophecy of Daniel 9:27* (San Marcos, TX: World of the Bible, n.d.), p. 22.

105. E. B. Pusey, *Daniel the Prophet* (Minneapolis, MN: Klock & Klock Christian Publishers, 1978 [1885]), p. 192.

106. Walvoord, *Daniel*, p. 229.

107. G. H. Pember, *The Great Prophecies of the Centuries Concerning Israel and the Gentiles* (Miami Springs, FL: Conley & Schoettle Publishing Co., 1984 [1909]), p. 345.

108. Feinberg, *Daniel*, p. 132.

109. Walvoord, *Daniel*, p. 231.

110. J. Dwight Pentecost, "Daniel," in John F. Walvoord and Roy B. Zuck, *The Bible Knowledge Commentary: Old Testament* (Wheaton, IL: Victor Books, 1985), p. 1364.

111. Miller, *Daniel*, p. 268.

112. Culver, *Daniel*, p. 157.

113. Wood, *Daniel*, p. 256.

114. Feinberg, *Daniel*, p. 133.

115. Pentecost, "Daniel," p. 1364.

116. Culver, *Daniel*, pp. 157-58.

117. Kenneth L. Gentry, Jr., *Perilous Times: A Study in Eschatological Evil* (Texarkana, AR: Covenant Media Press, 1999), p. 33.

118. Gentry, *Perilous Times*, p. 32.

119. DeMar, *Last Days Madness*, p. 328.

120. According to Miller, *Daniel*, p. 268.

121. Keil and Delitzsch, *Daniel*, p. 367.

122. Leupold, *Daniel*, p. 431.

123. Culver, *Daniel*, pp. 161-62.

124. Wood, *Daniel*, p. 257.

125. Gentry, *Perilous Times*, p. 32.

126. Wood, *Daniel*, p. 259.

127. Pember, *Great Prophecies...Concerning Israel and the Gentiles*, p. 351.

128. Wood, *Daniel*, p. 259.

129. See for example, DeMar, *Last Days Madness*, pp. 326-27.

130. Gentry, *He Shall Have Dominion*, p. 319.

131. Pember, *Great Prophecies...Concerning Israel and the Gentiles*, p. 351.

132. Miller, *Daniel*, p. 270.

133. John C. Whitcomb, *Daniel* (Chicago, IL: Moody Press, 1985), pp. 133-34.

134. DeMar, *Last Days Madness*, pp. 334-35.

135. Gentry, *Perilous Times*, pp. 31-33.

136. Gentry, *Perilous Times*, p. 33.

137. DeMar, *Last Days Madness*, pp. 334-35.

138. Pentecost, "Daniel," p. 1365.

139. Robert H. Gundry, *The Church and the Tribulation* (Grand Rapids, MI: Zondervan, 1973), p. 191.

140. DeMar, *Last Days Madness*, p. 101.

141. Price, *Prophecy of Daniel 9:27*, pp. 24-25.

142. DeMar, *Last Days Madness*, p. 333.

143. Gentry, *Perilous Times*, pp. 29-30.

144. Raphael Patai, *The Messiah Texts* (Detroit, MI: Wayne State University Press, 1979), pp. xxxii-xxxv.

145. Gentry, *Perilous Times*, p. 29.

146. J. Randall Price, "Daniel's Seventy Weeks, Dispensational Interpretation," in Mal Couch, ed., *Dictionary of Premillennial Theology* (Grand Rapids, MI: Kregel Publications, 1996), p. 77.

147. Tim LaHaye & Thomas Ice, *Charting the End Times* (Eugene, OR: Harvest House Publishers, 2001), pp. 28-30.

148. LaHaye & Ice, *Charting the End Times*, p. 30.

149. Arnold Fruchtenbaum, *The Footsteps of the Messiah: A Study of the Sequence of Prophetic Events* (Tustin, CA: Ariel Ministries Press, 1982), pp. 4-5.

150. DeMar, *Last Days Madness*, p. 228.

151. DeMar, *Last Days Madness*, p. 328.

152. Philip Mauro, *The Seventy Weeks and the Great Tribulation* (Sterling, VA: Grace Abounding Ministries, 1988), p. 74.

153. Gentry, *Perilous Times*, p. 18.

154. Gentry, *Perilous Times*, p. 27, fn. 63.

155. Louis E. Knowles, "The Interpretation of the Seventy Weeks of Daniel in the Early Fathers," *The Westminster Theological Journal* vol. VII (May 1945), pp. 136-60.

156. Gentry, *Perilous Times*, p. 27, fn. 63.

157. Knowles, "The Seventy Weeks," p. 136.

158. Knowles, "The Seventy Weeks," p. 137.

159. Knowles, "The Seventy Weeks," p. 136.

160. Knowles, "The Seventy Weeks," pp. 138-39.

161. Knowles, "The Seventy Weeks," p. 139.

162. See the views of Irenaeus in *Against Heresies*, book V, chapter 25.

163. Irenaeus, *Against Heresies*, book V, chapter 25, paragraph 4.

164. Knowles, "The Seventy Weeks," p. 139.

165. Kalafian, *Prophecy of the Seventy Weeks*, p. 83.

166. Knowles, "The Seventy Weeks," p. 142.

167. Hippolytus, *Fragments from Commentaries, Daniel*, paragraph 22; *Treaties on Christ and Antichrist*, paragraphs 61-65; *Appendix to the Works of Hippolytus*, paragraphs 21, 25, 36.

168. Hippolytus, *Fragments from Commentaries, Daniel*, paragraph 22.

169. LeRoy Froom, *The Prophetic Faith of Our Fathers*, vol. 1 (Washington: Review and Herald, 1950), p. 277.

170. Knowles, "The Seventy Weeks," p. 141.

171. Jerome, *Commentary on Daniel*, trans. Gleason L. Archer, Jr. (Grand Rapids, MI: Baker Book House, 1958), p. 95.

172. Kalafian, *Prophecy of the Seventy Weeks*, p. 80.

173. Knowles, "The Seventy Weeks," p. 157.

174. Knowles, "The Seventy Weeks," p. 160.

175. Knowles, "The Seventy Weeks," p. 160.

176. Jerome, *Daniel*, p. 81.

Chapter 14—Historical Problems with Preterism's Interpretation of Events in A.D. 70

1. R. C. Sproul, *The Last Days According to Jesus* (Grand Rapids, MI: Baker, 1998), p. 228.

2. Gary DeMar, *Last Days Madness: Obsession of the Modern Church*. 4th ed. (Atlanta, GA: American Vision, 1999), pp. 94, 52.

3. Martin Goodman, "Diaspora Reactions to the Destruction of the Temple," *Jews and Christians: The Parting of the Ways A.D. 70–135*, ed. James D. G. Dunn (Grand Rapids, MI: Eerdmans, 1999), p. 29.

4. Andrew Chester, "The Parting of the Ways: Eschatology and Messianic Hope," *Jews and Christians*, pp. 261-62.

5. Sproul, *Last Days According to Jesus*, pp. 117-19.

6. Sproul, *Last Days According to Jesus*, p. 121.

7. Sproul, *Last Days According to Jesus*, p. 122.

8. Sproul, *Last Days According to Jesus*, p. 124.

9. Sproul, *Last Days According to Jesus*, p. 126.

10. Doron Mendels, *The Rise and Fall of Jewish Nationalism* (Grand Rapids, MI: Eerdmans, 1997), pp. 356-57.

11. Mendels, *Rise and Fall*, pp. 357-58.

12. Frederick J. Murphy, *Early Judaism: The Exile to the Time of Jesus* (Peabody, MA: Hendrickson Publishers, 2002), p. 386.

13. Martin Goodman, "Diaspora Reactions to the Destruction of the Temple," p. 27.

14. Goodman, "Diaspora Reactions," p. 27.

15. Overman, *Matthew's Gospel and Formative Judaism: The Social World of the Matthean Community* (Minneapolis, MN: Fortress Press, 1990), pp. 41-43.

16. Rabbi Eliyahu Dessler, *Iyunim*, "Studies," as cited in *History of the Jewish People: The Second Temple Era* (Jerusalem: Hillel Press, 2000), p. 195.

17. Gerard Israel and Jacques Lebar, *When Jerusalem Burned*, trans. Alan Kendall (London: Vallentine, Mitchell & Co., Ltd., 1973), p. xii.

18. William Horbury, "Messianism among the Jews and Christians in the Second Century," *Augustinianum* 28 (1988), pp. 83-84.

19. Dan Bahat, ed. *Twenty Centuries of Jewish Life in the Holy Land: The Forgotten Generations* (Jerusalem: The Israel Economist, 1975).

20. Goodman, "Diaspora Reactions to the Destruction of the Temple," p. 28.

21. Dunn, *Jews and Christians*, p. 253.

22. James C. VanderKam, *An Introduction to Early Judaism* (Grand Rapids, MI: Eerdmans, 2001), p. 45.

23. For these citations and documentation see Charles E. Hill, *Regnum Caelorum: Patterns of Millennial Thought in Early Christianity*, 2nd ed. (Grand Rapids, MI: Eerdmans, 2001), p. 63.

24. Chester, "The Parting of the Ways," p. 258.

25. E. P. Sanders, *Jesus and Judaism* (Philadelphia, PA: Fortress Press, 1985), p. 87.

26. Overman, "Matthew's Gospel," pp. 30-32.

27. Cf. Markus Bockmuehl, "Why Did Jesus Predict the Destruction of the Temple?" *Crux* XXV: 3 (September 1989), pp. 11-17. Holding to the same interpretation for Jesus' predictions yet without the element of judgment is E. P. Sanders, *Jesus and Judaism*, pp. 85-88, who notes "the naturalness of the connection between expecting a new temple and supposing that the old one will be destroyed" (p. 85).

28. Cf. Joachim Jeremias, *Jerusalem in the Time of Jesus*, trans. F. H. and C. H. Cave (London: SCN Press, 1969), pp. 193-94, 377-78.

29. Overman, "Matthew's Gospel," p. 21.

30. Christopher Rowland, "The Parting of the Ways: The Evidence of Jewish and Christian Apocalyptic and Mystical Material," *Jews and Christians: The Parting of the Ways A.D. 70–135*, ed. James D. G. Dunn (Grand Rapids, MI: Eerdmans , 1999), pp. 213, 220-22.

31. David K. Lowery, "Evidence from Matthew," *A Case for Premillennialism: A New Consensus*, eds. Donald K. Campbell and Jeffrey L. Townsend (Chicago, IL: Moody Press, 1992), p. 177.

32. As cited in *History of the Jewish People: The Second Temple Era*, adapted by Rabbi Hersh Goldwurm from the translation of Yekutiel Friedner's *Divrei Y'mei HaBayit HaSheini* (Jerusalem: Mesorah Publications and Hillel Press, 2000), p. 200.

33. Gerard Israel and Jacques Lebar, *When Jerusalem Burned*, trans. Alan Kendall (London: Vallentine, Mitchell & Co., Ltd., 1973), pp. xi-xii, 177.

34. DeMar, *Last Days Madness*, pp. 52-53.

Chapter 15—Historical Problems with a First-Century Fulfillment of the Olivet Discourse

1. Cf. e.g. Lloyd Gaston, *No Stone Upon Another: Studies in the Significance of the Fall of Jerusalem in the Synoptic Gospels*, NTSup 23 (Leiden: E. J. Brill, 1970); and James Calvin de Young, *Jerusalem in the New Testament: The Significance of the City in the History of Redemption and in Eschatology* (Amsterdam: J. H. Kok N. VanKampen, 1960).

2. See chapter 1 for an explanation of historicism.

3. See chapter 1 for an explanation of preterism.

4. That the scope cannot be limited to a present audience is obvious from the fact that such usage cannot mean only those who heard the message or who were currently part of the present generation, since some who were not present and who were yet to be born must be included, while others would certainly have died before the events were fulfilled and, this would be part of that generation, especially since it is still *future* from the perspective of the speaker.

5. A comparison of the Greek texts of the three accounts reveals, e.g., that while Matthew and Mark use the term "great tribulation," Luke uses the term "great distress." This is because "tribulation" may serve as a technical expression of "the time of Jacob's trouble," an eschatological event, while "distress" may refer to a less specific time of persecution, such as that attending a military conquest. Cf. further on this Lukan distinction, J. Dwight Pentecost, *Things to Come: A Study in Biblical Eschatology* (Grand Rapids, MI: Dunham Publishing Co., 1958), pp. 276-77. As we will see below, this permits Luke's chiastic structure to have both a historical series and an eschatological series, whereas Matthew and Mark's chiasm is strictly eschatological.

6. Cf. Desmond Ford, *The Abomination of Desolation in Biblical Eschatology* (Lanham, MD: University Press of America, 1978), pp. 75-76, has purposed an alternative solution to the question. He argues that Jesus linked the destruction of Jerusalem with the end of the age and promised *both* to His generation. Was Jesus, therefore, wrong, for the end of that age (A.D. 70) did not bring the predicted coming of Messiah? Ford responds negatively because he believes that Mark 13:30 can be understood as belonging to the same genre as Jonah's "Yet forty days and Ninevah will be overthrown" (p. 75). He says, "We submit that the exegesis of Mark 13:30 is only complete if we allow for the possibility that Christ, as a Hebrew of the Hebrews, may have used an absolute statement with less than an absolute meaning, in harmony with those Scriptures He so implicitly trusted. It is possible that he believed that if the early church proved faithful to its missionary commission, and if the chastened Jewish nation repented, the end would transpire in that same Age. It is the linking of the gospel proclamation to the world with the end of the Age that provides the hint of the contingent element" (p. 76).

7. Luke's omission of this signal event is one of the reasons it is believed that at this point in his narrative he is presenting the fall of Jerusalem in A.D. 70 rather than the eschatological end of the age.

8. For this reason, consistent preterists must interpret Christ's coming as having occurred in A.D. 70. To do so, however, requires the employment of a nonliteral and historical hermeneutic, since the events cannot be reconciled with either the literal interpretation of the Old Testament citations and allusions in the Olivet Discourse or the actual events of the destruction.

9. Jesus' handling of the biblical text followed the exegetical methods common to Judaism and drew its perspective and presuppositions from Jewish backgrounds. "Jesus' use of both quotations and allusions from the Old Testament reveal that He was skilled in these various forms of rabbinic exegesis that were normative in His day (literalist and midrashic)," E. Earl Ellis, *The Old Testament in Early Christianity: Canon and Interpretation in the Light of Modern Research* (Grand Rapids, MI: Baker Book House, 1992), p. 121. Ellis, in a discussion of

Jesus' method of interpretation, demonstrates examples in the Gospels of Jesus' use of Hillel's Rules, *proem* and *yelammedenu*-type midrash, cf. appendix I, pp. 130-38. Furthermore, because the Judaism of Jesus' day was Torah-centric, to gain a hearing among His people, Jesus' teaching had to also be Torah-centric. The distinctive difference in Jesus' methodology was His employment of a creative element in His hermeneutics that arose from His concept of the Old Testament as a pre-messianic Torah, for examples of this messianic interpretive paradigm in application to Jesus' parabolic style have been ably demonstrated by Robert H. Stein, *The Method and Message of Jesus' Teachings* (Philadelphia, PA: The Westminster Press, 1978), pp. 112-47. In this regard, Jesus' eschatology, which followed the literalist approach of the Apocrypha, Pseudepigrapha, and Qumran in looking for a future fulfillment of the restoration of Israel in a millennial age, following the judgment of the Gentile nations, served as the basis for the Johannine, Pauline, and Peterine epistles—see E. Earl Ellis, *Prophecy and Hermeneutic in Early Christianity* (Grand Rapids, MI: Eerdmans, 1978), pp. 147-72, and Pasquale de Santo, *A Study of Jewish Eschatology with Special Reference to the Final Conflict* (Ph.D. dissertation, Duke University, 1957), pp. 397-402. We should add here the statement of Lamar Cope, "'To the Close of the Age': The Role of Apocalyptic Thought in the Gospel of Matthew," *Apocalyptic and the New Testament: Essays in Honor of J. Louis Martyn. JSNT Supplement Series* 24 (Sheffield, United Kingdom: Sheffield Academic Press, 1989), p. 123: "So it seems to me that we need to acknowledge that Christian faith did arise out of the seedbed of late Jewish apocalyptic movements, but we should also recognize that its finest insights about God, human life, and discipleship are anchored in a radical understanding of the grace of God which negates the dark side of apocalyptic." In response to Cope, I would say that the Christian faith, especially as reflected in the early Jewish-Christianity of the New Testament, is better recognized as a continuation of the eschatological thought of the biblical prophets, sharing with apocalyptic literature where it has also drawn from this same source. The "darker" side of apocalyptic, i.e., divine retribution/punishment, is essential to the formation of the "grace" theology which Cole would have it eclipse. Both of these elements are part and parcel to the prophetic message, and thus indispensable ingredients to the eschatological faith of Christianity. Therefore, it is essential in understanding Jesus' eschatological treatment of the Temple, to underscore His continuity with a Torah-centered Judaism whose eschatological hope was primarily drawn from the biblical prophets and whose influence governed the hermeneutical development of the early church.

10. P. W. L. Walker, *Jesus and the Holy City: New Testament Perspectives on Jerusalem* (Grand Rapids, MI: Eerdmans, 1996), p. 42, as cited by Gary DeMar, *Last Days Madness: Obsession of the Modern Church* (Powder Springs, GA: American Vision, 1999), p. 61.

11. David K. Lowery, "Evidence from Matthew," *A Case for Premillennialism: A New Consensus*, eds. Donald K. Campbell and Jeffrey L. Townsend (Chicago, IL: Moody Press, 1992), pp. 172-73.

12. Robert H. Gundry, *Mark: A Commentary on His Apology for the Cross* (Grand Rapids, MI: Eerdmans, 1993), p. 754.

13. Gentry, *Mark*, p. 754.

14. Martin Hengel, *Zealots* (Edinburgh: T. & T. Clark, 1989), pp. 185-86, 209-10, 217-24.

15. Kenneth L. Gentry, "The Great Tribulation Is Past: Exposition," in Thomas Ice and Kenneth L. Gentry, Jr., *The Great Tribulation: Past or Future?* (Grand Rapids, MI: Kregel Publications, 1999), pp. 46-48.

16. Gentry, "The Great Tribulation," p. 48.

17. For a list of these, see Craig A. Evans, *Mark 8:27–16:20*, Word Biblical Commentary 34b (Nashville, TN: Thomas Nelson Publishers, 2001), pp. 318-19.

18. Evans, *Mark 8:27–16:20*, p. 319.

19. Randall Price, *The Desecration and Restoration of the Temple as an Eschatological Motif in the Tanach, Jewish Apocalyptic Literature, and the New Testament* (Ann Arbor, MI: UMI Publications, 1994), pp. 355-67.

20. The Hebrew term *taqehes sheqetz* is related to *pigul* in that the latter refers to *dead* carcasses (cf. Isaiah 65:4), while the former only to *living* animals (cf. Leviticus 7:21; 11:10-13,20,23,41; Isaiah 66:17; Ezekiel 8:10).

21. Cf. Herman J. Austel, *"≈Qevi*,*"* *Theological Wordbook of the Old Testament* 2:955, who argues for both a reference to the "idols" and "something associated with the idolatrous ritual." He adds: "Not only are the idols an abomination, but they that worship them 'become detestable like that which they love' (Hosea 9:10), for they identify themselves with the idols."

22. This association is expressed in Leviticus 11:43; 20:25 where the root *shqtz* is paralleled with *tame'*, and in its close association with the meanings of the *Pi'el* forms of both *tame'*("make unclean") and *ta'ab* ("abhor")—see Bruce K. Waltke, "Abomination," *New International Bible Encyclopedia* I (Grand Rapids, MI: William B. Eerdmans Publishing Co., 19), p. 14.

23. Hermann J. Austel, *"μmv*,*"* *TWOT* 2 (1980): 936-37.

24. Francis Brown, S.R. Driver, and C.A. Briggs, *Hebrew and English Lexicon of the Old Testament* (London: Oxford, 1907), s. verse *"μmv*,*"* pp. 1030-31.

25. While *shomen* could here be translated as "the transgression *that causes horror*," expressing the psychological nuance as a result of the idolatrous act, it seems preferable to retain the idea of cultic [or spiritual] "desolation" as a result of idolatry, in keeping with the concept of *pasha'* as desecration, and allow *m'remes* to carry the nuance of physical desolation.

26. Edwin Hatch and Henry A. Redpath, *A Concordance to the Septuagint*. vol. 1, (Graz: Akademische Druk V. Verlagsonstalt, 1954), p. 215.

27. Cf. *BAGD*, s.v. "bdevlugma," p. 134: 1) literally, anything that must not be brought before God because it arouses His wrath (cf. LXX 1saiah 1:13; Proverbs 16:15; Luke 16:15; Epistle of Barnabas 2:5), 2) as in the Old Testament of everything connected with idolatry (cf. LXX Deuteronomy 29:16; 2 Kings 11:6, 33; 1 Kings 23:13; 2 Chronicles 28:3; Revelation 17:4f), also cf., X. Léon-Dufour, *Wörterbuch zum Neuen Testament* (1977), pp. 409-11.

28. W. Foerster, *"bdevlugma*,*"* *Theological Dictionary of the New Testament* 1 (1964): 598. His references for the "abominations" are: (LXX Jeremiah 13:27; 39:35; 51:22; Ezekiel 5:9,11; 6:9, etc.), and for the parallel with "lawlessness": (LXX Jeremiah 4:1; Ezekiel 41:18; 20:30; Amos 6:8; Psalm 5:7; 13:1; 52:1; 118:163; Job 15:16).

29. See LXX Proverbs 29:27; Ecclesiasticus 1:25; 13:20.

30. J. Zmijewski, "bdevlguma," *Exegetical Dictionary of the New Testament*, eds. Horst Balz and Gerhard Schneider (Grand Rapids, MI: Eerdmans, 1978–1980), 1:210.

31. Kenneth L. Gentry, Jr., *Perilous Times: A Study in Eschatological Evil* (Texarkana, AR: Covenant Media Press, 1999).

32. Gentry, *Perilous Times*, p. 60.

33. Evans, *Mark 8:27–16:20*, pp. 319-20.

34. Darrel L. Bock, *Luke* (Volume 2: 9:51–24:53), *Baker Exegetical Commentary on the New Testament* (Grand Rapids, MI: Baker Books, 1996), p. 1675.

35. For my arguments for this as well as alternative explanations, see my *The Desecration and Restoration of the Temple as an Eschatological Motif in the Tanach, Jewish Apocalyptic Literature and the New Testament*, p. 365.

36. Jacques Doukhan points this out when he states, "The seventy weeks' prophecy must be interpreted with regard to history in as realistic a way as Daniel did for the prophecy of Jeremiah." Jacques Doukhan, "The Seventy Weeks of Dan. 9: An Exegetical Study," *Andrews University Seminary Studies* 17 (Spring 1979), p. 8.

37. Bock, *Luke* 9:51–24:53, pp. 1680-81. This interpretation is also supported by D. L. Tiede, *Prophecy and History in Luke-Acts* (Philadelphia, PA: Fortress, 1980), pp. 87-96; Craig A. Evans, *Mark*, pp. 313-14, and John A. Jelink, "The Dispersion and Restoration of Israel to the Land," *Israel the Land and the People*, ed. H. Wayne House (Grand Rapids, MI: Kregel, 1998), p. 243.

38. Gundry, *Mark*, p. 755.

Chapter 16—Why Futurism?

1. Greg L. Bahnsen, "The Great Tribulation—Part 2" audiocassette recording #01298 (Auburn, CA: Covenant Tape Ministry, n.d.), side 1.

2. Arnold Fruchtenbaum, *Israelology: The Missing Link in Systematic Theology* (Tustin, CA: Ariel Ministries Press, 1989, 1992), p. 570.

3. Fruchtenbaum, *Israelology*, pp. 574-75.

4. Fruchtenbaum, *Israelology*, p. 575.

5. John F. Walvoord, *Israel in Prophecy* (Grand Rapids, MI: Zondervan, 1962), pp. 44-45.

6. Concerning the Suzerain-Vassal treaty format see Meredith G. Kline, *The Structure of Biblical Authority* (Grand Rapids, MI: Eerdmans Publishing Company, 1972); and Eugene H. Merrill, *Deuteronomy*, vol. 4 of *The New American Commentary* (Nashville, TN: Broadman and Holman, 1994), pp. 27-32.

7. George M. Harton, "Fulfillment of Deuteronomy 28–30 in History and in Eschatology," Th.D. Dissertation, Dallas Theological Seminary, August 1981, p. 16.

8. Harton, "Fulfillment," pp. 17-18.

9. Harton, "Fulfillment," p. 18.

10. Harton, "Fulfillment," p. 20.

11. Harton, "Fulfillment," p. 21.

12. Harton, "Fulfillment," p. 22.

13. Harton, "Fulfillment," p. 24.

14. Harton, "Fulfillment," p. 24.

15. David Larsen, *Jews, Gentiles, and the Church* (Grand Rapids, MI: Discovery House Publishers, 1995), p. 23.

16. Larsen, *Jews Gentiles, and the Church*, pp. 23-24.

17. Harton, "Fulfillment," p. 233.

18. J. Randall Price, "Old Testament Tribulation Terms" in Thomas Ice and Timothy Demy, eds., *When the Trumpet Sounds* (Eugene, OR: Harvest House Publishers, 1995), p. 61. The Hebrew terms, as provided in Dr. Price's chart, have been removed.

19. Paul Benware, *Understanding End Times Prophecy* (Chicago, IL: Moody Press, 1995), p. 244.

20. See the chapter in this book: "The 70 Weeks of Daniel."

21. Kenneth L. Gentry, Jr., *He Shall Have Dominion: A Postmillennial Eschatology* (Tyler, TX: Institute for Christian Economics, 1992), p. 471.

22. J. Randall Price, "The Desecration and Restoration of the Temple as an Eschatological Motif in the Tanach, Jewish Apocalyptic Literature, and the New Testament" (Ph.D. dissertation, University of Texas at Austin, 1993).

23. John F. Walvoord, *Israel in Prophecy* (Grand Rapids, MI: Zondervan, 1962), p. 26.

Chapter 17—Some Practical Dangers of Preterism

1. Kenneth L. Gentry, Jr., "A Preterist View of Revelation" in C. Marvin Pate, gen. ed., *Four Views on the Book of Revelation* (Grand Rapids, MI: Zondervan, 1998), p. 87.

2. For an explanation of the Hindu concept of *Maya* see John B. Noss, *Man's Religions*, 5th ed. (New York: Macmillan Publishing Co., 1974), pp. 99, 197, 199, 229.

3. Clifton E. Olmstead, *History of Religion in the United States* (Englewood Cliffs, NJ: Prentice-Hall, 1960), p. 342.

4. Mark A. Noll, *A History of Christianity in the United States and Canada* (Grand Rapids, MI: Eerdmans, 1992), p. 197.

5. Richard Kyle, *The Last Days Are Here Again: A History of the End Times* (Grand Rapids, MI: Baker Book House, 1998), p. 85.

6. Gary North, "Publisher's Preface" in Kenneth L. Gentry, Jr., *Before Jerusalem Fell* (Tyler, TX: Institute for Christian Economics, 1989), p. xi.

7. Gentry, "A Preterist View of Revelation," pp. 86-89.

8. Gentry, "A Preterist View of Revelation," p. 87 and pp. 86-89.

9. For example, Gary DeMar, *Last Days Madness: Obsession of the Modern Church*, 4th ed. (Powder Springs, GA: American Vision, 1999), pp. 223-26.

10. North, "Publisher's Preface", p. xii.

11. DeMar, *Last Days Madness*, p. 70.

12. David Chilton, "Looking for New Heavens and a New Earth" in Gary DeMar, *Last Days Madness: Obsession of the Modern Church*, 3rd ed. (Atlanta, GA: American Vision, 1997), p. 485, fn. 2.

13. DeMar, *Last Days Madness*, p. 70.

14. See J. Stuart Russell, *The Parousia: A Critical Inquiry into the New Testament Doctrine of Our Lord's Second Coming*, new ed. (1887; reprint, Grand Rapids, MI: Baker, 1984), pp. 119-22; Don K. Preston, *Into All the World: Then Comes the End* (no publishing information, 1996).

15. North, "Publisher's Preface," p. xii.

16. David Chilton, *Paradise Restored: An Eschatology of Dominion* (Tyler, TX: Reconstruction Press, 1985), p. 225.

17. Ken Gentry, "A Brief Theological Analysis of Hyper-Preterism," in *The Counsel of Chalcedon* (vol. XVII, no. 1, March 1995), p. 20.

18. R. C. Sproul, *The Last Days According to Jesus* (Grand Rapids, MI: Baker, 1998), p. 158.

19. This is a well-known fact within the world of preterism. It has been documented on the website ourworldtop. cs.com/preteristabcs/id88.htm. See also Edward E. Stevens, "Tribute to David Chilton" in *Kingdom Counsel* (vol. 8, no. 2 and vol. 9; Oct. 1996–Dec. 1997), pp. 17-18.

20. The following Internet address documents Hibbard's move toward full preterism: http://members.aol.com/healinglvs/ healinglvs/pt-08.htm.

21. Sproul, *Last Days*, p. 155.

22. Chilton, *Paradise Restored*, p. 224.

23. Chilton, *Paradise Restored*, p. 224.

24. Gary DeMar and Peter Leithart, *The Reduction of Christianity* (Forth Worth, TX: Dominion Press, 1998), p. 213.

25. Ray Sutton, *That You May Prosper: Dominion by Covenant* (Tyler, TX: Institute for Christian Economics, 1987), p. 242.

26. Sutton, *That You May Prosper*, p. 243.

27. Gentry, "A Preterist View of Revelation," pp. 51-52.

28. Gentry, "A Preterist View of Revelation," p. 52.

29. Kenneth L. Gentry, Jr., *He Shall Have Dominion: A Postmillennial Eschatology* (Tyler, TX: Institute for Christian Economics 1992), p. 394, fn. 2.

ABOUT THE EDITORS
AND CONTRIBUTORS

Malcolm O. Couch, Th.D, Ph.D., is an author and founder and dean of Tyndale Theological Seminary and Bible Institute in Fort Worth, Texas.

Gordon Franz, M.A., Ph.D., is an archaeologist who has lead many tours to the Holy Land and is an adjunct instructor for Talbot School of Theology and resides in Fair Lawn, New Jersey.

Arnold Fruchtenbaum, Th.M., Ph.D., is founder and director of Ariel Ministries in Tustin, California.

Mark Hitchcock, Th.M., J.D., is an author, a Ph.D. candidate at Dallas Theological Seminary, and pastor of Faith Bible Church in Edmond, Oklahoma.

Thomas D. Ice, Th.M., Ph.D., is a founder and executive director of the Pre-Trib Research Center in Arlington, Texas.

Tim F. LaHaye, D.Min., D.D., is a founder of the Pre-Trib Research Center, bestselling author, and popular speaker from Rancho Mirage, California.

John MacArthur, M.Div., D.D., is a bestselling author, president of The Master's College and Seminary, and pastor-teacher of Grace Community Church in Sun Valley, California.

J. Randall Price, Th.M., Ph.D., is an author and founder and director of World of the Bible Ministries, Inc., in San Marcos, Texas.

Larry Spargimino, M.Div., Ph.D., is an author and minister at Southwest Radio Church Ministries in Bethany, Oklahoma.

Andy Woods, Th.M., J.D., is a full-time Ph.D. student at Dallas Theological Seminary in Dallas, Texas.